READING

IN

ELEMENTARY

CLASSROOMS

READING IN ELEMENTARY CLASSROOMS
STRATEGIES AND OBSERVATIONS

Patricia M. Cunningham
Wake Forest University

Sharon Arthur Moore
University of Northern Iowa

James W. Cunningham
University of North Carolina, Chapel Hill

David W. Moore
University of Northern Iowa

Longman
New York & London

For Our Children: Wendy, Aaron, David, and TBA

Reading in Elementary Classrooms
Strategies and Observations

Longman Inc., 95 Church Street, White Plains, N.Y. 10601
Associated companies, branches, and representatives
throughout the world.

Developmental Editor: Lane Akers
Editorial and Design Supervisor: Joan Matthews
Production Supervisor: Ferne Y. Kawahara
Manufacturing Supervisor: Marion Hess

Figure 5.1 is reprinted from James P. Barufaldi, George T. Ladd, and Alice Johnson
Moses, *Heath Science*, copyright © 1981 by D. C. Heath and Company, Lexington, Mass.,
pp. 246–248. Reprinted by permission of D. C. Heath and Company.

Figure 5.2 is reprinted from Ralph C. Preston and Eleanor Clymer, *Communities at Work*,
copyright © 1964 by D. C. Heath and Company, Boston, pp. 182–185. Reprinted by permission of D. C. Heath and Company.

"April Rain Song" is reprinted from THE DREAM KEEPER AND OTHER POEMS, by Langston
Hughes. Copyright 1932 by Alfred A. Knopf, Inc. and renewed 1960 by Langston Hughes.
Reprinted by permission of Alfred A. Knopf, Inc.

Portions of Part II originally appeared in Patricia M. Cunningham, Sharon V. Arthur, and
James W. Cunningham, *Classroom Reading Instruction, K-5: Alternative Approaches*,
copyright © 1977 by D. C. Heath and Company, Lexington, Mass.

Library of Congress Cataloging in Publication Data

Main entry under title:

Reading in elementary classrooms.

    Bibliography: p.
    Includes index.
    1. Reading (Elementary) I. Cunningham,
Patricia Marr.
LB1573.R279   372.4   82-7814
ISBN 0-582-28390-6   AACR2

Manufactured in the United States of America
Printing: 9 8 7 6 5 4   Year: 92 91 90 89 88 87 86

Contents

Preface

Reading in Elementary Classrooms focuses on both the theoretical knowledge and the practical abilities required to successfully teach reading in today's elementary school classrooms. In Part I, *Reading . . .*, teachers and soon-to-be teachers are presented with up-to-date information about the reading process and how children can be led through the stages of reading. Chapter 1 presents the current thinking on the prerequisite readiness knowings children must formulate before they can begin the long journey toward becoming readers. In Chapter 2, a program of word identification which integrates the teaching of sight words, context clues, and decoding is presented. Chapter 3 presents a theory of concept development and comprehension, as well as instructional strategies for developing concepts and improving readers' comprehension. In Chapters 4 and 5, the focus is on *what* children read. Chapter 4 presents a rationale for the use of literature for children and a variety of literature response activities which engage children's minds and bodies in a consideration of that literature. Chapter 5 presents a unique and comprehensive treatment of reading in the content areas for elementary children. In Chapter 6, principles of diagnosis and evaluation are combined with practical suggestions for testing and observing children's growth in reading in ways which are both valid and reliable. Chapter 7 addresses the omnipresent concern of discipline. Ways of organizing and managing instruction so that the teacher is free to teach the many different levels of children found in most elementary school classrooms are summarized in 13 *DO*'s for good discipline. Chapter 8 addresses the question, "What is reading?" In this chapter, the theoretical underpinnings underlying the preceding and following chapters are summarized as readers discover how the *what, why*, and *how* of reading interrelate.

Part II, *. . . In Elementary Classrooms*, is an attempt to show how the principles and strategies discussed in Part I operate in real classrooms filled with real children and teachers. In Part II we take you to Merritt Elementary School where you will spend six years with a class of children as they progress from kindergarten to fifth grade. You will meet Miss Launch, the kindergarten teacher whose instruction allows you to see how the seven readiness ingredients presented in Chapter 1 could be implemented in a kindergarten or first-grade classroom. You will then, along with the 24 children, be promoted to Mrs. Wright's first grade. There you will see most of the children begin the process of becoming readers as Mrs. Wright uses language experience, personalized reading, and basal readers to help the children get off to a successful start. In second grade, you will share along with Miss Nouveau the growing pains of being a first-year teacher. Miss Nouveau makes the mistakes most first-year teachers make, gets discouraged enough to almost quit, and ends up concluding her first year of teaching having learned more than the children. In contrast, Mrs. Wise, the third-grade teacher, is teaching for the last year before retirement when she gets our class of children. Mrs. Wise uses a combination of approaches with a strong emphasis on children's literature and writing in order to help her young charges continue their reading growth. In fourth grade, you will spend the year with Ms. Maverick and her student teacher, Donald Ditto. In this classroom, you will see how reading can be integrated with science and social studies units. Finally, your last year at Merritt Elementary will be spent with Mr. Dunn. Mr. Dunn prepares his students for the big change to middle school by emphasizing content-area reading and research skills.

As you read these chapters, we hope that you will see that good reading instruction can be carried out in a number of different ways and that most good teachers use a combination of approaches to help various children become capable, independent readers. We hope that you will see that the emphasis of instruction changes as children move from readiness, to beginning reading, to intermediate reading, and to reading-to-learn stages. We hope that you will be able to see how teachers engage children with whom they are not currently working in useful activities as the teachers work with individuals or small groups. We hope you will see how instructional strategies build and change as they are used over time and how teachers diagnose and evaluate how children are progressing toward their instructional goals.

In Part II, we have attempted to make extensive year-long visits to classrooms available to you so that you can observe firsthand how children grow in reading and how teachers promote this growth. In order to do this, we had to make some compromises with reality. For one thing, we do realize that it would be most unusual in today's mobile society for a class of children to stay together for six years in one elementary school. We hope that you will accept this improbable situation which we created so that you could watch how children grow and interact, and watch the different children's responses to a variety of teaching styles and approaches.

In order to show a variety of approaches to reading instruction, we have had each of the six teachers approach reading instruction in a unique fashion. We also had to place these varied approaches as carried out in a particular grade level. We hope that you will *NOT* infer that children should have a different approach to reading each year. While variety is certainly desirable in any instructional program, this much variety is not necessary and perhaps even not wise. But, teachers are people and have different ways of functioning with which they are more or less comfortable. We believe that a variety of ways of organizing and carrying out reading instruction can be effective and wanted to show you this variety. Thus, each teacher at Merritt Elementary School uses a different approach to teaching reading—not because a different approach should be used each year but rather because this allowed us to share with you six unique and effective teaching programs!

We also hope that you will not tie the approaches to the grade level at which they are presented. Any teacher could do a literature/writing program modeled on the program Mrs. Wise followed in third grade or a basal program like the one Miss Nouveau developed in second grade. While the language experience approach used by Mrs. Wright is probably not appropriate when a reader has achieved some sophistication in reading, it is appropriate for a beginning reader of any age. A fourth-grade teacher who had a child who was not reading at all could use the language experience approach with that child. While Ms. Maverick's integrated curriculum approach does require some reading facility, it could be used by any teacher whose children have achieved that facility. Mr. Dunn's reading program is also appropriate for any class in which most of the children have mastered the basic reading skills.

Throughout Part I and Part II, we have included activities which readers can complete to extend knowledge and to take the principles presented to the application level. "Try It Out" activities ask readers to perform activities which demonstrate that they understand and can apply what they are reading. "Add to Your Survival Kit" activities suggest things readers might find, create, or construct which will help them "survive" in the real world of schools. "Find a Child" activities suggest that readers apply what they are learning by actually trying out a suggested strategy or idea with a child. "Read Some More about This" activities send readers to other sources to gain more information or another viewpoint on a subject under discussion.

Most books are read from beginning to end and, indeed, our book can be read in that fashion. The theoretical and practical framework for reading instruction is laid in Part I. Readers then get a chance to see these principles and strategies in action in the classroom in Part II. You may, however, choose to read Part II first. In fact, we tried to create the book so that Part II does not depend for its understanding on Part I. Some people like to get a look at the whole puzzle first and then begin to analyze the pieces. If that is your learning style, you might read Part II first and then read Part I. Finally, it is possible to skip around and integrate the chapters from Part I and Part II. Some chapters are tied closely together. Chapter 1 on readiness, for example, could be read just prior to or just after reading about Miss Launch's kindergarten program in Chapter 9. Chapter 5 presents some notions about reading in content areas in elementary schools and Chapter 14 shows how Mr. Dunn focuses on helping his children become independent learners in the content areas. In order to facilitate the correlation between Parts I and II, Part II contains *locators*. Locators are words in the margin which, when looked up in the index, will help the reader locate the other information in the book about that topic. In both Parts I and II, the cross references "[see pp. 000–000]" will help the reader work back and forth between the theoretical and practical information in Part I and its classroom application in Part II.

We hope you will enjoy both parts of our book. We have all taught and have found that while teaching has many problems, it is never dull, or boring, or unexciting. We have tried to have fun as we went through the long process of writing this book and have tried to create a book that is not dull or boring. We hope you will find that this book reflects the complexity and also the excitement that is integral to schools and to teaching reading.

P.M.C.
S.A.M.
J.W.C.
D.W.M.

Part I

Reading...

1 | Readiness and Beginning Reading

This chapter, perhaps more than any other in this book, is one in which the ideas can be used readily by all. Though you may consider it unlikely that you will be teaching very young children, still this chapter should be of interest to you. Almost every person reading this book will be either a parent or have very close associations with young children. Perhaps you babysit a great deal or maybe you are the favorite aunt or uncle of a child. In any of these instances, you will find the information in this chapter to be useful. The foundations for children's success in reading begin with experiences prior to school attendance. These experiences are structured by the important adults in the child's life. As an important adult in a child's life, we urge you to incorporate some of the learnings from this chapter into your dealings with children.

We believe that the reading process is a continuum. There are not sharp demarcations which mark the end of readiness and the beginning of reading. Rather, there is a fading from phase to phase so that slowly, nearly imperceptibly, the change occurs from preparing for successful reading to being a successful reader.

Children who learn to read early, before going to school, are children who share certain characteristics (Clay, 1976; Durkin, 1980). The young children in Clay's and Durkin's research viewed reading as a valuable experience because they saw the important adults around them reading regularly for various purposes. Their questions about words and letters were answered. They had been read to frequently from a variety of printed materials. As a result of being read to, they learned to anticipate and predict from the text structure and their own experiences what would occur next. To these children, it was natural that reading had to make sense, and that if it didn't make sense you could look back at the text and figure out why.

For these reasons, we also believe that all readiness and beginning reading activities must be done with print or directly related to understanding print. Many of the materials used to teach readiness and beginning reading are divorced from the reading process or are so obscurely related that children will not readily recognize the relationship. To teach visual discrimination, it is far preferable to use letters rather than pictures of teacups with missing handles or geometric shapes. The relationship between children's ability to discriminate abstract geometric shapes and letters and words has not been verified (Durkin, 1980). In fact, it seems that recognizing geometric shapes is part of building children's concepts about the world around them rather than aiding discrimination of letters and words. Therefore, it only makes sense that both visual and auditory discrimination occur with words, rather than shapes, or tones on a musical scale.

We also believe that all children can learn to read. That is not to say that all children will read equally well, but rather, that given what we know today about learning theory and how children learn language, there is no reason why all people in this country cannot be at least functionally literate.

The rest of this chapter will be devoted to explicating these three beliefs: (1) the reading process is a continuum, (2) readiness and reading activities must be done with or directly related to print, and (3) all children can learn to read. If you will bear with an analogy that, admittedly, does break down upon too close an examination, you will see these three beliefs elaborated. Imagine reading as a stew. If you can close your eyes and imagine a steaming bowl of stew in front of you, you might see chunks of vegetables of many types, and perhaps some meat, floating in a savory broth of indistinguishable components. Of course, it is true that these components are not totally unidentifiable, because your experience with stews and your knowledge of broths indicate many of the ingredients are, by the second or third day of serving, so well blended that the ingredients complement one another and heighten one another so that you are no longer as aware of the garlic, only of the garlic's enhancement of the other spices, the meat, and the vegetables. Just as meat, vegetables, and spices blend together to make a good stew, so do certain factors blend together to make good readers. It is, we propose, a blending of seven "readiness ingredients" which help to make the successful reader.

SEVEN READINESS INGREDIENTS

To cook up a readiness and beginning reading program which will result in a satisfactory dish (good readers), include these seven reading ingredients in your curriculum.

1. Children who are successful readers know what reading is for.
2. Children who are successful readers need to have an adequate background of information so that what they read makes sense.
3. Children who are successful readers expect that what they hear read to them and what they read for themselves will make sense.

4. Children who are successful readers know the conventions and the jargon of print.
5. Children who are successful readers can auditorily and visually discriminate letters and words.
6. Children who are successful readers have an interest in reading and a desire to learn how to read.
7. Children who are successful readers have had experiences with both story and expository text structures.

This chapter, as well as Chapter 9, will be devoted to explicating the factors which contribute to making good readers.

READ SOME MORE ABOUT THIS

Obtain a copy of Delores Durkin's *Teaching Your Children to Read* (1980) and read what she believes are the critical factors for helping children become successful readers right from the beginning (pp. 60–74). How do they compare with the "seven readiness ingredients" listed here?

---

1. Children who are successful readers know what reading is for.

The two major reasons which exist for reading in schools are to learn and to experience. Readers communicate with writers over time and space. Children who understand that the writer of the message is not and need not be present have gone a long way toward understanding the value of writing. Most of their communications with others are immediate and face-to-face. They may not associate the school tasks of reading and writing as having any relevance in their daily lives. If children come from homes in which adults place value on activities such as reading the Bible or writing to relatives, then these children are much more likely to be successful beginning readers (Clay, 1976). They have intuited and internalized the value of print.

Teachers and parents can do much to help children understand what reading is for. Even before they can make letters and words, children should be encouraged to "write to Grandma" to tell her of their doings. Such "scribble writing" doesn't mean much to Grandma in terms of message communication, but the fact that the child views this as a communication opportunity and experience means a great deal to the child. And if Grandma writes or calls expressing her pleasure at having received the "letter," the child is much more likely to continue these communication efforts.

Some children realize, eventually, that Grandma cannot read what they have written and ask for help. At this point the teacher, parent, or sibling can "write it the right way" for the child after the scribble writing has been put on the page. Ask the child to read back what was written; children will not typically say they cannot read it, for they know that they are the ones who expressed the written ideas. Asking them to read their own writing (or yours) helps to reinforce the idea that writing is talk which has been written down so that the writer can share ideas with others.

Another type of writing that adults frequently use is the making of lists. Shoppers make lists of things to buy; workers make lists of things they must do and often write them in the sequence they are to be accomplished. The reasons for making lists as well as the format of the lists vary with individuals and their needs. Encourage children to make lists of things they are going to do in the morning at school, or lists of things they are going to do after they get home from school, or lists of things they are going to help mom find at the grocery store. Children may use their scribble writing and then cross off items as these are accomplished.

It is likely that most adults who claim that they do not read actually do engage in reading. They don't consider reading letters from friends or relatives, checking items off the grocery list, following a recipe for a dinner menu, or assembling a toy from the directions as reading. And yet, for the majority of adults in this country that type of reading-to-do predominates. Even if children don't see adults pick up books or magazines for pleasure reading, they undoubtedly do see the adults engaged in reading activities. Just pointing out to children that the above mentioned activities are reading, too, may help to demonstrate what reading is for.

As classroom teachers, we were only too aware of the fact that many of our students came from homes in which they rarely, if ever, saw someone choose to read a book or magazine just for the experience of reading. An activity one of us tried was highly successful and very easy to accomplish. A book was tucked under the teacher's arm as the class went off to lunch everyday. The implication was clear: teacher wanted to read that book so much that it was even carried to lunch! The same book was then read during the class silent reading period. That further reinforced that reading was a valued activity. Children would sometimes inquire as to what was being read, at which point the teacher had the opportunity to share why reading was so important.

The home or classroom message board is another way to show children that writing can be read and why it is important to read. Children will quickly respond and try to read a message that is for them, particularly if the message is of intrinsic interest, such as are they allowed to watch TV after school and for how long. Activities like these go a long way toward helping children establish an understanding of why people engage in reading and writing.

Young children have difficulty conceiving of print as a communication from someone over time and space and that, unlike verbal communications which are always altered with retellings, written messages remain unchanged for all who read them. Each time a parent or teacher reads to a child, it is a good idea to talk about the author and the illustrator of the book. If several different books by the same author are read, then the adult can easily remind the child of the other books and talk about the author. Chapter 4 contains sources of information that adults can use to obtain personal information about authors or other books by the same author. Children enjoy knowing, for instance, that Ezra Jack Keats enjoys writing children's books as well as receiving letters from children who have read his books. Many of the children who write to him send pieces of fabric or colored paper or other bits of things which are important to them. Sometimes Keats will include a piece sent by a child in one of the collages he uses to illustrate his books. Knowing about Keats helps children to identify the author as a person who exists even if not in their immediate environment.

Adults should also include informational books as part of the child's literary diet. If adults use books as references for increasing their own adult scope of knowledge, then children see yet another form of the necessity for reading being modeled. "Let's look it up" should be a frequently heard phrase both in the home and in the classroom. Adults who admit that they don't have all the answers but they might be able to locate that information from a piece of printed material are demonstrating to children that printed matter is a resource for learning available to those who know how to read.

These two critical purposes for reading—to learn and to experience—must be communicated to children if they are to become successful readers. The ways for communicating those purposes are many, but it is a sure bet that demonstrating these purposes is better than merely talking about why we read.

ADD TO YOUR SURVIVAL KIT

Make heading cards for your file box for each of the seven readiness ingredients. On note cards compile activities which can be done at home and/or school to encourage the understanding of each ingredient by young children. You may use the ideas listed in this book or in other sources, but be sure to include bibliographic information on the cards if the ideas are not original. Try to find or develop at least five activities for each heading.

---

2. Children who are successful readers need have an adequate background of information so that what they read makes sense.

In order for children to become successful readers, they must have had enough experiences so that the materials being read to them or that they read for themselves make sense to them. What they listen to or read must contain mostly familiar concepts and vocabulary. Consider this excerpt from "A Critical Look at Marco-Analyses of Text" (Tierney and Mosenthal, 1980):

> The concept of a formal representation of text implies a representation that is rule governed. Such a representation means to formally describe something inherent in the text. This attempt encourages a use and an approach to text structure that treats a text as if it were an absolute. Van Dijk's notion of a text grammar theorizes the legitimacy of formally represented texts while the systems described by Meyer and Thorndyke assume the legitimacy of such representation. Unfortunately, in reading research it is a deceptively satisfying notion to hypothesize a formal description of, or template for, a text which can be used for comparing and evaluating recalls. The fact is, there are problems with the idea of a formal representation of text—at least in so far as macro-analyses are concerned (p. 126).

Did you understand all of that? Even if you had a definition for all of the words in this passage, you may well not have had the specialized definition required to read the passage. You may even have had moments while reading the excerpt that you thought, "Oh, yeah. Now I get it," only to be plunged back into confusion with the next phrase. A similar thing can happen to children when they listen to or read about topics for which they have little background. It is one of the major responsibilities of schooling to help students develop concepts and the terms which represent those concepts.

Classroom teachers and parents spend a great deal of time involved in activities designed to help students understand their world and to be able to classify and organize the information they have. Much of the learning as well as the teaching is unplanned and coincidental! It should be natural for a parent who is grocery shopping with a child to comment on the colors of the vegetables as well as their variety and uses. The alternative is to either ignore the child or to become irritable when the child begins to fidget during the long and boring experience. The fact that the parent finds the task just as boring doesn't occur to the child, and the way for both of them to help the time pass more quickly is to discuss the various items encountered on the way to the checkout counter. The child who has these kinds of grocery store or kitchen-shelf discussions is less apt to experience difficulties learning to read. When the child with these experiences reads about artichokes, the image of an artichoke can form in the child's mind along with any other associations which are connected to the word. Helping children to know words at a direct level of knowledge, one at which the terms have been experienced, is the major point of the field trips which teachers plan for their students. Parents have been involving children in field trips all their lives. How much interaction takes place before, during, and after these trips determines the amount of learning about the world which occurs.

TRY IT OUT

Go to a place where parents might be with children for a period of time such as the grocery store, the doctor's office, a department store, a bus, the airport, etc. Make notes about the kinds of conversations the adult is having with the child. What opportunities for concept development are exploited? What opportunities for concept development are missed?

Primary-grade teachers instruct children in basic concepts and terms which represent those concepts such as colors, numbers, and days of the week. Knowledge of these concepts helps children organize their world, and without these concepts children's language abilities are severely limited. For example, children may be listening to or reading a story about someone swinging a carton of soda pop on a hot summer day. Only if the children have had experiences with carbonated water, agitation, and heat will they be able to predict, even anticipate with glee, what will happen in the story.

Field trips are not the only way that concepts are developed in school. Before reading the soda pop story, the teacher most likely would have brought in a bottle of carbonated water and tried out all sorts of things with the bottle. Children would discover that the fizziness increases with agitation or with warmth. The combination of the two together can be, well, explosive. After such experimentation, you can bet what all children will be anticipating as they read or listen to the story! These opportunities to try out and test hypotheses do not only occur in the structured setting of teacher and students experimenting. In classroom learning centers, children have an opportunity to practice previously learned material as well as to try out new kinds of information.

Other important adults in the child's life can help the child develop concepts, too. Many children are permitted to bring home their basal readers after the class has finished the book. Children are often eager to

read the book to anyone who will listen. The adult who would like to enlarge the child's understanding of the story and the ideas behind the
story can easily do so. While the story is being read, ask the child to look
at the pictures and explain how the pictures contribute to understanding the story. Encourage a discussion of the ideas as they occur. Ask the
child to predict what might happen next and to explain how one could
guess that. If the child doesn't want to be bothered with such things during reading, ask him or her to first just read to you and then you'll read
again and talk about the story. Almost all of us have sat with a child
who has brought a reader from school and wants to read that book to
someone, anyone. Observe this experience the next time you are involved. Does the child "plow through" the story, word by word, page by
page, not stopping to discuss the ideas or the pictures? It is particularly
frustrating to sit with a child like this, as one of us did recently. All
attempts to get the child to talk about what he was reading, to anticipate what might happen next, or to include the pictures in the story line
were thwarted. "Obviously," his looks and manner said, "this person
doesn't know how reading is done. One begins at the beginning and goes
to the end!"

Television, too, has its role in developing children's concepts about
the world around them. Though the negative aspects of TV have been
heralded through the years, nevertheless, it cannot be denied that children come to school with larger vocabularies and a broader range of experiences, vicarious though they are, than did children prior to the introduction of television. No doubt the "radio-age" children entered
school with larger vocabularies and more vicarious experiences than did
their parents. Any experiences which children have that are varied and
involve language are bound to influence what children are able to
understand. The school can help bridge the gap between their vicarious
and direct knowledge of the world.

Parents and teachers alike can engage children in activities which
will help them to form insights about the concepts they have. Activities
such as picture sorting, simplistic though it may seem, help children to
organize and reorganize information into new relationships and patterns. Discovering these new ways to organize the world is an important
part of concept development. Young children often beg for homework,
having been impressed with the knowledge that homework is for "big
kids." The teacher can assign as homework the requirement to look
through magazines and catalogs or other materials to find pictures of
foods. The children return to school with their tattered pictures of food.
Having jumbled all of those pictures together, the teacher can divvy
them up among small classroom groups. The groups may be given one
assignment or they may have different assignments. The task for a
group might be to sort the pictures of food by color. Any food which is
more than one color can go into its own grouping or it can be sorted by

the predominant color (a harder task). Either way is all right as long as the children know the rules. The next task might be to take another group's already sorted pictures and put them into the categories that are labeled "breakfast," "lunch," "dinner," and "snacks." Yet another possibility would be to categorize them into food groupings: fruit, vegetable, meat, milk and dairy products, and grains. The groupings can go on indefinitely, since there are many ways to "know" the same foods. All the pictures can be put into a learning center so that children can categorize the foods in other ways and share those groupings with each other and the teacher.

A major goal of the readiness and beginning reading program is to develop both the depth and breadth of youngsters' vocabularies. The more words they understand, the better listeners and readers they will be.

3. Children who are successful readers expect that what they hear read to them and what they read for themselves will make sense.

If anything is the bottom line in reading instruction, this is it. The whole point of teaching children to use word identification and comprehension strategies is so that they will be better equipped to understand what they encounter in print. The strategies themselves are only the means to the end. The end is helping children learn to regulate and monitor their own understanding of what they hear read to them and what they will later read for themselves.

Prior to school attendance, most children have been dealing with the auditory mode of communication almost entirely. Admittedly they may "read" words in context such as "Coke," "STOP," "Sugar Pops," etc., but few of them have had reading experiences with connected discourse. Because of this lack of experience with connected discourse and because many beginning readers are put through a program which focusses on word identification, many children do not expect that the reading they will do must make sense. It is common to hear a child read, "The girl rode her house." The children who would read this way are the ones who frequently encounter words they do not know in text and who haven't been helped to develop the internal monitoring system which tells them, "Hold it! Girls don't ride houses!" In fact, for these children, the expectation seems to be that they will *not* understand what they read, since reading is "saying the words."

There are many ways that teachers and other interested adults can help children to develop an internal monitoring system for understanding. Such activities can begin with listening and later be transferred to reading. As many parents know, this listening for making sense is well developed in some children. Who has not read on oft-told tale to children and been told, "You skipped a part;" "It doesn't say that;" or, "Here comes the good part." These children have been building readiness for making sense with each repetition of a story. By the same token, these children will not likely sit passively by if the story is one they don't understand; they may complain, they may wander off, or they may ask questions. It doesn't make sense, and in their world, to date, they have been trying to make things make sense.

One strategy which can be used with a group of children, some of whom have the internal "making sense" monitoring system and some of whom don't, is to mangle stories as they are read to children. Initially, the mangling should be very broad and obvious, such as calling "Cinderella" "Snow White" or adding in a whole sentence from another story which clearly does not belong with the one being read. Your good monitors should pick that up and point it out to you spontaneously. If they do, ask them what is wrong? why? how did they know? Their answers to these questions will help to model this monitoring for the other children in the group. Later on, the mangles can become less obvious ones such as changing the word *horse* to *house* as was done in the "girl rode her house" example. If children do not "get" the mangles or hesitate to correct the teacher, then a new strategy must be employed. Tell the children that you are going to make three mistakes as you read a familiar story to them. As each one is found (you may have to pause and ask for it), make a tally on the board. That way they can keep track of how many have been found.

Another activity children enjoy is also done with familiar stories at first so that the task is clearly understood. You might say, "Humpty Dumpty sat on a _____." Pause to let the children finish the line. If they cannot, ask them what are some things one sits upon: chairs, benches, etc. If out in a field where such things as chairs do not normally exist, what might one sit upon? Such "thinking aloud" done with the group again helps to model the "making sense" process. To get children started, you might even suggest some unacceptable alternatives for children to consider and reject. "Humpty Dumpty sat on a _____. Well, he could sit on a glass. He could sit on a fire."

When doing listening activities with children, it is sometimes difficult to get the children most in need of these listening activities to respond. Children who don't need the activity for listening comprehension are always the ones with the answer! Every-pupil-response activities involve all in the lesson. Provide each child with a set of picture cards to select from and display. For example, give all the children in the listening group a set of three pictures: house, horse, apple. Each child would hold up the appropriate card to finish these sentences:

The girl went in the _____.
The girl rode her _____.
The girl ate the _____.

The girl petted the ___.
The girl painted the ___.

After children can respond well to these ending words, say, "Now we are going to listen for words which are not at the end of the sentence. I will say the sentence and when I come to the word you need to find a picture for, I will say 'blank' and go on with the sentence." The teacher might then read sentences such as:

The girl named her ___ Bay Beauty.
The red ___ looked so good she ate it.
The tall ___ had a big door.

These activities are called *oral cloze*. Oral cloze helps prepare children for reading by teaching them to use context in order to figure out unknown words. The value of such a strategy is evident when one considers that young children who learn to read prior to coming to school rely heavily on context to figure out unknown words (Taylor, 1977).

Teachers or parents can try a variation of the above ideas by having children respond to the sentences with cards picturing happy and sad faces. You might say, "Today I am going to read some sentences to you. If I read them right, you tell me I am right by showing me your happy face card. If I say a silly sentence, you tell me I am wrong by showing me your sad face card." The teacher or parent can then read sentences such as the following, helping children correct their mistakes if they occur:

The girl ate her horse.
The girl painted the house.
The girl named her apple Bay Beauty.
The girl rode her horse.

FIND A CHILD

Construct some oral cloze activities such as the ones described here. Find a child or a small group of children and go through a set of sentences with them. What do you observe and learn?

One genre in children's literature which lends itself particularly well to helping children develop the idea that books contain ideas which should make sense are the wordless picture books. As their name indicates, these books contain no text within the story itself (though some of them may be prefaced with text). Wordless books help children extract meaning from their reading by focusing attention on the illustrated story elements. Children cannot merely "say the words" since there are none; they have to attend to the information in the pictures. These books are, for the most part, illustrated with story structures such as characterization, plot, conflict, resolution, etc. Helping children to rely on getting meaning from these books by carefully attending to the details in the pictures is no easy task. What you are asking them to do is attend to a series of pictures which convey information sequentially without the added cue of words. In fact, with Mercer Mayer's *A Boy, a Dog, and a Frog* (1967), children tend to explicate each picture as it occurs, rarely tying in the information from one page to the next. They tend to describe the pictures, characters, and actions on each page as if that page were an entity unto itself. This same phenomenon of not associating one page with those before or after also occurs when some children read books *with* words; wordless books can help to break that pattern.

The adult who goes the route of using wordless books with children will probably want to find very short wordless books or books which have several short stories in one book (such as Steiner's *I Am Andy*, 1961). A later step can consist of asking the children to tell you about each page so that you can write it down for them, helping them to relate the pages to one another so that a sparse tale is told (even if it is not the one the author intended!)

One of the best ways to help children understand that reading must make sense is through classroom cookery. In the narrative chapters of this text you will find many recipes which can be prepared in an elementary school classroom. Children learn, first hand, that what one reads can be produced in the form of edible products. They must attend to the sequence, exact wording, and the implied information (such as turn on the oven before putting in the cookies) if they are to be successful. Cookbooks for children are proliferating, so there is ready access to a variety of types and levels of difficulty for the teacher or other adult who wants to approach meaningful reading from a very pleasurable avenue.

The activities mentioned above are not an exhaustive review of the posibilities for helping children develop an internal monitoring system. Throughout this textbook, the emphasis is on helping children expect meaning and make sense of what they read.

4. Children who are successful readers know the conventions and jargon of print.

Remember when you were last at a fine restaurant. You arrived at the entrance and waited for someone to seat you. You did not jump to fill your own water glass; someone came to your table and filled the glass for you. When you left, you gave money to those who had provided services for you. All of these activities, as well as others you could name, are conventions (arbitrary sets of rules) which are appropriate when dining at a nice restaurant. Children must also be aware of and know when to use the conventions of print. The English language has developed a set of arbitrary rules about how the print is located on a page and how one gets from one page to the next. In the English language, we move our eyes from left to right and then return to the beginning of the next line of print and move from left to right again. We also begin, usually, at the top line of print and go to the bottom line of print. We begin at the front of a book and go to the back. All of these conventions about print are ones children need to be able to use fluently and automatically if they are to be good readers. They don't even have to know the words left and right to be able to use that information. Good readers are not even aware that they are employing that knowledge.

Another aspect of reading that children need to be taught is the jargon (special language) of reading. Imagine hearing this being shouted at you when you are out with a friend:

> "Lower your spinnaker. You've got too much luff in your jib. Coming about! Heel to starboard."

Did you understand the conversation? Would you have been whacked on the head by a sail "coming about"? The language in the conversation is specific to sailing; if you are sailing with someone it is important that you understand what is expected of you both to help out and for safety purposes. Just so, young children need to learn about the special language used in teaching reading. Here is another scenario:

> It is the first day of school. The teacher says to the class, "Get out your books. *Turn* to *page* 59. At the *top* there is a *line* for your name. Do all the *sentences* on this *page*. Write down all the *words* you do not know."

The italicized words are ones children may well not know unless they have had many experiences with books and other reading materials. To some children this language is confusing because they already have a meaning for the word being used: a *top* is a toy, a *letter* is what comes in the mail; a *sentence* is what daddy is serving! For some of the language used to teach reading, children do not have any meaning. For example, try to define a *word* or a *letter*. Young children do not necessarily know that a word is a letter or group of letters set off by white space on both sides and that the letter or group of letters conveys meaning. For us, all of this seems so obvious that it is difficult to imagine a time when we, too, did not possess that knowledge. But each of us learned about the language of print, and it is a major responsibility of the teacher of readiness and beginning reading to help ensure that the children being taught understand print conventions and jargon. The understanding of both of these areas is called metalinguistic awareness.

Recently the literature of reading education has become more and more concerned with the concept of metalinguistic awareness in order to determine how children learn and can be taught the conventions of print and the jargon of reading. Morris (1980), Templeton (1980), Waterhouse et al. (1980), and others have addressed these concerns. Metalinguistic awareness refers to what children know about the conventions of printed language and the words used to describe language and its use.

The more clearly children understand print conventions and the words used to talk about reading, the easier it will be for them to learn to read. For example, learning that print is "talk written down" and that it can be produced by people not in the immediate environment is an important concept.

An example of this leap of intuition and comprehension was made by a three-year-old whom we observed. David was fascinated by the typewriter, as what child is not. He was typing over and over, *m, a, m, a* since that is what he calls his mother and he had wanted to be able to write her name. Later on, snuggled down in his mother's lap, listening to a story, he suddenly started up and pointed to a word on the page of the book. He exclaimed, "That says *m, a, m, a*. It says 'mama'." He learned that someone else could form the letters of the word he knew and put those letters into a book and use the word as David had. It was a revelation. From this stage on, children will typically begin asking questions about words and letters on the printed matter which exists in their world.

It is clear that the more children know about the jargon and conventions of language, the more equipped they will be to undertake reading instruction. It is to this concept of metalinguistic awareness that studies such as Durrell's et al. (1958) owe their results. Durrell et al. found that children who can name the letters of the alphabet are more likely to succeed in reading instruction. This finding has resulted in the requirement by many teachers that letter names be learned before children are allowed to read words. Many people assumed that a causal relationship existed when, in fact, letter name knowledge was merely correlated with reading success. Durrell's et al. findings were correct. The interpretation of these findings has led to questionable instructional practices. Rather than knowledge of letter names *causing* the children to be successful, it appears that they are successful beginning readers due to other basic underlying information about the language of language and the conventions of print which result in *both* knowledge of letter names *and* in the likelihood of success with beginning reading. The implications for instruction, then, seem to be clear. Teachers concerned with readiness will allow a multitude of opportunities in a variety of settings so that meta-linguistic understandings will be developed and enhanced.

Instruction concerning print conventions and the jargon of print should always be in the context of real reading materials. Common sense shows that this must be true, for anyone who has heard young children sing "The Alphabet Song" is aware of just how confused they are concerning the letter names. Remember the middle part of the song which children run together as one word, "elemenopee"? This is further verified if you ask children to name the letters rather than singing them; the lyrics of the song may just as well be nonsense words for all the meaning that is attached or for the limits of their ability to say the letters without reverting to the song.

Through the use of many experiences with books and other printed matter, children can learn that English is read from top to bottom, left to right, front to back. When adults are modeling this for children, they should try to have children sitting beside them, rather than across the book as is most often done in school rooms. Why? Children can develop strange misconceptions about language otherwise. For example, a mother brought her child to the university reading clinic for diagnosis when the child was a first grader. During the parent interview it was found that the child's experiences should have enabled her to learn to read easily. But, in fact, the child was "failing" first grade. Subsequent testing and working with the child confirmed that she was bright and articulate, but whenever she was handed a passage to read, she was unable to struggle through even a small part. One part of the testing day consisted of the child examining books on her own so that observations could be made concerning her attitude toward books and the way she approached them for reading. It was at this point that the examiner recognized the problem. Left to her own devices, the child picked up a book, *upside down*, and began to read aloud fluently to the examiner. Further questioning of the mother indicated that through all the years of reading to her child she had placed the child across from her and the child, through the many repetitions of the printed forms she saw, had learned to read upside down. A rare case perhaps, but one which illustrates that how letters are oriented on a page influences how children will learn. This orientation problem is confounded by the similarity of letter forms such as *d, p, b,* and *q.* To young children, the distinctive features of the way the ball is facing and where the stick is do not seem very important; in their world to date things remain the same no matter how they are oriented in space. A chair is still called a chair even if it is upside down. But now, these funny squiggles on paper change their meaning if they are turned around.

The concepts of "What is a word?" and "What is a letter?" are important ones to be learned. It cannot be assumed by the teacher that readiness or beginning reading-level children will know those terms. And yet they are used frequently in the classroom for they are part of the language of reading. The easiest way we have found to teach a child these two major concepts is with the child's own name. This is a word which is intrinsically motivating to the child; it is the most meaningful word in the child's language store. When the adult writes the child's name, say, "Here is your name. This word tells what your name is. Can you read this word?" Repetition of these sentences with other important words you write for the child or which the child finds in other sources (such as cereal boxes) will help to demonstrate the concept. It is a good idea to draw your finger underneath the word you have written or to underline the word in other printed matter. Include all the letters and go slowly from left to right as you ask, "Can you read this word?"

Later on you can use the child's own name again to teach the concept of letter. Ask, "What is this word?" as you draw your finger beneath the child's name. "I wonder how many letters there are in this word. Let's count them; one, two . . ." as you point to each letter. Again the process can be repeated over and over with other words of importance to the child (such as *mama*). You can write the child's name and the name of the child's best friend. Place one word under the other. "What is this word? Do you know this word? Which word has more letters? Let's count and find out." After counting the letters in each word by having the child draw a line under each letter, write the numeral to the side. Putting word cards in a learning center for children to play with and, therefore, learn from is also good. For example, if you place ten cards in the learning center with one word on each card, the child can be asked to find five words and bring them to the teacher. The child can also be asked to count the number of word cards in the center. If you place two or three words on the same card, the child can be asked to find the card with three words. Emphasize this concept of *word* by using words within sentences of your language experience stories: How many words are in this sentence? Find the word with seven letters in this sentence, etc.

Being able to recognize that particular groupings of letters comprise a word is called the speech-to-print match. Any activities which reinforce the idea that these letters, surrounded by white space, make a word I can say, help children to understand the concept of words. So begin clapping out words with children, give them a pencil to circle words in a sentence, and encourage them to count how many letters there are in words they want to know.

In this phase of reading, it is perfectly all right for the child to use a finger and point. In fact it is to be encouraged since this pointing reinforces the speech-to-print match. Sometimes, when you sing a song with the children, put the printed form of that song before them. Familiarity with the song aids the speech-to-print match. Another way to help children use their knowledge of the world at this stage is to ask them to bring in, as homework, words they can read from ads or food containers. The assortment might include *Pepsi, Triscuits, soup, potato chips*, and so forth. Again add these words to your learning center and ask children to count the letters. They can even group the words by word length. This means that they will need to count the letters and group all words of five letters together. This is more difficult than you might think because children will often try to group them by measured length. If they do, you know that they do not yet have the notion of what is a letter, or at least that they cannot apply their knowledge in a novel situation. It is important for children to realize that the size of the letter has no influence on word length as indicated by the number of letters.

TRY IT OUT

Make a list of the jargon associated with learning to read. Begin with: *word, sentence, letter.* Compare your list with others in your class.

Make a list of terms associated with the conventions of printed language. Begin with: *top, bottom, left-to-right.* Compare your list with others in your class.

Choose any one term or word from each list and try to devise a way that you could help children to grasp the concept which the word or phrase represents.

Give the children a notebook and pencil their first day of school and tell them that this notebook is for any writing they want to do. Surprisingly, few children will say they *can't* write; they think they can and they want to. Punching holes in unlined paper and putting string or yarn through the holes allows pages to be easily added to the book. As children's awareness of letters and words grows, you will begin to see evidence for that knowledge appearing in the children's notebooks. Ask them to "read" to you occasionally what they have written in their notebooks. Not only will they have the idea that what they have written is supposed to make sense, but it will also encourage them to experiment to try new forms and to learn new words. When children bring their notebooks to you, you have a built-in opportunity to teach them at the level they are on and help clear up misconceptions about print orientation. The teacher or other adult who uses this "invented spelling" approach to help children recognize the value of print and to provide teaching and reinforcement opportunities should read very carefully the articles by Read (1971, 1975) and Chomsky (1971, 1979). The invented spelling approach to readiness and beginning reading can be a joyous, exploratory adventure with words or can become a nightmare of frustration for children. The key to which way the situation develops is entirely up to the adult and how the adult receives and reacts to the children's writings. A noncritical, helpful, accepting attitude is necessary; the adult must be willing to allow the periods of invention which the child will go through while learning about print. Strict, rigid adherence to conventional print appearances will not only affect the success of the invented spelling approach, but might well result in a residual, detrimental effect on future efforts. This approach, perhaps more than any other described in this book, is largely dependent upon the attitudes of the adults involved. For more explanation, see how invented spelling was used as a component of the writing program in Chapter 9.

Another writing approach widely used by classroom teachers is the language experience approach (LEA). The language experience approach depends upon the language and thinking of children in order to produce reading materials. Children say something which the teacher writes down and the children then read it back. They learn that what they say can be written down and that it can be read by themselves or by others.

Structured language experience is so called because a sentence stem is provided for children. With structured language experience lessons, modeling of complete sentence patterns is provided. The teacher can prepare the lessons based on the classroom stimuli or can refer to many of the books by Bill Martin which use patterned language. Children who are unable to give complete sentences can nevertheless be taught to read complete sentences from their own experiences with the structured language experience approach.

When children have progressed to the point of being able to provide complete sentences, the teacher can use another form of language experience such as approaches advocated by Stauffer (1970) or Allen (1966). With these lessons children speak a complete thought related to the topic and the adult writes down what the child actually says, employing conventional spelling, but using the child's syntax and grammar. The importance of this is rather obvious; if indeed the teacher is trying to teach reading using the child's own language, then it is necessary that the child's language be used or children may well not be able to read back their dictated sentences.

Another type of language experience discussed in this text is the content-area language experience lesson. Chapter 5 details how these lessons are derived and the values of them. Both Miss Launch and Mrs. Wright employ content-area language experience lessons in their classrooms and examples of typical productions are available there. Briefly, the content language experience lesson is written in a highly structured way. The teacher poses specific questions focusing on an aspect of a content area. The resultant productions are written in paragraph form, using the more detached, objective third-person format of content-area textbooks or informational trade books.

All types of language experience lessons fulfill different objectives to achieve the same end: good readers of various types of printed matter.

One of the major values of the language experience approach over many others touted for readiness and beginning reading is that heterogeneous grouping is not only possible but desirable. Each child can use the same language experience lesson and come away with entirely different, and personally relevant, learnings. For example, if the teacher has in the group children at various stages of readiness and beginning reading, some children are learning left-to-right, top-to-bottom orientation. Some children are learning the end-of-the-line-to-beginning-of-the-next-line sweep of the eyes that occurs in reading connected discourse. Some children are still learning that a word is a group of letters surrounded by white space. Some children are beginning to notice that many of the words begin with the same letter. Some children are picking out individual words they are able to read, while others are able to read most of the passage by themselves. They all are learning that what they have said can be written down and read by others. And they are all learning that reading makes sense. Through the language experience approaches in their various forms, metalinguistic awareness is facilitated.

5. Children who are successful readers can auditorily and visually discriminate letters and words.

Even very young children can look at two pictures of animals and say whether it is the same animal in the pictures or two different animals. That is what discrimination is, being able to tell whether two things are the same or whether they are different. When adults work on visual discrimination with children, they help them learn to attend to certain physical features of the object which signal whether or not the two things are different. When we help children to determine whether or not two words are different, the same process is used. Though a chair remains a chair no matter how it is turned, letters of the alphabet are not so obliging. A *p* becomes a *q* or a *d* becomes a *b* depending on the positioning of that letter. Such subtle differences are not readily apparent to children since they have not been expected to use that kind of cue before.

The process of helping children learn to attend to these distinctive features of letter forms is best accomplished with words rather than teacups with missing handles, as we said earlier. Begin visual discrimination exercises by showing pictures of two different animals; ask children if they are the same or if they are different. Ask them to describe all the ways that the two animals are different. What did they look at? Now tell them you are going to do something very sneaky and show them two words, the names of children in the class. You want them to tell you whether the pairs of words are the same name or whether they are the names of two different children. Place two cards, one above the other, as shown here:

> George

> Sam

Children can tell they are different. Ask them to tell all the ways the two words are different. They should mention number of letters as well as that the letters are shaped differently. Other children's names can be paired in the same way, but every once in a while put up two cards with the same name on them.

> George

> George

Now children should be able to tell why those are the same word. When they are very good at telling apart or seeing the sameness of words, put up two which begin with the same letter and see if they can tell the differences.

> George

> Gloria

They should note that though the two words begin with the same letter, the words are indeed different, as looking at all the other letters will confirm. You can make these differences in the two words even fewer if you have children with names such as:

> Joan

> Jean

Now the only difference is with a single letter. When you run out of children's names, use other pairs of words such as *mall* and *malt* which are alike except for one letter. That one letter difference can be at the beginning, in the middle, or at the end of the words. It should be moved around with your word pairs so that children are forced to pay attention to the letters.

When your children become proficient with word pairs placed above one another, the same process should be started with the words placed side by side.

Are these the same or are they different? How do you know? Using the same words in the same sequence, go through this process so that they begin to examine words on the same line with the care they did when the words were above one another.

This process of teaching children to visually discriminate words does not occur in a single lesson nor in one day's time. Some children will understand and use the distinctive features earlier than others. But the practice with visual discrimination of words should continue for all children using a variety of sources until children can tell if two words are the same or different without much examination time at all.

Another visual discrimination activity we like to do with children is to ask them to find words on a language experience story. Hold up a word card that contains the same word as one which occurs several times in the passage. Children don't even need to know what the word is, only what its distinctive visual features are. Show the word card and have children play the "Search" game: "Look at this word. How many times is this word in the story we have here? Search for the word. Go!" A variation of the Search game is to give each child a copy of a story and to have them circle the word each time they find it. Sometimes we will say, "This word you see here is in the story six times. Try to find and circle all six times the word is used."

It is very important for the adult who is trying to teach children to visually discriminate letters and words to emphasize *only* the visual elements. There should be *no* mention of letter names or sounds at this point.

Auditory discrimination instruction occurs in the same way. Children are not taught the names of letters nor do they practice the association of letters with the sounds they represent. Auditory discrimination of words is limited to telling if two words are the same or different. Again, you can use the names of children in your class to begin. Say, "Listen to these two words. *George, Sam.* Did I say the same words or did I say two different words?" Finer and finer distinctions in the sound can be made by pairing similar words. Can children hear if they are the same or different? *Joan* and *Jean, mall* and *malt*; where are they different? Children should be able to tell you if it is the beginning, the middle, or the end parts which are different.

Auditory discrimination practice with rhyming words is used frequently in primary-grade classrooms. In fact, using trade books to help children attend to rhyming patterns has always been successful for us. One of our favorites is *The Hungry Thing* (Slepian & Seidler, 1971). The hungry thing is a monster-type character who comes to a town demanding that people "Feed me." Being polite, they ask what he would like to have and discover that he won't eat "noodles," but he will eat "foodles." Children love the nonsense rhymes and want to "feed the hungry thing" some of their favorite foods, such as "bice beam" or "lizza." Many other books and poems exist which can be used to help children attend to the sounds they hear in words. The chapter on word identification contains myriad activities which can help children discriminate words more effectively.

Though auditory and visual discrimination materials abound in the commercial market, it is undoubtedly better to rely on materials you have created for the children, or materials which they have produced. The most important consideration is that auditory and visual discrimination activities only involve deciding if the stimuli are the same or if they are different. There is no attempt at this stage to instruct children in letter-sound relationships, nor is an attempt made to teach letter names.

6. Children who are successful readers have an interest in reading and a desire to learn how to read.

Fine children's books abound, and in Chapter 4 various ways that teachers can help children learn about books are provided. But an interest in reading begins prior to school attendance, and if children come to school without an interest in words and books, then reading becomes an essentially meaningless set of exercises.

How do parents and teachers know if children possess ingredient six? They should notice that children will ask, "What does thay say?" or that children will ask others to write words for them. Frequently these children will copy words they see on boxes or words others have written for them. Children who have an interest in reading will recognize that some of the funny squiggles in words look like the funny squiggles in other words, and they will comment upon the similarities. Children who have an interest in reading will ask people to "read me a story." They have many pleasant associations with the concept of reading and want to experience other instances of pleasure. These children will notice books and other reading materials in places they visit and will often ask mom to buy them a book at the grocery store when they see a display of books. They will enjoy trips to the library and will request other visits. These children will make statements such as, "I can read that word," when they approach a stop sign at an intersection. They will notice the word "Coke" on a billboard on the highway and comment upon their ability to read that word.

Determining this aspect of readiness is easy, and if people in the child's life have encouraged ventures into reading and have responded to the child's questions about letters and words, then these children will be much more likely to come to school ready to learn from the activities the school has planned. Adults need to be supportive during these initial forays into the land of reading, since, as we all know, it is easy to become confused when confronting the world of words. When the child sees the word *SLOW* on the road sign and says, "I know that word. It says *stop*." The adult can respond in various ways. Saying, "No. That says *slow*," does give the child information, limited though it is. The child may think, "Now how did my dad know that?" If, instead dad had responded with, "I can see how you think that. A stop sign is also on the side of the road and both of them are short words that begin with the same letter, *s*. But that word is *slow* because we have a big curve to go around. We don't have to stop for it. Also, *stop* is written on a red sign and *slow* is always on a yellow one." Following this, have a game of counting how many stop signs and how many slow signs are encountered on the trip.

There are many things which adults can do for children to help develop this desire to know more about reading and to want to learn to read. When dad is preparing his special spaghetti dinner for the family, he might ask different children to assist him. Seeing dad read the recipe and follow the cooking directions on the package of spaghetti helps to demonstrate that dad uses reading regularly. When mom is trying to assemble the new book shelves for the living room wall, she can have a child help her to follow the directions and illustrations. Big brother may request help in learning his lines for the school play and sis might have received a new game she is trying to determine how to play by reading the directions. Any reading-to-do which occurs in the home is an opportunity to demonstrate to children that reading is important and worthwhile.

READ SOME MORE ABOUT THIS

A practical, readable book you should be familiar with is *28 Ways to Help Your Child Be a Better Reader* (Gambrell & Wilson, 1977). After reading this short book, see if you can come up with any other ways for parents to help children enjoy reading.

It has been mentioned that trips to the library should be regular parts of the young child's life. The adult who takes children to the library should demonstrate the value of reading by also checking out books for adult consumption. Make a big deal about going to the library; it should be an event. When the child gets up in the morning, start the day off right by saying excitedly, "Guess what we get to do today? We're going to the library!"

Birthdays and other gift-giving occasions can be marked by giving children books as presents. Let children have a bookshelf for book storage (rather than relegating them to the bottom of the toy box) and comment on how many there have been added to the collection.

Children love to receive mail, and what better way can there be to reinforce the fun of reading than to receive magazines or books regularly through a subscription. Even if children are unable to read the book or magazine on their own, they can still benefit from recognizing that reading must make sense and from sorting out the conventions and jargon of print. Indeed, the ideal situation would be for all family members to be having some type of printed matter arriving through the mail on a regular basis. This demonstrates vividly to children that reading is a valued activity worthy of both time and money.

This modeling aspect of adults valuing reading cannot be underrated and is one of the primary preschool functions which the home can perform. If, in addition, the modeling is accompanied by responsiveness to children's inquiries and attempts concerning words, then it is likely children will be ready to begin reading instruction at school.

7. Children who are successful readers have had experiences with both story and expository text structures.*

Many children come to school having had many experiences with stories. They have been read to, and they have examined countless story books from the library or in their own collections. These children have a sense about what makes up a story. They don't need to be taught that there are characters, that things happen which cause trouble, and that the characters have to figure out a way to get out of the trouble. Indeed, some more sophisticated children have a refined sense of story so that they know there has to be a "bad guy," or that in fairy tales events occur in threes, or that the first attempt to resolve a situation almost always is unsuccessful. These experiences with stories have prepared the child for reading and understanding stories.

The structure of stories, however, is quite different from the structure of exposition. Expository materials such as science or social studies

* A story is defined here as narrative fiction which includes characters, setting, conflict, and resolution.

texts and children's informational trade books are structured different-ly. The organizational pattern varies with the information being pre-sented and the style is objective and detached. As mentioned earlier, stories contain certain elements which are identifiable to many children. These elements do not even have to be formally taught, since repetition of the story elements is in itself a form of instruction. Children may not be able to articulate that stories have characters, but try to read them a story without any characters. They would notice! Children who have had experiences with stories can predict events or resolution attempts in stories. Many teachers will stop at critical places in a story and ask chil-dren to hypothesize about potential upcoming events.

But children who have not had frequent encounters with expository texts do not have an automatic response mechanism for anticipating or predicting when reading or listening to science or social studies informa-tion. If children have had experiences with story structures only, just imagine how confused they might become with a passage dealing with volcanoes. They might be several paragraphs into the passage before they realize that there is no plot being developed nor any characters appearing. In that space of time, they have probably missed some very important concepts. These children may well not know that a descrip-tive passage about volcanoes requires that they be able to group the in-formation in the passage into categories. If they are not able to group the characteristics, then it is unlikely that they will be able to recall the important information from the text.

When the teacher gives children an information text written in a cause-effect format, they would not necessarily realize that the effect part was missing. They would have great difficulty if the teacher were to stop reading a science experiment and ask, "What do you think will happen?" Because they may not have put the pieces together in a logical way in order to be able to draw a verifiable conclusion.

Our point, of course, is that children can be taught these structures which occur in expository texts, but that they have not had enough ex-periences with those structures so that they are naturally understood. What if a parent were never to read a story to the child, but always read informational trade books and sections from children's encyclopedias? How well would that child be prepared to deal with the initial reading demands that school imposes? We hypothesize that such a child would be ill prepared since the child would not have a story sense; the child would not realize that characters encounter obstacles which they must seek to resolve. By the same token, children who come to school with no or only limited experiences with expository structures are quite likely to have difficulty when they are required to use those structures to learn new information.

Of course, reading to children from a variety of materials will go a long way toward helping to prepare them for the varied reading demands they will meet in school. Another way to encourage the development of internal expository text structures is for adults who are using them with children to use the same techniques with those structures which they would use with stories. Ask children to predict and to anticipate. Expect them to be able to recount sequences in a process. Encourage them to be able to cite evidence for a particular point of view or to use the text information to support conclusions drawn.

Content-area language experience lessons help children to transfer their knowledge of expository text structures to a new piece of writing, and, in the process, reinforce those structures in the mind. Content-area language experience encourages an objective, factual, third-person account of information. The teacher can provide good models of informative expository materials which are not boring by turning to many of the informational trade books available in the library.

Some children, of course, come to school without an understanding of story structures. The classroom teacher then has a responsibility to help develop that story sense in children as well as to familiarize them with expository text structures. Frequent reading to children from a variety of materials, sending books home with the children for parents to read to them, and letting children listen to tape recorded books are all ways to encourage reading and to develop familiarity with various text structures.

THE ROLE OF PARENTS IN THE READINESS AND BEGINNING READING PHASE

Parents of children who are at the readiness and beginning reading stages are among the most interested parents in a school system. They are eager for their children to do well and want to be involved in that success. It may be a real temptation for them to purchase workbooks at the discount store and sit the children down with those books and try to teach them to read. The dangers inherent in such instruction are not readily apparent to parents, but they should be considered. Parents may attempt to teach reading skills to children in the way they themselves had been taught, which probably was with isolated skill instruction rather than in the context of printed matter as we have been suggesting. Such isolated skills work will probably be difficult for most children to accomplish and will be frustrating for both the parents and the children. Clay (1979) suggests that parents not engage in specific home teaching because the frustrations encountered could do damage to the goal of producing good readers. If parents would confine their activities to the ones put forth in this chapter and others along these lines, the goals of both home and school would be accomplished.

In this chapter we stated that one of the major roles for parents was providing children with many and varied experiences with reading materials. Another, and even more important role for parents, is one they assume naturally. Language expansion is a necessity for communication. When adults deal with children, they often find it necessary to enlarge the utterances of the children. If Mickey says, "cookie," Aunt Pam can tell from the intonation as well as the content of the word what Mickey is actually saying, and so expands the word to, "You want a cookie." This expansion models syntax for the child as well as reinforcing vocabulary which may be necessary for understanding. For example, if Mickey says, "car," Aunt Pam may expand that to, "You want to drive your car?" demonstrating understanding of the idea he was trying to express as well as introducing a word the child may not yet be using (but one he does understand). This idea doesn't have to be taught to parents; they happen onto it in order to survive daily with their children. Parents realize that they wouldn't be doing a favor for the child or themselves if they permitted him or her to remain at the one-word utterance stage. It is a natural response of adults to help children translate their language into sentence form.

This language expansion continues with children, probably for as long as they live at home. Even parents of adult children may be tempted to help them formulate their thoughts and to express those thoughts. Teachers should be encouraging parents in those activities which will stimulate language growth and development.

WHEN DOES READINESS END AND BEGINNING READING BEGIN?

That is indeed a good question, and you have probably already anticipated our answer. There is no one point at which you can look at a child and say, "Ah ha! He is now at the beginning-to-read stage." There is far too much overlap among the learnings. So while we can identify a child who is reading from one who is not, we cannot pick the exact point at which that reading happened. We know that acquisition of the seven reading ingredients facilitates the reading process. We know that children need to be able to attend to a task for a period of time and to be able to listen and learn through listening. But as to when it miraculously converts to reading. . . .

The best readiness and beginning reading program is one in which children and teachers are interacting with and about a variety of printed materials. Many programs which purport to be readiness materials are actually much more limited than we would advocate. We see reading happening with heterogenous groups so that those who are less ready have more advanced stages modeled for them by others within their group. Also, with the kinds of activities we advocate, such as language experience, all of the children in the group can learn what they are ready to learn from the same lesson. It is true that the kinds of learnings we feel are crucial for children at the readiness and beginning reading phases are not too "packageable." It would be impossible to buy a program which would provide the kind of instruction we have recommended in this chapter. This kind of instruction relies heavily on the children, their language, and their interactions. A good teacher will be alert to all these factors and weave them together with the seven readiness ingredients to produce a classroom of children who are indeed ready for reading instruction and who *will* become good readers.

2 | Word Identification

What do you do to identify words as you are reading? Your response to that question would probably be something like, "I don't do anything. I just know them!" For the average adult reader, almost all words encountered in reading are recognized immediately. You don't know how you recognize them and can't explain the process any better than you can explain how you recognize and associate names with most of the people you know. When you first met most of the people you now know well, you were probably introduced to them and told their names. If you have a poor memory for names, you probably didn't immediately identify the person's name at a second meeting, and had to be told the name again, or had to think for several seconds about where you had met the person. From remembering the particular experience, perhaps you could then dredge up the name from the deep, dark recesses of your memory. After several such encounters, however, you do learn a person's name well enough so that when you meet you identify that person effortlessly. You don't have to be told the name again and again or go through any intervening process to figure it out; you just know it! So it is with words. In our first encounter with a word, we are usually either introduced to it and told its name or we figure it out using context or letter-sound clues. After several encounters with a word, during which we might have to be told the word again or use some mediation device to remember it, the word becomes like a good friend: we just know it. In reading, a word immediately and effortlessly recognized in all contexts is called a *sight word*. For fluent readers, almost all words encountered in reading are sight words. The words which are not sight words are those we seldom or never encounter in our reading.

What do you do when you are reading and come to a word you don't immediately recognize or for which you don't have an appropriate meaning? If you are a good reader, you probably skip that word and continue reading until you finish that sentence and perhaps a few more. The clues contained in the words preceding and following the unknown words often allow you to identify the unfamiliar-in-print word or to fill in the meaning for an unknown word. While the identification of meaning for an unfamiliar word is not the focus of this chapter, an example should help to clarify how the context—surrounding words—often pro-

31

vides meaning for an unfamiliar word. A student who didn't have a clear meaning for *translucent* could probably figure out a meaning when reading, *The new frosted window pane was translucent. Light could pass through but you couldn't see through it.* The ability to use context clues to figure out meanings for unfamiliar words is crucial to reading comprehension and a strategy for teaching this skill is described in Chapter 13 [see pp. 427–428].

Context can also be used to identify a word you would recognize in its spoken form but are unable to decode in its written form. In this sentence several _____ have been left _____, but most readers will have _____ difficulty in filling in these words because the _____ words provide clues to the identification _____ the missing words. The previous sentence may be completed in several ways. Add the clue of word length (In this sentence, several _____ have been left _____, but most readers will have _____ difficulty in filling in these words because the _____ words provide clues to the identification ___ the missing words.), and the missing words become more predictable. Add first-letter clues to length (In this sentence, several w_____ have been left o___, but most readers will have l_____ difficulty in filling in these words because the r_____ words provide clues to the identification o__ the missing words.), and most readers would be able to read without difficulty the sentence: In this sentence, several words have been left out, but most readers will have little difficulty in filling in these words because the remaining words provide clues to the identification of the missing words. Because of the redundancy involved in any language, it is not necessary to be able to identify all words immediately and effortlessly in order to read with comprehension. As long as almost all of the words can be identified accurately and quickly, the use of context clues, word length, and first-letter clues to identify a few words that are unfamiliar in print will not disrupt fluent reading.

There are, however, some words which are not sight words and which cannot be identified by using context, word length, and beginning-letter clues. When this happens, the good reader further analyzes the letters in the word and applies additional letter-sound knowledge to figure out the word. Using letter-sound knowledge is generally referred to as *phonics* and the figuring out process is generally called *decoding*.

We now have a picture of our good reader moving rapidly through a book, magazine, newspaper, or other text and simultaneously recognizing most words immediately while applying context, word length, and letter-sound clues to mediate the identification of words not immediately recognized. This feat is astonishing enough without considering that as this word identification is happening, meaning identification (comprehension) and critical/creative response is also occurring. You now have some notion of what a complex process (we all take for granted) the ability to read is.

In teaching children to read, we try to teach them in such a way that their early attempts at reading are as similar as possible to the way good readers read. Because we know that good readers recognize most words immediately, we teach beginning readers many common words as sight words so that they, too, can immediately recognize many words. The mediated word identification skills, figuring out words using context and letter-sound relationships, are taught and practiced as tools to use when words are not immediately recognized. Because good readers perform the different processes of word identification as they are comprehending and reacting to what they read, we teach and practice word identification skills in the context of real reading so that beginners will, from the onset of reading instruction, integrate word identification and meaning identification.

In this chapter, a program of word identification instruction will be outlined which takes children from the point where they cannot identify any words to the point where they can recognize immediately or use context and letter-sound clues to mediate the identification of any word they encounter. Children will be taught to identify words in the context of real reading and will be asked to constantly pay attention to meaning and to use meaning as a check on whether or not they have correctly identified the words. The child who reads the sentence, "The dog bit the boy," as, "The dog bet the boy," is using word identification skills in isolation from meaning identification. The good reader has a constant internal checking system—"Is this making sense? If not, I have done something wrong. I had better look again at some of these words."—and uses words to identify meaning and meaning to identify and check the identification of words! The program outlined in this chapter will attempt to help children focus on word identification without losing sight of what reading is all about—meaning identification.

There are many different ways of teaching beginning reading. Some teachers use language experience or individualized reading as approaches to beginning reading. Most teachers use one of the published basal reading systems. Different teachers and different programs have varied sequences and put different emphasis on the word identification components of sight words, context, and letter-sound relationships. In order to show you, the reader, how word identification can be taught rather than tell you about teaching word identification, we have chosen to give a possible outline of the content and sequence of a complete word identification program. This outline was not, unlike the tablets of Moses, divinely written. Rather, it is a model. It is hoped that as you read through the four phases, an understanding of how word identification growth toward independence can be systematically nourished and developed. You will then be better able to teach and adapt any scope and sequence of word identification instruction to the needs of specific groups of children. In our model the learning goals and activities in each phase are discussed as if all children in the group will be ready for all goals at the same time and will successfully and simultaneously learn all skills in a phase and then move smoothly on to the next phase. Anyone who has ever worked with children knows this euphoric state of events will never be achieved. For convenience and economy of presentation, the goals are assumed to be taught, practiced, reviewed, and learned. In reality, teachers will find that some children already know what is to be taught, some children are not ready to learn it, and some children will never learn some parts of the process. By imagining a group of beginners moving through the phases toward independent word identification, however, you should gain an understanding of what an integrated word identification program involves and how it can be taught. In later chapters, you will see how programs and expectations can be modified to suit individual learners.

Figure 2.1   Word Identification—One Possible Sequence of Instruction

Phrase One:*
  Accurate and immediate identification of 25 to 30 concrete sight words
  Auditory and visual discrimination of rhyming words
  Use of context to identify unknown words
Phase Two:*
  Accurate and immediate identification of the most frequently occurring 150 words
  Letter-sound associations for initial consonants and digraphs
  Use of context and initial consonant/digraph letter-sound relationships to decode unknown words
  Use of initial consonant/digraph letter-sound relationships to decode words which rhyme with known sight words
  Ability to read known words with *s, ed*, or *ing* ending
Phase Three:*
  Accurate and immediate identification of the second most frequently occurring 150 words (for a total of 300)
  Letter-sound associations for initial blends
  Use of context and initial blend letter-sound relationships to decode unknown words
  Use of initial blend letter-sound relationships to decode words which rhyme with known words
  Letter-sound associations for *final* consonants, digraphs, and blends, and use of context plus these associations to decode unknown words
  Letter-sound associations for vowel and vowel combinations
Phase Four:*
  Accurate and immediate identification of the remaining 132 most frequently occurring words (for a total of 432)
  Ability to decode compound words
  Ability to decode two-syllable words
  Ability to decode polysyllabic words

* Goals within phases would be worked on simultaneously.

Because most teachers use one of the published basal reading systems, it is important for you to know that every one of these series will have its own scope and sequence of words and word identification skills. These scopes and sequences will differ from each other and from the one we present here in both minor and major ways. Fortunately, most basal reading series teach word identification in a manner that is generally compatible with the view we present here. If you look ahead to teaching reading with one of these series, this chapter can be of use to you in several ways. First, our approach can be used to provide additional or alternate means for teaching words and skills in the order they are presented in the basal series. In this case, you would ignore our order and would only use our suggestions in those cases when the suggestions in the basal teachers' manual seem insufficient or inadequate. Second, our approach could be used as is to supplement the basal program. You will find that it is not unusual for schools to use a supplementary word identification program along with a basal series. In this case, both our word identification program and that of the basal reading series would be followed, giving the students two different routes to learning word identification. Third, our approach could be used as is to supplant the word identification strand of the basal program. The basal program would be used but the word identification activities would not. Instead our approach would be taught separately from the basal. Fourth, our approach can be used as a model to teach the words and word identification skills presented in the basal. In this case, our order would be followed as far as the four phases are concerned, but what words and skills are taught and in what order *within* each phase would be determined by the basal series. Since the first and fourth uses of this chapter would require some modification by you, we have included some boxed activities periodically to enable you to make some of these modifications.

PHASE ONE

We will assume that our beginning readers have had some experiences with reading and writing and that through these experiences, they have mastered the crucial readiness skills. They know what reading is for and what it feels, looks, and sounds like when it is happening. They understand the conventions of print such as left-to-right, top-to-bottom orientation and are beginning to understand some basic jargon such as *letter, word*, and *sentence*. Their listening comprehension, while still in need of much development, is adequate to understand the simple stories common to most beginning reading programs. They can "read" some simple stories which they have memorized through their language experience lessons and/or through repeated listening to favorite books. It is now appropriate to begin to focus on teaching the children some sight

words and some word mediation skills. Phase One has three major goals
for the students to accomplish:

1. Accurate and immediate identification of 25 to 30 concrete sight
   words
2. Auditory and visual discrimination of rhyming words
3. Use of context to identify unknown words

Concrete Sight Words

In learning to identify a printed word, there are two distinct steps.
Almost all beginning readers know there is such a thing as cookies. To
learn to read the word *cookies*, they have mastered the first step. This
first step involves knowing there is such a thing as the word represents
and having a general idea of the meaning and/or function of the word.
The second step is the recognition that this printed word, *cookies*, stands
for that already known word. Most beginning readers use the word
what, but neither know it as a separate word nor know its meaning/func-
tion. If this seems improbable, consider the following ways in which the
typical young child uses the word *what*: "What's that?" "Whatcha
doing?" "Whatcha want?" In order to learn to read words such as *what,
of, this*, and *for*, children must not only learn that the written symbol
stands for the word, they must learn that the word exists, and they must
have an intuitive notion of its meaning/function. Consequently, these
function words, which occur very frequently in reading and writing, and
thus are important to learn, are very difficult for most young children to
learn to read, because they must first learn what the words in their
spoken form are, and then learn to associate that with the written
symbol.

On the other hand, words such as *cookies, monster, car, truck, jump,
blue, happy*, and *angry* have meaning for almost all young children.
The term *concrete words* will be used here to mean words which are
"real" to children. Many of these are objects, but actions, colors, and
feelings are also real and thus concrete to most children. These words,
because they are real and interesting to children, are relatively easy to
learn (Harris & Sipay, 1980). The words may be selected from language
experience stories or from those concrete words which will occur in their
preprimers. Children should also learn their own names and the names
of brothers, sisters, friends, and classmates.

To begin a class store of known concrete words, you may want to use
the "Words on the Wall" strategy to help children learn to immediately
recognize these words. To do this, select five words you want the children to learn and write them with a permanent marker on scraps of construction paper. (This is ecologically and economically sound, and seeing
the words on different shapes and colors helps children to remember
which is which.) Show the words to the children and have them pro-

nounce them and make several sentences with them. If the words are picturable, add or draw a small picture as a further aid to memory. Next, place the words where all the children can see them. Many teachers use the wall above the chalkboard (thus the name, Words on the Wall), but you can use a bulletin board or attach them to strings suspended from movable ceiling tiles. How and where you put them is important only in that you put them where they can stay permanently, where children can see them, and where they can be arranged alphabetically by first letter. (Eventually, you will have 100 to 200 words on your wall vocabulary and you will want children to be able to find them easily!) So, if the first five words you are putting on the wall above your chalkboard are *boy, girl, blue, monster*, and *snake; boy* and *blue* would be above the left side of the board, leaving space for the addition of some words beginning with the letter *a. Girl* would be about one-third of the way down. *Monster* would be in the middle and *snake* would be two-thirds of the way to the right edge.

Once you have the words placed on the wall, ask children to number a sheet of paper for a "spelling test." Then call out the five words, putting each in a sentence. (All children should do well on this test since they can find the words and write down the correct letters. This sense of success is very satisfying to young children and, believe it or not, their spelling test will become one of their favorite activities. One first-grade class often chose a spelling test as their "fun indoor activity" when it rained and they couldn't go outside!) When all five words have been written, have one child point to the words with a pointer or meterstick and have children correct their own tests or exchange papers and check.

Each day, at a regular time, call out the five words and have the children write and check them. By the end of the week, children will be much faster at finding and writing the words. Some of the brighter children will have learned to spell the words. It is now time to add five more words to the wall. Most teachers add new words on Monday. On the day words are added, these five new words are the ones used for the spelling test. During the rest of the week, however, any five words from the wall can be called. Words with which children need much practice can be called out almost every day.

For holidays and other special times, teachers usually add special words to the wall vocabulary. *Pumpkin, ghost, witch, cat*, and *candy*, with appropriate pictures, liven up the wall as the end of October approaches. If it snows for the first time on Monday, forget about the words you had planned to add and add *snow, snowball, snowman, sled*, and *boots* to your wall.

In addition to helping children learn to read sight words, the wall vocabulary is a great help when children are writing. Most first graders love to write but it is difficult to write if you can't spell words like *of, was*, and *one*. Having them "spell them the way they sound" is not a very good idea for these common words because, as you remember, many of the most frequent words are not spelled the way they sound. Children who do spell them the way they sound practice them wrong and often stay confused about how to spell them. With a wall vocabulary of the most common words, children know where to find them when they need to write them and thus practice them correctly. Some children will even learn to spell these words, an ability not usually acquired by even the brightest first graders. In addition to helping with writing and spelling, the wall vocabulary can be a source of words to use as a jumping off point for teaching letter-sound generalizations. In fact, during the rest of this chapter, we will assume that the classroom has a wall vocabulary consisting of the 30 concrete words and some of the most common words and will demonstrate how to use this to build initial consonant letter-sound relationships.

Having a cigar box or other container in which each child is to keep cards with the concrete words learned gives children a sense of growth and accomplishment. Often, children find or draw pictures on the reverse side of the card which illustrate the word printed on the other side. Children can play riddle games and sorting games with these cards. Often children like to practice writing or typing their "picture words" and this helps them make the association between the known word and the printed symbol. Most teachers do not find it difficult to help children build a store of known concrete words. Which words to include in this store will be determined by considering the experiences and interests of the children and the instructional demands of the beginning reading program. For purposes of showing how word identification skills are developed, we will assume our beginning readers have learned to immediately and accurately identify these 30 words:

Concrete Sight Words

boy	girl	monster	Spiderman	big
people	window	man	money	cat
bat	milk	elephant	baby	red
blue	dog	hat	children	jump
walk	ball	hamburger	fly	fish
green	little	snow	house	snake

ADD TO YOUR SURVIVAL KIT

Select a basal reading series that you now use in teaching reading or one that you are likely to use (we will refer to this series as *your* reading series). Remember our definition of a concrete word. Make a list of the concrete words introduced in the preprimers of your reading series. Consider how you could use that list instead of the list above during Phase One of teaching word identification.

Rhyming Words

One of the most predictable features of the letter-sound relationships in English is that most words which end with the same letter patterns rhyme. Once children know what *to rhyme* means, they are ready to learn to discriminate by listening to hear if two words rhyme. Children might make an every-pupil-response card by drawing a happy face on one side of a sheet of paper and a sad face on the other side. The teacher says pairs of words "trying to make them rhyme." If the teacher is successful in making a rhyming pair, the children hold up their happy face. The sad face is displayed if the teacher fails to make the words rhyme and needs to try again. The first nonrhyming pairs presented to children should be very different. It is difficult, at first, to hear that *cup* and *map* do not rhyme, but it is easy to get the idea with pairs such as *cup/Wisconsin* and *bird/party*. Gradually, the teacher should introduce nonrhyming pairs which are closer in sound. Children may also want to give pairs and let the other children respond with happy or sad faces. While working with auditory discrimination of rhyming words, it is better *not* to have the children looking at the words or to try to simultaneously teach visual discrimination. All rhyming pairs, even those such as *meet/eat* and *rain/plane* which are not spelled alike at the end should be accepted. Children are ready to learn that many words which look alike at the end rhyme when they can correctly and consistently respond to spoken pairs of rhyming and nonrhyming words.

ADD TO YOUR SURVIVAL KIT

There are many games and fun activities which you can use with children to develop auditory discrimination of rhyming words. Add five of these to your survival kit. If you find them in magazines or books, be sure to include the source. If you are creative and make up some of your own, give yourself credit for the brainstorm.

Once children have achieved auditory discrimination of rhyming words, they should be lead to notice that words which end with the same letters usually rhyme. They can learn this principle inductively by observing the known concrete words *cat, bat*, and *hat*. The words should be placed under one another on the board and the children, after reading them, should be asked to listen and to decide if the words rhyme. (They will, of course, quickly decide that these words rhyme since this prerequisite auditory discrimination ability has been firmly established!) The teacher will then direct the children's attention to the last two letters in each word and help the children observe that the words end with the same two letters. Next the teacher might write the known word *red* and under it the unknown word *bed*. She would pronounce these words and the children would decide that the words rhymed. They would then observe that the words ended with the same two letters. Now, the teacher might put the words *red* and *cantaloupe* on the board and ask the children if they are "just the same in the middle and end." Based on the children's response that the words were different in the middle and end, the teacher would ask the children to guess "whether or not this strange word (*cantaloupe*) is going to rhyme with the word *red*." After many lessons of this kind in which children make observations about the middle and ending letters of words and then guess if the words would rhyme when spoken and, conversely, make observations about whether or not spoken words rhyme and then guess whether or not they would look alike at the middle and end, children should conclude that "often words which look alike in the middle and end rhyme."* The lessons just described were examples of inductive teaching. When you teach inductively, you show examples and ask questions in such a way that the learners will induct the principle which the examples illustrate. Inductive teaching helps youngsters to use what they know as a basis for generalization. You will see many more examples of inductive lessons throughout this book.

Context

You will remember from the introduction that when a good reader comes to an unknown word, the first line of attack is to skip that word and continue reading. If enough of the other words are known, the word can often be figured out. Since the use of context—surrounding words and sentences—is a word identification skill used by good readers, its use should be taught to and practiced by young readers (Artley, 1977; Heilman, 1981). Exercises in which children are shown a sentence in which one word is covered and are asked to guess what the covered word is demonstrate to children that you can make guesses, that often several words are possible, and that the guesses must fit semantically (meaning) and syntactically (sentence structure) (Goodman, 1967). Here is a sample context lesson:

> Children are shown this sentence written on a sentence strip or on a transparency. The blocked-out word is taped over. The teacher reads the sentence and says "blank" for the covered word:

* While it is true that most words which share middle and ending letters rhyme, it is not true that most rhyming words share middle and ending letters. The words *train, plane,* and *reign* rhyme but do not share middle and ending letters. Since there are numerous ways to spell a particular sound pattern, the teacher (NOT the children) should come up with the rhyming examples and the teacher should be alert that the principle being taught is that many words which share a middle and end rhyme, NOT that words which rhyme are spelled alike.

Joey rode to school in his father's ███ .

Children guess at the covered word. All acceptable guesses are recorded on the board. (Unacceptable guesses are discussed and the reason they are unacceptable are clarified. *Horse* would not be acceptable since while you might conceivably ride to school *on* a horse, it is not likely you would ride to school *in* a horse.) These guesses might include: *car, truck, bus, van, jeep,* and *Cadillac*. When all reasonable guesses have been listed, the taped-over word is revealed and the children visually match their guesses with the word, deciding which of their guesses was the actual word. (It is possible that the taped-over word may not have been among the guesses but this is unlikely if the teacher has selected words common to the experience of the children. If this should happen, the children would note that sometimes you just don't guess correctly even when your guesses fit the sentence.)

Along with examples in which there are a limited number of possibilities, examples in which there are only one or two possibilities should be included: "Billy went to school ███ his brother." "I got a new bike ███ my Grandmother." "███ did you put my sweater?" These function words which do not have meaning in and of themselves but show the relationships between concept words are often examples of only one word which fits the sentence. Because the function words are difficult for many children to learn to read, it is particularly important for the children to realize that, in some cases, you can say "blank" and have only one reasonable guess about what will fit in the sentence. Being able to often guess them correctly from the context of the other words will make up, to some extent, for the difficulty children experience in learning to immediately recognize these important and ever-present words. The ability to make reasoned guesses about unknown words is an important reading skill and children should practice it and see its usefulness from the beginning. In later phases, children will learn how to combine their "it makes sense" notion with their knowledge of letter-sound relationships to further narrow the range of possible guesses.

FIND A CHILD

Get permission to work with a first grader who is being taught to read in a basal reading series. Use sentences from the book that student is currently reading to teach the use of context in the manner just described.

PHASE TWO

Now that our beginning readers have a store of some concrete sight words, can auditorially discriminate rhyming words, know that words which share middle and ending letters often rhyme, and can make reasonable guesses at unknown words based on the context of the other words, they are ready to move into Phase Two. Phase Two has five major goals:

1. Accurate and immediate identification of the most frequently occurring 150 words
2. Letter-sound associations for initial consonants and digraphs
3. Use of context plus initial consonant/digraph letter-sound relationships to decode unknown words
4. Use of initial consonant/digraph letter-sound relationships to decode words which rhyme with known sight words
5. Ability to read known words with *s, ed*, or *ing* ending

It is important to note here that all goals within a phase are worked on simultaneously. Phase Two will take a long time since there are many difficult words to be learned and many initial consonant and digraph letter-sound relationships to be learned and applied to the identification of unknown words. At the end of Phase Two, however, children will have achieved a great deal of independence in word identification and should be able to read most books written at the preprimer and primer levels.

150 Most Common Sight Words

Which words would you guess occur most frequently in English? If you immediately thought of words such as *the, a, and, to, you*, and *on* you know that there are some words without which it is impossible to write a sentence, much less a paragraph. It is logical that if children are to become independent readers, they should immediately and automatically recognize these common words (Dolch, 1948). In addition to the fact that these words are the most common, there is another reason why these words are often taught to children as words to recognize immediately rather than words to figure out based on letter-sound relationships. In words such as *cat, take, mark*, and *Bob*, there are predictable relationships between the letters and the sounds. (A simple way to decide if words are regular is to ask yourself if other words which share the same middle and ending would rhyme with them. Thus *cat* can be considered regular since *at, mat, that, bat* and many other words ending in *at* rhyme with *cat*.)

Now look again at the common words *the, a, and, to*, and *you*. Which of these words can be considered regular words? Well, *the* does not rhyme with words that end like it such as *be, me, she,* and *he. A* does not rhyme with *Ma* and *Pa. To* does not rhyme with *go* and *no.* There are no words which end like *you.* The only word which can be considered regular is *and* (*band, sand, land*). It is unfortunate but true that the *most* common words are the *least* regular. This fact is not part of a devious plot to confuse young readers but rather occurred because the pronunciations of words change as they are used. The words most frequently used are the most changed from the time the spelling system was standardized. Thus, there are two good reasons to teach the most common words as words to be recognized immediately rather than as words to be figured out. Because these words occur so often, readers should not have to stop and decode them, often losing their "train of thought" in the process. Many of the most common words are not regular and thus cannot be figured out.

How do you decide which words are the most common? There have been several studies to discover which words were most common in material to be read by children and adults. For many years, the Dolch list of 220 words was considered the standard list. This list, however, was based on a count of frequently occurring words in basal readers in use 40 to 50 years ago and thus does not necessarily reflect current basal readers. For this textbook, we will use the A and P Sight Word List (Otto & Chester, 1972) to determine the most common words. This list was based on a computerized study of material read by children and is more current and comprehensive than some other lists. The A and P Sight Word List originally contained 500 words. We have eliminated numerals, proper names, and inflected variants of already included words to come up with a list of 432 frequent words. The most common 150 words (in order of frequency) are listed on page 44.

ADD TO YOUR SURVIVAL KIT

Instead of using the first 150 words from the A and P Sight Word List, make a list of the first 150 words introduced in your reading series. Compare the two lists.

While, by the end of Phase Two, children should know as sight words all 150 words, the words do not have to be taught in the order presented here. In fact, it is best to teach the words as they occur in the classroom. Language experience stories, for example, are a good source of sight words. Imagine that children have dictated and can read the story:

Bobby had a birthday.
He is now six years old.
His mother bought cupcakes for everyone.
We all were glad Bobby had a birthday.

The Most Common 150 Words (in order of frequency)

the	one	them	time	me	only
a	this	write	more	went	old
to	all	their	down	put	away
and	had	about	my	around	children
of	from	by	no	new	help
in	be	like	go	know	why
you	can	see	get	come	work
is	but	so	now	who	through
he	there	if	long	its	here
it	not	these	find	came	place
that	when	make	look	right	before
was	how	into	made	air	three
on	were	him	just	sound	home
for	your	other	big	think	house
are	do	word	very	tell	again
they	each	would	back	after	another
I	will	water	first	Mr.	number
with	up	little	way	man	our
his	many	two	over	may	must
said	we	has	too	much	off
at	then	did	than	does	name
as	her	people	good	say	mother
have	or	an	use	same	asked
she	out	which	day	been	picture
what	some	could	where	take	most

In this story, the words *had, a, he, is, his, for, we,* and *were* are on the 150 most frequent words list. Because the children have experienced Bobby's birthday, dictated the story, and memorized the reading of it, the function words, *had, a, is,* etc. become real to the children. The teacher can now have the children make cards for some or all of these words. These cards can be put in a word bank and used for many activities including sentence making. Now, it is hard (if not impossible) to make a sentence with just the italicized words listed here, but you will remember that your beginning readers know 30 concrete words. They should also have these words on cards and can combine words to make such sentences as:

A boy had a red ball.
He is a big boy.

Children should also have cards with their names and the names of relatives, friends, and classmates. Thus, sentences such as these can be made:

Bobby is a big boy.
Carol had money for a hamburger.
His money is for Grandma.

Of course, you will want to add the words from the 150 most common words list to your Words on the Wall. Be sure that when you add easily confused words, such as *want* and *went*, that these words are written on different colors and shapes of your scrap construction paper. Some of these 150 most common words are picturable, so you may want to draw or add a picture to help children find and remember the word as you did when you were adding concrete words.

The ways of helping children meaningfully review and practice sight words are numerous. One obvious way, often forgotten, is to send the children on word searches in books, magazines, and newspapers. The most frequent words are ubiquitous and children can cut and paste to make a collage of a word. A collage of the word *the* cut from various advertisements will help children see it in all different sizes, colors, and type faces and will propel children toward the sight word goal of being able to recognize it immediately and effortlessly anywhere!

Children should also read stories in which the words being taught occur. These can be language experience stories, simple stories written by the teacher, or preprimers and easy-to-read books. Children who only know a few words can read silently to look for these words, underline them lightly in pencil, and then, as the teacher reads the story, chime in on their underlined words. Many teachers have young children do imitative reading [see Chapter 11, pages 327–373] in which children listen/read along with the taped reading of an easy-to-read book until they can read the whole book independently. The common words will, of course, occur in these easy-to-read books and children get practice reading them in the context of real books.

There are some words which always present particular problems for children, especially slow readers. These words (*what, want, went, with, this, that*, and *they*, for example) are particularly difficult for children to learn because they are confused about the "knowing that the word exists and what it means/does" step and because the words look a lot like other words about which they are equally confused. For these words, a "drastic strategy" is needed. This drastic strategy (Cunningham, 1980) should be used in combination with other activities suggested in this chapter. The steps in the drastic strategy are:

STEP 1. Write the word you wish to teach on a card for each child in the group. Then, tell a story which uses the word many times. Since your chosen word is a common function word it occurs again and again in speech and it should not be difficult to spontaneously create a story in which it is used many times. Children tend to enjoy these stories most and become involved if the stories include each of them as characters. For the four-letter word *what*, for example, you might construct the following story:

> Last Saturday morning I woke up early. "*What* time is it?" I wondered as I looked at the clock. "*What*! It is already nine o'clock. I wonder *what* made me sleep so late? *What* am I going to do today?" I wondered. "The wonderful thing about Saturday morning is that it is the only morning of the week when I can get up and decide *what* I want to do. I know *what* I will do," I decided. "I will go into town and see *what* is going on at the street fair." Quickly I got up and got dressed. I had no trouble deciding *what* to wear. On Saturday I always wore my jeans. I got on my bike, and as I was riding into town, I saw Billy, Tom, and Joe. "*What* are they doing here?" I wondered. "I thought they were going to the baseball game this morning. I wonder *what* happened to that game?"

Tell the listeners to hold up their *what* cards every time they hear the word *what* as the story is told. Pause as you come to the word so the students can determine that it is a separate word, and during the course of the story can learn how it functions to connect the other words.

STEP 2. Step 2 is similar to Step 1, except that the children make up the story. Each child has a chance to make up a story in which the word *what* is used as many times as possible. Each time the word *what* is used, the other children hold up their *what* cards.

STEP 3. Now that the children are aware of the word as a separate entity and aware of its function in language, they can begin to try to associate the printed symbol with that spoken word. In Step 3, go around to each of the children in turn, and after having alerted them to take a good look at their word *what* so that they can make it again, cut each word into letters, hand the separate letters to each child, and instruct each of them to arrange their letters to make the word *what*. When you get back to the first child, loook at what the child has accomplished. If the child has correctly rearranged the letters to make the word, mix the letters up again and instruct the child to make the word *what* a second time.

Often, however, some children will not be able to make the word *what* correctly. One child may put all the letters in just a random order. If this occurs, put the letters in the correct order, tell the child to look at them closely and try to remember which letter comes first, second, third and then last, and, after giving the child a few seconds to look at the word spelled correctly, mix up the letters and ask the child to make the word *what*. Some children may put all the letters in the right order but put some upside down or backward. Remind these children that letters often become something else when turned upside down or backward. A *W*, for example, can become an *M*. A *d* can become a *p*. Arrange the letters going in the proper direction and ask the child to study them. Once again mix up the letters and ask the child to make the word *what*. Occasionally, a child will make the word *what* and spell it *t a h w*. This child is probably not dyslexic! In fact, what has happened is quite simple and predictable. The child probably began at the right side of the desk or table and then put the letters in the right order but arranged them going from right to left. If this occurs, put a mark, a piece of tape, or an object on the left corner of the desk and remind the child that when we make words, we start on the left side and go to the right side. Ask the child to begin where the visible marker has been placed and then make the word going in that direction. In other words, go around to each child. If the child has arranged the letters to form the word *what* correctly, say, "Good," mix the letters up, and say, "Do it again." If the child has not done it correctly, give the child information about what has been done incorrectly, let the child study the correct form again, and then mix the letters up and ask the child to try again.

The goal in this step is to have each child arrange the letters of the word correctly at least three times. When this step is finished, children should put their letters in an envelope reserved for this purpose. Write the word on the outside of the envelopes and save them. In time, each child will have an envelope on which is written all the four-letter words they have worked on so far and in which can be found all of the letters needed to reconstruct these words. This becomes a valuable seat-work activity.

STEP 4. Write the word on the board. Ask each child to look closely at the word and try to take a picture of that word in the same way that a camera takes a picture. Instruct the children to close their eyes and see if they can see the word *what*. Have them open their eyes, look at the word *what*, and see if this is what they did indeed see when they had their eyes closed (Horn, 1919). Repeat this "close-your-eyes/open-your-eyes" procedure several times. Next, have the children take a sheet of scrap paper, erase the word from the board, and ask them to write the word *what* without looking at it. When each child has tried to write the word *what*, write the word *what* again on the board. Have each child compare what was written to what was on the board, and give information about what was omitted, turned the wrong way, or put in the wrong place if that information is needed. Have them then fold the papers so that they are not looking at what they wrote the first time, and again, erase the *what* from the board and ask them to write it. Repeat this procedure several times. As in Step 3, the goal is to have each child correctly write the word *what* without looking at it, at least three times.

STEP 5. Now that the children are aware of the existence and function of the word *what* and have had practice connecting the printed symbol with the spoken symbol, the word should be put back into a written context so that children can recognize it when they are actually reading. This can be easily accomplished if you write several sentences on the board which contain the word *what*. Each time the word *what* needs to be written, have a child come to the board and write that word since he or she has now learned to do so.

STEP 6. Give the children mimeographed sheets or, better still, real books which contain a story in which the target word *what* is used many times. Ask the children to look at the first page, or the first paragraph of the story, and underline lightly in pencil every time they see the word *what*. When they have done this, read the story to them, stopping each time you get to the word *what* so that they can read the word.

In the sample lesson described, *what* was assumed to be the first word taught using this drastic strategy. As more words are taught, the previously taught words are constantly reviewed. Sentences can be constructed using the four-letter words and known concrete words. Students can be sent on word hunts, lightly underlining in pencil all the known words in a selected story.

Initial Consonant/Digraph Letter-Sound Associations (*b, c, ch, d, f, g, h, j, k, l, m, n, p, r, s, sh, t, th, v, w, y, z*)

Among the most regular and predictable letter-sound relationships are those between the initial consonant letters and the sounds they represent. The consonants *b, d, f, h, j, k, l, m, n, p, r, v, w, y,* and *z* almost always represent the same sound when they occur as the first letter in a word. The consonants *s, t, g,* and *c* usually represent the same sound unless followed by the letter *h*, in which case the *sh* and *th* digraphs have fairly predictable sounds. *G*, as the first letter in a word, may represent the sound heard at the beginning of *go* and *get* or the sound occurring at the beginning of *Gina* and *giraffe*. *C*, by itself, may represent the sound heard at the beginning of *cat* and *Carl* or the sound heard at the beginning of *city* and *Cindy*. *C* followed by *h* usually represents the sound at the beginning of *chair* and *champion*.

There is no hard and fast rule about which initial consonants should be taught first, but, since the letter-sound generalization will be based on known words, the first associations taught should be those for which students have some known words. It is probably best not to teach similar looking and sounding letters (*b, d; m, n*) as the first ones. Because *s, t, g*, and *c* have more than one predictable sound, they will be taught last.

ADD TO YOUR SURVIVAL KIT

Because it is best to teach initial consonant/digraph letter-sound associations when students know sight words beginning with the association being taught, look through the lowest levels of your reading series to make sure that at least two or three sight words have been taught for each association before it is introduced. Make this search for each of the letter-sound associations in Phase Two. If any association is introduced before sight word exemplars have been taught, develop appropriate sight words to teach to supplement those in your reading series.

Let's assume that children know the words *boy, baby, ball, big*, and *be*, and the words *man, monster, money, my*, and *make*. It would be logical then to teach the predictable, different-looking and -sounding letters *b* and *m* as the first two initial consonants.

Before one can associate a particular letter with a particular sound, one must first be able to hear the sound and discriminate it from other sounds. Often, teachers *assume* that children can hear the difference and begin right in at the association level, trying to get children to identify which words begin with which letters before children can discriminate that sound from other sounds. It is generally felt that it is best not to isolate the sound from words. Because you can't pronounce a consonant by itself, the sound is always distorted when it is isolated: *b* represents the sound heard at the beginning of *boy*; it does not "say *bŭ*." Furthermore, children who are taught to say the isolated sounds (*bŭ ă tŭ*) often have trouble recognizing that as the word *bat*.* In these lessons, the children will learn to discriminate the beginning sounds from other beginning sounds and will learn to associate the sound with the appropriate letter, but neither the teacher nor the child willl say, "*b* says *bŭ*." Rather, children will demonstrate their letter-sound knowledge by identifying the letter(s) with which words begin and naming several words which begin with designated letter(s). To teach children to discriminate the sound represented by the letter *b* at the beginning of words from the sounds represented by other letters, choose one word all the

---

* There are reading programs which do teach children to make the isolated sounds of the letters and blend them back together. These synthetic programs sometimes result in short-term gains and long-term problems and are not recommended by the authors of this textbook.

children know beginning with *b*. If there is a child in the room whose name begins with a *b*, such as *Bobby* or *Billy*, that child should become the model to which the children are matching. (*Brenda* and *Brook*, however, would not be used since they begin with the *br* blend and might confuse children at this point. They will get their turn to be the model later when you teach the *br* blend.) Have each child make an every-pupil-response card on which he or she draws a smiling face on one side and a sad face on the other side. Tell the children that you are going to try to think of words which begin like *Billy*. (If you don't have a child whose name begins with a "pure" *b* sound, use a picture of a common object such as *baby* or *boy*.) If you succeed in thinking of a word which starts like the model, they should hold up their smiling faces; if you don't succeed they should hold up their sad faces.

Then say pairs some of which begin alike (*Billy, button*; *Billy, bag*; *Billy, balloon*) and some of which do not (*Billy, cookie*; *Billy, giraffe*; *Billy, zebra*). In the beginning only use matches which are pure *b* sounds. That is, don't use *blue* or *break* which have a *b* blended with another letter. Also, make your different pairs quite different. *B* and *p* sound more alike than *b* and *m*. Later, these sound-alike pairs will of course be included but in the beginning stages, you want to make the contrasts as clear as possible.

After you have said each pair say, "ready, set, show," at which signal the children will show you their happy or sad faces. (Do not allow children to show them before it is time since, if you do, children who require more think time will just wait and follow the lead of the faster children. Every-pupil-response activities are valuable because each child is actively involved in making a decision each time. If you allow children to "jump the gun," you forfeit the effectiveness of the every-pupil-response technique.) As the children display their sad or happy faces, respond ONLY to the children who have the right response. "Yes, Johnny, *Billy* and *Bertha* begin alike so you held up your happy face" gets the message across as well as, "No, Cathy, you should have held up your happy face since *Billy* and *Bertha* begin alike." In addition, it accentuates the positive. Children want your recognition. If you only give it when they respond correctly, they are more likely to work at responding correctly. Perhaps Johnny held up his happy face by accident and does not really know how to discriminate beginning sounds. Your recognition of his success will suggest to him that he can succeed and he will work harder to succeed.

You should continue with these exercises until almost all children are responding correctly almost all the time. (We say "almost all children" because this is a whole-class or small-group activity and in teaching anything, there will be children who cannot learn it at that time. You may decide to go on to the association level without Johnny's having demonstrated that he can do the discrimination, but you will make a note that Johnny didn't learn the discrimination and thus probably won't learn the association and will need individual or small-group help later.)

Once the children demonstrate that they can hear the difference between words which begin like *Billy* and words which don't, they are ready to learn that most words which begin with the letter *b* like *Billy* also begin with the sound that *Billy* begins with. You will now need your known words *boy, baby, ball, big,* and *be* (*Billy,* too if he is in your class and was the model you used.) Put the words on the board and ask children to notice "if the words look alike in any way." They should notice that the words all begin with the same letter. Next, have them listen, as you read the words, to hear if the words sound alike in any way. They should observe, based on the discrimination practice you have provided, that the words sound alike at the beginning. Based on their observations of the examples provided, the class should generalize that if words begin with the letter *b,* they will probably sound like *boy, baby, ball, big,* and *be* at the beginning and that if words sound like *boy, baby, ball, big,* and *be,* they will probably start with the letter *b.*

Once the children have, with your help, stated this prediction, have them make a new every-pupil-response card. (Collect and save the others for future lessons. Many wonderful teaching strategies have been scrapped because teachers depended on young children to keep up with the necessary materials.) For this every-pupil-response lesson, have them make cards with a *Bb* on one side and a sad face on the other side. You will now say words and at the ready-set-show signal, they will show their *Bb* side if they think it will begin like *boy,* etc. with the letter *b* and their sad side if they think you have not succeeded in coming up with a *b* word. Once they have displayed their cards, write the word on the board and let them decide if they were right or wrong.

Continue with this activity until almost all children, almost all the time, are showing you the *Bb* side when you say a word which begins with the letter *b* and the sad side when you say a word which begins with another letter. Simultaneously, you will want the children to be doing three other things to help them make the association between the letter *b* and the sound usually associated with it at the beginning of words.

Send the children on an object/picture/word hunt for words which begin with *b* and objects or pictures representing objects beginning with the letter *b.* Make suggestions to the children about pictures which they are likely to find beginning with *b: baby, ball, basset, bat, bookcase, bed, bib, bag, bonnet,* and *book* to name just a few. Pictures and words can form a collage bulletin board. The objects can be placed on a table near the bulletin board. Children will now have many tangible things to help them make the association between the letter *b* and its common initial sound.

Not all children learn with pictures and objects, however. Some children are very action and taste oriented. That is easily solved. For each consonant taught, have the children learn an action and eat a commonly liked food. Children who get up and pretend to bounce a ball when they are shown the letter *b*, and who remember that when they were learning the letter *b* they ate bananas, have very powerful letter-sound associations.

When children can name for you words which begin with the letter *b* and correctly decide whether or not a spoken word begins with the letter *b*, it is time to teach the next letter. We will quickly outline some lessons for teaching the letter *m* once the letter *b* has been learned. Of course, children must first learn to discriminate the sound associated with *m* at the beginnings of words from other sounds. This will be accomplished as it was for the letter *b*. Choose known model words. Children will listen and, with their every-pupil-response cards, show happy or sad faces depending on whether or not you have succeeded in saying a word that begins like *Mike* (for example). Once the children are making the discrimination, display the known words *man, monster, money, my, make*, and *Mike* and lead the children to observe that they will begin with the same letter and sound. Children will then listen for words and respond with their *Mm* cards if they think the word will begin like *man, monster*, etc. and with their sad faces if they think the spoken word will begin with some other letter. Simultaneously, the children will go on hunts for *m* objects/pictures/words and an *Mm* bulletin board display will be created. Organize an action, such as marching, to be done as a further association with *m*. Marshmallows might be a great food to eat and thus associate with the letter *m*. As activities to learn the letter *m* are carried out, continually review the letter *b*. Children might listen to the following list of words and respond with their *Mm, Bb*, or sad face cards as appropriate: *mountain, Maggie, building, Jupiter, song, manager, bargain, mouse, bite*, and *carry*.

In this manner, you would teach each of the initial consonants and digraphs (*sh, th, ch*). For each, the children would first learn to discriminate the sound from other sounds. This step should go much more quickly as more sounds are taught but should not be omitted since discrimination is essential for learning the associations (Durkin, 1980). Next, they would learn to associate the sound with the letter by observing known words; hunting objects, pictures, and words; doing an action; and eating a food beginning with that letter. As new letters are introduced, all old letters would be reviewed.

The order in which the letter-sound relationships are taught should be determined by the availability of known words beginning with the letter as well as, while the first few letters are taught, some concern that pairs of letters which look or sound very similar not be taught too early. For some letter-sound relationships, the children may not have learned sight words beginning with those letter-sounds. You will want to teach some words as sight words before introducing the associations. (*Zebra, zoo,* and *Zeb*—if he is in your class—could be taught before the letter *z* is introduced.) Words with the variant pronunciation of *c* and *g* such as *cents, Cindy, city, giraffe, gym,* and *Gina* will need to be taught as sight words before these letter-sound relationships are taught.

While there is much disagreement about when these variant but predictable letter-sound relationships should be taught, it seems logical to leave *s, t, g,* and *c* for the last consonants to be taught. By then children will have developed more facility at learning letter-sound associations and will have a larger store of sight words. Following the sound of *s,* the sound associated with *sh* could be taught. *T* and *th* would be taught in the same way. Next *g* would be taught and students would note from their known words *get, go, Gary, giraffe, gym,* and *Gina* that *g* is a "sneaky" letter and that when they are trying to figure out a word that begins with *g* they should try the sound heard at the beginning of *go* first and if that doesn't result in a word they know, to try the sound heard at the beginning of *giraffe.* Practice might be provided by your writing a sentence and trying the two sounds and letting the children decide which one made a word they knew and made sense in the sentence. Finally the letter *c* should be taught, with its two common pronunciations and the special sound represented by *ch.*

TRY IT OUT

Plan an inductive lesson to teach the letter *c.* Be sure to take children through the discrimination stage and to have known words for both sounds of *c* and for *ch.* Can you think of an action the children might do when *c* has the sound heard in *cat* and another when it sounds like it does in *cents*? What about an action for the *ch* digraph? Don't forget food as you are planning your lesson. Chocolate, cherries, and cheese are just three of the wonderful foods that make the *ch* letter-sound relationship delicious.

Context Plus Initial Consonant/Digraph

As children are learning the consonant and, later, the digraph letter-sound associations, they should also be learning to apply this knowledge to figuring out unknown words as they are reading. Often, teachers say, "They know the sounds and rules, they just don't use them." When you look at what these children have been taught, you will see that they have been taught to "know the sounds" (association) but have not been taught to "use them" (application). It does a child no good to know that *d* is the letter that starts *dog* if, when he or she comes upon an unknown word beginning with *d*, that knowledge is not used. As the consonant letter-sound associations are taught, we suggest two activities to teach children how to apply these associations as they are reading. The first application activity involves leading the children to extend their knowledge of context gained in Phase One to include their knowledge of consonants.

If children have been successful at the context lessons outlined in Phase One, they are now very adept at generating possible guesses for a taped over word. It is easy to extend this knowledge to include their growing letter-sound knowledge. Have children make guesses for a sentence containing a taped-over word as before. For the sentence, "Bobby ate all the ███████," the children's guesses might include: *cookies, pizza, cake, spaghetti, chicken, blueberries, grapes, candy, pie, donuts*, and *apples*. Then suggest that since we are learning about how words begin we could uncover just the first letter (or two if the word begins with a digraph, *sh, th, ch*). Imagine that when the tape is removed to uncover the first letter, that letter is a *b*. The only guess which remains a possibility is *blueberries*. Erase all other guesses and the children should now guess "things that would fit the sentence and begin with the letter *b*." Since this application lesson follows the discrimination and association *b* lessons, children should be able to generate many *b* words. Write only words which begin with *b* and fit the sentence on the board. If someone suggests *baby* you would respond, "*Baby* begins with the letter *b* but it also has to make sense in our sentence. *Bobby ate all the baby* is silly and doesn't make much sense." If someone suggests *carrots* you would respond, "Carrots makes sense in our sentence but it doesn't begin with the letter *b*. Remember, now, all our guesses have to begin with the letter *b* and make sense!" When a number of sensible *b* words have been guessed and written on the board (*blueberries, beans, bananas, barbecue, butter, bread, broccoli*, etc.) uncover the taped word and have the children determine by visually matching their guessed words and the uncovered word which, if any, of their guesses was correct. Occasionally, the children will not guess the covered word. In this case, after helping the children to observe that their guesses do not match the taped word, tell the children the word, or let them generate more guesses, or give them additional clues.

These context plus initial consonant/digraph lessons should be carried out regularly as new letter-sound relationships are learned. In addition, as children are reading and come upon an unknown word, they should be encouraged to say "blank," finish the sentence, and think what would make sense and start like that. As children learn more and more letter-sound associations, they will be able to figure out more and more words and will begin to realize that knowing the letter-sound association helps them read! As they begin to see why they are learning the letter-sound associations they will be more attentive and motivated to try to learn them.

Initial Consonant/Digraph Substitution

A second way to help children apply their knowledge of consonant sounds toward figuring out unknown words is to help them combine their knowledge that words which share middle and ending letters often rhyme and their knowledge of letter-sound relationships. Let's assume that children have learned letter-sound associations for the consonants *b, m, l, r,* and *w.* For this lesson, have each child in the group write the known words *red, cat, will,* and *jump* on cards. Then write sentences which contain an unknown word which rhymes with one of the known words and begins with one of the known consonants. Lead the children to find their card which has a middle and end like the unknown word and to use their rhyming and consonant knowledge to decode the unknown word. For example, write the sentence, "I saw a *rat* at the farm." Read the sentence saying "blank" for the italicized word. Then ask the children if they can think of some things they might see at the farm which begin with the letter *r.* The children might suggest *rabbit, raccoon, radish, rake,* and possibly *rat.* Listen to the suggestions, explain why any which start with *r* but don't make sense are impossible, and do *not* write the suggestions on the board. When the children have made a variety of suggestions, help them note that there are lots of things which begin with *r* and might be found on a farm. Then tell children that there is another tool they can use to help them figure out the unknown word. Direct their attention to the four word cards they have made and ask them if any of their words share the same middle and end as the unknown word. The children will observe that *cat* ended with the letters *at* and so did the unknown word. Ask if anyone remembers anything special about words which share the same middle and ending letters. The children (or teacher, if necessary) will state that "words which share the same middle and ending letters often rhyme." "What would a word that started with *r* and rhymed with *cat* be?" you ask. Based on their prior work with rhyming words during readiness and Phase One, the children should be able to come up with the rhyming word, *rat.* They will then read the sentence with the word *rat* in it and decide that it does indeed make sense.

As the lesson continues, write more sentences containing words which rhyme with *red, cat, will,* and *jump* and begin with *b, m, l, r,* or *w.* The sentences should be ones in which the underlined, unknown word can be many words just based on making sense and beginning letter. Then lead the children to use their four word cards to find a rhyming word and figure out the underlined word. Here are some possible sentences:

Carol went to *bed.*
My father works in a *mill.*
The *mat* is dirty.

My aunt will be *wed* in May.
Billy had a *lump* of clay.

As more consonant/digraph letter-sound associations and more sight words are learned, children continue with lessons such as the one described in which they find from several known words a word which shares a middle and ending with an unknown word, and then try the rhyming word to make sure it makes sense in the sentence. In addition, as children come across an unknown word which rhymes with a known word in their reading and ask you for help in figuring out the word, lead the children to think of a word they know which has a middle and ending like that one and thus, eventually make all known, regular words clues to the decoding of unknown, regular words. In Phase Three, children will be given direct instruction in thinking of a known word which shares middle and ending letters with an unknown word without the aid of the tangible word cards.

TRY IT OUT

Assume that children know all consonant and digraph letter-sound associations. Select five known words which have many rhyming matches. Make up 20 sentences containing unknown words which begin with known consonants/digraphs and rhyme with the five known words. Can you see how, once children have learned initial consonant/digraph substitution, they can decode hundreds of words by comparing them to their known words?

Known Words with *s, ed, ing* Endings

During Phase Two, children will be meeting many words in their reading which have the endings *s, ed, ing*. It is important that they learn early to recognize their known words in this form. To teach this, you will use an inductive teaching strategy as you have to teach other letter/sound generalizations. Imagine for example, that you show the children a picture of a cat, and write the known word *cat* next to it. Then, show them a picture of several cats and write *cats* next to it. Follow this with one house and the word *house*, several houses and the word *houses*, and one ball and the known word, *ball*, several balls and the word, *balls*. Children will soon generalize that the *s* on the end makes the word mean more than one. When they have made this generalization, tell them that you have several pictures some of which show only one thing and some which show more than one thing. Their task will be to guess (and, of course, show their appropriate every-pupil-response cards) whether the picture which they will be shown *after* the word is written and *after* their guess will have one or more than one object. The children will soon learn to guess more than one when the written word ends in *s* and one when it does not (don't confuse the issue at this point by showing words such as *bus* and *guess* which end in *s* but don't mean more than one).

Similarly, you can demonstrate the *s, ed, ing* endings on verbs by showing children what happens to the known word *walk* when it is used in sentences such as:

> Billy *walks* to school every day.
> He *walked* to school yesterday.
> Now, he is *walking* home.

With this model in front of them, then ask the children to guess what letters can be added to the known word *jump* so that it can fit in each of the sentences:

> Susie is _____ rope.
> Cathy _____ rope every afternoon.
> Billy _____ rope with them yesterday.

Based on their knowledge of spoken language, children should be able to orally generate the correct form and then, based on the *walk* example, figure out what letters should be added. Practice exercises such as these with new verbs learned as sight words should enable children to read known words with *s, ed*, and *ing* endings.

PHASE THREE

By the time children reach Phase Three they are readers. They know a large number of sight words and can use context, initial consonant/digraph letter-sound associations, and word endings to decode unknown words. In Phase Three this ability to recognize words immediately and automatically and to mediate the identification of unknown words will be extended. Major Phase Three goals are:

1. Accurate and immediate identification of the second most frequently occurring 150 words (for a total of 300)
2. Letter-sound associations for initial blends
3. Use of context and initial-blend letter-sound relationships to decode unknown words
4. Use of initial-blend letter-sound relationships to decode words which rhyme with known words
5. Letter-sound associations for *final* consonants, digraphs and blends, and use of context plus these associations to decode unknown words
6. Letter-sound associations for vowel and vowel combinations

300 Most Common Sight Words

Using strategies outlined in Phase Two, students should learn the following 150 words bringing the total number of immediately and automatically recognized common words to 300.

part	need	white	ran	far
food	still	soon	page	today
saw	keep	let	world	cold
different	together	hard	eyes	inside
live	sun	hearts	high	run
well	us	side	ever	cried
any	got	until	might	fast
school	Mrs.	should	four	answer
even	great	sometimes	few	best
under	father	own	move	light
line	along	dog	sure	red
because	night	door	miss	means
thought	took	once	feet	hand
next	sentence	enough	tree	green
small	story	near	knew	gave
every	land	kind	often	across
want	never	oh	add	yes
something	always	top	better	learn
earth	play	didn't	room	can't
last	began	draw	such	change
men	give	told	vowel	both
read	below	country	almost	turn
left	also	white	ground	warm
hear	head	large	sea	without
show	grow	I'm	heard	between
end	set	year	try	short
don't	paper	letter	money	stop
found	it's	fish	box	family
eat	morning	car	cut	form
boy	I'll	city	thing	black

ADD TO YOUR SURVIVAL KIT

Instead of using the second 150 words from the A and P Sight Word List, make a list of the second 150 words introduced in your reading series. Compare the two lists.

Initial Blend Letter-Sound Associations

Teach children to discriminate and associate letters and sounds for the initial blends *br, cr, dr, fr, gr, pr, tr, bl, cl, fl, gl, pl, sl, sc, sk, sm, sn, sp, st, sw,* and *tw.* Carry out inductive lessons similar to those outlined for teaching consonant digraph letter-sound associations. Be sure children know some sight words which begin with these blends. If they do not know some sight words, teach these before introducing the blend. If you need a sight word for the *sp* or *fr* blend, consider *Spiderman* or *Frankenstein*!

ADD TO YOUR SURVIVAL KIT

Make sure that at least two or three sight words have been taught for each initial-blend letter-sound association before that association is introduced in your reading series. Make a search for each one of the blends in Phase Three. If any association is introduced before sight word exemplars have been taught, develop appropriate sight words to teach to supplement those in your reading series.

Content Plus Initial Blend

Carry out lessons to help children learn to use context and initial blends to decode unknown words similar to those suggested in the "Context Plus Consonant/Digraph" section.

Initial-Blend Substitution

As each blend is taught, children should be given practice in using that blend letter-sound relationship to decode new words. You will remember that in Phase Two, initial consonant/digraph substitution exercises were carried out during which children made five word cards and then decoded an unknown word which started with a known consonant/digraph by deciding which of their five known words (written on cards) the unknown word looked like in the middle and end. They should have been given much practice with this substitution since they were learning all the consonant/digraph sounds presented in Phase Two and, by this time, should be very adept at finding the matching card and pronouncing the rhyming word. Assuming that they have achieved this ability, the blend substitution will take them a step further toward decoding independence. In reality, what the reader does when faced with an unknown word not apparent from the context is not to shuffle through index cards looking for a similar word but to shuffle through the mind looking for words stored there. Thus, in Phase Three, as students learn the blend letter-sound associations, they will be given practice in using all the words they know and the known blends to decode words. (If children have not become very adept at using the tangible index card word store when blends are introduced, they should first practice with an index word store as outlined in Phase Two and when they are performing well with the tangible store move to the activities which will be described here to help them use all the words they know as matches for unknown words.) Imagine that children have learned the letter sound associations for *br, cr, fl, sp,* and *st.* A lesson which will help them use these known letter-sound associations and all known words to decode unfamiliar words would look like this. Write a sentence which contains an unknown regular word beginning with one of the known blends:

Billy and Cathy had a spat.

The children read the sentence and decide that there are many words which start with *sp* and would make sense in that sentence: *spoon, sparkler, spanking,* to name just a few. Then ask the children if they know any words which end in the letters *at.* Children suggest several words and the teacher writes them on the board. If the children suggest words which don't end in *at,* you should write these, help the children to observe that they don't end with *at* and erase them. When several words ending in *at* are suggested (*bat, cat, at, hat, rat*) and written on the board, the children read the *at* words and then figure out the probable pronunciation of the rhyming word, *spat.* Once decoded, the word *spat* should be read in its sentence to see if it makes sense. While the word *spat* is not a common word, someone in the group is apt to know what it is; if not, you can provide the meaning for the word. ("It's like a not-too-serious argument. Have you ever had a spat with your friend, or brother or sister?") By this time, children know many words and, in order to find words they don't know as sight words for the decoding practice, it may be necessary to use some fairly uncommon words. Often, however, one child in the group will know the meaning and, if not, you can spend some time on meaning development once the word is decoded. The lesson might continue with sentences such as:

Cathy can do a flip.
I can't get the flap open.
I think the spout is clogged.
Please bring me my crown.

For each sentence, children read the sentence and, having determined that you can't be sure about the unknown word just from the context and the way it begins, think of some words which share a middle and end with the unknown words. If possible, children should give more than one similar word since you don't want to give children the wrong idea that there is just one word which will help them figure out the unknown word. If children correctly guess the unknown word before thinking of rhyming words, have them think of some rhyming words to check that guess. The final step in the process is to read the sentence with the decoded word and decide if the word makes sense and sounds right in the sentence. This is a particularly important step because there are some words which can have variant pronunciations and children should be given enough practice in simultaneous word identification and meaning identification that they become automatic at using the sense of what they are reading to monitor their decoding. You, as a good reader, automatically read the sentence, "As she took a bow, the bow fell from her hair," and give the proper pronunciation and meaning to each *bow.* You have *read* sentences like this all your life and probably never noticed that you *read* the two *bows* differently. It is obvious to all that word identification is an aid to meaning identification. It is not as obvious that meaning identification is an essential aid and check to word identification.

Perhaps, as you were reading the previous paragraph, a problem with rhyming word substitution decoding occurred to you. If, for example, you were asked to think of words which shared middle and ending letters with *bow*, you could think of *show, slow, mow* and also *cow, how,* and *chow. Bead, knead, dead,* and *head* all share the same middle and ending letters and they don't all rhyme. Remember that we have been teaching children that words which share middle and ending letters *usually* rhyme. Usually—not always! There are some cases in which the middle and ending letters can have two regular, predictable pronunciations. When children become good at blend substitution by thinking of words they know which share middle and ending letters with the unknown words, these variant pronunciations should be introduced. Here is a lesson which introduces the variant pronunciation for *ow.* Write this sentence on the board:

The boy had a crow.

Having established that there are lots of things the boy could have had which begin with *cr*, ask the children to suggest words which end with *ow*. Hopefully, they would suggest words with both pronunciations. If this happens, the teacher would list the words in two columns, like this:

show	how
grow	now
slow	cow
row	pow

The children would see that there are words which end in *ow* which rhyme with *show* and words which rhyme with *how*. How can we determine which one our unknown word will rhyme with? If children have had much practice in reading the sentence to see if the decoded word makes sense they should immediately come up with a plan to read the sentences with the word rhyming with *show* and with *how* to see which one sounds right. In this way, the correct pronunciation and meaning for *crow* should be easily determined (Durkin, 1980).

It is possible that children will only suggest words with one rhyming pattern. Perhaps, they will suggest *how, now, cow*, and *pow* and no others. The pronunciation arrived at will then be tried in the sentence and the children will conclude that they don't know what it means or that it doesn't make sense. After a pause, someone (preferably the children, but, if necessary, the teacher) should suggest that "I know a word, *show*, that ends in *ow* but doesn't rhyme with *cow*." Other words which rhyme with *show* would be suggested and the variant pronunciation of *crow* would be determined to make sense in the sentence.

If, on the other hand, children only suggested words like *show, slow*, and *grow*, the correct pronunciation of *crow* would be arrived at immediately and would make sense. Rather than point out the variant pronunciation immediately, you should go on to the next sentence which might be:

My dad bought a new plow.

By the end of the lesson, children should have concluded: "Sometimes you think of a word which has the same middle and ending letters as the unknown word but the pronunciation you try for the rhyming word doesn't make sense. Then, you should think if you have other words which share those middle and ending letters and which have a different sound." This lesson should be a further indication to you as teacher and to your students that word identification and meaning identification support one another and that all word identification instruction should be in the context of real reading so that children get in the habit of using them simultaneously.

TRY IT OUT

Plan a lesson in which you teach children the variant pronunciation for *ead*. You may want to use the words *tread* and *plead* in your sentences.

Final Consonant Digraph/Blend Letter-Sound Associations

Most children, as they learn the initial consonant/digraph/blend letter-sound associations, induct the final letter-sound associations. You may want to be sure that students do this, however, by providing practice in which students guess a word based only on context:

John fell on the _____.

Then, make some more guesses when the initial letters are revealed:

John fell on the st_____.

And, further narrow their guessing by being shown the final letter(s):

John fell on the st__mp.

Now, there is the faint possibility that John may have fallen on the *stamp*, but it is much more probable that he tripped over and fell on the *stump*.

Exercises in which children use final consonant/digraph/blend letter-sound associations and context to decode words can be carried out at the same time as those used to teach initial blend plus context. (Children are not taught to substitute final consonant/digraph/blend sounds on known words because it is generally what follows the vowel which determines its sound. The known word *car* or *cake* does not help to decode *cast* in the same way that the known words *last* and *past* do.)

Vowel Sounds

The least predictable letter-sound relationships in English are those represented by the vowels (*a, e, i, o, u*). Most of us were taught that vowels had short and long sounds. In reality, each vowel letter represents many different sounds and which sound it does represent is determined primarily by the surrounding letters. In the preceding two sentences, the letter *e* occurred in the following words:

least	vowels
predictab*l*e	reality
letter	each
relationships	different
*E*nglish	does
represented	determined

A glance at this list should demonstrate to anyone that learning just short, long, and "r-controlled" vowel sounds is not going to take care of all the sounds represented by the letter *e*. Children have a great deal of difficulty learning to associate sounds with the vowels because these associations are complex and are quite different for one-syllable words and polysyllabic words.

If consonant/digraph/blend substitution exercises have been done consistently with children, if, when faced with an unknown one-syllable word, they can think of words which share middle and ending letters, and if they are acquiring an ever increasing store of known sight words, it is not necessary to teach vowel sounds. Any regular one-syllable word can be decoded by thinking of words which share middle and ending letters. Since it is the letters which follow the vowel which determine its sound, thinking of words which share middle and ending letters will result in the successful decoding of the word without knowing rules for the vowel sounds. For irregular words, thinking of a similar word won't work but neither will the rules!

If you feel it necessary to teach vowel sounds as an alternative decoding route for your children, simply follow the principles outlined in the inductive lessons for teaching consonant/digraph/blend letter-sound associations. Choose vowel letter-sound relationships for which your students have some known words. Be sure that they can auditorially discriminate the vowel sound to be taught. Have them observe from some known examples (*make, taste, tame*) the letter-sound relationship and then apply that to unknown words. As with all letter-sound relationships, present the words to be decoded in the context of a sentence and check the arrived-at pronunciation against the "that makes sense" criteria.

READ SOME MORE ABOUT THIS

There are many good sources of information about what the most commonly occurring vowel and vowel combinations letter-sound associations are and ways to teach them. You can read more about this in:

Durkin D., *Teaching young children to read*, Boston: Allyn and Bacon, 1980.

Heilman A., Blair Timothy, and Rupley William, *Principles and practices of teaching reading*, Columbus, Ohio: Charles E. Merrill, 1981.

Karlin R., *Teaching elementary reading*, New York: Harcourt Brace Jovanovich, 1980.

PHASE FOUR

By the time students have completed Phase Three, they can immediately identify or mediate the identification of one-syllable words. By the end of Phase Four, children should be able to immediately identify or mediate (using context and letter-sound relationships) the identification of most words in their listening vocabularies. Phase Four goals are:

1. Accurate and immediate identification of the remaining 132 most frequently occurring words (for a total of 432)
2. Ability to decode compound words
3. Ability to decode two-syllable words
4. Ability to decode polysyllabic words

432 Most Common Words

Using strategies outlined in Phase Two, students should learn the remaining 132 words bringing the total number of immediately and automatically recognized common words to 432.

those	bird	himself	ten	happy	space
am	town	fly	five	being	bed
horse	cannot	cat	watch	happened	complete
front	fire	hold	road	everything	carry
seen	call	face	winter	gone	slowly
ready	plant	wind	milk	order	woman
eggs	talk	window	goes	sleep	hole
body	that's	done	gold	strong	remember
whole	animal	half	rain	anything	ship
blue	important	true	river	try	stand
stood	really	walk	garden	let's	tiny
table	soil	dark	Indian	snow	friend
moon	ball	sing	piece	tall	kept
song	hot	summer	boy	round	ride
miles	sky	outside	fine	care	tail
baby	study	behind	nothing	store	seeds
beautiful	ago	open	catch	built	against
second	spell	book	everyone	hit	covered
above	stay	six	legs	maybe	wood
leaves	toward	glass	grass	class	bright
girl	feel	ice	listen	fun	game
sat	young	start	someone	street	rest

ADD TO YOUR SURVIVAL KIT

Instead of using the last 132 words from the A and P Sight Word List, make a list of the third 150 words introduced in your reading series. Compare the two lists.

Compound Words

Use the compound words children have learned in Phase Two and Three as sight words (*something, sometimes, another,* and *without,* for example) to show children that sometimes a big word is made up of two little words and that when you are reading and encounter a long unknown word, you should look to see if it is made up of two words you know. Then present them with sentences which contain a compound word composed of two of their known words. Some examples are:

Bob can be the *shortstop*.
Carol was on the *lookout* for trouble.
Dad forgot to put his *headlights* on.
Judy hit her brother, Billy, with a *snowball*.
Plants grow in winter in a *hothouse*.

There are numerous compound words which are composed of the known sight words. Children love to read them because they enjoy the success of being able to figure out "big words." Of course, there are some words (*father* and *together,* for example) in which there are two or three words which do not make compound words. Children should also be shown these in a sentence and use their "it has to make sense" monitoring system to observe that *Fat her was late coming home* doesn't sound right. Once again you see the importance of children's learning to simultaneously use their word identification and meaning identification strategies. If children have a list of known words (Words on the Wall or word banks), they will enjoy making up compound words and writing sentences with them for the other children to read.

Two-Syllable Words

Many two-syllable words can be decoded by using a consonant/digraph/blend substitution strategy on each part of the word. The word *garnish,* for example, can be seen as having a first part which rhymes with *car* and a second part which rhymes with *fish. Secret* can be decoded by considering that the first part rhymes with *he* and the last part with *pet.* (We will refer to the parts rather than to the syllables of words because syllabic divisions are arbitrary points determined by dictionary writers and often have no reality in speech. For example, in the words *baker, donut, sober,* and most other two-syllable words separated by a single consonant or digraph, the sound of the single consonant or digraph is, in reality, a part of both syllables. In order to decode words of two or more syllables, children do need to segment the words. But it is probable that this segmentation is based on seeing familiar parts in the unfamiliar whole rather than on the application of syllabication rules.) Once children have a large bank of known one-syllable words and can apply the initial consonant/digraph/blend sounds, they can decode many two-syllable words by thinking of a known word for the first part and a known word for the second part. As we did when we began consonant/digraph/blend substitution with one-syllable words, we will begin the two-syllable-word teaching process by having students use a tangible word store (words on index cards) and then help them make the transition to using all the words they know as possible matches for the unknown words.

STEP 1. Have each student begin a tangible word store by writing the following five words on cards: *he, went, her, can,* and *car.* Present students with sentences in which there is an underlined two-syllable word, the parts of which share middle and ending letters with one of their known words. Have the students read the sentence, find a similar word for each part of the underlined word, decide on a probable pronunciation for the underlined word, and check that pronunciation by rereading the sentence to see if it makes sense. Using the words *he, went, her, can,* and *car,* students should be able to decode the underlined words in:

> They held up a *banner* at the game.
> Carol married a man who is *German.*
> A snake is a kind of *serpent.*

There are many other words which can be decoded by comparing the parts to the five known words. You might want to use many sentences and include in them such words as *charter, meter, garter, barber, cancer, merger, garment, percent, repent, panther, tangent, Herman, barter, decent, farther, recent,* and *slander.* Some of the words will probably be unfamiliar to your children (or words they have heard but don't really know what they mean). For these words, you will want to spend a little time beginning to build meaning. Be sure to have the children relate their own experience to the new word. Once the word has been explained, questions such as, "What garment are you wearing today? and, "Have you ever done anything you later had to repent for?" help children remember words by making the word a part of their experience.

STEP 2. Have children make five more cards for the words *in, at, then, it,* and *is.* Using all ten word cards, have them decode the underlined words in sentences such as:

> This soup tastes a little *bitter.*
> I have a friend who moved to *Berlin.*
> All the kids said Paul was a *hermit.*

Make up more sentences containing words which can be decoded by consonant/digraph/blend substitution on the ten known words. You may want to use such words as: *scatter, blister, bitten, bandit, cretin, ginger, remit, batter, center, winter, margin, latter, misspent, whisper, whisker, splatter,* and *matter.*

STEP 3. Have children add the words *let, fish, sun, big,* and *and.* Have them read sentences and decode underlined words using such words as *market, hunger, secret, disband, clannish, setter, catfish, blunder, punish, letter, varnish, garnish,* and *pigment.*

STEP 4. Enlarge the word store from 15 to 35 by adding the words *on, Bob, dance, care, face up, us, side, found, rain, ate, am, rose, Tom, or, top, but, go, them,* and *boy.* Do this gradually over several days' lessons. As new words are added, have students read sentences containing underlined words which can be decoded using words added to word banks so far. As you increase the list from 15 to 35, write the known words on a chart or let the children make their own lists. Abandon the cards as you increase from 15 because more than 15 cards is just too many to manipulate and look through. Having the words on a chart or list will make them readily available to all. When all 35 words have been added to the list, the following 200 words can be decoded. Children enjoy forming two teams and competing to see who can decode the most words. Children should be given the 200-word list in advance of the contest so that they have time to figure out the words with the help of the 35 known words and their team members. Words with one star require three matching words and are worth twice as many points as unstarred words. Words with two stars require four matching words and the points are quadrupled. Many teachers like to have the team which pronounces the word make a sentence with that word and give additional points for an acceptable sentence. Children can use the dictionary to look up the meaning of words not in their listening vocabulary as long as they do this before the contest. Here are the 200 words decodable from the 35 one-syllable words:

1. German	11. Herman	21. bandit	31. trigger
2. barber	12. repent	22. center	32. blunder
3. percent	13. panther	23. scatter	33. catfish
4. cancer	14. serpent	24. fitter	34. setter
5. garter	15. bitter	25. bitten	35. misspent
6. garment	16. ginger	26. Berlin	36. banish
7. merger	17. margin	27. hermit	37. disband
8. meter	18. latter	28. blister	38. hunger
9. charter	19. winter	29. punish	39. farther
10. banner	20. batter	30. market	40. secret

41. decent	*81. entertain	121. stutter	161. garnish
42. regret	82. luster	122. chopper	162. pigment
43. donor	83. embrace	123. clutter	163. enjoy
44. donut	84. probate	*124. ignorance	*164. enjoyment
45. order	85. retrace	125. sputter	165. demand
46. donate	86. refrain	126. entrance	166. deface
47. orbit	87. pinto	127. cutter	167. detain
48. homer	**88. entertainment	128. instance	168. hitter
49. remain	*89. employment	129. propose	169. border
50. organ.	90. restate	*130. observance	170. porter
51. joker	91. robber	131. gutter	171. bandstand
52. motor	92. compose	*132. resistance	172. grandstand
53. regain	93. disgrace	133. profound	173. fender
54. bonus	94. whisper	134. employ	174. tennis
55. rotate	95. scarlet	135. pittance	175. tender
56. combo	96. splinter	*136. repentance	176. spender
57. retain	97. slender	*137. Tupperware	177. Buster
58. sober	98. fritter	138. repose	178. locate
59. relate	99. chosen	139. butter	179. crocus
60. voter	100. enclose	140. disclose	180. clover
61. yoyo	101. dispose	141. boyish	181. focus
62. commit	102. Sounder	142. tomboy	182. poker
63. prevent	103. grounder	143. annoy	183. Rover
64. command	104. confound	144. complain	184. permit
65. debate	105. decoy	145. comment	*185. persistent
66. litter	106. founder	146. spoken	*186. performer
67. grocer	107. resound	*147. November	187. open
68. blender	108. unsound	*148. December	*188. override
69. mainland	*109. underground	149. compare	*189. understand
70. member	110. flutter	150. refrain	190. winner
71. confide	*111. attendance	151. matter	191. dinner
72. clobber	112. stopper	152. chatter	192. thinner
73. misplace	113. supper	153. platter	193. dropper
74. decide	114. mutter	154. sitter	194. cluster
*75. remember	115. shopper	155. recent	195. fluster
76. goblin	*116. remembrance	156. slander	196. pertain
77. compare	*117. buttercup	157. whisker	197. manner
78. landslide	118. rebound	158. splatter	198. disdain
*79. monogram	119. shutter	159. letter	**199. independent
80. popper	*120. performance	160. varnish	200. prefer

STEP 5. You will remember from our blend substitutions on known words that when faced with an unfamiliar word the reader does not have visible before him or her a list of known words. Rather, the reader must search through his or her cognitive word store and find matches.

Once children are adept at using a tangible word store, help them decode two-syllable words by thinking of words they know which will help them decode the parts. You might want each student to look through books and write down several sentences which contain six- or seven-letter words which are not immediately recognizable. Each child can then put his or her sentence and underlined word on the board and let the other children in the group suggest words they know which might help them decode the underlined word. Their known words would be written on the board and once a tentative pronunciation is arrived at, the sentence would be read to make sure the word made sense. If the word didn't make sense, alternative matches should be tried. If no sensible match could be made, the children should consult the dictionary to see if the unknown word is one they don't have in their listening vocabulary. As children are reading and come to you with a, "What's this word?" question, you will want to decide if the word is one which can be decoded based on known words, and if so, ask the child, "Do you know any words which share middle and ending letters with parts of this word?" This will provide children with practice using their decoding skills in the context of real reading.

Polysyllabic Words

There are some word parts (*tion, ous, able,* for example) which only occur in polysyllabic words. Polysyllabic words have unstressed syllables which result in every vowel and various vowel combinations occasionally representing the ə sound as represented by the second *a* in *imaginative*, the first *i* in *sacrifice* and the *o* in *compartment*. There is predictability to the letter-sound relationships but it is a complex predictability in which the sounds of letters are influenced by the surrounding letters and the position of those letters in the word. In previous parts of this chapter, we have suggested that students might be taught to decode unknown words by comparing and contrasting these unknown words to their store of known words. The same applies to the decoding of polysyllabic words. There is, however, a different problem to be overcome when teaching students to decode polysyllabic words. Unknown polysyllabic words must be compared and contrasted with known polysyllabic words. If you will look at the 432 most common words we have taught as sight words, you will realize that very few of these have more than two syllables. In fact, the only words of three or more syllables we have taught as sight words are: *another, different, together, important, beautiful, everyone, everything, anything,* and *remember.* If students are to decode polysyllabic words by comparing and contrasting them to known polysyllabic words, then we must make sure they know some polysyllabic sight words. In order to teach children to compare unknown polysyllabic words to known words and to also teach them some polysyllabic sight words, a game entitled "Mystery Word Match" was developed.

To play Mystery Word Match, divide the children into two teams. The teams earn points by comparing the mystery word to clue words and correctly guessing the mystery word. Guessing the word is originally worth ten points. Each time the team asks a question which gets a "no" answer, one point is subtracted and it becomes the other team's turn to ask questions and try to guess the word. Always write the mystery word in a sentence using lines to indicate how many letters are in the word. Write two or three clue words underneath the sentence containing the mystery word. The play is carried out by the students trying to find out which parts of the clue words are used in the mystery word. They ask, "Does the mystery word begin like _____?" "End like _____?" "Have a middle like _____?" Here is an example of how the game is played:

TEACHER: (Writes: I have made a _____.) As you can see our mystery word has ten letters and completes the sentence "I have made a . . . ." Does either team want to guess the word?
(Team members chuckle [hopefully!] at the absurdity of trying to guess the word with that impoverished context as the only clue.)
TEACHER CONTINUES: Here are the clue words: *absolute, relative, attention.* (Teacher writes each clue word on the board and then pronounces each. Students pronounce each, define and/or use in sentences.) Billy's team won the toss. They can go first. The mystery word is worth 10 points.
BILLY'S TEAM MEMBER: Does the word begin like attention?
TEACHER: No, it does not. Joe's team for 9 points.
JOE'S TEAM MEMBER: Does the word end like attention?
TEACHER: Yes it does. (Writes *tion* on last four lines: _____ tion.) You may go again.
JOE'S TEAM MEMBER: Does the word begin like absolute?
TEACHER: No, it does not. Billy's team for 8 points.
BILLY'S TEAM MEMBER: Does the word have a middle like absolute?
TEACHER: Good for you. (Writes *solu* on the appropriate lines: __ __ solution.) You may go again.
BILLY'S TEAM MEMBER: Does the word have a beginning like relative?
TEACHER: Yes it does. (Writes last two letters in *resolution*.) The team may confer and name the word. (Team confers and triumphantly pronounces *resolution*. Teacher records 8 points for Billy's team. Game continues with next mystery word.)

This game is entertaining, and the students are exposed to many polysyllabic words. While playing they learn to use the clue words to figure out other words. This game is intended to both build a store of polysyllabic words to which to compare and contrast other polysyllabic words and to give practice in the compare-and-contrast decoding skill.

There are infinite combinations of mystery and clue words which can be used. Often, the mystery word can be gotten from two clue words, one of which is like the beginning of the mystery word and one of which is like the ending. Students particularly like the two-clue word matches because if they guess right, they are almost assured of winning the 10 points. If the team which goes first guesses incorrectly, the opponents will almost surely win. Do not be concerned that in two-clue word matches syllable boundaries are ignored since decoding proceeds faster if the reader recognizes larger-than-a-syllable units. Remember to always introduce the mystery word in a sentence so that the pronunciation can be checked in the context of the sentence and so that the decoding practice more closely resembles real reading. It is fun to make up mystery and clue word matches. Here are a few to get you started:

I will admit that I had high _____.

            limitations
            explorer
            respectable

This is a clever _____.

        indecisive
        prevention

Currently I am without _____.

          deploying
          embarrass
          apartment

My friend was suffering from _____.

            incomplete
            editor
            suggestion

I think _____ must look like this.

     merchandise
     paragraph

ADD TO YOUR SURVIVAL KIT

Make up some mystery word match starters. Be sure your clue words have the same sounds in the same place as the mystery word. Be sure that some of your mystery words can be figured out from only two clue words since you want students to see large familiar chunks in words.

PRINCIPLES OF MEANINGFUL WORD IDENTIFICATION INSTRUCTION

As you come to the end (no doubt, thankfully!) of this long and detailed chapter, you are perhaps a little overwhelmed by the fact that teaching and learning word identification is such a long, complex process. It is! In fact, a big chunk of each day in first-, second-, and third-grade class-rooms is spent teaching reading and a big chunk of that reading in-structional time is spent on helping children become accurate and quick word identifiers. It is perhaps apparent to you now that you could easily "lose the forest for the trees" and get so involved in the enormous task of teaching word identification that you forget that meaning identification is what reading is all about! We have tried, in this chapter, to pre-sent a program which provides children with systematic, structured in-struction in the crucial word identification skills without ever allowing the teacher or the children to forget that making sense and enjoying is "the name of the game." Because we feel so strongly that word iden-tification instruction must always be a means to the end of comprehen-sion, we would like to end this chapter by summarizing some principles of word identification instruction which attain the goal of helping chil-dren identify words without interfering with the large goal of identify-ing meaning. The principles which we hope have been exemplified in this chapter and throughout the book are:

1. Because reading is a complex act during which word identifica-tion, meaning identification, and print processing occur simultaneously, and because anything which is not automatic requires attention, chil-dren should be taught to immediately and automatically (without decod-ing or stopping to think) identify common words as sight words. This frees up attention which would have to be allotted for decoding to be used for meaning identification.

2. Because many words not known as sight words can be figured out quickly (and almost automatically) by skipping the word, reading on, and then thinking about what that word might be which would make sense in the *context* of what is being read, readers should be taught and encouraged from the beginning to use context to decode unknown words.

3. Before letter-sound associations can be learned, children must be able to discriminate the particular sounds being taught. Once the chil-dren can make the letter-sound associations, these associations only help them to be better readers if they apply these associations to the de-coding of unknown words. Thus children should be taught to use context and letter-sound associations so that they can apply the knowledge they have. Another application-level strategy is the use of initial letter-sound associations to decode words which rhyme with known sight words.

4. Good readers have an internal meter which lets them know if they have identified most of the words correctly. This "making sense"

meter stops them when they misread "The boy is in the house," as "The boy is in the horse." Students develop an internal meter by reading words in context so that they can make sense and by being reminded by the teacher that "if it doesn't make sense, you had better go back and re-read." Because word identification instruction is always carried out in the context of sentences and stories, and because children are constantly asked to make sense of what they read, neither the teacher nor the children can get confused and think that "reading is saying the words right."

3 | Reading Comprehension

Say these words to yourself or to someone else:

process	consider	involve
obtain	solution	reference
correlation	axis	residual
correspond	table	factor
adjustment	certain	first
inconsequential	continue	configuration
magnitude	vector	second
place	subject	centroid

Were you able to pronounce them all? Yes? Well then, you should have no trouble understanding this sentence:

> The centroid solution involves placing the first reference axis through the centroid of the configuration of vectors; obtaining a table of residual correlations, which are subject to certain adjustments; placing the second factor through the centroid corresponding to the table of residual correlations; and continuing the process until the magnitude of the residuals can be considered inconsequential (Ferguson, 1971, p. 416).

Now, can you cover the sentence and explain in your own words what it means? No?

While word identification is important if readers are to comprehend, we hope this exercise has shown you that word identification is far from all that is required. The question to be answered in this chapter is: What, besides word identification instruction, can teachers do to improve students' abilities to comprehend when they read? We answer the question by presenting and discussing four guidelines for reading comprehension instruction:

Develop concepts for topics and words.

Use instructional level materials.

Teach comprehension lessons in instructional level materials.

Provide time and motivation for individual reading.

TRY IT OUT

A *directed reading-thinking activity* (DR-TA) is a type of comprehension lesson plan which you will learn more about in this chapter and elsewhere in the book. In one version of a DR-TA, called an *expectation outline*, students predict an outline of what they expect to learn from their reading. Based only on what you have read so far in this chapter, develop an outline of your expectations for what you will learn in the rest of the chapter.

DEVELOP CONCEPTS FOR TOPICS AND WORDS

Let us return for a moment to our introductory paragraph about the centroid solution. Why were you unable to comprehend this paragraph? If you could answer us, you would probably say something like, "Well, I don't know what it is all about and what's a centroid anyway?" In order to understand what you read you must have some understanding of "what it is all about" and you must have appropriate meanings for the key words. We will refer to the "what it's all about" as a *topic* and to your understanding of the individual words which all relate to the topics as *word meanings*. So your reading comprehension problem with this paragraph involved two closely related phenomena: (1) you lack a background of experience with the topic, and (2) you don't have well-developed meanings for some of the words that relate to that topic, such as *centroid, reference axis, vectors,* and *residual correlations*.

During the past decade, a body of important research which can be placed under the label of *schema theory* (Anderson, 1978; Anderson, 1977; Rumelhart, 1980) has demonstrated the importance to comprehension of what a reader knows about a topic prior to reading. This prior knowledge of a topic can be thought of as a schema. As you read, the words on the page trigger prior knowledge stored in your head. Strange (1980) explains the interaction between what is printed on the page and what is "printed" in your knowledge store when you read, "The Indian rode off into the sunset."

When we read the sentence about the Indian, all our previous knowledge about Indians becomes useful ... knowledge about the dress of Indians, culture of Indians, white men and Indians, Indian social structure, etc. that is cued for use by the word *Indian* in the text. We don't know how much of this previous knowledge is necessary for understanding this text until we read further. As we read the word *rode* we cue our knowledge about transportation. People ride on trains, planes, horses, etc. We also have experience about Indians and transportation and so predict that this Indian was riding on a horse.... Schemata are not static however, and can be changed in a number of ways. Say that we add to our sentence "on a motorcycle." Motorcycles are part of our transportation schema, but not of the Indian and transportation schema.... There is nothing in our Indian schema, however, that actually prohibits riding on motorcycles, so we change our schema for this sentence, deleting horse and accepting motorcycle. Riding motorcycles is also added to our Indian schema, making this happenstance a slightly more probable interpretation the next time we read about Indians and transportation. (p. 393–394)

This example of what happens when reading about Indians and riding should make it clear that reading is an interactive process in which what you know allows you to understand what you read, and what you read adds to what you know. If you know little or nothing about a topic, you cannot understand and remember what you read about that topic. If you don't understand and remember what you read about an unfamiliar topic, you will have no more information stored in your mind to relate to that topic the next time you read about it! This is the unfortunate situation most of us find ourselves in when doing assigned reading on a topic we know nothing about. One of the authors of this textbook "memorized" her way through college chemistry. Memorizing is what you do when you can't understand but must be able to recall facts to pass a test. Unfortunately, once the exam for which the information was memorized is gone, so is that information!

In the remainder of this section, we are going to help you develop your understanding of how concepts are learned and then suggest a variety of activities you can engage your students in which will help students develop concepts.

How Are Concepts Learned?

Children do not come to school blank slates on which experience can write. Rather they come to school with thousands of well-developed concepts built through experience. If you have ever been around young children, you know that their first words relate directly to objects and realities they have experienced. *Daddy, mama, milk, cookies, hot, up, bye-*

bye, fall down, and *No!* are among the first words of many children. These words were, in most cases, not taught to the children. Rather, the children learned the words by hearing them used while they simultaneously experienced them. Furthermore, young children cannot define the words they know. Rather, they show us that they have the concept of cookies by pointing to the cookie jar and saying "cookies"; pointing to the TV when a commercial for Oreos comes on and saying "cookies"; and by pointing to the crumbly mess on the floor, which has obviously been stepped on and rolled in, and saying "cookies!" Later, these same young children will add hundreds and thousands of words to their vocabulary and demonstrate by their use that they have a concept for these words. Children who come to school generally have concepts for *deep* (as in a deep hole and the deep end of the pool). They also have the concept of *not deep* which some children can describe using the concept word, *shallow.* Most children who come to school have concepts for the common colors such as *red, blue,* and *black.* They may not, however, have any concept of less common color words such as *turquoise* and *chartreuse.* Children come to school with thousands of concepts and with a variety of concept words they use to describe these concepts. Most of these concept-words they have learned by being in the presence of the object or reality, and hearing these words used to describe the object or reality. We will refer to this actually being there to experience an object or reality as *direct experience.*

Not all concepts which young children bring to school with them, however, were learned through direct experience. Many young children have a concept for *mountain* even if they have never been in the presence of a mountain. Most young children can recognize *zebras, elephants,* and *monkeys,* including children who have never been to a zoo, circus, or other place where they might have been in the presence of these animals. Some children who have never *sailed* or been in a *canoe* have the concepts represented by these words. How did they learn them? Did someone explain to them what a mountain was? Was the dictionary definition of monkeys read to them? Did some adult attempt to explain or define a canoe? In most cases, when children have concepts for objects and realities they have never directly experienced, they have seen these objects or realities portrayed on television, in movies, or in picture books. We will refer to this visual experience in which the learner sees the object or reality and hears the appropriate words used to describe the object or reality as *indirect experience.* All children in our media culture come to school with many concepts learned through indirect visual experience via TV, movies, and pictures.

There is another way in which concepts are learned but we suspect that young children do not learn concepts this way. Sometimes, we tell or define a word. If, for example, a young child overheard you use the word *cancel* and asked, "What does cancel mean?" you might respond by telling or explaining: 'Well, cancel means to have something but then decide not to have it anymore. Sometimes, school is canceled because of bad weather." In this case, the child has not experienced *canceled* directly or indirectly but has only heard it defined and described. We refer to this way of learning words as *symbolic* because the only route the child has to understanding is through words which symbolize but are not reality. Symbolic encounters with words are generally not very potent and the word thus encountered is seldom learned unless some direct or indirect experience is added to the symbolic explanation. If, for example, the same child on the following day arrived at his music lesson only to discover that it had been canceled because the music teacher was sick, then the child would have had direct experience with the concept of canceled and is apt to remember what canceled means the next time he encounters that word. The same concept could be learned indirectly if the boy was watching a television show in which the baseball game of the main character was canceled due to rain.

Most concepts, then, which young children bring with them to school are those which they have experienced directly. They were in the presence of the object or experienced the reality and the appropriate words were used. Many concepts were learned indirectly. In indirect experience, you may feel as if you are there but, you really aren't. Indirect experience leads to concept development when the object or reality is portrayed through some media and the appropriate words are used. Some concepts may be learned symbolically. The distinguishing feature of symbolic experience is that *only* words (spoken or written) are used. Words are, of course, used in conjunction with the direct or indirect experience. But in symbolic experience, words alone are used to symbolize the object or reality. It should be obvious why those concepts which we have never experienced directly or indirectly but have only heard about or read about are the least well-developed concepts and the words used to represent these concepts are often forgotten. Thus our first principle for concept development is: *Whenever possible provide direct or indirect experience for concept development.*

So far, we have been explaining concept development as if it were a "one shot" affair. This is seldom the case. Most words for which we have well-developed concepts have been encountered on a number of different occasions. Some of these encounters have involved direct experience, some indirect experience, and some have involved only words or symbolic experience. Think of the concept represented by the word *hot* for example. Maybe, you first experienced the reality of *hot* when you burned your hand on the fireplace grate. As you screamed and your sister held your hand under cold water, she repeated, "I've told you never to touch anything near the fireplace. Even when the fire is out, that grate stays hot for a long time. You see how hot things burn. Never, never touch hot things again." This experience and the word *hot* are not likely to be forgotten anytime soon. But, at this point, you have only a limited concept of *hot*. This concept will be broadened as you hear that word in relationship to many direct experiences—a hot summer day; the soup's too hot, blow on it; Dad got hot when his team fumbled the ball. You may also see a hot desert on television and a picture of your mother wearing the sometimes fashionable hot pants. Your concept of *hot* will be broadened by hearing the word in relationship to these indirect experiences. You may also broaden your concept of *hot* by reading that a suspect was arrested with hot goods and by hearing someone comment that their team's center was hot under the basket last night. These symbolic encounters with hot further broaden and delineate your concept for the simple word *hot*.

You might think of concepts as developing like an onion—one layer at a time. Each experience, whether direct, indirect, or symbolic gives shape and adds layers to your developing concepts. This leads us to the second principle teachers should keep in mind when helping children develop concepts: *Provide many and varied experiences, direct, indirect, and/or symbolic with the concept being developed.*

Let us return for a moment to the experience of burning your finger on the hot fireplace grate. Our focus when discussing that encounter was on your experience with the concept of *hot*. This word, *hot*, however, was not the only concept word being learned. The experience and ensuing conversation was also helping you build concepts for *fireplace* ("never touch anything near the fireplace"), and *grate* ("even when the fire is out, that grate stays hot"). The concept of *hot* was also being presented in contrast to the *cold* water under which your sister was holding your hand. Thus, the topics of *fireplace. grate*, and *words which describe temperatures* were all being simultaneously developed through this one direct experience.

We seldom if ever know a word without knowing other words which relate to the same topic. Take the word *clock*, for example. People who know the word *clock* don't just know it as a piece of machinery for keeping time. People who know the word *clock* also have the concept of where different clocks are generally found (alarm clocks in bedrooms, grandfather clocks in living rooms, clocks in classrooms, clocks in cars, clocks in airports, etc.). Most people know uses for clocks and words associated with time keeping. Some people know the names for different parts of different kinds of clocks. We could say that you have a clock schema which contains all the information you know on the topic of clocks. We could also refer to your clock schema as your background of experience with clocks.

Concept development thus refers both to developing meanings for individual words and to developing meaning for the topic to which those words all relate. As you learn more about a topic, you add word meanings to your store of information about that topic. Likewise, as you learn meanings for words in the context of a particular topic, you add to your store of information. Because knowledge of word meanings is crucial to comprehension, we must focus on helping children build meanings for words. Because word meanings never exist in isolation but always in relationship to other words which make up the topic those words share, we must develop concepts for words in the context of and simultaneously with topics. This leads us to our final principle for concept development: *Teach word meanings in topical word-sets*. This principle is easily carried out in content-area classes such as science and social studies. These content areas have topics (weather, nutritious foods, China, democracy, for example) which are being developed and the key words for which meanings must be learned will, if they are key words, relate to the topic being studied. When teaching reading, however, words often need to be taught to children which have no relationship to one another, but which children must have meanings developed for if they are to understand what they are about to read. How can teachers of reading carry out the principle *Teach word meanings in topical word-sets* if the words which need to be introduced do not form topical word-sets? The answer to that question would appear to be that teachers of reading can foster concept development of topics and words by building topical word sets based on the words to be introduced prior to reading. There is a general knowledge of the world which reading comprehension requires and which is, generally speaking, not taught in schools. This knowledge is varied and relates to such general topics as animals, buildings, kinship, occupations, and numerous others. Reading teachers could preview the book to be read by a particular group looking for topics which are most universal in nature. Some of the topics one might find are:

animals
buildings (types of)
clothing
locations (countries, continents, states, regions)
feelings (ways we feel)
food
furniture
kinship (mother, cousin, half-sister, etc.)
movements (ways we move our bodies)
occupations
sports
tools
transportation (means of)

These topics will not be obvious at first since the stories are not *about* them. With practice, however, you will soon begin to notice when two or more otherwise different stories have animals or furniture mentioned somewhere in them.

Once five to ten topics of a universal nature are chosen for a several month period of reading selections, these topics should be introduced to the students in the reading group one topic at a time. Let's say that *food* is the first topic to be introduced because there are several different foods mentioned in the next two or three reading selections to be covered. A piece of chart paper, which has "Food" written at the top, should be taped to the wall, put on a bulletin board, hung from the ceiling, or otherwise displayed for the reading group to see. Students then talk about what food is and give some examples of foods they like or can prepare. They are then told that until further notice, every time they read any selection regardless of their purpose(s) for comprehending, any word they find which is related to food can be added to the chart entitled "Food." In a few days, after adding words to the food chart through several selections, a second topic with its chart is introduced in the same manner. Now, students will be adding words from their reading to both topical word-set charts. Then a third topic and chart are introduced and students are adding words to three topical word-sets. Three topical word-sets at any one time may be enough for first graders or severely disabled readers while as many as nine or ten may be able to be used with good readers in fifth or sixth grade. [See pp. 425–426 for more about topical word-sets.]

Concept Development ALL DAY, EVERY DAY

Because the concepts we have are crucial to our perceiving and thinking as well as to our listening and reading comprehension, concept development should be going on ALL DAY, EVERY DAY in the elementary classroom. Field trips which take children out of the classroom and guests and objects brought into the classroom provide direct experience for concept development. Teachers make maximum use of these concept development opportunities by preparing the children ahead of time for what they will experience and by leading them through discussions and other language-oriented activities after the experience. This helps children sort through the information learned and store it away with other information for later use in perceiving, thinking, and comprehending. [See Chaps. 9 & 13.] Reading to children and involving the children in literature response activities [see pp. 122–131] following reading are concept development activities. Picture books, particularly because of the indirect experience provided by the illustrations help children develop rich concepts for unfamiliar words and more information about various topics. Films and filmstrips are another source which many teachers use to help children develop concepts for things that they have not directly experienced [see p. 435]. Even the pervasive "show and tell" period (which some teachers refer to as "bring and brag") can present concept development opportunities. Questions related to the objects brought to share such as, "What is this object made of?" "Is this object more than one foot long?" "Where would we find these objects?" "Can anyone think of other objects that are usually this color?" "Which objects have a narrow space in them? Where?" help refocus the children's attention from who brought what to concept development as it relates to these objects the children are directly experiencing. Group discussions and writing which take place during language arts time can foster concept development as children clarify concepts by talking and writing about them. Science and social studies time should have as their primary goal helping children develop rich concepts for events, places, people, and phenomena.

In addition to taking advantage of all the opportunities presented throughout the elementary school day for concept development, teachers also need to plan lessons so that children build concepts for particular topics and words. There are numerous ways to do this. In the remainder of this section, we will share with you some of our favorites.

Scavenger Hunts (Vaughn, Crawley, & Mountain, 1979) This is a way of gathering objects and pictures to represent concepts which need developing. Imagine that you are about to begin a science unit on weather. You look through the text your students are going to read; preview films, filmstrips, and other teaching aids; and make a list of the unfamiliar vocabulary you will teach as you increase their store of information on the topic of weather. Your list includes; *evaporation, condensation, cirrus clouds, cumulus clouds, stratus clouds, precipitation, temperature, humidity, barometer, thermometer, cyclone, tornado, hurricane, meteorologist, wind vane, rain gauge*, and a variety of other words. Of these words, some can be represented by pictures (indirect experience) and objects (direct experience). Other words such as *evaporation, condensation, precipitation, temperature*, and *humidity* cannot be represented directly or indirectly. Take all the words on your list which can be represented by pictures or objects—*cirrus clouds, cumulus clouds, stratus clouds, barometer, thermometer, cyclone, tornado, hurricane, meteorologist, wind vane*, and *rain gauge* and add to these some familiar, picturable words related to the topic of weather such as *snow, rain, ice, lightning, fog, frost*, and *rainbow* until you have a list of 20 to 25 picturable words which relate to the topic of weather. You now have your list of things for things for which your students will scavenge!

Assign your students to teams of four or five and provide each team with the list. Explain that on _____ (a date a week or two from when the list is provided) the teams are to bring a picture and/or object representing as many of the items on the list as they can find. To the students' inevitable question, "How can I bring a hurricane?", your response will be, "You can bring a picture of a hurricane!" Two points are given for each object and one point for each picture. Pictures can be illustrations, photographs, tracings, or drawings as long as they actually represent the word. Allow the team time to discuss what the different words mean and who might be able to find an object and/or picture representing each. Of course, if some of the words are truly unfamiliar to your students, the question, "What's a rain gauge?" will arise. Depending on the maturity of your students and on whether this is their first or their tenth scavenger hunt, you may choose to respond by explaining what each word means or by saying, "I guess you will have to look it up somewhere. It's hard to find a picture or object which represents something if you don't know what that something is!" This response should send your teams to their dictionaries or other reference sources!

Allow the teams to meet several times during the time they are scavenging. They should check things off the list as pictures and objects are found. Do not, however, allow any pictures or objects to come to school before the appointed date. Teams should be cautioned to keep secret what they find and where they found it. On the appointed day, each team assembles and shows their pictures and objects. The teacher totals the points for each team (two for each object, one for each picture—only one picture and object per word per team). The team with the most points is the winner. Now, winners like to get a prize, and what better prize than being allowed to create the bulletin board. "What bulletin board?" you ask. Why the weather bulletin board, of course. You certainly are not going to let all these pictures go to waste! The winning team should design the bulletin board so that each word is printed in large letters and the different pictures which represent it are displayed with the word. (A word without any pictures might be displayed by its lonely self—a challenge to someone to find a picture). "What about the objects?" you ask. Well, any objects which are valuable, dangerous, or live must, of course, be taken back home. But the rest can be displayed on the table you push underneath the bulletin board! Of course, you will need to say in big bold letters someplace: WEATHER BULLETIN BOARD CREATED BY WINNERS OF WEATHER SCAVENGER HUNT and include a list of the winners' names.

You are now ready to begin your unit on weather. What's more important, your students are now ready. Having spent the last week or two collecting objects and pictures related to the topic of weather has increased their general knowledge of that topic (perhaps they talked to the local meteorologist, or watched the weather report, or even read an intriguing section of the reference book from which they traced their picture of cirrus clouds!), and has greatly increased their interest in the topic of weather. You also have a marvelous bulletin board with representations of the portion of your meaning vocabulary words which can be represented by objects and pictures. Some of your meaning vocabulary which could not be directly or indirectly represented can be easily understood with reference to the pictures and objects: *precipitation* is a form of moisture such as *rain* or *snow; temperature* is measured with *thermometers.*

Now that the children have enjoyed their first scavenger hunt and have begun their actual study of weather, what next? Well, perhaps you plan to study Mexico in social studies soon and your Mexico topic includes such words as *pinata, pyramids, castintets*, and *tacos*; or maybe you are developing a topical word-set on animals with one of your reading groups and words such as *polar bears, cobras*, and *gerbils* are part of that topical word-set. The children will certainly be ready for another scavenger hunt. This time, having learned how to hunt for objects and pictures, how to find out what unfamiliar words mean, and how to create a bulletin board, they will be much more ready to get right to work on locating these representations.

Vocabulary scavenger hunts are our most highly recommended concept development strategy for a variety of reasons:

1. The principle of providing direct and indirect experience with unfamiliar words is adhered to as the students collect objects and pictures.
2. The principle of providing for a variety of different experiences is adhered to since there will be many different pictures and/or objects representing each word and since the students will be talking about these with other team members and resource people as they look for them.
3. The principle of developing word meanings as they relate to topics is adhered to as the objects and pictures being sought all relate to the same topic.
4. Students become involved and interested in the topic to be studied.
5. Students sharpen their reference skills.
6. Once the teacher makes the list, the students are collecting the representations and making the bulletin board. Thus the students, NOT the teacher are doing most of the work!

Word Drama Another favorite method of ours for use with elementary students is word drama, because it provides direct experience for a few students and indirect experience for everyone else. Its only weakness is that it is a method for introducing a word's meaning; other strategies need to be used to provide the necessary repetition for long-term learning of the word. When used with a set of related words, the different word dramas or skits for the different words together provide deeper and deeper understanding from a variety of standpoints of the topic underlying the word-set. The method may be used with any word from a unit or topical word-set that is an action or the manner of an action. It can also be used with any word representing an attribute of such an idea or object. The method proceeds in either of two ways, depending in part on the age and sophistication of the students: Either the teacher or small groups of students make up the skits. To make up a skit, take a word from a word-set and develop a scenario in which students can extemporaneously act and speak to certain specifications so that the meaning of the word being taught becomes clear. The skit is acted out in front of the class and then both the skit and the word being taught are discussed by the class. For instance, imagine that you wish to teach a class of first graders the concept word *curious*. Consider how acting out the following skit might serve as a good introduction to the word *curious*:

> A girl and a boy pretend to be a boy and his mother walking down a street. Two children pretend to be playing hopscotch at one place along the street. Two other children pretend to be adults having a conversation about which one should pay to have a wrecked car repaired at another place. Two more children pretend to be brothers and/or sisters arguing over whose turn it is to help clean up after dinner. As the "mother and son" walk down the street, the boy keeps listening to each conversation, or watching the game, asking questions to try to find out who's winning or what someone said. All this time, the mother keeps trying to get him to come along for she is in a hurry. The mother and everyone else keeps remarking how curious the boy is or that he is too curious.

When the actors finish the skit, the teacher asks the audience what *curious* means. So far, the actors have direct experience with the word *curious*. They were actually in a situation where curious behavior occurred and heard the word *curious* used to symbolize this behavior. The audience has indirect experience; they watched but were not directly involved in a curious experience. Most children, however, have had direct experience with *curious* even if they did not attach the concept word *curious* to the experience. The teacher can help children remember the direct experience they have had by asking, "What have you been curious about?" "Have you ever been in a situation where someone got into trouble for being too curious?" "Do you know someone who is an exceptionally curious person?" While not providing children with the direct experience of *curious*, these access questions help children pull out from their experience a situation in which they experienced *curious* and connect the concept word *curious* with that experience.

TRY IT OUT

Write a skit for a word which can be dramatized. Then, write some questions you could ask children following the skit which would help them remember any direct experience they might have had with the concept and connect the concept word to this experience.

In the Manner of the Adverb In this variation on word drama, you provide your students with indirect experience in the manners of actions. You write a manner in which an action can be performed (an adverb such as *happily, greedily,* or *languidly*) on the board. Then you allow individual students to give you directions such as:

Walk in the manner of the adverb.
Talk in the manner of the adverb.
Answer the doorbell in the manner of the adverb.
Sit at your desk in the manner of the adverb.
Deal with a student in the manner of the adverb.

When students give you a direction which is irrelevant to the manner of acting you are attempting to convey, you just say, "It doesn't apply," and wait until you get one you can act out. After a while, stop to discuss the adverb to see if the understanding of the concept word is developing. At this point you can act out more directions from students or use other strategies to convey meaning of the concept and concept word.

TRY IT OUT

Imagine that the adverb you want to teach is *languidly.* Can you walk in the manner of the adverb (e.g., languidly)? Can you talk in the manner of the adverb? Can you get out of bed in the manner of the adverb? Think of some directions to which you would reply, "does not apply" or "can't be done."

Word Posters In this method, students are asked to select one word from the unit topical word-set and illustrate it with a poster. You can have students sign up for words so that no two posters are about the same word or you can let repetition occur where it will. Both approaches have their advantages and disadvantages. In either case, the students may use whatever textual or human sources available to determine an understanding of the word chosen and then they look for or draw pictures which illustrate the word. In addition, a student may use a short caption for each picture to add to the poster's clarity in representing the concept-word. Word posters are a meaningful homework assignment.

Feature Matrices   Although this method provides only symbolic experience, it does enable students to begin to develop understandings of concept words through first understanding their attributes. This method is based on the idea that words, like people, have features. Some of these features are shared with many other people; others are unique. Have you ever been fascinated by the notion that people are so much alike, yet each person is distinct? The *feature matrix* (Johnson & Pearson, 1978) is a teaching strategy that helps students become aware of the relationships among words and the uniqueness of each word.

The teacher selects a category for the feature matrix that relates to the unit being studied. Once the category is selected, students list five or six members of the category. These category members are listed down the side of the blackboard, overhead transparency, or chart paper.

The teacher then lists, across the top, five or six features that some members of the category share. Now teacher and students are ready to fill in the matrix together. (+ is used to indicate that the member has that feature; − indicates the member does not have that feature.) If our category were animals, the beginnings of our feature matrix might look like this. Can you fill in the missing pluses and minuses?

Category—Animals

Members	Swims	Long Neck	Fins	Claws	Hooves			
Bear	+	−	−	+	−			
Horse	+	+	−	−	+			
Giraffe	−	+	−	−	+			
Whale	+	−	+	−	−			
Porpoise								
Zebra								
———								
———								
———								

Next, the students expand the matrix, adding more members and more features. This is a good activity to do in pairs or small groups. When each group has an expanded matrix, it can trade with another group. Each group can then ask the other questions that focus attention on the shared properties and uniqueness found in the members of a category. One reads across the matrix to discover the unique combination of features for a word or concept and down the matrix to discover which members share which features.

List, Group, and Label   Like feature matrices, list, group, and label lessons (Taba, 1967) provide only symbolic experience and help children define the attributes words share. In addition, list, group, and label lessons help children see how words can belong in a variety of groups (categories) depending on the feature of the word being focused on. A teacher begins a list, group, and label lesson by asking students to list all the words they think of when they think of a certain topic (*weather, Mexico,* or *animals,* for example). The teacher records on a chart or on the board the words the children think of. When a good sized list has been generated, the children are asked to think of some words that "seem to go together in some way." Children thus form groups (younger children tell words in their groups—older children write the words in their group). As different children volunteer what is included in their group they are asked, "Why did you put those words together?" and "What would you call or label that group?" List, group, and label lessons can be done as "unit openers" to diagnose how much children know about a topic and to help them to begin thinking about a topic. They can also be used as a culminating activity to evaluate how much children have learned. [See pp. 333–334 and 451 for sample list, group, and label lessons.]

The Dictionary   Look at the following word and notice how incredibly fast a meaning pops into your mind:

purple

Now think of the definition of *purple.* Aren't you finding that, instead of having a definition of purple memorized, you are having to use your understanding of purple to make one up! In other words, your understanding of words can be used to construct definitions but your understanding of words is not a set of definitions. In fact, your understanding of words is really a set of nonverbal sensations (images, etc.) and semantic associations. Generally, the only words for which you have memorized definitions stored in your memory are those words which you do not understand. For years, one of us kept trying to understand *existentialism* as a philosophy or school of thought. He never understood it, but then, and to this day, he always remembered the definition: "The philosophy that existence precedes essence." Perhaps had he ever come to understand *existentialism,* he would have forgotten that definition. Having students memorize definitions of words as a means of building their meaning vocabularies cannot succeed, because understanding a word means that you do *not* have a definition stored in memory for it. Reading dictionary definitions can *remind* us of meanings we already understand or can refine or add precision to meanings we already have. Expecting a definition to provide the package of semantic association necessary to understanding a word meaning to the point of usefulness is like expecting a photograph to be an adequate substitute for getting to know someone!

Think back to your elementary school days. Do you remember looking up words and copying their definitions? If the word had several definitions (as most words do), which one did you copy? The first one? The shortest one? What did you do if the dictionary definition contained a word for which you didn't know the meaning? Most of us have had the experience of looking up words, copying the definition (first or shortest), and then memorizing it for a test regardless of whether we understood it. As soon as the test was over, however, most of the really unfamiliar words were forgotten. Those words for which you already had some associations were remembered, of course, and their meanings were probably broadened by the experience of checking the dictionary definition. That brings us to our dictionary principle. *Have students use the dictionary to check or add to a word's meaning. Do not allow students to copy definitions!*

There are a variety of ways to promote *active* use of the dictionary which do help students broaden their concepts and also teach students what a valuable resource the dictionary is. Students should learn to turn to the dictionary to find out what an unfamiliar word on the scavenger hunt list is. Often, they will find a picture of the unfamiliar object which can be traced or drawn. Students might also need to look up a word used in a feature matrix to clarify a particular feature of that word. In Chapter 13, you will see Ms. Maverick leading her students through a lesson in which they try to guess the meaning of an unfamiliar word based on the context surrounding that word. The final step in this lesson is for the students to check the appropriate dictionary definition to see how close their definition based on context matches that in the dictionary.

Insult or compliment is an activity (Lake, 1977) in which students sort groups of descriptive words into two categories, "Words I would be insulted by" or "Words I would be complimented by." The list contains some familiar words and some less familiar words. In order to decide how to classify the words, students will need to look up some of the words in the dictionary. You can organize the same activity for food words in a food topical word-set. Foods (*quiche, escargot, pasta*, and *mousse*) could be divided into "Foods I would love to find on my plate tonight" and "Foods that would send me rushing to the nearest fast-food restaurant."

Unfamiliar words can also be put into sentences which capitalize on the fact that they are similar in some ways to other words. "Is a *trapezoid* the bar a trapeze artist practices on?" "Is *treble* the part the soprano sings?" "Is a *mousse* a small furry animal?" Students answer each question "Yes" or "No" and then prepare to defend their answers.

All of these activities (and many more creative teachers use) reflect our principle that the dictionary must be used for checking and adding to meaning and cannot be considered a source through which students learn meanings by copying definitions. These activities result in *active* dictionary use as opposed to passive copying. A student who looks up *captious* to decide if she would be insulted or complimented if this word were used to describe her and finds words in the definition which are unfamiliar, will look up those words, or ask for help, or do something to find out the meaning and thus know how to classify it. Likewise, a student who is trying to decide what to look for on a scavenger hunt will not accept a meaningless dictionary definition. The key to active use of the dictionary is to create a dictionary activity which requires students to do something with the information they find there.

ADD TO YOUR SURVIVAL KIT

Find in reference sources (books and journals) three activities which promote active use of the dictionary. Explain how these activities help students check or broaden meaning and how these activities foster the notion that the dictionary is a valuable resource tool rather than a boring source of copying drudgery.

Concept Development from Reading

So far in this section, we have talked about concept development as an activity which goes on continually in an elementary classroom and promotes reading comprehension. It is, of course, equally important to realize that students gain quite a bit of information about the world and develop concepts from reading. But how can we help children build concepts as they read? Concept development through reading can be promoted if teachers will help children learn to: (1) connect the known to the new, (2) predict and anticipate what might be learned, and (3) monitor how well the information that is being read is being understood and integrated.

Connecting the known to the new requires that students integrate what they know about a subject with what they encounter while reading. In the previous section, many activities were suggested which help children build concepts prior to reading. Some of these activities can be extended to help children connect what they already know to the new information. The feature matrix, for example, is generally completed prior to reading and indicates what an individual or group already knows about the subject. After reading, students can return to the feature matrix they had completed and add to or revise their decisions based on knowledge gained from reading. The list, group, and label lesson can also be used prior to and after reading. A simple strategy for helping children connect the known to the new is to ask them prior to reading to write down one thing they know about the subject and one question they hope the selection will answer. Similarly, students can be presented with a list of statements and decide prior to reading if they think the statements are true or false. After reading, they would update their stores of knowledge in accordance with the new information gained.

Predicting and anticipating what might be learned is closely related to connecting the known to the new. Good readers establish prior to reading what they do and do not know about a topic being covered. They anticipate that much of their prior knowledge will be confirmed but that some new information will be found in the text. Then they read actively to discover what is new. Teachers can help children form the habit of anticipating and predicting by leading them through activities which require them to predict and then, during and after reading, by helping them discover which of their predictions were "on target." Questions such as, "From the title, what do you think this selection will be about?" "What new information do you think you can learn from this selection?" "What do you think will happen next?" lead children to approach the text with an active mind set. Good readers read with an active "will it tell me what I think it might tell me" mind-set rather than with a passive "read and see what it says" attitude. By having predictions to confirm or disaffirm, readers are more apt to add to the store of information in their heads which makes up their concepts for topics and words.

Monitoring how well the information that is being read is being understood and integrated is how good readers decide if they are learning what they need to learn. Most of you can remember a time when you were reading along and suddenly realized your eyes had been looking at the print but your mind was off in another world somewhere. What did you do? If gaining the concepts contained in the text was an important goal for you, you probably backed up to the place where you had been attending and then reread that part which you had not attended to. Have you ever read something which seemed to contradict something you had read three paragraphs earlier? Have you noticed how your eyes can go immediately back to the place where the first piece of information was so that you could resolve the contradiction? Sometimes, when your eyes dart back to the original source of information, you find a typo which resulted in your confusion and sometimes you find that you misread a word. Occasionally, you find that there is indeed a contradiction between what the author said in one place and her statements three paragraphs later. In the following section, *Use Instructional-Level Materials*, you will find a discussion of why having students placed in materials they can comfortably read is crucial for the development of their internal monitoring system. The development of this internal monitoring system is fostered by the teacher as he or she demands that children demand sense from what they read. Questions such as, "Was there anything in what you read which didn't make sense to you?" "Were you able to get out of reading that what you thought you needed to get?" "Where did you have to go back and reread and did that rereading help clarify your confusions?" help children monitor their own concept development.

USE INSTRUCTIONAL-LEVEL MATERIALS

Take the following common-sense quiz:

When learning to play golf, is it better to use clubs that feel comfortable or uncomfortable in your hands?

When learning to bowl, is it better to use a ball that is too heavy for you or one that you can carry comfortably?

When learning to drive a car, should you be allowed to adjust the seat or should you have to sit at the distance for the average person your age?

When learning to ski, should you begin on a slope you can handle or on one beyond your ability?

When learning to read, should you be given material that is hard or comfortable for you to read?

Challenge may be good for your character but there is no evidence that it is good for your reading ability. Cooper (1952) found that the easier the assigned reading book was for children to read, the greater their reading gain for the year. This finding held true for both boys and girls, for students in grades two through six, and for below-average, average, and above-average readers. Ekwall (1974; 1976) found that students reading test passages difficult for them exhibited signs of frustration and anxiety which could be measured by a polygraph machine. Jorgenson (1977) found that the easier the assigned reading book was for children to read, the better their behavior in the classroom. If these research findings do not convince you that students learn to read better when given confortable materials, consider some reasons why it is so.

Students Read More Words Per Lesson

For most children, the more difficult the material the slower they read. This relationship tends to hold true during both oral and silent reading.

Moreover, when reading difficult material orally students tend to make more oral reading errors and therefore, are interrupted more often for correction by the teacher or other students. These interruptions also reduce the number of words a student gets to read during the lesson. If it is obvious that one way students get better in reading is to successfully read more words per lesson, then it should be equally obvious that students will successfully read more words per lesson the more comfortable the material they are given.

What the Teacher Does Matters More

Even though both research and experience support the fact that those who read comfortable materials in reading class achieve better in reading than those who read difficult materials, some teachers still seem to feel more needed when students are reading challenging material. They have sometimes expressed to us that the more words children miss when reading orally or the more problems they have with comprehension, the more "teaching" they get to do. The assumption is that the more teaching they do the more the students will learn. At first, this assumption seems plausible but, under examination, it can be seen to be an illusion.

Suppose that you are teaching some young people to bowl. Imagine that you have provided them with bowling balls which are in every case several pounds too heavy for them to use comfortably. You will indeed be busier as a bowling instructor than if you had given them balls of a more appropriate weight. You will probably be called on more often to help them carry the balls than you would if they were lighter. You will probably teach more students how to have the pins reset when their balls go into the gutter both times in a frame. You will probably spend more time providing first aid to bruised thighs and feet from students having hit their legs with the ball during their motions, or from students having dropped the ball before getting to the lane. Since you will have fewer strikes, it will take longer to finish bowling the practice games. The question is whether the extra time and effort required on the bowling instructor's part matters? Are the students better bowlers than they would have been had you, the instructor, been able to take less time with peripheral matters and more time with the actual bowling lessons? Is it possible that you could have spent less total time and energy and produced better bowlers?

In teaching reading, teachers may be busier if they have to tell the students a lot of words they do not know and to explain what the selection is about because they do not understand what they are reading, but the question is whether the extra time and effort required on the teachers' part matters? Will what teachers do matter more when they focus on a few words, skills, learnings, or tasks and teach them carefully and in depth or when they try to teach many words, skills, learnings, and tasks with little pattern, repetition, or depth of study? It should be obvious by now that what the teacher does matters more when the teacher can spend all the time with students helping them learn a few things well. This situation can only occur if the material used with the students is easy enough to allow the teacher to focus on just the aspects of reading the text which are probably new for the learners.

Students Concentrate More on the Purpose of the Lesson

Every reading lesson should have a purpose. Students are learning one or more sight words through their repetition in the passage, learning to apply one or more decoding skills, reading to learn meanings for one or more words, reading to gain some knowledge, or reading to learn one or more comprehension strategies. If students are reading comfortable material, they can concentrate on the words, skills, learnings, or tasks which are the focus of the lesson. If the material is hard to read, however, they must also concentrate on many words and sentences (in order to read them) which are not the focus of the lesson.

Imagine that the focus of a golf lesson is to learn how to put backspin on the ball when shooting short-iron shots. If the student has golf clubs with shafts that are too long, he or she might have to concentrate on modifying the grip and backswing and therefore not concentrate on the angle at which the club face hits the ball. In reading, like golf, it makes sense that the learner needs to concentrate on the purpose of the lesson. It also makes sense that the harder the materials being read are, the less likely the reader will be able to avoid distractions and concentrate on that purpose.

The fact that students do concentrate *more* the more comfortable the material they are reading has been repeatedly substantiated by recent research studies (Britton, Holdredge, & Westbrook, 1978; Britton, Ziegler, & Westbrook, 1980; Britton, 1980). These studies found that students took longer to react to distracting clicks presented to them during silent reading when they were reading easy material. The easier the material was, the more time it took to react; the harder the material was, the less time it took to react. Britton and his associates have concluded that reading easy material uses more *cognitive capacity* than does reading hard material.

Students Like Reading Better

Admit it! When you are beginning to read an assignment for a course you are taking and you expect that reading to be challenging, don't you count how many pages you have to read? And when it is a large number, don't you groan a little before beginning? When you are reading for enjoyment, do you *choose* to read difficult material? Do you like reading material which is hard to read? When you are reading something hard such as an article about something you know little about and you have a choice, don't you generally stop reading it? School children can be expected to have less tolerance for discomfort than adults. Can it be surprising that some children who are used to reading hard materials complain about reading, ask when reading will be over, count the pages to each assigned selection, and groan or sigh?

The students in schools who read the most and who like to read the most are also the students for whom reading is and has been the most comfortable; the students who read the least and who like to read the least are the students for whom reading is and has been the most difficult. All good readers who love to read have had a lengthy period of extensive, comfortable reading; few if any poor readers who hate to read have had such a period. If students who like to read do better in reading, is it not obvious that comfortable material fosters a like for reading more than difficult material?

Students Develop an Internal Monitoring System

In Chapter 8, "What is Reading?", we will demonstrate that *print processing* is all the things that a reader must do (other than visual word identification) that the listener need not do to construct an internal representation of the external text. Print processing will be described as consisting of moving the eyes appropriately, coordinating print with sound, coordinating print with meaning, and coordinating the print-sound link with the print-meaning link. Do you ever remember being taught to move your eyes in a certain way in school? Do you remember being taught to coordinate your voice or subvoice with print perception? Do you remember being taught any of the print processing abilities? Yet, if you are a good reader, you developed print processing ability; and if you are a poor reader, you probably did not. How do good readers develop print processing ability when print processing is not taught? They learn print processing by using what might be called an *internal biofeedback system.*

Biofeedback Until the 1960s, the ancient claims of Oriental sages that they could control internal bodily functions such as heart rate or temperature were considered superstitious folklore by Western medical science. In the mid 1960s, however, techniques were developed through which almost anyone could learn to control blood pressure, brain-wave patterns, heart rate, etc. These techniques have collectively been called *biofeedback*.

Although the elementary and secondary school health textbooks of a generation ago pronounced that these internal bodily functions were *automatic* and thus beyond a person's conscious control and manipulation, it seems that the only reason people cannot ordinarily control such functions is that they have no awareness of immediate changes in them. It is not the problem, then, that we cannot control these functions, but that without feedback on how those functions are changing at any one moment we do not know when and in what direction we are controlling them. Biofeedback is a technique of learning to control these internal functions previously thought to be automatic. Biofeedback works by using electronic monitoring to provide a person with immediate and continuous feedback on the functioning of the organ or process to be regulated. Most persons receiving this feedback begin to be able to manipulate the functioning in the desired direction. Provided with a meter giving a constant and precise reading of one's blood pressure, one can concentrate on the meter and modify the blood pressure. Of course, it is not known what the person does internally to change the blood pressure only that concentrating on the meter makes it possible.

Internal Monitoring and Print Processing Readers develop print processing the same way athletes and patients learn to regulate involuntary motor functions such as heart beat rate or blood pressure: they use a monitoring or feedback system. When a doctor or a physical education director arranges for a patient or an athlete to use biofeedback, that person is not teaching the patient or athlete to regulate internal processes. Rather she is providing the patient or athlete with a meter or some other monitor so that the patient or athlete learns to regulate internal processes by causing the meter or other monitor to fluctuate up or down. Readers, too, can only learn to control print processing if they have a monitor to consult while reading. The only monitor students can consult during reading is their internal response to what they are reading. If students are not getting the meaning they know they ought to be getting, they begin subconsciously to manipulate their eye movements, their voice/subvoice, their rate of reading, their rereading, etc., until they begin to get a sensible interpretation of the text. How does this internal monitoring system develop? From reading lots of comfortable materials over a considerable period of time. How do students know what internal responses they should be getting from reading if they have not been in the habit of getting them? Only students who know what good reading comprehension is like can use that knowledge as a monitor to help them develop the print processing adult reading material often demands. The only students who know what good reading comprehension is like are those who have read enough comfortable material to experience it truly and frequently.

Readers who have experienced good reading comprehension enough to have a real sense of what it is like concentrate on monitoring their comprehension with internal questions like these:

Does this make sense to me?
Does this sound like language to me?
Am I achieving my purpose(s) for reading this?
Do I feel like I am reading?

Asking internal monitoring questions like these and concentrating while reading on getting positive responses to them works like biofeedback in helping the reader to learn to control the many print processing abilities. Of course, it is not known what the reader does internally to change his eye movements, print-sound coordination, etc., only that concentrating on internal monitoring makes it possible.

Because having students read interesting materials is important, it seems prudent to follow this suggestion: Use the most interesting and appealing materials which are comfortable for the students to read.

TEACH COMPREHENSION LESSONS IN INSTRUCTIONAL-LEVEL MATERIALS

Regardless of how well and how meaningfully beginning reading and word identification have been taught; regardless of how well students have been placed in instructional-level materials; and regardless of how well concepts for topics and words have been taught, when reading few students will comprehend as well as they might, and some will not comprehend very well at all unless they have been taught to do so by a teacher. A teacher guiding students through the comprehension of an interesting piece of written language at the students' instructional level is the core of any program to improve reading comprehension. No teaching machine, no set of "teacher proof" instructional materials, and no teacher management system can replace a competent, confident, dedicated, and supported teacher actively engaged in leading students "by the mind" through reading comprehension lessons.

Unfortunately, there is evidence that few teachers spend much time directly teaching students to comprehend. Classroom observations by Durkin (1978–1979) revealed that less than 1 percent of reading instructional time in fourth grade was given to direct comprehension instruction while nearly 18 percent of the time was spent assessing whether students had comprehended something they had been assigned to read. Moreover, teachers who rely on lesson plans printed in teachers' manuals of basal reading series are not apt to be providing very much in the way of direct comprehension instruction (Beck et al., 1979; Durkin, 1981).

A comprehension lesson is the direct guidance given to students before, during, and after comprehension of written language. All comprehension lessons have at least four steps:

Comprehension Lesson Steps

STEP 1. Establish purpose(s) for comprehending.

A reading comprehension lesson without having clear purposes for comprehending would be absurd—like a piano lesson without touching the piano, or a golf lesson without touching a club, or a painting lesson without brushes, paints, and canvasses! And it is necessary to have the students read with a purpose directly related to the strategy the lesson is designed to teach. There are many possible purposes for comprehending, because there are four strategies and innumerable passages one might try to teach students. (A method of generating purposes for comprehending based on the range of possible strategies to teach will be described after this section.) Whatever the instructional goal of the lesson, students must clearly, precisely, and completely understand their purpose for comprehending (and this is not always easy to accomplish). For example, telling students to read to get the main idea is jibberish to any student who does not understand what a main idea is. Any comprehension lesson in which a student does not really know what she is reading for cannot possibly teach that student the strategy on which that purpose for comprehending is based. Sometimes a demonstration or the presentation of a number of examples is necessary before students understand what they are to do, learn, produce, etc., while or after reading.

STEP 2. Have students read for the established purpose(s).

The most important part of this step is that the students develop and use self-monitoring while they read. In the beginning, this goal may necessitate that the teacher actually interrupt the students during reading and ask them questions about their awareness of their performance: "Are you doing what I asked you to do?", or "Will you be able to tell me what I asked you to be able to tell me when you finish reading?", or "Will you know _____ when you get through the way I asked you to?", etc. Later, it may be necessary for the teacher to remind the students only at the beginning of their reading that they are to stop regularly and test themselves to see if they are accomplishing their purpose for comprehending.

STEP 3.   Have students perform some task which directly reflects and measures accomplishment of each establishment purpose for comprehending.

In most instances it will be obvious and commonsensical what task one would use to measure the established purpose. For example, if students were given the purpose in Step 1, "Read so that you can define *chartreuse*," obviously they should be asked to define *chartreuse* in Step 3!

STEP 4.   Provide direct feedback concerning students' comprehension based on their performance on that task.

The only way students can be informed about the quality of their comprehension for the assigned purpose (and the quality of their self-monitoring based on that purpose during reading) is to receive clear and abundant feedback concerning the precise nature of their response to the task. A caution is that there will rarely be *one and only one* "right" response and students must not be taught that they are trying to guess exactly what the author or teacher would have done or said. In some respects, any response without problems is an acceptable one; if nothing can be found wrong with a response, it is acceptable however different from the teacher's or author's. As much as possible, the group of students should provide feedback to individuals rather than the teacher conducting a monologue of praise and criticism.

In addition to having these four mandatory steps, many comprehension lessons begin with an optional readiness step:

READINESS STEP.   Cue access to or develop background knowledge assumed by the text.

To avoid insulting the reader and to save words, most authors leave unsaid that which they feel the reader can easily reconstruct. For example, in the sentence,

> The promotion of the Generalissimo was conducted by bullets rather than by gavels.

the author assumes a great deal of knowledge on the part of the reader about the way governments operate. A reader who does not have that knowledge or who has it but does not make use of it will suffer a lack of comprehension. For this step, ask yourself what background knowledge the author of the text has assumed that your students might not have. If you conclude that the students have the assumed background knowledge, cue them that they will need to use that knowledge while reading to relate the new to the known; if you conclude that the students lack so much background knowledge that it cannot be built for them within a reasonable time, do not use the selection; and if you conclude that the students lack some background knowledge (including concept-word meanings) but that you can build it within a reasonable time, provide that instruction before asking students to read the selection.

Generic Comprehension Lesson Plans

A number of generic comprehension lesson plans have been developed over the years and have been given various, often arbitrary, names. Several of these lesson plans are described in detail in other parts of this book, but some of them will be introduced and briefly discussed here. In each case, you will be referred to other sections for additional, more complete information.

A *directed reading lesson* (also called a *directed reading activity*) begins with a readiness step, continues with purpose setting and silent reading, and has students recite, answer questions, or perform an activity, then receive feedback. The DRL (or DRA) also often includes an attempt to motivate students before the lesson, some oral reading following the feedback step, and follow-up activities such as skills instruction or extension. [See pages 427–429.]

A *guided reading procedure* is actually a two-part lesson in which the first part follows the four mandatory steps of any comprehension lesson. In the second part, students reorganize or reconstruct the original message of the text, answer inferential or critical questions about the text, and take a short-term and, later, a long-term test. [See Chapter 13.]

A *directed reading-thinking activity* leads students to develop their own purposes for comprehending by having them make predictions before reading based on the title, headings (if any), and illustrations (if any). Students then read to verify or refute the predictions. The feedback step is conducted by having the students search the text to find statements that verify or refute their predictions. [See pages 370–372.]

Possible sentences also leads students to develop their own purposes for comprehending. They select two or more words from a list of key words from the selection to be read and construct a sentence using those words which is possibly though not necessarily true. The students do not have to know that it is true, only that it is possible. As in a DR-TA, the feedback step is conducted by having the students search the text to find statements that verify or refute their predictions.

A *listening-reading transfer lesson* is a parallel lesson in which a directed listening lesson is followed by a directed reading lesson, both of which have the same general purpose for comprehending. Students are told between the two lessons that now they should do the same thing when they read that they did when they listened. [See pages 448–450.]

A Method for Generating Purposes for Comprehending

The crux of any comprehension lesson plan is the purpose-setting step. Because the choice of a purpose for comprehending is so central to a comprehension lesson, this section presents a method for generating comprehension purposes. The method is based on the notion that there are four comprehension strategies.

1. The first comprehension strategy is *understanding what is stated*. When employing this strategy, the reader resists going off on tangents caused by overemphasizing some parts of the message and ignoring others (Thorndike, 1917). The reader is careful to separate his own feelings, beliefs, and knowings from those expressed by the author of the text. The goal of this strategy is the literal understanding of the total passage as well as all of its parts.

2. The second comprehension strategy is *attending to what is important*. A reader should always attempt to be true to both the WHAT and the WHY of reading. If the first comprehension strategy seems especially oriented to the WHAT, the second strategy is more oriented to the WHY. Here, the reader uses the purpose(s) for reading this particular text to determine what in the text is important and should be considered in depth and what is not important and can reasonably be discarded from consideration. The goal of this strategy is to give the greatest attention to the most important aspects of the text given the purpose for reading and the least attention to the least important aspects.

3. The third comprehension strategy is *inferring what is not stated*. When employing the first comprehension strategy of understanding what is stated, it may become clear to the reader that there is knowledge and reasoning which the author did not give but which she obviously expects a reader to use. Or it may become clear to the reader that his purpose for reading would be better served if he used knowledge and reasoning to draw conclusions or make generalizations not stated in the text (and perhaps not thought of by the author). The goal of this strategy is to add to the interpretation of a text whatever information or creative ideas are either necessary or desirable given the text and the purpose for reading it.

4. The fourth comprehension strategy is *restructuring what is produced through understanding, attending, and inferring*. It could be said that the second comprehension strategy is basically leaving out of one's interpretation of a text that which is redundant, trivial, or not germane given the purpose for reading and that the third comprehension strategy is basically one of adding to one's interpretation of a text that which is necessary or desirable given the purpose for reading. Obviously, these two strategies change the elements of the internal text from being all those and only those of the external text. As soon, then, as one or both of these strategies is used by a reader, the reader must restructure the new

set of elements into a whole because the text would otherwise have gaps and additions which were not integrated. The goal of this strategy is a coherent interpretation of the text given the deletions and additions made through the employment of the other comprehension strategies.

A purpose for a comprehension lesson is constructed by taking one or more of these four strategies, making it specific to the text used, developing a description, a model, or an example of the task the reader(s) will perform after reading, and producing an imperative sentence or sentences.

Imagine, for example, that a group of second graders were asked to read "The Bremen Town Musicians" during a reading lesson. Applying the four reading comprehension strategies, these are some of the purposes for comprehending which can be generated from the story:

Read so you can list everything that happened in the story in the right order. (Understanding)

Read so you can explain where the four animals were going and what they were going to do there. (Attending)

Read so you can describe what happened to the robber who returned to the house to see if it were all right for the robbers to come back. (Attending)

Read so you can describe what a town musician was and what one did. (Inferring)

Read so you can explain why the owners of the four animals all wanted to get rid of them. (Inferring)

Read so you can retell the story in your own words. (Understanding and Restructuring)

Pretend you are the robber who returned to the house. Read so you can act out what the robber told the other robbers. (Attending and Restructuring)

Pretend that the owners of the four animals came together after the animals left. Read so you can tell what each of the owners said to the others. (Inferring and Restructuring)

Read so you can tell in 50 words or fewer why the animals set out for Bremen and what happened to them on the way. (Understanding, Attending, Inferring, and Restructuring)

Again, once one or more of these purposes have been constructed and placed in Step 1 of the comprehension lesson plan, then the other steps logically follow.

Guidelines for Teaching Comprehension Lessons

An almost infinite number of specific lesson plans can be generated using the optional readiness step and the four mandatory steps of comprehension lessons in conjunction with the method for generating purposes for comprehending. Several guidelines for the actual planning and teaching of these specific comprehension lesson plans are now in order.

Use fewer purposes per lesson the younger or more disabled the students are. Younger or severely disabled students will need to focus on one purpose per lesson; more experienced or less disabled students can read for a few purposes per lesson when those purposes reflect the same strategy; and good readers can read for several unrelated purposes in the same lesson.

Repeated readings for different purposes are appropriate for some students. When students are especially young or disabled, reading the same selection two or more times, each time for a different purpose, can be very beneficial.

Spaced practice is better than massed practice. This guideline simply means that it is more effective to teach a lesson each Monday for five weeks on the same strategy than it is to teach a lesson every day for one five-day week on that strategy. Teachers should have a spiral to their lessons where each week sees several strategies being taught or re-taught.

Purposes for comprehending should be based on both the text and the needs and abilities of the students. Purposes for comprehending must never be imposed on a text to the extent that the text is bent or distorted by the purpose. This is merely to say that not all strategies can be taught with a specific text. The purpose for comprehending must respect the text in the sense that what the students read for is relevant and important to the text. While any text lends itself to being read for a variety of purposes, some texts will be far better than others for teaching particular strategies.

Purposes for comprehending must likewise never be imposed on students without regard to their current readiness or their current needs. While any group of students will have a variety of strategies they need and are ready to learn at any one time, some strategies will be far more appropriate and useful than others to teach. (For help in determining students' needs and abilities relative to comprehension strategies, see the section "Diagnosing Comprehension" in Chapter 6.)

Be sure you are teaching, not just testing, comprehension. It is not the four mandatory steps that ensure students will learn to comprehend better. Rather, it is the way those steps are carried out. Purpose setting will merely be an assignment unless the teacher makes absolutely certain the students understand the purpose(s) for comprehending and are clear about the specifics of the task they will perform after reading. Moreover, the teacher should tell the students anything she can to help them to successfully read for the purpose(s). During reading the teacher should help the students in any efficient way. When the students are engaged in the task following reading, the teacher must give direct help to students when they are unable to overcome a problem. And the feedback provided to students about their performance must be informative and helpful, not just whether they were correct or incorrect. Students do not perform the task to demonstrate they read the material; they perform it so they and you can see if they are learning to employ the strategy from which the comprehension purpose was generated. When teaching comprehension, students do not fail, lessons do.

PROVIDE TIME AND MOTIVATION FOR INDIVIDUAL READING

No one ever becomes very good at something solely by being given good instruction. Excellent pianists, violinists, painters, sculptors, golfers, tennis players, etc. have always had good teaching, training, or coaching but they have also always had much individual practice. In each case, several minutes of practice must occur for each minute of instruction or the talent does not develop. This relationship has at least one parallel in schools: Math educators often advocate that children spend three minutes practicing computation for every one minute of instruction in computation.

When teaching reading, teachers should realize that regardless of the quality of the reading instruction a child receives that child is not apt to develop into a good reader without considerable additional reading outside of reading class time. Those of you who are good readers will recall reading many unassigned books during your elementary school years.

From your own experience, and from our rationale for using comfortable materials during reading lessons, it should be obvious that easy materials must be provided if students are to choose to read for enjoyment and relaxation, and if their reading ability is to improve from such reading. In addition, interest is much more a factor when students are reading at their own pace and of their own volition. Books of a wide variety of types and subjects must be available if all students are to become involved in individual reading.

Developing individual reading is every bit as important as developing concepts for topics and words and teaching comprehension lessons in instructional level materials. Because it is so important, and because so little attention is devoted to it in some classrooms, the next chapter is "Reading and Responding to Literature for Children." As you will soon discover, there are many opportunities and ways to provide time and motivation for individual reading.

4 | Reading and Responding to Literature for Children

In the galaxy of literature, a world of books exists for children. These books contain some of the very best writing currently being produced. Children may read a variety of materials, including the books and magazines of adults, but the field labeled "children's literature" consists of books that are expressly written for children and which achieve literary and artistic excellence (Sutherland, Monson & Arbuthnot, 1981). Various awards are presented to the authors and illustrators of children's literature, encouraging them to strive for this excellence. These awards include the John Newbery Medal, the Randolph Caldecott Medal, the National Book Award, and The Boston Globe-Horn Book Award. However, not all literature for children consists of books which have been in contention for any of these awards. Most all of you probably grew up reading the Nancy Drew or Hardy Boys series books. Though they are not "quality" books as defined by the award givers and book reviewers, they are nonetheless books which children read and enjoy and search out. Because of the existence and popularity of these types of books, we have purposely used the terms *literature for children* and *children's books* in this chapter. We are discussing classroom uses of books which children can and will read, as well as books judged by adults to be quality pieces. We subscribe to the idea that children need a balanced literary diet. After all, what was the last piece of literature you read? Was it a classic or was it the latest best seller?

Children's tastes in literature are varied, and, fortunately, the world of literature for children is broad and encompassing. You may not be aware of just how broad and encompassing this world is. In fact, there are entire books written about literature for children which detail the varied genres, describe the books within those genres, and describe the authors and illustrators of those books.

There are children's books for all ages and interests. The genres of books include poetry, folk literature, fantasy, modern and historical fiction, alphabet and counting books, wordless books, mystery, biography, and informational books. Three of these literature types, folk literature, fantasy, and informational books, may not be familiar to you by the title we have used. Because of this, we will describe these three rather carefully. At the same time, by seeing how broad these three genres are, you can see that all genres may be broader than you suspect. As we said, there is a world of literature available for children.

Folk literature encompasses fairy tales, folk tales, epics, myths, and fables. Though modern fairy tales such as *The Princess and Froggie** may be written, we normally think of fairy tales as part of folk literature. Folk literature consists of tales for which there is no identifiable single author or for whom authorship is in doubt because the stories have been in existence for so long. Folk literature was first part of the oral tradition and was only written down much later. For that reason, modern fairy tales are part of the genre known as fantasy.

Fantasy is also a broad genre. It includes both classic fantasies (such as *Alice's Adventures in Wonderland*) and modern ones (such as *Charlotte's Web*) as well as science fiction and science fantasy. The distinction between these last two may be somewhat blurry. But, essentially, science fiction books contain scientific facts which have the possibility of being extrapolated into reality; science fantasy books involve the supernatural or are so futuristic that currently known scientific facts do not allow the extrapolation which occurs. A good example of science fiction is *The Endless Pavement*, whereas *A Wrinkle in Time* embodies the essence of science fantasies.

Another type of book which is quite rich is informational books. This category contains factual materials for science, social studies, cooking, and other content areas, as well as "concept books" dealing with the relationships of time, space, and amount (such as *Inside, Outside, Upside Down*). When we think of informational books, often an image of dull, pedantic, sterile writing comes to mind. If that once were characteristic of informational books, it certainly is so no longer. The illustrations and photographs of many current informational books enrich the text and are often of high quality; the writing is lively and entertaining. These books explain something to children or teach them how to do something. For example there are many, many children's cookbooks such as *Pickle in the Middle and Other Easy Snacks* and *More Science Experiments You Can Eat*. Other books explain science concepts to children in a clear, yet interesting, way such as *Flash, Crash, Rumble, and Roll* and *What's Inside?* Children learn about life in prehistoric times with *In the Time of Dinosaurs* and learn how to write with the symbols of another language in *You Can Write Chinese*. *Just a Box* describes various ways children can use boxes to make toys and furniture. And then there are books such as *Still More Tell Me Why* which provide answers to many of the questions children commonly ask.

---

* References for this children's book and others in this chapter are located at the end of the chapter.

A major value of informational books in the classroom is that a teacher can use these books to expand topics introduced in children's textbooks. Indeed, the content of content reading is not just textbooks; the content includes informational books and periodicals, also. Content reading helps children to understand and better organize the world in which they live; informational books provide a wonderful way to do that. They are often more interesting than children's textbooks because the authors of children's informational books know that their products will be purchased and read by children if the children enjoy them. The textbook has a teacher who guides children through the information, providing necessary help to understand and organize that information. Informational trade books must depend on the author's writing style to be appealing and interesting as well as informative.

Rather than describing in detail other genres of literature for children, this chapter focuses on the use of literature in the classroom. As we have mentioned, there are many excellent compendiums of children's literature, and you no doubt have encountered or will encounter one in your course on children's literature. We urge you to keep that reference text, for you can use it frequently as you attempt to provide a wide and varied literature program for your students. In addition, we have listed in Appendix A several sources of books and articles that further describe children's books, their authors, and ways to use books in the classroom.

READ SOME MORE ABOUT THIS

In order to become familiar with compendiums of children's literature, divide your class into three groups and have each group be responsible for one of the following texts. Each group should come back to the class and describe the scope of their book and the range of information that it contains. Be sure to examine the book's table of contents, appendixes, and indexes. What categories of children's books are dealt with? What information can one obtain by using the book as a reference source? How much information is given about authors, individual book titles, and ways to use books with children?

Anderson, W., and Groff, P. *A new look at children's literature.* Belmont, Calif. Wadsworth, 1972.

Huck, C. *Children's literature in the elementary school* (3rd. ed., updated.) New York: Holt, Rinehart and Winston, 1979.

Sutherland, Z., Monson, D., and Arbuthnot, M. H. *Children and books*, 6th ed., Glenview, Ill.: Scott, Foresman, 1981.

(If any of these books are not available, locate any three compendiums used in the teaching of children's literature classes.)

WHY USE LITERATURE FOR CHILDREN?

Literature from the genres we just described as well as other genres is essential to your reading program for several reasons. This section will discuss reading to learn and reading to experience, as well as using literature to improve students' reading abilities and attitudes toward reading.

Reading to Learn

Literature for children expands their knowledge and awareness of the world. It allows children to learn about people, events, and locations that are beyond the possibility of face-to-face contact. Literature expands children's horizons by presenting to them people such as Marco Polo and Geronimo, events such as the Crusades and the first landing on the moon, and locations such as the Amazon and the North Pole. Young readers can be transported to other times and other places and learn about new things. They can follow Kit from Barbados to Connecticut and learn about the Puritans' way of life in *The Witch of Blackbird Pond*, and they can live with Sam and learn about survival in a mountain wilderness in *My Side of the Mountain*. Additionally, children can learn that they are not alone in their wishes, successes, and rejections. The insights gained about characters' dilemmas and solutions to dilemmas give children different perspectives which allow them to broaden their understanding of situations and human relationships.

Literature not only expands children's awareness of the world through vicarious experiences, but it deepens that awareness. When children emotionally identify with story characters they can experience the events more deeply than if they only read about the events in a textbook. Children who read *Roll of Thunder, Hear My Cry* learn well what life was like for rural Blacks in the South during the Depression. This learning takes hold and becomes meaningful because readers share Cassie's anger at her and her family's persecution; readers do not simply read a catalog of problems that Black people in those circumstances had to face. As readers enter into the world suggested by an author, they strip away objective detachment and participate emotionally in that world. Such participation deepens understandings and appreciations for what they read.

Reading to Experience

Much literature for children qualifies as works of art, and centering children's attention on such works provides them the opportunity for aesthetic reading. An aesthetic experience is a perception of beauty. We experience the aesthetic in literature when we become absorbed in the combination of sensations, ideas, and emotions conveyed by a particular literary work. In aesthetic reading, how the author constructed the message is more important than *what* the message actually is. It has a liberating effect because we transcend our perception of individual aspects of a literary work and perceive all aspects in a synthesis of senses, understandings, and feelings. For instance, countless children have read or listened to *The Elephant's Child* primarily at the aesthetic level. They become quite absorbed by the language cadence and rhythm, the imagery, and their identification with the young elephant who runs away to "the great grey-green, greasy Limpopo River." Young children generally appreciate this story for its exquisite writing more than for its message about curiosity.

Another way to explain the nature of an aesthetic experience is to point out that aesthetic reading requires that we encounter the literary work, itself (Rosenblatt, 1968). In practical reading, we can read an exact paraphrase that can be as useful and have as much impact as reading the original. Reading an exact paraphrase of a biology textbook has the same effect as reading the original. However, in aesthetic reading we need to experience the actual literary work. For example consider the following poem by Langston Hughes (1932):

April Rain Song

Let the rain kiss you.
Let the rain beat upon your head with silver liquid drops.
Let the rain sing you a lullaby.

The rain makes still pools on the sidewalk.
The rain makes running pools in the gutter.
The rain plays a little sleep-song on our roof at night —

And I love the rain.

Any attempt to paraphrase this poem would destroy its essence because the delicacy of the language would be lost. Clearly, aesthetic reading involves qualities of language beyond the direct, specific meanings denoted by words.

Reading literature also can be just plain enjoyable. The Dr. Seuss books, *Winnie-the-Pooh*, and *Frog and Toad Together* are examples of books which exist mainly for the joy of reading. But you should realize also that reading literature for pleasure is as important as reading to increase abilities or to develop knowledge of the world. That is, escaping into a good mystery or fantasy book can provide the release many of us need in order to cope with the pressures of the outside world. Children can use some escape, too. They can identify with Max in *Where the Wild Things Are*, who is sent to his room but who escapes through his imagination to the land of the Wild Things. After holding a wild rumpus there, Max leaves the land of the Wild Things and returns to his real-life home and finds dinner still hot and waiting for him. Like Max, children often need to escape to other worlds and let their imaginations run free. Children can make their escapes on their own or through books. But whatever the case, the relaxation, escape, and enjoyment that children derive from literature can be a healthy and worthwhile outcome.

Reading to Improve Abilities

As we said in Chapter 3, students require practice with independent-level materials in order to improve their reading abilities. When they read, good readers attend to such things as letter-sound relationships, punctuation, and the gist of a passage. Good readers fluently integrate all these sources of information. Because of this, young readers require practice with quantities of reading material at their independent levels so that they can become good, fluent readers. Making literature available for children to self-select and read on their own provides them the opportunity for such practice.

Reading quantities of literature helps students anticipate upcoming parts of stories. Good readers seem to have an abstract conception of what a typical story is like. They know that stories have elements such as settings and characters, that the characters have goals, and that there are outcomes and reactions to outcomes as characters pursue their goals (McConaughy, 1980). In order to become adept at anticipating which of these story elements is coming up next, children need to read and listen to multitudes of well-formed stories. Such stories abound in the world of literature for children.

Another outcome of children's literature on reading abilities is that children become accustomed to whole stories and books. Materials published specifically for reading instruction frequently consist of excerpts of children's literature, but entire works generally are not reprinted. Thus, if young readers are to become proficient with complete books, then they need a program that allows them to deal with such.

Reading to Promote Attitudes

Many reading programs devote exclusive attention toward teaching students *how* to read. That is, young students work daily on developing their word identification and comprehension skills by reading short instructional passages and by completing worksheets that are related to the passages. The problem with these programs is that they neglect to show students *why* they should read. The skills work frequently is done at the expense of developing interests and attitudes toward reading, and the result is students who can read but who have no desire to do so. Including literature for children as a regular part of your classroom reading program helps ensure that this does not happen.

Furthermore, providing students with a quantity of interesting, compelling books motivates them to learn how to read even better. If books are seen as an enjoyable way to learn new things and experience new feelings, then they become friends and something to seek out rather than enemies or obstacles to avoid. Students who look forward to reading and story-telling time because they appreciate what they get out of it are motivated to become better readers and listeners. And students who are motivated have a far better chance of developing their reading and listening abilities than students who are not motivated.

READ SOME MORE ABOUT THIS

Choose five books from an author in column one or three books from an author in column two and read them carefully, noting both text and illustrations. Make a note card for each book labeled with each of the four factors discussed above: reading to learn, reading to experience, reading to improve abilities, and reading to promote attitudes toward reading. Describe how these factors apply to each book. Bring the books and your note cards to class and share your findings in small groups.

Column One (Primary Grades)	Column Two (Intermediate Grades)
Franklyn M. Branley	Judy Blume
Leo & Diane Dillon	Beverly Cleary
Ezra Jack Keats	Jane Louise Curry
Leo Lionni	Roald Dahl
Mercer Mayer	Leon Garfield
Gerald McDermott	Jean George
Bill Peet	Mollie Hunter
Maurice Sendak	Madeleine L'Engle
Uri Shulevitz	Eve Merriam
Isaac Bashevis Singer	Katherine Patterson
Judith Viorst	Richard Peck
Brian Wildsmith	Ellen Raskin
Margot & Harve Zemach	Shel Silverstein
Herbert Zim	Laura Ingalls Wilder

INCORPORATING LITERATURE FOR CHILDREN IN THE READING PROGRAM

You can view the use of literature in your classroom reading program along a continuum. To make an analogy, let's say that you are on The Reading Railroad and are traveling on the literature tracks. You get on at NewTeacher Station and settle in your seat for the trip. As you click down the tracks, you begin to talk with some of your fellow travelers about their destinations. You had no idea that there were so many possible stops on these tracks! The people you are with are getting off at four literature stations: NoLit, SomeLit, LottaLit, and AllLit.

NoLit Station

The first stop on these tracks, according to one group of teachers, is NoLit Station where they will be leaving the train. Unfortunately, they say, all their reading instruction is based on the adopted reading series materials. In addition, there is no time for them to read to children in their classes or to allow children free reading time since their adopted reading program provides so many workbooks and ditto sheets for the children to complete that the day is over before many children even finish their assignments.

They tell you that in their classrooms children go to the school library weekly or biweekly depending upon the school regulations and that the children take their checked-out books home to read. However, not all children do take their books home and some books simply remain in their desks until the next library visit. "No," they answer your question, "we don't have classroom libraries. Classroom collections are difficult to maintain and to keep updated, so we have given our books back to the school library."

"Response activities?" they repeat blankly in answer to your question. "What are they?"

SomeLit Station

"Well," contribute the teachers from SomeLit Station, "we include some, but not much, literature for children in our reading programs." The teachers getting off at SomeLit Station like literature and wish that they had more time to use books in their classrooms, but they feel they can justify only a little time for children to become involved with it.

The SomeLit teachers like to draw on literature for some of their skills development as when, for instance, the basal calls for teaching children to interpret figurative language. They teach that skill to children and then ask them to locate examples of figurative language in the books they have checked out of the library.

Their students, too, follow the school's schedule of weekly or biweekly visits to the school library, but SomeLit teachers do permit some time, about 15 minutes, for children to examine their new books after the library trip. The SomeLit teachers encourage their students to take the books home from school and remind them the day before library day that they need to return their books if they intend to get more. They don't turn their classroom libraries over to the school; the books gathered by previous teachers in that room are lined up on shelves on the side of the classroom. Although the books are a little tattered and many are woefully out-of-date, the SomeLit teachers ask if you have any idea how expensive it is to buy books! However, they do occasionally receive some new books whenever their class places a large enough book club order so that the class is entitled to a free book.

SomeLit teachers like to read to children, they tell you, but with all that there is to be accomplished with the school's adopted reading series, they can permit only one or two sessions per week for this reading. Occasionally they will choose novels to read to the children, but generally they select books, short stories, or poems which can be completed in a single reading. The SomeLit teachers feel good that they are able to allow children a time to read every week: children are permitted to choose free reading or working on their weekly news periodical on Friday afternoons for 20 minutes.

Basically, SomeLit teachers believe that if they are going to allow children time for reading then they should check on how much the children learned from it. Consequently, oral and written book reports are the general practice, though children occasionally put on a skit or display other creative responses to books read. They have not had very good luck with letting children discuss books, since they feel that more time is spent with the discussion than the reading warranted.

LottaLit Station

"But you don't have to stop there!" interrupt the teachers who are bound for LottaLit Station. "There are lots of worthwhile ways to use children's books in the classroom reading program." LottaLit teachers, too, follow their basal reading program, but they often will use the basal stories as jumping off points to get children into whole books. If, for instance, a reading group has a story in their basal which is an excerpted chapter from a novel, then they will plan ahead and locate enough copies of that book for all the children in the reading group. They will then take a break from the basal and allow children to read the novel for their reading-group experience. These teachers feel compelled to ensure that their students are taught all the skills their basal lays out, but they don't feel that they must have the children read all the stories in a particular reader. They know that the skills can be taught in a variety of ways and with a variety of materials.

The LottaLit teachers have talked with their librarians and have an arrangement whereby children can check out new books whenever they return the ones they borrowed last visit. This allows some children to go to the library daily because they go through a lot of books. These teachers also have an arrangement which allows children to check out one more book than they would normally be allowed to have. The children keep that book at school for their free-reading period which is held daily. The children from LottaLit classrooms are often seen in the library before school and during recesses. LottaLit teachers believe that it is important to have a classroom library which will encourage independent reading by children. They don't change the materials much, but they are constantly looking for ways to increase their libraries, such as having children bring some of their own books to school to lend to the room library for a few weeks. Their libraries include a variety of books at many different reading and interest levels, and they try to make the area attractive to children by having rugs and floor pillows for the children to use while reading. These teachers try to attract children to the area with displays of books on different topics or by featuring an author or illustrator of the month.

Children are encouraged to read materials from the classroom library after they finish their assigned work, but LottaLit teachers ensure that all students have daily free reading by planning the free-reading period as a regularly scheduled event. Lottalit teachers have made and purchased many tapes of books. Children who can't read very well but would like to "read" a good story follow along in the book as the taped voice reads the story.

The teachers at LottaLit Station frequently read aloud long books so that children have the opportunity to see characters develop through a long work and also because the teachers know that children enjoy a long piece and look forward to coming to school to find out what will happen in the next chapter. Of course, these teachers always read at least once a day to their students, but most weeks they find that they have read more than once a day.

Children have the opportunity to select, within a certain range, the type of response activities they will do after reading. Sharing these responses is always encouraged. The teachers may give them three activities to choose from unless the students can come up with one of their own which they would prefer. The types of responses that are offered generally include one written, one oral, and one artistic response.

AllLit Station

"How interesting," the AllLit group of teachers chimes in. They tell you that literature *is* their reading program. They use basal readers and all other adopted texts as supplements to the overall literature program. They consider adopted materials simply another type of reading material of which they have multiple copies. AllLit teachers occasionally require multiple copies of some reading matter so they can work with small groups of children. The emphasis in their reading program is on reading entire works, rather than the one-chapter excerpts which tend to be found in basal readers. Groups of children get together for reading because of a common interest rather than being grouped by the teacher for skills work. The AllLit teachers provide reading instruction and monitor children's reading progress through individual conferences and by keeping individual checklists of skills which good readers should possess.

An important aspect of the reading program at AllLit Station is that children continually share what they are reading through discussion with the teacher and with other children. Children may choose to write or give oral book reports, but they are not required. The teachers encourage ways of sharing books which involve an integration of the language arts of reading, writing, listening, and speaking. Children may turn a story into a play and perform it for a small group since it is unlikely that the whole class would be interested in the same topic. AllLit classrooms include many types of response activities to literature since that is a major component in their evaluation of children's reading progress.

AllLit teachers have made some sort of arrangement with the school librarian so that children can go to the library whenever they need to or want to during the school day. Children check out as many books as they wish because they use the library for obtaining both reference and pleasure-reading sources. The AllLit teachers encourage children to go to the library before school starts and during recesses as alternative activities to occupy their time. Far from having given their classroom libraries back to the school library, the AllLit teachers have built up their classroom collections to include borrowings from the county and school libraries, donations, books borrowed from students within the class, and books from the teachers' own personal collections of children's books. They change these books periodically so that there are always some appealing new additions. The classroom library is attractive and inviting with plants, a bathtub filled with pillows, and a seat from an old car. These teachers feel that attractively displaying the books is part of the lure, and so they have bookstands and shelves in order to display the front covers of many of the books in their libraries.

These teachers take every opportunity to read to children during the course of the school day. There is scheduled reading time built into their lesson plan books, but, in addition, they take advantage of all the transition times which occur. They keep a book of poems handy so that while the children wait in line to go to the lunchroom, they can read the poems to them.

AllLit teachers find that beginning the day by reading to children helps to set the tone and that ending the day by reading to children helps them to go home feeling good about school. By the same token, the children they teach read frequently. There is no planned free reading time because AllLit teachers see to it that reading is what the day mainly consists of.

But now it is up to you. You look around the group and study the various teachers getting off at NoLit, SomeLit, LottaLit, and AllLit Stations. They have given you much to think about. "Well," they ask as they all turn to you, "what's your destination?"

TRY IT OUT

The hypothetical teachers who were getting off at the various literature stations differed in the ways they incorporated children's books in their reading programs. The teachers from NoLit, SomeLit, LottaLit, and AllLit Stations differed mainly along six aspects: (1) content of their reading program, (2) school library, (3) classroom library, (4) teacher reading time, (5) children free-reading time, and (6) response activities. Divide your class among six groups and have each group report how the hypothetical teachers at each station differed according to a specific aspect of their literature/reading program. In addition, consider ways to combine these aspects and produce a new station somewhere along the line.

ENCOURAGING QUANTITY READING

"The more you read, the better you read" is a common expression among reading and language arts educators that has much merit. As you might guess, we would get off the literature tracks somewhere around LottaLit Station. After all, reading is something that is learned. It does not occur automatically like breathing or sleeping. And for children to learn something well, they should be immersed in it. This section describes specific ways to encourage reading among children in order to provide such immersion. The methods we present here all are designed to get quantities of literature into children's hands. Furthermore, you will see that these methods emphasize reading story- and book-length literature rather than reading isolated words, phrases, sentences, or short paragraphs.

Fluency Activities

During fluent reading, students decode words automatically and smoothly. The sources of information that are available in texts such as prior context, sound-symbol relationships, and spelling patterns are utilized simultaneously and effortlessly during fluent reading. Thus, attention can be devoted to reacting to the ideas of a passage. The three teaching practices described below are designed to help students experience this process and reinforce use of it. These three practices all emphasize repeated readings of a single passage. By repeatedly reading one passage, students become familiar with it, they know what to expect, and so they learn to read the passage fluently. And once the students know what fluently reading literature is like, they can attempt to read other literature the same way.

Imitative Reading A story is recorded in an appealing fashion for children to listen to and follow along in the text. The children listen to the tapes as often as necessary so that they can eventually read it on their own. When they feel ready to read the story without the use of the tape, they should make the attempt. If their fluency is not acceptable, they should continue listening to the tape and reading along. This should continue until their independent oral reading of the story is fluent and expressive.

Reading to Younger Students Older readers can receive needed fluency practice in independent level materials when they become teacher's "helper." They do this by going to a lower-grade classroom to read aloud to a small group of children. Students should practice the passage before going to the classroom in order to assure them of a successful experience. They should know the passage thoroughly so they can make maximum use of intonation, pauses, and eye contact with their listeners.

Tape Recorder Reading First, a student practices reading a passage silently, and then it is read orally and tape recorded. Next, the student and teacher, or aide, listen to the taped reading and note strengths, weaknesses, and specific areas to be improved. Again, the student practices reading silently and then retapes the passage until satisfaction is reached. The teacher and student can listen to the final recording and compare it with the original as a means of evaluation.

Sustained Silent Reading

Sustained Silent Reading (SSR) involves students in reading self-selected materials for a certain time period (Hunt, 1971). SSR requires extensive, varied reading materials because all students and adults read during this time. Thus, a wide selection of books, magazines, newspapers, and pamphlets are needed.

SSR is based on the assumption that in order to appreciate reading, students require free-reading time, a quiet place, abundant materials, and an adult role model (Moore, Jones & Miller, 1980). The basic goal is to induce students to read large quantities of material. As students read a lot of books, their interest and their proficiencies should improve. Too often, elementary school children read only short passages and terse directions. In fact, many of your students may have had very little experience reading whole books, which SSR provides.

To begin an SSR program in your classrooms, collect a large assortment of reading materials. (We describe how to build a classroom library in the next section entitled "Acquiring Literature for Children.") Once reading materials are obtained, set aside a certain time of the school day for SSR. Some teachers set it immediately after breaks in the day such as lunch or recess because SSR typically settles children down. Specify an exact amount of time for this activity, and keep your class to that time. It can be gradually increased as your students become better and better able to stay with a sustained reading task. Some teachers start off primary-grade children with five minutes a session and then try to increase gradually to 15 minutes by the end of the year.

Before beginning an SSR session, have your students select the material they will read. Then inform your class that everybody is to read silently for the specified time. It is important that you read, too. Teachers who grade tests, file papers, or do other administrative tasks during reading time communicate to students that SSR really isn't very important. After the reading time is up, you all return your reading materials and then proceed to the next activity of the day.

No formal response activities should be assigned during or following SSR. After all, continued attention to a specific passage is a response by itself. Furthermore, at one time or another, most of us have experienced a powerful, compelling book or movie and then immediately afterwards been asked, "Well, what did you think of it?" Do you recall how frustrating and maddening that question can be? Quite often we need time to sift through our reactions in order to figure them out. And even after we've figured them out, often we'd like to just let them simmer inside awhile for our own gratification and not share them with others. Children work the same way. They share experiences with each other all the time—including experiences with books. Because of this, students should have the opportunity for reading on their own without always having to formally respond to what they read. SSR provides that opportunity.

This section explained the general rationale and procedures for implementing SSR. Part II of this text provides elaborated versions of how SSR can be implemented and maintained at various grade levels. The following section presents ways to acquire children's books and periodicals for SSR and other reading activities.

Acquiring Literature for Children

Most classroom teachers endorse the idea of having a large quantity of literature for children in their classrooms. However, the problem is acquiring a sufficient quantity of such materials. Especiallly during an era of cutbacks in educational financing, stocking a classroom with bright, new books purchased with school district money can become a distant dream. Nevertheless, we encourage you to search for book monies among the labyrinth of school budgets and outside grants. School administrators generally don't advertise that they have extra funds available, but if you present a specific, already-prepared book order that requires only a signature and a school purchase order, then you might be pleasantly surprised. However, if that doesn't work, or if it does work but you need still more books to adequately fill a classroom library, then you should consider the following.

Book Drives Book drives call for students to bring in reading materials from their homes and their neighbors' homes to be donated to the school. The results of such drives can be amazing. Hundreds of books can be acquired this way, and students' interest in reading can be heightened. A good way to enliven your book drive is to organize a contest: the individuals or classrooms that bring in the most books receive a prize. Classroom prizes can consist of such things as a special movie, a free day, or a party. Prizes for individuals might consist of a special toy or model that is displayed in the front office. Certificates can be run off and presented to students who bring in specific numbers of books. In addition, advertising book drives contributes greatly to their success. Letters can be sent to your students' homes, announcements made in the local newspaper and on the radio station, and school board members can be notified.

Before beginning a drive, set aside a particular time of the day for collections, and designate a large area for the books to be deposited. This is especially important if you are conducting a school-wide drive. Have ready many cardboard boxes so that the books can be culled and sorted according to categories of reader level and topic. Older students, teachers, or parent volunteers should conduct the sorting. Book drives typically net a large quantity of materials, and the quality and appropriateness of those materials need to be monitored for proper distribution. In fact, clear descriptions of the types of books that you desire can help limit the amount of improper materials you receive. Guidelines are appropriate that specify complete, readable children's books and that disallow adult books and magazines as well as tattered materials.

Borrowing from Libraries   Along with book drives, sharing books between classrooms and borrowing a quantity of books at one time from the school library are ways to bring literature into your classroom. Rotating books this way allows you to get the most mileage out of what currently is available at your school. Furthermore, a close working relationship with your school librarian can do wonders toward acquiring and promoting children's literature. Most schools have scheduled times for classes to visit the library and check books out, but inviting the librarian to come into your classroom to promote books that have just arrived can be done, also. Another important service that the school librarian can perform is to compile books that relate to a certain unit or theme that you are exploring with your class. Literature can be collected at your city or county library and brought into your class for a certain period of time, too. Up to 20 books at a time usually may be acquired this way.

Involving Parents   The PTA and other groups of concerned parents can be mobilized. Parents often want to help out in some way but they don't know what to do. Asking them to gather, borrow, and buy literature for children certainly directs them toward a worthwhile goal. When Christmas arrives and you prepare to receive presents from your class, you might suggest books. Perfume, handkerchiefs, and neckties are nice, but you probably would do better with a good, new piece of children's literature to share with your class.

If you buy children's books on your own and place them in your classroom library for a time, don't forget that those purchases are tax deductible! Another way to stock your classroom library is to have children bring in books from their personal collections to share with the class. Children enjoy reading their favorite books to their peers and then placing that book in the library.

Building Children's Collections   Helping students acquire books for their own personal collections at home also deserves attention. Book fairs can be held wherein representatives from one or more book companies come to your school and display their books for sale. Although book fairs are designed ostensibly to sell books, they also seem to sell enthusiasm and interest in reading. Watching young students move among all the new books as they prepare to make a purchase confirms this second outcome. Additionally, the money earned from book fairs can go toward purchasing materials for your classroom library.

Another, more common way to help students build a personal collection is to participate in book clubs. In book clubs, students' orders are sent away to a specific company. The bonus books you receive with a minimum order are good additions to the classroom library, too. You can make available to students and their parents subscription information for periodicals such as *Cricket, Jack and Jill,* and *Boy's Life.* (Appendix B contains a list of such periodicals and ordering information.) Few techniques are better at encouraging children to read than the regular receipt of their own personal magazine in the mail.

And finally, Reading Is Fundamental, Inc. (RIF) is a national non-profit organization that has worked since 1966 to provide books for children. RIF is made up of local volunteers who supply books for children to select and keep for themselves. Each local RIF project raises funds to buy books, and in most cases those funds are matched by federal dollars. The RIF address is:

Reading Is Fundamental, Inc.
Smithsonian Institution
475 L'Enfant Plaza, Suite 4800
Washington, D.C. 20560

LITERATURE RESPONSE ACTIVITIES

In this section we describe response activities that are designed to help students refine their interpretations and value judgments of literature. These activities include oral, written, and artistic forms of expression. These forms, in turn, comprise media such as letters and essays, posters and illustrations, plays and pantomimes.

Perhaps the greatest contribution of response activities is that they allow students to determine for themselves how thoroughly and imaginatively they comprehended a piece of literature. In order to produce an overt response to what has been read, students need to "step back" and sort out their thinking. And if they find their level of comprehension to be inadequate, then they can rethink and reread the passage in order to obtain a deeper insight. Without response activities to stimulate higher-order reading, students often become stranded at superficial, lower levels of comprehension.

Response activities also get students into the habit of processing literature at higher-order levels of thinking. That is, as you regularly help students interpret and evaluate literature, they can learn to interpret and evaluate it on their own. Students then become used to expecting insight from what they read, and they are not satisfied until such insight is obtained. In essence, response activities lead students to a better understanding of literature.

There are numerous ways to help students react to what they read. The following are some that we have found to be effective. It is important to realize that they represent types of activities; they do not exhaust all the ways children can react to books. They are grouped according to three response formats: story retellings and re-creations, oral and written compositions, and visuals.

Story Retellings and Re-creations

Retelling and re-creating stories help children to react to literature and share what they have read or listened to. Retellings and re-creations consist of activities such as puppetry, story acting, lap stories, flannel boards, and acetate stories. Three outcomes of these activities seem to be especially valuable.

Children who engage in story retellings and re-creations are internalizing the structure of stories. They put episodes into proper sequence, identify the plot and characters, and elaborate characterization and episodes. If children do not yet have a well-developed story sense, then dramatic retellings provide another model, in addition to their own reading, for what the elements of a story are.

Retellings also allow children to orally interpret what they have read or listened to so that the story comes alive for them. Teachers rarely need to tell children to "talk with expression," when they are dealing with puppets or flannel cutouts.

A third major benefit of these activities is that they can act as a comprehension check in a classroom wherein the teacher uses on-going diagnosis to plan instruction. If children can retell stories using the modes we are suggesting in this chapter, the odds are quite good that the children possess understandings of literary elements such as characterization, character motivations, setting, and sequence of episodes.

Puppetry Children can and will make puppets out of any material known to person. We found that having some books on how to make puppets and having boxes that contain raw materials such as socks, papier-mâché, colored paper, colorful materials and textures, and other "junque" provide enough for children to come up with puppets for story retellings. Two sizes of stages are appropriate for puppetry, a large one behind which several children at a time could crouch and present their stories, and a small one for use in a classroom behind which one or two children could hide in order to present.

Story Acting With very few simple props such as an umbrella and various animal ear-and-tail parts, children can readily dramatize stories such as *Mushroom in the Rain*. That children enjoy participating in classroom plays is not a secret to any of you. Many teachers allow frequent productions given by various groups of children who particularly enjoyed a story that was read to them or that they saw on TV.

Classroom dramatization can be the comprehension check of a story that a group read rather than asking 15 questions or having children complete a ditto sheet. Children in a certain reading group are charged with turning a story into a play. However, the play is not one for which the actors memorize their parts. Rather the group gets together and discusses who the characters are, what the sequence of events is, and how the characters respond to situations. The children then list the sequence of episodes they are going to present and which characters they will have in each episode. Further discussion allows them to decide on potential dialogue. They should try out their story first to see if it will "play in Peoria" before presenting it to the class.

A word of caution: one thing that kills classroom dramatization is memorizing dialogue. Though this activity might be appropriate in a few instances, we think that there are more benefits to children and much less stress if they engage in dramatization as described here.

Lap Stories The lap story requires a small painted or covered board which will fit in your lap and sheets of unlined paper to tear into the shapes of story characters. If you desire, clay can be used for molding. First, discuss the story to review the sequence of major events. Next ask, "Who is in this story?" and as a child names a character, give the child a sheet of paper or a lump of clay. Direct the child to create the character by tearing the paper or molding the clay into a representative form. No drawing or cutting is allowed. However, if children are tearing paper, they can be given colored markers to add details after the tearing is done. Though clay can, of course, be used to make the characters, we feel it is best to have children tear paper into shapes because it seems to reduce anxiety about art. We've had children say, "I can't draw a bear," but practically everyone can *tear* a bear, and the children know it! For this activity we want to decrease the emphasis on art and increase the emphasis on storytelling.

After various children have been given paper or clay for the creation of characters, ask them, "What else do we need for this story?" Children should identify needed major props such as the bridge for *The Three Billy Goats Gruff* or three porridge bowls, three chairs, and three beds for *Goldilocks and the Three Bears*. Children may also want to include nonessential props such as the forest or other items of furniture. The only limitation you have is based on how much your lap can hold and how much your hands can manipulate. We have gotten ourselves into a pretty pickle on occasion by allowing all the children to create items for the lap story, only to find an insufficient lap to hold it all!

The third step involves your beginning the story background and acting as narrator. You tell the story and manipulate the torn forms on your lap board to depict the various episodes of the story. The children who created the characters each speak at appropriate points. If a child cannot remember what the character says, it is perfectly legitimate for others to help out as long as that child does, indeed, speak for the character. Give an appropriate conclusion to the story, if necessary.

To recapitulate, the steps in lap stories are:

1. Discuss the story and characters.
2. Have children make the characters and props.
3. Retell the story, with your students providing the appropriate dialogue.

After many lap stories have been done, you can let one of the children take over your role as narrator, since you will have acted as a role model several times. With younger children, we have found it helpful to prepare the paper in advance for certain stories. For *The Three Billy Goats Gruff*, for instance, three sizes of paper are provided so that the goats don't end up being the same size. When the lap story is done, the characters and props can be placed in a large envelope, labeled with the story name, and placed in a learning center or story box. Then children can get the envelope and retell the story whenever they wish, without you as narrator. Even when the paper shapes become tattered, we have found that it is no great problem. For one thing, they represent very little time or money investment. Also, children can easily replace the tattered forms with new ones. Finally, we take the salvageable shapes from several envelopes (tossing out the ruined ones) and put them together in a "Make a New Story" envelope to derive even more use.

Lap stories are more easily done with small groups of children, but they also work very well with entire classes. The only caution is to seat the children close enough to you so that all can see and enjoy the story.

Flannel Board Stories Another type of story retelling which is quite common in the elementary school classroom is with the use of the flannel board. Story retellings can be done with a surface covered with a material with a nap (such as felt or flannel) and objects representing characters and props which will stick to the surface of the flannel board. The size of the surface used for flannel boards ranges from very large, heavy easels which are virtually untransportable to small stationery boxes with hinged lids which children can use individually at their seats.

Some people make their characters and props all from colorful felt pieces and glue on contrasting felt or draw with colored markers for details. Others cut out paper characters from books or draw paper characters which they seal with clear adhesive paper in order to protect the figure and to give it more substance. A small piece of felt or sandpaper is glued onto the back of these paper figures so that they will adhere to the surface of the flannel board. Again, these characters are manipulated by the teacher as narrator with children providing the dialogue, or children use the flannel boards by themselves to retell familiar stories.

Acetate Stories The success of acetate stories seems partly due to the fact that children enjoy gimmicks and machines. Acetate stories include the creation of miniature transparencies of story characters and props. Older students are able to make acetate stories for you to tell stories to children in the lower grades. You need to locate a book with small illustrations which aren't too "busy." We do this because we can't draw! If you, however, possess artistic skills, you may want to draw your own set of acetate pictures. What we do, though, is place a sheet of acetate, such as is used to make overhead transparencies, over the illustrations in the book you want to use for story retelling. It is important that the pictures are not too large; an overhead projector enlarges what it projects and you may have a wall full of dragon without room for any other characters or props on the screen.

When the acetate has been carefully placed over the desired picture, trace around the shape of the illustration with a thin-line, permanent-ink marker. It is important to use the permanent-ink markers because water color ink will not adhere to the acetate. After the shapes and internal details are outlined, fill them in with thin-line, permanent-ink markers in various colors. After the acetate pictures have dried (it takes only a few moments), peel back part of the backing from a sheet of clear adhesive plastic. Place the side of the acetate you just colored on the sticky side of the clear adhesive plastic. Cut around the edges of your characters and props so that you have the tiny acetate figures to go with a story the children know. What remains is a little transparency which can be projected on a screen for you and your children to use in story retellings.

FIND A CHILD

Choose a story which you especially like. Following one of the story retelling and re-creation formats described in this section, have a group of elementary school children engage in a story telling activity.

Written Compositions

We present below two types of writing that seem to help students better understand and appreciate literature. The types are divided between (1) writing about literature and (2) writing literature. As you will see, writing about literature calls for students to analyze a particular aspect of a book and then discuss it from an outside, objective point of view. Oral and written compositions about aspects of literature such as a sequence of events or students' favorite parts can lead students to categorize and clarify their thinking. At the same time, writing literature brings students inside a writer's world and allows them to personally appreciate the intricacies of the writer's craft. Those who play a musical instrument seem to appreciate and understand what an expert musician has accomplished better than those who do not play.Likewise, if your students write literature, then they can become attuned to the contents and arrangement of literature produced by others. The "writing literature" topics which we suggest below all are in response to specific pieces of literature, but having students create completely original stories certainly is valid, also.

The following topics are divided between writing about literature and writing literature. They are general examples of the types of compositions we suggest students apply in response to the specifics of individual stories.

Writing about Literature
- Describe a part of the story that is like something you have experienced. How are the experiences the same? How are they different? For example, children might recount adventures they and their dogs have had and compare them with the adventures and tragedy in *Where the Red Fern Grows.*
- Interview people who have read the same book and obtain their reactions to it. Then describe the similarities and differences between their reactions. Did people like the same parts of the story? Would they recommend that others read it?
- Explain to the author why you liked reading that author's book. Identify the episode that was the most exciting (or most emotional, most unexpected, funniest, etc.). Suggest topics or situations that the author should write about next.
- Choose everyday objects that best represent the main characters. Explain why a certain piece of furniture, animal, toy, or plant has qualities similar to the character's qualities.
- Explain to the main character the basic problem that he or she had to deal with. Describe how you would have handled that problem if you had been faced with it.

Writing Literature
- Compose a passage that parallels an original one. For example, after reading *Dawn*, children can compose a passage entitled *Dusk*. After reading *Alexander and the Terrible, Horrible, No Good, Very Bad Day*, children can write *Alexander and the Wonderful, Fabulous, Not Bad, Very Good Day.*
- Take a character from a story and place him or her in another setting. For instance, describe an adventure that begins with Humpty Dumpty walking down a busy downtown city street.
- Compose an episode that should have been included in the story. The episode can be designed to come before the actual beginning of the story, during any part of the story, in place of an episode that was already included, or after the story ends. Did Cinderella really live "happily ever after?"
- Compose a diary or a journal as one of the characters would while living the events of the story.
- Retell a story from the viewpoint of another character. For instance, pretend you are a troll, and tell how the three Billy Goats Gruff kept disturbing you so you simply had to get rid of them.

Visuals

Creating visuals such as collages, posters, and book jackets helps students learn to form mental images of what they read. Furthermore, students manipulate and develop ideas through visual, artistic forms of expression just as they do through oral and written forms. Creating visuals is the mainstay of many response activities in primary-grade classrooms because young students often can put into a picture what they cannot put into writing. The following visuals provide a nonverbal outlet that often is the most effective way for students to represent their ideas on paper.

Illustrations   Students often draw pictures of characters, scenes, or locations they encounter in literature. The criteria for deciding what to illustrate can depend on what your students consider to be their favorite, most important, or most exciting topic. In addition, posters and bulletin boards frequently are designed by students in response to what they read.

Collages   Assembling a group of pictures, cloth, wood, and other materials in response to what has been read is a favorite activity of older students. They especially seem to enjoy hunting through magazines, catalogs, and newspapers for just the right pictures or printed phrases that symbolize a character or general theme of a novel.

Maps Showing where a character went in a story requires careful reading. After deciding what locations to represent, students map them out on paper, label them, and often illustrate them for greater detail. Maps can depict story characters' travels in any area. For example, the locations within a single house as well as the locations within a community, state, nation, or world can be mapped.

Time Lines Time lines comprise a set of illustrations that portray the key events of a passage. Different groups of students can be responsible for individual illustrations, or one student can complete the entire project. The illustrations may be separated on different pieces of paper for others to arrange in correct sequence, they can be placed in different segments of a single sheet, or they can be drawn on poster paper to make a mural.

Comic Strips This activity combines aspects of several other activities described here. Students depict a series of story events into a time line and produce dialogue for the story characters within that time line. Retelling a story through this comic strip format is a somewhat advanced task.

Book Jackets Designing a book jacket that differs from the original directs students' thinking toward the central focus of the book. In order to choose a character or scene to portray on the cover, students need to judge what deserves emphasis. This is a high-level reading task.

Display Ads Creating a display ad is similar to creating book jackets; however, display ads openly attempt to convince readers to buy a certain book. They generally include more information about a book than its jacket does, and they include brief pieces of persuasive writing along with examples of what to expect.

Game Boards Older students frequently enjoy designing games based on a specific story. A traditional game board format can be used as players spin or throw dice to see how many places they move en route to the finish. Along the way, penalties and advances can be included that reflect events in a story. For example, a game board can be based readily on *Call It Courage*, wherein Mafatu has many positive and negative experiences with his tribe and with life on the desert island where he is marooned.

Choosing Appropriate Activities

While deciding upon appropriate literature response activities such as the ones described, you should consider several points. First, matching the right activity with the right book and the right student is an uncertain undertaking. The best method we know for making proper matches might be termed "enlightened trial and error." You simply try certain activities that seem right for certain students and then pay attention to the results. If your students work comfortably with the project and if they gain insight into the material they have read, then you have evidence that a worthwhile match was made. If the results you obtain are not so positive, then another activity that focuses on the same desired learning outcome should be tried. You will note that no mention was made here of stating behavioral objectives or of comparing pre- and post-test results. The nature of response to literature simply does not fit these views of instructional decision making.

Our second point about response activities is that they can be viewed as products for instruction or as products for testing. For example, questions can be instructional when they are used to expand students' thinking about certain aspects of a story. Take the children's novel *Queenie Peavy*. Queenie experiences a range of emotions when her father, whom she has idealized, returns home from jail showing neither affection nor responsibility. Asking students, "How did Queenie feel about her father after he returned from jail?" can stimulate quite a bit of thinking and discussion. At the other extreme, students' answers to that question can be written down and then graded with no constructive feedback. When response activities such as questioning are used as a product only to be graded and not discussed, commented upon, or elaborated in some way, then they are being misused.

Third, overt responses are important because they elicit active thinking and allow students to receive feedback, but time spent reading is important, too. Discussing ideas, writing down ideas, and creating artistic responses can be counterproductive if actual reading time is reduced too far. Many have expressed this concern, but Allington stated it perhaps most succinctly in the title of his 1977 article, "If they don't read much, how they ever gonna get good?" And we mustn't forget: continual, sustained reading is a response all by itself.

Another point about requiring overt responses such as the ones described in this section regards balancing them with opportunities for aesthetic responses. Many teachers present a piece of literature to their class and then place that book in the classroom library. This gives students the opportunity to enjoy and respond to the book on their own terms. After a while, response activities are assigned with that book. This way, one piece of literature can serve as the stimulus for both inner, subjective responses and overt responses.

Finally, the activities described in this chapter extend many of the suggestions contained in the preceding chapter on reading comprehension. Literature for children clearly fits into our suggestions for using instructional level materials during reading lessons, providing time and motivation for individual reading, teaching concepts and their verbal labels, and using comprehension lesson plans.

SURVIVAL KIT

We have described many activities that are appropriate for helping students react to what they read. But there are many other activities available. Locate the following references. Copy down their activities that differ from the ones we have described but seem appropriate for helping students react to what they read.

Fisher, C. J. 55 ways to respond to a book. *Instructor*, 1979, 88, 94–96.

Mavrogenes, N. A. 101 ways to react to books. *English Journal*, 1977, 66, 64–66.

FOCUSING ON SPECIFIC LITERARY ELEMENTS

In order to enter fully into a piece of literature, students require an awareness of the fact that stories typically contain elements such as a plot, characterization, symbolism, conflict, and theme. Moreover, students require some internal mental criteria for evaluating these elements. This is not to suggest that young students be taught labels such as "plot" or "theme" or that each literary work be analyzed and evaluated according to certain criteria. Such an approach denies the relatively unsophisticated abilities of young students as well as personal, subjective responses to literature. But some attention to important literary elements is necessary so that students can obtain a better handle on what they read or listen to. Emphasizing the subjective, aesthetic experiences students obtain from a piece of literature needs to be balanced with emphasizing students' awareness of the elements of literature that stimulate those experiences. While the response activities in the preceding section indirectly deal with specific literary elements, this section describes a more direct teaching procedure that focuses students' attention to selected elements.

The teaching procedure described here includes four steps for students to follow: (1) observe, (2) replicate, (3) create, and (4) independently apply. First, students observe how you respond to a piece of literature according to some specific format; second, they replicate that format by interpreting new stories the same way on their own; third, they create original passages that are based on the format; and fourth, they are given the opportunity to use that response format and independently apply it to unfamiliar stories. To illustrate this four-step procedure for guiding responses to specific literary elements, we will describe a way to react to story characters. (We chose characterization because it is a compelling literary element.) The format that we discuss here for responding to story characters consists of justifying why specific terms best describe them. Other formats might consist of comparing characters with each other (e.g., how are Cinderella and Snow White alike?), to identify characters' greatest strengths, or to select some dialogue that best represents the main character. The point is that we are specifying one element of literature (i.e., characterization) and focusing on it through a specific format (i.e., justifying why certain vocabulary best describes the character).

Observe

To begin this teaching procedure, your students observe how to apply one specific format to a certain literary element. In this case, present some terms that students can use to describe characters. *Curious* and *daring* could be the descriptive terms you are teaching. Next, tell your class that you will read a short passage to them and that you will show them how curious and daring describe a certain character. After allowing children to enjoy a story such as *The Elephant's Child* on their own terms, you later might describe the main character by pointing out how the young elephant was curious and what he did that showed he was daring. You might write a brief composition about this topic for your students to copy. Following *The Elephant's Child*, other stories that contain daring and curious characters can be read to your students while they still observe how to apply this format. This is the observation part of the lesson.

Replicate

After your students understand the activity they have been observing, move to the replication stage. At this stage, students either listen to or read stories, and their task is to replicate what you have been modeling. That is, they read or listen to passages and describe the character the same basic way you have been describing your characters. In this case, your students should become accustomed to locating the evidence in the stories that support their descriptions of the various characters. Ask your class questions such as, "How do you know the character was curious?" "What did he do that showed he was daring?" Continue at this step until your students are able to independently identify instances of daring and curiosity in story characters. As you can see, the observation and replication stages are parallel processes: the same basic format is being employed. The difference lies with who is employing it, you or your class.

Create

After your students can identify instances of daring and curiosity in story characters, have them produce a story on their own about a daring and curious character. This is the creation stage of the lesson. You might provide a picture of a character in a certain situation so that your students have something to begin with. The creations might be composed by students in a large group, small group, or individual setting. It depends on the amount of support they require. Whatever the case, students who can create original stories that follow some certain format most likely can employ that format on their own while they read. In other words, students who can create stories about daring, curious characters most likely can identify and discuss daring, curious characters in the literature they read.

Independently Apply

Finally, at the independent application stage of this procedure, your students interpret a piece of literature with few specific instructions from you. For example, after your students become proficient with a variety of descriptive terms that can be applied to story characters, you might read to them Judy Blume's *Superfudge*. Then, at this application stage of the lesson, give your students the open-ended task to describe Fudge, the main character. This task can be quite difficult for students because they need to decide on their own how to describe the character. Unfortunately, this level of task is also the one at which many response-to-literature activities begin. By this we mean that students often read or listen to a passage, and they then are required to react to it in some way. An open-ended question such as, "What did you think of the main character?" might be asked, and then students are left basically to their own devices to answer it. Discussion often follows such questions, but it does not always precede it. As you can see, the primary value of the teaching procedure described here is that it provides students with the devices for interpreting literature before they read.

Two additional points about this procedure need to be considered before we leave it. First, we presented a single pair of descriptive terms as a structure for responding to characters in fiction. But this procedure can be used to teach whatever format you choose for responding to any literary element. For example, if you chose to emphasize plot, the four essential components of the procedure still would be the same. First, you would highlight the plot of a story according to a desired format (e.g., crucial events could be summarized on strips of paper, and the strips then posted in correct order). Then students would identify the plot the same way in other stories on their own; next, students would write their own examples of stories with plot after first listing important events on paper strips; and, finally, open-ended opportunities for application would be provided so that students learn to identify the plot of stories without being directed to.

Our second point about this procedure involves the mode of presentation and the size of the student group which you deal with while following this procedure. That is, the literature to be interpreted can be read to students or they can read it themselves. Occasionally, you can obtain records, tape recordings, films, and filmstrips of pieces of literature. Some material can be challenging to students, and some can be at their independent level. The important thing to realize is that all of these media and different levels of difficulty can be utilized to teach one format for interpretation. If you are helping your students interpret figurative language by having them substitute the implied meaning into passages (e.g., "it was raining heavily" for "it was raining cats and dogs"), then all figurative language encountered in media such as basal readers, easy-reading supplementary material, and difficult trade books can be translated through this lesson format.

Moreover, students can take part in these lessons as members of the whole class, small groups, or as individuals. For instance, the whole class can translate the figurative language in a story that has been read to the class, or else students can work in small groups. Small groups of children can choose their own materials to read and then identify the figurative expressions. Students also might work individually with a story in order to translate the figurative expressions on their own. This procedure allows you to accommodate a wide range of individual differences as students apply the identical format to a variety of materials that are at their appropriate reading levels.

TRY IT OUT

The teaching procedure described here is appropriate for refining students' understanding of most elements of literature. In order for you to practice these four steps, choose a literary element (such as characterization, plot or figurative language) and plan a series of four lessons to simulate this procedure in your college classroom. Select books with clear examples of the element you are teaching and go through the four stages: observe, replicate, create, and independently apply.

We close this chapter on reading and responding to children's literature with a caution that has appeared throughout this chapter. That is, one of the roles of elementary school classroom teachers is to help students understand and appreciate the literature they read. Indeed, the majority of this chapter is devoted to describing formal, direct ways to realize that goal. However, we caution you not to "kill the butterfly." The beauty of books and the beauty of butterflies comes from viewing their intricacies, their form, and their color in their entirety. Consequently, take care to preserve children's feelings for the wholeness and overall impact of pieces of literature. Well-written and well-illustrated books, like butterflies, fall apart when their parts are dissected and overanalyzed. Literature can be presented with no teacher intervention, and children will enjoy and respond to it on their own. Anyone who has seen a child cry at the ending of *Charlotte's Web* knows what we are talking about. Because of this, knowing when *not* to require overt responses to literature is as important as knowing which response activities are most appropriate when they are required.

5 | Content-Area Reading, Writing, and Learning

Imagine trying to teach content-area subjects such as science, social studies, or health without using language. You couldn't do it! Indeed, if you take away the language of a content-area subject, then you have taken away the content area. As Postman (1979) rather concisely explains: "Biology is not plants and animals. It is language about plants and animals. History is not events. It is language describing and interpreting events. Astronomy is not planets and stars. It is a way of talking about planets and stars" (p. 165). In short, teaching and learning in the content areas require language.

When you present content subjects to your students, you have countless opportunities to extend their reading and language abilities. For example, if you are presenting a unit in science on the weather, then your class can read newspaper weather reports, listen to radio announcements, talk about how rain occurs, draw pictures of various cloud formations, and write about experiences during various types of weather disturbances. You can use the textbook along with informational trade books, Weather Service brochures, and pamphlets. Charts can be developed to show wind currents and pressure systems. Maps that indicate weather patterns can be interpreted, and tables that report the temperatures of various cities can be consulted. Experiments with water evaporation can be conducted and reported. Filmstrips and movies that explain weather changes can be watched and then discussed or written about. These suggestions only hint at the myriad language activities that can occur while studying content-area subjects. What is important to realize is that reading and language instruction can occur simultaneously with content instruction (Herber, 1978). That is, as you develop students' understanding of facts and ideas related to a content subject, you can also develop students' abilities to read, write, speak about, and listen to those facts and ideas.

Four categories of students' reading abilities are directly addressed during content-area instruction. To begin, students' stores of information about topics, concepts, and their verbal labels are developed. Content-area subjects systemmatically provide a great amount of information about the world. As students learn about new topics and concepts and acquire new verbal labels, they apply what they have learned to new, advanced reading tasks. In fact, even if schools did not set aside time for formal content-area instruction, you would still need meaningful, content-related material for your students to read so they could increase their stores of concepts. Content reading material, printed matter that explains and organizes some specific aspect of human knowledge, is necessary to help develop students' understanding of the world. After all, a lot is learned by reading. And if children only have books that contain familiar mundane concepts, then those children's stores of concepts and their verbal labels will be limited.

A second outcome of reading and language instruction during content assignments is that children learn to cope with expository materials. Youngsters tend to expect reading passages to be organized according to a traditional story mode with characters, a plot, a setting, and so on. Stories typically contain characters for emotional identification, exciting plots that move from one episode to the next, and settings that can be easily visualized. Conversely, expository materials typically present a detached, objective treatment of a topic and follow such organizational patterns as simple listing, cause-effect and comparison-contrast. Because content materials generally are written in an expository mode, students need help making the transition from the structure and function of narrative fiction to that of expository nonfiction.

A third outcome during subject matter reading lessons is that general reading abilities are reinforced and refined as students deal with specific content tasks. For example, when your students discover the meaning of terms such as *fungus, spore,* and *bacteria* by carefully noting their use in the context of a science passage, the value of using context is reinforced. This reinforcement is essential because students have difficulty generalizing abilities they have gained in one setting to another setting.

While students reinforce general reading abilities in subject matter areas, they also refine specific abilities needed to cope with each area. It is true that all reading passages include words and that in all reading we must identify and understand the relationships among those words. But the demands of reading vary slightly from discipline to discipline. We use one mind set when we read poetry, another when we read arithmetic word problems, another for adventure stories, and even another for reading explanations of scientific phenomena. When we read materials from different content-area subjects, we enter a particular "language environment" (Postman, 1979). These language environments differ because they deal with various areas of the world. Consider the following: literature inquires into personal actions and motivations of people, science analyzes how the physical world functions, arithmetic deals with abstract number relationships, and social studies examines the role of individuals in a society. These areas of inquiry differ according to the questions they ask about the world and the basic vocabulary they employ. Students require guidance with these differences in language as they deal with each content area.

A final outcome of reading-language instruction during content-area assignments is that students discover how to read to learn. It is a traditional but incomplete statement in the field of reading education that students "first learn to read and then they read to learn." The first part of this statement, that students "first learn to read," means that young children initially acquire basic word identification and comprehension abilities. The second part of the statement, that students "read to learn," means that their purpose for reading is to understand and remember the content (i.e., the facts and ideas) that is presented during subject matter reading assignments. The notion that the above statement misses is that students must learn *how* to read to learn.

Students learn how to read to learn when class time is spent helping them independently determine important from unimportant information, connect previous knowledge with newly encountered information, and organize content so that it can be stored in memory and easily retrieved. In learning how to read to learn students acquire the ability to study material on their own. And this ability is best obtained while students deal with actual content materials which they are expected to understand and remember.

In the remainder of this chapter, we present activities that you can employ to help your students achieve the four outcomes we have just described. Three sections are included: (1) Single-Text Activities, (2) Unit Approaches, and (3) Writing to Learn.

READ SOME MORE ABOUT THIS

Compare two viewpoints about how content-area reading instruction should occur. Obtain a copy of Paul McKee's *The Teaching of Reading in the Elementary School* (1948) and read Chapter 12, "Introduction to the Program in the Reading-Study Jobs." Then read Chapter 1, "Rationale and Definitions," in Harold L. Herber's *Teaching Reading in the Content Areas* (1978). How do the suggestions they provide for content-area reading instruction differ from each other? How are they similar?

SINGLE-TEXT ACTIVITIES

This section provides suggestions and sample lessons for guiding students when a small group or entire class is reading the same content-area passage. Rather than explaining our activities in the abstract, we have reprinted two passages from content-area textbooks so that we can give you specific examples. We chose a science and a social studies passage as the basis for these sample lessons with the belief that they are sufficiently representative for you to generalize these lessons to other types of content material. It is simply beyond the scope of this book to accurately present sample lessons for all the different types of content texts. The following lessons are meant to illustrate what you can do when you present content reading materials to your students.

Fire Rocks

The passage, "Fire Rocks" (see Figure 5.1) appears in a chapter entitled "The Earth's Rocks" (Barufaldi, Ladd, & Moses, 1981) which occurs in the middle of a science text. You should read "Fire Rocks" now in order to follow this discussion.

As you can see, the passage has a generous number of pictures and illustrations. Furthermore, key terms have been printed in bold-faced type and phonetic respellings are provided. Let us assume that we are preparing a lesson on "Fire Rocks" for a class of "average" fourth-grade students.

The first step in planning a content-area reading lesson is to perform a content analysis so that you can determine which concepts in a reading passage are important for your students to learn. In such an analysis, you compare the requirements of your subject matter curriculum with what the available printed material actually contains. First you determine what your students are expected to learn about a certain topic, and then you decide which of those expectations can be satisfied through reading. For example, if your students are to learn the job roles of community helpers, then you determine which job roles your particular text covers. After completing a content analysis, you will know what concepts you want your students to obtain from a particular passage. With regard to "Fire Rocks," we have decided that our students should be able to describe the relationships among the four key terms in this passage, *magma, lava, igneous rocks*, and *volcanoes*.

The next step in planning a content-area reading lesson is to prepare students for the new learnings they will gain from the passage. Preparation for new concepts is especially crucial when students begin to study unfamiliar domains of content materials. All students can benefit from surveying the text, discussing upcoming information, directly experiencing concrete objects that relate to the text information, and viewing A-V materials prior to reading the text. With regard to "Fire Rocks," it seems that most of our students need to realize that material that is extremely hot can "bubble up," thereby causing an eruption. Additionally, the pronunciation of the four key terms, especially *igneous*, needs to

"Fire Rocks"

Do you know how hot pudding looks when it is poured into small dishes? In a short time, the top of the pudding cools and becomes solid. What happens when someone breaks through the surface of the pudding with a spoon? Do you think it will still be hot on the inside? Even though the top layer of the pudding has cooled, the part under it could burn your tongue!

 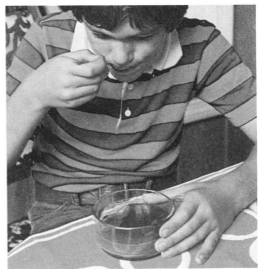

The earth's surface is somewhat like the surface of the pudding. It too has had time to cool and has become solid. Under this thin layer, however, the temperature is very high. In fact, the temperature is so high under the earth's surface that the matter there is hot and melted. We find that it is a thick liquid rock called **magma** [MAG-muh].

FIGURE 5.1

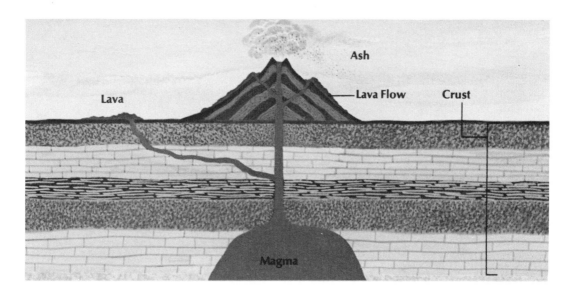

Inside the earth, the pressure is sometimes so high that the hot magma is forced through cracks in the earth's surface. When this happens, we have a volcano! A volcano is an opening in the earth's surface that allows liquid rock and gases to escape. The deposits of ash and rock that build up around the opening are part of the volcano as well. The hot, liquid rock that escapes from the opening may flood the land for kilometers around.

Once at the surface, the hot rock is called **lava** [LAV-uh]. Lava cools quickly and becomes solid rock. Some volcanic mountains form from the lava that builds up over the years. Others form quickly and suddenly. When magma, almost as thick as tar, bursts through the earth's surface, there are large amounts of volcanic dust and great noise.

FIGURE 5.1 (continued)

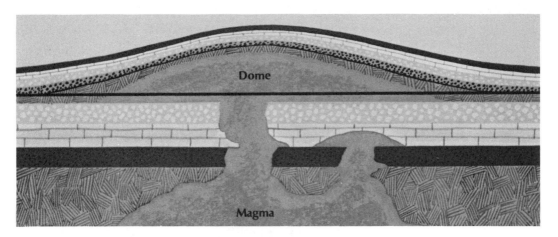

Often, however, magma stays under the surface in huge pockets or in cracks in the crust. Here the liquid rock cools slowly. In fact, it takes thousands or even millions of years for this magma to become solid rock.

All rocks that were formed from fiery-hot magma, whether they cooled above or below the earth's surface, are called **igneous** [IHG-nee-uhs] rocks. Igneous means "fire-formed." Why, do you think, is this a good name for these rocks?

FIGURE 5.1 (continued)

be taught. In order to demonstrate how heat can cause an eruption, the pudding example from the first paragraph could be made real. Bring to class a hot plate and the necessary ingredients for making pudding and do some classroom cooking. As your class observes the pudding bubble, they can get a clear and direct idea of what causes eruptions. Now that you have established some good background information, on to the text!

First, as we noted, students need to be able to pronounce the new terms. Write the four words on the board, and help your students pronounce them (with special attention to *igneous*!), but don't give away their meanings yet. That's one of the reasons why you're having your students read the passage! Key terms frequently need to be explained before your students meet them in a passage because they are not always defined by the context of the passage. However, "Fire Rocks" provides a clear description of the key vocabulary, so this lesson is designed to help students grasp their individual meanings and relationships to each other.

Now that our fourth graders are ready for the passage, we need to set specific purposes in order to guide them through it. *Possible sentences* (Moore & Arthur, 1981) is one activity that provides such guidance. After listing the key terms on the board and teaching their pronunciation, tell your students that "these words are in the passage we're going to read. Your task right now is to put any two of these words together into a sentence that we might meet in the passage." The dictated sentences then are written on the board. Copy the original sentences exactly as they are dictated, even if they do not contain accurate information. Maintaining the exact wording is necessary for evaluating these sentences later.

At first, students will be hesitant about composing sentences with unfamiliar terminology, but they soon get into the swing of things and produce some intriguing combinations. If you receive bizarre suggestions that are designed to waste time, then you should remind contributors that you will accept only "possible" sentences. We don't wish to stifle creativity, but we do want thoughts directed to a specific passage during this lesson. For example, using *lava, magma, igneous rocks*, and *volcano*, students might make up the following possible sentences:

1. *Lava* looks like *magma*.
2. *Lava* comes from a *volcano*.
3. *Volcanoes* are made up from *igneous rocks*.
4. *Magma* and *igneous rocks* are very hot.
5. If you climb a *volcano*, you will see a lot of *magma*.

Students may repeat words that are already placed in a previous sentence, but eventually each word on the list should be included in at least one sentence. After dictating enough sentences to keep this activity motivating yet manageable, students read or listen to the "Fire Rocks" passage for the specific purpose of verifying their classmates' statements. Of course, since two words are placed into one sentence, students are in fact checking on the relationships between the key terms of the passage.

Then, with their books either open or closed, the possible sentences are verified: Which ones are accurate? Which ones need to be changed? Which ones cannot be validated because the passage did not deal specifically with them? Finally, the original sentences that prove to be inaccurate should be fixed up or else totally erased in accordance with the information gained from the reading. For instance, the possible sentences dictated above might be modified to form the following:

1. *Lava* is *magma* that has come from underground and cooled off.
2. *Lava* comes up through a *volcano* and flows down its sides.
3. *Volcanoes* produce *igneous rocks* that come from *magma*.
4. *Magma* is very hot, but *igneous rocks* cool off.

As you can see, possible sentences are especially appropriate when the key terms in a passage are well defined and where the relationships among them are rather clear. This activity provides a specific purpose for reading, includes a writing component, and follows up on the specific purpose.

After conducting a possible-sentences lesson with "Fire Rocks," a good concluding activity would be to have your students learn to reproduce the diagram of volcanic activity that is provided. This activity would help cement students' understanding of the relationship among the key terms by having them visualize the concepts, and it would help teach your students to interpret diagrams. First, have your students inspect the diagram and discuss its various parts in order to be able to reproduce it without having it in front of them. Then have your students close their books and reconstruct the diagram on drawing paper. Only a certain amount of time should be allowed for the reconstruction. After the time is up, your class members open their texts and determine how accurately their diagrams reflect the original. Close the texts again and this time allow sufficient time for all students to finish this project. This inspect-reproduce-evaluate-reproduce procedure is identical to the way students frequently are taught to study words for spelling.

A good follow-up word-study activity would be to point out the similarity between *igneous, ignite,* and *ignition.* Place these three words on a chalkboard one over the other with the *ign* in a column. Then direct a class discussion toward the similar meaning and spelling of these terms. The meaning of *igneous rocks* that was acquired from the passage could be reviewed, the notion of *igniting* charcoal or a forest could be discussed, and the role of a car's *ignition* presented. Underlining the *ign* in each word while you talk about its meaning can lead you to note that *ign* is a common element in the three words that refer to fire. Word groups such as this one and numerous others such as *history, historical, historian,* and *grass, grassy, grasslands* are derived word forms based on a common root word. Derived word formations are a prominent feature of English and deserve frequent attention during content-area instruction.

What were the possible learnings from this lesson on "Fire Rocks?" Regarding content-area knowledge, the major goal was to teach the relationship among four earth science concepts. Additionally, volcanic action was described. With regard to language and learning abilities, general abilities were applied to specific situations. Students were led to use context to determine the meanings of unfamiliar words. Clear sentence writing was maintained. Students were helped to visualize what they read, interpreting diagrams was conducted, and a note on the meaningful structure of common terms was presented. In summary, content-area information and reading abilities were addressed simultaneously.

FIND A CHILD

The preceding lesson on "Fire Rocks" exemplifies a way to guide students through a content-area reading passage. Choose a content-area passage and develop a lesson that includes preparation for reading, specific purposes, and follow-up that is similar to the lesson described here. Conduct your lesson with a child who is reading at an appropriate level for your passage.

Manufactured Building Materials

"Manufactured Building Materials" (see Figure 5.2) is a section midway through a unit entitled "Houses for the Community" (Preston & Clymer, 1964) in a social studies text. It follows a discussion of wood and stone which are natural building materials. For this second example of a content-area reading lesson, we are presenting a longer selection in order to demonstrate several activities. The activities are designed for our same class of "average" fourth graders, but we trust that you will be able to generalize the following lesson structure to situations with different reading materials and different age groups.

Again, conducting a content analysis is the first step in designing a content-area reading lesson. Analysis of this passage indicates that the composition and uses of four types of building materials are the major

Manufactured Building Materials

Wood and stone are natural building materials. They need only to be cut before they are ready for use. Not all building materials are natural. Some are manufactured.

To "manufacture" means to make something new out of natural materials. Some kinds of soil, chemicals, and rock are mixed together and treated in special ways. This manufacturing gives builders many materials to work with. Builders use both natural and manufactured materials.

Brick

One of the first building materials early men made was brick. Long, long ago, in a faraway place, men learned to make bricks from clay. Clay is a kind of soil that is sticky when it is wet. Clay holds its shape. Men dug clay from the ground and mixed it with dry grass. They shaped it into blocks and dried the blocks of clay in the hot sun. When the blocks were dry, they were bricks. They could be piled up to make walls. The hard, dry bricks were easier to work with than stone.

Today men are still making bricks. They make bricks in much the same way as before. But bricks are now made in factories. They are baked in hot ovens to make them very hard. They last much longer than the sun-dried bricks of early times.

FIGURE 5.2

In a brick factory men mix sand with clay. Sand makes the clay stronger. Water is added to make the clay and sand easy to work with.

Now the mixture is ready to be made into bricks. It is put into a machine. The machine pushes out the mixture in long strips of clay. The long strips are cut into bricks. All the bricks are the same size.

Forming the Bricks

The wet bricks are piled in a drying room. Some of the water dries out of the bricks there. Then the bricks are put on little cars that carry them into ovens. The ovens are called kilns. The bricks bake for four or five days. They bake in the kilns until they are hard.

When the bricks come out of the kilns, they cool in the brickyard. Then they are ready to be used.

Tile

Tile is made from clay in much the same way that brick is made. Sheets of clay are pressed and shaped. They are baked in kilns until they are hard. Tile can be given a smooth finish or a rough finish. It can be colored with chemicals.

Into the Kiln

Tile is made in round shapes for underground pipes. It is sometimes curved for use as a roof covering. Walls can be built with hollow blocks of tile. Tile squares, both large and small, are used as floor and wall coverings.

FIGURE 5.2 (continued)

Concrete

One kind of building material can be poured into place! It is not cut to size and nailed into place as boards are. It is not piled up as bricks or stones are. Workers can pour it into any shape and size they need. When it is dry, it is as strong and hard as stone. This building material is concrete.

To make concrete, builders mix sand, small stones, and water with cement. Cement is the secret of making concrete. It makes the sand and stones hold together.

Sometimes a builder buys cement in strong paper bags. Then he mixes the concrete himself. At other times he orders a truckload of concrete. Water, sand, stones, and cement are mixed right in the truck. By the time the truck gets to the new building, the concrete is made. It is ready to be poured.

Concrete is easy to work with while it is wet. It can be poured flat and smooth for floors and walls. It can be poured into rounded shapes for roofs.

CEMENT

Cement is made from limestone and clay. These materials are broken up and mixed together. Then they are heated several times. In the end they make a fine powder called cement.

FIGURE 5.2 (continued)

Because it is strong and lasts a long time, concrete is used for many buildings. The basements of most buildings are made of concrete. Big buildings often have concrete walls and roofs, too.

Concrete Blocks

Concrete blocks are like large bricks made of concrete. They are made in a factory by pouring wet concrete into square forms. When the blocks harden, they are taken where they are needed.

A hollow space is left in most concrete blocks. The space keeps them from being too heavy. These blocks are easier to fit together than stones. They are faster to build with than bricks because they are bigger. Concrete blocks are used in making the walls of many buildings.

Mortar

A special kind of concrete is used in laying stones, bricks, and concrete blocks. This material is called mortar. Mortar is a mixture of cement, sand, and water. It is smoother than other concrete because it has no stones in it. Mortar is spread between bricks or stones when a wall is built. When the mortar dries, it holds them in place.

FIGURE 5.2 (continued)

content learnings to be gained from this passage. The key terms consist of the following: *manufacture, brick, clay, kiln, tile, concrete*, and *cement*. Now, in order to prepare students for this passage, we would remind them that we are learning about materials for building. This reminder would help connect the earlier sections on wood and stone to this section. The distinction between manufactured and natural building materials should be made. In order to help make the information in this section more real for our students, a half-hour tour of the school building and a look at buildings across from the school might be undertaken. The purpose of this quick field trip would be to attune students to the fact that different buildings are made of different materials. After this tour, the class could list buildings and the dominant materials used in their construction.

Another way to develop students' background information for this passage is to bring in samples of the materials that are discussed. Ask your students, friends, and relations for a brick, piece of tile, chunk of concrete, and concrete block. It's amazing how some concrete (!) examples can help students better understand what they are encountering in content texts.

Now that your students' prior knowledge of the topic has been brought forward and developed, help them set a specific content-related purpose for reading. In our first example, we demonstrated how to set reading purposes by using possible sentences; in this case, we will demonstrate how purposes can be set and then followed up through the *directed reading-thinking activity* (DR-TA) (Stauffer, 1969).

In a DR-TA, students first survey an assigned reading passage. Surveying calls for students to skim all the special features of a text: title, headings, and marked words; illustrations, photographs, and diagrams; maps, graphs, tables, and charts; and questions and directions both interspersed in and at the end of the passage. A survey of "Manufactured Building Materials" would last only a short time as the class noted the bold-faced headings *Brick, Tile, Concrete*, and *Concrete Blocks* and viewed the photographs and illustrations along the sides of the pages. Briefly discuss these sources of information before moving on to the next step.

The second step of a DR-TA is to have students predict what the different portions of the passage include. This should be done one portion at a time. For example, after students see that "Manufactured Building Materials" comprises four subsections, you first elicit predictions about the information contained in the "Brick" subsection. Tell students that that passage describes what bricks are made of and how they are made. Then ask the question, "What do you think bricks are made of?" and list the responses on the board. Next ask, "How do you think bricks are made?" and list those responses, also.

After recording the predictions on a chart or chalkboard, direct your students to read the "Brick" passage in order to see whether their predictions are accurate, inaccurate, or not discussed in the passage. Next, have your students indicate that they finished reading the section by putting their books face down. After everyone has finished reading, return to the board and maintain the predictions that can be verified, erase those that are refuted, and put a question mark by the ones not covered by the text. This stage calls for careful reading and directed discussion as students provide evidence from the passage to support their evaluation of each prediction.

With the "Brick" section completed, now move on to "Tile" with the same question-predict-read-evaluate procedure. Note that in "Tile" you might include the question, "What is tile used for?" along with, "What is tile made from?" and, "How is tile made?" Purpose-setting questions can vary with every piece of material that is read. After dealing with "Tile," you would then continue the DR-TA through "Concrete" and "Concrete Block."

There are several ways to follow up and extend the learnings obtained from a DR-TA of "Manufactured Building Materials." Higher-order questions should be asked such as, "Which material do you think is the cheapest?" and, "Which material do you think is the safest?" Your students might interview their parents about which building material they prefer for their residence. A class bulletin board or individual and small-group posters could be designed with building materials listed on top, and photographs, illustrations, and drawings of appropriate buildings placed underneath. You might encourage independent individual and small-group inquiries into aspects of this topic not covered by the text. This way students learn to set their own purposes and read for personally compelling reasons.

Because "Manufactured Building Materials" follows such a clear pattern of organization, graphically depicting that pattern would be appropriate. Three devices that depict patterns of ideas are presented here: *webs, structured overviews*, and *outlines*.

Webs A web is a good beginning way to help young students learn to organize what they read because it is the least structured of the three ways we present here. Think of a spider's web as you design one. The pattern is not always totally symmetrical, yet the parts are always connected. To begin a web, place the title of the section in a box in the middle of the chalkboard. Then ask for the titles of the main divisions of the topic and place them around the center with lines connected to the center. Finally, consider each division separately, and list the main points under each. Figure 5.3 contains an example of a web for "Manufactured Building Materials." As you can see, the main ideas are well connected, but emphasis is placed on getting them listed and elaborated. Arranging concepts in a parallel order is not done during webbing as it is with structured overviews and outlines.

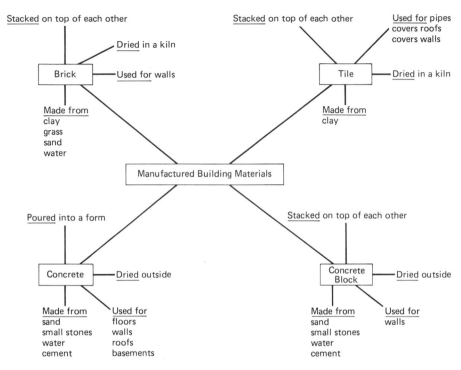

FIGURE 5.3   Web of "Manufactured Building Materials"

Structured Overviews Structured overviews were introduced by Richard Barron (1979) as a prereading activity. However, Barron's later research has suggested that structured overviews should follow the reading and be designed by students with teacher assistance. There are several steps in this activity. First, identify the key terms in a passage that you want your students to learn. Second, arrange those terms into a schematic diagram (i.e., a structured overview) that depicts their relationships. Parallel terms are placed at the same height in the diagram, and major concepts are represented on top of minor concepts. Third, words and phrases are added to the diagram that help clarify it and make it more complete. By now you will have a thorough knowledge of the passage you are going to present, along with a model structured overview for yourself. Having this model for yourself will help you assist students as they create their own. The fourth step calls for listing the target words and phrases and presenting them to your students either on the board or on a ditto sheet. Their task in step five is to record each individual word or phrase on a separate index card, and then in step six to work either individually or in small groups and design their own structured overviews. After arranging their cards to their satisfaction, students copy the arrangement on paper and connect the words and phrases with lines. Finally, in step seven terminate the activity and provide feedback. You might construct a single structured overview at the

Words and Phrases Listed for Students to Organize

Covers other material	Tile
Stacked on top of each other	Brick
Poured into a form	Concrete block
Pipes	Concrete
Roofs	Clay
Walls	Sand
Floors	Small stones
Basements	Water
Dried in kiln	Cement
Dried outside	

Model Structured Overview of "Manufactured Building Materials"

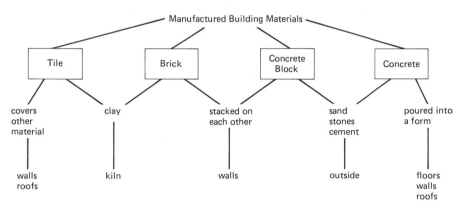

FIGURE 5.4   Structured Overview of "Manufactured Building Materials"

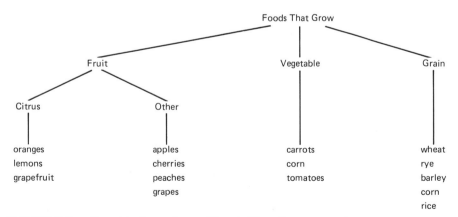

FIGURE 5.5   Graphic Organizer of Foods That Grow

board with class input, or certain groups can reproduce their overviews at the board for your subsequent discussion. Some follow-up is important as a model for future efforts.

You can see an example of a structured overview of "Manufactured Building Materials" in Figure 5.4. We included another overview entitled "Foods That Grow" in Figure 5.5 to give you an idea of what you might present to students in order to introduce them to this activity. At first, you should model the entire structured overview procedure with familiar concepts for your class so they can see how to go about designing one.

Outlines   Traditional outlining, like webbing and creating structured overviews, can promote deep thinking about the organization of a passage. And when students work at identifying organizational patterns, they tend to learn the information better than when they simply read a passage one time (Anderson & Armbruster, 1980).

Showing students how to construct outlines is best done after first identifying the major and minor points of a passage as we did with webs and structured overviews. After listing the major and minor points of a passage, place the major points on the board in the order in which they appear in the text. Include a title, and then label the major points with Roman numerals I, II, and so on. Next, elaborate each major topic with its minor points, labeling those points with upper-case letters, numbers, and lower-case letters according to the degree they are subsumed under each other. Figure 5.6 includes an outline of "Manufactured Building Materials."

Figure 5.6   Outline of Manufactured Building Materials"

I. Brick
   A. Made from
      1. Clay
      2. Grass
      3. Sand
      4. Water
   B. Used for
      1. Walls
   C. How used
      1. Stacked on top of each other
   D. How dried
      1. Kiln
II. Tile
   A. Made from
      1. Clay
   B. Used for
      1. Walls
      2. Roofs
      3. Pipes
   C. How used
      1. Stacked on top of each other
      2. Covers other material
      3. Made into pipes
   D. How dried
      1. Kiln

III. Concrete
   A. Made from
      1. Sand
      2. Small stones
      3. Water
      4. Cement
   B. Used for
      1. Walls
      2. Floors
      3. Roofs
      4. Basements
   C. How used
      1. Poured into a form
   D. How dried
      1. Outside
IV. Concrete Block
   A. Made from
      1. Sand
      2. Small stones
      3. Water
      4. Cement
   B. Used for
      1. Walls
   C. How used
      1. Stacked on top of each other
   D. How dried
      1. Outside

All of these organizing devices can be demonstrated first with familiar topics before applying them to information your students acquire from their books. In fact, webbing can be done readily with primary-grade children following their word or picture sorts. For instance, after sorting animal words or pictures into piles of those that fly, swim, and stay on land, you might transfer that information onto a chart or chalkboard web to graphically depict the categories. In addition, the amount of structure you provide your class can be faded out with time. At first it is best to walk your students completely through the construction of several examples of one device, but then you can gradually let your students assume more and more responsibility for the assignment. Instead of your arranging all the terms in a device, let some students decide which ones go where. The idea is to provide careful, clear models at the beginning of a school year and then gradually wean your students so that they can produce the devices themselves. Furthermore, instead of listing all the major and minor points on the board before organizing them, you might leave out some important ones and let your class search the passage to discover them.

Our suggested lesson for guiding students through the "Manufactured Building Materials" passage contained many elements. The composition and uses of brick, tile, concrete, and concrete blocks were presented for students to add to their store of content knowledge. Reading abilities were targeted as students set their own specific purposes for reading in the DR-TA. Helping students graphically organize the information in this passage would contribute to their ability to learn other information independently. Again, content-area information and abilities to acquire content-area information are promoted together.

TRY IT OUT

Take a content-area reading passage and organize it according to one of the devices described here (i.e., web, structured overview, or outline). Note how carefully you think about the passage in order to create the device.

Adjusting Single-Text Activities

All classes include students of different reading abilities, so you can expect some students to have difficulty with a single class text and others to read it with ease. Even though young readers may know how to perform reading strategies such as looking for root words or comparing known concepts to unfamiliar concepts, those strategies will not work with material that is too difficult. To illustrate, your students might be able to locate the root words in *unhappy* and *agreement*, but they may be quite unable to locate the roots in *predigestion* and *invertebrate*. This may be because the latter terms are totally unfamiliar. At the other extreme, you may have a few students who can read your textbook independently. These students have such an enriched background and such well-developed reading abilities that they require more of a challenge than your book provides. Because of the wide range of individual differences found in most classrooms, content-area reading assignments should be differentiated. Students require guided reading of the type we described under "Fire Rocks" and "Manufactured Building Materials," but they also require adjusted assignments. Determining the correct balance between guiding large groups through a text and adjusting the guidance for individuals depends largely on the maturity and reading abilities of your students. This section suggests ways to adjust guidance while using a single textbook.

Listening to Text Material A class textbook may be tape recorded for students with reading difficulties to listen to and follow along. (Listening posts do much toward reducing the noise level if this procedure is followed!) When you record a passage, include the page numbers and headings in the recording so that students who listen can follow along more readily. A chapter outline may be provided to guide students through the text as they listen. You can be the one to tape record the text, or parent volunteers, older students, good readers in the class, paraprofessional staff, or aides can produce the recordings. Inserting questions and directions into a recording helps set purposes for listening. For example, purpose setting questions might be included before each section of text and then restated at the end of the section for students' responses. Following this format, students would turn the tape recorder on and off as they worked through the assignments.

If tape recording the text is not possible, then you might simply gather certain groups of children together and read the text aloud to them, discussing it as you go along. Another activity is to place students into "study buddy" teams. Good readers are paired with poor readers, and the text is read and discussed. The buddies could help teach essential vocabulary to each other by noting the word meanings and then sharing experiences in order to elaborate those meanings.

Finally, radio reading (Greene, 1979) may be employed. In this activity, one student orally reads a passage to a small group or to an entire class who are listening and who do *not* have their books to follow along. Before reading, the student announcer should practice with the passage. The purpose of the activity is to have one person convey information to his or her peers just as a radio announcer conveys information to a listening audience. Of course, the short intense announcing style of "Top 40" AM stations should not be the model here. After reading a certain portion of a passage, the student announcer checks for understanding. The group may summarize what has been read and questions may be asked. If necessary, certain parts of the passage may be reread in order to clarify an unclear message.

Besides providing students the opportunity to listen to oral renditions of a text, teaching activities can be conducted that allow poor readers to learn text information if they listen to the follow-up discussion. The *guided reading procedure* [see Chapter 13] is one such activity. The GRP calls for all students to read a short passage; brainstorm everything they can remember; list the remembrances on a board; reread; verify the accurate remembrances, remove inaccurate ones, and add new information; and then distinguish the main ideas from the supporting details.

In order to adjust single-text activities, you can have some students read a text and others listen. You can also differentiate the actual tasks that you want students to do. That is, different children may be directed to read for different purposes, different amounts of text may be assigned, and varying degrees of structure may be offered.

Different Purposes   The purposes for reading may differ according to your students' reading ability. This can be done by assigning different directions, questions, vocabulary tasks, or writing assignments to different groups. For instance, if you are studying a passage on forestry in a social studies text, a group of good readers and writers could be assigned to read and learn how paper is made. Another group's task might be to read in order to list all the products that come from forests that are mentioned in the passage. And another group could read in order to design a conservation poster warning about the dangers of forest fire. You should note that all three of these tasks could be completed after reading or listening to an identical passage. Although the tasks vary somewhat from complex to simple, it is important to realize that varying students' purposes for reading does not mean that good readers always get higher-order tasks and poor readers get literal, lower-order tasks. It is best to involve all students at all levels of thinking.

Different Amounts of Text   Besides adjusting students' purposes for reading or listening to a text, the amount of information to be covered may be modified. Content-area assignments do not have to cover one chapter at a time. For example, one group of students may be assigned a short section that stands by itself within a chapter, and another group may be assigned three short sections. The pictorial aids that are provided in textbooks can be considered a section for certain students to master, also. Authors use pictorial aids such as graphs, charts, pictures, and maps to express what might take hundreds of words. Focusing one group of students on a single pictorial aid and another group on two pages of running text illustrates a way to differentiate the amount of information to be covered. Whatever types of adjustments are made, whole-class discussion should follow the directed reading so that all students are exposed to important information.

Different Degrees of Response Structure   The amount of structure that is provided students as they respond to the same textbook may be varied, too. A good way to vary the response structure is by alternating your students' tasks between answering questions and verifying statements. For instance, during a unit on food the question may be asked, "How are citrus fruits alike?" This is an open-ended question that may require rather sophisticated reading and composing abilities. A more highly structured and manageable task consists of the following:

Mark the ways that citrus fruits are alike:

_____Their trees have leaves at all times of the year.
_____ They are sweet.
_____ They grow in the southern parts of our country.
_____ Cold weather does not hurt them.
_____ They need plenty of water.

As you can see, providing statements to be verified can require that students deal with information that is identical to an open-ended question, but the response form is much more manageable. We hasten to add, however, that a steady diet of marking answers does little to improve students' writing and other language abilities.

The preceding activities allow you to differentiate assignments as you use a single class textbook with a large group of students. These activities are provided for your occasional use in order to help you cope with a situation wherein one text is the only material that is available for a classroom of students. However, it is important to realize that a few students will have difficulty with a textbook no matter how much preparation and guidance you supply. Listening to taped versions of the textbook may be insufficient for some children because the material may be beyond their listening comprehension level. These students require simpler materials or even the opportunity to create their own materials through a language experience approach. At the same time, a few students with well-developed abilities and background require even more complex material in order to be challenged. Matching children with instructional- and independent-level content-area reading materials, then, is a prime consideration. The following section deals with some approaches for making that match.

UNIT APPROACHES

The single-text activities we detailed in the preceding section allow you to guide students' reading and learning processes rather efficiently. Such guidance is important. However, students also require guidance with more than one text if they are to become independent, mature readers. As we noted earlier, a class of students always contains readers at different levels of achievement, and allowing individuals to work with materials at their respective reading levels is a necessity. In addition, students can learn to ask their own questions and pursue their own reasons for reading when they have a variety of materials available. And as students work with books on their own, they can learn to monitor their understanding and learning of the material independently. Providing a variety of materials also allows students to delve into topics that they find personally meaningful and interesting. A final, important reason for providing varied reading materials is that informative trade books, periodicals, and other such materials can elaborate concepts that are only introduced in a class textbook. Content-area textbooks frequently only mention information because they cover many topics in a subject area. However, trade books and magazine articles tend to elaborate one single topic rather thoroughly. Because of this elaboration, students can be led to deeper and broader understandings of concepts presented in textbooks. As you can see, there are some compelling reasons for providing varied reading materials as you and your students study content-area topics.

Several approaches for using varied reading materials during content-area instruction have been designed since the turn of this century when John Dewey advocated such a procedure (Joyce & Weil, 1972). In general, these approaches are based on setting purposes for investigation and then having students explore a variety of information sources in order to satisfy those purposes. For example, you might ask your class how mountains were formed, how many kinds of animals there are, or what people you depend on in a community. Information about such topics then can be obtained from a great assortment of materials: textbooks written at easier and more difficult levels, trade books, supplemental reading books, magazine features, pamphlets and brochures, newspaper articles, encyclopedias, and kits. Additionally, films, filmstrips, records, pictures and photographs, guest speakers, and field trips can be used as references. Students can be introduced to such units of study through single-purpose or multiple-purpose units.

Single-Purpose Units

Having the whole class pursue one specific purpose is a good way to begin using varied reading materials during content-area instruction. In this approach, you begin by introducing a topic for study and then presenting whatever you have available to develop basic concepts related to that topic. Concrete objects, pictures, movies, and discussion can be helpful here. Next, one specific purpose for a group investigation is set. Students then work with a variety of printed materials and other matter as they attempt to satisfy that purpose. As your class gathers information, a group project is constructed in order to report the information they locate. For example, in Part II of this text Ms. Maverick conducts a unit of study on the state in which she and the children live. In order to guide her students through this unit, she posts a large blank map of the state, and encourages children to designate areas on it that they have visited or else know about. Some children talk to their parents about places in the state, some recall places on their own, and some read the literature provided by the state for information. Learning about their state provides direction and motivates students to read and learn about one rather specific topic while pursuing numerous materials. Filling in the blank map is the group project that allows students to report their information in a structured manner.

If you were studying reptiles, then you might ask children to go through all the available materials to satisfy three purposes: (1) list reptiles, (2) describe reptiles, and (3) describe the areas where each reptile is found. These purposes then allow you to differentiate the materials that your children are using, but it keeps everyone on the same track.

Some structure might be added by telling your students how to describe their reptiles. For instance, you could tell them to draw their reptiles and to indicate each animal's size, color, and whether it is dangerous or not. Of course, additional information could be gathered, but those three things provide specific ways to describe a reptile. As in the case of the state map, a group product such as a chart or bulletin board of reptiles can be constructed so that students share with the class what they have been reading and learning on their own.

Multiple-Purpose Units

The second general way to use varied materials during content-area reading assignments involves each student or small groups of students pursuing multiple purposes. This approach provides greater independence than when students pursue a common question; however, it is more difficult for students because they must learn to ask researchable questions and to locate independently most of the materials to answer their questions. Furthermore, with this approach students acquire the ability to report their findings by themselves with little support from a group.

It seems best to gradually allow students to embark on individual or small-group research projects while the class pursues one specific topic. This means that you begin an overall topic just as you would if you intended to maintain only a few questions at a time. Then, as you see that some children are ready and willing to look into related areas, you encourage them to do so and offer some direction. To return to our reptiles example, you may be presenting whole-class activities such as movies, filmstrips, discussions, and directed reading lessons about these cold-blooded creatures. Students also may have time each day to search their textbooks, library books, encyclopedias, and articles for the names, descriptions, and habitats of various reptiles. However, as certain children or groups of children complete their search, then you might suggest that they study more about a particular animal. If crocodiles or rattlesnakes have caught their fancy, then you could help the children form some specific questions about them and suggest how to organize and report the information that is located. (The lessons you do as a whole class on note taking and on the one-paragraph essay that we discuss in the next section will come in handy as these students work independently.)

You can formally design individual and small-group unit activities after a whole-group project if the children appear to be ready. Readiness for this step depends upon the maturity and reading and writing ability of your class. For instance, after listing reptiles, describing them, and classifying them according to where they live, the following individual and small-group projects might be undertaken: create a poster describing one reptile in detail, write a story about a friendly lizard, draw a map that shows where reptiles are found, draw an illustration of a snake that emphasizes its scales, and describe various dinosaurs. As you can see, these projects all deal with one general topic, but students are pursuing multiple aspects of that topic.

READ SOME MORE ABOUT THIS

Read "The Half-Open Classroom: Controlled Options in Reading" by Richard A. Earle and Richard Morley (1974) in order to learn one method for moving from a single-text teaching approach to a unit teaching approach such as described here. Additionally, read one or two of the following references in order to supplement your understanding of the unit teaching approach. (Note that some of these references will give you an historical perspective on unit planning.)

Burton, W. H. *The guidance of learning activities* (Section three: The organization of the setting for learning). New York: Appleton-Century-Crofts, 1952.

Heilman, A. W. *Principles and practices of teaching reading*, 2nd ed. (The unit approach, 327–334.) Columbus, Ohio: Charles E. Merrill, 1967.

Kilpatrick, W. H. *The project method.* New York: Teachers College Press, 1919.

Shepherd, D. L. Reading, language arts, and the content areas. In H. A. Robinson, Ed., *Reading and the language arts.* (Supplementary Educational Monographs, vol. 25, no. 93.) Chicago: The University of Chicago Press, 1963.

Stauffer, R. G. and Harrell, M. M. Individualizing reading-thinking activities. *The Reading Teacher*, 1975, 28, 765–769.

WRITING TO LEARN

We are devoting a separate section to content-area writing activities because we believe that these activities are especially valuable for helping
students simultaneously learn content information and increase their
language abilities. When your students write about what they have
read, they become engaged with the ideas and facts that were presented.
They decide what is important and which relationships among ideas are
worth writing about. These decisions are made regardless of whether
the assignment is to paraphrase an original passage or to respond to it
through some creative, innovative assignment. For instance, your students may read about the Navajo Indian reservation for the purpose of
comparing life on a reservation with life in a city. With this purpose as a
guide, your students may ask themselves questions such as: "Is the location of the tribe's reservation important?" "If the location is important,
how much should be said about it?" "Should we say that it's in the western United States or that it's in the northeastern corner of Arizona?"
"Should we explain how the Navajo reservation surrounds the Hopi Indian reservation?" Clearly, these few examples indicate that even when
you provide explicit, clear directions and purposes, writing still requires
active thinking about a topic.

Because writing represents ideas and holds them on paper, this
activity also provides your students a good opportunity to examine and
evaluate their thinking about what they read. Reviewing their own
writing allows your students to confirm their knowledge about a topic.
The statement attributed to E. M. Forster, "How can I tell what I think
until I see what I say?" summarizes this role of writing. For example,
after your students write down what they think is important about the
location of the Navajo reservation, they can review their thinking and
judge for themselves how well they really understand that bit of information. After young, primary-grade students dictate a passage about
a class pet, they are genuinely intrigued the next day when they "see
what they said" about the animal.

Finally, writing helps students generate new insights about a topic.
As your students work on composing a passage about a topic—either individually, in small groups, or as a whole class—they frequently discover relationships among ideas that had never occurred to them before. Indeed, as your students write or dictate a passage about something in
their own words, they are reorganizing their past experiences. Whenever ideas are written in a form that differs from the original text, then
they have been reorganized. This process is an essential feature of
comprehension.

In this section, we present six activities that are designed to improve
your students' abilities to write in order to learn.

Content-Area LEA

In *content-area LEA*, the emphasis is on organizing information about a certain topic and then reporting that information in an expository mode. This activity is most appropriate for primary-grade children and for older children with language difficulties. The procedure for conducting a content-area LEA lesson is nearly identical to the regular language experience approach (LEA). Students interact with some stimuli, they dictate a passage, and then they learn to read the passage fluently. However, there are some notable differences between regular and content-area LEA.

Content-area LEA is always based on a specific content-related topic. For example, students may dictate a passage about a fire station they have visited or about the eating habits of a class pet. Often, teachers will photograph various plants or a sequence of actions such as making popcorn and have students elaborate each picture through dictation. If you are studying dinosaurs, or transportation, or Hawaii, then have a group of students dictate a passage about some aspect of that topic.

Besides being based on content-related topics, the passage should be dictated in an expository mode. This mode consists largely of detached, objective listings, comparisons, or sequences of objects or events. Young students frequently have difficulty explaining things this way because they are still very egocentric. Thier egocentrism leads them to perceive objects and events only in relation to themselves. Thus, helping students to perceive objects and events in a detached objective fashion is a major goal of these lessons.

In order to meet the goals of content-area LEA, you should have a clear topic and set of questions prepared before each lesson. For instance, a class' gerbil may be the topic. In order to elicit exposition, you might focus only on what the gerbil eats. You would then ask questions such as: "What does our gerbil eat?" "What does he not eat?" "What kinds of food are these?" The responses to these questions would then be written in paragraph form. The resulting dictated paragraph might consist of something like the following:

What Sammy Eats

Sammy eats lettuce, sunflower seeds, and carrots. Sometimes he eats little nuts. He can only eat vegetables. Sammy cannot eat meat or chocolate cake.

The dictated passage might be elaborated on another day to discuss what Sammy drinks, his size relative to other animals, or his sleep habits.

Of course, the original passage should be reviewed on succeeding days so that students can learn to read it fluently. Questions might be asked about the passage to elicit further thinking about what Sammy can and cannot eat. This way, students are encouraged to focus on the animal and not only on what they do to him. Moreover, as the facts are listed and discussed, students become accustomed to passages that do not follow a story format. By constructing expository, informative passages, students became adept at the style of writing that they will encounter over and over in their content-area classes.

TRY IT OUT

In order to determine the difference between regular and content-area LEA, take one stimulus such as a picture, kitchen utensil, or some natural phenomenon. Then elicit one passage from your peers that follows a personalized story-type mode and another passage that follows an expository mode.

Translation Writing

Translation writing is similar to the language experience approach because students respond to a stimulus, produce a written passage, and then work with that passage. However, there is a fundamental difference between these two activities. That is, translation writing is based on a specific reading passage, while LEA is based on whatever stimuli you choose. The goal of translation writing is for students to produce a passage that roughly parallels an original text, but in LEA students produce an original passage to begin with.

Very simply, translation writing is the process of converting information from text into a "translated," rewritten version. Only short sections of a passage should be selected at first until students become familiar with this activity. Furthermore, care must be taken that the passage is at an appropriate level of difficulty for students to translate. There are several steps for doing translation writing in your classroom.

First, present the essential vocabulary of the passage to be translated and elaborate the concepts which they represent. This readiness step is no different than if a regular comprehension lesson using the passage were to follow.

The second step is to present short sections of the passage to your students in one of several ways. Those who can read the text on their own should be encouraged to do so. Able and less able readers may be matched so that students with reading difficulties may listen to the good reader. The teacher may prefer to read the passage aloud to a group. A tape recording of the passage may be made. Upper-grade students may come into the classroom to read the passage aloud. Whatever the case, it is important that all students read along as the passage is presented because this activity is designed to attune students to the structure and format of their textbooks.

The children next convert the text passage into their own words either individually or in groups. This is accomplished by dictating their passage to someone as is done in a typical language experience lesson. A good way to record the dictation is to place each sentence on a strip of paper or tagboard. This way, each separate idea can be reviewed individually. After translating a portion of the book, students listen again to that portion in order to evaluate what they have dictated. The translated version then can be modified if inaccurate information were included or if important information were left out.

Finally, after a group of students has completed a translated version of a portion of the class text, that version should be saved. The translation can be copied into students' notebooks or placed into a group folder. These versions then can be used for review and for future classes to read. [See pp. 446–447.]

The One-Paragraph Essay

Students in the intermediate and higher grades frequently are required to report in a written essay format what they have read. The problem students face with such assignments is that composing the essay often is more difficult than comprehending the original passage. If the assigned readings are at students' instructional or independent reading levels, then they generally can report a large number of facts. However, placing those facts into an organized pattern such as simple listing, cause-effect, comparison-contrast, or sequence of events is often a major difficulty. Guiding students through the one-paragraph essay is one way to help them overcome this difficulty.

The one-paragraph essay begins with a general question, but then is followed by information that carefully structures the response. The general question is followed by a thesis statement so your students have a clear idea of what they are writing. After the thesis statement, the number of items to be included in the essay is provided. Finally, the number of sentences your students are to write in order to explain each item is specified. For example, if in social studies you are studying how city people acquire food, then the following question might be asked: "What jobs must be done in a grocery store before it opens?" This question calls for a simple listing, so the thesis statement might be: "Several jobs must be done in a grocery store before it opens." Then, tell your students that they should list three jobs, and inform them that about two sentences each should be written to explain each job.

If you are studying the ocean, the question "Why is the ocean salty?" may be posed. Then provide students with this thesis statement: "Scientists give two major reasons why the ocean is salty." You should note that the number of items to include in the essay is provided in the thesis statement of this example. Next, tell your students to describe each reason with about two sentences each. The following explanation might then be produced:

Why Is the Ocean Salty?

Scientists give two major reasons why the ocean is salty. Rivers flow into the ocean. Rivers carry salt. The salt stays in the ocean because of evaporation. The sun evaporates the water but the salt stays there. The rivers keep bringing the salt to the ocean, and the sun keeps leaving it there.

As can be seen, the one-paragraph essay provides structure for students' writing. For those students who need help with organization beyond that provided by the thesis statement, number of needed items, and number of sentences per item, you might list each item in the appropriate order. In the example above, you would tell your students to first discuss the river carrying the salt, and second the sun evaporating the water. Students who are unable to write independently should have the opportunity to dictate their passages whenever possible. At the other extreme, your advanced writers might be provided only the thesis statement and their task would be to decide how many items to discuss and how elaborately to discuss them.

Note Taking and Summarizing

We discuss note taking and summarizing together because these two traditional writing activities involve a similar process. That is, teaching students how to write notes and summaries enables them to identify and attend to the important information in a passage (Weener, 1974). Indeed, directing students' attention this way may be even more valuable than the actual products (i.e., the written notes or summaries) which are composed. Having a set of notes or a summary helps you store information on a particular topic and allows you to review it later, but learning how to create notes and summaries helps you attend to the important information while reading about any topic.

As complex study strategies, note taking and summarizing cannot be taught in one or two sessions. Students need a variety of experiences and clear guidance. Modeling is perhaps the essential element to teaching these strategies. As reading passages come up during content lessons, you should occasionally "walk" students through the process of taking notes or writing summaries with the aid of a listening guide. In such a "walk through," you provide a rough outline of the passage that omits selected details and/or major points. Your students have a copy of the outline at their desks, and you have one on an overhead transparency. You then read aloud brief portions of the passage, and students follow along in their text. The length of the portions depends on factors such as your students' attention span, background, reading ability, and interest. After reaching a logical stopping point, stop and fill in your outline guide on an overhead projector with the light off. Students fill in their identical outlines at their desks. Next, turn on the overhead projector light and compare what you have written with what your students have written. This allows your class to see what good notes are like. If necessary, your students should fix up their notes so that they approximate yours. Then turn off the light and read the next portion of text to your class as they read along. This read-compose-compare-fix up procedure then continues throughout the passage.

Of course, the modeling format described here should be mixed with opportunities to compose notes and summaries independently so that your students do not come to overdepend on your help. Furthermore, the amount of structure provided by the listening guide is to be faded out with time. This means that you provide most of the information in an outline at first, but gradually remove more and more of the points during the year until your class begins with practically a blank page. As a final word, the rough outline you provide as a listening guide during this activity need not follow the rigid format of traditional outlining. Major and minor points are to be listed, but labeling each point with uppercase letters, numbers, or lowercase letters need not be enforced.

Content Journal Writing

Having students maintain class journals is becoming widespread largely because of the belief that students need the opportunity to write in an expressive mode. Expressive writing involves self-examination, exploration, and discovery (Britton et al., 1975). It is a record of personal thoughts and experiences. Diaries, letters to friends, and rap sessions typically consist of expressive language. This is in contrast to the formal language most often used in classrooms which calls for detached, objective treatment of a topic. For example, students writing expressively about reptiles might record personal experiences with those creatures or speculate how snakes move so quickly. Formal writing about reptiles most likely would include exposition on their distinctive body structures, eating habits, environment, and so on. The writing activities that we presented previously in this section address students' abilities with expository types of writing, but content journal activities are designed for expressive outcomes.

A content journal is like a diary because it records personal responses to what has recently happened; it is like a set of class notes because it contains information about specific subject matter (Fulwiller, 1980). The entries into content journals can be based on reading assignments, class presentations, or both. Specific suggestions on what to write should be provided when students first start keeping journals, but these suggestions should eventually become vague. By moving from specific to intentionally vague suggestions, students are better allowed to respond to class topics on their own terms. An essential ingredient in content journal writing is that students learn to reorganize information by connecting what they already know with the new content.

Students should write in their journals on a regular basis. Many teachers set aside time for journal writing just as they do for free reading. Some have students write in their journals before the subject-matter period, and others prefer writing afterwards. If students are maintaining personal diary-type journals in addition to a content journal, then the writing times should be coordinated so that a good thing is not overdone. Teachers can read the journals or listen to selected entries and then discuss them during individual student conferences or as a class activity. Oftentimes, students will spontaneously share their entries with other students. Time for formal sharing should be provided, but students should not be forced to read if they prefer not to.

Evaluating the quality of content journal writing is difficult because insights about a topic one records during journal writing may be profound to one person but trivial to another. Furthermore, language skills one uses to express new insights are most likely the best that one has at that time. Journal writing is a totally individualized activity wherein students work at their daily writing level. They are writing for themselves and not for someone else. As long as students conscientiously maintain their content journals, then they are meeting expectations. Thus, content journals can be graded on a pass/fail basis, according to the amount of writing that is produced, or not at all.

As a final point, students should be encouraged to review what they have entered. As they review their compositions, they are practicing reading. Studying one's own writing can be as valuable as studying someone else's. In addition, reviewing allows children to rehearse the information they have acquired, and it helps them evaluate their current writing proficiency in relation to the past.

Varying the Writing Task

As we noted in our discussion of teaching with various materials, students require experiences with different types of printed matter in order to develop their understanding of a topic and improve their reading abilities. The same case can be made for writing outcomes. Students require different types of writing assignments in order to develop their understanding of a topic and improve their writing abilities. In order to design different writing assignments that are based on the same topic and purpose for reading, you can readily vary two aspects: audience and form (Daigon, 1980).

Typically, the audience for students' writing consists of the teacher who assesses the quality of their writing. However, you can see to it that on occasion your students direct their writing to an audience that is more directly and meaningfully involved with the purpose for writing. For instance, in social studies your class might be studying protection. The specific purpose for reading and writing might be to learn and then describe how people protect themselves from crime. The audience for writing can then be varied by having students direct their compositions to a convicted thief, a policeman, the city mayor, or a younger brother or sister. Specifying an audience this way tends to enliven writing assignments. Furthermore, when you create an audience other than yourself, your role as rater and "giver-of-grades" is lessened, and your role as helper is enhanced.

Although students realize that you really are the one who will be reading their compositions, most students will suspend that knowledge and write as if someone else were going to read their writing. Moreover, submitting your children's writing to an actual audience other than yourself is a valuable exercise. Thank-you notes to visitors who have spoken to your class about crime, suggestions to the school principal for safely maintaining the building, and notes to parents about the value of safety frequently result in replies that students find quite rewarding.

Writing assignments also can be varied according to the form students use to convey their message. The form of writing includes styles such as essays, poems, stories, personal letters, formal letters, notes, directions, news stories, and dialogues. Each of these forms leads students to think about their topic in a slightly different manner. To illustrate, your purpose for writing may be to describe how people protect themselves from crime, and your audience may be a class of younger students in the school. Your form for this assignment could be a list of notes on an illustrated chart. Just as easily, you could have the audience be a child in India and the form be a personal letter. By altering the audience and the form of writing tasks, you help students learn to manipulate their language about content-area topics.

TRY IT OUT

This chapter offered reasons for providing reading and writing instruction while presenting content-area information. Numerous teaching activities and their rationales then were suggested. The key terms that represent the information from this chapter are listed below in random arrangement. Copy each term onto a separate card and organize those terms into a web, structured overview, or outline in order to review your understanding of this chapter.

Reading abilities addressed
  during content-area instruction
Content journal writing
Different purposes
Learn how to read to learn
Content-area LEA
Unit approaches
Single-text activities
Reinforce and refine general
  reading abilities
Note taking and summarizing
Single-purpose units
Different amounts of text
Translation writing
Analyze the content

Follow up
Writing to learn
Set purposes
Learn the structure and
  function of exposition
Multiple-purpose units
Listening to text material
Prepare for new learnings
One-paragraph essay
Adjusting single-text activities
Different degrees of response
  structure
Varying the writing task
Develop topics, concepts, and
  their verbal labels

6 | Classroom Diagnosis and Evaluation

In order to teach anything, the teacher must have some knowledge about what the learners already know or can do. As the skill or content is being taught, teachers need to know how well it is being learned. Learners also need to know how well they are progressing. Diagnosing what students know and can do and evaluating how well students are moving toward teaching and learning goals is a part of the teaching process. In this chapter, we will present diagnosis and evaluation as a normal and integral part of teaching and learning. We will recommend planned observation and teacher-made tests as the primary vehicles for diagnosis and evaluation and we will suggest ways that teachers can assure that their observations and tests are both reliable and valid. Because reliability and validity are confusing to many people, and because reliability and validity are essential to diagnosis and evaluation, a description of each will be included here. Throughout the chapter, as suggestions for observing and testing are made, you will be reminded of the importance of reliability and validity.

A person is said to be reliable if that person can be depended on, time and time again, to do whatever he or she is expected to do. Nunnally (1967) states that "reliability concerns the extent to which measurements are *repeatable* by the same individual using different measures of the same attribute or by different persons using the same measure of an attribute." An assessment measure is said to be reliable if it can be depended on, time and time again, to do what it is expected to do. If a measure is very reliable, it will yield approximately the same results today as it will tomorrow or next week. You can rely on the consistency of the response. A scale is a reliable indicator of your weight if you neither gain or lose pounds and each time you weigh yourself it indicates the same weight.

Test makers achieve reliability in a number of ways, one of which is by including many different items to measure each ability. A student may miss one of the items due to confusion, inattention, or fatigue and get most of the other items correct. Another student may correctly guess the answer to an item but show the true deficiency by responding incorrectly to the remainder of the items. The scores of both students will be fairly reliable if there are a number of different items testing the same ability, because judgment is not likely to be made based on the one chance mistake or guess.

Teachers achieve reliability in a similar manner. Judgments are never made based on one observation or on one test item. Rather, teachers make decisions based on several observations or testings. In addition, once decisions are made, teachers continue to observe, evaluate, and constantly rethink their decisions based on new information.

The concept of validity is somewhat harder to explain than the concept of reliability. Nunnally (1967) states that "in a very general sense, a measuring instrument is valid if it does what it is intended to do." Validity of measurement refers to the match between the concept or skill to be measured and the means by which it is measured. A measure is valid to the extent that it measures what it was intended to measure. This distinction may seem academic and superfluous since we ought to be able to assume that any instrument will measure what it is intended to measure. This assumption, however, is often questionable. An example should clarify both the meaning of validity and the difficulty of achieving it.

Imagine, for example, that a reading skill important for beginning readers is associating consonant letters such as *b*, *m*, and *s* and the sounds commonly associated with these letters. Creating a valid test of this knowledge would appear to be quite simple. One could create a test which contained some pictures and ask students to write the letter they thought the picture began with. Is this a valid measure of their knowledge? When the tests have been scored, will the teacher know which students have this initial consonant knowledge and which don't? The answer is "perhaps." Imagine, for example, that some students don't know, or can't remember the names for, or have different names for some of the pictures. A student who looks at a picture of a dog and calls it a puppy, and writes the letter *p* under the picture has the wrong answer and the right knowledge. Imagine another child who writes the letter *b* under the picture thinking that he or she has made the letter *d*. This student too has marked the test item incorrectly but has the knowledge that the test was designed to evaluate. Another student may be able to spell *dog*, and thus writes the letter *d* under the picture. If this response was generated by a memorized spelling, the correct response does not indicate that the child has achieved the desired letter-sound associations. In order to create a valid test of students' consonant letter-sound knowledge, the test creator would have to be sure that most of the stimulus pictures were familiar to the children, called by the desired name, and not familiar enough to have their spellings memorized.

There is, however, a much more serious problem with the test procedure just described. This problem is related to the issue of why it is desirable for students to be able to associate consonant letters with sounds. This knowledge, in and of itself, is useless. It becomes useful only when the student can *use* this knowledge and the context of what is being read to decode an unfamiliar word. What we really want students to do is to *apply* their knowledge of letter-sound relationships as they read. The previously described test procedure is aimed at testing the student's letter-sound association knowledge, not the application of this in real reading. So, if the desired skill is the ability to use this knowledge in reading, how can this be measured validly? The answer to this question is obvious and simple. Put the children in a "real" reading situation in which they demonstrate their ability.

Imagine that you want to know which students have learned consonant letter-sound associations and can apply them as they are reading. How would you find this out? You would probably carry out a lesson that looked like this:

> Boys and girls, this morning I put some sentences on the board. While I wasn't looking, a leprechaun sneaked in and covered up some of my words with these shamrocks. He must want us to play a guessing game since this is St. Patrick's Day, a special day for leprechauns. Let's read each sentence together saying "blank" when we come to the covered words. Then let's guess which word the leprechaun covered up. (Students read the first sentence and make four or five guesses for the word.) We certainly have a lot of guesses. How can we decide which is right? Yes, we could uncover the whole word, but look here, the shamrocks are cut so that the left corner of each comes off. The leprechaun must want us to have some extra clues. Let's tear the left corner off. (Corner is torn off revealing the initial consonant of the word.) Aha! He did give us some extra clues. Now, which of our guesses are still possible? Yes, that word begins with an *l* so it could be *lake* but not *pond, ocean,* or *river*. Let's try the rest of them in the same way. First, we will guess without any clues about how the word begins. Then, we will make new guesses based on the clues our leprechaun left us.

The lesson continues and, once the sentences on the board are completed, each child is given a duplicated sheet on which you have written three sentences. Each sentence has a word with a shamrock drawn over all but the initial consonant. Tell students that the leprechaun left them each a surprise (leprechaun picture to color and puzzle are at the bottom of each sheet.) Then ask students to read each sentence, saying "blank" when they come to the shamrock and trying to figure out what will go in that blank that makes sense and begins with the clue left by the leprechaun. When they think they know what goes in the blank, they can come up and whisper-read the sentences to you and then, telling no one else what their guess was, they can color the leprechaun and complete the puzzle. As the children whisper in your ear, you will make notes about two abilities, the ability to use context to come up with a response that makes sense and the ability to use initial consonant letter-sound associations to figure out unknown words.

Because these observations occur as a natural part of the lesson, children are able to demonstrate their true ability unconfounded by the anxiety, panic, and inability to understand directions that often result from the knowledge that one is taking a test. Because you have structured the observations so that decisions are based on the correct or incorrect response of the children, you view these responses in an objective, unbiased way. Because these observations are conducted in the context of "real reading," you can observe not only whether students have learned certain associations, but also whether they can apply what they have learned as they read. You have achieved validity by objectively measuring what you chose to measure in a natural context which simulates as closely as possible the tasks children are actually required to perform as they read. You will achieve reliability if you make tentative decisions about how well different children are learning to use context and initial consonant letter-sound knowledge based on the three sentences read to you, but suspend judgment in any final sense until you have had a chance to observe the childrens' responses for another day or two.

We hope that you now have an intuitive sense of reliability and validity and understand that only if you measure what you want to measure in a reliable manner can you put much faith in your diagnosis and evaluation. In the remainder of this chapter, we will list some questions that most elementary teachers want and need to answer and suggest ways in which you can reliably and validly go about answering them. We will not tell you how to diagnose and evaluate every reading goal. That would exhaust all the remaining page space in this book as well as us, the writers, and you, the readers. Even if we had unlimited page space and patience, we could not tell you how to diagnose and evaluate everything for every child. There are an infinite number of goals when you consider all the different approaches to reading, facets of the reading process, and idiosyncracies of individual learners and teachers. Even if we could tell you how to diagnose anything you might ever need to diagnose, we wouldn't! We believe that as you read the examples in the remainder of this chapter you will learn the principles of diagnosis and evaluation and be able to demonstrate your knowledge by applying it to diagnosing and evaluating new reading goals.

QUESTION: **Is the Child Ready to Read?**

As you remember from Chapter 1, readiness and beginning reading instruction occur simultaneously. But most teachers need to know when to shift the emphasis of instruction from readiness to the learning of words. How can a teacher reliably and validly determine when a child or group of children is ready to learn to read? To establish validity, you must decide what it is children must know and be able to do and then measure this in a way that is very similar to the actual reading task. To establish reliability, you must measure what you are measuring more than just once. So, what is it your beginning reading instruction will require children to know and do so that they can succeed? Some reading programs have children "sound out" most of the words they meet in the very first reading book. In order to be successful with this kind of instruction, children must (1) be able to name all the letters in lower- and upper-case form, (2) have developed the ability to segment the sounds heard in words into letters, (3) associate some letters with some sounds, and (4) blend sounds together to form words. At the other extreme, some teachers begin reading instruction using a language experience approach in which children first learn to read sentences, then words, and develop their letter-sound relationships *as* they learn to read. Children can be successful with this kind of beginning reading instruction even if they lack the four letter-sound abilities listed above. In fact, children can begin reading and develop these letter-sound relationships as they become readers.

You have probably inferred (and rightly so!) that we would begin reading instruction with a whole-language approach such as language experience, and build knowledge of letter-sound relationships based on known words as we were developing beginning reading ability. Thus, we would want to ask and answer questions related to the seven ingredients outlined in Chapter 1. We believe that every approach to beginning reading requires these seven factors and that an approach which begins with letter-sound relationships requires these seven plus several more. Since the development of these letter-sound relationships is complex and takes a lot of time, we would prefer to begin reading instruction when the child demonstrates some facility with our seven knowings rather than postpone it until the letter-sound relationships are learned. But, the point is not what we would do for beginning reading instruction. The point is what *you* would do. Once you know what your beginning reading approach requires of children, you will know what to measure.

For us, there are seven questions. Does the child know what reading is for? Does the child know enough about the world to make sense of what is written in beginning reading materials? Does the child expect that reading will make sense? Does the child know the conventions and jargon of print? Can the child auditorially and visually discriminate words? Is the child interested in learning to read? Can the child follow the structure of simple stories and exposition?

Many of these questions can be answered as we provide the child with listening and reading experiences and then observe how the child responds. Children who can make up a story to go with pictures in a book have an intuitive sense of story structure. Children who enjoy being read to and who "pretend read" some books clearly have an interest in learning to read. Children who read the language experience story and move their hand from left to right under the top line, start again on the second line and proceed to the bottom have learned the convention that, in English, print is read left to right and top to bottom. On the other hand, a child who points to letters rather than words while reading a language experience story and points to the letter *o* in horse while saying *big* trying to read "My horse is big," does not yet know the difference between letters and words and the function of space between words.

To help children realize that reading is important not just for school but for life, many teachers send children home with the "homework" assignment of finding out what their parents have to read to do their jobs. It is often astonishing to children to discover that truck drivers, auto mechanics, and housewives need to read many things in order to be successful in their jobs. To assess this knowledge, children might be asked to find a picture in a magazine which shows someone working and be ready to tell the group what that person might have to read.

In addition to these indicators of how well children are developing the seven essential understandings, there is a more global and direct indicator of when children are ready to read. If language experience stories and shared reading of familiar stories is a major vehicle for developing readiness, some children will begin to learn words. Children who suddenly begin to say, "Look, teacher, I can read this word," and can, are probably ready for some word identification instruction. As you read about Miss Launch and Mrs. Wright [see Chaps. 9 & 10] you will notice that language experience and shared reading are used extensively and that, for some, these experiences are building the essential readiness; for the children who are ready, these experiences are the beginnings of actual reading. When we ask the question, "Is the child ready to read?" we are really asking, "Does the child have the essential understanding so that I can begin to emphasize learning sight words and decoding skills?" The child who is successfully reading the language experiences and familiar stories and who is "picking up" some words demonstrates readiness for reading by doing it!

QUESTION: Is the Child Learning Letter-Sound Relationships?

This question is really many questions and each of them can be asked and answered at three levels. Imagine, for example, that you want to determine if the child "knows the blends." Well, there are many different blends and these blends occur at the beginnings and endings of words. In addition, some children may be able to hear the difference between the different blends (discrimination); others may be able to hear the difference and also know which letters represent which sounds (association). The application of these letter-sound associations to figuring out unknown words is the highest level of "knowing." So, for each letter-sound relationship, there are three distinct levels of knowing, discrimination, association, and application. Which level should the teacher test for? That diagnostic question can be validly answered if you will ask yourself the question, "What do I want to know?"

Imagine, for example that you are just introducing the initial blend sounds to the children. You will, as a first step, develop their auditory discrimination for these blend sounds by having them listen and then decide if two spoken words begin with the same blend or if a spoken word begins like a known word. Children who can hold up smiling faces when asked to listen for words which begin "like Frankenstein" when *frown* and *frankfurters* are spoken and hold up sad faces when *crowded, flatter*, and *football* are spoken have demonstrated that they know how to auditorially discriminate the *fr* blend from other beginning sounds. You will want to evaluate their ability to consistently respond to tasks which require them to listen for same and different sounds before you try to teach them to make the association between the letters *fr* and the sound heard at the beginning of Frankenstein.

Once this discrimination level has been accomplished and you have helped children learn to associate the letters with the sounds, you will next want to evaluate their ability to make this association. Again, children might respond in an every-pupil-response fashion to demonstrate they can make the association. Children who have been taught the blends, *fr, fl, br*, and *bl* should be able to hold up the appropriate card (*fr, fl, br*, or *bl*) when the words *flipper, blanket, frantic, bracelet, brand, freak, blender*, and *fling* are pronounced.* You will notice that we have used *two* words for each blend we want to diagnose. This helps to achieve reliability. Doing the same task on another day with two more words for each would further ensure reliability. We have not chosen words the child is likely to know how to spell such as *blue* or *from* because if the child responded with the appropriate letters for a word he or she could spell, our diagnostic measure would not be a *valid* indicator of that child's letter-sound associations for blends.

Now, since all the work you have done to develop the discrimination and association levels has been wasted unless the child applies this knowledge to decoding unknown words while reading, you will want to diagnose and evaluate this application-level ability. The leprechaun les-

* Being able to say *fru* when shown the letters *fr* is also an association-level task but not one we recommend for reasons stated in Chapter 3.

son presented earlier in this chapter was an example of diagnosis conducted at the application level. In order to tell if children are applying what they have learned to real reading, you must diagnose these abilities in the context of real reading! Some teachers include a diagnostic measure at the end of each reading lesson by having the children come and whisper something to them before going to their seats. If you wanted to diagnose the children's ability to use blend letter-sound associations to decode words which rhymed with known words [see pp. 59–62] you might end your lesson by having each child come to you and whisper-read these three sentences:

> She has a *flat* boat.
> Fill it to the *brim*.
> My friend is named *Fran*.
> I drew a *blob*.

As the children whisper-read the sentences, you would make notes about each child's ability to produce a word which made sense, began with the appropriate blend, and ended appropriately. A child who read the third sentence as, "My friend is named Fred," is making sense and is using the appropriate initial blend but is not utilizing the known words, *an, can,* or *man* to correctly decode *Fran*. A child who read the first sentence as, "She had a flit boat," is using the initial blend but is not making sense or using known rhyming words such as *at, cat,* and *hat*.

Perhaps you are wondering how teachers can keep all this diagnostic information about all the children in their head! The answer is they don't—they keep it in their notebooks. The teacher who was diagnosing the children's ability to discriminate the *fr* blend would have put check marks in the "discriminates *fr* blend" column for all the children in the group who were showing the appropriate every-pupil-response card. Children who were wrong more often than chance would allow would have minuses in that column for that day's diagnosis. Children whose responses were often but not always correct would have question marks. Likewise, the teacher who was diagnosing children's ability to associate *fr, fl, br,* and *bl* with appropriate sounds would have noted their success in the *fr, fl, br, bl* columns. After the whisper-reading described above, the teacher would have noted abilities in the "uses context to make sense," "applies blend sounds," and "uses known rhyming word" columns.

The example we have just presented to you in which the teacher teaches discrimination and then assesses how well the children have learned it, teaches association and assesses it, and then teaches application and assesses it indicates the appropriate order in which to diagnose assuming the teacher is teaching letter-sound relationships which most of the students are not apt to know. But, what if a teacher of more advanced readers wanted to know about their blend letter-sound relationships? What would you do if you were teaching fourth graders who read at the second-grade level and you wanted to know if they knew their blends? In this case, it seems appropriate to reverse the order of diagnosis. Since, if the children can apply these blend letter-sound relationships as they are reading, they must be able to make the appropriate associations and discriminations, you would begin your diagnosis with these older children at the application level. All children who began the italicized words in the following sentences with the appropriate blends are applying the blend letter-sound relationship as they read and they would be unable to do that if they didn't have the association-level knowledge. (You will notice that in these sentences, we are using words which are not likely to be known as sight words to children reading at second-grade level.)

He was a *bloodthirsty* man.
The old doll looked very *fragile*.
My mama cooks *flank* steak.
I am having trouble attaching these *brackets*.

All children who pronounce the italicized word so that it began with the appropriate blend would be assumed to have application level knowledge of the blends. (This would include children who pronounced *brackets* as *braces* who are both making sense and using the initial blend sound. What would you know about a child who pronounced *fragile* as *friendly*? What about a child who pronounced *bloodthirsty* as *block*? What about the child who pronounced *flank* as *fried*?) If you found children who lacked the application-level blend knowledge (such as the child who pronounced *flank* as *fried*), you would want to see if they could make the association between the blend letters and sounds. For readers who were unable to demonstrate that they had this association-level knowledge, you would drop back another level and test their auditory-discrimination-of-blends ability.

If you look back at the letter-sound relationships discussed in Chapter 2, you will be able to tell what questions about letter-sound relationships teachers are likely to want answers to. Which questions you are asking and answering depends on where in the sequence your readers are. If you are going to teach letter-sound relationships which you don't expect children will have learned, you will begin teaching these at the discrimination level. Your evaluation of this teaching and learning will follow as a natural extension of your teaching, and your notes made during several days about children's abilities will let you know when you can move to the association level. Likewise, you will evaluate and record whether children can make the desired letter-sound associations before moving to the application level. You will evaluate this application-level ability by a task which involves real reading. For children who may or may not have the targeted letter-sound associations, you can use your time and theirs most efficiently if you begin your diagnosis at the application level and move to the association and discrimination levels as necessary.

FIND A CHILD

Select a letter-sound relationship such as an initial consonant, digraph, or blend; or final consonant, digraph, or blend. Construct an application-level, real-reading task which will let you know if an older reader has achieved the targeted knowledge. Next plan an association-level task and a discrimination level task you can use if your reader fails the application-level task. Be sure to include several items on each task to achieve reliability. Find a child and see if you can diagnosis his or her knowledge of your targeted relationships. Make a chart on which to record your results.

QUESTION: **Is the child comprehending?**

Comprehension is a complex phenomenon and, while children's progress toward the goal of becoming thoughtful, critical, responsive readers can and should be assessed, it cannot be approached in the same way that word-identification abilities are assessed. Word identification is a *closed system*. That is, there is only so much to be learned and, eventually, when you have learned it all, you are finished with it. Most of you could on page 75 correctly pronounce the word *centroid* even though few of you had a meaning for it. One of the authors once gave a word-identification test to a very bright fourth grader named Scott. The test had words at different grade levels and Scott proceeded right through to the college level, pronouncing words such as *splendiferous, expeditious*, and *catalyst*. As Scott was returning to his seat, he was overhead to say to the next child who was coming up to be tested, "You had better hope she just asks you to pronounce them and doesn't ask you to tell her what they mean!" Scott, like most good readers at the intermediate level, had mastered word identification: He could pronounce any fairly regular English word. He knew, however, that he had yet to master comprehension!

Because comprehension is an *open system*, it can never be mastered: No matter how well someone currently comprehends, there are always new topics and words to learn concepts for, new benefits to be gained from additional individual reading, and new abilities to be developed from guided reading or study of good writing. For this reason, a major guideline in Chapter 3 suggested that to improve children's reading comprehension the teacher should place them in the hardest material they can read comfortably and guide them through the reading of that material with a comprehension lesson plan. This process would never end. Even doctoral students in English literature attend classes or seminars wherein professors guide their reading/study through certain selections!

Because comprehension can never be mastered, the approach to comprehension assessment must be an open-ended one. Rather than asking, "What comprehension abilities has the student mastered?" we suggest that you place students in different kinds of reading situations and ask, "Is the child comprehending?" This is based on the assumption that comprehension is always specific to a particular reading selection and a particular task or purpose for reading. We will suggest a manageable set of important dimensions along which reading situations can differ and then we will suggest procedures for assessing comprehension by answering the question, "Is the child comprehending?"

Two Text Dimensions

Of course, the reading selections available for use with students can differ in many ways, but here we will concentrate on two that seem most practical and valuable for teachers of reading. The first dimension we will discuss is *passage length*. A reading passage can vary in length from a single sentence, to a paragraph, to a section, to a complete passage (a short story, an article, a chapter, etc.). All other things being equal, the longer a passage is the more sophisticated a reader must be to comprehend it. Paragraphs include sentences but a paragraph is not just any set of sentences—the sentences must logically relate to one another. Sections include paragraphs but a section contains the relationships between and among paragraphs as well. Likewise, passages are made up of sections *and* the relationships between and among them. Because each new level of passage length requires that, in addition to being able to process the lower levels of passage length, the reader must cope with a new set of conceptual relationships, determining how well the child can cope with various lengths of passage can be important. Teachers are already aware of the need to consider passage length when teaching reading. Teachers of young children will be aware that most reading instructional materials for these children guide them through the reading selection one or two pages at a time. All teachers of poor readers will have seen how sensitive these students are to how many pages there are in what is about to be read.

The second dimension we will discuss is *genre* or *mode of discourse*. There are many different, general types of writing that literary critics have identified. The three major types are prose, poetry, and drama. Each of the three major genres of writing contains subgenres. Prose, for example, includes both narrative and exposition. Teachers are already aware of the need to consider genre or mode of discourse when teaching reading. Classroom teachers will be aware that content textbooks (exposition) usually present more problems to students than do stories or biography (narrative). These same teachers will be aware that poetry is usually more difficult than prose and drama is easier than prose for most students.

Three Task Dimensions

As with reading selections, reading tasks can differ in a number of ways, but we will focus on just three. The first task dimension we will discuss relates to the strategy required by the lesson. You will remember from Chapter 3 that there are four reading strategies and that purposes are set for lessons which require one or more of these strategies. Some reading purposes are quite literal and require only the strategy of *understanding what is stated.* (Read to find out where the story begins or what happened first are purposes which only require understanding what is stated if these facts are clearly stated.) In addition to understanding what is stated which all comprehension requires to some degree, some comprehension purposes require that the reader perform the second strategy of *attending to what is important.* (Read to get the main idea, or summarize, or outline are purposes which require both understanding and attending to what is important.) Other comprehension purposes require that the reader understand what is stated and also perform the third strategy of *inferring what is not stated.* (Read so that you can predict, or explain, or conclude are purposes which require inference if the expected responses are not literally stated in the text.) *Restructuring what is produced through understanding, attending, and inferring* is the fourth comprehension strategy and will be discussed under the *mode of response* task dimension.

As teachers set purposes for reading, they should consider what reading strategies those purposes require. The children's ability to successfully fulfill the purpose will be an indication of the extent to which they are able to perform that strategy.

The second task dimension we will discuss is *text availability*. This is simply a distinction between open-book and closed-book comprehension activities or responses.

The third task dimension is *mode of response*. It is this task dimension that takes into consideration the fourth reading strategy of restructuring. The way that teachers have students respond during or after reading determines how much restructuring they must do. There are three general modes of response: *recognition, cued recall*, and *free recall*. In recognition, the responses are already structured or restructured and the task of the student is to mark true or false, yes or no, or select the correct response from among distractors. In cued recall, the student is not given any structured responses to evaluate or recognize but the student is given questions or other cues which provide some signaling as how to restructure what is recalled. In free recall, the student must restructure with no cues at all. A favorite free-recall activity is asking students to "retell the passage in your own words."

Procedures for Assessing Comprehension

Because comprehension is open-ended, it is not possible to assess what comprehension abilities have been mastered. Each act of comprehension can be seen as having the different dimensions discussed above and the teacher asks of each act, "Is the child comprehending?" Consistent weakness by a student or group of students in comprehending when a particular text or task dimension is present should lead the teacher to either (1) instruct the student(s) in how to better cope with that dimension, or (2) seek out easier materials employing that dimension. Teachers can be as informal as they like in presenting students with different comprehension situations, remembering who successfully comprehended, and what the specific dimensions of that comprehension situation were. Here we present one possible method of keeping track of student success with the different dimensions.

A teacher could develop a comprehension assessment sheet like the one in Figure 6.1 and duplicate enough copies for each student. The text and task dimensions are checked in advance of the diagnostic lesson as part of the planning for that lesson. Then, either during the lesson or following it, the teacher answers the question, "Is the child comprehending?" by writing "almost all," "most," "some," or "almost none" in that blank. Figure 6.1 describes what one student's comprehension assessment sheet might look like after three diagnostic lessons.

Such a record-keeping system allows teachers to become students of their students' comprehension. Only then can teachers achieve the goal of comprehension instruction: that students comprehend almost all of a variety of texts under a variety of task dimensions in increasingly more difficult material.

QUESTION: What Is the Child's Instructional Level?

You probably remember from Chapter 3 that in order to become better comprehenders students must be given instruction in materials at their instructional level and must practice reading in materials at their independent level. Thus, a question that every teacher of reading must answer for every child is, "What is the child's instructional level?" This question is easily asked, but not so easily answered. Because it is crucial that you have some understanding of the concept of instructional level

Student	Jane Martin

| | Text Dimensions | | | | | | | | Task Dimensions | | | | | | | | Is This Child Comprehending? |
| | Length | | | | Genre | | | | Strategies required | | | Text availability | | Mode of Response | | | |
Date	Sentence	Paragraph	Section	Complete passage	Drama	Narrative	Exposition	Poetry	Understanding	Attending	Inferring	Open	Closed	Recognition	Cued recall	Free recall	Almost none? Some? Most? Almost all?
10/3	✓						✓		✓	✓			✓	✓			Most
10/18		✓				✓			✓	✓	✓		✓			✓	Almost none
11/9	✓					✓			✓		✓		✓			✓	Some

FIGURE 6.1   Comprehension Assessment Sheet

and how to find each child's instructional level, we will attempt to provide you with a thorough but practical explanation.

The concept of an instructional reading level was first popularized by Emmett Betts in the 1940s. Betts (1946) suggested that instructional-level material was that material in which the student could respond to comprehension questions following reading with at least 75 percent comprehension and correctly pronounce 95 percent or more of the words. Betts further suggested that teachers could determine the instructional levels for their students by selecting passages from the different levels of the basal reader, asking a child comprehension questions to assess comprehension ability, and listening to each child read aloud in order to assess the child's word identification ability. Teachers were encouraged to begin testing children in the basal reader level they thought might be instructional level and to continue having children read passages and answer questions until the 75 percent comprehension criterion or the 95 percent word identification criterion was failed. The test made and given by the teacher to determine instructional level was called an IRI (Informal Reading Inventory).

In the 40 years since Betts popularized the notion of reading levels, there has been continual controversy about how teachers could most efficiently and accurately determine children's reading levels. Some (Powell, 1970; Spache, 1972) have suggested that the 95 percent word identification criterion is too high and that children can read with comprehension and fluency if they can identify as few as 90 percent of the words. Others (Cooper, 1952) think the 95 percent criterion is too low and would like to raise it to 97 percent or 98 percent. What to count as an error has also been the subject of controversy. Pikulski (1974) points out that the child who reads, "The boy sits on the chair and waits for his mother," as, "The boy is sitting on a chair waiting for his mother," has made more oral reading errors than the child who reads the same sentence as, "The boy s-s-s (examiner pronounces word *sits*) on the champ and water for his mother." Who is the better reader, however? Because fluent readers have an eye-voice span [see pp. 241–243] which allows their eyes to be several words out in front of their voices, they often make nonmeaning changing substitutions, omissions, and insertions as they read orally. Goodman (1970) would explain the reading of the first child described here by saying that the child saw and correctly identified the words in the sentence but "recoded" them into speech in a more natural way. Goodman suggests we consider deviations from printed text as miscues and rather than counting them, analyze the miscues made, and decide how the reader is doing with the material by considering what kind of miscues are being made. "Did the miscue change the meaning?" is the major question Goodman would like us to consider.

In addition to the controversy surrounding how many errors to allow and what should count as an error, there has also been controversy about how to measure comprehension. Goodman and Burke (1972) suggest that rather than ask children questions, we have them retell the selection read and score their retellings according to a retelling outline in which points are given for recalled information about characters, events, plot, and theme.

Others who would assess comprehension by asking comprehension questions disagree about the type of questions to be asked. Many authors (Betts, 1946; Botel, 1968) suggest that comprehension questions be balanced between those which reflect literal comprehension ability, inferential comprehension ability, critical reading ability, and vocabulary knowledge.

Examples of each type which might be asked after reading a selection about a boy and his dog are: *Literal*: Where were the boy and his dog going? *Inferential*: Why was the boy taking the dog with him (assuming this was not directly stated)? *Critical*: Do you think the boy really had the best interests of his dog at heart? *Vocabulary*: What is *rabies*?

Since most children and adults can, without having read the selection, give an adequate answer to the question about rabies, the use of vocabulary questions is questionable. Tuinman (1971) labels this type of question as "not passage dependent" and suggests that only those questions be included which cannot be answered unless the reader has read and comprehended the selection.

It has also been argued that questions (such as the one about the boy having the best interests of his dog at heart) which can be answered either way depending on the personal, critical evaluation of the reader do not adequately measure comprehension of material read. In fact, a child who responded either "yes" or "no" to the third question and who knew what rabies was would automatically receive 50 percent credit toward the commonly used 75 percent comprehension criterion.

Finally there is controversy about the whole notion of being able to place a child in a book at instructional level since most basal readers contain a variety of text types and text difficulty within each book. Because a reader's knowledge about a particular subject and familiarity with the way in which information is presented affects comprehension, it is impossible to accurately determine and tightly control the level of every selection in a basal reader. Most basal readers contain in each book some selections which are much more difficult or much easier than is desirable for a particular reader.

About the only idea over which there is no controversy is that if you sit a child down with books at preprimer through eighth-grade level, there will be books most of which can be read with few errors and understood fully (independent level), books in which some errors are made and comprehension is fairly good for most selections (instructional level), and books in which the student makes many oral reading errors and/or understands little of what is read (frustration level). Determining this level, given a group of children and a series of graded books, is at best a chancy endeavor. So, what's a teacher to do???

In the remainder to this section, we will share with you our "best guesses" about how to determine instructional reading levels for a class of children. While we hope that in the next ten years, reading comprehension and readability research will provide more definitive answers to the important questions of measuring comprehension and controlling the difficulty of material, we know that most of you must somehow, in the meantime, continue providing good reading instruction for children. So, here are some guidelines we would use to determine as efficiently and accurately as possible instructional reading levels.

1. Decide what materials you can use for group instruction.

There are a variety of ways to approach reading instruction. Most teachers use a combination of approaches. The basal reader is used for some of the instruction for some of the children in almost all classrooms in America. Many teachers use language experience, writing, individualized reading, content-area reading, high-interest low-vocabulary books for some of the reading instruction for some of the children. Regardless of the approach used, most teachers bring together groups of children and lead them through comprehension-oriented lessons as part of that reading instruction. If children are to become better comprehenders, they must be given instruction in materials at their instructional levels. Thus, regardless of which approach to reading instruction is used, most teachers need to know which of the books they have available in multiple copies are at the instructional levels of which children.

Often, teachers choose books from different levels of different basal reading series and also high-interest, low-vocabulary books as what they intend to use for group instruction. Let's imagine that for an imaginary class of fourth graders, we decide to use the 3^1, 3^2, 4, and 5 books from a basal reading series and a second-grade high-interest, low-vocabulary book. Since this second-grade high-interest, low-vocabulary book is the easiest material of which we have multiple copies and since we don't want to put anyone in a book written at first-grade level and interest, we will decide to do language experience and imitative reading with our children whose instructional level is below the second-grade high-interest, low-vocabulary book.

Since we plan to put all our fourth graders who read at fifth-grade level and above in the fifth-grade book and supplement this group instruction with many independent and content-area reading experiences, we do not need multiple copies of books above the fifth-grade level. We now know that we plan to use the second-grade high-interest, low-vocabulary books and the 3^1, 3^2, 4, and 5 books of the basal series for small-group, comprehension-oriented lessons.

2. As the children have a week or two to "get back into the swing of school" and to practice reading from library books and other materials, determine "probable instructional levels."

Often, beginning teachers, in their haste to get organized and started, make their assessment of children's reading levels during the first week of school. If you do this, you will almost surely underestimate the levels at which they can read. Many children have not "cracked a book" in three months! During the first week or two, plan time each day for them to read. Some teachers like to give children the level of the basal they completed the previous year and let the children reread favorite stories. Where the child was reading the previous year is valuable information and may shorten the time for diagnosis. All children's instructional levels should be reevaluated at the beginning of each year, however, for three important reasons: (1) During the three long summer months, some children read enough to maintain their June level; others become bookworms and read so much they may actually skip a level or two; others never look at a book, and may need some more practice in another book at the level they just finished before moving to the next level. (2) Even with the best teaching, some children are misplaced. If a child was placed too high or too low last year and you continue based solely on last year's completed books, that child will spend another year placed too high or too low. (3) Instructional level is not a single concept. Instructional level refers to how well children can function at a particular level given your type of instruction. In order to *validly* place children at the appropriate level for your instruction, you must decide what your instruction will look like and your diagnosis must be a simulation and reflection of your instruction.

As children are "refinding" their reading abilities, you should make your best guess at each child's instructional level. If you have a record of books completed the previous year, you can base your guess on these records. If not, observe what books the child is reading during the first two weeks of practice reading and make a tentative judgment. Imagine that for our class of fourth graders, we have determined the following probable instructional levels:

5th grade or above:	Carol, Paul, Sam, Susie, Ralph
4th grade:	Janet, David, Sharon, Jim, Pat, Debbie, Carla
3^2:	Gary, Jill, Abraham, Sal
3^1:	Susie, Dick, Paula
2nd or lower:	Samatha, Clayborn, Sarah, Clayton, Benjamin, Harry, Derrick

> **3. Try out the children with materials at their probable instructional level and observe them as you direct them through the first two or three selections in the book.**

You will remember that diagnosis must be both *valid* and *reliable*. Validity refers to how well you are measuring what you actually want to measure. In determining instructional level, what you want to measure is how well children can read a particular book given your instruction and expectations. The best way to find that out is to put them in the book you think they can best function and then observe how they do. The major things you want to observe are their silent reading behaviors and rate, comprehension, and word indentification. Imagine now that you have Gary, Jill, Abraham, and Sal in the 3^2 book. You have done concept and meaning vocabulary development prior to reading and you have set a purpose for their silent reading. How will you decide if this is the appropriate instructional level for each of them. First, observe their silent reading. Children at the third-grade reading level should be moving their eyes and turning pages! If you notice that a child is pointing to each word or is "mouthing" each word you will want to make a note of this, because while these behaviors are not unusual for a child reading at first-grade level, they are often signs of frustration-level material for children reading at third-grade level and above. Note also which children finish reading way ahead of the others and which take much longer to finish. While there is no such thing as the "right reading rate," children who read very slowly and who finish long after the others have finished may be experiencing frustration.

When the children have finished reading, have them complete an activity which reflects the purpose you set for comprehending [see pp. 99–103]. While this activity should generally be completed as a group for instruction, you will probably want each child to complete it individually so that you can evaluate how well they can comprehend for a particular purpose in the probable instructional level book. Next, have each child read to you (or to a tape recorder) one page from the selection which has already been read silently (teachers often let children select the page they want to read). As you listen to the child read, count any oral reading errors made. In general, children should not make more than 1 error in 20 words when reading orally (not counting errors which don't change meaning). A child who does not make more than 1 error in 20 words probably has sufficient word identification ability to read at that level.

This procedure of observing children's silent reading behavior and rate, comprehension for a stated prupose, and word identification ability as evidenced by oral reading should be continued for one or two more selections in each book. If the information you receive from observing the children read the second selection confirms what you saw on the first selection, you probably do not need to lead them through another selection. If, on the other hand, the information from the first two selections is contradictory for some children, you will want to lead them through a third selection in order to make a *reliable* judgment of their probable instructional level. Figure 6.2 shows the notes made about Gary, Jill, Abraham, and Sal as they read the first three selections in the book.

As you can see from the chart, three selections were needed in order to obtain a reliable portrait of how well these students could read in the 3^2 book.

	Probable Instructional Level	Signs of Frustration			Silent Reading Rate			Comprehension for Stated Purpose			Word Identification		
		Selection			*Selection*			*Selection*			*Selection*		
		1st	*2nd*	*3rd*	*1st*	*2nd*	*3rd*	*1st*	*2nd*	*3rd*	*1st*	*2nd*	*3rd*
Gary	3^2	none	none	none	nor-mal	nor-mal	slow	good	good	good	good	3 errors on 50 word page	good
Jill	3^2	none	none	none	fast	nor-mal	nor-mal	good	some	good	good	good	good
Abraham	3^2	mouthing	none	mouthing	slow	slow	slow	some	very little	very little	good	good	good
Sal	3^2	none	none	none	nor-mal	fast	nor-mal	good	good	good	good	good	good

FIGURE 6.2   Silent Reading Rate

4. Move children up or down a level depending on how well they did in the probable instructional level book and try them out again.

Instructional level is generally considered to be the *highest* level at which a child can read comfortably with good comprehension and adequate word identification. Based on your observation of Gary, Jill, Abraham, and Sal, you know that Gary, Jill, and Sal can comfortably read and comprehend and have adequate word identification to read in the 3^2 book, but you haven't yet found their instructional level. Perhaps they can comfortably read, comprehend, and have adequate word identification in the fourth-grade book. Abraham, on the other hand shows by his mouthing, slow rate, and poor comprehension that the 3^2 book is at his frustration level. You must try him out in easier material until you find his instructional level. So for your next round of diagnosis, you will place Gary, Jill, and Sal along with any of the children for whom the fifth-grade book was too hard in the fourth-grade book and teach lessons using two or three selections from the fourth-grade book to make decisions about silent-reading behavior and rate, comprehension, and word identification. Imagine that when you do this, Gary and Jill demonstrate that this fourth-grade-level book is frustration level for them. Then you know that 3^2 was indeed their instructional level. Sal, however, does well in the fourth-grade-level book. Is fourth-grade-level his instructional level? Perhaps, but you will have to try him out in the fifth-grade book to see.

Since instructional level is the highest level at which children can comfortably function, you must find each child's frustration level. The level just below frustration level is considered instructional level. For Abraham, you have found that 3^2 was frustration level, you must now move back down until you find the level at which he can comfortably comprehend and has adequate word identification. Abraham, along with any of the children who did well at the probable instructional level of second grade, should be tried out in the 3^1 book.

For most children, trying them out in their probable instructional level and then moving them up or down one level based on their performance at that level will result in their being appropriately placed in the instructional level book. Figure 6.3 is a chart showing what the two groupings revealed about our imaginary class of fourth graders.

5. Do individual diagnosis with children for whom you are still unsure after group tryouts at two levels.

As you can see in Figure 6.3, 22 of the 26 children have been appropriately placed at their instructional level after meeting for group instruction in the book at their probable instructional level and in the book higher or lower than the first book. For four children, however, the

Figure 6.3   Probable Instructional Level

	Level First Try-out	Next Try-out at Level	Test Individually in	Instructional Level
Carol	5	4		4
Paul	5	*		5
Sam	5	*		5
Susie	5	*		5
Ralph	5	4	3^2	3^2
Janet	4	3^2		3^2
David	4	5		5
Sharon	4	5		4
Jim	4	3^2		3^2
Pat	4	5		4
Debbie	4	5		5
Carla	4	5		5^2
Gary	3^2	4		3^2
Jill	3^2	4		3^2
Abraham	3^2	3^1	2	2
Sal	3^2	4	5	5
Susan	3^1	2		2
Dick	3^1	2		2
Paula	3^1	2		2
Samantha	2	**		below 2
Clayborn	2	**		below 2
Sarah	2	3^1		2

Figure 6.3 (continued)

	Level First Try-out	Next Try-out at Level	Test Individually in	Instructional Level
Clayton	2	3^1		2
Benjamin	2	3^1		2
Harry	2	3^1	3^2	3^1
Derrick	2	3^1		2

* These children did fine at level five and since we have decided that the level-five book is the highest we will use for small-group instruction, we do not need to test them in harder material.
** These children were at frustration level in the second grade high interest-low vocabulary book and since we have decided to use language experience and imitative reading with easy-to-read books with children whose instructional level is first grade, we don't need to test them in first-grade books. We do need, however, to do more diagnosis and determine what is keeping them from reading better.

probable instructional level was not very accurate and these children will require some additional diagnosis. Ralph needed to be tried out in the 3^2 book which was found to be his instructional level. Through individual diagnosis, Abraham was placed in the second-grade high-low book, Sal was placed in the fifth-grade book, and Harry was placed in the 3^1 book.

6. Once you know the instructional levels for your students, decide how to schedule and manage the various groups.

In our imaginary fourth-grade classroom, we have selected the books of which we had multiple copies and which we could use for small-group instruction. We have then tried to match the books to the children so that children were getting some of their reading instruction in material at their instructional level. After small-group and individual tryouts, we find that we have the following children at the various levels:

5th—Paul, Sam, Susie, David, Debbie, Carla, Sal
4th—Carol, Sharon, Pat
3^2—Ralph, Janet, Jim, Gary, Jill
3^1—Harry
2nd—Abraham, Susan, Dick, Paula, Sarah, Clayton, Benjamin, Derrick
Below 2nd—Samantha, Clayborn

This is six different levels and many teachers find it difficult, if not impossible, to teach that many different groups. There are a variety of solutions to this problem. Harry, for example, is the only one who needs to be instructed at the 3^1 level. The teacher might: (1) try him out in the 3^2 group and given him extra support and help, including assigning him a partner in that group who will work through the comprehension questions and skills with him; (2) let him read with the group in the second-grade high-low book and also read individually in the 3^1 book; or (3) trade Harry during reading time for a child in the fourth grade across the hall who reads at the 3^2 or 2 level if that child happens to be the only one in the other fourth grade at the 3^2 or 2 level and if the teacher across the hall has a group at the 3^1 level. Samantha and Clayborn, who read below second-grade level, will need some individual attention from the teacher but might be able to meet with the children in the second-grade high-low book for skills instruction or listening instruction. It is also likely that Samantha and Clayborn are getting some additional reading instruction from a special reading teacher or other resource teacher.

The issue of how to manage instructional time and resources to meet the needs of all the different reading levels found in a heterogeneous class will be further explored in Chapter 7 and in Part II of this book.

QUESTION: What about commercially produced tests?

When most people think of diagnosis and evaluation, they think of tests. In this chapter, we have tried to present diagnosis and evaluation as an ongoing and continuous part of teaching and learning. Teachers decide what it is they are trying to teach and then devise ways to reliably measure it so that the measurement is instructionally valid. How do tests fit into this scheme? There are basically two kinds of commercially produced tests: Standardized norm-referenced achievement tests indicate how well groups of students are achieving compared with a larger population, such as the nation or the state; criterion-referenced tests attempt to measure how well students are learning certain abilities and skills. What is the proper place of standardized norm-referenced and criterion-referenced tests as teacher tools for diagnosis and evaluation?

Except as a screening device, standardized norm-referenced achievement tests have NO place in diagnosis and evaluation of individuals. Standardized reading tests tell you how well groups of children are achieving. They do not tell you anything about individual children even though, unfortunately, they do print out scores for individual children. How can this be? If a child scores 3.1 on a standardized reading achievement test, doesn't that mean that the child is reading at the first month of third grade? Shouldn't that child be placed in the 3^1 book and be given instruction at that level, and wouldn't that be easier than all the diagnosis described under the "What Is the Child's Instructional Level?" section? The answer to all those questions is an unqualified "No."

Consider, first, the number 3.1. What this number means, according to the creators of the standardized test, is that this child reads as well as the average child in the first month of third grade. But, how well is that? This is in no way tied to the basal reader level 3^1 which indicates the book in that series average third graders might read in the first half of third grade. In fact, the average third grader in the first month of school might be placed in a particular basal reader's 2^2 or 3^2 book. The number 3.1 only means "reads as well as the normed population's average readers in third grade, first month."

Furthermore, all tests have what is called "standard error." Standard error is the term used to describe how much the child's "true score" is apt to vary from the test score. Standard error comes from sources such as the fact that some children get really "up" for tests and perform much better for the test than they ever could on a day-in, day-out basis while other children panic and don't do nearly as well as they do on a day-in, day-out basis. Standard error also exists because some children don't feel well on the day of the test. Moreover, some test-wise children make great guesses. Others are easily frustrated and quit when they get to a hard item. Finally, some children are just plain lucky! All standardized tests have standard error and the test manual will tell you how much the standard error is for each part of the test. A standard error of four months is not unusual for a subtest of an achievement test. That means that if a child scores 3.1 and the test has a standard error of .4, the child's true score is likely to be someplace between 2.7 and 3.5. That child probably reads somewhere between where the average reader in the seventh month of second grade and the average reader in the fifth month of third grade. This is not very informative to the teacher who must make instructional decisions for that child!

So, what is the value of standardized achievement tests? Standardized achievement tests were designed, as their test makers state, to measure the achievement of *groups* of individuals. If the test tells me that an individual has a score of 3.1 and that test has a standard error of four months, I know that the individual's true score is probably between 2.7 and 3.5. But, if the test tells me that my group of third graders scored 3.1, I can believe that score is quite accurate because the child who scores four months below actual ability because he had a cold is balanced by one who scored four months above actual ability because she was lucky that day! Standardized achievement scores tell us something about groups. They do not tell us anything about individuals. Teachers and parents must not expect these scores to be accurate for individuals.

Now, what about criterion-referenced tests which don't give us a number such as 3.1 or 5.2 but rather tell how well a student has learned something? These, we believe can be used if there is a match between the teacher's instruction and the test's measurement. There are, for example, many readiness tests which are supposed to indicate whether or not children are ready for reading. Should a teacher use one of these instead of or in addition to teacher observation and teacher-made tests? That would depend on what the test was testing. Many readiness tests evaluate children's knowledge of letter names and sounds. If one of your readiness goals is to have children learn all letter names and sounds before you begin reading instruction, then information from this test might be valuable in helping you make your decision. If, however, you intend to begin your reading instruction in a more global way with sentences and words, and, as you go along, develop letter-sound knowledge, a readiness test which considers as prerequisite some abilities you intend to build as you go along would indicate that many children who might be ready for your kind of beginning reading instruction are not ready. It is also possible that a readiness test might ignore some things you think are essential. Few readiness tests attempt to assess whether or not children know what reading is for and expect reading to make sense.

Most basal reading series include placement tests which teachers can use to place students on the appropriate instructional level. Should you use these tests rather than construct your own? Again, you must consider your instruction and the test and decide how valid that test would be for the type of instruction you believe children should have. Often, the passages children are to read on commercially produced IRIs are very short, 100 words or less. Is a test which measures a child's ability to read 100 words from the fourth-grade book and answer orally four comprehension questions a good indicator of how well that child will read entire stories and answer questions in writing?

There is another problem inherent in paper and pencil tests which must be considered when the decision of whether to use them is being made. You will remember that letter-sound relationships knowledge was discussed as occurring at three levels: discrimination, association, and application. The association level required that given the word, the child could identify appropriate letters associated with some sounds, or that given the letters, the child could come up with words containing sounds represented by those letters. This level you can test with a paper and pencil test. But, the application level required that the child use this association-level knowledge in real reading. This you cannot measure with a paper and pencil test. Paper and pencil tests are limited, by their nature, to association-level tasks. Teachers who say, "They know the skills, they just don't use them," are really saying they have learned the association but not the application. Application-level assessment usually requires interaction between a teacher, a child, and something to read.

Criterion-referenced tests were created by persons, and the items on these tests generally reflect, within the limitations of paper and pencil tests, the instructional beliefs of the creator. Teachers should consider the match between their instructional beliefs and the test items and, when this match is a good one, use criterion-referenced tests to measure learning at the association level. Teachers who believe that an unused association is a worthless one will teach and evaluate also at the application level.

7 | Organization, Discipline, and Reading

"I could teach any child to read well if I only had one child at a time," is a statement often uttered or thought by elementary teachers. Barring major flu epidemics, this is *not* the normal pupil-teacher ratio. Elementary teachers must teach a whole class of children, whose instructional levels and needs vary considerably. Thus, in order to be an effective teacher of reading, you must be able to have some of the children engaged in worthwhile activities that allow you to work with other children. And that, as any experienced teacher will tell you, is no mean feat! We have seen many caring, well-trained teachers unable to carry out effective reading instruction because they could not establish a classroom climate in which children worked independently for short periods of time while the teacher worked with individuals and small groups. Establishing routines, schedules, activities, and rules for the morning language arts time so that the teacher is able to work successfully with some children while the others are constructively and quietly busy is directly related to the success or failure of reading instruction. Teachers, principals, and parents refer to the whole melée of things which result in a relatively quiet, smooth-running classroom as *discipline*. It is the major concern of school personnel and the general public.

In this chapter, we shall share with you 13 "*do's*" used by successful teachers to achieve the goals of good discipline and good reading instruction. Since we believe that "an ounce of prevention is worth a pound of cure" is especially true of classroom discipline, the chapter begins with some "*do's*" which help prevent problems. Because even with the best preventive program some problems will occur, the *do's* at the end of the chapter are included to help you deal with these problems. The 13 *do's* are:

1. Do arrange your classroom to facilitate whole-class, small-group, and independent work.
2. Do establish routines for routine things.
3. Do have and post a reasonable schedule.

4. Do bring your kitchen timer to school.
5. Do make maximum use of small-group or individual instruction time.
6. Do provide interesting, varied, doable, and worthwhile activities for the ones you are not working with.
7. Do let the children share the work and responsibility.
8. Do think positively.
9. Do practice consistency.
10. Do ask yourself, "Is that pretty normal?"
11. Do have end-of-the-day meetings.
12. Do remember that nothing will work for every child.
13. Do follow the school bus home.

1. Do arrange your classroom to facilitate whole-class, small-group, and independent work.

In the old days, desks were screwed to the floors in straight rows. A raised platform and podium distinguished the teacher space from the pupil space. This classroom arrangement was conducive to teacher lectures, pupil recitations, and whole-class instruction. Currently, most classrooms have furniture which can be moved and most classrooms are arranged so that a variety of activities can go on throughout the school day. In the old days, the teaching materials consisted of textbooks for each subject, notebooks, and pens. Classrooms of today have a variety of teaching materials. The effective elementary teacher knows that the arrangement of classroom space, furnishings, and materials can support or detract from good reading instruction. While there are other considerations beyond supporting reading instruction which must be kept in mind when arranging your classroom, here are some arrangement suggestions which most teachers agree are crucial to successful reading instruction.

Regardless of whether you have your class divided into basal reading groups or call children together for other kinds of groups, you will need a space where you can work with your groups. Ideally, this space would have a chalkboard on which you and the children could write. If not, you will want to provide chart paper or an overhead projector and screen because being able to write words and sentences and have the children *watch* you as you write is essential to good reading instruction. This space may have a carpet on which the children (and you, occasionally!) sit. Alternatively, you may have chairs which stay in this small-group space or children may carry their chairs with them to the group. Regardless of what the children are seated on, they should be seated in a half-circle or horseshoe arrangement with their backs to the rest of the class. Seated this way, they can (1) all see what the teacher is writing; (2) face each other as they are responding and discussing; and

(3) not be distracted by what the children elsewhere in the class are doing. The teacher would then be facing the small group and the rest of the class and would have better control of the children not in the group. In order to make efficient use of the limited time available for small-group instruction, a box of supplies (computer and index cards, markers, scissors, etc.) would be kept handy for use only in this area. Teachers' manuals and other instructional materials needed for reading would also be stored in this area.

Occasionally, we have seen classrooms in which the teacher seats the children at tables or clusters of desks according to which group they are in and then goes to each area to work with each group. This arrangement does not seem to be a good use of classroom space because it does not meet the criteria already mentioned (space always available for writing, group with back to rest of class, teacher facing, materials handy in one area); and because children need to move from place to place and the movement to and from the reading group space allows for purposeful, orderly movement. Another problem with this arrangement is that the children with whom the teacher is not working are sitting very close to one another during their independent working time. This closeness promotes unnecessary chatter and occasional conflicts (He tore my paper! She kicked me!). In an ideal arrangement, when a teacher was working with one group, the other children would be dispersed around the seating area and at learning centers.

Learning centers also require space in the classroom. There are as many different kinds of centers and ways to make space for centers as there are creative teachers thinking up ingenious ways to keep children busy, involved, and learning. In Chapters 9 through 14, you will see a great variety of types of learning centers and ways to create space for them.

Occasionally, you will be doing instruction which will include the whole class. Your ideal whole-class seating arrangement would be one in which (1) all children can easily see you and the largest blackboard; (2) you can maintain eye contact with all children as you move around and position yourself next to various children; and (3) the children all face one another, and thus can easily hear one another and interact in a discussion. This ideal arrangement would probably be an open rectangle or horseshoe in which the children's desks or tables are all along the outside and which is open to the area where the chalkboard is located. This would leave a large open area in the center, which could be used for various activities and might contain a table on which needed supplies are kept and completed papers are filed. In this ideal arrangement the teacher would have good attention and interaction when desired because everyone is looking at everyone else and the teacher can move easily around the group and still maintain eye contact with all children. Troublesome children can be placed at either open end of the rectangle or horseshoe and a better behaved child can be seated next to them. Thus, while not isolated from the other children, they have fewer opportunities for creating disturbances and, since they will be seated at the front, they will be close to the teacher working from the chalkboard area. (This assumes, unfortunately, only two troublesome children per classroom!) If the children in the different reading groups are not seated next to one another, there are empty spaces throughout the seating area when any group is with the teacher. It is easier to work quietly and not be distracted when you are not too close to lots of other people.

In many classrooms there is not enough room to make one large horseshoe or rectangle and have room left over for anything else. If this is your situation, you may want to make two horseshoes or rectangles, a smaller one inside the larger. This arrangement keeps the advantage of all children being able to see the teacher and the chalkboard and allows the teacher easy movement to all children. You do, however, lose the important advantage of all children being able to maintain eye contact with one another. (The children on the inner horseshoe or rectangle can't see the children on the outer one; the children on the outer one can only see the backs of the inner horseshoe or rectangle children.) Also, the children cannot hear each other as well. Some teachers solve this problem by having a "discussion-time arrangement" for which the children on the inner horseshoe or rectangle bring chairs along the front open area and, with their backs to the chalkboard, face all the children in the outer horseshoe or rectangle. This creates a supportive discussion arrangement with a minimum of movement and hassle.

Having a place for everything and teaching the children to put everything in its place is not an easy task to accomplish, but it is of crucial importance. In classrooms where teachers are free to spend a good portion of their time working uninterruptedly with individuals and small groups, the children know where to get what is needed and put things where they belong afterward. Your major task in considering room arrangement is that you must establish where needed materials can be put so that they are accessible to the children and easily put away. Some teachers keep a box of needed supplies handy for each small group of children who are seated near one another. Along with supplies such as pencils, erasers, scissors, and paper, the box often contains worksheets and assignments for the children who share the box. Finished work may be filed in folders kept in the box. A child is assigned each week to make sure all supplies are returned and to check to see that papers are filed in the right folders.

Labeling everything goes a long way toward solving the keeping up with materials problem. Many teachers hang shoebags on bulletin boards, walls, or doors and label the pockets of the shoebags according to what is in there and what should be returned there. Pictures of what belongs where along with the word labels help very young children to be responsible workers. Parts of games or puzzles should always be numbered or color coded so that their replacement is as simple as possible.

In spite of all your organizing and labeling, there will be things found during the day which the person who finds them doesn't know where to put them. Thus, every classroom needs a "Where Does This Thing Go?" box! Objects, papers, game and puzzle pieces whose place cannot be located easily are placed in this box. At the end of each day, the teacher and children clean out the box and jointly decide where the things go. All this organizing, arranging, and labeling takes a large initial investment of time and energy from the teacher and the children, but the long-term gain in teacher energy and time as well as independence and responsibility for the children makes it a wise investment.

2. Do establish routines for routine things.

In every classroom, pencils are going to need to be sharpened and the children are going to need to go to the restroom. These constantly reoccurring activities are not what schooling is all about, but they must be carried out efficiently and unobtrusively and with as little teacher direction as possible so the teaching and learning that schooling is all about can occur. There are still a few schools in which children are lined up all at the same time and walked down to the boys' and girls' restrooms! In most schools, however, teachers recognize that this practice is degrading, wasteful of children and teacher time, and not very effective. Regardless of what time your schedule says they should all go to the restrooms, someone will need (or say they need—and how can you tell?) to visit the restrooms at other times. If the procedure for going to the restroom is to interrupt the teacher and ask permission, not much reading instruction is going to go on. Activities such as pencil sharpening and going to the restrooms are considered to be routines and, as such, children should learn to carry them out in a routine, unobtrusive way.

Many teachers routinize going to the restroom by hanging somewhere in the room a chart which says "Boys" and one which says, "Girls." In a pocket created by stapling a strip of paper along the bottom of each chart are cards on which each child's name is written. When a child needs to go to the restroom, that child looks at the chart to see if there is a card displayed in the slot where children put their cards when they are in the restroom. If there is no card there, the child knows there are no other children out of the room and, after placing his or her name card in the appropriate slot, goes to the restroom. Upon returning, the child removes the name card from the slot and places it back in the pocket at the bottom of the chart. This system has several advantages:

1. No more than one boy or one girl is ever out of the room at the same time.

2. The teacher can tell by glancing at the chart who is in the restroom (this is crucial in case of fire drills or other unexpected critical situations).
3. The children can go to the restroom independently and are expected to behave responsibly while out of the room.
4. If a child fails to behave responsibly, his or her card can be removed from the pocket and that child will have to seek the teacher's permission and/or have another child accompany him or her to the restroom.
5. Much time is saved for teaching when the teacher does not have to line up and escort or grant permission to 30 children twice each day to use the restroom.
6. A child who feels he or she must "take a walk" and get out of the classroom for a few minutes has a legitimate way to do this as long as the privilege is not abused.

Pencil sharpening can also be routinized. Most teachers allow children to go to the pencil sharpener as long as there is no one there or they are not in a group which is supposed to be attending to the teacher. (Going to the restroom also should not take place except in dire emergencies when the group is working with the teacher. Children who know when they will be with the teacher will plan ahead and go to the restroom during their independent working time.) Some teachers are disturbed by the noise made by the pencil sharpener when they are working with a small group. This is especially true in classrooms where the pencil sharpener is permanently attached very near to the only feasible small-group working area. If you do not want children going to the pencil sharpener during small-group time, provide a store of pencils they can borrow and then replace when they have had a chance to sharpen theirs. If you have a box of supplies for children who sit near one another to share, "loan" pencils could, of course, be a part of this box. There are also small, cheap, quiet little pencil sharpeners which might be included in the supply box and which would also minimize the pencil-sharpening hassle.

Pencil sharpening and restroom going have been used as two examples of everyday events which occur in classrooms and which should be routinized. Anything which goes on regularly and which is apt to require teacher time and energy if not routinized should be routinized. Other examples of situations needing routines include learning to walk quietly, to close the door without a bang, to carry chairs and slide them in and out quietly, to get the teacher's attention without shouting. These can all be routinized if the teacher and children figure out a reasonable, workable system and then practice the system until everyone understands what is expected. All routines should be role-played by children and teacher when they are first begun so that there is no doubt that *all* children understand the procedure. Not all children will follow the procedure, but most will if the teacher expects them to and compliments them regularly on how independent and responsible they are becoming. For those children who *won't* follow the rules, advice is provided in the *Do remember nothing will work for all children* and the *Do follow the school bus home* sections.

3. Do have and post a reasonable schedule.

In order to make the best use of instructional time, teachers and children must know what is to be accomplished and the approximate time frame in which this should be accomplished. Certain activities (an opening-together time, break time, story time) will probably occur at the same time and for approximately the same duration every day. Other activities may vary from day to day. The important point is that the teacher and children have a clear notion of what is going to happen when so that they may plan ahead. You can't behave responsibly and go to the restroom or sharpen you pencil *before* the teacher meets with your group if you don't know when the teacher is going to meet with your group. It is very frustrating for children to get started in an activity and be abruptly called away from that activity to meet in a small group or with the whole class. So, a schedule should be posted and gone over together each morning so that everyone knows what they must do when. Many teachers make a changeable schedule by cutting slots in a piece of poster board and inserting in the appropriate time slots strips of paper which indicate what will be happening when. Standard activities which occur at the same time each day can be permanently written on the poster board and the others inserted at the beginning of each day.

As you plan your schedule, be sure to alternate times when children must work independently because you are engaged in small-group or individual instruction and times when you are interacting with the whole class. Many teachers, after an initial whole-class activity, try to pull out for an hour or more and work with small groups and individuals and then follow that with 45 minutes of whole-class time. This means that the children not working with the teacher are expected to carry on independently and responsibly for 60-plus minutes and then everyone is expected to be attentive for a long period of whole-class time. It would be much better scheduling for the teacher to plan two 20–25 minutes of small-group or individual instruction time, followed by a 20–25 minute whole-class time, one more 20–25 minute small-group or individual time, and then one more 20–25 minute whole-class time. With this schedule, the same amount of small-group or individual and whole-class instruction can take place, but children are not required to work independently for long periods of time nor are they required to attend to a whole-class lesson for 45 minutes. A further step can be taken by the teacher to ensure that children are responsible, independent workers if a five-minute transition time is planned between the two small groups which meet first. During this five minutes, the teacher circulates to see that children are succeeding with their activities; the group with whom the teacher has finished working begins their independent activities; and the group with whom the teacher is about to work finishes their independent work and goes to the small-group area. Small problems which need the teacher's attention before they become big problems can be attended to and children who have been behaving responsibly and independently can get a special smile, wink or pat on the head from their pleased teacher! If you are having difficulty imagining how the teacher is keeping up with all these changes in activity and adhering to established time allotments, you will understand the necessity of the next *do*.

4. Do bring your kitchen timer to school.

Most people don't think of the timer they use to remind them when the eggs are boiled or the cake is baked as a teaching tool, but it is. In fact, teachers who use their timer throughout the day in the classroom would part with their chalk before they would part with their timer! How do you use a kitchen timer to help you be a more effective teacher of reading? One obvious use for the timer is to help keep you, the teacher, close to the schedule you have made and posted. Consider what happens in the minds of children if the teacher makes and posts a schedule and then fails to stick to it. "Boys and girls," reminds the teacher, "I will be working with this group for 25 minutes. You will have 25 minutes to complete what you are working on. At 10:35 we will all begin to put away our independent and small-group work and materials and by 10:40 I hope we can all be seated on the rug ready to make plans for our field trip on Thursday." Now the teacher, with the best of intentions, gets involved with the small group. The time flies by and before the teacher notices it, 40 minutes have passed. Frantically, being 15 minutes behind schedule, the teacher hurries the group being worked with and the others to the rug area. Materials are not put away and the transition between activities is not smooth because the promised five-minute finishing up, gear-shifting time was not provided. Furthermore, the children who have taken the teacher seriously and tried to pace their independent work so that they can finish in 25 minutes have worked hard and proudly finished, and then must sit around and wait for 15 minutes. The slowpokes and procrastinators, on the other hand, have been rewarded with an additional 15 minutes of working time! The teacher and children must have a reasonable schedule to follow if the children are to become responsible, independent learners. The teacher must stick to the schedule or the children can't and won't. A timer serves the same function in the classroom as it does in the kitchen. When you are engrossed in making your white sauce (working with your small group or individual), the timer reminds you that you have a cake in the oven (other children in the room) in need of your attention.

In addition to helping you keep to the schedule you have made, the timer can be used to make routine chores fun! Trying to get the desks, floors, and other areas cleaned up, and the chairs on top of the desks (so the custodian can sweep) and all children over to the rug for an end-of-the-day meeting can be most frustrating for a tired teacher at the end of the day. A teacher who uses the timer wisely, however, will say, "I'm setting the timer for four minutes. Let's see who can beat the clock and get their area clean, chair on desk, and be seated on the rug before the timer rings." Children love a race and will work quickly and dilligently to beat the clock.

Teachers who use timers to time their whole-class, small-group, or individual activities find that the children in the activity are more attentive. "Okay, kids, we have a story to read and a lot to talk about today in 25 minutes so let's get started and try to move right along. If we happen to have a few minutes at the end, I have a riddle I would like to see if anyone can guess the answer to." This is a group opener which catches everyone's attention and motivates everyone to do their best and speediest work. Teachers often complain that "there just aren't enough hours in the day." While it is true that there is much to accomplish in a limited time in every elementary classroom, it is also true that there is a great deal of wasted time. Time is wasted whenever the teacher has to prod children to "find your place," "pay attention," "listen to what the question is." Much inattentive behavior can be minimized by the imposing of time limits, the promise of something fun to do if we should happen to have leftover time, and the visible, audible timer ticking the minutes away. Smart teachers will make sure that the planned activities can be completed within the allotted time if children are relatively attentive and that, much of the time, there is a minute or two left for the riddle or for a quick game of "Hangman" or "Simon Says". Finally, to the child who is not succeeding well and finds it most difficult to sit and attend to any activity, the timer says, "This too shall pass." Many inattentive, unruly children who would create some kind of disturbance after trying to attend for 20 minutes can "make it" when they look at the timer and know they only have to last 5 more minutes. The small-group or individual instructional time is always limited, so it must be intense. This leads us to *do* #5.

5. Do make maximum use of small-group or individual instruction time.

Many of the suggestions already made in this chapter will help you be efficient in your use of small-group or individual instructional time. An appropriate seating arrangement and the establishment of routines will minimize the number of times you are interrupted by the children who are supposed to be working independently. Having all needed materials and supplies at your fingertips in the small-group area will save you minutes spent looking for or going to get materials. Using your timer to help you stick to the allotted group time and to help the children be attentive during that limited time will also increase what you can accomplish. There are some other "tricks of the trade," however, which successful teachers use to stretch their teaching time. One of these is the use of every-pupil-response cards.

Imagine that you are meeting with a group of children who have read an informational text about insects before coming to the group. You want to quickly establish what factual information was provided about insects and then move on to helping the children choose an insect about which they want to learn more. You could tell the children to "listen as I describe some feature of some of the insects you have just read about. Raise your hand if you can tell me what insect I am describing." Then, you could describe various insects and call on children who volunteer to demonstrate that they have comprehended what hey read. Now, consider another way of accomplishing the same goal of reviewing the literal information contained in the text about insects. "I am giving each of you eight computer cards. On each card, I want you to write the name of one of the insects we have read about. When you have your cards made, I will describe an insect and, when I give the signal, show me the card which has the name of the insect you think I am describing." As you describe each insect, all children in the group listen and shuffle through their cards so that when you say, "Ready, Set, Show!", they can display the name of the described insect.

How does this every-pupil-response activity make maximum use of instructional time? In the "raise your hands and I will call on you" mode, each child gets to respond once or twice and, since children know that when they have "had their turn," you probably will call on someone else for awhile, they are apt to stop thinking. Children who are not very confident, able, or assertive may never try to have their turn and may never be thinking! Every-pupil-response activities increase the attention and number of responses made by each pupil. Thus, while the amount of time you are teaching has not increased, the amount of time each pupil is actively thinking and learning may have tripled or quadrupled! Furthermore, if you told children *before* they read the story the nature of the every-pupil-response activity they were going to engage in after reading (and maybe even had them make the cards with the insects' names on them!), they would probably have read the story more actively in an attempt to be sure they could make the appropriate responses. Thus, you have actually increased their learning even when they were reading the story on their own.

TRY IT OUT

The type of cards made by children to perform every-pupil-response activities after reading depends on the nature of the comprehension follow-
up the teacher desires to do. If, for example, the children have read a
story in which there are four major events, the teacher may have the
children write *first, second, third, last* on cards. Then, as they are told an
event, they would respond by showing the card which indicated the
sequence of the event in the story. Choose a story or informational text
you might have children read. Decide what your comprehension follow-
up should be and then decide what cards your children would make for
an every-pupil-response activity.

Another way that savvy teachers get the most out of their instructional time is to give children *think time*. It may seem contradictory to
suggest that you save time by pausing (and forcing the children to
pause) for five seconds before allowing children to raise their hands or
make any response, but you do. Think time is particularly important
when you are asking children to evaluate what they have read and/or go
beyond the information given in the text. I can quickly respond, "Abraham Lincoln," if you ask, "Who freed the slaves?" But five seconds is
probably the minimum time required for consideration of such questions
as, "Was Abraham Lincoln considered by his contemporaries to be a
great president?" or, "How could history have been changed if Abraham
Lincoln had not been assassinated?" Many teachers find that they can
greatly increase the inferential and evaluative thinking abilities of
their students by simply prefacing an appropriate question with, "This
next question requires you to think about what you read. The book
didn't answer this question directly. So, after I ask the question, I am
going to count slowly and silently to five and only when I nod my head
to show I have counted off five seconds do I want to see any hands
raised. Remember this is a thinking question and so I want each of you
to take five seconds of think time. I won't call on anyone whose hand is
raised before I nod my head."

Think time saves time because all children have a few seconds to
consider the question and thus more children are actively engaged in
learning as you are engaged in teaching. Time is also saved because the
responses you get after five seconds of think time are better and children
are able to think at higher levels without the teacher feeling as if he or
she is "pulling teeth!"

Finally, as you consider how to make maximum use of small-group
or individual instructional time, remember that you have the power to
decide which parts of the reading lesson children need to be sitting with

you for and which parts they could do before or after their instruction as part of their independent seatwork. Many teachers spend most of their instructional time getting children ready to read and following up the reading with discussion and other comprehension activities. The silent reading is done by the children on their own. This practice is a particularly efficient use of time since people do read at different speeds and, if the group is supposed to read the story silently while sitting in the group, some children are sure to finish quickly and others are sure never to finish before the teacher moves on to the follow-up activity. It is hard to be involved in a comprehension follow-up if you haven't finished the story! Once the directions for their completion are clear, worksheets accompanying the story can be done individually or by working partners (more about that in *Do provide interesting, varied, do-able, and worthwhile activities for the ones you are not working with*). The discussion of what was done on these worksheets and why particular responses are correct or incorrect should probably occupy group time since this student-student and teacher-student interaction is crucial to improved comprehension.

There are many decisions which must be made about what can be done most efficiently and effectively in what setting. Which decision is made will vary with the age and ability of the students as well as their instructional needs and independent working ability. The good teacher, however, knows that you can't be with them helping them do everything and decides for which of the many activities the teacher-group interaction is most crucial.

6. Do provide interesting, varied, do-able, and worthwhile activities for the ones you are not working with.

A suitable classroom arrangement of furniture and materials; the establishment of routines for routine events; a reasonable, posted, adhered-to schedule; a working, used timer; and efficient, active small-group or individual instruction go a long way toward establishing a classroom climate in which maximum teaching and learning can occur. But, if the children are not provided with interesting, varied, do-able, and worthwhile activities with which to engage their time and themselves when they are not working with the teacher, maximum teaching and learning will not occur. It is not reasonable to expect that children will sit quietly at their places and complete workbook pages, ditto sheets, and boardwork for most of the morning. Workbook pages, ditto sheets, and copying from the board can be a part of what children do and, if these activities are indeed do-able, children should be expected (and indeed required) to complete them. The problem many teachers and children face is that sitting and working with paper and pencil is all children do when they are not working with the teacher. Since there is so much of it to do, many children won't attempt to do any. If the same seatwork assignments are made to the whole class and there are children reading on many different levels in that class, the seatwork is too hard (not do-able) for some children whose reading levels are below the class average, and worthless for many of the brighter children. Often, when children complete one worksheet, they get another one to do! Children soon learn that if they finish too soon or they will get more of the same. In our experience, the biggest problem faced by elementary teachers as they try to provide instruction for the varied levels of children they have in their rooms is not what to do with the children they're working with, but what to do with the ones they're not working with! Throughout Chapters 9 to 14, you will find a variety of ways teachers at different grade levels solve this problem. In this section, we shall list a few universal precepts which good teachers of all grade levels follow in order to keep children working when they are not working with them.

Assign each child a limited amount of doable work and demand that this work be completed by a given time. The keys to accomplishing this goal are to be found in the words, *limited* and *do-able*. You cannot demand that children do something they can't do! Even if the work is do-able, if there is too much of it to do and if children must spend all morning sitting in one place doing it, it won't get done. In addition to being limited and doable, as often as possible the tasks to be completed should be interesting and worthwhile. Now, where is the teacher to find these limited, doable, interesting, worthwhile tasks and how is the teacher to make sure that they are completed? Given that there are many different reading levels in the classroom and that all of what children need to do related to their reading lesson cannot be done while the children are sitting with the teacher, it seems apparent that seatwork assignments should be made in the reading group, should involve reading, preparing to read, or following-up reading, and should be brought, COMPLETED, to the reading group at the specified time. If children are placed at the appropriate reading level and if their seatwork involves work with materials at this level, all children should be able to do this work. If the work involves reading or reading-related tasks, and if the teacher used what the children have done for small-group activities, children are more apt to see the work they do as interesting and worthwhile. Furthermore, a child who has not completed the work will be immediately and obviously "discovered" when that child arrives for the group follow-up empty handed. Many children who don't give a thought to the teacher not finding their work in the stack of papers to be corrected, would be embarrassed to face the teacher and their group without the assignment. Children who continually fail to complete this doable, limited, worthwhile work should be denied privileges or dealt with in ways suggested in the *Do remember no system will work for every child* and *Do follow the school bus home* sections.

Another device used by successful teachers to get work completed is to assign children to working partners. Working partners work together to complete an assignment. They are jointly responsible for the completeness and correctness of their responses and may complete one or two copies of the assignment. The secret to having partners successfully sharing the work and the learning is to make working with a partner voluntary on the part of the partners, and for the teacher and students to consider working with a partner a privilege. It is important that the partnership be a voluntary one (either partner can choose to work alone) because there are days when each of us wants to be left alone and doesn't feel up to intense interaction and because if one partner is leaving all the thinking and work to the other partner, the burdened partner will soon demand equal participation or dissolve the partnership. Since working in partners is a privilege granted by the teacher to independent and responsible learners, it can also be revoked by the teacher if the partnership is not working quietly and/or is not producing a quality product. When you revoke the partnership privilege, be sure that this revocation is temporary and that the partnership has a chance to try again. "I'm sorry, Carol and Joan, but your work this week is sloppy and shows very little thought. For next week's work, you will each complete your own. Week after next, I will give you another chance to work together." This is a way of revoking the privilege but letting the partners know why it has been revoked and that they will have another chance. Generally, Carol and Joan will not like doing their work by themselves next week while the others work in partners and will try harder the following week to demonstrate they can work together. Teachers who have children completing their seatwork through joint efforts find that a better product is produced in less time, that the children learn from each other, and that the completion of the assignment is less of a chore.

Not all of the activities which occur during the morning independent working time need to be reading-group related. In fact, using some of the morning time to work on science or social studies projects increases the amount of time for science and social studies and helps in a different way to solve the problem of keeping them busy. Especially for children in third grade and above, much of their morning time should be spent in reading, researching, writing, and creating which is content-area related. Since these content-area projects are usually interesting and fun for the children, they don't need to be constantly prodded to keep working. Since the child-created product of this project will probably be shared with the teacher and class during the science or social studies time, the teacher does not have an enormous stack of daily work to check for each child. We hope that you are seeing throughout this section that when the teacher decides to assign a lot of pencil and paper seatwork, that teacher is committed to spending an inordinate amount of time creating and checking that work and "keeping on children" to make sure that it gets done. If you consider all the things you would like children to accomplish throughout the school day for which there is never enough time, and then use some of the morning independent working time to accomplish some of these goals, more gets done and less must be graded and recorded.

Finally, successful teachers always have interesting, varied, and worthwhile activities in which students can engage their minds and bodies when the assignments are complete. One fourth-grade teacher began a crafts project with her students every other Friday afternoon. After soliciting needed materials from friends and parents, she spent a good block of time making sure that every child knew how to weave or macrame or do whatever the project required. For the next two weeks, the children could work on their craft whenever they were through with their assignments. Each child's in-progress masterpiece was hung at a particular spot in the room when not being worked on. In addition to keeping the children meaningfully and busily occupied, the room was a colorful melage of objets d'art and the parents were always impressed with what their children brought home every other Friday and with how talented their children and the teacher were! If a child successfully completed one of whatever the craft was before the two weeks were over that child could begin another one. At the end of two weeks, all projects, finished or unfinished, were taken home and something new was begun. If a child continually failed to complete his work well, that child found his masterpiece missing! To that child's complaint that "someone stole my basket," the teacher responded, "She surely did and if you get down to business and get your work completed today, she may return it tomorrow!"

The continual arts and crafts projects going on in this room not only kept the children busy, got them to finish their work quickly and well, and delighted the parents, it also provided the children with opportunities to work and think with their hands. In our stuffed curriculum, learning to think and create with your hands has become an endangered species. Why not use some of the children's independent working time to put back into the curriculum some of the simple pleasures of less harried times?

Of course, there are other activities which are different from seatwork and don't require continual checking from the teacher which children can become involved with when other tasks are through. In Chapters 9 through 14, you will see teachers at different grade levels utilizing creative writing centers, art centers, listening centers, reading centers, and many other types of centers in which the children can choose what they want to accomplish, explore, and learn in more open-ended ways. The important point is that children must want to finish their assigned work well and quickly so that they can do some other things.

They will naturally want to be independent and responsible learners if there are intriguing pursuits awaiting their eager minds and bodies.

7. Do let the children share the work and responsibility.

One of the questions a successful teacher continually asks is, "Could one of the children do this?" As often as not, the answer is, "Absolutely!" When one of the authors was a first-year, first-grade teacher, she had a terrible time remembering to send the milk and lunch count to the office. Every morning at 9:15, the intercom would come on and this impatient voice would inform the teacher that they were waiting for *her* count. Frantically, she would interrupt her teaching and get a count which as often as not was incorrect since it was done so hurriedly. This occurence created problems later in the day at snack and lunch time and the teacher was often at odds with the lunchroom staff as well as the office staff! Try as she did to remember, this beleaguered, beginning teacher would always get caught up in greeting the children and trying to get her instruction underway quickly (she had been taught that every minute counts!) and, most mornings, the click of the intercom coming on would remind her and set in motion the frantic, inaccurate count. One morning, Eric, who was an extremely precocious first grader said, "Teacher, why can't I just take the count every morning as the children come in and then you wouldn't have to get so upset and get yelled at by the office lady and the lunchroom lady?" "Eric, do you think you would be able to do that?" asked the hopeful but dubious young teacher. "Oh, sure, no problem," replied the confident and concerned young Eric. Thereafter, every morning, Eric sat at a table by the door and as the children entered, they told him if they were buying milk and/or lunch. Eric made a tally mark next to a dittoed sheet containing each child's name and milk and lunch column. He then added up the tally marks, wrote the *correct* numbers on the slip, handed it to the teacher to sign and took it to the office. The first graders, their teacher, the office lady, and the lunchroom lady lived happier ever after. The teacher also learned that there were many jobs which the children could do better than the teacher and that the children derived a lot of pride, identity, and satisfaction out of doing them!

In classes which function smoothly and in which a lot gets accomplished, the teacher and everyone else is working hard! In classes where the functioning is rocky and rough, and not enough seems to be getting done, the teacher is usually found to be trying to do everything. Some jobs (cleaning the chalkboard, keeping up with materials, being in charge of a center, for example) can be done by everyone in the class and well-organized teachers keep a large job chart posted, rotate jobs every week or two, and make sure the jobs get done; and the children feel proud of their accomplishments. Other jobs are beyond the talents and capabilities of all children, but not of some children. Is there a tall child who is the only one who can open and close the windows? Is there an Eric who even in first grade can take care of the lunch count? Is there a person who is such a good leader and so well liked and respected by all that he or she could be substitute teacher whenever the teacher has to leave the room momentarily and who could keep order without bullying the other children?

In addition to all the help the teacher now has in keeping the classroom running smoothly, sharing the work and responsibility with the children has an important bonus. The children who work to keep the classroom orderly and interesting feel more pride and ownership in *their* classroom. Because they work in it, it belongs to them. Because it belongs to them, they will care for it and take better care of it!

8. **Do think positively.**

In any classroom at any point in time there are positive things going on and children behaving in positive ways, and there are negative things going on and children behaving in negative ways. Successful teachers deal with the negative things but they focus on the positive things. If your children were asked to clear their desks and get ready to listen and discuss, and 24 of them have and 2 of them haven't, that is a 24 to 2 positive ratio! Show children that you appreciate their quick responses to your directions. Statements such as, "Billy sure is ready to go today. He had his desk cleared before I finished telling everyone to," or, "I asked all of you to clear your desks and 24 of the 26 of you did. What a good class I have!" focus on the positive things children do and show them you appreciate their quick compliance while, at the same time, suggest to the two who didn't comply that you noticed and expect them to.

One third-grade teacher we know kept a dittoed list of all her children's names in her top desk drawer. At the end of each day, she reflected for a few minutes about what she had said nice to whom during the day. As she remembered positive interactions, she put a check mark next to that child's name in the appropriate dated column. "Let's see, I told Carol she wrote a great story, and I told Bill I had seen his picture in the paper, and I told Jill and Carrie they had made the best bulletin board ever...." After several days, when she noticed some children with no check marks next to their names, she contrived to find some positive things to say to them. (There is *something* positive about every child, although with some you may have to stretch it as in, "I love the color blue your shirt is made of." or, "You have the biggest freckles I have ever seen!")

Another teacher divided her bulletin board into enough spaces to display *every* child's work. Each child had a yarned off and labeled space on that bulletin board on which something (work, story, art, etc.) that child had done was displayed. Sometimes the teacher chose what to display; sometimes, she let the children choose. Regardless, that bulletin board said, "This room belongs to every one of you. You can all do some things well and these things are worthy of being put on display." The children in this room, knowing that some things would be displayed, developed pride in their achievements and took more care with their work!

Many successful teachers send "brag notes" home. Throughout the day, they take a few minutes to write a note to the parents of some child telling the parents what the child should be bragged about for.

Dear Mr. and Mrs. Jones,

You should be so proud of Billy. He has been paying such good attention during reading group and I am seeing real progress in his reading. I shall let you know how he continues to grow. Meanwhile, if you choose to, you could let Billy have a special treat or extra privilege this weekend in recognition of his good attention and growth.

Sincerely,

Unlike the teacher notes many of us remember from our childhoods, brag notes are always positive and because they are, they get home!

9. Do practice consistency.

Emerson's belief that "consistency is the hobgoblin of a little mind" was not meant to apply to discipline in the classroom. Good teachers strive to be consistent in their day-to-day dealings with their students. If something is wrong today, the same something is probably wrong tomorrow. If Johnny's doing something is wrong, then Billy's doing the same something is probably also wrong. If break time is scheduled for 15 minutes it should probably last 15 minutes, not 10 minutes when the teacher is pushed to accomplish something and 30 minutes when the teacher needs some extra time to rest. Consistency is important because children need to know what is acceptable and what is not acceptable. If that acceptable behavior changes according to the teacher's mood and state of fatigue, or if what is acceptable for some children is unacceptable for others, the students are never sure about what will and will not be allowed. As long as it is possible that something might be allowed, the children will continually try to see what they can "get by with." In order to achieve consistency, most teachers have a limited number of classroom rules, strive to help the children see the importance of these rules, and enforce these rules quickly and consistently.

It is easier to enforce rules quickly and consistently when both teachers and children know what is acceptable and what is not. If, for example, the rule is "quiet talking only during working time" and the teacher disbands a partnership because they were "too loud," the children can always argue that they "were not too loud." One teacher made her rule more definitive. "If I can make out what you say, you are talking too loudly." That teacher enforced her rule by saying, "Carol I heard you say to Judy, 'I thought I'd crack up when he came over to talk to me.' Our rule is that during working time if I can make out *what* you have said it is too loud. You and Judy will have to work alone for the rest of the day."

10. Do ask yourself, "Is that pretty normal?"

Even in the smoothest running classrooms, things will not always go right! Teachers and children have their bad days. Three rainy days in a row will have you all wondering if you could survive another rainy day. When you are disturbed at something your children are doing or something that is not going well, ask yourself the question, "Is that pretty normal?" If you are out of the classroom for a few minutes and upon your return you find some children "messing around" and talking and laughing instead of working away diligently, is that pretty normal? Would the same thing happen in a university class if the professor left the room momentarily? The answer is probably, "Yes, that's pretty normal." If so, the teacher should respond by getting the children back on track but should *not* react as if the kids are bad kids. If you decide that what is occurring is pretty normal (what any group of people, children or adults, might do in similar circumstances), simply get everyone back on track with a firm but not angry attitude. The teacher who returns and finds some children not working might simply flip the lights to get their attention and then cheerfully announce, "Okay, you've had your unscheduled break. Now, the old ogre is back, so it's back to the grindstone." The teacher would then wait until everyone had settled back down again before resuming small-group or individual instruction.

If, on the other hand, the teacher returned to find a fist fight in progress, that is not pretty normal and should be dealt with differently. The participants involved might be taken from the room and dealt with by the teacher and/or principal, parents might be called, privileges would certainly be revoked. Since a fist fight is not what you could expect from a group left unattended for a few minutes, the teacher has a right and a duty to feel angry and to punish the offenders.

If, in the heat of a two-team vocabulary contest, the participants or spectators get a little noisy and carried away (as might the participants and spectators at a close basketball game), that's pretty normal. The teacher doesn't let it continue because order and relative quiet are important to learning in school settings, but the teacher gets everyone calmed down without getting angry or acting like they are bad, abnormal kids. On the other hand, fights or verbal abuse are not tolerated at basketball games and should be seriously dealt with if they occur as part of classroom contests.

Good teachers ask themselves, "Is that pretty normal?" As often as not, the answer is yes and then, while it may still need to be curtailed, it is not a discipline problem. By asking that question, teachers have fewer discipline problems with which to deal and the ones they have are clearly not normal and need to be dealt with.

11. Do have end-of-the-day meetings.

Another activity used by successful classroom teachers to keep things running smoothly and to deal with little problems before they become big problems is to have the children and teacher sit down together at a specified time each day (usually just before lunch or just before dismissal) and discuss how well the morning (day) went and what problems arose. In these meetings the teacher and children can make comments and suggestions about how "our class" can get more done and get along better. Children who have problems during the day can bring up those problems to the whole class and ask the class to help solve them. In fact, many teachers defuse small conflicts by suggesting that the child complaining to the teacher bring that matter up at the meeting. If Carol says to the teacher as they are going to reading group, "Bobby kept borrowing my eraser without asking during our working time," the teacher can respond, "Hmm, I know that must have been annoying, maybe you will want to talk about that problem during our meeting this afternoon." Chances are that by the time of the meeting, Carol will have gotten over, forgotten about, or made up with Billy about the eraser incident. Meantime, the teacher has sympathized with Carol and suggested that it might be important enough to bring up for class discussion. Often, all the complaining child wants is to be heard and have the problem appreciated. If Carol does bring it up at the meeting, a lively productive discussion about property rights, sharing, and politeness is apt to ensue. Meeting time is also a time when teacher and children share information, thoughts, and feelings and when good group discussion and problem-solving skills are built. Because it is important that the children be able to talk to and hear one another, the appropriate seating arrangement for a meeting is a circle or closed rectangle or horseshoe.

12. Do remember that nothing will work for every child.

As you are reading this chapter, you are probably thinking of children who could not work with a partner, would not put away the materials in a learning center, could create a disturbance in the hall if they went to the restroom by themselves. Often, when we work with teachers and suggest some of these management, discipline, and organization ideas, a teacher will say, "Well that would be fine if I didn't have Johnny," or, "I have three children who couldn't possibly be expected to complete their work and then go on to another activity without disturbing everyone." To which we respond, "Nothing will work for everyone." The question is, "Will it work for most of your children?" Some children do find it very difficult to handle independence and behave responsibly. These children must be given opportunities to behave responsibly. (Everyone starts out able to go the restroom on their own and being allowed to work with a partner.) But, children who do not behave responsibly lose that privilege for a specified period of time. Look at it this way. Assume you have some children in your classroom at the lowest level of responsibility, independence, and maturity. If you set your classroom rules and climate so that no one is allowed to take any responsibility or have any independence, you will have to be constantly monitoring what everyone does. The children who could learn to behave responsibly don't get the chance and the irresponsible ones are still irresponsible at the end of the year. If you structure your classroom so that independence and responsibility are expected, and privileges are temporarily withdrawn when children do not behave responsibly, you are freer to teach; the majority of the children become very responsible, independent, and proud of it; and the children who are not responsible may become more responsible as they see that they are losing independence and privileges by behaving irresponsibly. Our observations in the classrooms of successful teachers tell us that these teachers guide children to be independent and responsible, expect them to behave that way, withdraw a privilege when it is abused, and then give the irresponsible child a second, third, and fourth chance (after appropriate periods of denial) and, in time, achieve a classroom climate in which most of the children behave well most of the time.

Setting a classroom climate in which independence and responsibility are cherished and strived for but only given to those who can handle them will not solve all the discipline problems of disruptive children. Successful teachers often find that it helps them to target the specific problems of a "bad kid" if they keep some anecdotal records of that child's behavior. They can then talk specifically about what the problems are with the child and/or the child's parents. Of course, the good teacher will look for good things to note as well as bad things.

Often, when you are having a persistent discipline problem with a child, it helps to talk about it with someone else. In some schools, psychologists, guidance counselors, and principals may be able to offer help, advise, and give possible solutions. A particularly good source of counsel for most teachers is another teacher! Pick a teacher whose classroom climate you respect and ask for that teacher's help in dealing with your problem. Chances are that there are some things to try you haven't thought of even if you think you have "tried everything."

13. Do follow the school bus home.

One of the authors once taught a fourth grader who no amount of privilege withdrawal, patience, or positive statements would sway. He was a "mean, bad kid!" The teacher knew she must talk with the parents and try to convince them to work with her to help the child become more agreeable and responsible. The teacher, however, knew better than to send "bad notes" home (they never get there!). She rejected the idea of mailing a letter because she wasn't sure how literate the parents were and because parents always react negatively toward the school and teacher when they get bad news in the mail along with the bills. The teacher's plan to call and ask the parents to come to school was thwarted when she discovered they didn't have a phone. She then waited to see them at PTA, but of course, they didn't come. Finally, in desperation, she decided she would drive out and make a home visit. The boy lived out in the country, refused to give the teacher directions to his home, and had a P.O. box address. Finally, one afternoon, in desperation, the teacher informed the boy that she would be there to see his parents that afternoon. The boy commented that she'd never find them. The teacher responded that she would too because she intended to follow the school bus to his house. The boy's final retort was that his folks weren't home from work when the bus got there and the teacher responded, "I can wait!" The boy then broke down and cried and he and the teacher had their first real discussion about the problems. The teacher never did have to follow the school bus home, but the boy and the teacher knew she would if she had to. All parents care about how their children are doing in school and although they may respond negatively to negative letters and phone calls, they are usually willing to help in any way they can if you can sit down with them face-to-face. Most children do not want their parents to know if they are being unruly and uncooperative. If they think that you can't get in touch with their parents, they think they are "home free" behaving any way they want to. Once you have organized and arranged your classroom; established a regular and reasonable schedule and routine; tried to provide doable, varied, interesting, and worthwhile activities; let children share the responsibility and tried to think and act in a positive manner; if you are still having persistent and unresolvable problems with one child, get ready to follow the school bus home.

READ SOME MORE ABOUT THIS

This chapter has only touched on some of the issues and suggestions about the important-to-all-teachers topic of discipline and organization. There are many good books and articles in journals which will explore other issues and give you other suggestions. Read some more about this topic. A few suggestions for your continued learning are included here. Try also to find some recent books or articles not listed here.

Bloom, Robert B. Teachers and students in conflict: The CREED Approach. *Phi Delta Kappan*, May, 1980, 624–626.

Charles, C. M. *Building Classroom Discipline*. New York: Longman, 1981.

Ginott, Haim G. *Teacher and Child*. New York: Macmillan, 1972.

Guide to sanity saving. *Instructor*, November, 1978, 59–66.

Tanner, Laurel N. *Classroom Discipline*, New York: Holt, Rinehart and Winston, 1978.

8 | What Is Reading?

When an adult is asked a question like, "What is walking?" or, "What is reading?" the first reaction is probably that the questioner is not sincere. Because adults are familiar with what walking and reading are, such a question seems to be either a trick or an insult. However, the question that entitles this chapter is neither a trick nor an insult but a straightforward question to which anyone who attempts to teach reading should have at least a temporary answer.

So, what *is* reading? Dictionaries are not much help for they tell us that one can read signs, cloudy skies, fortunes, persons, thermometers, punch cards, law, minds, or even the Riot Act. While we certainly use the word *read* to refer to these actions and understand it when used in such contexts, we most certainly also know that the *reading* we want to teach in schools is something different from these other more metaphorical kinds of *reading*. From the outset, then, there are two obstacles which stand in the way of developing a useful and accurate answer to the question, "What is reading?" The first obstacle is our familiarity with reading: the fact that we have done it a lot for a long time lulls us into thinking that we understand it. The second obstacle is that the word *read* is used so loosely and metaphorically by all of us in our everyday language: *reading* means so many things in a vague way that it means very little in a precise way. In this chapter, we will attempt to overcome these two obstacles and answer the question, "What is reading?"

THE WHAT OF READING

If dictionaries and our everyday conversations reveal that, in some sense at least, one can read everything from thermometers to law, placing us in a "schooling" frame of mind restricts our notions of what can be read. Asking a group of adults or even school children the question, "Once you have learned to read in school, what are all the different things you can read?" will ordinarily elicit responses such as "books," "newspapers," "letters," "directions written by a teacher on the chalk-board," "recipes," "instructions on products," and so on. Seldom if ever will you get a serious response such as "fortunes," "skies," or "punch cards." People, from the time they begin school, seem to be aware and to never forget that the kind of reading we teach in school always involves written language, whether handwriting, print, calligraphy, Braille, paint, or neon.

Because stripping the word of its metaphorical senses means that the act of reading always involves written language, it seems appropriate to examine the nature of written language in pursuit of a clear understanding of what reading is. Because written language is both language and writing, this examination will proceed on two fronts.

Written Language Is Language

Imagine that a race of telepathic beings exists somewhere in space and that they discover a planet whose inhabitants exhibit definite signs of intelligence but no capacity for telepathy and no other system of communication. Furthermore, imagine that this race of superior beings is benevolent and believes that a system of communication would greatly enhance the quality of life for the beings on this planet. At first, our space explorers are at a loss for how to help the planet's inhabitants because telepathy is the only system of communication which has ever occurred to them—they transmit mental pictures, smells, sounds, tastes, and textures as well as emotions directly to the mind of the object of communication. Finally, they capture one of these poor, frightened primitives and completely examine him for some possible tool of communication. They discover that these beings have two pairs of mucous membrane folds in a cavity in their throats. They also discover that these creatures, especially when afraid, can manipulate the lower pair of these folds so that when they exhale or inhale air through their throats, these folds vibrate producing various types of sound which can be heard for short distances. Finally, they conclude that maybe these vibrating folds could be used to send messages that would be received by the ears of other primitive beings. But, how would it work? How can vibrations transmitted through the air ever transmit the picture of a state or an event? Well, some system will just have to be worked out, they conclude, even if it only allows for meager communications.

Concepts The telepaths think logically about what things make up reality. They decide that there are objects (a *person*, an *animal*, a *tree*, a *tomato*, a *star*, a *rock*, a *cave*, etc.), that these objects have certain attributes (a *pretty* person, a *tall* animal or tree, a *red* tomato, a *bright* star, a *heavy* rock, etc.), and that objects have these attributes to varying degrees (a *very* pretty person, a *barely* red tomato, a rock *too* heavy to be picked up). They also conclude that there are actions (to *jump*, to *grow*, to *break*, to *fly*, to *think*, to *feel*, etc.), and that these actions are conducted in certain manners (to jump *high*, to grow *quickly*, to break *cleanly*, to fly *far*, to think *seldom*, to feel *likewise*, etc.) and to certain degrees (to jump *very* high, to break *almost* cleanly, to fly *too* far, to think *only* seldom, etc.). In addition, they conclude that objects also have locations (*in a house, on a hill, under water, at the well*, etc.) and that actions have both locations and times at which (*three o'clock, yesterday, now, on Sunday*, etc.) or during which (*Spring, January, while visiting*, etc.) they take place.

These telepaths then teach some group of the primitives certain arbitrary sound patterns which arbitrarily stand for objects, actions, etc., in the environment of the planet.

The lesson of this fable for us is that both our spoken and our written language are based around a *lexicon* of *concept-words*. These concept-words stand for objects, attributes of objects, actions, manners of actions, locations of objects or actions, degrees of attributes or manners, and times or durations of actions (Frederiksen, 1975).

Relations between Concepts Let us return to our fable. After our space traveling telepaths have taught the primitives concept-words for the phenomena which surround them, they critically observe what happens. Sure enough, the primitives communicate with each other but the communications are more meager than even the telepaths had feared. The primitives seem only to point to some object or action and to utter a single word which names or describes it. These one-word utterances seem to convey so little meaning of a practical nature that, at first, the telepaths wonder why they have bothered. Then one creative telepath suggests that perhaps it would help if they had some system for combining these one-word utterances so that the primitives could make some communication about an object or an action not present at the time of communication. Of course, this would require that two concept-words be uttered together somehow; the object or action would have to be mentioned since it is not present, and then the other concept to be related to that object or action would have to be mentioned. The telepaths teach a few primitives to say two concept-words together and it seems to help. These are among the most successful:

    food   bring
    water   drink
    run   fast

Unfortunately, other concept word pairs are more ambiguous. These are among the most confusing:

water   run
food   animal
drink   food
poison   water

When the same creative telepath suggests that three or four or even more concept-words can be said together, it results in both better communication,

water   fast   drink

and in more ambiguous, and more dangerous, communication.

hit   table   head (a report or a request?)

The telepaths quickly see that saying two or more concept-words together certainly increases the quality of the communication system they have provided the primitives, but they also see that some other sounds and procedures for making sounds need to be developed to eliminate the ambiguity and confusion which often results from stating two or more concept-words together in no order. After working long hours with problems of logic, the telepaths develop a set of rules and some additional sounds for the primitives to use. These rules and sounds mark a limited set of relations which can exist between concepts. The telepaths assume that the primitives understand these relations between concepts when two or more concept-words are used together and there is only one interpretation. The problem arises when concept-words are used together and there are two or more possible relations which the hearer of the message can infer. The concept-word pair, for example,

burn   house

can be interpreted as both a report and a request. In order to eliminate much of this possible ambiguity about the relations between concepts in a message, the telepaths develop five cueing systems and teach the primitives how to use them. The five systems are:

1. *Word order*—so that "Mary hit Bill" and "Bill hit Mary" no longer mean the same
2. *Function words*—words like *of, is, to, a*, etc., which do not represent concepts as *house, jump, blue*, etc. do; rather they represent relations between words as in "...house *is* blue...."
3. *Inflections*—word endings such as *s* or *es, ed, ing, ly*, etc., which mark tense, plurality, form class, etc.
4. *Words that mark tense*—words like *will* and *shall, has* and *had, was* and *were*, etc.

5. *Intonation*—the use of pitch (height or depth of tone), juncture (pauses and stops), and stress (volume and duration) in the voice for emphasis and clarity of meaning

The lesson of this part of the fable for us is that our language (spoken and written) has *grammatical information*: surface features of language which cue the relations between concepts. The purpose of this grammatical information is to mark relations between concepts which would, in many instances, be ambiguous or unclear if the concept-words were merely expressed together in no order. Writing and speaking share the first four grammatical cueing systems (word order, function words, inflections, and words that mark tense) but, instead of the intonation (pitch, juncture, and stress) of spoken language, written language has capitalization, punctuation, italics, and spacing.

When making a statement, the communicator uses a lexicon to stand for concepts, and grammatical information to stand for the relations between concepts. The communicator then combines the lexicon and grammatical information to produce oral or written statements. In the following written statement, the lexicon has been written in italics; all unitalicized written symbols and word order make up the grammatical information:

The *white stallion* was *gallop*ing through the *swift*ly *mov*ing *creek*.

Eliminating the lexicon would leave a grammatical shell:

The _____ was ____ing through the ____ly ____ing ___.

Eliminating the grammatical information would leave an unordered lexicon of concept-words:

creek
gallop
move
swift
stallion
white

Coherence As we return to our fable, the telepathic space explorers are revisiting the planet to see if the primitives are still using the communication system they developed for them. To their surprise, they find that not only are the people still uttering statements, but that all speakers seem to have developed the practice of uttering a series of statements one after another, in a sequential whole. Instead of expressing a series of perfectly formed, but unrelated utterances such as,

> The candy tastes too sweet. A boy jumped the fence around our yard last night. Lightning sometimes strikes trees. Drinking was difficult during that era.

they are expressing a series of perfectly formed and related utterances such as:

> The robber ran from the store. The owner of the store ran after him. The robber turned and shot his gun toward the owner of the store. The owner fell dead in the street.

Wow! they exclaim, we expected them to continue to use the concept words and grammatical information, but we did not expect them to tie statements coherently together in their communications. The primitives have learned that if the statements they utter together all concern the same topic they can communicate a coherent, logical network of ideas to the listener. Moreover, the telepaths discover that the primitives have developed a system for marking some of this *coherence*. The primitives mark coherence by: (1) the order in which the statements are expressed, (2) the words that link statements together ("The car hit the curb *before* the light became red"), and (3) the reference ("He felt the needle; *it* was very sharp").

The lesson of this part of the fable for us is that our language (spoken and written) has *cohesion* (Grimes, 1975; Halliday & Hasan, 1976). Cohesion is the system of statement order, words linking statements, and different kinds of reference (pronouns being the most common kind) used by speakers and writers to indicate the coherence of the underlying message they are attempting to communicate. *Coherence* is the property of a message which makes it one message rather than two or more. For example, pretend you overhear this conversation:

> JANE: Did you read what the governor said about teachers' salaries? Your tie is crooked.
> MARK: Thanks, I'll straighten it. I sure did and I will never vote for him again for anything!

Such a conversation is not unusual in everyday life, but what message is being transmitted by Jane to Mark? Is there just one message? Obviously, there are two different messages being discussed simultaneously. Because each of Jane's two remarks (one a question; one a statement) represents a different message, lack of cohesive ties is appropriate. In fact, cohesive ties between ideas which lack coherence result in jibberish:

> JANE: Did you read what the governor said about teachers' salaries *because* your tie is crooked?

MARK: Thanks, I'lll straighten it *while* I sure did and I will never vote for him again for anything!

Two parts of the same message always have some logical relationship, i.e., *coherence*, and when this message is represented in spoken or written language, the speaker or writer will probably elect to use *cohesion*, i.e., the order in which the statements are expressed, words that link statements together, and words of reference (pronouns, especially), to make the coherence in the message more obvious.

Generally speakers and writers do not communicate different, unrelated messages at the same time. They transmit one message. Because it is one message, all parts are logically related, i.e., have coherence. In this case, cohesion will help the listener or reader reconstruct logical relationships in the message. In the following passage, cohesive ties are marked with italics (the statement order also provides cohesion). Every italicized word either refers back to a previous word or statement or links two statements together logically. The unitalicized words provide the new information in each statement:

> Soil-dwelling termites live in large nests *and* eat wood. *Their nests* are made of packed *soil and* can be as *large* as 15 feet tall. *Because soil-dwelling termites live* in *soil, they* are most likely to *attack wood* close to the *ground.*

Prominence While the telepaths are fascinated by finding, on their return, that the primitives are able to communicate coherent messages by using cohesion to link spoken statements together, they are puzzled by another finding. Sometimes when the primitives communicate there seem to be several parallel and related messages presented at the same time, as if one were attempting to hear a speaker address a topic through the left ear while attempting to hear another speaker address the same topic through the right ear. A primitive soldier might be explaining something to a younger primitive, for example. After saying something general about weapons, the soldier calls a spear a weapon. Then spears are described and their uses explained. Then something else is said about weapons and then swords are discussed. The telepaths are confused. Is the soldier's conversation about weapons or is it about spears and swords? Eventually, they conclude that it is about both, and that language allows a discussion of the same topic at different levels of *prominence*. They notice that sometimes speakers have only one level of prominence; everything they say seems to be equally important. Sometimes, however, speakers may have certain points to make which they stress but they may present other information which, though less important than their main points, serves to give a broader or more precise picture.

The lesson of this part of the fable for us is that language has *staging* (Grimes, 1975) which represents different levels of prominence of ideas in the message being expressed. Staging is all the devices (titles, topic sentences, headings, indentation of paragraphs, changes of topic between paragraphs or sections, examples, parentheses, etc.) used to give more prominence to some statements and less prominence to others. The statements receiving the most highlighting represent the ideas which are the highest level of the message; the statements receiving the least highlighting represent the ideas which are the lowest level of the message. Staging is what allows someone to outline what someone else has said or written. Outlining is just dividing a text into the levels of the message being presented. Figure 8.1, for example, is a partial outline of this chapter. The highest level of prominence of this chapter is represented by the title: the principal and foremost task of this chapter is to define reading. The next highest level of prominence of this chapter is represented by Roman numerals I, II, and III: reading is defined in terms of what is read, why it is read, and how it is read. The next level of the chapter is represented by capital letters A, B, and C. (The breakdown of the second and third sections of this chapter is not included.) In the first section, the what of reading is explained in terms of the dual nature of written language as both language and writing. The next level of prominence is represented by Arabic numerals 1, 2, 3, 4, and 5. These four levels of prominence of ideas are being simultaneously communicated to you, the reader, in Chapter 8. The highest level is the most prominent— the entire chapter is an attempt to answer the question, "What is reading?" The lowest level is the least prominent—fewer pages are given to describing concepts, relations between concepts, coherence, prominence, and sense of audience.

Figure 8.1   Partial Outline of Chapter 8

What is Reading?
   I.   The What of Reading
        A.   Written Language Is Language
             1. Concepts
             2. Relations between concepts
             3. Coherence
             4. Prominence
             5. Sense of audience
        B.   Written Language Is Writing
             1. Print to sound to meaning
             2. Print to meaning
             3. Coordinating the two links
        C.   The What of Reading Defined
  II.   The Why of Reading
 III.   The How of Reading

Sense of Audience Not only do the telepaths who return to the planet of the primitives find them stringing statements together to express coherent messages and using staging to discuss a topic or tell a story at different levels of prominence, but they also find that the primitives have developed the strange ability to modify *how* they express themselves depending on who is listening.

At first, the telepaths find this custom beyond their understanding. In their own telepathic communications, they send or withhold their thoughts but they have no means of presenting their thoughts differently for different audiences. To understand this phenomenon, they spend a great deal of time observing the primitives speaking to one another. They observe that, in every case, the primitives combine concept-words with grammatical information to make statements. Moreover, they observe that the primitives often string these statements together so that their order suggests a coherent message and that, furthermore, the primitives make this coherence still more obvious by using cohesive ties such as conjunctions and pronouns. In addition, they notice that the primitives sometimes express sophisticated messages where different parts of the message are staged high or low depending on the prominence the speaker wants to give to those parts. The telepaths notice, however, that the primitive speakers choose different concept-words as well as different types and amounts of grammatical information, cohesion, and staging depending on who is to receive the message. They observe, for example, that on the same day the same primitive describes the same hunting incident differently to three different audiences. When the primitive was speaking to his young children, he said:

> Always remember, my children, that a sword can save your life. Today, daddy was running through the woods when he came upon a mother tiger and her babies. As soon as she saw me, she jumped on me and I pulled out my short sword. She held me to the ground and started to bite my neck. I stuck the sword as far into her heart as I could. She died right then. I brought the baby tigers home for you to play with.

When the primitive was speaking with his friends, he said:

> Well, I almost said good-by today! A tiger and her young cubs were in the forest and I just about ran over them. The old mama came after me and I grabbed my blade. She pinned me down and went for my throat but I gave it to her good—right in the heart. She died that second, saving my life for sure. I took the cubs home for the kids.

When the primitive was speaking to the honored Chief Sword Maker of the tribe, he said:

> Honored Sir, my gratitude, your cutlass saved my life today. I was dashing through the forest when suddenly I encountered a tigress with young cubs. As she leaped, I took the cutlass from its scabbard. I entered it deep into her heart as her teeth neared my throat. The cutlass killed her instantly. The cubs will make good pets for my children.

To the telepaths, observations such as these reveal that primitive speakers have a clear *sense of audience*. The telepaths realize that primitive speakers take situational factors very much into account when selecting what concept-words, grammatical information, cohesion, and staging they will use to transmit the concepts, relations between concepts, coherence, and prominence of their messages.

The lesson of this final part of the fable for us is that our language (both spoken and written) has *registers* (Halliday, 1978). Speakers and writers make choices regarding the language they will use to communicate their meaning. A register is a pattern of these choices reflecting the purpose of the message, the medium of the message, the characteristics of the intented audience of the message, the situation in which the message is communicated and received, and the social, political, and cultural relationships between the communicator and the comprehender. There are as many different registers in language as there are considerations to be made when communicating to a particular audience. Readers and listeners must always be aware that any piece of expressed language exists in a rich context and gives clues to the nature of this context.

Written Language Is Writing

Written language is writing and, as such, is different from other non-written forms of language. Even though both written and spoken language share concepts, relations between concepts, coherence, prominence, and sense of audience, they differ in that spoken language has a sound-meaning link whereas written language has both a print-sound-meaning and a print-meaning link (Baron, 1976).

Print to Sound to Meaning What can be written can be said. Some written languages generally have one symbol for each word (e.g., Chinese), some generally have one symbol for each syllable (e.g., Japanese), and some generally have one symbol for each sound (e.g., Spanish). Regardless, each of these written languages represents one or more spoken languages and can be turned into spoken language (read aloud). This feature of written languages enables readers to make use of the same concept-words, grammatical information, cohesion, staging, and registers with which they are already familiar in their spoken language experience.

Languages in which there is some systematic relationship between print and sound have an additional advantage: these relationships can be used to turn an unfamiliar-in-print word into a familiar-in-speech word. In English, for example, young children are often taught by one or another phonics method to decode printed words into sounds. Once learned, the ability to decode helps the developing reader to read words not previously encountered in print although they are old friends in speech. Because spoken language has a sound-to-meaning link, written languages which have a systematic print-to-sound link allow students who are learning to read to take greater advantage of their existing knowledge of spoken language.

Print to Meaning Read the following two sentences aloud to someone else and ask if they are the same:

>   Eye red the sine be sighed the rode.
>   I read the sign beside the road.

Clearly, if these two sentences are spoken, they are the same, but if they are read they are considerably different. When hearing the first sentence, you are instantly aware of what the sentence means, but when reading it, you are instantly aware that something is seriously wrong. This reveals that you as an adult good reader are responding to written language's print or *orthography* (how the words of a language are spelled, drawn, printed, etc.) at the same time that you are responding to its sound or *phonology* (how the words of a language are pronounced). Likewise, reading a pair of sentences like,

>   I shot a boar.
>   I shot a bore.

illustrates, as did our *Eye red/I read* pair above, that readers do not merely change letters or words into sounds and then listen to those sounds for comprehension. In short, print does not just represent spoken language, it also represents meaning directly.

Coordinating the Two Links The fact that we attend to both orthography and phonology gives readers two important advantages. First, good readers are getting meaning at the same time from two sources: words represent meanings quite apart from their sounds (*eye/I;*

red/read; sine/sign; etc.) and words represent sounds which themselves have meanings. When reading, these two messages reinforce and complement each other. Sometimes the orthography is ambiguous but the phonology is not:

> By the factory, the flowers were red,
> But flowers die when they take the *lead*.

Sometimes the phonology is ambiguous but the orthography is not:

> hear, here.

Because good readers can use both, their comprehension does not suffer just because the message on one channel is unclear—they just ignore that channel and attend to the other one.

Second, not only do good readers get two parallel messages when they read, but good readers of English and other alphabetic or syllabic languages have a way to check the two messages against each other. As adults we take this ability to check orthography against phonology and phonology against orthography for granted, but beginning and developing readers can use this checking mechanism to see if they are really doing the right thing. Let us imagine that a second grader were reading,

> Mary gave her father a shirt.

Pretend that our second grader does not know the word *shirt* when she sees it and that she is not able to decode it if it is presented to her in isolation on a card. Likewise, pretend that if *shirt* were replaced by a blank, she would not guess it. If there were no relationship between orthography and phonology (in Chinese, there is very little), our second grader could not use her knowledge of the *sh* digraph to help her guess a word she cannot read. In this case, our second grader guesses that the word is *shirt* because it is the only thing she can think of that Mary might have given her father that starts with the sound usually represented by *sh*. In the sentence,

> Jon gave his father a camera.

our second grader might guess *car, case, camera, comb,* and *cooler* from context but settle on *camera* because the word on the page looked like it would more likely spell *camera* than the other possible gifts. Because orthography can be used to shore up phonology and phonology can be used to shore up orthography, our second grader can understand what gifts Mary and Jon gave their fathers.

The *What* of Reading Defined

When we read, we always read written language. The *what* of reading, therefore, is written language, and defining the *what* of reading means defining written language: Written language is a system of visual symbols representing a message.

The following graphic is a diagram of the components of messages and the corresponding components of language:

Components of Messages	Components of Language
Concepts ———————————	Lexicon of concept-words
Relations between concepts —————	Grammatical information
Coherence ———————————	Cohesion
Prominence ———————————	Staging
Sense of audience ———————	Registers

Moreover, written language is a system of visual symbols representing spoken language. What can be written can be read aloud; what can be said can be written down.

Therefore,

Written language is a system of visual symbols representing both a message and how that message would be expressed in spoken language.

THE *WHY* OF READING

Because written language represents both a message and how that message would be expressed in spoken language, one can read to oneself or to others. When one is reading to oneself to get a message, there are a variety of reasons why it is desirable to get that message. These insights lead us to consider four general reasons why people read: we read to do, to learn, to experience, and to perform.

Reading to Do

Decide what the following different kinds of reading have in common:

Reading a menu
Reading a recipe

Reading the directions on a fire
  extinguisher

Reading the instructions for installing indirect lighting

Reading the directions on a pattern

Reading the directions on a cake mix

Reading the names written on bathroom doors

Reading a section of the yellow pages

Reading a form for applying for a job

Reading traffic signs

Is it clear that in all these cases the reader is reading so that the reader can later do something? The primary purpose is not to learn information or to read for enjoyment or relaxation but to be able to accomplish one or more tasks. This type of reading—reading to do—(Diehl & Mikulecky, 1980) is often called *functional reading*. Of course, this is the kind of reading which employers often demand of their employees and which life demands of each of us. In fact, a subset of functional reading seems so necessary that it is often called *survival reading*.

Reading to Learn

Reading textbooks and listening to lectures and formal discussions are the principal means for learning subject matter from the primary grades through graduate or professional school. Comprehension of written language is important for success in school. And even if McLuhan's media revolution ever occurs so that new books are not being produced, reading will be necessary so that the millions of primary sources already written can be consulted to understand our history and culture. Reading will continue to be *the* major means for acquiring knowledge for the forseeable future and students will continue to need to know how to read to learn. Moreover, reading to learn is valuable outside institutionalized education. Many people read during leisure time for self-improvement so that they can acquire knowledge they want to have. Curiosity is surely as important a reason for reading to learn as is the ambition to succeed in school or in the job market.

Reading to Experience

Reading is to the mind what exercise is to the body.

SIR RICHARD STEELE

How many a man has dated a new era in his life from the reading of a book.

HENRY DAVID THOREAU

While reading can obviously be a means to the achievement of practical, academic, or intellectual goals, many find reading worthwhile for its own sake. Reading can be a most relaxing and enchanting pastime.

Unlike television and film, reading allows the person control over how people and places will look, sound, feel, smell, etc. Unlike recordings and radio, reading allows a person control over how fast or slow to receive the message, when to receive the message, and when to stop it to return later to the exact point where one left off. Reading does not require equipment, or a power source, or a special location or situation. It is the most practical and portable medium as well as the most versatile and creative. Many people read to experience without any intention of remembering or applying what is read. For them, there is hardly anything better than a few hours with "a good book."

Reading to Perform

Several occupations require reading to perform. Teachers, preachers, broadcasters, and actors often read to others to instruct, entertain, or inspire them. Parents, too, often read to their children for their pleasure or their education. Any time one reads to another, that person is taking advantage of the fact that written language represents both a message and how that message would be expressed in spoken language.

The *Why* of Reading Defined

There are many hundreds or even thousands of specific reasons a person might read some particular piece of written language, but all of these specific reasons can be classified under one of four general reasons for reading: reading to do, reading to learn, reading to experience, and reading to perform. The first three general reasons are based on the fact that written language represents a message; the fourth general reason is based on the fact that written language also represents how that message would be expressed in spoken language.

Of course, while one usually reads with a primary purpose in mind, it should be noted that sometimes we read for more than one major purpose at the same time; these four general reasons for reading are not mutually exclusive. In addition, it should be mentioned that while reading with no purpose(s) in mind prevents comprehension from occurring, there is the possibility of *serendipity* in reading. Sometimes we discover pleasure in reading when we only intended to read for information; sometimes we discover knowledge in reading when we only intended to read for pleasure; and so on.

The *why* of reading influences the nature of the message gained from the *what* of reading. Imagine, for example, that you are working on a term paper for a course. You might skim hundreds of articles and books for opinion or research pertinent to the topic. In many cases, you will draw a conclusion from one of those articles or books which is a perfectly proper one to draw and is quite pertinent to your term paper topic, but which was really incidental information as far as the author of the original source was concerned. Have you comprehended? We think so, for you did not misrepresent what was in the original, you just ignored the rest of the original as irrelevant to your purpose for reading. For another example, imagine that you are reading a novel on a sunny afternoon at the beach. At one point, when you become anxious about the fate of a particular character (and this summer day is no day to be anxious), you skip momentarily to the end of the book to see if the character is still around (she is). At another point, you skip a long section which describes the countryside (and descriptions bore you), and throughout the book, you develop elaborate explanations for why the characters behave as they do even though this text is sparse on explaining motivations. Have you comprehended? We think so, for you did not deny the text, you just ignored and or embellished some of it so that you could better enjoy your day.

During reading or listening, comprehenders construct an internal, cognitive text which corresponds in certain ways to the external text they are reading or listening to. This internal text is being composed during reading or listening comprehension. Some people imagine scenes or characters during comprehension of a passage and remember these images whenever they think of that passage. In essence, they have "illustrated" their internal text! Other people do not form an internal text at all during reading and, consequently, have little or no memory for what they have read or heard. In any case, this internal text must be true to the concepts, relations between concepts, coherence, prominence, and sense of audience of the message being comprehended; but the *what* of reading or listening does not dictate entirely the nature of the internal text. Comprehenders select what parts of the message they will retain in their internal text and what parts they will not. Comprehenders make inferences about aspects of the text and then add these to the internal text even though they were not in the external text. Comprehenders synthesize parts of the message and store them in their chunked form rather than in the separated form they had in the external text. Comprehenders make evaluations and judgments concerning the truth or beauty of the message and store these critical responses in their internal representation of that message. The characteristics of the internal text are determined by what will be done with that internal text later. When reading a recipe, for example, it is probably not a good idea to exclude exact measurements or ingredients from the internal text!

In general, therefore,

The why *of reading is to construct an internal text with certain characteristics or to read aloud for an audience so that they can construct internal texts with certain characteristics.*

THE HOW OF READING

Reading always involves either producing spoken language which represents the text (oral reading), or producing an internal text representing in certain respects the external text on the page (reading comprehension), or both. As we have discussed, an internal text might only represent the part(s) of the external text which the reader considered relevant to the purpose for reading. And an internal text might contain inferences and other embellishments consistent with the external text but not contained in it. But how does the reader construct this internal text? The *how* of reading requires the reader to simultaneously perform three complex behaviors: word identification, language comprehension, and print processing.

Word Identification

Read the following sentence for comprehension:

> *¢+#*@   )*#   &##$.

Having trouble? Surely you have the concept of *a large and natural stream of water*; the concept of *extending far down from a surface*; the relationship of *plurality*; the relationship of *attribution*; and surely you are familiar with the grammatical pattern (word order) of *object-function word-attribute*. Still not comprehending? Actually, the three words above have been written in code. The code is a simple one: for the letter *r*, * was substituted; for *i*, ¢ was substituted; for *v*, +; for *e*, #; for *s*, @; for *a*,); for *d*, &; and for *p*, $. Working back from these symbols gives the trite message:

> Rivers are deep.

Having any trouble comprehending now?

This code has very little in common with real language codes, but this much is the same. It does not matter how much you know about language, how well you can recite language rules, how easily you comprehend oral language, how much you know about the world, or how fast you can think: *If you cannot figure out what concepts, relations between concepts, and written arrays of letters represent, you cannot comprehend*. By some method the print *must* be decoded into meaning or comprehension cannot take place. Either the student must have meaning associated with the orthography (spelling) of a word (as in words we understand when we read but which we are uncertain how to pronounce such as *epitome* which one of us pronounced for years as /ĕpĭ tōm/) or the student must have meaning associated with the phonology (sound) of the word and must be able to turn the print into sound so the student can access that meaning. Ideally, the reader would have meaning associated directly with the orthography, meaning associated directly with the phonology, and phonology associated directly with the orthography so that the two channels of print-to-meaning and print-to-sound-to-meaning could complement and corroborate each other.

In teaching beginning reading, we ordinarily are teaching students to identify words in print which they already use in their speech and already comprehend when they hear them (the sound-to-meaning link is present; the print-to-meaning and print-to-sound links are missing). When readers develop to the stage where the material they read contains words for which they have no meanings even when they hear them, then students must learn both the pronunciations and the meanings of the new words. For example, no first-grade teacher feels the need to explain the meaning of the word *walk* (meaning "to move on foot at a moderate speed") when it appears for the first time in a story in the reading book, while a fourth-grade teacher would not hesitate to explain the meaning of *zest* (meaning "something added to give flavor") if it appeared in the reading book. Why could you not comprehend "*¢+#*@)@# &##$"? Because you had neither a print-to-meaning link nor a print-to-sound link for any of those three words.

Obviously, then, comprehending language requires that comprehenders somehow make the link between the concept words and the concepts they have in their heads, between the inflections, words that mark tense, and function words, and the relations between concepts which these symbols can cue.

We now present two definitions:

Word identification accuracy is the pronunciation of a written word in the same way a person pronounces it if that person uses it in spoken language (making the print-to sound link).

Word identification speed is the rate at which the person accurately identifies words (speed of making the print-to-sound link).

When is word identification accuracy most important? It is most important when the reader has a sound-to-meaning link for a word but no print-to-meaning link. As we have said, beginning readers understand many more words when they hear them than when they read them. Consequently, word identification accuracy is important in beginning reading because the print-to-sound-to-meaning link is the only channel available to beginning readers to get the meaning of many printed words.

When is word identification accuracy least important? It is least important when the reader has a print-to-meaning link for a word but no sound-to-meaning link. (In fact, in this latter case, word identification accuracy is of no value at all.) Pretend, for example, that a person has never heard the name Raskolnikov. Would the reading of *Crime and Punishment* be impaired? Probably not. The reader would soon develop a print-to-meaning link that this strange-looking name was the main character and would go from there.

What purpose, then, does word identification accuracy fulfill in mature reading? When one encounters a word while reading that has been heard and understood but not seen in print before, word identification accuracy provides the reader with the sound of that word so understanding can occur. Mature readers seldom have such experiences. Indeed, mature readers have more words in their reading vocabularies (print-to-meaning links) than they do in their listening vocabularies (sound-to-meaning links). Word identification accuracy does provide the reader with the luxury of having two parallel channels, print to meaning and print to sound to meaning, to check and balance against each other. Word identification accuracy, then, is generally beneficial but not necessary for mature reading comprehension.

If perfect word identification accuracy is not necessary for comprehension to occur during reading, then neither is it sufficient. Read the following poem to yourself for comprehension:

ehT redips
tnatibaH fo eltsac yarg,
gnipeerC gniht ni rebos yaw,
elbisiV egas naicinahcem,
tselufllikS naicitemhtira. (W. E. gninnahC)

If you did not give up, you certainly found it possible to accurately identify the pronunciation of each word in the poem. However, the slowness with which you obtained this word identification accuracy may have placed a heavy burden on both your memory and your patience. Can you imagine reading a lengthy essay where each word was spelled backward? Even if you were able to persevere to the end so that you accurately identified every word, would not your comprehension be likely to suffer, perhaps severely? Would you not find that you had forgotten the beginning of a sentence by the time you had decoded its end?

Word identification speed is almost as necessary as word identification accuracy. In fact, in those instances where word identification accuracy is important, word identification accuracy without sufficient speed will be of small benefit unless only a word or two is being decoded.

Language Comprehension

Reading is the second story of a two-story building of which the first story is language. Reading builds on general language ability. Severely hearing impaired students ordinarily will not be able to read a text with comprehension if they are unable to understand that text when someone signs and/or lip reads it to them. Severely visually impaired students ordinarily will not be able to read a Braille text with comprehension if they are unable to understand that text when someone reads it aloud to them. Students having no visual or auditory impairments ordinarily will not be able to read a text with comprehension if they are unable to understand that text when someone reads it aloud to them.

Reading can be easier than listening to something being read aloud because the reader can read as slowly or quickly as is necessary, and can reread difficult portions. Listening and other receptive language modes, however, do not allow rate control or reprocessing to take place. Consequently, being able to manipulate rate and to use selective rereading to enhance comprehension are fairly sophisticated skills which young or disabled readers rarely have. In general, then, it is true that readers will not be able to comprehend when reading any text they could not comprehend when it was presented to them through another more familiar language mode.

The reason that language comprehension ability is required before reading comprehension can take place is simple. A message has the same concepts, relations between concepts, coherence, levels of prominence, and sense of audience regardless of whether that message is transmitted via print, speech, signing, or Braille. If someone cannot understand a message presented in their most familiar language mode, how could one be expected to understand that message in the mode of reading? Different language modes usually rely on the same concept-words, grammatical information, cohesion, staging, and register to transmit the components of a message. If someone cannot deal with certain language components in the most familiar language mode, how could one be expected to deal with them in the reading mode?

Moreover, it is not enough to have conceptual knowledge and knowledge of language conventions and structures to match the components of language. Language comprehenders must also have prior knowledge of the world in which to relate the message as a whole (Anderson, 1978). For example, the statement,

Memories are mirrors.

would probably be incomprehensible to a fifth grader ever if that student had appropriate meanings for the words *memory* and *mirror*. It is not the concept words, grammatical information, cohesion, staging, or register, but the lack of knowledge of metaphysics which makes that statement difficult to understand or interpret. No amount of ability to deal with the components of language can overcome a lack of prior knowledge about the topic when it comes to language comprehension.

Language comprehension, as related to reading, is what reading comprehension and comprehension of written language read aloud have in common. In all these cases, the comprehender must have sufficient knowledge of both the components and the topic of the message to construct an internal text with certain characteristics. There are four language comprehension strategies:

1. *Understanding what is stated*—Processing language so that the message in the internal text matches in part or whole and never contradicts the message of the text being read
2. *Attending to what is important*—Processing language so that the parts of the message of the text being read that are contained in the internal text are more important (given the levels of the prominence in the message and/or the purpose(s) for comprehending) than those left out of the internal text
3. *Inferring what is not stated*—Processing language so that the parts of the message in the internal text that are not contained in the text being read are consistent with the text being read
4. *Restructuring what is produced through understanding, attending, and inferring*—Composing a language product using language components that can serve as a representation of the internal text

Print Processing

Pick a partner. Each person take turns watching the eyes of the other reading silently. Watch until each of you sees clearly that when reading for comprehension a reader's eyes move rapidly in a series of jerks and stops (called *saccades* and *fixations*; together called *saccadic movements* or *eye movements*). In the same partnership, take turns counting approximately how many times the other person's eyes stop or fixate on *each* line. Then count how many words per line there are in the lines which were read while you counted. See how many words one reads per fixation on the average. Just one? Or more? Notice also that when watching the eyes of someone read that reader's eyes occasionally (every few lines) return to a spot a few words, or even a few lines, backward and re-read what is there. This perfectly natural behavior is called a *regression* and all good readers make regressions when reading for maximum comprehension.

Now with the same partner, take turns having one person read aloud from an easy passage. At a random spot, the one listening quickly covers the text while the one reading attempts to keep reading. In most instances, such a demonstration will reveal that a reader can continue reading from one to seven words after the text has been covered! Peripheral vision and guessing from context will rarely allow more than one word ahead to be read, so what is happening? Now, each of you read aloud from an easy passage and notice while you are reading where your eyes are when you are pronouncing the words. Are you looking at each word as you say it? No, your eyes are a number of words ahead of your voice, and this distance is called the *eye-voice span* (EVS). Good readers have eye-voice spans when they are reading aloud for comprehension. There is evidence that good readers have *eye-subvoice* spans when reading silently for comprehension. (The subvoice is the vibrations of the vocal cords which take place during silent reading. Sometimes the subvoice is called *internal speech*.)

Why do readers have eye-voice and eye-subvoice spans? Because these spans enable readers to use the context clues following a word as well as those preceding it to make the judgment as to that word's meaning and pronunciation. Read the following sentence aloud:

I read yesterday that inflation will always be a problem.

How did you pronounce *read*? Like *red* or like *reed*? Like *red*? Of course, and you did so without thinking. Yet how would you probably pronounce *read* if it were presented to you in isolation on a card? Like *reed*, right? It is clear that you used the word *yesterday* to determine the meaning and pronunciation of *read* before you said it. Your eye-voice span allowed you to use *yesterday* to provide context clues to the meaning and pronunciation of *read* even though *yesterday* followed *read*. This advantage of eye-voice span has no counterpart when listening to a text being read orally. If I were to read the sentence in our example to you, you would have to wait to hear or see the word *yesterday* before using its information, and your processing of *read* would have already occurred.

Eye movement behaviors and eye-voice/eye-subvoice spans are part of a set of abilities which reading uniquely requires. We call these abilities *print processing*. Print processing is everything you have to do to read silently with comprehension that you do not have to do to comprehend the same text being read aloud or signed, exclusive of word identification accuracy and speed. Imagine two tasks. In the first task we take all the words of a passage, randomly order (scramble) them, and write one word to a card. We present these words to a reader one at a time for less than one quarter of a second, and then allow two seconds for the reader to pronounce the word. (Obviously, words used more than once in the passage are presented more than once in the task since *all* words were reordered and written on cards.) In the second task we read the text to the reader and then present a comprehension task closed book, orally, and the reader answers orally. Do you believe that there will be readers who can pronounce 95 percent or more of the words from the text presented in isolation this quickly who will perform better on comprehension after listening to the passage than after reading it, even with identical comprehesion tasks and equal efforts? Reading the passage to yourself requires everything the first task requires (word identification accuracy and speed) and everything the second task requires (language comprehension ability) plus eye movements, eye-voice or eye-subvoice span, and the other print processing abilities. A person who can identify the words from a passage and who can understand that passage when it is read might still have problems in *reading* comprehension due to print processing problems.

There are four areas of print processing: eye movements, coordinating print with sound, coordinating print with meaning, and parallel processing.

Eye Movements   While the eyes do not need to move when one is listening to someone else read aloud (the eyes can be closed) or when one is identifying words one at a time on cards flashed (the eyes can remain completely still as long as they are open), the eyes must move when one is reading written language silently or aloud. In English, the eyes must be moved "through" the print from left to right, top to bottom, and front to back. The eyes must move from line to line without skipping any line. Because the eyes move in a series of saccades and fixations (jerks and stops), the reader must subconsciously determine just how many letters or words the eyes should jerk or jump over next and how long the eyes should fixate during each stop. Moreover, because readers make good use of rereading to enhance comprehension and memory of what is read, they must monitor while reading by asking questions such as: "Does this make sense?" "Am I understanding this?" "Am I accomplishing my purposes for reading this?" They must then use this monitoring to decide whether, when, and what to reread. They must also be able to remember where in the lines just read certain words or statements were located so that they can return to them efficiently without losing time searching. Although eye movements are not necessary for accurate and fast word identification of words in isolation or for language comprehension, they are crucial for reading comprehension and oral reading.

Coordinating Print with Sound   Whether reading orally or silently, readers need to keep their eyes ahead of their voices or subvoices so that they can make good use of context clues following words to help determine their meanings and pronunciations. Proper coordination of the eyes with the voice or subvoice enables the reader to make maximum use of postcontext without getting so far ahead as to become confused. In addition, readers must use grammatical capitalization, punctuation, and italics as well as knowledge of language patterns and understanding of the message so far to break the print into syntactic phrases and to determine the emphasis to place on words and phrases. When we listen to someone read aloud, the speaker's intonation helps to mark emphasis and phrase boundaries, but the reader must infer these.

Coordinating Print with Meaning Because English has many words which sound alike but are spelled differently (homophones), readers can make use of the orthography of words to get additional information over and above what they could get hearing a passage read aloud. (A *pat* answer and an answer from *Pat* are less confusing in print than when heard.) Moreover, print allows the reader to use spacing between words, between sentences, between paragraphs (indentation), and between unheaded text sections (extra spacing) to break the passage into meaning segments such as words, sentences, paragraphs, and sections. This spacing does not ordinarily exist in speech where wordsareruntogetherwithhardlyapause.

Parallel Processing Reading has a print-to-meaning link and a print-to-sound-to-meaning link whereas listening to someone read a text aloud only has a sound-to-meaning link. Readers not only must coordinate print with sound and print with meaning, but readers must coordinate the print-to-meaning channel with the print-to-sound-to-meaning channel to check the two parallel message channels against each other. Readers must also be able to use one channel exclusively if the other channel is unclear or ambiguous.

The *How* of Reading Defined

When reading, a reader should always attempt to be true to both the *what* and the *why* of reading. Being true to the *what* entails making appropriate responses to the components of the language message and to the print itself. Being true to the *why* entails keeping in mind what is already known about the topic and what the purpose is for reading. The process of integrating the *what* and the *why* of reading is the *how* of reading. The *how* of reading is a combination of three complex behaviors: word identification, language comprehension, and print processing.

Therefore,

> *Reading is accomplished by identifying words, processing print, and comprehending language so that either an internal text or spoken language is produced which is consistent with both the text and the purpose for reading it.*

WHAT IS READING?

If we are watching someone maneuver a car around a curve, up a ramp, and onto an interstate highway and are asked what that person is doing we will probably answer, "Driving." To call what that person is doing *driving* is to imply that it is one action; well, it is and it isn't. The person is glancing at the rear-view and side mirrors, looking from side to side out the side windows, watching the road ahead through the windshield, turning on the signal light, turning the steering wheel, touching the brake pedal, pushing in the clutch pedal, downshifting, pushing the gas pedal, and predicting the location of the other cars on the interstate when this car gets to the top of the ramp. These, in fact, are many actions, some with their own names. Together we call them *driving*, by which we mean the coordinated collection of behaviors by which a vehicle is caused and guided to move.

When we use the word *reading*, something similar is taking place. By reading, we mean one action which is a coordinated collection of other actions. This collection of actions must reflect the *what, why*, and *how* of reading.

Therefore,

> *Reading is the process of using word identification, print processing, and language comprehension with written language to construct an internal text or to perform it for an audience so they can construct internal texts.*

Since reading is a complex act, teaching reading is not a simple process. The teacher who is reading to the class and then leading the class in a comprehension follow-up activity is teaching reading because that teacher is improving language comprehension. Similarly, the teacher who takes children on a field trip, or brings real objects into the classroom so that children have direct experience with new and unfamiliar concepts is teaching reading because concept development is part of language comprehension. The teacher who cooks with children and teaches the children to read and comprehend the recipe is improving language comprehension and showing children that functional reading is an important *why* of reading. These children will learn that when reading a set of directions such as a recipe, their internal text must contain many specific details. On the other hand, a teacher who is helping children locate pertinent information in a reference source shows children that when your purpose for reading is to find some specific facts, you can skim the rest and do not need to include all of what you read in your internal text. These children are also learning that reading to learn is an important *why* of reading. The teacher of beginning readers who teaches children to immediately recognize common words as sight words and to decode unknown words using context and letter-sound relationships is teaching reading because accurate word identification is a part of reading. The teacher who provides time for children to read easy and interesting books is assuring that the children will develop their word identification speed through practice in easy material, and is allowing them to develop their print processing skills as they read to experience and enjoy.

The teacher of reading must be a juggler. Anyone could probably teach reading if there were only one ball to keep in the air. But the teacher of reading must juggle many balls, some bowling pins, and an occasional banana! In Part I of this book, we have presented to you the objects to be juggled. In Part II, we shall let you spend a year in the classrooms of six master jugglers, Miss Launch, Mrs. Wright, Miss Nouveau, Mrs. Wise, Ms. Maverick, and Mr. Dunn. These teachers will all be teaching reading but they will be teaching reading in a variety of ways which place more or less emphasis on the various objects to be juggled. These teachers will use a variety of approaches to reading which reflect (1) the age and reading maturity of the children they teach, (2) their own beliefs about how reading is most effectively taught and learned, and (3) their own particular teaching styles. The goal of Part II is not to have you find the "best" approach and then mimic it in your own classroom, or to suggest that a particular approach is most suited to a particular grade level. Rather, the goal of Part II is to show you the great variety of ways and styles of teaching which can produce children who read well and broadly.

So, let's now take a look at Merritt Elementary School as our imaginary class of children who start in Miss Launch's kindergarten and finish fifth grade with Mr. Dunn experience it. Our cast of main characters includes:

THE STAFF

Mr. Topps: The super, supportive principal we all would like to teach for, Mr. Topps is tops.

Miss Launch: Launching kids into the world of school and reading and preparing them for reading with the seven ingredients, Miss Launch teaches kindergarten.

Mrs. Wright: A first-grade teacher who uses language experience and a variety of other approaches, Mrs. Wright is seldom wrong.

Miss Nouveau: As a first-year teacher, Miss Nouveau is tempted to quit before Christmas, but she gets better and better and learns to successfully use the basal reader as the core of her combination approach to beginning reading.

Mrs. Wise: As her name suggests, Mrs. Wise knows all—or almost all. Individualized reading of library books and writing are the core of Mrs. Wise's program.

Ms. Maverick: Ms. Maverick is a maverick classroom teacher. She believes in integrating the teaching of skills such as reading, writing, and computation with the teaching of science and social studies content. Her student teacher, Donald Ditto, couldn't agree more!

Mr. Dunn: Mr. Dunn finishes the students at Merritt and prepares them for the realities of middle school, high school, and life by focusing on reading to learn.

THE KIDS

Betty	Rita	Pat
Manuel	Mitch	Mandy
Horace	Alex	Mike
Jeff	Butch	Alexander
Chip	Carl	Daphne
Paul	Mort	Roberta
Joyce	Hilda	Steve
Daisy	Danielle	Tanana
Larry	Anthony	

Our story begins at the beginning. Miss Launch is having her beginning-of-school parent meeting. Let's look in on her, her parents, and (through her monthly journals) her year of kindergarten instruction.

Part II

...In

Elementary

Classrooms

9 | Miss Launch

THE PARENT MEETING

Over at last! Miss Launch glanced at her watch and noted with surprise that it was only 9:00 P.M. It seemed much later to her. As she moved about the room collecting materials and getting out other supplies for the next day, she thought over her first parent meeting in this new school. The previous school where she had taught kindergarten for three years had not held these meetings, and she had *not* looked forward to this one!

She had talked to them for approximately half an hour, and then some parents had asked questions. To her surprise, many parents had stayed longer for a private chat. But now, even they had gone, leaving her to her reflections.

She knew that this would be one of the most important encounters she would have with parents this year, and that this meeting would set the tone for all future parental cooperation. Mr. Topps had also told her to relax—these meetings went much more smoothly if they were informal and casual. To Miss Launch, with her penchant for food, that meant cookies and coffee!

While the parents were assembling in the classroom, she had announced that refreshments were in the rear of the room as was a sign-in sheet for their names. She would need to contact absent parents at a later time to discuss her kindergarten program with them.

Miss Launch firmly believed kindergarten to be an essential and integral part of the total school program. She had told the parents that kindergarten was *not* play time for which she was the babysitter. Further she had emphasized that the foundation for all future school success was laid in kindergarten.

She had outlined some of the experiences that the children would have in her room and the reasons for them. This had been an important part of her presentation, for she wanted and needed parental support and cooperation. She had pointed out to the parents the various centers for learning. In addition to the traditional block, art, and house corners she had included other areas that she felt would enhance the educational program for the children. There was an animals area, an area for pup-

251

pets and plays, one for reading, and a things-to-do corner that would include activities ranging from math, to science, to cooking and other topics. Much of the learning would take place in these centers.

Learning, however, would also occur outside of the classroom. Miss Launch had told the parents that she had planned two field trips a month to various places in the school and community. Follow-up activities for these field trips would include making thank you cards, drawing pictures, and dictating stories.

Miss Launch also had informed the parents of her concern with oral language development. She said that there would be many and varied opportunities for the children to talk. One of the mothers questioned why talking was important.

"Miss Launch, I don't know much about how they do school now, but when I was in school they didn't take learnin' time for talkin'. I don't see how that can help Chip learn to read! Readin' and talkin' are two different things as I see it!"

Miss Launch had replied calmly to Mrs. Moppet. "Not so different as you might think! Children are already speaking many thousands of words when they enter kindergarten. They will be able to read all of those words within the next few years. In addition, they will be reading other words which they do *not* yet know. But almost without exception, those new words they will learn to read will also be words which they have used in speech. If they do not learn to *say* new words, or if they do not learn to use old words in new ways, then they will only read at the level at which they now speak. That is why I do so much with oral language development. In reading I want to build from what the children know to what they need to know. That is another reason, by the way, for the two monthly field trips. Not only will the children become more familiar with their community, but these trips will also expose them to new words and new ideas which they need later for reading."

She had gone on to say that there would be much dramatization and story telling. Some of the children's stories would be written on chart paper, some might appear in individual story books, and still others might become part of one of the classroom books of original stories. Each day, before the children left, she would sit with them and discuss all the activities engaged in that day. She felt this discussion would help them develop a sense of sequence, the recognition of main ideas, and a memory for things they had accomplished, all important requisites for reading. Besides, she had said, when parents ask children what they had done in school all day, she wanted to prevent the old "Oh, nothing!" response that children often give!

Miss Launch explained that she wanted to give the children many experiences in identifying, sorting, and classifying. These activities help children develop vocabulary and see conceptual relationships. They would work with letters, colors, numbers, their own names, and myriad other concepts that would help them build the foundation for success in reading.

She planned to read to the children a great deal, and she expected them to "read" to her. For some children this reading would consist of picture interpretation, while for others, actual words would be read. Everyone would be reading during their classroom SQUIRT (Sustained *QUI*et *R*eading *T*ime) period. They would all start out reading for one minute. By the end of the school year they would be able to read silently for much longer. She had also planned many literature response activities for the children. These activities would be extensions of stories read to them, and they would be tied into other classroom activities such as music, art, and cooking.

Miss Launch indicated that she would use a variety of techniques to prepare children for the very important idea that one reads with the expectation of understanding what is read. They would construct charts of their animals' activities, of the weather, and of other things they knew about or could observe. They would be dictating stories and "reading" them to one another and to her. They would cook in the classroom, and follow simple recipes. While she did not believe that kindergarten is the place to establish reading groups and use commercial reading programs, she did believe that each child should have constant exposure to things that can be read. Children would then be able to ask questions about reading and would have the opportunity to explore reading activities without pressure or without being labeled as belonging to a particular reading group.

Horace's mother held up her hand. "Could you explain that in a little more detail, Miss Launch? I'm not quite sure that I understand what our children will do if they are not ready to read. And how will you know if they are ready?"

MISS LAUNCH: Mrs. Middleman, isn't it? Well, Mrs. Middleman, children first of all need to develop a desire and purpose for reading. Reading is a difficult task at best, but without proper motivation, it is even more so. We're all going to read, read, read in this class and not just during SQUIRT. I will read to the children and they will "read" to me and to one another. Even if they're only reading pictures, they are still acquiring abilities they will need to be good readers. They can determine the sequence of story events, what the important ideas in the story are, and what might happen next in the story. We will write and, I hope, receive letters. We will label things around the classroom and set up a post office for messages. We'll make books of all kinds—some will only have pictures like Mercer Mayer's "Frog" books and others will have words. We'll follow recipes for purposeful reading. In addition, we'll be working with rhyming patterns and the shapes of letters. As I said earlier, I feel that a firm background of oral language is the most important contribution I can make to your child's future success in reading, so I will do much with that. I have lots more planned, but I hope that you have the general idea. As to the determination of readiness, we don't yet have tests that can accurately tell us when children are "ready to read." There are many factors—physical, emotional, and intellectual.

MR. MARTIN: You've mentioned cooking in kindergarten a couple of times now, and I can't for the life of me figure out what cooking has to do with this prereading program you've set out. Can you explain it to me?

MISS LAUNCH: Would you believe that it's really because I like to eat? (Chuckles around the room). Actually, I can justify it educationally, though I must admit that I enjoy the food, too! (Chuckles again). Cooking in this room will be done for several reasons. First, since children eat what they prepare, they learn that it is important to follow directions carefully; second, the food produced is the incentive to do the work well, so there is meaning to doing it; third, there is always more language produced as we discuss why a particular sequence is necessary, and why certain ingredients are added, what they do together; and fourth, new concepts are observed and dealt with, such as the evaporation of liquid, or the nature of change as we observe it with popcorn. And, maybe I should add a fifth one—because it's fun, and if learning can result from an enjoyable activity as well as it can from a pencil and paper task, well, I'm all for it!

MRS. SMITH: My friend's son was in kindergarten last year, and he had all kinds of those papers done with purple ink and he had a reading readiness workbook, too. I think that with those you can tell what the children are learning.

MISS LAUNCH: I feel that workbooks and ditto papers stifle creativity and encourage conformity. And not only that, they do not necessarily teach the important things that children who are getting ready to read need to know. It's very important to instill an interest in reading and a desire to learn how to read. The best way to do that is with books—lots and lots of books! I assure you, however, that I will know what your children are learning. I use charts to keep track of children's progress with learnings that are important. I keep anecdotal records on children. I also keep samples of children's productions, such as their writing, so that I can observe vocabulary and language understandings. These are the ways which give me the greatest possible information about your child, or, as in your case, children. I assure you that I will know as much as is necessary about Roberta and Betty.

Miss Launch then explained that there would be at least two parent conferences this year, and that at the end of the year parents would receive a written appraisal of their child's performance in various areas.

She then summarized the scheduling she had completed for the staggered entrance of the children in school.

Miss Launch asked if there were any further questions.

MR. GRAHAM: I have no questions as such, but I just want you to know that I am amazed that so much can be done with kindergarteners! You have a very ambitious year mapped out! Is there anything we can do to help you?

MISS LAUNCH: Is there ever! Thanks so much for asking, because my next statement was to be a pitch to solicit your help. I can use parents and other relatives to help with taping stories, typing books children dictate, field trips, cooking, and all sorts of things. I'll be sending a request-for-help letter home soon, giving you the opportunity to volunteer. Some of the jobs can be done at home so that even if you don't have a lot of time, you can still help me out. As to all that the children can do, I have found that many adults tend to underestimate the capabilities of children, and for that reason we do not help them to attain their full potential. I hope to help them do so without the attendant pressure that we sometimes place on children.

As Miss Launch evaluated the evening, she found that the meeting had gone rather well. Many of the parents had remarked to her that they were pleased that the emphasis would be on learning through creative means. She was certain that she would have a great deal of support from the parents whenever she might need it. She hoped she had convinced them that kindergarten was "real school." Oh, well, if not now, then by the end of the year they would be aware of it! She glanced around the room. Yes, all was in readiness for tomorrow morning. She allowed herself the luxury of a stretch and a yawn; then she turned off the lights and left for home.

MONTHLY LOGS

September

September is always a bit of a shock to my system. Each year I am taken aback at how small and shy the entering kindergarteners are. I quickly realize that I am using the children of the previous spring as my criteria. How much they do grow and change in one year's time!

I asked Mr. Topps if I might stagger the children's entrance into kindergarten. I felt that each one of this group of 25 children would be better able to make the adjustment if he or she entered with a small number of other children. I could give more personal attention to each child while I tried to deal with some of the school socialization processes—such as how to use the water fountain and what "line up" means! Those can be difficult areas for children to deal with for the first time. Fortunately, most of them are already "housebroken"!

The following chart shows how I managed the staggered attendance. It was somewhat confusing for the parents, but since they each had a copy of the chart there were very few mix-ups. I suggested that they go through the schedule and ring their child's group with red or some other color to make it readily visible so that they could see, at a glance, the days their child would attend. We also allowed the twins, Roberta and Betty, to attend the same sessions so their parents wouldn't have two sets of classes to keep track of. This attendance procedure has the added advantage of gradually acquainting children with the school. Even the half-day sessions we run can be tiring for children who are unaccustomed to remaining in one place for more than ten minutes.

Kindergarten Attendance Plan

Group 1	Group 2	Group 3
Mike	Joyce	Pat
Steve	Mort	Jeff
Rita	Butch	Alex
Mitch	Carl	Paul
Daisy	Larry	Manuel
Chip	Mandy	Daphne
Betty	Horace	Hilda
Roberta	Anthony	Danielle
Alexander		

	Monday	Tuesday	Wednesday	Thursday	Friday
1st Week	Group 1	Group 2	Group 3	Group 1	Group 2
2nd Week	Group 3	Group 1, 3	Groups 1, 2	Groups 2, 3	Groups, 1, 2, 3

Another reason that I like the staggered attendance is that children come to know a few classmates well in a short time, rather than being lost in a large group. It's important to feel a part of a group, no matter how small.

Starting the year is the difficult task, and as I look over the list of all I have set out to accomplish, I wonder somewhat at my audacity. This year I am going to make much more of a concerted effort to systematically teach children about language and the reasons for reading. I know that a certain road is paved with good intentions and that if I don't structure myself, I will probably not do all that I now plan to. Therefore, I have taped a list of factors inside my plan book so that I will be reminded to include specific activities for these factors as I do my planning. These seven readiness ingredients [see Chapter 1] are:

1. Children must know what reading is for.
2. Children need to develop an adequate background of information so that what they read makes sense.
3. Children must expect that what they hear read to them and what they read for themselves will make sense.
4. Children must understand the conventions of printed language and the jargon of print.
5. Children must learn to auditorily and visually discriminate letters and words.
6. Children must have an interest and a desire to learn to read.
7. Children need experiences with both story and expository reading materials.

Readiness Ingredients

Due to the extraordinary mixture of children I have this year, I really don't know how I could have managed with all 25 on the first day. Working with groups of eight and nine at a time was so much easier for me, as well as for them. One child was so withdrawn that I was immediately aware that his problem was more than fear of coming to school for the first time. Paul wouldn't speak to me or any of the others for three class sessions, and then he merely uttered his name in a group game. When this happened, we were so excited that we gave him a "silent cheer" (that is, we raised our hands into the air, shook them up and down, and formed our mouths as though we were cheering). Paul cried often during those first two weeks, but they were strange, silent tears that rolled down his cheeks. There was no sobbing or screaming—just a sad, sad look and those tears running down his cheeks. (I have asked the school social worker to investigate the home situation. Something is drastically wrong; perhaps we can discover what it is and then remedy the situation.) Alex and Daphne began to sniffle when they saw this (tears are among the most contagious of childhood afflictions), but Hilda simply told them to be quiet, that she had looked around and it was obvious that there was nothing to be afraid of! The sniffling subsided, but Paul continued his silent crying despite all my efforts to comfort or distract him.

I read to the children every day, and sometimes the whole morning is built around one book. First the story is read to them, and then we do other activities to tie the book into the other curricular areas. As an example, one of the first books I read to them was Mirra Ginsburg's *Mushroom in the Rain* (1974). After reading it, we talked about their favorite parts of the story and they drew with crayons or painted at the easel the one thing they had enjoyed the most. We hung these up and let children tell what the part was and why they had chosen it. The fox

Literature Response Activities

section was the most popular of all, for children like to be scared just a little. Then we dramatized the story by playing the parts of the various animals. I sometimes had to play, too, to have enough actors for all the characters. When I asked the children what we could use for a mushroom, they cleverly decided to use an umbrella that they would open out more and more as the various animals came under! In addition, we counted the number of animals in the book. We looked for certain colors ("Find all the red things on this page"). We made up a song that we could sing to the tune of "Are You Sleeping?":

Is it raining,
Is it raining,
Little Ant?
Little Ant?
Hurry to the mushroom!
Hurry to the mushroom!
Drip, drop, drip.
Drip, drop, drip.

Is it raining,
Is it raining,
Butterfly?
Butterfly? (*etc., for all the animals up through the rabbit. Then:*)

Here comes Foxy!
Here comes Foxy!
Poor Rabbit! (*two times*)
"No, he is not here, Sir." (*two times*)
"Go away." (*two times*)

See the rainbow (*two times*)
In the sky. (*two times*)
Now the sun is shining (*two times*)
Warm and bright. (*two times*)

We tested the hypothesis that mushrooms grow in the rain and we planned additional adventures for the characters in the book. We talked about who else might have come to the mushroom, what might happen next, where Ant would go when the rain finally stopped, and what other scary things might happen to the other animals. After we did a lap story with *Mushroom in the Rain*, I placed the characters, props, and the book in the puppets and plays center so they can retell the story individually or in small groups over and over [see pp. 123–126].

Routines We have only had two weeks of regular school this month because of the staggered entrance of the children, but in those two weeks we have established a daily pattern or schedule. Establishing a routine which children can depend upon is a critical aspect of school. The morning group arrives at 8:30 and leaves at 11:30, so I only have three hours in which to do a lot of things. The schedule, which is altered only for special events, field trips, etc., is:

    8:30 Attendance, sharing, read a story or poem
    9:00 Work time—centers, SQUIRT, oral language lessons, etc.
  10:00 Physical education—outside if possible
  10:30 Snack, rest, story
  11:00 Work time
  11:15 Group together for summary of day, etc.

During the third week, at work time the children were to find pictures of red things in magazines and catalogs. Larry, who is already reading, I've discovered, found the word *red* also. We pasted the things they found on a chart labeled "Red Things." Most of the children could already identify the colors without help, but some could not. I paired Joyce (who could) and Chip (who couldn't) so she could help him find red things. Daisy, Jeff, Paul, and Butch also worked with other children to find red objects.

Concept Development— Colors

Also during work time, I've been having the children practice their phone numbers and addresses. It is essential that they learn those as soon as possible, so that if they should ever get lost, they can be reunited with parents quickly. As Chip has no phone, he has learned the phone number of a neighbor. We'll practice dialing their numbers on toy telephones.

We began the first field trips of the year right in our own school area. It is important for children to be come oriented to the building, the grounds, and the personnel as soon as is possible. The first day the children came to school, we spent part of the morning walking through those parts of the building we *had* to know—the restrooms, the office, and the janitor's room—so that *when* (not *if*, but when) a child throws up I can stay with the child while someone else asks the janitor to bring a mop. We have our own kindergarten-sized playground equipment, and that also had to be shown. We went to the office on subsequent days and met the secretary, Mrs. Mainstay, and the principal, Mr. Topps. I prepared for these trips by first going there myself and making sure that someone who knew precisely what it was I wanted the children to learn about that particular place would be on hand. I prepared the children by telling them the highlights of each place, alerting them what to look and listen for, and urging them to try to remember everything so that we could talk and make up a story when we got back to the room. Upon our return, I asked them to tell what we had seen and done. As each child made a contribution, I wrote it down on chart paper with the

Concept Development— Field Trips

child's name after it, so that he or she could see the very words contributed. Then I cut the words apart and with the children's help, I glued them back on another piece of paper in the proper order of occurrence. Finally I read it all back to them and they agreed that they had done a fine job!

Cooking

Our cooking experience for September came near the end of the last week in the month. I began by talking with the children about one of their favorite foods: peanut butter! "Yippee Skippy," they yelled. I asked them what they thought peanut butter might be made from. They all guessed, with no trouble, the main ingredient. "What else," I queried. They said that there was nothing else because that's why they called it peanut butter. After all, they reasoned, butter was only made of butter and hot dogs were made of hot dogs! Oh, boy! It's going to be a long year! I reached into the bag next to me and took out two peanuts in the shell. Some of the children were clearly fascinated since they thought peanuts came in cans. They watched me shell the peanuts (two nuts to a shell, we noted) and place them in a little ceramic bowl. I then began to mash the peanuts with a pestle and showed them the results periodically. When I had the four peanuts pretty well mashed I showed the bowl to each child. "Does that look like what you put on your crackers?" I asked. They all agreed that it did not, and we discussed why.

"It's too dry looking," said Larry. "Maybe they call it peanut butter because they put butter into it."

"Good guess," I responded. "You're right that it does need something greasy in it. The recipe I have says that we just put plain oil into the mashed peanuts, add a little salt, mix it up, and spread it on crackers or bread." Then I asked if they would each like to make their own peanut butter to have at snack time. They were, to put it mildly, agreeable to the suggestion. We made a recipe chart for the cooking area and I put them into pairs to work on their peanut butter during the morning work time. I paired them so that more independent and mature children would work with those who needed help. Larry and Paul were put together and did a really nice job. Here is the recipe chart that the children dictated.

How to Make Peanut Butter for Two People

We Need:

10 peanuts for each person
2 teaspoons of oil
1 sprinkle of salt

We Do:

Take the peanuts out of the shells

Mash the peanuts in the bowl
Put the oil into the bowl
Mix the oil and peanuts with the salt
Put the peanut butter on a cracker for snack time

TRY IT OUT

When Miss Launch took the children on the field trips, she was helping to develop several of the seven readiness ingredients from her chart. Look at page 257. Miss Launch was developing numbers 1, 2, 3, 4, and 7. She knew that going on the trip would help to develop children's background of information. She knew that writing a language experience chart after the trip would help children understand that one reason for reading is to enjoy a pleasurable experience through the words that tell about the trip. They also saw that what she wrote was only about the trip, and did not include information not related to the trip or "silly words." They observed her moving her hand from left to right, top to bottom on the page, noting that she always went back to the beginning of the next line. Because the chart was an account of their trip, they had experience with reading expository text.

Similarly, the cooking activity described above was designed to help develop some of the seven readiness ingredients. List which of the seven ingredients you think were being developed.

October

October is over—I didn't think Halloween would *ever* arrive, and neither did the children! Every day they asked if it were here yet! Well, at least I was able to channel some of that interest toward school activities. Many of the books I selected to read to them and ones they chose themselves were about Halloween, witches, or monsters. One of my favorites, *Where the Wild Things Are* (Sendak, 1963), was one of those with which we did literature response activities. The children made monster masks and we had a "wild things" parade. We also had a word **Meaning** gathering for scary words—I asked them to tell me all of the scary **Vocabulary—** things they could think of. Since this was our first word gathering, the **Topical** children had trouble getting started. After only a few suggestions by **Word Sets** other children everyone joined in. Even Paul gave me one—*night*. When they started to bog down, having given me several words and phrases, I asked them for scary colors, then for scary smells, sounds, and looks. This is their completed list—I am sure Dr. Herbert Sandberg of the University of Toledo, who explained word gathering at a meeting I attended, would approve.

Scary Things

blood	monster	bad dream	nightmare
ghost	bloody	black cat	Boo!
howl	scream	witch	mummy
giant	storm	red	fire
dogs	growl	night	orange
purple	blue	scared	afraid

something touching me in the dark
when my night light burns out
footsteps in the dark
my mom's closet without the light on
my window with the curtains open
noises outside in the dark

After we had completed the list, I read the words back to the children, running my hand under each word or phrase as I said it so that they would have more opportunity to observe left to right progression with the return sweep to the next line. "Now," I told them, "we are

Poetry going to write a poem!" I had read many poems to them and they did enjoy poetry. Now it was our turn to produce. I used a concrete format since it is the simplest one I know. I drew a random number and arrangement of lines on the chalkboard and the children helped me to fill them in with words and phrases. To show them what I wanted us to do, I had them count the number of lines I had drawn and I told them that I was going to use some of the words from our *scary things* chart to help me make up the poem. There would only be 1 word written on each line so since we had counted 21 lines, I needed to write 21 words. This is what they saw:

    —— ——
    —— —— —— —— ——
    —— ——
    —— —— —— ——
    —— ——
    —— —— —— ——

The children were intrigued, particularly when they saw me begin to write words on each of the lines. This is my finished poem:

> I <u>felt</u>
> <u>something</u> <u>touching</u> <u>me</u> <u>in</u> <u>the</u> <u>dark</u>.
> I <u>knew</u>
> <u>my</u> <u>window</u> <u>curtains</u> <u>were</u> <u>open</u>.
> I <u>screamed</u>.
> <u>Bad</u> <u>dream</u> <u>go</u> <u>away</u>.

We counted the number of words that were on each of the lines. Mort pointed out that the first line in the second row had nine words on it! At that point we talked about how some words have one letter (pointing out "I" in the poem) and that some words have more than one letter. The word *something* has nine letters. I wrote *Mort* on the board. "What is that word?" I asked. He did know his name and told me that it said *Mort*. "This is one word and that word is your name. But your name has four letters in it." Of course, it was necessary to do the same with the names of several other children since all of them wanted their names written. But it was also important to count the letters in the names of several children in order to show children the concept of *letter* versus *word* in lots of examples. Obviously they didn't all get it this time around, but with lots of examples throughout the year they should all have the idea by the time they hit first grade (I hope!). With a little help, this is what the class was able to come up with:

One Night
Black cat scream, black cat howl!
Why do you make that noise?
Growl, purr, growl, purr
Dog and cat
fight.

I copied both my poem and their poem onto sheets of chart paper and hung them near the scary things chart. I find it fascinating that Danielle will steer her wheel chair over and pore over the poems with Roberta and Alex. They seem fascinated with the idea that there is one word on each of the lines and they try to count how many letters are in each of the words. Occasionally Mort will wander over and watch them for a while. I heard him say, "But how do you *know* which ones are words and which ones are letters? I don't get it. I think you're making it all up." Clearly, there is a range of abilities within *this* classroom!

We also did a concrete poem on the color *black*. First we had a word gathering of black words, sounds, and smells to get them prepared.

Black
Black, black is the night,
blacker than black
is
my   window.

While we were gathering *black* words (which was, of course, the color chart they were working on that week) a discussion took place. The children were coming up with all kinds of black things, when Butch contributed three words: *Joyce, Danielle,* and *Jeff*. Some of the children turned around and looked at those children as if they had never seen them before, and Alex said, "Hey! They are kinda black!" Others started murmuring as well—this *was* a revelation!

Larry said, "No, I don't agree. They are called Blacks, but I think they look more brown than black."

The three were asked what color *they* thought they were and Joyce said, "Well, what color do you think *you* are?" Jeff and Danielle said nothing. After a little more discussion they all agreed that Joyce and Danielle were brownish, but that Jeff was closer to black. So his name went up on the chart of black things, and though he tried to hide it from them, he smiled! Later I saw him tracing out the letters of his name on the chart. He was the only child to get listed on the chart!

Sight Words— Names

By now I had labeled a lot of things around the room: window, door, mirror, desk, table, chair. Children seem to enjoy finding labeled objects which have letters like those in their names. I was working with each of the children so that they would recognize their own names. I wrote each name about three inches high on unlined paper. I then took each child's hand and traced over the name with two fingers. All the time we did that, I said the name over and over with the child. Then, after we had done that a few times, I let them go to the scribble section of the chalkboard where they could write it, using the paper as a model. I stayed with each child until the name was mastered and then went to work with the next one. With that technique, almost all of the children can recognize their names when they see them in manuscript writing, and several can write their own names without looking at a model. As a further incentive, I labeled the bulletin board with their names and then asked them to make a picture of themselves and tell me where to hang it. Mort, Paul, and Daisy were the only three who needed extra help. Mort got confused because of all the names which began with *M*, as did Daisy with three *D* names. Paul just didn't have a clue! Another activity they like is to dip their one-inch brushes into clear water and write on the board with those. They have fun, they learn, there is no erasing to do, and, at the end, the chalkboard is clean!

Volunteer Help

Perhaps you'd be interested in the letter which the parents received from me at the beginning of October to solicit help.

Parental response to the letter was overwhelming. For the most part, parents want to be involved in their children's education and will volunteer if there is something specific that they feel confident in doing. In some cases, parents prefer to or *must* do things at home. For example, Chip's mother must stay home to take care of an elderly aunt and uncle who live with them. She thus offered to cut out things for me if I would send the materials to her, since they don't have any magazines or newspapers. *Where* it's done matters not to me! I'm just delighted that parents are willing to do it at all!

Dear Parents,

As I told you at our September parent meeting, I am most eager to provide your children with a year full of good learning experiences. In order to give them the kind of program I have envisioned, I am asking for your help in many ways. Would you please put a check mark beside those things which you would be willing to do for us this year. The space for "other" is one in which you might suggest to me any possible aid or special talent you would like to contribute.

Thank you so much for your prompt attention to this matter. Your children and I will gain much from your participation in their education.

Sincerely,

Helen Launch

....

Please detach here and return.

I would be willing to help in the following ways:
____ coming to school one hour a week
____ typing at home (or school)
____ cutting out paper at home (or school)
____ transporting children for field trips
____ helping with the monthly cooking project at school
____ donating scrap materials (cloth, pretty paper, etc.)
____ tape-recording stories, music, etc.
____ making puppets
____ contributing art materials
____ contributing materials for house corner
____ contributing books, records, pictures, etc.
____ contributing scatter rugs, pillows for floor, etc.
____ other:

Name: _____
Telephone: _____

Field Trips

Our two field trips this month were to those places which supply us with food—the store and the farm. I had gone to these places prior to the children's visit, and I made extensive notes to myself about the kinds of things I wanted them to notice and learn about. I spend a lot of time listing for myself what the concepts and vocabulary are that I anticipate will be developed. After each visit, then, we make charts of things seen and learned.

Since the store didn't open until 9:00 A.M., I made arrangements for the manager to show us around at 8:45. I planned to spend half an hour there so the children would be able to observe some shoppers, but the store wouldn't be too crowded. I prepared the children for this trip by discussing with them the various services and goods the store has to offer. Daisy was the greatest contributor, for she had spent a good bit of time in stores with her mother. I put down anything the children said, so after the trip they could look at their list and add to it. From the amended list we made up a story about the store which hung on the bulletin board surrounded by all of the children's pictures. Here it is:

Language Experience

We went to the store. (Daphne)
We saw lots and lots of food. (Daisy)
The fruits and vegetables are called *produce*. (Larry)
Lots of meat. (Chip)
There were sweet things to eat. (Carl)
The store man showed us many things. (Pat)
We had fun and learned a lot. (Rita)
My mother and Larry's mother drove. (Roberta)

In addition the children drew pictures and wrote "scribble writing" thank you letters [see pp. 5–6] which I mailed to "the store man" along with a copy of their story and a personal note of thanks from me. Some of the children were even able to write a few real words.

Meaning Vocabulary

We did the same kinds of activities for our visit to the farm. So many children do not associate the farm with the store that I made a special effort to talk about where butter, milk, meat, and vegetables come from. When I first asked them where milk comes from, Butch replied, "From the carton." But where did the milk for the carton come from, I persisted. Jeff told me that it came from the store! In my whole morning group, only four—Larry (no surprise!), Steve and Anthony (the science buffs), and Daphne (who lives on a farm)—knew that cows are milked and that is the source of milk.

A concern I have when taking my children on these trips is that the guide speak loudly enough for all to hear. Because I prepare them so well for their trips, they have plenty of questions to ask and are willing to listen to the answers, but too often the guide is not prepared to wait until they are all quiet and close enough to hear, or careful to speak loud enough to overcome background noises.

Cooking

We received several pumpkins from both the farm and the store, so it only seemed reasonable to try out some of the recipe and craft ideas in *The All-Around Pumpkin Book*, by Margery Cuyler (1980). Following her directions, we cooked pieces of pumpkin and put the peeled, softened pumpkin meat through a sieve to make pumpkin sauce. Two of their favorite recipes were roasted pumpkin seeds and pumpkin milk (believe it or not!). Here's the recipe for pumpkin milk, which they did in groups of six:

Pumpkin Milk

We Need:

2 cups of plain yogurt
3/4 cup pumpkin sauce
1½ tablespoons honey
1½ teaspoons nutmeg
1½ cups milk
2 tablespoons wheat germ

We Do:

Put everything in the blender and turn it on
Turn the blender on whip
When it is all mixed up it will be all orange
Turn off the blender and pour the pumpkin milk into 6 glasses

I thought it turned out remarkably well. All the children except Anthony tried it. However, I was a bit chagrined to overhear Butch muttering, "I'd rather have a beer."

ADD TO YOUR SURVIVAL KIT

Begin to collect simple recipes that you could make with young children in the classroom. Make a booklet containing at least 15 of them.

November

Finally! Colors are finished! Our room looks like a rainbow gone crazy. Because some of the children had decided that Joyce and Danielle were "brown things," I changed the order of the colors we were working on. We did brown the first week in November. They remembered their "discovery," and when we began to gather brown things for the chart, their names were the first things mentioned. They helped me spell them, too, which made it even more important to them. We did purple and white things during the second and third weeks. Larry is able to read a great many of the things we have listed on our charts. I'm amazed that he can read so well. He often chooses the reading corner in which to spend his free time.

The reading corner is furnished with an old bucket seat from the car **Library** of a friend of mine. (My friends are well trained—they never throw any **Corner** unusual items away without checking with me first! Over the years I have asked them for odd items, from popsicle sticks to eggshells!) The children love the car seat—two can sit together cozily, reading or looking at books. There also is a small rug remnant, some pillows donated by parents, and a small table with three chairs. A shelf contains a variety of books, ranging from those with pictures only to those with quite a long story line. The children choose books they want me to read to them, and often we do literature response activities with these books.

Interest Centers

The blocks area is another one that the children enjoy and use frequently. It lends itself to all sorts of language experiences as the children build and discuss what they have done and why. Sometimes they ask me to write signs for them or write down stories that the constructions trigger. By the end of November we had enough of those stories to make a book which we placed in the reading corner. The children were really pleased that I valued their work enough to put a cover around it and give it a title. Nearly everyone in the class had contributed something to the book, and even those who hadn't had worked in the block corner and could enjoy the stories and illustrations.

The art area has paint, easels, clay, crayons, colored chalk, *lots* of paper, odds and ends for constructions, and various other materials for art work. I have a section of the bulletin board reserved for paintings and a small table nearby for displaying constructions. Very often, art work acts as a stimulus for story writing. One of the children might ask me to write down his story about the horse he or a classmate had made of clay. I am often asked to label their work; not only is there further language concept development, but this labeling also seems to add value to the work.

I have never called the house corner the doll corner or doll house as some of my colleagues do, for lots of boys don't want to play there if it has that name. They learn too soon to shun the so-called feminine play things. By calling it the house corner there is a greater opportunity to draw boys in. They experiment with all sorts of housekeeping experiences, even arguing over whose turn it is to vacuum the floor. Of course, they get real cooking and dishwashing experiences from the cooking sessions we have.

Visual Discrimination

It was been another busy month, of course, with the field trips as well as some of the activities that I have been doing with the children to help develop visual discrimination of letters. We have learned to play some new games. I wrote out six copies each of the capital letter forms *P, H, A,* and *R.* I made each one about six inches high so that the children could readily see them from across the room. They are on sheets of oak-tag and covered with clear plastic adhesive paper so that they are durable. The first game was one that the whole class played together. I shuffled the cards and dealt out one to each of the children. I told them to find the other children who had the same letter shape. When two children got together they had to stay together while searching for other children who matched them. If they thought that they had found one that was a match, they carefully looked at the parts to see if they were correct. After all groups had been formed with no leftovers, I checked them: Perfect the first time, just as I had known it would be, for the abler ones helped those who could not yet match! (I had set the timer for three minutes. They enjoyed the timing—it gives games a little added excitement.)

It was interesting to observe the differences among the children as they formed their groups. Paul stayed put and was found by Mandy and Horace, who also had *P*'s. They dragged him along with them until they found or were found by the other *P*'s. Daisy dashed wildly around the room, ostensibly looking for the other *A*'s, but in fact making it only more difficult for them to track her down. Mort sat in a chair, apparently not wanting to exhaust himself, being fully confident that the *H*'s would get to him in time. Chip and Manuel held hands and went from group to group checking the letters, even though Chip was an *A* and Manuel an *R*. I suppose they just needed the extra confidence that they gave one another. The children begged to do it again, so we shuffled the cards and went through the same process. This time, Hilda tried to organize the thing a little more by shouting out, "A! A! A!" apparently as a clue to those who might know the name of the letter. Larry formed his hand into the letter *P* and said "Do you look like this?" Ingenious children I have!

For another game I used the same cards and placed three cards of the same letter on the chalkboard tray with one that was different. I arranged the cards like this for ease the first time: *A A A N*. I then asked Rita to come find the ones that were the same. She choose the first three. "Terrific! Let's all give Rita a silent cheer!" (The silent cheer is a good reward for children and it's also easy on the teacher's eardrums.) I continued the game with other children making the letter combinations harder or easier depending on a child's capabilities. I then put the cards into the things-to-do center and suggested that they were available to play with.

For the time being, every time we do a language experience story, I underline each word as I read back the completed story to the children to emphasize the concept of a *word*. Our latest one dealt with one of our more disastrous cooking experiences!

Language Experience

> We had a messy time cooking today. (Anthony)
> We made cranberry-orange relish to take to our
>   Thanksgiving dinner with the first graders. (Danielle)
> We got juice and seeds all over the floor. (Alex)
> It tasted yucky. (Butch)
> Nobody wanted to eat any but Miss Launch. (Carl)
> Miss Launch face look sad. (Paul)

We continue the quest to distinguish between letters and words, as well

Metalinguistic Awareness

as trying to emphasize the return sweep to the next line of print. Paul, Mort, Daisy, and Chip are still unable to figure out how children like Roberta, Danielle, and Larry can always tell which marks mean words and which ones mean letters. Most of the group are able to figure out questions such as, "How many words are in the first sentence?" if they can come up to the chart and put a finger on each word in the sentence as they count. The story here allowed me to get into another concept with them. Danielle's sentence continued onto another line. When I asked, "How many words are in Danielle's sentence?" most of the children said eight. A few, Betty and Larry and some others, disagreed. There were 14 words, they contended. Alexander, who thought he had finally caught Larry in an error, volunteered to come to the chart and check it out. It took a lot of convincing, with Danielle chiming in for support, to try to convince some of them that Danielle's sentence was indeed 14 words long. Eventually, I know, all of them will understand the difference between words and letters.

SSR   This month I began SQUIRT. Most of the teachers in this school set aside a time period during which the children and the teacher silently read in materials of their own choice. I explained to the class that I was going to set our timer for one minute and during that one minute, everyone was to be looking at a book. We went to the school library to select books just for SQUIRT. I aided some in their selections so that Larry, Roberta, and Danielle had books they could read and Paul and Daisy had some bright picture books on topics they found interesting (a children's cookbook for Daisy!). At SQUIRT time it all went rather well, considering that this was a first for them. After it was over, I pulled aside the children who had had an especially difficult time sitting with a book for one whole minute. We discussed how they could look at the pictures to try to figure out what the story was about, or they could look at the pictures and try to name the colors they saw on the pages, or they could go through and think of the names of as many things as possible on each page. I encouraged these children to try to decide if they liked the book enough to want me to read it to the whole class. I had to do this several times with various children in the room (not always the same ones), but by the end of the month the children really could sit still with a book for one whole minute. Mr. Topps was really pleased when he came into the classroom to read with us!

TRY IT OUT

Which of the seven readiness ingredients was Miss Launch trying to develop when she was doing the cranberry-orange relish language experience story? What was she trying to accomplish by having SQUIRT every day with the children?

Daphne's grandparents, with whom she lives, are farmers. In fact, it was their farm we had visited in October. They told me that they very much enjoyed having the children to the farm and that they felt somewhat guilty that they did not have enough time to come to the school and volunteer some of their time. Despite my protest that it was fine, they insisted that they wanted to help out in some way. Could I use two bushels of apples from their orchard? I love questions like that!

Need I tell you that every one of our cooking activities for the month **Cooking** of November involved apples? I did have to alter the cooking plan that I had made for the year, but it was worth it. One of their very favorite recipes came from *The Taming of the C.A.N.D.Y. Monster* (Lansky, 1978).

Candy Apples

We Need:

1 apple for each person
1 popsicle stick for each person
A bowl of honey
Toasted wheat germ on waxed paper

We Do:

Pull the stem off your apple
Push the stick in where you took out the stem
Dip the apple in the bowl of honey and turn it 2 times
Hold the apple over the bowl of honey until it stops dripping
Roll the apple in the wheat germ and eat it up!

December

Despite the holiday rush and clamor, we did manage to accomplish some things this month. It does seem to me, though, that the break can't come a minute too soon, for we have been in a holiday whirl since Halloween!

I have quite a collection of books without words or with only a few **Compre-** words which I have been using with children in small groups. I use **hension—** these books to encourage them to discuss what they are seeing in the **Wordless** story and to help them develop the story line as it occurs. The first books **Books** I used were *I Am Andy* (Steiner, 1961) and *The Elephant's Nest* (Burton, 1979). These books each contain several very short stories. I had a small group consisting of Butch, Alexander, Betty, Anthony, Jeff, and Hilda do the story "The Big Pocket" with me. First I told them that we were going to look at a book which had no words but had some stories in it. "How can there be a story without any words?" asked Hilda. "Stories have words." I assured her that it would all come clear. I showed them the title page (Hilda said, "Ah ha! I knew there would be words!") and then turned to the next page which showed a kangaroo with babies jumping out of her pocket. At the end of the four pages, there are four babies who have leaped out. I did not try to tell the story to them, rather as I showed each page I asked them to tell us what was happening. Before I would turn to the next page I asked them to guess what might be coming up next. After seeing three kangaroo babies hop out of the pocket they readily guessed that another would jump out on the next page. When I asked my same question at the end of the fourth page, they thought they had the pattern. "Another one will jump out," they told me.

What a surprise it was when the baby elephant jumped out of the mother kangaroo's pocket! They immediately guessed, in response to my question of "What will happen next?" that there would be a total of four elephants jumping out of her pocket. But the next page showed a baby giraffe climbing out of the kangaroo's pocket. They were surprised to find during the course of the story that the parents of the giraffe and the elephant came by to pick them up and take them home. We continued the free-flowing discussion through the examination of all the pictures in that story. "Now, we are going back to the beginning of the story and this time you are going to tell me what is happening in the story."

They wanted to go ahead of the pictures we were looking at, but I would not let them do that. I wanted them to listen to one another and stay with what was on each page. The next day I called the same group to me, showed them the book, and asked them to tell the story with me again. After this retelling (which went much better than the others), I told them that now we were going to tell the story with the tape recorder on, and every time we finished with one page, someone would ring the bell as a turn-page signal. The upshot of it all was that I prepared a written text to go along with the book and the tape recorded story and placed it all in a learning center. I've done quite a few of the wordless books this way and are they ever popular!

TRY IT OUT

Which of the seven readiness ingredients were being developed with the activity with wordless books?

Functional Reading A device I started this month to help the children identify their own names and also to help develop responsibility is a *job chart*. There are always many tasks to be done in a classroom, and by this time of the year I try to involve the children even more than previously. There are enough jobs for everyone, even though several children have the same job simultaneously, as the cleaners do. So that children have a variety of jobs during the year, the job assignments rotate weekly. There are jobs that can be done by the children only if their teacher instructs them. For instance, they must be told how much water to give the plants. One tip that I found helpful was to color-code plants to soup cans used for watering. Draw a line inside the soup can with permanent marker to indicate how much water is needed for a plant. A small square of color on the plant container that matches the line drawn in the can will clue children so that they will have a hard time going wrong. Be forewarned, however, that if you have a color-blind child like Butch, you may have a drowned cactus and a droopy ivy! Using this kind of a coding system is the beginning of learning to follow "written" instructions. Though no words are used, children learn to decode the meaning of the symbol being used (in this case, color) in order to follow some specific instructions.

Here is the job chart for one week. Every week new assignments are made:

Water plants	Chip	Paul	Anthony		
Room cleaners	Betty	Butch	Daisy	Rita	Hilda
Messengers	Manuel	Daphne	Alexander		
Mail	Larry and Danielle (they knew all of the names)				
Line leader	Mort				
Group work leaders	Roberta	Horace	Carl	Alex	
Feed animals	Pat	Mike	Steve		
Special helpers	Mitch	Joyce	Mandy	Jeff	

We did another very easy poetry format this month. First, I asked the children if they knew what opposites were. Horace volunteered, "That's when my Mom puts money into the bank." **Poetry**

"Pretty good guess," I replied. "That is called a *de*posit."

Larry said, "You know, they're words that mean just the different thing, just the, well, *opposite*, like hot and cold, wet and dry, up and down." **Meaning Vocabulary**

"Very good, Larry. Can you think of any other opposites, children?" They came up with several pairs: warm and cool, summer and winter, big and little. I asked them to choose a pair so that we could make up a poem. They chose *up and down*. I told them that this time we would start and end the poem with those words and fill in with others. We would put the words in one long column, one word per line. There was an uneven number of words, for the middle word, the transition word, had to have something to do with both of the opposites. Here is what they came up with:

Up,   (Larry)
Sky,   (Joyce)
Clouds,   (Pat)
Flying,   (Mike)

Swing,   (Hilda)
Falling,   (Butch)
Dirt,   (Mitch)
Rocks,   (Steve)
Down.   (Larry)

I read their poem to them, phrasing it to make the most of the poetic elements. Notice that the middle word is the one where the transition is made between the opposites. The words from the top to the middle build images for the top word; the words from the middle down build images for the bottom word.

Language Experience

This month we did one of our recipes as a language experience chart very much like the ones which are in some of the children's cookbooks which I showed to the class. They had almost all seen cookbooks of their mothers, but they had not really noticed how the recipes were written.

Cooking

Happy Holidays Egg Cones (for two people)

Ingredients:

2 cups water
3 eggs
1 tablespoon chopped celery (Miss Launch does)
1 teaspoon pimento
2 pinches of salt
2 tablespoons mayonnaise
2 leaves of lettuce
2 ice cream cones

Utensils:

pan
hot plate
bowl
fork
table knife
spoon for mayonnaise
spoon for mixing

Preparation:

1. Put 3 eggs in pan
2. Add 2 cups of water to pan
3. Put pan on low heat on hot plate
4. Cover pan and let it cook for 20 minutes
5. While eggs cook, put lettuce on counter and cut with table knife into small pieces
6. Put lettuce pieces in the bottom of the ice cream cone
7. When eggs are done cover with cold water

8. Let eggs cool for 5 minutes
9. Gently crack eggs on counter and peel off shell
10. Put eggs in bowl
11. Mash eggs into little pieces with the fork
12. Put in: celery, pimento, salt, and mayonnaise
13. Mix everything together
14. Spoon ½ of egg stuff into each ice cream cone
15. Ready to eat!

This was one of our better experiences this year. The children learned so many things while putting together this recipe. For example, we looked at raw eggs and hard cooked eggs and talked about how the cooking changed them from a liquid to a solid. We measured the water after the first batch of eggs had finished cooking. Evaporation was discussed when they noticed much of the water gone. This recipe format allowed the introduction of quite a few new words, such as *ingredients*. There was much more measuring than in other recipes we had tried. All in all, it did go well. It amazes me to realize the number of concepts being developed. I guess they are ready for all of our recipes to involve cooking now.

January

The children seemed really glad to be back at school—two weeks is a long time to be away. I find, too, that they have become bored at home and come to miss the routine we have so carefully established. Furthermore, most of them are anxious to share their holiday "goodies" with the other children. Pat got her wish and received some new books, which she assured me she could read. I asked her to bring them in and show them to us and perhaps read them to the class. Pat brought in one of those early-reading books, *Ten Apples Up on Top* (Le Seig, 1961), that she had received for Christmas. First she read it to me, and then I let her read it to her small group. I had to agree with her—she *was* reading.

Reading to others is one of the favorite activities of the children, even of those who cannot read! It works this way: when one of the children indicates to me, as Pat did, that there is a book she would like to share with her group, I ask the group leader to get the group together. (Group leaders are appointed each month and are listed on the job chart.) The group leader informs the others in the group when they are to work together, and is also responsible for this work being turned in to me. In addition, the group leader must get the group together for special things, such as when a member of the group wants to "read" to them. At an appointed time the group meets together and listens to the story. Most often the children "read" pictures to one another and make up a

Reading to Perform

story. This story, while generally plausible, is often quite different from the original.

Children are getting the idea that what is in books should make sense to them and to others. By "pretend reading" the books over and over, many of them are even able to identify some of the words which occur over and over. Certainly the motivation of reading to their peers has helped some of the children to become more interested in reading and in words. They also are becoming exposed to a variety of book types. Anthony always brings a science book to class so the children are learning about all sorts of real things in an expository format, and not just listening to stories.

Field Trips There was a flood of stories to be dictated and typed for the children after our field trip to the fire station this month. *Now* everyone wants to be a fire fighter! They tell gory stories to be written down about how brave fire fighters save helpless women and little babies—the influence of television, I think, for the Fire Chief certainly did nothing that would have aroused such stories.

Our second trip, a visit to a restaurant, couldn't compare with the excitement of the trip to the fire station. The children were fascinated with the huge appliances in the kitchen, and informed the chef that they, too, were cooks. He asked them what they could cook and they proceeded to catalogue our entire year of cooking for him, complete with the description of the mess we had with the cranberry-orange relish!

SSR SQUIRT, too, continues to roll along smoothly. We are up to three minutes of reading time, now. We will hold at that level for a while since Butch and Mort are at the upper limit of their ability to sit still. Larry and Danielle, however, continue to read after the class time is up. They both are reading almost a book a day. Danielle's father told me that he thinks Danielle is such a good reader because she was in the hospital for so long after the car accident in which she was hurt and her mother was killed. Her father, the nurses, and all her visitors read constantly to her, and had her try to guess about story events, and sat beside her so that she could always see the words as they were reading.

I am still having problems with Alexander. He often removes his hearing aid so that he can get out of work by claiming he doesn't know what to do! And of all the children, he is one of the most in need of the language activities we do. He still doesn't talk in sentences; mostly he grunts and points. I suspect he can understand more than he appears to because his mother told me that they communicate this way at home often. He points and she fetches! He is really getting to be a pill! He is so low in language because he missed so many important concepts since his hearing loss wasn't discovered until two years ago! He really has the language development of a three-year-old child. Even Paul may be **Visual** ahead in this area!

Visual Discrimination I've been working hard, also, on ingredients four and five: learning the language of print and helping children discriminate auditorily and visually between words. They really have become quite good at matching letters to one another and at being able to tell which letters are different in a row of letters. Now I will put up four words on the chalk tray and they have to locate the different one and group the three which are alike to one side. I also will write selected words from our language experience charts on cards and put these cards in the chalk tray. Putting my hand underneath the word *snail* on the chart, I will say, "Carl, this word is *snail*. Can you find another word that says *snail* in the chalk tray? If you can, bring it here and we'll check it letter for letter." Carl, finding the word, brings it to the chart and we check first by counting how many letters are in the card he has brought and comparing that to the number of letters in the word on the chart. Next I have him check to see if the first letter looks like the first letter of the chart word; then we check the second letter, and so on. If each letter matches the letters on the chart word and all are in the same order, ta da, a match! Hooray for Carl!

Sometimes, after I write a language experience chart, I tell the children that I am going to cover up the chart with another sheet of paper and we're going to play the "How Many Words?" game. I peek at the first sentence so that I can say it aloud to the children. As I read it to them, they are to clap with each word I say so that they can tell me how many words are in a sentence. They tell me the number (or numbers!) and I remove the paper covering so that we can count the number of words. Then I clap with them so that they have a model for what we are doing, and we do another sentence on the chart the same way.

Metalinguistic Awareness

I have also been doing a lot with listening to tell if two words are the same or different. Earlier in the year I only used two words that were very different to help them get the idea of same and different. For example, back in the fall, I would say, "Listen and tell me if I am saying the same word or if I am saying two different words." Then I would use pairs like *Hilda Hilda, Carl Anthony, story chair*, and *door lights*. With such dissimilar word choices for the "different" category, the children quickly advanced so that I could use words which were different but which began or ended with the same letter. That has been tougher. Rhyming words seem particularly hard for them to label as different. So that is what we are working on right now. I will say, "Listen to these words and tell me if they are the same or different: *chair pear, juice juice, cook look, cup cup, paste paste, dot hot, cream dream, fix mix*." If we keep plugging away, I guess they will all eventually get it. Some, of course, understand well the learnings just described. By working with small groups, I can adjust my instruction accordingly.

Auditory Discrimination

I was reading recently about allowing children to have notebooks from the first day of kindergarten and first grade. There are lots of articles available now on "invented spelling." The idea is that by allowing

Writing

children to have their own writing utensils and paper from an early age we encourage them to view writing and reading as important activities, and that children will practice both reading and writing so that they get better at it. Another major point that was made was that children know a lot more about words and letters than most adults realize. By letting them do a lot of writing, we allow them to explore letters and words as we focus on what they can do. If, for example, a child writes:

Midg nm Sm —"My dog's name is Sam"—

we can tell that child knows, among other things, that letters go from left to right when words are made, that many sounds have been matched with their letter forms, that letters are grouped to make words, and that there is an understanding that words are written so that others can read them. Clearly there are many things still to learn; however, it is easier to teach from a base of what is known and introduce the new information.

Language Experience

Jeff burned himself during a cooking adventure the other day, so I took him over to the plant shelf, broke off a piece of a leaf, and rubbed the cut end of the leaf over the burned area. Immediately a crowd grew around the scene, fascinated children observing that the juice of the plant had made the burn feel better. "What is that?" "How did you know to do that, Miss Launch?" "Wow! Magic!"

Ah, ha! The teachable moment my college teachers were always talking about! "Let's sit down and do a chart about this plant," I suggested. "Plants are really wonderful things. Not only do they look nice in our room, but some of them can be used for food, some for medicine, and some to make clothes and houses. What are some questions you have about this plant?" For the next five minutes they asked questions and I wrote those questions on the chart.

Some of their questions were related to the name and characteristics of the plant (color, size, etc.), some dealt with the care of the plant, and some of their questions were concerned with how new plants were grown. After all their questions were on the chart, I cut them apart and we grouped them according to the type of question they had. Based on this grouping, I sent Danielle, Paul, and Horace to the library to bring back books on plants. I sent a note with them to Miss Page, the librarian, telling her we were trying to get information about the aloe plant. With books before us, we came up with the following chart about aloe plants.

The Aloe Plant

Our plant's name is "aloe vera." (Anthony)
Aloe vera means "true aloe" because there are more than one kind of aloe. (Larry)

Aloe vera is a succulent because it has fat leaves and likes water. (Danielle)

It can grow one or two feet. (Paul)

It is all green. (Chip)

It likes lots of light. (Carl)

You can make new plants by planting the baby shoots called suckers. (Steve)

Aloe is special because it can help the burn places on you. (Jeff)

I was impressed with how much they really got into the aloe plant. Now they keep asking me if the other plants we have are special in any way. We may be making our own book about our classroom plants.

Another really successful cooking experience was tied to one of the **Cooking** many books I read to the children each week. I had brought in several versions of the old story, "Stone Soup", and we compared how the stories were alike and how they were different. After those discussions, I told them that we were going to make some stone soup in the slow cooker. Their reactions ranged from Butch's "Yuk!" to Hilda's "How fascinating!" Everyone was told to bring in a vegetable, any vegetable, the next day.

"But what do we need, Miss Launch? How can we cook if we don't know what we need?" asked a worried Betty.

"Well, in the book they didn't have a recipe. They just put in whatever was brought to them." That, clearly, was not very satisfying to Betty.

The next day most of the children had remembered to bring in a vegetable and Daisy brought a loaf of Italian bread! Oh, well, it should go well with the soup! Next we went out to the playground and each person was to find one small stone that we could put in the soup. Alex was appalled! "But they're dirty. People have been walking on them and I even saw Mort and Butch spitting on the rocks!" "Yuk, too," I thought, though I dared not show it! "We will carefully wash each rock in hot, soapy water so that they are nice and clean for the soup," I told him.

And wash we did. The rocks were then placed in the bottom of the slow cooker and I added 12 cups of water and 12 beef bouillon cubes. Joyce's job was to turn the cooker to low heat.

We began role playing the story with three children pretending to wonder what else they could put in the soup and how good it would be if only there were a carrot or two. We went through each of the vegetables the class had brought in this way. Whoever had brought the vegetable had to wash it and cut it into pieces to put it into the soup. I helped cut off the tops and bad places, but the children did most of the work. When all the veggies had been added, we put on the lid of the slow cooker and left it until nearly time to go home. Daphne gave it a stir with a big wooden spoon and put the lid on one more time. I took it home with me to continue cooking and brought it back for snack time. Needless to say, the soup was pretty good, much to Alex's amazement. Daisy's bread was just the right touch and all of the children plan to make stone soup at home with their mothers' help.

February

Following Directions

This month I began to have the children follow "written" directions. The written directions consist of a series of pictures which show the children each step to take in finishing a figure. They particularly enjoyed the one shown here.

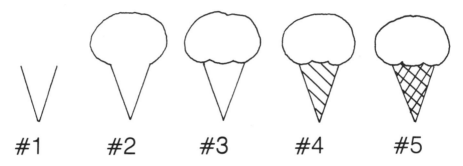

I begin the exercise by handing out paper with an oblique line already drawn so that they know what size to make their drawing. My instructions are given from the chalkboard, where I draw a similar kind of picture in various stages. I ask them what to do to make the picture on the board look like drawing #1. What do we do to make it look like drawing #2? And so on, until we have a completed picture. Some of the more mature children like to create their own sequences for their friends to do.

Comprehension Pictures

This month, too, I have been trying a technique that John Warren Stewig suggested using when I attended an International Reading Association meeting at which he spoke. He suggested using different artists' interpretations of the same subject and asking children to go through the following three-step sequence. First, ask them to describe the object being viewed in clear, concrete terms. Next, have them compare and contrast objects being viewed. Last, they are to value one of the objects, explaining why they prefer one interpretation over another. I used the three books, *One Fine Day* (Hogrogian, 1971), *Mushroom in the Rain* (Ginsburg, 1974), and *In the Rabbitgarden* (Lionni, 1975). Each of these has an illustration of a fox. I held up one at a time and allowed the children time to describe what they saw. I tried to elicit clear, concise statements that showed thought, observation, and conclusion. I asked them to tell me how all three foxes were alike. Typically they said that all had four legs, a nose, a mouth, and so on. Then we got into contrasting elements which brought on comments about size, color, and ferocity. In the valuing step, I asked them to tell me specifically what kinds of things made them prefer one of the foxes. Then I asked which one seemed to be the most gentle or the most fierce.

Stewig says that the same thing can be done by using varied interpretations of the same story so that children can see the various ways in which different artists deal with *The Three Pigs*, for instance. We have been doing this twice a week for three weeks now, and I plan to continue that schedule for the remainder of the school year. One thing that I have noticed lately, though, is that whenever I am reading a story that has a character similar to one of those in Stewig's visual//verbal literacy lessons, the children will comment. Mandy recently said, "Look at that snake [in *Why Mosquitoes Buzz in People's Ears*! (Aardema, 1975)] I don't like him as much as the one in *In the Rabbitgarden*. Doesn't he look scary and mean, Rita?" The children agreed that they much preferred the gentle snake of *In the Rabbitgarden*. Some stated that the snake in *Crictor* (Ungerer, 1958) was their favorite because he could come to school!

Our poetry writing is coming along so well! I read Mary O'Neill's **Poetry** *Hailstones and Halibut Bones* (1961) to the children and discussed with them that Miss O'Neill thought colors could represent things and feelings, as well as thoughts. Then we did a poetry format (again as a group) that has this configuration:

> I feel _____
> I see _____
> I hear _____
> I smell _____
> I taste _____
> I feel _____

The unifying factor here is the repetition of the phrase "I feel." To help the children recognize the five senses the poem deals with, I told them that I would give them several days to work on a collage of pictures from magazines, newspapers, and other sources that portray the five senses. They were to find as many pictures as they could that would finish the phrases I listed. It was a messy assignment, but the children helped to create several poems and collages. In addition the children were proud because the collages described *them* as individuals. I had the children work individually on this project, so I did have to help out some of the more unsure children such as Paul and Chip. Paul struggled—with my help—to find one example for each phrase; Chip kept asking the others to save any pictures of peanuts that they found for him—he wanted to finish each phrase the same way! When some of the children wondered if they could finish the phrase with just one word or a picture, I told them that they could. Others complained that they couldn't do that—they needed to say more! I told them that the only rule was that they finished the phrases, no matter how many words they used.

Writing   The writing notebooks are, all in all, rather successful. Each child has a notebook and I ask them each to write in their notebooks for a while during their work time. Some of the children merely draw, but even Paul has gotten to the point where he will, if I remind him, go to one of the bulletin boards and copy down words he sees there. There is no spacing between words, he hasn't a clue what he is writing, and he frequently leaves out letters from the words he is copying. Hilda, on the other hand, has become so intrigued with her notebook that I have trouble getting her to work in the math center or go to recess! She carries it everywhere. She is attempting to write about the people around her, and is learning more about letters and words with each page she fills!

Last month's interest in the plants did indeed result in a book we made for the classroom and the school library about the plants we have. Steve, who has a remarkable eye for drawing nature objects, did the illustrations. Actually, he did the outlines in pencil and then he asked certain students to do the coloring in. We made one book for our room and another for the library, since Miss Page had been so helpful when we requested information. That interest in a book on our plants caused Mitch to suggest that we make a book about the animals we have in our room. We went through the same process: what are the questions we have about our animals and how can we categorize those questions?

I suggested that the first page in our book ought to be about how the animals are alike and how they are different. That way, I told them, we help people get ready to pay attention to what we want them to know. I also suggested that I work with small groups of children, one group for each animal, and one group to do the page where we compare the animals. They were agreeable, naturally, so I assigned children to groups and then pulled a piece of paper out of a box with the name of the section each group would work on. Here are the groups:

Guinea Pig	*Guppies*	*Turtle*
Alex	Betty	Alexander
Butch	Daisy	Joyce
Anthony	Hilda	Horace
Danielle	Manuel	Pat
Rita	Mort	Steve

Snail	*Introduction*
Carl	Chip
Jeff	Daphne
Larry	Mandy
Mike	Mitch
Paul	Roberta

It took most of the month to meet with each group, look at and read reference materials, and to make notes about what the children observed about the animals. When I told Mr. Topps that we were working on a massive project, he offered to have Mrs. Mainstay type the final book copy with the primary typewriter! He suggested, too, that this time we type the book on dittoes so that we could make enough copies for all the children to take home. Terrific! Here is what the introduction finally looked like:

The Animals in Our Room

We have many animals in our room. It is to hard to count them all because the guppies won't hold still. Besides, they keep having babies. We have four kinds of animals. We have two guinea pigs, one turtle, fourteen snails, and a lot of guppies.

Guppies are the littlest animal we have except for some of the baby snails. The next biggest animals are the snails. Our turtle is the next biggest animal, but he is much smaller than our guinea pigs.

Some of our animals have legs and some do not. Some of our animals have fur. Some of our animals have shells. Some of our animals have scaly bodies.

All of our animals need air, just like us. But the guppies and snails get their air from the water! The guinea pigs would die if they tried to breathe in the water.

All of the animals have to eat food, but their food is real different. People could not eat guppy food and guppies might get sick if they ate people food. Guinea pigs like vegetables even more than we do!

If you like to read about animals, you will like this book. It tells about all of our animals.

By: Chip, Daphne, Mandy,
Mitch, and Roberta

I went back to *The Taming of the C.A.N.D.Y. Monster* for this recipe: **Cooking**

Whole Wheat Pretzels

Ingredients:

2 one-pound loaves of frozen whole wheat bread dough
boiling water
1 egg
1 teaspoon water
salt shaker
shortening

Utensils:

cookie sheets

small bowl
pastry brush
shallow pan for boiling water

Preparation:

1. Thaw the frozen bread dough in the refrigerator
2. Let two people divide the dough into pieces
3. Each loaf should be made into 14 pieces
4. Each person gets 1 piece of dough
5. Roll your piece of dough into a long rope the size of the paper on the counter (8 inches)
6. Five people need to grease 5 cookie sheets
7. Make your rope into the letter your name starts with
8. Put your letter on a cookie sheet
9. Let the letters sit for 20 minutes
10. Mix up the egg with 1 teaspoon water
11. After the letters sit for 20 minutes, brush on the egg and water
12. Sprinkle the letters with salt
13. Put the pan of boiling water on the bottom rack
14. Turn the oven on to 350°
15. Put the cookie sheets in the oven and bake for 20 minutes
16. Let them cool before you eat them

March

I started this month with a game that the children really enjoyed. An odd thing has been happening to me recently. I noticed that I don't even look at my seven readiness ingredients in the front of my plan book anymore. It has become so automatic to think of everything we do in terms of those seven that I was well into the preparation of the cards for this game when it suddenly occurred to me that this simple game was facilitating some of my seven ingredients. In fact, all around me are opportunities to exploit learning! Back to the game, however.

I told the children that we would be playing a game that might take all morning to finish, but that it didn't matter because they could play the game while they worked.

Concept Development

Surprise, surprise! Each child was going to have the picture of an animal pinned on his or her back, and they were to guess the animal. They could ask only two questions of each classmate, and the questions could only be answered yes or no. The purpose of this restriction was to encourage a maximum use of language on the part of the one guessing, and to discourage unnecessary hints and clues. The children seemed very excited by the idea and were ready to begin immediately! I reminded them that they were to continue their work while trying to guess, and that it would be a good idea to think carefully before asking questions so that the questions wouldn't be wasted. I gave the following demonstration: "Mandy, will you please pin the picture of an animal to my back?" She did so, and I turned so that my back—and the picture—were toward the children. There was much giggling from some of the children.

"Okay. Steve, do I have hair? No? Hmmmm. Steve, do I have six legs? No? Thank you. Let's see now—Rita, do I have wings? No. All right, do I have scales? Ah, ha! Now we're getting some place. Mandy, do people catch me to eat? No, that means that I'm not a fish. Do I crawl? I thought I might. Horace, am I a snake?"

The children were amazed that I guessed the animal so quickly. I explained that animals are in groups and that I was trying to find which group my animal was in. One large group that includes bears, cats, dogs, beavers, and people was the one I was asking about first—they all have fur or hair. When I knew that the animal didn't have fur or hair, I knew that it had to be an insect or an amphibian (living both on land and in water) or a bird or a reptile (an animal with scales). "Listen carefully" was my last injunction before pinning on the animals. And the game was on! Larry, Hilda, Roberta, and Steve guessed theirs rather quickly, for they had paid attention to what was told to them and tried logically to figure out what to ask next. Daisy used up all her questions by running from person to person asking questions like, "Am I a deer? Am I a goat?" rather than trying to find the category and proceed logically. It took most of the children the entire morning to determine what they were. Paul managed to find out that he was a dog, though his guess was based on luck, rather than system. Mitch never figured his out because he kept trying to start arguments with those who answered his questions. He wanted so much to own a horse that he was convinced that a horse must be the animal pictured on his back. Whenever the children would give him an answer that didn't fit his mind-set, he would argue with them, insisting that they must be wrong! Carl guessed "deer" fairly early, partially, I think, because he likes deer so much. And so it went—an interesting exercise for the children. They've already asked to play it again soon.

So many things are going on with this particular activity. Children are engaging in an identifying-sorting-classifying game which helps to develop further their understanding of animals and animal characteristics. They are developing logical thinking processes as they work on this background information. I think I'll do this again next week with forms of transportation or foods.

The children have been working all year on matching uppercase letters to uppercase letters, and recently they have been matching lowercase letters to lowercase letters. At last we're ready to begin matching upper- and lowercase letters. One of my tricks is to tell them that while they were outside an elf came in and mixed up all those nice letters we **Letter Names** had been playing with—could anyone help us to get them straightened out again? Of course, there are always several volunteers! We concentrate on three pairs at a time, which is a workable number for them. Also, I always begin with those upper- and lowercase letters which tend to resemble one another except for size (such as *Ss*) to further insure success.

I also play a game of "Memory" with the letters that we are currently working on. I shuffle the six letter-cards and place them face down in a two-by-three array. The children take turns selecting two of the letter cards to be revealed. They are then turned over. If they match, they keep the cards. If they do not match, the cards are turned back over to be chosen at a later time by someone who can remember the position of the letters.

Another game for group work after all of the upper- and lowercase letters have been studied is a game like "Go Fish." We have two different groups of cards, one each for upper- and lowercase. The cards are shuffled together, and three cards are dealt to each player. If the player has a match of letter forms, the cards are put on the table. After everyone is given a chance to do this, the player to the left of the dealer asks another player if he or she has a particular letter. If the answer is yes, the card must be relinquished. The player continues to ask for cards until he is told to "Go Fish" by a player who doesn't have the card asked for. The first player then picks a card from the remainder of the deck which has been placed in the center of the playing area. The first player to have all his or her cards matched and on the table is the winner.

An individual activity for matching is played with the bottom of an old ditto master box. All 26 letters of the alphabet, uppercase form, are written on the bottom of the box. The lowercase forms are on separate cards which can be placed over the uppercase forms. In the lid of the box is the answer key showing which forms match, so that children can check their own work and correct errors immediately.

Diagnosing Letter Name Knowledge I have begun to check letter name knowledge with the children, too. I have been calling them to me one at a time and showing letter cards with both the upper- and lowercase on the same card and asking the children to name the letter. I use a system of putting the known and the unknown in separate piles. Later, then, I write down on that child's card which letters he or she still doesn't know so that I can begin direct instruction. Up to this point, the letter names that the children have learned have been through exposure to lists of their classmates names, letters and words they have matched on the chart stories, and writing in their notebooks. Eleven of the alphabet letters were easily learned by most of the children just because those letters begin the names of the 25 children. Paul is the only child who knows only two letters: *P* and *C* (for Paul and Carl). Larry, Danielle, Pat, Roberta, Hilda, Joyce, and Mandy can name all the letters. Rita, Betty, Horace, Alex, Steve, and Anthony know most of the letter names with the exception of the weird ones like *Q, U, V, X, Y,* and *Z* which occur infrequently (at least in the words we have been using). The other children are at varying points in the number of letters they can name.

I used to begin in September to teach the names of the letters to the kindergarteners in my class. Boy, what a frustrating experience both for them and for me! Trying to associate the names of the letters with those funny shaped symbols that could be called different things depending on how they were turned (*b, d, p,* and *q*) drove them and me buggy! When I tried to make it easy on myself by teaching everybody every letter, starting with *Aa*, many of the children were terrifically bored and an equal number just couldn't quite get it. I began to notice that on their own many children would go to one of the labels on objects in the room or to the list of children's names and ask someone what the name of the letter was. It occurred to me that such opportunities could be expanded and encouraged without actually trying to teach the names of letters until later in the year. I find that by starting now to assess where the children are in letter name knowledge, I still have plenty of time to teach the names of the letters to those who can learn them. Even if I began teaching them systematically to Paul in September, I cannot imagine that he would be further ahead in the number known. I am convinced that by now he would have a real sense of failure because of his inability to learn the letters, had I taught them. As it is, now he doesn't know them all, but at least he is receptive to learning them. Some kindergarten teachers may not even bother teaching letter names, but I think it will help them to have some idea of what their first-grade teacher is talking about when she spells a word for them! Letter name knowledge may not cause children to be better readers, but knowing the names is a characteristic of good readers.

Anthony's mother has been riding me all year about making sure that I am teaching the children all they need to know to go into first grade. She and I have had a few points of departure this year in our assessments of his abilities. He is her brilliant, only child and she wants to make certain that he will be ready to attend M.I.T. when the time comes! I showed her my seven reading ingredients which are critical prereading factors. She, not accepting this, has been taking books home from the school she teaches in for him to read with her. No wonder he is so intractable some mornings. She has told me that they have one hour of reading every night, and that she has been having him copy the words he doesn't know over and over. I told her that he had many opportunities and materials to explore and read at school. However, since he is so focussed on science she feels that we are not providing enough science stuff here. I haven't been able to budge her or she me. Oh, well!

Things are not going badly at all. SQUIRT is up to four minutes and **SSR** the children are still writing in their notebooks. Some of the children have been going through the collection of recipes we have made this year and have been copying those recipes into their notebooks. Other students have been working on stories about events in their lives. Steve and Anthony have been trying some science experiments and writing down what they do and how it turns out (I am unable to read most of it, but they generously share what their markings mean).

Volunteer Help

The third graders from Mrs. Wise's class have been writing books for the children as well as coming down to take dictation so that the kindergarteners can get *their* stories into print as well. The third graders have been studying book binding and have made some very handsome books for the children to take home or to put in our classroom library. To thank them for all their help, we invited them to come help us eat the results of another of our cooking experiences from Lansky's book.

Cooking

Peanut Butter Cookies

Ingredients:

4 egg whites
1⅓ cups honey
3 cups peanut butter
1 cup toasted wheat germ
grease for cookie sheets and measuring cup

Utensils:

fork
spoon
cookie sheets
bowl
measuring cups

Preparation:

1. Turn oven to 325°
2. Mix up the egg whites
3. Mix in the honey and stir up good
4. Grease the measuring cup and spoon peanut butter in to the top
5. Put the peanut butter into the bowl and mix it in
6. Do steps 4 and 5 until all 3 cups of peanut butter are in the bowl
7. Mix in the wheat germ real good
8. Put the cookie dough on the baking sheets a teaspoon at a time
9. Mash each cookie down a little bit with the fork
10. Bake in the oven for 8 minutes

Needless to say we bought our peanut butter. Do you know how long it takes to *make* three cups of peanut butter???

April

Spring, Spring, Spring!!! I love it. We've been outside a lot lately which **Rhyming** has been good for the children as well as for me. We do some of our work **Words** out there when we can, such as our lesson with rhyming words for which I use one of my favorite books, *The Hungry Thing* (Slepian, 1971). The children in the book meet the Hungry Thing and find that he will only eat silly rhymes for real words, so that if they want to feed him "noodles," they tell him he is eating "foodles"; "soup with a cracker" is "boop with a smacker," and so on. As we read the story, the children try to guess what the Hungry Thing is eating througout the book. When we finish the book I tell them it is our turn to feed the Hungry Thing. I tell them to think of their favorite food and then to try to find a silly rhyme for it so that the Hungry Thing will eat it. It's fun to play with words, and if children realize that when they are small, I think they will be more likely to enjoy words as they grow up.

The poetry we composed this month used an "I wish" format. I told **Poetry** the children that they were to think of four different things they wished for. The poem was to have lines beginning with the words "I wish," but the first and the last lines were to be identical. Here is the large-group poem that we did before breaking up into small groups for more poetry writing using this format.

> I wish spring was here. (Steve)
> I wish that the sun was warm. (Manuel)
> I wish that the frogs would make noises. (Butch)
> I wish I could go out without my coat. (Alex)
> I wish spring was here. (Steve)

The children have been creating greeting cards all year long, but **Writing** some of the birthday cards for Jeff were just too much! Someone got the notion that even if he couldn't give Jeff a present, he could *wish* to give him a present. I don't know who began it, but I was swamped with requests like "Please write, 'I wish I could give you this for your birthday!'" In walking around later, I noticed that they were cutting pictures out of our catalogs and magazines. The picture of a bike, swimming pool, motorcycle, or some other luxury would appear at the bottom of the written message, which was then passed over to Jeff for his birthday. Jeff was grinning from ear to ear all day long!

Each of these activities has children using whole words, but I find that they are increasing in their ability to name the letters and are becoming quite proficient with rhyming games. All around the four walls of the classroom I have put charts, one for each letter of the alphabet. The chart (huge) has upper- and lowercase forms of the letter, a picture on the consonant letter charts, and the names of various children and classroom pets where they are appropriate. I decided not to put pictures up on the charts for the vowels since the vowel sounds are so variable and I would need so many for each chart. Occasionally I will put up some highly interesting word (such as *marshmallow*) from our language experience stories.

Also I am still trying to help the children develop their reasoning and questioning abilities by such things as the "feely" box. I have constructed the feely box by cutting a hole in one end of a shoebox and attaching to the hole a sock with the toe end cut off. I placed a comb in the box and permitted the children to reach in through the sock and into the box where they could feel the object but not see it. Each child was permitted a few seconds to feel the object and then report what the object might be. I changed the objects frequently so that the children would have many opportunities to use the sense of touch. The next project was somewhat harder for the children, for I had arranged the experiences in order of difficulty. This time a single child would feel the object, describe it in three different ways, and then guess what it was. The third kind of experience was to let a child see an object, describe it to the other children, and let *them* guess what was being described. The fourth task was even more complicated, for this time the child felt an object, described it to the other children, and they had to guess what it was that he or she had felt. Occasionally, as a variation, I would let several children feel the same object so that they could help one another with the description. The rest of the group had to try to guess what it was that was being felt. This worked out very well, particularly when Paul, Chip, or Joyce, who have a great deal of difficulty verbalizing, described the object. However, it is obviously easier for the group if the clues given are clearly stated, a skill these three were unable to demonstrate yet.

The three gained from listening to the descriptions given by the more verbal children, however, for they experienced the same object and could compare their own perceptions with what was being said. The fifth task with the feely box was to have a child feel an object and then give a one-word clue, and so on. A particularly interesting game was one that took place this week. Steve reached into the box and felt the object. He said, "Prickly." There were guesses of *porcupine, cactus*, and *pins*. The next clue was, "Woody." The children were stumped for a moment, until Larry guessed that it might be a plank from the workshop. The next clue: "Tree." Something from a tree that is wooden and prickly?

"Oh, I know, I know!" exclaimed Hilda, who had been putting all the clues together. "It's bark from the tree!" She sat back smug and confident.

"No, that's not it. 'Seeds'."

The crestfallen Hilda began muttering, "Seeds? Seeds. Seeds! It's a pine cone! Am I right this time, Steve?" Steve's nod reassured her that her deduction skills had been well utilized.

The most difficult of all was the last project—identifying the object within a wrapped box by asking questions of me. They found this to be a very challenging task. They knew that it could not be a chair, for instance, for the package would not accommodate that large an object. The questioning techniques of the children had increased with the readiness activities which they had been doing for the few weeks prior to this exercise, and they soon guessed that the object was a shoe. I got the idea for this project from one of the other kindergarten teachers at a recent meeting. The teacher said she had presented a wrapped package to the children for them to determine the contents. The task was too difficult for them because they had not had exercises leading up to this game. As a result, the children were unable to figure out what was in the box, the teacher was frustrated and embarrassed, and she had tried to figure out what had gone wrong. She concluded that the activity was incomplete and useless until she set up the other activities.

We had a lot of fun "constructing" this recipe. The cheese filling recipe is adapted from *The Taming of the C.A.N.D.Y. Monster*. The children and I named it together after we had completed our sandwiches.

Cooking

Apple-Cheese Pinwheels

Ingredients:

1 slice whole wheat bread per person
4 apples (cored and sliced in halves)
4 tablespoons margarine
3 pounds American cheese
4 egg yolks
2 cans evaporated milk (13-ounce size)
2 tablespoons flour

Utensils:

cup
table knife
rolling pin
graters
whisk
wooden spoon
double boiler
hot plate
can opener

Preparation:

1. Put water in the bottom of the double boiler and put on the hot plate
2. Turn the hot plate on medium
3. Grate the cheese with the grater but watch your fingers
4. Put the egg yolks in a cup and mix them up
5. Put the top pan on the double boiler and put in the butter

6. When the butter is almost melted put in the cheese
7. Keep stirring while the cheese is melting
8. When the cheese and butter are melted, slowly add the egg yolks and mix them in good
9. Add the milk and the flour and stir in good
10. Keep cooking until it gets thick then turn off hot plate
11. Cut all 4 crusts off your bread
12. Use the rolling pin and make your bread real skinny
13. Spread the cheese mix on your bread
14. Grate a little bit of apple all over the cheese
15. Start at one side and roll your bread up into a pinwheel

Boy, did they learn a lot while making this recipe. And they are so much better at following directions and measuring and stirring carefully. Dare I try a whole meal next month?

May

Field Trips   We had two really nice field trips this month. The trips were preceded, as usual, with a listing of words they could think of that were associated with the location. We also generated questions for the inevitable question period guides always have. Afterward, we did a whole-group language experience lesson and some children dictated or wrote individual remembrances. Same old stuff we always do prior to and following these trips, but such activities are crucial to concept development.

The first was a day trip to the zoo with the children from both kindergarten sessions, as well as many parents. They took sack lunches. Everyone returned exhausted but exhilarated (and only a few of the children got sick on the bus).

For the last field trip—I asked the two first-grade teachers if they would permit our children to visit their rooms to acquaint them with the teachers and also to give them some idea of what they could expect to see in first grade. Both teachers agreed, and gave the children a fine overview of the first-grade program. Mrs. Wright had one of her students act as guide around the room, and she had others who explained the various things that they were working on. The kindergarteners were quite impressed with the "big" first-graders who were so helpful to them, and all of them said that they wanted to be in Mrs. Wright's room next year.

After the children had finished their tour, I asked them how they would feel about doing something similar for the kindergarten class who would be arriving next fall.

"You mean you're going to have *more* kids here? I thought you just taught us," said Daphne.

"Now you know that there is an afternoon class, too, Daphne. You know that I teach other children."

"Yes, but we thought . . . I thought . . . I mean . . ."

"I will remember all of you. You don't have to worry about that. We care about one another, and when we care about people, we don't forget them. But you can't stay with me forever. You are ready to go on and learn more. You don't want to do the same things again. First grade is so exciting! You'll love it, but remember to say 'hello' to me once in a while! But, you still haven't answered. Shall we do something for the next kindergarten class like what the first graders did?" Amid cries of "Yes! Yes!" there was one, Larry, who commented that that would be difficult, since we didn't know who the children would be.

"How about this?" I began, and outlined the plan for creating a mu- **Routines** ral depicting the various kindergarten activities. The children would put it up on the bulletin board and leave it there. When the fall classes came in they would see some work done by "big" kindergarteners telling them what to expect. The children loved the idea, and so did I. One of my pet peeves has always been that I begin the school year without any art work from children on the walls—now there will be.

SQUIRT has been highly successful this year. We're up to five min- **SSR** utes a day as a class. However, some children continue reading after the timer rings. Mandy told me that she enjoys the idea of everyone reading at the same time.

I did decide to risk making a meal at school and it actually came off **Cooking** well! I had considered an early lunch for them to prepare, but I decided after one of our book sessions that nothing would do but to fix breakfast. The impetus for this decision, as you might have guessed, was Dr. Seuss' *Green Eggs and Ham* (1960)! The room was set up in stations for the big event. There was the measuring and mixing area, the scrambled eggs area, the toast area, the juice and milk area, and the clean-up area. Five children were in each of the areas, with clearly defined responsibilities.

The scrambled egg recipe was quite easy, although it did involve some high-level counting skills. For each person to be served, they measured and mixed: 1 egg, 1 tbsp. milk, and 2 tsp. diced ham. When it was all mixed together, they added the special ingredient: ½ tsp. blue food coloring! (We had quite a discussion about what color we should add to the yellow eggs.) The eggs were cooked in three electric skillets at the scrambled eggs area. Many cries of "Yuk!" and "Gross!" were heard and brought others to the scrambled eggs area to exclaim anew at the mess they saw before them.

Meanwhile, the people in "juice and milk" were pouring out servings into paper cups and the people in "toast" were making four slices at a time. After the toast came out of the appliance, they used a plastic glass and pressed the top into the slice of toast, cutting out a circle. They made two heaps of toast: circles and slices with holes. The clean-up people, who would not have anything to do until after the breakfast was over, came to the toast area and placed one circle and one slice on each one of the paper plates. They carried the plates to "scrambled eggs" where a spoonful of green eggs and ham was put into the hole of the bread slice. They got their beverages and then their plates, and we all ate heartily! I didn't think Chip would ever stop eating, and I was sure that Daisy wouldn't, though she informed us that she had a huge breakfast before arriving at school! Even Mort seemed to show a flicker of interest—I suppose because it was not our normal routine (he seems so bored by routine).

Readiness Ingredients

My routine, lately, has involved sorting out materials and tossing away some of the accumulation. In doing so, I came across my very tattered copy of the seven readiness ingredients. Before it was put in the pile of typing I wanted Mrs. Mainstay to do for me, I looked over the list yet again and thought back over all the activities I had been led to do using those seven factors as my guideline.

1. *Children must know what reading is for.* Children were exposed to so many different reasons for reading that I don't think a single one of them is leaving here without a fairly clear idea that we read to do, we read to learn, we read to perform, and we read to experience [see Chapter 8]. Messages were sent and received. Charts of stories and information were compiled. Books by the hundreds were encountered. Directions were followed from print. And on and on and on.

2. *Children need to develop an adequate background of information.* I tried to make sure that each and every field trip and other major happenings were accompanied by the production and reading of printed materials. We discussed the vocabulary and concepts represented by that vocabulary every time we had an experience [see pp. 76–80]. Children were encouraged to reason and ask questions about unfamiliar information.

3. *Children must expect what they hear and read to make sense.* I tried to get the children to anticipate and predict logically what might be happening next. Often, when I would read to them, I would ask, "What do you think is going to happen next?" before I would turn the page. When we used nonsense books, like *The Hungry Thing*, they were aware that we were playing with words, and that even there was some sense to what was going on.

4. *Children must understand the conventions and jargon of print.* Constantly I worked with the children in determining the differences among terms like *sentence, line, letter,* and *page.* I tried to point out individual words and phrases in the chart stories, making the return sweep with my hand to the next line of print. Though Paul does not yet have this down pat, I think that he is beginning to understand what we've been doing all year.

5. *Children must learn to auditorily and visually discriminate letters and words.* Obviously I structured many activities for the children in these two areas. However, I found that through constant exposure to printed materials, many of the children learned these skills sort of

serendipitously. I did help to expedite that learning by organizing words alphabetically and by letting them play with plastic letters and write in their writing notebooks.

6. *Children must have an interest and desire to learn to read.* If *nothing* else, I think this particular goal has been introduced and reinforced over and over. That does not necessarily mean that all of the children leaving here are paragons of accomplishment of this goal. Nevertheless, they leave me this year much more along this road than any other group I have taught.

7. *Children need experiences with both story and expository reading materials.* There is no doubt in my mind that I have done more with this factor than I have in previous years. Probably half of our experience charts were content related. We had lots of books from various disciplines because of the various interests of the children. Anthony and Steve kept us supplied with science materials. Daphne and Carl led us to many new story books. Joyce, Jeff, and Danielle alerted us to the literature by and for young Black Americans. Poetry and cookbooks came out our ears. And on it went.

However, now that I look over these capsule descriptions I can see how many things we did that I didn't even list in any of those areas. Not only that, but most of the activities, such as the writing notebooks, fulfilled several of my goals at the same time. I wonder if it is possible to delineate all of the learnings which occurred in this room this year, or is there such an interaction of children, needs, and ingredients that it would not be possible to construct two-dimensionally? I think I'll leave that one for contemplation at my beach retreat this summer!

THE CURRICULUM COMMITTEE

Miss Launch sat at the large, oval table, trying to restrain herself from tapping her pencil on the tabletop. She had been sitting at this table every week for the last three months. It did look as if the group were going to recommend that the school system purchase one of those reading readiness kits for each and every kindergarten classroom within the school system. Miss Launch had been very quiet during these meetings, feeling that as the newcomer she should allow those who had been with the school system longer to do most of the talking.

Reading Readiness Kits

As nearly as she could tell, the group of kindergarten teachers, all of those who taught in the school system, were divided into three general groups. Miss Launch felt sorry for Sue Port, the Curriculum Supervisor, who had to chair the meetings. She had always found Ms. Port very facilitative and helpful. But these meetings must surely be a strain on her good nature! The groups who were trying to come to some sort of consensus were those who favored purchasing the kits, those who wanted to be left alone to do their "own thing," and those who felt as she, Miss Launch, did about the seven reading ingredients.

"All right, people," interrupted Ms. Port, "let's try to get some consensus on this matter. Let me summarize what we have all agreed on!" There was general laughter around the room since they all knew that this would be a short summary!

"Our curriculum guide is 15 years old and though it has some good aspects to it, it seems that some of the information and guidelines are outdated. It also seems that the guide is better the longer you have taught! This indicates to us that the guide is not very helpful to beginning teachers since more experienced teachers have to fill in with materials and knowledge they already possess—not a problem for them, but it surely is to some others. The feeling among many of you is that you like the, shall we say, vagueness of the present guide since it allows a lot of freedom for individual teaching styles. But there is no choice, which is what I've been trying to get through to you these past many weeks; we are mandated by the school board to produce a new curriculum guide by the end of the summer. Frankly, I'm getting worried! I see three factions in this group. Let me outline them for you so that we can try to bring this together today.

"We have one group of teachers who would like us to purchase one or more of the reading readiness kits on the market. This group argues that the kits are complete with materials, teacher's guide, and objectives. I brought a few examples of kits today so that we could examine them more closely.

"Another group seems to want to develop a new curriculum guide which will be a kind of super teacher's manual and to meet through the summer over salad lunches to put together the materials you'll need for the first few weeks. We would then meet regularly during the school year to produce additional materials and to add to the teacher's manual based on the actual teaching done with it.

"The third group is inclined to forget the whole thing," she paused as laughter interrupted, "but knowing we can't, they would like us to add a couple of things to the old guide and then ignore it so that they can continue teaching as they have always done."

"Wow," thought Miss Launch, "she's not pulling any punches today!"

"That's not quite fair," spoke up the most vocal member of the third group. "We have been teaching for a long time and nobody seems to have complained about what we've been doing. Why change now just to be changing? I know for sure that I can do a better job with the children I teach than if you made me use one of those kits over there! Those kits don't contain all the aspects that I deal with in my program."

"You know, Willa," said Ms. Port, "you just might be able to pull off the greatest program in the world. However, much as I'd like to think it, this school system just is not filled with Willa Tichners. What about some of our less able teachers? What about some of our teachers who just got out of college? What about teachers like Miss Launch who came to this school system from another, very different one? Don't we owe those people a chance to share in your expertise?

"One problem we face is that we have to have some consistency within our school system so that kindergarten means essentially the same thing no matter where one goes. Why, even within the same school I've noted great differences, substantive differences, in the kindergarten program. Another fact to face is that the instruction in kindergarten should help to facilitate the child's beginning reading experiences, not hinder them. If we have some common goals toward which we are all working, then we should be facilitating beginning reading. Right now, we only hope we are. We have some ideas about specific teaching emphases based on our experiences with the spring kindergarten screening we do. However, I've always felt *that* information is somewhat suspect because the situation in which the children are assessed is so strange to them. They are taken into a big room, the cafeteria or gym, and meet with many different people to perform many different tasks. You all know how hard it is to get a five-year-old to perform on command! So we know if they can see or hear, but I wonder how much valid information we get on their academic knowledge such as knowing the letter names or knowing their colors.

"I'm open to suggestion as to where we go from here. Yes, Miss Launch, is that your hand I see snaking up?"

"Well, I've kept rather quiet through all of these discussions, but I wonder if I might be able to offer, just as a starting point, the guidelines I used to help me teach this year. Maybe we could look at the kits up there using these objectives, so that at least we would all be talking about the same things."

With Ms. Port's encouragement, Miss Launch put the seven readiness ingredients on the chalkboard in the room and then sat down and discussed each of them briefly. She noticed murmurs and nods of agreement among teachers from all three factions. No one could argue against any of them, since they did seem to be essential to beginning reading success. However, the discussion did turn lively when they began to examine the kits using the ingredients as guidelines!

"Hey, where are all the books? If we are to encourage children to read and listen to a variety of materials, and to immerse them in books so that they develop a desire to learn to read, then we're going to need more books than the five they have in this kit. Five books is an insult! Why put in any?"

"Look how flimsy all this stuff is! My kiddies would have these thin cardboard pictures destroyed in a week, even though they're pretty careful. And those puppets! Do you believe they are trying to pawn those off for classroom use? I give them three days!"

"Speaking of the pictures, just look at them closely. What's that a picture of? A dog? A beagle? A puppy? Pet? Stuffed animal? It's really hard to tell. The pictures are small and not very clear, too much distraction in them."

"Listen to this manual, you guys. This whole kit as well as the other two really hit phonics hard! These are not whole-language kits like their ads say; they're phonics stuff! And it's not even as good as the phonics materials I make on my own; this is too hard for my students and they need a lot more repetition than these kits provide for. It says here we can "add additional materials" from our own sources, if necessary! I thought this was supposed to be complete?"

These comments continued for some minutes as the teachers found that even with their aura of professionalism, the kits were not complete sets of materials which would make teaching a breeze for the school year, and more importantly, they didn't even come close to providing for all the learnings that adherence to Miss Launch's seven ingredients called for. Ultimately, it was clear to Ms. Port that the consensus had indeed been found. Though much discussion about the details of pulling off the new curriculum guide remained to be gone through, basically the teachers agreed that Miss Launch's seven ingredients should be the core of the new curriculum guide. They realized that they could produce their own kits of materials which would be much more complete than any they could purchase for the same money. The guide could contain lesson plans for trying to accomplish those objectives which did not lend themselves to kit production. And, they agreed, this compromise would allow all of the groups to feel that they had had an impact on the final new guide. The "kit people" would have their kits, the ones who wanted and needed the structure of a new curriculum guide would have their super teacher's manual, and the group who wanted to be allowed to do what they had always been doing would not be tied to doing any specific set of lessons (as they would have been with the kits) but could have a lot of freedom to develop lessons which would accomplish one or more of their seven goals.

Miss Launch and Ms. Port left the room together, the last of the group to trail out. "Thank you for your help today," said Ms. Port. "I think they see now that good learning and teaching can't be totally packaged nor can it exist without structure. That was the breakthrough today. You've left your mark on this school system. I'm glad you're one of us!"

Miss Launch waved to the departing back of the smiling Ms. Port, marveling at what she had just said. "Me? I left a mark? I'm just trying to teach some kids the best way I know how."

10 | Mrs. Wright

THE PARENT MEETING

Mrs. Wright sat in her first-grade classroom awaiting the arrival of the parents for their meeting. She remembered her first parent meeting and felt the same tightness in her stomach as she remembered that first night. One problem, of course, had been that although she was perfectly at home with groups of youngsters, she had been quite uncomfortable talking to adult audiences. The major problem was not knowing what to talk to them about! Mr. Topps had explained to her that the purpose of these beginning-of-school meetings was for each teacher to greet the parents and give them an overview of the program their children would be participating in during that year. He had gone on to say, "Of course, first-grade parents are always most curious about the reading program. They want to know how you are going to transform their little ones into bookworms!" Mr. Topps had then volunteered to be present at her session, but Mrs. Wright had declined. The only thing worse than trying to explain her reading program to parents was having to explain it when she herself didn't understand it! And the only thing worse than both of those would be to have the principal there as a witness to her ignorance!

The first parents began to arrive. "Oh, Mrs. Wright, it is so good to see you again. Do you remember me? I'm Pat's mother, and I was Kate's mother. Well, I mean I still am, but she's in the third grade now. She did so enjoy your class." Mrs. Wright realized that she had reminisced for 15 minutes and rose to greet the parents who were now streaming through the door.

"Welcome, parents, to first grade," Mrs. Wright began. "I have only had your children for a week now but I must say they are an exceptional group! I am sure we will have a busy, exciting year, and as the year goes on, I will want to talk with each of you about the progress of your children individually. Tonight, however, I would like to describe our first-grade reading program and respond to any questions you may have.

"If you will look around the room you will see some experience charts. These charts were dictated to me by your children and reflect the experiences we have had in this first week of school. This chart, titled

'George the Gerbil' is one we did on the first day of school. First, we sat very quietly and observed George for several minutes; then we talked about our observations. Finally, several of your children told me some things they had observed and I wrote them on the chart."

George the Gerbil

George lives all alone in his cage (Daphne)
George is brown and furry and cute. (Betty)
George is always on the go. (Roberta)
George likes to eat vegetables. (Manuel)
He looks a little like a miniature rabbit. (Horace)
Gerbils are rodents. (Larry)

Mrs. Wright turned to the second chart on the wall. "This chart was written today," she continued. "It outlines all the things we do in order to get lunch in the cafeteria. To make this chart, we first made a list on the board and then decided which we had to do first, second, and so on."

How to Get Lunch

1. Remember to bring your lunch money. (Betty)
2. Give your lunch money to the teacher. (Pat)
3. Line up and walk quietly through the halls. (Alex)
4. Go to the cafeteria. (Steve)
5. Wait in line again. Then pick up your napkin and fork. (Mike)
6. Get your tray off the stack. (Mandy)
7. Walk by and let the ladies put food in your tray. (Rita)
8. Pick up your milk. (Carl)
9. Go way over to the other side and sit down. (Hilda)
10. Eat your lunch. (Mitch)

"As you can see, I write the sentences just the way your children say them and put each child's name after the sentence. In this way, most children have an immediate initial success with reading. They can remember what they said and can find the sentence with their name after it. They can then 'read' that sentence.

"We will be using whole-class experience charts to record classroom events and for reading material all year. Starting next week, I will divide your children into four groups and do structured language experience lessons with them. These lessons are structured in that all the sentences in them begin with the same words. We will write a story entitled, 'Foods We Like to Eat,' in which all the sentences will start with, '*I like to eat . . . .*' The children will read these stories and will learn the important reading readiness abilities as they learn to read these repetitive stories. Be on the lookout next Thursday; your children will all be bringing home a book they can read.

"As the year goes on, your children will be dictating individual stories to me and to some fifth graders who will come and help record their dictations. In fact, if any of you could volunteer an occasional morning to help record their dictations, I would love to have your help. It is really quite simple and enjoyable. You just never know what will pop out of a first-grader's mouth, as I'm sure you are more aware than I! Don't worry about their revealing family skeletons. They sometimes do, but they spin wild tales of fantasy and your skeletons would be lost in the tall tales. I'll make a deal with you. I'll promise not to believe anything fantastic they tell me happens at home if you promise not to believe their tales of what's happening at school!

"Many of you may be thinking that although it might be a good idea to write stories, that shouldn't comprise the total reading program. 'How are they going to learn the words they must know?' and 'What about phonics?' are questions you must have. Well, you can be sure that I will be teaching sight words and phonics. If you look up here above the chalkboard, you will notice the names and pictures of six of your children. We will add six more each week until we have all your children's names and pictures up here. Then we will begin to add other words. This wall vocabulary is the primary method I use to make sure all children are learning the most common words as sight words. Each day, we have a "spelling test" on these words. Of course, all the children do well on this test since they can look right up here and then write down the word. But, as we gradually add words and then practice writing them correctly every day, your children will learn to immediately recognize each other's names and the words such as *and, the, of,* which occur over and over in reading and writing. Many of your children will learn to spell some of these words and almost all of them will learn them as sight words. **[Sight Words— Wall Vocabulary]**

"We will also use our wall vocabulary to begin to teach children phonics, or the letter-sound relationships. As you see, we have Mike and Mandy in here whose names both begin with the letter *m*. We also have several other children whose names begin with the letter *m*. Since the children will know the names which begin with *m*, *m* is probably the first letter-sound relationship we will learn [see pp. 48–53]. Don't be surprised if your children tell you that they ate marshmallows and learned to march, because food and actions are good ways to remember letter-sound relationships. **[Decoding]**

"In addition to making sure your children can associate particular letters with particular sounds, I will also do activities with them so that they learn to use these letter-sound relationships as they read. We will cover up words in sentences and guess, based on the other words, what the covered up word might be. We will then reveal the first letter and revise our guesses based on this additional clue [see pp. 53–54]. Many words can be correctly figured out just by thinking about how the word begins and what would make sense in that sentence. I will also help the children use the words they know to figure out words which rhyme with these known words. *Mike*, for example, will help us decode *bike*, *hike*, and *like* [see pp. 53–56].

"You will be able to tell how many words your children are learning by watching their word banks grow. Here is one left by a child who moved away unexpectedly last year and didn't take his with him. As you can see, he had quite a stack of words that he knew when he moved in February. These word banks contain known words from group and individual stories. Each child comes to that back table there and tells me his or her story. Sometimes the stories are thought up by the children, but more often, they are inspired by a picture, a display on the flannel board in the corner, or an activity going on in the room. As the child dictates the story to me, I type it. I then read the story aloud to make sure it is accurate. Then we talk about things like how many sentences a story has, which is the longest sentence, which is the longest word, why there is a period here and a question mark there. In this way, the children learn about the conventions of writing.

"Each child then goes back to his or her seat, reads the story, and often illustrates it or pastes a magazine picture above it. Children usually read their stories to other members of the class. The last part of the project is for the child to underline each word he or she knows in the story.

Sight Words   "The next day, when this child comes back to dictate another story, I use a little card like this with a hole cut in it to isolate an underlined word. If the child can pronounce that word, it is a known word. I then write the word on a computer card and that card goes in the word bank. At first most of the words in the word bank are tangible, important-to-children words like *snake, hamburger*, and *football*. Later, however, as certain words are used again in the stories, the child learns to recognize intangible, frequently used words like *the, and, to*. In this way, each child learns a sight vocabulary which includes those words usually found in basal readers.

"Well, it seems that I have talked most of our 30 minutes away and haven't left you much time for questions. But, let's use what little time we do have for questions."

A TALL MAN: This experience story method has some advantages, but will the children ever read real books in class?

MRS. WRIGHT: Oh, yes. I got so carried away explaining about language experience, I forgot to tell you about the rest of the program. The children certainly read. In fact, most of the teachers in this school have something call SQUIRT—Sustained Quiet Reading Time. During **SSR** SQUIRT time, everyone reads. I read something I am interested in. We have our SQUIRT time in here right after lunch. We start with five minutes. I use this little timer here to time it. Gradually, as the children become more able to sustain their silent reading, we increase the time by one minute at a time. Last year, my first graders got up to 13 minutes. I am so glad you asked about reading books, because I wouldn't want you to think we were having daily water fights after lunch when your children came home talking about SQUIRT. In addition to this daily SQUIRT time, once the children are able to, they read independently from many basal readers and library books. During the second half of the year, we have story parties every Friday. The children fix a snack and get together in threes or fours and read a favorite story to each other. This gives them meaningful practice in oral reading.

MRS. PENN: Mrs. Wright, I know we are about out of time, but I just want to say that this year you have my second child, Pat, and two years ago you had Kate. I think this is a fine way to teach reading. In fact, I requested that Pat be in your room.

Mrs. Wright ended the discussion by assuring the parents they were welcome to visit the class at any time, got the names of a few volunteer parents, and gave silent thanks that she had mastered parent meetings during her years of teaching.

September

Now I know why October is my favorite month—all month long I celebrate my survival of September! My supervising teacher from long-ago student-teaching days used to say, "I could teach first grade until I am 80 if someone would teach the first four weeks for me." Of course, that was in the days before there was kindergarten. Now, most of the children have been to kindergarten and know something about lining up and listening. I got my group this year from Miss Launch.

They are as ready and eager as a motley crew of six-year-olds can be. And a motley crew they are. I am most worried about Paul. It is a rare day which Paul doesn't return to his seat, put his head on his desk, and sob. I have tried to contact his parents but there appears to be no father at home and his mother works odd hours. Miss Grant, the social worker, says his home situation is awful, so I will continue to do what I can for him here. Daisy needs to be put on a diet! Her mother will be in next week for a conference. I wonder how I'll broach the subject to her. I guess it depends on her overall reactions to the other concerns I have about Daisy. I'd like to say, "Your daughter is a spoiled, selfish child," but I'll restrain myself!

Poor Chip! I have managed to stop most of the taunts and snickers directed at his tattered clothes, but I know Butch and Mort still bother him on the playground. He goes his own way, however, and pays as little attention to them as possible. I do admire the child.

Last Friday he contributed to a language experience chart. We were talking about fishing and Chip's sentence was, "You fry them up and they sure good." Joyce wanted to correct his sentence and I informed her that that was Chip's way of saying it and that was the way I was going to write it!

Larry, Danielle, Roberta, and Pat are reading! Miss Launch tells me that Larry and Danielle were reading when they came to kindergarten and that Roberta and Pat learned during the year. Next month, when I begin the individual story writing, I will begin to confer with those four about their reading. Larry has more general knowledge than anyone else. He is always adding some little-known (to the other children) fact to our stories. The others listen in awe and amazement. Yesterday Hilda said, "Larry, how do you know that?" He responded, "I read it in a book," as if that were the most natural thing in the world, and I guess it is for him.

Alexander has a hard time sometimes dealing with me and the other children. The hearing aid he wears is supposed to give him enough hearing capacity to function normally if he is seated close to you, but his oral language and listening abilities are like those of a four-year-old. Miss Launch says I should have seen him when he came to kindergarten last year. He could hardly talk and wouldn't listen. Apparently, they didn't discover his hearing problem until he was over two years old and had yet to say "mama" or "daddy"! I have assigned Steve to be his buddy for the time being and have talked with the children about what an important invention hearing aids are. One hundred years ago, Alexander would not have been able to hear at all! We try to treat Alexander as special and lucky but he still gets frustrated sometimes and lashes out at us. Once in a while, I think he pretends (or chooses) not to hear— usually when I say, "Time to clean up," or, "Where is your paper?" It is hard to know what to do. I want to treat him as normal but he does need special consideration yet I can't let him get out of things, using his handicap as an excuse. Mr. Lang, the speech and hearing specialist, will work with Alexander on Wednesdays and Fridays. I think I will ask him for advice.

Structured Language Experience

I have formed the class into four heterogeneous groups and I am doing structured language experience lessons with them. Structured language experience is different from other ways of doing language experience in that the lesson is structured so that all children's sentences begin with the same words. Because food is of universal interest to children, I did the first story with each group on the topic, "Foods We Like to Eat." Each child was given a "homework" assignment over the weekend to cut out and bring in a picture of one food they liked to eat. Everyone but Mort, Alexander, and Mike brought at least one picture of food to school on Monday. (Daisy brought a whole folder full of pictures of fattening foods.) I sat Mort, Alexander, and Mike down with some magazines and scissors first thing Monday morning and told them to cut out a picture of some food they liked and bring it when I met with their groups. (Mort didn't bring one! He said he just didn't care what he ate. I cut out a picture of pie for him and his response was, "Yuk, I don't like pie!" My patience is wearing thin with him already!) When the children came to meet with me, we spent a few minutes talking about each pic- ture they had brought. We answered such questions as: What is it? What color is it? Do you eat it cooked or raw? For breakfast? Lunch? Dinner? Is it a fruit? Vegetable? Meat? Bread? Dessert? How big would it be? Does it grow in the ground? Who else besides ____ likes it? This talking time is important to their oral language and listening develop-ment, and discussing the pictures helps them build concepts and in-crease the depth and breadth of their meaning vocabulary.

Concept Development

After this brief discussion of each food, I told the children that each group was going to make a chart telling what everyone likes to eat. (Anthony commented that "that way, if any visitors come and want to bring us a gift, they can see what foods we like!' He, at least, under-stands that reading and writing serve a communicative function in the world!) I wrote *Foods We Like to Eat* on a sheet of chart paper and had each child tell me a sentence starting with "I like to eat...." I picked children who talked in sentences first and left Paul and Chip until last so that they would have several models to follow. It worked, both Chip and Paul spoke a complete sentence. This was the first time I had heard either of them say more than a few words. The chart we made with this group looked like this:

Foods We Like to Eat
I like to eat carrots. (Betty)
I like to eat tacos. (Manuel)
I like to eat fried chicken. (Horace)
I like to eat ice cream. (Jeff)
I like to eat chocolate cake. (Chip)
I like to eat pizza. (Paul)

As you can see, I left an empty line between each sentence. This makes them easier to read and allows space for sentence matching later. After we had read the chart in chorus several times, I let volunteers read it to the group. All the children, by now, knew that each sentence started with "I like to eat," and most children could read their own chosen food. But, most of the children could not yet read all the names of the other foods. Since I wanted each child to have a successful reading experience, I used the "stand up, sit down" strategy to ensure everyone could read all the sentences on the chart. As each child began reading, I pointed to the name in parentheses after each sentence and said, "Will the person whose name this is please stand up." As each person stood up, that person displayed his or her picture as the reader read that person's sentence. Even Paul was able to successfully read the chart when I guided his hand and said, "Betty is standing up and showing her picture of carrots. Manuel is standing up and holding his picture of apples." I

Conventions

was amazed to notice that Paul pointed to individual letters rather than to words and that he didn't seem to know to make a return sweep at the end of each line but rather wanted to read left to right and then come back across the next line, right to left! In the old no-kindergarten days, many children didn't know this left-right, return sweep convention of print but I find it hard to imagine how a child could sit through Miss Launch's kindergarten for a year and not have learned that.

On Tuesday, we practiced reading the chart together a few times and then I wrote each child's sentence on sentence strips. I told the chil-

Jargon

dren to watch and see whose sentence I was going to write first and that I wouldn't necessarily write Betty's sentence first just because it was at the top of our chart. (The underlined words in the preceding and following sentences indicate some of the "jargon" children must learn if they are to be successful readers.) I then wrote the word I and asked, "Whose sentence will this be?" Six children chorused, "Mine!" By scrutinizing all the sentences on the chart, we determined that all the sentences began with the word I and that you couldn't tell by the first word whose sentence it would be. I then wrote like and only got three responses of "mine" to "Whose sentence is this?" By the time to and eat had been written, the children saw that since all the sentences had the same first, second, third, and fourth words, you would have to wait until the fifth word was written before you could tell whose sentence it would be. As I wrote pizza, I paused after the writing of the p to see if Paul would notice I was writing his sentence since pizza was the only food which began with the letter p. Paul didn't, but Horace did and he poked Paul and said proudly, "It's yours, Paul. She wrote a p so she's writing your sentence first." In this manner, I wrote everyone's sentence on a sentence strip. It took quite a while to do this but the children were intrigued by trying to guess whose sentence it would be and they learn the conventions and jargon of print by being there while writing is happening and by talking about what is happening [see pp. 14–21].

Once I had all the sentences written, I gave the appropriate one to each child and cut the sentence into words. Each child then used the model sentence on the chart to rearrange his or her words back into the sentence. Horace, Betty, Manuel, and Jeff got theirs all in the right order and turned the right way the first time. I said, "Good; do it again," as I rescrambled their words. Chip's sentence read: *cake. chocolate eat to like I.* "You did it right, Chip," I complimented, "You just didn't start in the right place. We always start our sentence on the left side." I put a piece of tape on his left hand and had him note that when we were in our group area, the windows were at his left. I started him out on the left side and he arranged his words correctly. Paul didn't have a clue! I helped him match his words to the words on the chart and the second time, he did have them in the right order but several of the words were turned upside down.

I am so glad they have gotten the primary typewriter fixed and have a new ribbon for it. Last year, you were wasting your time trying to use it. I explained to Mr. Topps that words look different in books from the way they look when you write them and that children needed to get used to reading the type if they were to transfer their ability to read charts to reading books. He realized that regular type is too small for most first graders to read easily and when I pointed out to him how different many of the letters look in type and writing, he responded, "You know, I never noticed that difference before. I'll get that primary typewriter in shape this summer." So, I now have a working primary typewriter again and I can type some of the stories and make sure my children learn to read words as I write them and as they are typed. Before school on Wednesday, I typed the "Foods We Like to Eat" story using the primary typewriter in the media center and made 24 copies, 4 for each child.

On Wednesday, we reviewed the chart story again using the stand-up, sit-down strategy and all the children read it quite easily. I then gave them each one copy of the typed version of the story and let them read that. I took another copy of the story and cut it into sentences which the children reordered and pasted to make the original story. (Later in the month, I cut the story into words rather than sentences for Horace, Manuel, and Betty. Jeff, Chip, and Paul continued sentence matching and reordering.)

Visual Discrimination

On Thursday, we made books. We cut 9 x 12 construction paper into half-sheets and stapled these together. I gave each child a typed copy of the story to cut and paste at the bottom of each page. (I put the fourth copy for each child in a folder and saved it so that we could reread the stories all year and make a big book of all stories to take home at

Christmas! If they don't read something over the two-week Christmas break, I'm afraid they will forget everything!) Once, they had pasted all the sentences in the appropriate order, they cut or drew a picture of each food, and then cut out all different kinds of foods to make a collage on the cover. On that Thursday of the first full week of school, every child took home a book he or she could read (even Paul!). They knew every page started with "I like to eat" and the drawn or cut picture on each page cued the appropriate food name.

I like to start the year with structured language experience lessons because it gets everyone (including me!) off to such a successful start. First graders come to first grade expecting to learn to read. When they take that booklet home at the end of the first full week of school and can read it they are delighted that they are reading. This successful beginning spurs them on and they approach all our reading tasks with confidence. In addition to the flying start first graders get off to, I like to do language experience lessons because they meet the needs of all different levels of maturity and readiness. Many of the children who came to me ready to read [see pp. 175–176] have begun reading as we do the charts. Many of them have learned to read as sight words some of the words used in the stories. Other children like Paul and Chip and Daisy are developing readiness as they participate in the stories. Paul now points to words rather than to letters as he is reading and reads left to right pretty consistently. Chip said the other day that he thought reading was just in books and that he didn't know you could write stories to tell people stuff! All of the children are developing the ability to visually discriminate letters and words as we do our word and sentence matching and reordering activities. As we do our structured language experience lessons, the ready children begin to acquire a sight vocabulary and begin reading, the unready ones get ready, and I get to observe, diagnose, and evaluate where on the readiness/reading continuum the different children are.

I have described the first structured language experience lesson with Paul's group. Of course, I did "Foods We Like to Eat" charts with the other three heterogeneous groups. Anyone who came into our class in September knew what the "in" foods with six-year-olds were. Mike was the one who had the idea for the second week's charts. "Let's talk about foods we hate," he suggested and so the second week's topic for each group was born!

The chart Daisy's group did during the second full week of school shows "Foods We Don't Like."

For the third week's topic, each child brought to school a toy. Our charts for the fourth week grew out of our science and social studies unit on pets.

As you can no doubt tell by looking at the children in the different groups, I have tried to make each group heterogeneous—a mixture of

Foods We Don't Like

I don't like carrots. (Joyce)

I don't like milk. (Daisy)

I don't like anchovies. (Larry)

I don't like onions. (Rita)

I don't like spinach. (Mitch)

I don't like chop suey. (Alex)

Toys

I like to play with cars. (Butch)

I like to play with playdoh. (Carl)

I like to play with trucks. (Mort)

I like to play with blocks. (Hilda)

I like to play with dolls. (Danielle)

I like to play with Legos. (Anthony)

Pets
I want a pet dog. (Pat)
I want a pet cat. (Mandy)
I want a pet monkey. (Mike)
I want a pet rabbit. (Alexander)
I want a pet parakeet. (Daphne)
I want a pet horse. (Roberta)
I want a pet snake. (Steve)

quiet and noisy, mature and immature. This assures that there are good language models and good thinkers in each group and helps cut down on discipline problems since "the problems" are seldom in the same place at the same time.

Wall Vocabulary   Our September schedule finds us doing Words on the Wall first thing in the morning. To start our wall vocabulary, I took pictures of all the children and mounted them on construction paper scraps. Each week I drew six pictures "from the hat" and, after having let the children watch me write the child's name above the picture, I taped these six names and pictures to the wall above the chalkboard. Eventually, I will have about 200 words up and I want the children to be able to find them easily so I am arranging them alphabetically by first letter. On Mondays, I added six more pictures and names (seven on the last Monday so that I could get all 25 children up in four weeks). Each morning at 8:45 the children number a sheet of paper from one to five and get ready for their "spelling test." I call out the names of five children. Since the children know each other's names and know where each picture is, they are all able to correctly write down the name. We then check the papers by letting the children whose names were called out stand up and spell their names. The children are delighted to see themselves displayed so prominently at the front of the room. Many of the children can read (without the picture) most of the names and a few are even learning to spell the names. Next month, I shall add some concrete words to the wall and then I will begin adding some common words such as *the, and*, and *of*. The children must learn to immediately recognize these common words in order to become good readers and they must be able to spell them if they are to become writers [see pp. 36–38].

At 9:00 I work with my first group. I vary the group I work with first, each day. I refer to the group by using one of the children in that group's name. I try to select an unremarkable child and refer to the group as that child's group hoping to confer a little status upon that child since the group is named after him or her. As they are currently grouped, I call them Paul's Group, Joyce's Group, Danielle's Group, and Daphne's Group. Roberta and Betty's mother called the other day to ask why the girls are in different groups and which one was in the highest group. I told her that no group was any better than any other, that these were not ability groups but rather groups heterogeneously formed to facilitate more participation. I told her both girls were doing well and commented on how different they were. She agreed that about the only things they shared were their brightness and common birthdates.

Schedule

While I am working with one group, the other three groups rotate through three centers: a story center, a magazine center, and a math center. In the story center they listen to a taped story and do a short follow-up activity. In the magazine center, they look through magazines and newspapers for particular pictures, words, or letters, cut them out and paste them on a large chart on the bulletin board in that center. They have looked for "Things to Eat," "Animals," and "Things That Are Blue," among others this month. In the math center, they classify, measure, and manipulate objects. We use half the allotted math time for these concrete activities and then do more formal math activities in the afternoon. Right now the children are all doing pretty much the same things in the centers. As the year goes on, I will individualize their activities more.

Concept Development

I set my timer and spend 25 minutes working with each group. When the timer goes off, I announce to all that we have five minutes to get to our next center or group activity. I then set the timer for five minutes, go around and help get the centers ready for the next group, and see that everyone gets where they belong. The children have gotten very good at using that five minutes to finish up, clean up, and get to their next place. They love to beat the clock and be where they need to be when the timer sounds. They then settle down for another 25 minutes. When I first started teaching, I kept my groups with me and the other children sitting much too long. Everyone got restless. I have to move right along to get all I need to do accomplished in 25 minutes, but that is about all the time they can attend and moving to a new activity every 30 minutes has certainly helped reduce discipline problems. I have a schedule posted for each group which shows where they should be. [See pp. 204–205.] Here is how this month's schedule looked for Paul's group.

	September Morning Schedule (Paul's Group)				
	Monday	Tuesday	Wednesday	Thursday	Friday
9:00	Story Center	Magazine	Math	Mrs. Wright	Whole-Class Activities
9:25	TRANSITION				
9:30	Magazine Center	Mrs. Wright	Story	Math	Whole-Class Activities
9:55	TRANSITION				
10:00	Break	Break	Break	Break	Break
10:15	Mrs. Wright	Math	Magazine	Story	Whole-Class Activities
10:40	TRANSITION				
10:45	Math Center	Story	Mrs. Wright	Magazine	Whole-Class Activities

October

To most first graders Halloween is second only to Christmas in generating excitement and distractions. I try to build on this excitement and channel their energies. Several of our Friday whole-class stories related to Halloween. We carved a jack-o'-lantern and then wrote down the steps in sequence. I read a newspaper article to them about some children being hurt on Halloween and we made a list of Halloween safety rules. We planned our Halloween party and made lists of what was needed and who would bring each item.

Rhyming Words

We also did a lot of work with rhyming words this month. I began by making sure that the children could hear if two words rhymed. All but Paul, Daisy, and Alexander now can tell if two words rhyme and can pick out the one that doesn't rhyme in a series of three words (such as *jump, boy, pump*). We then began to make charts of words that rhyme.

We chose Halloween-related words: *cat, witch, moon, trick, treat, owl,* and *candy*.

We made these charts over several weeks and reviewed the words frequently until most of the children could read down the list of rhyming words. We also observed that most, but not all, of the words ended with the same letters as the word they rhymed with. Finally, we used our rhyming word charts to write a group poem. I made up the first sentence of each couplet and the children composed the second. In several cases, we had several suggested second lines. We wrote them all down and decided when we had the poem written which choice we liked best. Here is the final version.

Halloween Night

On Halloween night you might see a cat.
    A black cat riding high on a bat.

On Halloween night you might see a witch.
    When she sees you she ducks into a ditch.

On Halloween night you might see an owl.
    Whooo, Whooo is all he will howl.

On Halloween night by the light of the moon,
    If you watch, you might even see a raccoon.

This month, during our whole-class phonics lessons (which we do on Wednesday and Thursday between 10:45 and 11:15, and on Friday sometime during the morning), we have been working on auditory discrimination. [See pp. 23–24.]

Auditory Discrimination

We take objects in the room and put the ones which begin alike together. We also sort pictures and play the "I'm thinking of" game. One child starts by saying, "I'm thinking of something in the room that begins like balloon." He then calls on children to guess the object; the correct guesser then gets a turn to think of something. (Each child whispers the object to me so that I can be sure the game is honest! Some children love to say "No!" even to correct guesses.) We vary the game by guessing things to play with or things to eat. In addition to building auditory discrimination, this also promotes concept development by developing meaning vocabulary and classification ability.

I also do some every-pupil-response activities in which the children make a happy face card and a sad face card and display the happy face if I (or a child) succeed(s) in saying two words which begin alike and the sad face if the two words do not begin alike. I have been observing and noting the children's responses to these every-pupil-response activities for the last several days and it appears that all the children except Paul, Daisy, and Alexander are responding correctly almost all the time. Now that they can make this discrimination, I shall begin helping them make the association between particular beginning consonants and their sounds. (I will continue to do work with auditory discrimination and hope that Paul and Daisy will catch on. With Alexander's hearing loss and delayed language development, I suspect he will have to rely more on sight words and context than on decoding skills, at least for awhile.)

Wall Vocabulary

We have added 20 concrete words (five each week) to our Words on the Wall this month. Among them, of course, were our Halloween words. We also added some of the common picturable nouns from the A and P Sight Word list, the source I will be using to make sure my first graders learn to immediately and automatically identify the most common words. The common nouns which are now part of our wall vocabulary are: *man, children, house, food, school, boy, sun, dog, girl, fish, tree, cat,* and *horse.*

The children are so proud of their growing wall vocabulary. They are pushing me to add more than five words each week. I won't, however, because I want every child to be able to find and write the words. If I add too many, Paul and Chip, among others, will not be able to keep up. Even though I am only adding five each week, my better students are being challenged because many of them are learning to spell all the words. This wall vocabulary will be most helpful next month when I begin to teach the students initial consonant letter-sound relationships. I think I will teach the letter, *Mm* first because already on our wall we have seven words which begin with *m* (*Mort, Mitch, Mike, Manuel, Mandy, moon,* and *man*).

Sight Words— Word Banks

It now takes two weeks, two days each week, to finish one structured language experience chart sequence. We still do our oral language and listening development and dictate the story on the first day. On the second day, we do sentence and word matching as well as practice reading the story. On the third day, the children cut and paste the words from a typed copy to make the whole story on their own. (Some children work in partners to do this. Manuel is very patiently helping Paul.) We use the group time on the third day to work with developing sight words and add words to each child's word bank. The word banks were made from shoe boxes which we covered and decorated. As the children watch me, I print all the words from the story on computer cards. (There is a computer center where my neighbor works and she brings me boxes full regularly.) There are never too many words because each sentence repeats many of the same words. Once the children have watched me print the words, they begin their cutting and pasting and I have each child come up one at a time. I shuffle the cards and then show them to them. If they say the word correctly, they get the card and I make a new one so I will have a complete set for the next child. Sometimes I don't get to all the children during the allotted 25 minutes but we have time to finish up on the fourth day when the children are making their take-home books. Many of the children regularly know all the words. In fact, it made Roberta so mad one day when she missed one that now she practices reading the chart backward to see if she knows all the words! I don't know if this is a good idea since she is reading right to left but she dismissed my suggestion that she practice it the right way by saying, "Mrs. Wright, you know that won't work. I know what those sentences say so, of course, I can read the words in the right order. If I can read them backward, I'll never get cheated out of another word for my word bank!"

On Wednesdays and Thursdays, I do not meet with any of the groups. I sit in the group-meeting area and have each child come to me to dictate a story. On Wednesdays, the people in Paul's and Joyce's groups come. On Thursdays, I meet individually with the people in Danielle's and Daphne's groups. While I am meeting with one child, the rest of the children rotate through the three centers. On Wednesdays, for example, from 9:00 to 9:25, Joyce's group is in the story center, Daphne's group is in the magazine center, and Danielle's group is in the math center. The children in Paul's group are meeting with me individually or preparing for our individual conferences. Between 9:30 and 9:55, I meet individually with the children in Joyce's group. From 10:15 to 10:40, I finish up individual story writing and conferences with those in Paul's and Joyce's group whom I haven't yet met with. Sometimes, I have some fifth graders come and let the children dictate their stories to them. This is a big help. On the days when I don't have

Schedule

Wednesday Morning Schedule (October)

	8:45	9:00–9:25	9:30–9:35	10:00	10:15–10:40	10:45–11:15
Joyce's Group	WORDS ON THE WALL	Math Center	Mrs. Wright	BREAK	Story Center or Mrs. Wright	WHOLE CLASS PHONICS
Daphne's Group		Story Center	Math Center		Magazine Center	
Danielle's Group		Magazine Center	Story Center		Math Center	
Paul's Group		Mrs. Wright	Magazine Center		Story Center or Mrs. Wright	

(TRANSITION appears between the 9:00–9:25 and 9:30–9:35 columns and between the 9:30–9:35 and 10:00 columns; TRANSITIONS appears between the 10:15–10:40 and 10:45–11:15 columns.)

help, I sometimes have to squeeze a child or two into the afternoon schedule. Here is what our October Wednesday schedule looked like. If you switch the places on Paul's group and Danielle's group, and Joyce's group and Daphne's group, you will know what our Thursday schedule looks like.

The charts for the other groups are similar to this one. Each group rotates in order through the story center, magazine center, meeting with me, and the math center. The difference is which center they begin in. On Mondays, for example, Joyce's group begins in the magazine center, meets with me at 9:30, goes to the math center at 10:15, and finishes the morning in the story center. While it may seem confusing, the charts make it all clear.

At 10:00, we have our morning break. Each week a different child has the responsibility of setting the timer for 15 minutes and giving us a 1-minute signal just before time is up. During this one minute, the children clean up and try to get to their next activity before the buzzer sounds. This is a good system for getting us all back to our morning work.

Individual Dictation

The individual story dictation is off to a good start. At first, many children did not know what to tell a story about. I encouraged them to look through magazines, find pictures they liked, and think of a story to go with the picture. Now many of them come to me with their picture, ready to talk. Also, during our afternoon science and social studies experiences, I point out possibilities for stories. Each child (except Paul) now has four stories.

For several (Chip, Joyce, and Mort), their stories are really only one sentence, or in Chip's case, only a phrase. Chip's language development is like that of a four-year-old. Alexander seems to be developing his oral language rapidly.

Joyce is strange! I think she has a good imagination because I occasionally watch her solitary playacting in the theater corner on Friday afternoons. She is very nonverbal, however.

Mort just couldn't care less about the stories! He seems bored with everything.

Paul is a mystery. Each time it is his turn I talk to him or look at a picture book with him. He nods his head and occasionally utters a word, but certainly no stories. He is spending part of the morning with Miss Launch in the kindergarten (as her helper). We both feel the language development activities she does every morning will help him.

Daisy will tell a story (which always begins with "I"). Part of the exercise is to underline all the words the storyteller knows—so Daisy underlines them all. When it comes time to put words in her word bank, I use my card with the hole in it to isolate the underlined words and see which ones she knows. She seldom knows a word except, of course, *I*. I discussed this with her mother and then went on to the subject of her weight, but her mother informed me that Daisy had a healthy appetite and was "just growing."

Many patterns are beginning to emerge in the children's storytelling. Roberta and Mike have wild imaginations—their stories always have a strange twist in them. Larry tells only factual stories. Steve is a nature buff—his stories are all about animals and living out in the wild. Hilda fancies herself a young Nancy Drew-type, and Alex always spins fantastic tales and swears they are true.

Here are two of the Halloween stories:

I like Halloween because you get lots of candy and stuff to eat. Last year I got two big bags. This year I hope to get three.

by Daisy

A True Halloween Story

My Aunt Sadie is a witch. Last Halloween she came to visit us and wore her witch's costume. Usually, she just wears regular clothes. She can cast spells and knows all kinds of magic. I was the only kid on the block with a real witch for Halloween.

by Alex

November

Most people think of November as turkey month. I think of it as teaching month. By November, I know what to expect from my different children and they know what to expect from me. Routines and schedules have been established and we are moving full-speed ahead toward developing readers, writers, and computers! Just yesterday, I noticed that some of the children who were unable to read at the beginning of the year are beginning to recognize words in the easy-to-read books they can choose to read during SQUIRT time. We have our SQUIRT time right **SSR** after lunch. We come straight back to the room and get a book. I sit in my rocking chair and the children sit on the rug around me. Everyone has a book and we begin SQUIRT as you would a race. One child (whose job it is for the week) waits to see that everyone is seated quietly with a book ready to open. That child then says, "Ready, Set, Go" and sets the timer for five minutes. I read a book or magazine which I am interested in but I also keep one eye out for "someone who is reading particularly nicely." When the timer sounds, I read the book of the person who was "reading very well today" to the whole class. In reality, I keep a chart of the children's names in my desk drawer and I put the date next to each child's name as I read his or her book aloud. Just before SQUIRT time, I glance at the chart to see whose book I haven't read yet (or in a long time) and then choose one of those children (assuming they are sitting and looking at their book which they almost always are) as the "best reader" and read their book aloud. I want to recognize all the children and I just can't keep all that information in my head so I keep it in my desk drawer. If anyone pilfered my desk drawer and made off with all my lists, I would have to quit teaching.

As I am reading the easy-to-read book, I make a tape of it for the story center. The children are quiet as mice as I read and they participate by clapping their hands as a turn-page signal. I now alternate activities in the story center so that the children get practice reading easy-to-read books and, on alternate days, improve their listening comprehension. On days when they are reading along with easy-to-read books, three people share a book. I have a number of easy-to-read books of which I have two copies since I ask parents to donate these to our class library as Christmas presents and I borrow a copy from the school or public library. The group listens to the book twice. During the first listening, they just listen and follow the words in the book. During the second listening, they are encouraged to read along on any parts they can.

On listening comprehension days, they are listening to books which are not easy-to-read. One child has the responsibility of running the tape recorder, holding the book and turning the pages so that everyone can see the pictures, collecting the listening comprehension exercises, and rewinding the tape for the next group.

Wall Vocabulary   We have added five Thanksgiving words to our wall (*Thanksgiving, turkey, pilgrims, Indians*, and *feast*) as well as 15 words which are among the most common according to the A and P list and which have occurred in our structured language experience charts. Many of the children have these words (*I, like, to, play, with, want, a, is, and, the, for, be, had, not*, and *see*) in their individual word banks already. I made sure to put *want* and *with* on different colored and shaped scraps of construction paper because I knew how confused children get with these similar looking, abstract words and I wanted them to have color and shape as a temporary aid to memory. I knew it was working the other day when I called out *want* and heard Alexander mutter "Want—now that's the one on the red skinny one not the one on the green tall one!"

Decoding   This month, we have been working to learn and apply some initial consonant letter-sound relationships. I taught *Mm* first because the children had so many words from the wall vocabulary which began with *Mm*. I made sure the children could auditorially discriminate the sound represented by *Mm* at the beginnings of words by having them make every-pupil-response cards. Then, as I said words, they showed their smiling face if I had succeeded in saying a word which began like *Mort, Mitch, Mike, Manuel, Mandy, moon*, and *man* and their sad face if I was unsuccessful. Everyone except Paul and Alexander (including even Daisy—I can hardly believe it!) responded correctly almost all the time. I then be-

gan to help them make the association between the letter *Mm* and the
sound heard at the beginning of their known words which begin with
Mm. (I don't know if Alexander will be able to learn letter-sound relationships given his hearing loss, and Paul is "not here" even when he is
here so much of the time. I will watch for indications that these two are
ready to learn letter-sound relationships and then reteach these to them
and anyone else who needs review in a small group later in the year.)
We ate marshmallows and learned to march as a food and an action
associated with the letter *Mm.*

Jj was the next letter-sound relationship taught because *Jeff, Joyce,*
and *jack-o-lantern* were part of our wall vocabulary. The letter *Bb* for
which we had the known words *Betty, Butch, boy,* and *be, Rr (Roberta,*
and *Rita),* and *Hh (Hilda, Horace, horse, house,* and *had)* were the third,
fourth, and fifth letter-sound relationships we worked on. For each, I
first made sure the children could auditorially discriminate the targeted
sound from other beginning sounds and then helped the children learn
the association between particular letters and particular sounds. For
each we ate a special food (*jellybeans, bananas, raisins, honey*) and
learned an action (*jump, bounce, run,* and *hop*). We often play a game in
which I hand different children a card with one of the letters we are
learning on it and that child does the action associated with that letter.
The other children must guess what letter the action-doer was given.
Even Paul can do the actions associated with the letters although he has
difficulty with the other association-level tasks we are doing.

We also make a bulletin board for each letter. The children spend
part of their time in the magazine center cutting out pictures of things
and words which begin with the targeted letter. (I suggest to them things
they might find. You can count on finding lots of *babies* and *bottles* in
magazines.) Children also brought in objects which began with the
targeted letter and we placed them on a table beneath the bulletin
board. Under the *Bb* bulletin board, we had *balls, balloons, belts, books,
beads, bows, bags, banks, bells, beans, bugs, boats, biscuits, bats,* and
bananas. (I sent Mike home with his *bra* telling him it began with *br!*)
[See p. 59.]

When most of the children can make the association between certain
letters and certain sounds (and show me they can by consistently holding up the correct every-pupil-response card), I do two different kinds of
activities to help them apply this letter-sound association knowledge to
decoding words. One application-level activity I do is to help children
make guesses at unknown words using context and initial consonants. I
use the overhead projector and let them help me read a sentence in
which one word is covered up. We say "blank" when we come to that
word. The children then guess what the covered up word might be by
suggesting words which make sense given the other words in the sentence (context). I write all reasonable guesses on the board. I then uncover

the first letter of the word. We erase all the guesses which don't begin with the now-visible first letter and make some more guesses which both make sense and begin with that letter. Finally, we uncover the word and, most of the time, discover that we have indeed guessed the correct word. The children are learning that they can make good guesses at unknown words if they will think of something that begins appropriately and makes sense in the sentence [see pp. 53–54].

The other application-level activity we do is to substitute the initial letters we are learning to make words which rhyme with known words. Yesterday, for example, I had them write *Chip, Pat, Mike, boy*, and *sun* on separate computer cards. I then read them some sentences saying "blank" for an italicized word. (I hope Roberta didn't break her *hip*. Butch is hoping for a new *bike* for Christmas.) All the italicized words rhymed with one of the words they had written on cards and began with the letters for which we had learned letter-sound associations. The children held up their card which showed a word with the same middle and ending letters as the italicized word and then pronounced the known word and the unknown rhyming word. Paul and Alexander can't do this at all and Butch, Jeff, Mort, Daisy, and Chip are having trouble with it. The others, however, are catching on fast. Once they learn to think of a word they know which rhymes with an unknown word, and once they develop a large sight vocabulary of known words, they can decode almost any regular one-syllable word. [See pp. 59–62.]

December

Finally—two weeks vacation! Am I ever ready for it after this month! We did manage to do some nonseasonal things this month. We added 15 more words to our Wall Vocabulary (although, come to think of it, 10 of these were Christmas-related words!). We ate donuts, fudge, lemonade, and pizza and learned to dance, fish, laugh, and pedal as we learned letter-sound associations for the letters *Dd, Ff, Ll, Pp.*

We have been making greeting cards and learning to read the words of many songs. Most children wanted to write a letter to Santa although Butch and Hilda insist that there is no such thing as Santa Claus. They are constantly teasing the other children about it. Yesterday, Butch had Rita in tears and I decided to try to call a halt to it. I told them that I didn't know for sure that there was a Santa Claus but that someone always left presents under my tree. Larry refuses to comment on the subject but he wears a knowing look.

Mort's mother came in one Friday morning and told us that in her family and many others Christmas is not celebrated. She then explained about Hanukkah, and the children wrote a whole-class experience story about Hanukkah customs. Typically, Mort was uninterested even while his mother was here.

Early in the month, we made a chart of words to help the children in card, letter and story writing, and reading. We have used these words for our consonant substitution practice and many children have added lots of seasonal words to their word banks. More and more now, they are taking it upon themselves to write their own words on cards and add them to their banks. They write their own stories sometimes by taking the words from their banks and arranging them in sentences. If they need a new word, I supply it. If they need a duplicate of a word they already have, they make a duplicate card. Soon I will begin to help some of the children sort their cards alphabetically and make their own personal dictionaries. Then they will be able to do much writing independently.

Larry is already writing his own stories. When he comes to me on Thursdays, we have a conference about the books he has read and he shows me the stories he has written. Often, his stories are summaries of the informational books he is constantly reading. Larry continues to amaze me. The children are getting very good at making intelligent guesses at unknown words and at using words they know to figure out those they don't. Many of them are reading their own stories and those of others quite fluently. They are devouring the easy-to-read books they check out each week from the library. Next month, I shall make lots of preprimers available for them to read and begin to individualize their morning activities more.

January

This has been a most satisfying month. The children have become much more independent and mature. Sometimes I think that I spend all fall laying the groundwork for these long winter months. When the children came back on Monday, I had put out four sets of preprimers. Two were from the series being used in this school and the other two I found in a corner of the book closet. These last two were a bit ragged around the edges, so I got Mr. Topps' permission to cut them up and I stapled the individual stories into construction paper booklets. I color-coded all the preprimer story booklets. I had 14 preprimers out but it looked like more than that, because 8 of them were cut up into little books. When the children first saw them, they were impressed with the pile. They immediately began to open them and Hilda shouted, "Hey, I can read this whole book." She proceeded to do just that and many of the others followed suit! An exciting start to a new year!

For a while, I let the children experience the excitement of being able to read so many books. I then called them all together. They shared tales of their holiday vacations and a few had brought some of their treasures with them. I was so pleased to see that many of them had easy-to-read books from the list I had sent home and that they were proud of

Basal Readers

them. I promised that we would have a story party that very afternoon so they could read their books to the other children. I then told them that the books on the table were for them to read and that, as they had already discovered, they could indeed read most of the words in them. "Some of the books," I explained, "have a family or two in them and this morning we will get acquainted with the members of the family." I then introduced the family in one series by showing pictures in the four books and talking about the characters. We then wrote a group experience story about this family. That afternoon we repeated this procedure with a family from a second series.

The children are now truly ready to read 14 preprimers. With the exception of the names, most of the words are sight words for them because they have occurred so often in their group and individual stories. They are able to figure out the remaining words by using consonant substitution and context-plus-consonant clues. I gave each child a folder in which I had stapled a ditto sheet to each side with the title and color code of each book. Under that were the title and page numbers of the stories in the book. We spent a long time identifying each of the 14 books and then finding the stories in them. During this time, we talked about what the stories might be about, and different children expressed the desire to read different stories. I then demonstrated how they would use this folder to keep a record of the stories they had read. They were to check off each story as they read it and write the date (copied from the board) next to that story. I further told them that they could read any story in any book and that since there were over 100 stories, I didn't think any of them could read all of them. (I saw several confident nods as I said this and realized that my challenge had been accepted.) I told them that they could read these stories by themselves or with a friend, and then let them get started immediately. About half the children chose books and read with a friend, and the other half read alone. I walked around and gave them assistance in finding and recording the stories they had read. Most of the children chose a book and read it from start to finish. Others browsed through the books to find a good story. Larry read the titles of the stories from the dittoed record sheet and then went looking for what he wanted! I think he will be back to his library books soon. But, as usual, he seems to have a natural instinct for not appearing too far ahead of the other children.

I have altered the schedule again this month. I am no longer meeting with all the children to do structured language experience lessons. Rather, on Monday and Tuesday from 9:00 to 9:25, I do language experience lessons (the sentences do not follow the same pattern) similar to what we do as a whole class on Fridays with Butch, Chip, Jeff, Paul, Alexander, Daisy, and Mike. We also do a lot of work with their word banks. They are having difficulty learning the abstract words and I am using the six-step drastic strategy [see pp. 45–48] to help them learn the abstract words which occur in their language experience stories.

On Mondays and Tuesdays from 9:30 to 9:55, I meet with Butch, Chip, Jeff, Mort, Mike, Paul, Daisy, Anthony, and Alexander. I had observed in our whole-class phonics lessons that these children were not learning the consonant letter-sound relationships very well. I have thus put them together and am starting again on the consonants. We are going more slowly through discrimination, association, and application levels and everyone except Alexander appears to be learning them this time around. I think I may exclude Alexander from this group because even though he doesn't know them, he doesn't seem to be able to learn them and he is getting quite frustrated. He likes to read the easy-to-read books. He can hear best using his hearing aid with the headphones. I think I will let him listen to a tape of a chosen book as many times as he needs to (imitative reading) until he can read it to me. Fortunately, he seems to be learning sight words in the 9:00 group and he is becoming better at using context to decode unknown words. Some children simply cannot learn letter-sound relationships and, with his hearing loss, it is possible that he is one of these children.

From 10:15 to 10:40, I have individual conferences with children. Then from 10:45 until 11:15, we do our whole-class phonics activities just as we have been doing on Wednesdays and Thursdays. (Our Wednesday, Thursday, Friday schedule is the same as it was in December).

During the individual conferences, I check up on the children's progress through the preprimers and, occasionally, have them read a selected portion of one to me. I record their dictated language experience stories, listen to them read their already written stories and help them add words to their word banks.

Word Banks

While the children are in the magazine-newspaper center, I encourage them to cut out pictures of things they like and paste them on index cards. When they come to me, they bring these cards and tell us what they call the item. I then write the word on the other side of the card. Many of the children now have a stack of these cards and are learning to read them without any help. They sit down with the word side of the card showing and try to think what that word is. If they think they know it, they turn the card over to see if they are right. If they don't know a word, the picture "tells" them the word.

I learned through experience to let each child tell me what each picture is called. There are very few things which have only one name. What is that thing in which you push a baby down the street? A stroller? A carriage? A buggy? A pram? The first year I taught, I had the children cut out pictures and paste them on cards and then wrote my word for that object on the cards. One day I observed a little boy going through his cards. He looked at the word *dog* and said *puppy*. He then turned it over, saw his picture of a puppy and smiled. On the next card, I had written the word *car*. He looked at the word, said *Volkswagen*, turned the card over and there was a car that just happened to be a Volkswagen. I stood there horrified as it occurred to me what he had just learned: *d-o-g* spells "puppy," *c-a-r* spells "Volkswagen." Well, we had to re-do everyone's cards—I discovered that each child had at least one card, more often many cards, for which his or her word did not match my word. Now I say, "That's a nice picture. What do you call it?" and write that on the card.

Mike gets the prize for storytelling this month. I had some fifth-grade girls in taking down the stories dictated to them. I reminded the girls to "write down exactly what the child tells you" because I didn't want them changing Butch's "She got her some money" to "She got some money." "Butch would read it as he said it," I explained, "and thus he would read *some* as *her* and *money* as *some* and run out of words before he read *money*. We are modeling standard English in here," I said, "But when they dictate a story, I use it to develop reading and sight word knowledge, so it needs to be written in their exact words." The fifth-grade girls agreed. In a few minutes I heard a lot of embarrassed giggles coming from the math center. Of course, Mike was in the middle of it all. I went over there and found:

Mike's Monster Story

One day I saw a monster—a big, big, ugly monster.
He had eyeballs hanging down on his cheeks.
The blood was dripping on my shoes.
It made me puke.
I ran home and puked in the toilet.
I looked out the bathroom window and there he was!
It scared me so much I crapped in my pants.
When he smelled that, boy, did he run away fast.

As I read the story, the children were very quiet. I wasn't quite sure what to do but I knew I had to nip this in the bud. I crumpled up his story and tossed it into the trash can. "Mike," I said, "you have lost your privilege of working with my helpers. From now on, you dictate stories to me only."

The embarrassed girl who had written down the story explained, "I didn't know what to do. You said to always write down exactly what they tell you." I met Roberta and Betty's mother in the grocery store that Friday and she had heard all about it. Betty had come home and informed her that Mike had "really done it this time." Roberta then told her mother the story (vividly, I'm sure), Betty being too delicate to use such words. Fortunately, Mrs. March didn't make much of it and just told the girls to ignore Mike. Betty would love to pretend Mike doesn't exist but Roberta is clearly intrigued with him and has been heard to say she would like to have his guts.

February

> Dere Mrs. Right
> I dream of you evry night
> Please be my valentine
> That wood be just fine.

As this anonymous Valentine shows, the children are becoming independent writers as well as independent readers! This month, as for other holidays, we have written whole-class and group stories around the Valentine's Day theme. We have also made charts of Valentine words and done our phonics substitution exercises starting with a Valentine word. In addition to the consonants, most of the children now know the sounds of the digraphs (*sh, ch, th,* and *wh*) and we are currently working on the blends. As we master the letter-sound association for each of these, we apply them immediately through substitution exercises and context exercises. I now can see the children beginning to use these word identification skills as they read.

I have added two more centers to our room. One is a writing center **Centers** for independent writing. There I have put different kinds of paper (stationery, bright-colored paper, chart paper), envelopes, and colored markers.

I also have a box of objects in the center for the children to pick any three objects from and write a story which includes them all. There is also a new supply of pictures about which they might want to write and the flannel board with Valentine cutouts. They also have paper, crayons, and colored pencils so that they can illustrate their stories. This is a very popular center but, because of space, I limit the number of children to four at a time.

I also have a new reading games center. Here I have put several games I made as well as some I bought. I taught Larry and Mitch to play these games and they are teaching the other children. These games are designed to give the children practice and review with the most common words and to help strengthen their knowledge of letter-sound relationships. I try to make sure that all games, including those I make, are really helping the children practice those abilities needed to become better readers.

Of course, I still have the listening, math, and magazine centers in which I constantly change the material. Now when the children come in each morning, they choose the centers in which they wish to work. We have a chart on the bulletin board with spaces for each center and each activity. We first decide which children are meeting with me and these children tack one of their three name cards in that block. They then get first choice on the other two blocks. The rest of the children then choose their three blocks for that morning's work. We set the timer for 25 minutes and when it rings, the children have 5 minutes to get finished up and move on to the next center. We follow this kind of schedule on Tuesday, Wednesday, and Thursday. Our schedule for last Thursday is shown here.

Basal Readers   Many children have begun reading the primers this month. I have made a chart for the stories similar to the one I made them for the pre-primers. Next month, I will put some 1^2 books out and also some 2^1 books. When the children start reading those books, they will be able to make their own charts to record the stories. Joyce finally wrote a whole story last week. She had pantomined a story about a witch and a frog during a creative dramatics session, and the next day I got her to verbalize her pantomine. She is very imaginative, a trait I hope I can continue to build on.

Mandy told the strangest story last week. She always sees things from a different point of view. Her story illustrates that.

The Real Story of the Three Billy Goats Gruff

Once upon a time there lived a troll under a brand new bridge that he had just finished building.

He had worked hard to make it a very nice bridge.

You might be wondering why a troll would need a bridge. Well, I'll tell you.

Trolls live under bridges just like we live in houses.

That's just the way they are.

He was just sitting under the bridge minding his own business when he heard this little noise up on top.

He went up on top and said very politely. "Excuse me. I think you must have the wrong bridge. This is where I live."

He couldn't help but notice the muddy footprints the little goat had made on his nice clean bridge.

The little goat was real smart-alecky and said, "Naaa! This bridge takes me across to the meadow and I'm going to go over and eat some grass. So there!"

That made the troll very unhappy—so unhappy that he said something he later was sorry for. He said, "Yeah! Well, get off my bridge or I'll eat you for dinner!"

That scared the little goat so much that he ran off the bridge and said, "Oh please don't eat me. Eat up my brother. He's much bigger."

The troll said that he would do that, but he only said it to scare the goats away from his bridge.

Typical Daily Schedule (February)

	Meet with Mrs. Wright	Library	Reading Center	Writing Center	Reading Games	Listen Center	Magazine Center	Math Center
9:00 9:25	Roberta Rita Mort Paul	Daphne Danielle	Betty Joyce Mandy	Alex Mitch Pat	Hilda Jeff Daisy	Chip Carl Steve	Mike Manuel Anthony	Butch Horace Larry Alexander
9:30 9:55	Mike Mitch Mandy Alexander	Joyce Larry Pat	Danielle Horace Roberta Rita	Daphne Hilda Betty	Carl Alex Mort	Jeff Daisy Manuel Anthony	Chip Butch	Paul Steve
10:15 10:40	Manuel Steve Larry Pat	Carl Betty Horace	Daphne Hilda	Roberta Mandy Danielle	Anthony Butch Mitch	Alex Joyce Mort Paul Alexander	Jeff Daisy	Chip Rita Mike

Later on, the middle-size Billy Goat Gruff came onto the bridge. The troll again went up and asked the goat to leave, for this was his bridge.

The goat laughed in his face and spit on his freshly cleaned bridge.

That made the troll so mad that he said, "If you don't get off of here right now, I'm going to eat you up!"

The scared goat started crying and said, "Oh, don't eat me. Eat up my big brother. He'll fill you up much faster."

The troll patted him on his head and said, "OK, I won't eat you. But stay off my bridge."

The troll cleaned his bridge again and then went down under for a nap. He was sound asleep when he heard an awful clumping on his bridge.

He was grumpy from being awakened, so he roared, "Who's walking on my bridge?"

The big Billy Goat Gruff said, "It's me! What are you going to do about it, Shrimp?"

Boy, the troll got so mad that he went up to yell some more at the goat, but the goat, who was *so* big, just knocked him into the water. The troll decided he couldn't stay there any longer, so he just moved away and built a new bridge where there weren't any goats.

by Mandy

Parent Conferences
This was parent conference month. All the children had someone come in except Paul and Jeff. The most amazing thing I learned was that Alex does have an aunt who is a witch and she did come to visit them for Halloween! His mother and I were talking about his vivid imagination and I used his witch story for an example. She hesitated and said, "Well, some people have skeletons in their closets, we have witches! My sister-in-law believes that she is a witch. I don't know what kind of an effect this is having on Alex. But, she is family, so, what can we do?" For starters, I will start to listen to Alex with a more open mind!

Manuel's parents both work during the day, so I met them here one evening. They were very nice and were so pleased that their only son is doing well. "I tell him all the time how important it is to have a good education," said Mr. Tomás. Chip's mother also came at night. I told her that Chip was a hard worker and was making progress.

Mort's mother said he is as bored at home as he is in class and she doesn't know what to do about it. Daisy's mother, on the other hand, said that her little darling had lots of energy at home and never fought with the neighborhood children. Now, that I just can't believe!

Daphne's grandmother came. I can see now why Daphne is so sedate and proper. In behavior, she and Betty could be twins! Roberta and

Betty's mother is very pleased with the way they are both doing and wants them kept together in the same room next year. I'm not so sure that is a good idea but she is their mother.

I tried to explain to Mike's mother how his constant movement has inhibited his learning this year. She agreed that he is a handful. I suggested that she take him to the doctor for a complete physical examination and she told me that she had done that when Mike was in kindergarten and the doctor had said he was borderline hyperactive. She wasn't sure what that meant and neither am I. I hate to put labels on kids but he certainly is at least the active half of hyperactive.

Mitch's mother informed me that he felt out of place because he is so much bigger than the other children. I never realized that bothered him. He is the biggest boy in the class and a little clumsy, but he is also almost a year older than the others due to his November birth date. I did suggest that Mitch is a bit overweight and that added to his size problem. She said she would watch his eating habits, and I said I would try to make him feel good about his ample size.

I also gained some insight into Butch's behavior. Butch is the oldest of four children and it is his job to look out for the younger ones. Butch's father is very proud of his son's toughness and bragged that Butch is "all boy!"

Danielle's dad is delighted with the adjustment she has made. I told him that, most of the time, I don't even think about Danielle's being in a wheelchair and that the other children just naturally help her get where she needs to go. Alexander's parents seem to feel that he is just doing fine too. I'm not sure that is true. He has made progress this year in every area but I wonder if he can ever make up for those first three years of his life in which he lived in a near-silent world.

March

This month our big project has been to make dictionaries from our word banks. The children are doing so much independent writing now that they needed to have their words organized in order to find them when needed. I made a booklet for each child in which I had stapled dittoed sheets with one letter in upper- and lowercase form and two or three familiar words beginning with that letter on each sheet. Each child went through all the words in his or her bank and wrote them on the appropriate page. **Word Banks**

The children also use the wall vocabulary to help them spell words as they are writing. We now have 137 words of which 70 are the common words from the A and P List. We still add five words on Monday and then have our spelling test every day. Now, however, I do not call out a list of five words. Rather, I say a sentence comprised of five or more of **Wall Vocabulary** the words on the wall. Since all the children's names are part of the wall vocabulary, I often make up a sentence which includes one or more of the children's names. The children are eager to know who I will make a sentence about (I check them off on a list in my desk drawer but they don't know that!) and everyone has learned to begin a sentence with a capital letter and end it with a period, question mark, or exclamation point. The wall vocabulary was a new idea I tried this year and I certainly intend to continue using it. Because the words are on the wall alphabetically, some have pictures, and they are added gradually, all children can successfully find and write the words. Thus, they can find them when they need them in their writing. I often see them looking up there when it is writing time. Some children have learned to spell many of the words (a feat not usually accomplished by first graders) and all children can read almost all the words. (Paul can read many of them, but still confuses words like *went* and *want*, and *them* and *they*.)

Decoding   The wall vocabulary is also very helpful as we are learning letter-sound relationships. We have finished all the consonants and digraphs. All the children can tell you what food we ate for each of these and can do the action associated with each of these. Most of the children can use context and initial consonant/digraph sounds to decode unknown words, and I have noticed recently that when they come to a word they can't figure out using context and initial sound they use the wall vocabulary to see if they can find a word which has a middle and end like the unknown word. We have been working this month on the initial blends. The first one I taught was *st* because *Steve* and *stop* are part of our wall vocabulary. I began by making sure that the children could auditorially discriminate the sound represented by *st* from other sounds and then did association-level activities similar to those we did for consonants and digraphs. The children found pictures and words in magazines and newspapers which began with *st* and we had a scavenger hunt for *st* objects. I divided them into teams and gave them a list of ten common objects (stamp, stick, stone, etc.). On the following day, the teams brought their objects to school. It wasn't much of a competition since each team had all ten objects but they enjoyed it anyway. "It's best when everyone wins and nobody loses," was how Betty summed it up. Our action for *st* is "stand still." Mike has developed a particular dislike for this action and in fact declares it's not an action at all!

I have taught *tr, pl, bl,* and *sn* because we have the known words, *tree, play, blue,* and *snow* on the wall. We do not have known words which begin with all the blends, however, so I will be sure and add some to our wall vocabulary before I teach those particular blends [see p. 59].

Of course, we are doing application-level context plus initial-blend activities to help children apply their knowledge of blend letter-sound relationships to decoding unknown words. We are also doing blend sub-

stitutions on known words. When we did the consonant and digraph substitution on known words, I had the children make computer cards with
known words printed on them and then find their word which looked
like the unknown word. I am now trying to get them to "search through
their minds" for the match which will help them decode. "You are
getting so good at matching rhyming words to your computer card words,"
I announced one day, "but you can also use the words you have stored in
your minds as matches. Let's try to use the words in our minds to decode
some words which begin with the blends we have been learning." I then
wrote, "I want you to *stand still* by the *stump*," on the board. The children quickly told me that *and* would help them decode *stand*, that *Bill*
and *will* would help them decode *still*. They had a little trouble thinking
of a word which would help with *stump* until I asked them what our
action for the letter *j* was. I am going to give them lots of practice with
using the words in their minds to figure out unknown words. Some of them
are already very good at this. In fact, Daphne astonished me the other
day. She had cut the word *trumpet* out of a magazine to put on our *tr*
collage. She brought it hesitantly up to me and asked quietly, "Is this
word *trumpet*?" "It sure is," I replied. "Well, I figured it out because the
first part rhymes with gum and the last part is pet," she announced.
This gave me the idea to include some two syllable "challenges" when
we do our blend substitution decoding. The other day, the more advanced readers successfully and triumphantly decoded *triplets, black-
smith*, and *snapper*! [See pp. 66–70.]

This month, I have tried to individualize the children's activities **Centers**
more when they are in the centers. Some of my best readers (Rita, Mandy, Danielle, Alex, and Joyce) are not very good at math. They have specific assignments in the math center each week.

In the magazine center, instead of working on large whole-class
charts, many children are working on individual assignments. Paul and
Daisy are cutting out pictures of objects and placing them in a book I
made for them. Each picture is pasted on a page labeled with the letter
the object begins with. The children bring the book to me periodically,
and I write the names they tell me under these pictures. They are
developing some facility with consonant letter-sound associations, but it is
slow!

Steve is making a nature book. He cuts pictures of woodsy scenes
from magazines and lists the wildlife he thinks he would find there.
Chip, Butch, and Jeff look for words they already know and then put
these words together to form sentences. Roberta and Horace are making
riddle cards—they cut out a picture, paste it on a card, and then write a
clue on the back of the card, such as "This is something you use to clean
the house and it begins with *m*." They love to share these riddles with
the other children.

Many children now use the magazine center to browse for pictures to inspire stories or to find new words for their dictionaries. As a result many of the dictionaries now include such immediately recognizable words as *McDonald's, Fritos*, and *Holiday Inn*.

Mike is having a very difficult time with the morning block of time now that it is less structured. Amost every other day I revoke his game center privileges because he won't follow the rules. I always give him another chance after a suspension, because if I don't he will never learn to play by the rules. I try to make allowances for Mike's extra energy, but sometimes the other children resent the extra freedom they think he enjoys. I guess they will just have to learn that treating everyone fairly does not necessarily mean treating everyone the same.

Basals I now have the whole range of books out. The children, for the most part, select those they can read and which interest them. Roberta, Rita, Danielle, Mandy, Larry and Pat are reading second-grade books and lots of library books. Daisy, Paul, Butch, and Chip are still reading in the preprimers (*when* they read!). The rest go back and forth between the primers, the 1^2 books, and library books. I have found that first graders enjoy the basals when they can easily read them and often read them on their own or with a friend.

April

April has been much like March, only warmer. The children are continuing to make great strides in their independent reading and writing skills. We are now up to 12 minutes of SQUIRT time daily. I am still worried about Paul and Daisy. They are reading a little in the preprimers now, but don't seem to be making much progress. Daisy will not do anything constructive unless I am sitting with her, but I can't be with her all the time. Paul is still in a daze. He doesn't cry as much now and he will talk to me if I ask him a direct question. He has no friends, however, and seems to be constanty preoccupied.

Concept Development All year I have been concerned with providing direct and indirect experiences to promote concept development and increase the depth and breadth of my children's meaning vocabulary store. Whenever possible, I bring real objects into the classroom and encourage them to bring objects in. We not only name each object, we also describe and classify it, decide which attributes it shares with other objects, and how it is different from other objects. Often these objects relate to the science or social studies unit we are studying and in addition to talking about these objects, we write about them in group-experience stories. I also use many films, filmstrips, picture books, and pictures to provide the students with indirect experience with words and concepts for which we don't have real objects readily available. Years ago, I started a picture file for one of my methods courses and I have added to it ever since. Currently my picture file categories include: food, animals, plants, clothes, occupations, vehicles, holidays, city life, South America, Asia, Africa, U.S., famous people, tools and utensils, and a huge and disorderly miscellaneous category. I have laminated with clear adhesive plastic most of the pictures I have collected and I find it an invaluable resource in concept and meaning vocabulary development.

ADD TO YOUR SURVIVAL KIT

Begin a picture file. Collect pictures of people, places, and objects you think might be helpful in concept and meaning vocabulary development. Laminate them with clear adhesive plastic. What categories will your picture file have?

I also do many categorization activities with my children to help them clarify and extend meanings for words. One I particularly enjoy doing is a list, group, and label lesson originated by Taba (1967) for use in the social studies curricula. To do a list, group, and label lesson, you begin by asking children a question which will elicit many responses. Last week, as we were beginning our science unit on nutrition, I asked the children to list all the foods they could think of. As they named various foods, I wrote these food words on the board. From time to time, I stopped to read what was already listed on the board and encouraged them to think of more foods. Finally, when we had filled almost the whole board, I said, "Let's just have Mike, Roberta, and Horace tell me their foods since they have their hands up. We will then have the whole board full of food." I then reread the whole list letting the children read along with me if they desired. I then left the list on the board for the next day.

List, Group, Label

On the following afternoon, I pointed to our list of foods and told the children that I was going to read the list again and that this time they should listen and think, "Are there any foods on the list which seem to go together in some way?" I then read the entire list and asked if anyone had a group of foods which seemed to go together.

Mitch said that cake, cookies, chocolate pie, ice-cream, and gingerbread went together. I wrote these five on a sheet of chart paper and asked him why he had put these foods together. He said, "Because you eat them all after the meal." I then asked him if he could think of a name or label for his group. He hesitated a moment and then said, "Desserts."

Steve put mushrooms, grapes, berries, rhubarb, and nuts together. I listed these five foods, on the chart paper and asked him why he had put those particular foods together. He said it was because they all grew wild.

I then asked him if he could give a name or label to that group. After some hesitation, he said, "Things that Grow Wild."

Chip put peanuts, chocolate candy, hamburgers, potato chips, soda, oranges, and tomatoes together. I listed them and in response to my "why" question, he said, "Because they are my favorite things to eat." When I asked him to give a name or label to this group, he couldn't. I said that that was fine, that we couldn't always think of names for groups, and went on to the next child.

While doing these lessons. I accept every child's response. During the listing process, everyone usually contributes something, but I call on the children with smaller vocabularies first so that they have a chance to contribute. I usually save the grouping and labeling steps for the next day so that the lessons don't take more than 25 minutes. When we form groups, each child who wants to organize a group tells me why those particular things are grouped together and then attempts to give a label to that group. This labeling step is difficult for many of my children and if they can't do it, I simply accept that and go on to the next volunteer.

As you can see, the children have different categories and different reasons for grouping things together. Therefore no child is allowed to add anything to another child's group. I also write the name of the child who labeled a group under that group. Objects from the list can be used over and over again as different children make groups. The children enjoy these lessons and I can see that they have had an effect on their vocabulary and categorization skills.

May

Well, the year is almost over. Just one more week of half-days of school for the children and lots of report writing for me. I always feel sad during this last week of school—so much yet undone. It has, all in all, been an exceptionally good year. During this last month, we had SQUIRT time for 14 minutes each day. The children were so proud that they could sustain their reading almost as long as the third, fourth, and fifth graders do. During SQUIRT, I always read something of real interest to me. This is part of the modeling process. Children should see adults reading for pleasure and information. This month, however, I found something I was captivated by and which I could share with the children. I read *Watership Down* (Adams, 1977) and each day at the end of SQUIRT, I would tell the children what was happening to Fiver, Silver, and the other rabbits. Finally, I got so involved I took the book home over the weekend to finish. When I sat down for SQUIRT on Monday with a new book, the children were dismayed. How could I finish the book without them? We talked about how we sometimes get so involved

SSR

with a book that it is hard to stop reading. I then related to them the last 100 pages of *Watership Down* and we went on with SQUIRT time. Reading something which interested me and which I could share with the children was so successful that I shall look for other books like that next year.

Well, we prepared books to take home again as we did at Christmas. This time we did some editing on the stories the children had written themselves. We decided that if people other than the children themselves are to read their books, we want to make the book as readable as possible. Therefore, spelling and punctuation must be correct. I put a sign which said "Editor-in-Chief" near my typewriter and we spent much of our morning time editing and rewriting or typing. The children saw the need to make these changes and cooperated willingly. The stories that went home were far from perfect but they were readable by others and I think quite remarkable for first graders. We also prepared their word banks and dictionaries to take home. Many children plan to add words to these over the summer and to show them to me in the fall.

We held an auction for the charts we have been making during the year. (I saved several to show at the end-of-year grade-level meeting. Miss Port, the Chairperson, has asked me to talk to the first-grade teachers in the district about language experience.) Each child was given 20 tokens (bottle caps) and Larry was the auctioneer. This was a huge success and, of course, just as at any good auction, we were all hungry at the end of it and needed refreshment! The parents provided this and we had a party.

We also had our annual book fair this month, sponsored and run by Ms. Maverick's fourth-grade class. The children bought many books, and we also sold many to parents during our end-of-year conferences. I hired Chip to help me clean up the room each night and paid him with books!

Of course, Miss Launch brought her class to see their new room and new teacher. Gosh, the kindergartners look so tiny. It always makes me stop and reflect on how much the children grow during first grade. Next year's class looked like a good group. I doubt, however, that they will be able to compare with this year's group. Just yesterday I remarked to Mr. Topps about the diversity of this class and how my next group of children couldn't be as interesting as this one. He nodded, smiled, and said, "Mrs. Wright, you say that every year!"

THE FIRST GRADE MEETING

Mrs. Wright had been secretly pleased when Sue asked her to explain her reading program to the June meeting of the first-grade teachers. When she had first begun using this approach, she had been very zealous and had tried to convert her fellow teachers to her method, and had been quite taken aback when a veteran teacher informed her that "every year there is some young teacher experimenting on the children with newfangled ideas." Since then she had quietly gone her own way and let the other teachers go theirs! The word had spread, however, that her method worked, and now she had been asked to address their group! Mrs. Wright was indeed pleased, and she was also prepared!

Mrs. Wright brought samples of the whole-class and structured language experience charts to the meeting. She had also borrowed some of the individual books, word banks, and dictionaries from the children, promising on her honor to return them promptly. She had brought charts showing the schedules her class had followed and slides of the wall vocabulary, the letter-sound bulletin boards, and the various room arrangements.

She began by explaining how she started the program. She showed some of the whole-class charts and pointed out that she recorded exactly what each child said and put that child's name next to it. She then explained how she divided the children into four heterogeneous groups and did structured language experience stories with them. She told the teachers that the children experience immediate success with reading because of the repetitive nature of the stories and because each take-home book is illustrated with appropriate pictures. She further pointed out that beginning the year with structured language experience lessons was good for everyone. "The children who were not ready to read were in the presence of reading and writing, and developed the essential readiness understandings. Those who were ready began actual reading as they learned some of the words from the stories. I benefited by being able to provide everyone with a successful start and by being able to observe, diagnose, and evaluate the various readiness levels of different children."

She showed the chart showing Paul's group's September schedule and explained how the children must learn, from the very beginning, to work independently. Several teachers' eyebrows rose as she said this, and Mrs. Wright elaborated on how she got them working independently.

"In the beginning of the year I had quite structured activities in the centers," she explained. "In the listening center, the children put on headphones, listened to a story and did a simple follow-up activity after the story. One child in each group was responsible for turning on the tape, rewinding it afterwards, and collecting the follow-up papers. In the math center, again the activities were quite structured. There were specific sets of objects to count, patterns of beads to string, objects to measure, or problems to solve. In the magazine center, children looked for specific objects or letters and pasted these on the appropriate charts on the wall. Each group had one person who was responsible for seeing that everything went smoothly in each center. This is another advantage to having the groups heterogeneously formed so that they have both very mature, capable children and some less capable ones. Before the children went to work in the centers, I took a few minutes to point out what their tasks would be, and as the groups changed centers each half-hour, I circulated and made sure that each group had begun their work before I joined the group with which I was working.

At the end of each morning, we discussed the morning's activities and noted new additions to the charts in the magazine centers. When there were problems, we discussed what had caused them and what we could do about them. Of course, some children had a difficult time working independently in the centers, but these same children would have had difficulty completing exercises at their desks. I find I actually have fewer discipline problems now than I did when each child spent the morning sitting at a desk copying the daily story from the board and completing dittoed sheets."

Several of the teachers were nodding their heads and taking notes, so Mrs. Wright continued. She explained how she usually began the individual story writing sometimes in October when the children were adjusted to the independent activities. She pointed out that she changed the schedule by not meeting with the groups two days a week to allow her time to meet with children individually.

She then showed them some slides of the Words on the Wall at different times and explained how this was her major vehicle for building sight word ability and for building letter-sound relationships. She told them how, after assuring that all children could make the auditory discrimination, she taught letter-sound associations by referring to known words. She could tell that the teachers liked the idea of having an action, a food, and a bulletin board of pictures, words, and objects for each letter-sound relationship taught because they all started making notes furiously when she mentioned this. She then showed them some sample context plus consonant/digraph/blend activities and consonant/digraph/blend substitution exercises and stressed that she felt it was important for the children to apply the letter-sound associations in their reading.

Finally Mrs. Wright talked about getting the children into the basals and handed out copies of the charts she had stapled in the children's folders in order to keep track of the stories the children had read. She emphasized that during the last half of the year many of the children were writing their own stories and that her conferences with each child now varied according to his or her wishes and needs. For some, she continued to write down their stories and help them add known words to their banks all year. For others, the conference became a time for discussing the basal stories and library books they were reading. Other times, she used this individual time to help children edit the stories they had written.

Mrs. Wright ended her talk by showing the teachers the slides illustrating the room arrangement at various times during the year. She also related to them how the work centers and the individual conferences were tailored to individual needs as the year went on.

After a break, the teachers got together for a discussion and question period. They seemed enthusiastic, but had many practical concerns. One teacher asked what the children found to write about—she had tried to have the children do some creative writing toward the end of the year and the children complained that there was nothing to write about. Mrs. Wright told them that the experiences the children have all day during science, social studies, and math are story material, and that she constantly pointed this out to the children. In addition to this natural stimulation for writing, Mrs. Wright suggested many "artificial" stimulations for writing—she told them about the flannel board cut-outs, the pictures, the boxes of objects and story starters which she used as motivators in the writing center.

Finally, she pointed out that the notion of "story" is really too limiting. Many experience stories are actually lists of facts or directions. She showed them the story the class had written after Mort's mother talked to them about Hanukkah, the chart of rules which was displayed in the games center, and the chart with the recipe of Christmas cookies. She told them about Steve, who always wrote stories based on facts of life in the wilderness. Finally, she told them about Joyce, who was so imaginative in her creative play but could never "think of anything to write about" and how she often capitalized on this interest.

Another teacher asked about children with dialects. Mrs. Wright, who was originally from another part of the country, pointed out that she thought all the other teachers spoke a dialect, and they admitted that they thought she spoke a dialect. The conclusion was reached that everyone speaks a dialect of English, but some dialects seem to be more generally acceptable. Since Mrs. Wright knew that what they were really asking was, "Do you write down a child's improper grammar?" she shared some of Chip's and Jeff's stories. Several teachers seemed appalled at the notion of actually writing down sentences like, "They sure good," and, "That bird don't never stop singing." Mrs. Wright tried to explain that the language experience approach is based on the principle that what a child says can be written down and read by that child and others.

She further pointed out that children learn language by hearing it spoken, and that in a language experience classroom there is a lot of speaking going on. The children who speak language patterns which many consider incorrect will have many opportunities to hear other children and the teacher speak, and may begin to modify some of their speech patterns.

To the question of whether sentences like, "They sure good," confused other children, Mrs. Wright responded that they were no more confusing than, "They sure are good," looks to Chip. After some laughter, Mrs. Wright went on to explain that the only time this would cause confusion was during the whole-class stories, and that this was one of the reasons she put the child's name after each sentence. In this way, each child could read his or her own sentence as it had been spoken. "When other children correct a child like Chip, I tell them that that is the way Chip says it."

Several teachers wondered if it didn't take a lot more time and preparation to teach in this way. Mrs. Wright responded that she really didn't think so once the class had been organized and begun. "I used to spend hours each week correcting workbooks and preparing ditto sheets and charts to introduce the basal reader stories. Now I spend that same amount of time getting the centers ready, changing the materials in them, and thinking of activities for individual children. Initially, I spent a lot of time worrying about the composition of my reading groups. Just at the time I had them set up and had everyone at the same place, one child would begin a growth spurt and another would reach a plateau. I just never was happy with grouping them according to ability. In addition, I used to spend endless hours on the phone explaining to Billy's mother why he wasn't in the top group with Johnny!"

Finally, a teacher asked if there was any research to support this approach to beginning reading instruction. Mrs. Wright reminded them that research consistently rated the teacher as the most important single variable in the classroom and that, according to research, there was no one superior method.

Mrs. Wright then drew on her own years of teaching experience and gave her reasons for preferring the approach she was currently using. "I like it because it is integrative," she explained. "The children talk and listen. They then write about what they have discussed, and read what they have written. The reading material is pertinent to the child. There are no comprehension, vocabulary, or sentence structure problems when a child is reading what he or she has written or dictated. The language experience approach builds on what all the children are already good at —talking! They have an immediately successful experience with reading and go home after the first week of school thinking, 'I can read!' This feeling of achievement is heightened when I decide that most of the children have a large enough sight vocabulary to read the preprimers independently. Reading their first real books is easy and fun, and they read them again and again to anyone who will listen."

Mrs. Wright ended the meeting by pointing out that although language experience was the core of her program, she actually used a combination approach. The children began with language experience stories, then moved into independent reading in four series of basal readers, and finally into a more individualized library book reading program. Throughout the year word identification skills were continually developed so that her children became independent decoders of words.

Miss Port ended the meeting by reminding the teachers that they could use their two professional days for classroom visits and suggested that they might want to visit Mrs. Wright's class. The response was enthusiastic and Mrs. Wright promised to put them to work when they came!

11 | Miss Nouveau

THE PARENT MEETING

Miss Nouveau arrived at the school two hours before her 8:00 P.M. parent meeting was scheduled to begin. Frankly, she was nervous and dreaded having to face all the parents in a large group. But, at least, she thought, Mr. Topps would be there to help. He had generously offered to come to her meeting in case she needed help answering questions about school-wide policies she might not even know about yet.

She was looking over her new bulletin board when Mr. Topps arrived at 7:45 P.M. He told her that the board was lovely and that the fall theme she had chosen brightened the room. She didn't tell Mr. Topps that she had been working on that bulletin board for two weeks, sometimes until 2:00 A.M. She wanted him and the parents to think that she was efficient and organized.

Miss Nouveau had made name tags for all of the parents to wear. In that way she could easily identify each parent, and she would know from the leftover name tags who had been unable to attend. When all of the parents had had a cup of coffee and were seated, Mr. Topps, as had been agreed to earlier, introduced her to the group.

"As you all know," he began, "I am Mr. Topps. I especially wanted to come this evening to introduce your child's teacher to you. Miss Nouveau comes to us this year as a first-year teacher. She did exceptionally well both at the university and during her student teaching, so that when this position opened up last spring, I was delighted to have Miss Nouveau among the applicants for the job. I know that you will be as happy with her as we are. If there is anything that you would like either of us to do, do not hesitate to call. Now, let's hear from Miss Nouveau."

"Thank you, Mr. Topps. This is an exciting moment for me. All my life I have dreamed of being an elementary school teacher.

"I want to explain to you the kind of program that I have planned for this school year. You see here on this table the reading books that your children will be using. It is the *Reading Can Be Fun* series published by Basic Publishing Company. In addition to reading these books, your children will be working with these workbooks. When they are not with me in one of the three reading groups, they will be at their seats doing follow-up skills in workbooks or other assignments that reinforce

341

the basal's skill development program or reading a book from the library shelf over there. My assignment of the children into these three groups has been based on the results of a test which accompanies the reading series called an Informal Reading Inventory (IRI). It measures your child's performance in oral reading and comprehension." Miss Nouveau, relieved that *that* was over, hurried on to a topic she knew more about.

"You know that physical factors are quite important in determining how well your children do in school. You can be most helpful in seeing to it that your children get to bed by 8:30 at night, that they come to school after having had a nutritious breakfast, and that they play out in the fresh air for a while every day after school. I intend to emphasize these basic health habits with the children this year. We will be studying nutrition, the value of recreation, and the importance of adequate rest. Starting on Monday, I am going to ask you to send a snack to school with your child. We will have snack-time every morning in order to help keep the energy level of the children high. The school nurse will test vision and hearing in October, and if there are any problems, I will be in touch with you."

Miss Nouveau looked at her watch and saw that what she had planned to take thirty minutes had only consumed fifteen minutes of time, so she asked Mr. Topps if there was anything he would like to add. There was not. The time had come for the part of the meeting that she had been dreading. She turned back to the parents and asked, "Are there any questions?"

All over the room, hands shot up. She called on Mrs. Moore first.

"You will be using the same set of books for all of the children? How can you do this? Aren't they at different reading levels?"

Miss Nouveau replied, "Yes, they are at three different levels. Some of them are reading below grade level and they are reading in this first reader; most of them are reading right on grade level and they are in this 2^1 book; however, some of them are reading above grade level and they are reading from this 2^2 book." She smiled proudly! "The difference in instruction among the three groups will be not only the book they're using and the pace at which they move through the books, but also the amount and kinds of material covered."

Mrs. Penn raised her hand to ask. "Why are you using *this* particular series?"

Mr. Topps intervened. "If I may, I would like to answer that one, Miss Nouveau, since the decision was made before you were hired. You see, Mrs. Penn, the teachers in this school who use basals met together last spring and selected this series from among the six state-approved adoptions. Most of the teachers at that meeting felt that this series allowed for the most flexibility while still retaining the structure and sequential development of skills which is a strong point of the basal reader approach."

Another hand went up, and Miss Nouveau called upon Mr. Tomás. "When the kids aren't with you, how will they know what to do? Won't they just waste time and not do their work?"

"I take time every morning to explain to the children what they are to do on their work papers. You see, they all do the same ones, so I can give those instructions to everyone. In their reading groups, they have been told what they need to do in their workbooks. They do have instructions, and they know what to do. But sometimes some children don't complete their work. When that happens, they just have more to do the next day."

Mrs. Penn glanced over at Mr. Topps for his reaction. Had he pressed his fingertips to his forehead because of a headache?

With all of the questions answered, Miss Nouveau thanked them for coming. She started to gather up some of her materials when she noticed Mrs. Penn at her elbow.

"Miss Nouveau, I just want to offer to help you in any way that I can. I used to be a teacher, so I think that I might be of some help to you. *Please* feel free to call on me. I really enjoy helping out, and I know what a difficult task you have."

"Oh, thank you, but I'm sure that won't be necessary. I think that I have things pretty much under control now. But I do appreciate your offer. I will call for help if I need it."

"Fine. See that you do. Good evening. It was lovely meeting with you this evening."

Mrs. Penn and Mrs. Middleman left the room together. They were talking quietly, but Miss Nouveau heard some of what was said.

MRS. MIDDLEMAN: Isn't she a dear little thing? So cute! And just look at that lovely bulletin board. My, she certainly is creative.

MRS. PENN: Yes, she is. But, you know, I always rather like to see the children's work up on the bulletin board. It's not as pretty or tidy but there's something wonderful about your own child's work displayed. Mrs. Wright did so much of that last year.

Miss Nouveau was crestfallen. All of that work, and they would rather see things that the children had done! "Maybe I should think about having the children do something to put up. Oh, but it will be so messy!"

MONTHLY LOGS

September

My major premise is wrong! I thought that all children loved to read or that at the very least they were eager to learn. How wrong! How wrong!

I just can't understand it. Butch sits in his seat (sometimes) just waiting out the day. If I ask him to practice the sight vocabulary words with which he is having trouble or to do one of the other assignments, he just looks at me and asks, "Why?"

"So that when you grow up you'll be able to read. You need to be a good reader to get a job."

"Oh, yeah," he replied. "Well, my dad, he don't read so good, but he makes two hunderd bucks a week!" That sounds like a great deal of money to a seven-year-old, but if he only knew!

One of the most frightening aspects of this teaching business is the weight of responsibility one feels. I was so excited to have my own classroom assigned to me and spent a lot of time here this summer getting my room ready for the first days of school. But the full realization of the responsibility didn't hit me until I saw the first children come into the room—my room—*our* room.

I fervently hope that I will never again live through a day like the first day of school. The children were quite well behaved (I suppose the novelty of returning to school) and I had prepared an excess of material for them, just in case. I had enough for two days—so I thought! By noon, I had used up everything I had planned for the first day. They worked so much more quickly than I ever imagined! By lunch time I was rattled. What to do? That afternoon I used up the next day's lessons!

Another horrible feeling of incompetence came when I realized that I had to put these children into reading groups, and I didn't have the foggiest notion of what criteria to use. How many *is* a group? Grouping had been talked about in my undergraduate reading course, but I now realized I really didn't have a well-defined idea of how to go about it.

Basals   At least I had the books straight in my mind. There are so many that I found it very confusing to see a huge stack of books in the office with my name on them. I must have looked shocked, because Mrs. Mainstay came over to me and asked if anything was missing. Missing? Good grief! I thought that perhaps they had given me someone else's books as well. I finally admitted to her that I didn't understand all of those markings on the books.

Because she has done the ordering of textbooks for so many years, she knows them well. She grabbed a pile, motioned for me to do the same, and we went into my classroom where she proceeded to explain the hierarchy in basal reading books. "Our series has three preprimers, a primer, and a 1^2 book which average children complete during first grade. An average second grader would read the 2^1 book during the first half of second grade and the 2^2 book during the second half. For average third graders, there are also two books, 3^1 and 3^2. For grades four and above there is one book for each year."

When she had finished, she told me that third-grade books would be available whenever I needed them. I thanked her but said I wouldn't need those: "My children are in second grade."

She smiled and said, "Well, once you get to know the children, you may see a need for the other books, too."

I gave all the children the IRI which accompanies the series. It **IRI** wasn't easy to get it done because the other children were so noisy and interrupted me so often. I think also that it was too much to try to do it all in two days. Next year (if I am alive and teaching!), I will spread it out across a week so that the children only have to work independently for a little while.

By the time of the parent meeting, I did have my groups formed, though that had not been as easy as I felt it would be. Larry gives every indication of being an extremely bright child, yet when I was scoring his IRI, I was amazed at the number of errors he made in oral reading. Instead of, "He could not get the car to start," Larry read, "He couldn't get the car started." Yet with all of those errors, his comprehension remained high! As a matter of fact, he did amazingly well, answering every question asked of him without error. I put him into the middle group anyway, because the requirements for the IRI include both oral reading and comprehension. I thought Mort would do better, too, but he was so inattentive that he made all kinds of silly mistakes. [See p. 189.]

Daisy and Mike didn't really meet the 95 percent oral reading accuracy criterion for the first reader but I didn't think I could manage another group so I put them there and I will send extra work home with them. Paul wouldn't read for me! I pleaded, threatened and bribed but he steadfastly refused. I put him in the lowest group but I don't know where he belongs. He won't read aloud or do his workbook. He is not mean and behaves; he just won't do anything. I must talk to Mrs. Wright about him.

I assigned children to reading groups and let them choose a group name. For some of the groups this took a long time, but eventually all three groups were named. Some things do puzzle me about these groups. Why are the Butterflies all girls and why is there only one girl in the Monsters? I wonder if there's any significance to that?

MONSTERS		*ASTRONAUTS*		*BUTTERFLIES*
Mike	Jeff	Horace	Mitch	Mandy
Daisy	Chip	Daphne	Manuel	Pat
Paul	Mort	Betty	Joyce	Roberta
Butch		Steve	Larry	Rita
Carl		Alex	Alexander	Hilda
			Anthony	Danielle

One thing that really concerns me is the name of one group. I tried to get them to change the name, but Mike, the leader in the group, convinced the others that they should keep it. I just hope that no one thinks that *I* named them! (They certainly chose a descriptive name!)

When the groups begin to work each morning, they can see the order of their assignments on the chalkboard. The first thing that each child must do is work on the writing lesson which I placed on the board. Children need this practice in handwriting and it keeps them busy until they come to their reading group. If they finish that and their other work, they are permitted to choose a book from the library shelf to read quietly at their seats. The reading group order changes every week so that I do not always see the Monsters after recess when they are so excited! Here is this week's schedule:

MONSTERS	ASTRONAUTS	BUTTERFLIES
copying and	reading group	copying and
ditto sheets	workbook	ditto sheets
reading group	copying and	workbook
workbook	ditto sheets	reading group

I haven't written a time schedule for them, for I find that I'm never quite sure when I will be done with one reading group and ready to call another, or how long it will take a group of children to finish their workbook assignments. [See pp. 204–205.]

I've been having trouble with some of the children not finishing their work. At the beginning of the month, they all worked so hard and cooperated with me very well, but as time went by, I found they didn't maintain that attitude. Roberta, for instance, says the workbook is stupid. When she refused to do it, I had no choice but to move her into the middle group where the work is easier. Lask week I began keeping those children who didn't complete their work in at recess, so that they could finish what had been assigned. They were not permitted to go out unless all of their work was finished. So on Monday and Tuesday, I had Mort, Mitch, Mike, Daisy, Paul, Jeff, Butch, and Roberta stay in and finish work. On Wednesday, Daisy, Butch, and Mitch didn't have to stay in, because they had finished their work. I thought my system was working until I checked over their work. I found it had been done very carelessly and that it needed to be done over again. By Wednesday, I noticed that Carl, too, dawdled over his work and seemed delighted when I told him that he would have to stay in. Thursday, the same children were told to stay in to work when I suddenly realized, after looking at my planbook, that I had to go outside since it was my day to supervise the playground! I got chills thinking what this group of children might do if left unsupervised in the classroom, so I did what I thought it best to do—I marched them down to the office and told them to sit on the bench and do their work there. From what Mrs. Mainstay told me later, there was little work accomplished. Mr. Topps came down to talk to me after school, as he does nearly every afternoon, and suggested that I might be able to find another solution for this problem. He reminded me of my own statement at the parent meeting that children require recreation and fresh air. I thought hard about it all night, and decided that any work left un-done at the end of the week would be sent home with the children to be completed over the weekend. That should take care of that problem!

I've had to send a note home to the parents about our morning snack time. It never occurred to me that there might be problems, but several children bring nothing. I don't know whether Chip, Paul, and Jeff forgot to bring something, but they look hungrily at the other children who do bring snacks. And Daisy! The first day she brought three cup-cakes, a bag of potato chips, and a can of cola (warm)! The rest of that first week was just as bad, so I have written to the parents asking them to please send snacks like fruits, vegetables, peanut butter and crackers, cheese, and so on. I also informed the parents that we would be putting all of the food together and letting each child choose something to eat from the accumulation.

SQUIRT is such a neat idea! I usually have the children reading for **SSR** five minutes a day when we do it. At first I read along with them as Mr. Topps told me I must, but I am getting so far behind on grading all of these assignments that I'm sure it won't matter if once in a while I check a few papers while they read. I always make sure that the chil-dren do the reading. Sometimes, however, I get so involved with my work that they read for eight or nine minutes. I am usually reminded by my clock watchers that we have gone past the five minute mark. Other days, we only read for three minutes. I figure that makes up for it, and besides there are so many things that we have to get done!

October

If only I can survive until January! I student taught during the winter quarter last year, and if we can only get to January I'll know what to do! Why did everything look so easy when my supervising teacher did it? Either I am doing something wrong or else I have a really rough group of children. I always wanted to teach second grade because the children are still so cute and they already know how to read. That seemed like the perfect grade to me, but how different it really is! Some of them can't read and some of them are definitely not in the "cute" category!

This class makes me wonder about the first-grade experience that they had. Whenever I walk by Mrs. Wright's classroom, it *appears* that she has good discipline, but I wonder if she does really. If she had good control of her class, how could a class like this one be giving me so much trouble? I know that Mrs. Wright is an excellent teacher—listening to the reading of Pat and Rita convinces me of that, but perhaps she is just not a disciplinarian. Well, whatever the reason, I've really had to crack down on these kids. I've started putting much longer writing assignments on the chalkboard just to keep the children from running around the room. That should keep them sitting a little longer! The problem with the added material is that they take less time to copy it than it takes me to think it up and carefully write it on the chalkboard.

Routines

Another thing we have been having trouble with is going to the bathroom and getting drinks of water. Every morning at 10:10 we go to the restrooms and water fountain. The teacher under whom I did student teaching called this "watering" the children. I never understood the real significance of that until Paul came back from the restroom one day soaking wet. Bit by bit, I got him to tell me that Mike, Butch, and Mitch had been dunking him in the toilet. (I hope it had been flushed!) I give the children five minutes in the restrooms, which should be adequate time for them without allowing too much extra time for "messing around." Obviously, for some of the children five minutes is several too many!

And the pencil sharpening! At the end of the day I require the children to turn in their pencils that need sharpening. After they leave I sharpen the pencils. Yuk! But what else can I do? They would probably be at the pencil sharpener all day long if I let *them* do it.

Basals

The children have also not been conscientious about their workbooks. Every night as I check them, I find that many of the pages are completed incorrectly, if they are completed at all. I think I'm going to have them bring their workbooks to reading group so that we can do them there. But, gosh, where am I going to find the time! As it is, I am spending 30 to 45 minutes with each reading group. *They* get tired, and so do I! But how else can I do everything that the lesson plan in the manual outlines? By the time that I have introduced new words, reviewed old words, gone through the phonics lesson, gone over the oral language lesson, had them do all the ditto sheets that accompany the story, read the story out loud and answer their questions (I gave up the silent reading section during the fifth week—just no time for it!), and then do the follow-up activities, the best part of an hour is gone. We haven't had a social studies or science lesson for two weeks because there just is not enough time in the day to do everything. I haven't read stories to the children in so long that I can't even recall the title of the last one. I love to read aloud, but something has to give with a full curriculum like ours.

The oral reading of the children is very poor! I wonder if that could be related to the fact that the first time they see the story is during oral reading? Maybe I should have them practice the story before they come to the reading group. I didn't want to let them take their reading books back to their seats because they might read ahead and spoil the fun of the stories coming up, but I think I'm going to risk it. If nothing else, these children must learn to read!

In addition to everything that has been happening within the room, they tested the children's vision and hearing this month. I was convinced that Mort had an auditory problem, for he seems to be tuned out a lot of the time. He doesn't hear me when I call on him and when he does hear, he doesn't immediately follow through on what I ask him to do. His hearing screening was normal, however. I guess he just doesn't pay attention. Jeff, Mandy, Larry, and Manuel were referred to ophthalmologists. Butch, I discovered, is color-blind. No wonder he couldn't do the work papers that required him to color according to the directions given at the top. I hate to admit this but I had him do them over three times before I finally gave up on him in disgust!

SQUIRT is not going very well. Sometimes I have them read for 10 **SSR** or 15 minutes. Butch and Mitch say they hate SQUIRT and have become very rambunctious during this time. I had been told about SQUIRT when I first came to Merritt and had heard that almost all the teachers did it and that the children loved it. That's certainly not the way a lot of my children feel about it. I don't think it's as great as it's cracked up to be but I sure can get a lot of grading done while they read.

TRY IT OUT

Refer to Chapter 7 for the 13 DO's suggested for classroom organization and management. How is Miss Nouveau doing? What can you suggest to her?

November

Butch, unable to complete his daily work, has been the bane of my existence lately. Two weeks ago he had accumulated so many work papers that by Thursday evening I could see that he would have a lot to do for the coming weekend. That Friday morning he arrived at school with a cast on his left arm, and I'm ashamed to admit that my first reaction was, "Oh, thank goodness it's his left arm. He can still do his work!" He came into the room grinning and showing off his autographed cast. During work time, I noticed that he wasn't working. I told him that he had better do some of his work or he would have even more to take home that evening. He simply looked up at me and said, "I can't. My arm's broke."

"Yes, I know it's broken, but that's only your left arm. You can still use your right one."

He grinned and said, "Yeah, but I'm left-handed!" Oh, no! I had never noticed—I had never thought to notice handedness before. I glanced around the room and saw that no one else was left-handed. There must be a conspiracy against me!

How is Butch going to do his work? I finally decided to let him do what he could (circling answers, and so forth) and paired him with Larry or Pat to do the rest of his work. He thoroughly enjoys having secretarial help. Sometimes I wonder—is it really broken?

I think I should resign at Christmas. I'm not doing these children any good and they are not doing any good for me. I go home every night at six or six-thirty simply exhausted. Even then I take work home with me so that I don't get to bed until after midnight. I barely can make it to school by 8:00 the next morning; I haven't been to a movie or on a date for weeks. I had no idea that teaching would be so difficult and so depressing. I thought that children were lovable, but I have found I cannot bear to be around some of them. I must be an ogre not to be able to love them all.

I have been talking quite a bit with Mr. Topps recently, and he has been making some very positive suggestions. He tells me that I shouldn't quit, but that instead I should talk with Mrs. Wise or some of the other teachers to get some ideas for control and organization. He helped a lot when he came in after school one day as I was grading workbooks. I marked them as usual—"x" on the wrong ones and a -12 (or whatever for the total incorrect answers) at the top—when he suggested that I might want to emphasize the positive with the children. He told me that when he had taught he always marked those that the children had done correctly with a "C" and wrote $+9$ (or whatever) at the top. He said that by emphasizing the elements which were correct, I would help the children focus on those elements. They would still see at a glance which ones they had missed, but those were not as obvious or as embarrassing. A lot of children, he said, come to fear the red marks on papers because we only use them negatively. They should learn to see the red marks for what they are—aids to understanding the material. I tried Mr. Topps' idea, and, though it took me a while to adjust to the system, I use it all the time now. An interesting comment was made the other day by Chip, whose papers had formerly been bloodbaths of red marks: "Wow! Look how neat my paper is! See all the things I did good, Manuel!"

Two of the children have started wearing eyeglasses this month. Larry came in with his first and all of the children wanted to get them! Mr. Topps told me that Jeff, whom I had referred for further testing, had not yet been to the eye doctor. When I questioned him about it, Mr. Topps indicated that Jeff's family couldn't afford the glasses. I was appalled! A child not able to get the glasses he needs! I remembered something in my notes from college and checked them when I got home that night. One of my professors had indicated that service organizations often provide funds for school children to get glasses or other medical attention. I got the phone number of the local organization from Mr. Topps and called that night to explain the situation. The club president was very helpful and told me that his organization would be glad to help Jeff get his glasses. I also discovered that his organization acted as a collection agency for old pairs of eyeglasses which people didn't use. They take these glasses to eye doctors who are able to reuse the frames and regrind the lenses to provide glasses more cheaply for those who need them. I told him that in return for helping Jeff, I wanted to do something to help his group, so my class and I began canvassing our neighborhoods to collect old pairs of eyeglasses for the service organization. I dittoed a sheet for people whom the children contacted so that the youngsters wouldn't have to remember all the details about why they were asking for glasses. They handed a sheet to whoever answered the door and asked if they had any old eyeglasses to contribute. My kids collected 15 pairs of eyeglasses! Boy, was I proud of them!

The workbooks are still causing me some problems. They take up so much time and I have to grade them all at night. Four pages per child is a lot of work for me to correct in addition to all the dittos they do. I sat down one night to try to find a solution, and I thought about it for a long time. Why is it that the workbooks are provided with these basal reading programs? I came to the conclusion that the authors wanted to provide practice for some of the skills they had introduced. Well, some of my groups already know some of the skills so I have taken a chance and decided to skip some of the pages if everyone in the group can already do them. I hope that is okay. Somehow it doesn't seem right to have those unfinished pages. **Basals**

I have also begun letting the middle and top groups work on their workbook pages independently in pairs. Two children work together to come up with their best responses. We then go over these responses together when they come to the group. During reading group we check the pages and analyze why an answer is right or wrong. I also have them explain the reasoning behind wrong answers. Sometimes their reasoning leads them to an answer which is wrong according to the workbook key but which makes much more sense from a child's point of view.

I have tentatively moved Larry from the middle group into the top group. He is one of the best comprehenders in the room and I have noticed that when he makes oral reading errors, they are "smart errors" like reading *can't* for *cannot*, or *little* for *small*. I learned in my undergraduate reading course that all good readers have an eye-voice span and that their eyes are out ahead of their voices. I never thought that this could apply to a second grader. I think, however, that this must be why he didn't meet the 95 percent word identification criterion on the IRI and I am just sure he can read as well as anyone in the top group. I have also moved Mort into the middle group. He also made smart errors on the IRI and he reads much better than any of the other Monsters. [See p. 189.]

Nevertheless, I am still discouraged about the conflict between what I had hoped to accomplish this year and what I am actually accomplishing. I am rapidly coming to the conclusion that a job as a waitress might not be so bad after all! Or maybe I can try to support myself with my writing. Since I love to write children's stories, I might be able to sell some of them for publication. I will talk with Mrs. Wise and see what she suggests, for I have found her name to be quite descriptive of her ability to analyze a situation.

December

SSR At the beginning of this month, we stopped SQUIRT. It seemed obvious to me that it just couldn't work. I had forgotten about Mr. Topps, however. He has a schedule of when the different classes do SQUIRT so that he can come and read along with the different classes from time to time. He thinks it is particularly important that the boys see reading as something which adult males do. About a week after we had quit, he walked in at what had been our SQUIRT time and sat down and opened up his book. He noticed, of course, that no one was reading or ready to read and looked perplexed. "Did I get your schedule mixed up with someone else's, Miss Nouveau?" he asked kindly.

"Oh no," I replied, "We're just running a little behind. Come on boys and girls. Get your books out."

"But why?" asked Alex, "You said we wouldn't have SQUIRT anymore."

Mr. Topps said, "Oh, is there is problem, Miss Nouveau? Maybe I can help. Let's chat after school." Then he sat down in a chair and began to read as if nothing were out of the ordinary. Of course the children and I began to read, too. We read for eight minutes, and Mr. Topps signaled me at that point that we should stop. I told the children to put away their books and return to work.

After school, clutching my keys, I knocked on the open door to Mr. Topps' office. He looked up and said, "You didn't have to come up here, Miss Nouveau. I would have come to your room on my way home later this afternoon."

"Well," I replied, "I would rather get it over with now. I know that I'm a disappointment to you—I am to myself. Would you like me to resign now or wait until Christmas?"

"Who said anything about resigning? Miss Nouveau, I think you have the wrong notion about my role in this school. I want to help you, because I remember well the agonies of *my* first year as a teacher! Now, what seems to be the problem with SQUIRT?"

"The children are restless and bored with it. Maybe second graders are just too young, or perhaps this particular group of children is just too undisciplined. Anyway, I can't seem to control them."

"We know they aren't too young, Miss Nouveau. They have been involved in SQUIRT since kindergarten. While I do agree that you have an unusual class, I have seen SQUIRT used with enough classes to know that it will work with your class, too. Let me just run through some of the hazards that one might encounter when using SQUIRT; perhaps being aware of some of these might prove useful to you in organizing the program. First of all, and probably most important, children must know that we adults value reading. That is why it is crucial that the teacher read something enjoyable while the children are reading and why I circulate among the various classes as often as I can and read with the classes during SQUIRT. Everyone who is in the room must be reading to make it work. ("Oops!" I thought.)

"Also, SQUIRT must be done every day and the sustaining power of the children must be increased gradually. We start at five minutes a day in second grade, permitting those who wish to continue reading longer to do so, of course. When you begin to see them sustaining their reading for five minutes with no difficulty and exhibit eagerness to read longer, then you increase the time to six minutes. In that way you build up their reading time gradually. You only create uncertainty when the children have no notion of how long they are to read. *Never* let them read 8 minutes one day, 3 the next, and 12 the next. ("Oh, no," I cringed.) Also, some of the children will become clock watchers if you don't cover the face of the clock during SQUIRT. ("Of course!" I nodded.) Most of the teachers have a timer which they can set and face away from the class, but if you don't have one, you simply slip a piece of paper over the clock face so that the children cannot see the passage of time. You want them to focus on reading, not timing. They will know, of course, because you have told them, how long they are to read, but it's much better when they can't watch the clock. ("So that's it!" I thought.) Do you have any questions about SQUIRT? I hope that some of the things I've mentioned might be useful. And, Miss Nouveau, please don't think of resigning. I've been really pleased to note your enthusiasm, sincerity, and dedication. I think that you have worked out some difficult problems for yourself, such as the workbook situation. I have a great deal of confidence in you, Miss Nouveau!"

Wow! Maybe things will get better for me. I think I had better call Miss Port and ask her for some suggestions. And Mrs. Wise has always been most helpful.

I have tried, up to this point, to write in my journal at the end of each week so that I could keep up with what was happening, but since my chat with Mr. Topps, so many things have been happening that the weeks rushed by until the holidays gave me a chance to sit down at home and continue my journal. I am so excited by the changes that I have made and the ones I am going to make! I called Miss Port the evening after I had talked with Mr. Topps. She told me that she had been planning to come and see me that week.

Miss Port and I talked for almost two hours one afternoon early in the month. At first, I was afraid to tell her about all the problems I was having. But, she asked me about my groups and my schedule and before I knew it, I had told her everything about how I couldn't get everything done even when I kept my groups for 45 minutes, and how the children didn't do their seatwork and workbook pages, and the parents complained when I sent them home with homework every night. I told her about the Monsters. "Heavens, my dear, you don't call them that, do you?" she inquired.

"Well, yes, I do. But I didn't name them. I learned in my college reading class that you should let them choose their name. No one ever told me they might choose such a descriptive name."

Miss Port suggested that I refer to them by using one of the children in the group's name. "You might choose the natural leader in the group or, on the other hand, you might choose a quiet child and call the group by his or her name."

"I think I would rather call it Paul's group than Mike's group," I replied. "Mike already thinks he is in charge of the group. And actually, neither Mike, nor Paul, nor Daisy belong in that group. I think Mike and Daisy belong in the primer and Paul probably could read the primer on a good day and nothing at all on a bad day. I know I should have another group for these three. But, how would I ever find time to meet with them? I am worried about Carl, too. He is with the Monsters (Miss Port flinched and I quickly corrected that to Paul's group!) but I think he could read with the Astronauts, which is Alexander's group." Miss Port suggested that I let Carl read with both groups for awhile and see if he could, indeed, catch up with and function well in the 2^1 book. "Now, why didn't I think of that?" I asked aloud.

"Because, my dear," Miss Port replied, "when we are under a lot of pressure and feeling anxious, we don't think very well. That is often the sad paradox of the beginning teacher." Miss Port suggested that I needed to do some things with the whole class, some things with individuals and some with my groups. "Take writing and listening, for example, you can often teach those with the whole class." Miss Port must have realized from the expression on my face that I wasn't teaching those and that the thought of something else to try to fit in was overwhelming because she hurriedly went on, "You are meeting with your groups everyday. Perhaps you could meet with them three days a week and use the other two days for whole-class and individual instruction.

"I wish I could," I responded, "but as it is, it takes me a week to read one story with each group and do everything in the teacher's manual. At that rate, we will just finish two books if I don't miss a day."

Miss Port then picked up the teacher's manual and a red pen. She **Basals** went through a lesson plan and circled the things in red that had to be done for each story. "The most important part of reading is reading," she lectured. "Having the children read the story silently and then having a follow-up comprehension-oriented discussion is the essential thing. These other activities are helpful suggestions for you to use when you and the children need them." As we looked at the manual, Miss Port helped me to see that sometimes, if the topic was familiar to the children (which it almost always is to the Butterflies, I mean Danielle's group), you didn't need to introduce all the new vocabulary words. She also pointed out how I could decide if the children needed to work on a particular skill and do that skill's lesson only with the groups or children in a group who needed it.

"But, what if I'm not sure?" I asked.

"Then you do a quick diagnosis at the beginning of the lesson and decide," she responded. "Mrs. Wright is a master teacher when it comes to using every-pupil response cards to determine what children know and don't know. You should talk to her about that. Or, better yet, I will come and keep your class one morning and let you go and observe Mrs. Wright. I think you will find she knows many tricks of the trade which will help you."

"I never thought of that either," I responded, "I would love to watch both Mrs. Wright and Mrs. Wise."

And that's how it came to be that Miss Port took my class on two mornings and I spent a morning in Mrs. Wright's class and a morning in Mrs. Wise's class. I can't begin to list here all the things I learned, but I can see now where many of my problems were coming from and I think I know how to begin to solve them. I have already solved the pencil **Routines** sharpening and bathroom problem, again thanks to Miss Port. As she was preparing to leave that afternoon after our long talk, I picked up a stack of pencils and began my nightly routine of pencil sharpening. Miss Port paid no attention to me until I was working on my eighth pencil, when she turned to me and said, "Good grief, you use a lot of pencils! What do you do—chew off the points?"

"Oh, these aren't mine. I sharpen the children's pencils."

"*You* sharpen? Do they all have broken arms? My dear, your time is more valuable than that! Let the children sharpen their own. I know— you're afraid that they'll stand there all day just sharpening and not have any pencil left. Yes, that will happen at first, especially since you have made it such a high priority. They think it must be something pretty special if you always do it. But they'll soon tire of it, and will only sharpen when they need to. You know, one of the best ways to ward off trouble is to create a routine. If things get bad, just make a routine like having them sign a sheet of paper every time they use the sharpener, or putting a ticket on your desk. Children will soon tire of the extra step and you can see more clearly who is still a problem. Now that we're on the subject of management, how do you handle the bathroom situation?"

I explained to her about the "watering" procedure, and my general dissatisfaction with it, primarily because some of the children claimed they didn't have "to go" when we went! But later, they needed to go by themselves. I also told to her the story of poor Paul's dunking.

"Then why don't you just let them go when they need to? How would you like someone to tell you when to go to the restroom? Try this. Have a symbol for the boys and one for the girls in the chalkboard tray. Whenever a child wishes to use the restroom, he or she comes to the front, picks up the symbol, places it on his or her desk, and goes to the restroom alone. The child returns the symbol to the chalkboard tray when he or she returns. When the symbol is in the tray one child may go to the restroom; when it is missing, the next child must wait. Now at first, there will be problems for going to the restroom alone will seem to be a big deal. But again, as with the pencil sharpening, the novelty will wear off if you don't make a fuss."

So far, so good. The children went through the stage that Miss Port predicted and are now settled down into this new set of routines. Without her warning of what to expect, however, I think that I would have chucked the whole thing when the negative behavior increased temporarily.

I was quite eager for the holidays to begin! Not, as originally, so that I could escape from here but so that I could have some uninterrupted time to plan how I would begin the new year. I want to make a new schedule and look through the books I got at the faculty Christmas party. Each teacher was to bring an "idea" book for another teacher. I bought a book which had many ideas for creative writing for Sally Jane Dick. It had so many great ideas I couldn't resist buying a second copy for me! Mrs. Wise drew my name and she gave me an excellent book which explains how to do story drama to improve listening and reading comprehension. I also got two unexpected presents. Mrs. Wright gave me a timer. She says it is her most valuable teaching resource. I can see why she says that having watched her teach. Mr. Topps also gave me an unexpected gift—a copy of the latest bestseller. "This book is totally worthless," he announced, "and your homework over the break is to relax, and not think about school long enough to read this." Never in my wildest dreams did I think I would ever have a principal like Mr. Topps!

January

I always thought that if I could survive until January, I could make it. This turns out to be true but not for the reasons I had thought. I student taught last year starting in January and I figured when I got to January, I could pull out my student teaching lesson plans! I did pull them out but they weren't very relevant to this class. Many of my children read much better than the children in the class in which I student taught and then there are always Mike, Paul, and Daisy! Besides, the children in my student-teaching classroom had had an excellent teacher prior to January and these children have had me! I'm getting better, however. Those visits to Mrs. Wright's and Mrs. Wise's classrooms and my several long chats with Miss Port have really helped. I now have a new schedule which I have posted and each morning, first thing, the children and I look at the schedule and decide who is going to be where doing what when! I couldn't possibly keep on schedule, however, were it not for the timer Mrs. Wright gave me for Christmas. I carry it around with me and use it as Mrs. Wright does to keep my groups to 25 minutes, to see who can get their old places cleaned up and get to their new places in the 5 minute transition time, and to time SQUIRT and snack time. It is so much a part of me, I feel like I am missing something when I leave for home and do not have it in my hand.

Organization

I am becoming efficient in other ways, also. Watching Mrs. Wright made me realize that if I were going to be a good teacher, I was going to have to use the space in my room more efficiently. I had been having the reading groups sit together all day. Of course, you can imagine the chaos in the Monster's (I mean Paul's group) seating area when I wasn't working with them. My children now sit in a big horseshoe which comes around from the board. I have Mike seated between the chalkboard and Betty. On the other end, I have Daisy between the chalkboard and Daphne. I wish I had an end for Butch, but he is not so bad now that he sits between Horace and Steve. I have made a little group-teaching area in a corner at the back of the room. I have taped seating areas around the rug there for the children to sit in. This keeps them in a semicircle and they don't get so close to one another. I keep all my basal readers and manuals and teaching supplies there and I don't spend as much time looking for stuff as I used to. It's a good thing, too, because I now only have 25 minutes with each group. That is not long enough but Miss Port, Mrs. Wright, and Mrs. Wise all separately insist that after 25 minutes you may still be teaching but the children are almost never still learning.

With Danielle's and Horace's group, I spend the first day of each lesson sequence getting them ready to read the selection, building background and vocabulary for the story, and setting a purpose. They then read the story silently at their seats while I am working with another group. This saves a tremendous amount of group time and solves the problem of the children reading at different rates and finishing at different times. Their oral reading is so much better after they have read the story silently. I don't have them take turns reading the story orally any more either. I do different things. Sometimes we do

Oral Reading

choral reading with one page in the story. Sometimes we do "Stop and Go Reading" which I read about in an article by Bill Hardin and Bonnie Bernstein (1978). In stop and go reading, a reader continues reading until a punctuation mark is reached and then immediately stops. The next person must see how fast he or she can begin reading when the preceding person stops. Sometimes, it takes five people to read one sentence as in "Stop," Billy said, "there is a big, black, ugly snake in the road ahead." The children love the "race-type nature" of stop and go reading. They pay excellent attention because their turn comes up quickly and unexpectedly. We often read one page of the story this way and it takes almost no time because their attention is so good.

Often, I pair up my children and have them take turns reading the pages of a story. I walk around and listen to each pair for a minute or two so that I can diagnose their oral reading and word identification abilities. If four partners read a four-page story, each person reads two pages. This is four times as much reading practice as they would get if they each read a portion of the story orally since a four-page story divided by eight readers is only one-half page each. I was always told in my reading courses at State not to do round-robin oral reading and I never thought I would. But when I started teaching, I was afraid they wouldn't read it if I didn't hear them read every page and I didn't know how else to make sure we covered the stories. Now I know that if you have them read silently for a specific comprehension purpose and then follow up on that purpose when you meet with the group and do oral reading occasionally with only small portions of the story in an interesting way, most of the children will indeed read the story.

Once in a while, I have children whom I suspect haven't read the story. I try to encourage them to do it and I don't let them participate in our group's activities if they indicate by their responses to comprehension questions or in oral reading that they haven't read the story silently. Last week, I had to send Roberta to her seat during group time to read a story she hadn't read. When I questioned her about it she protested, "It was a dumb sissie story." I told her I was sorry she didn't like it but that she had a responsibility to her group to come prepared. I then sent her to her seat to read the story while I did some story dramatization with her group. Roberta, who loves to act in stories, was furious but she hasn't come to reading group unprepared since. I have also had some trouble with Alexander's not reading his stories and I have him sit with me in the group area while I meet with Paul's group until he has his story read. He is not too happy about this and promises to read his stories faithfully if I will let him sit at his seat like everyone else in his group. One real advantage of having this group area and not going to the groups who are seated together all day as I used to is that I can, as necessary, send the children to their seats from the group and I can also keep a child from another group with me in the group area to make sure the reading and workbook pages are getting done.

With Paul's group, I feel the need to guide their silent reading page by page. Rather than set a purpose for the whole story as I do with the other groups, I set a purpose for each page. "Read to find out where Billy was going. Now, read to find out what upset Billy," etc. We read the whole story silently with a purpose for each page and then do some choral reading, stop and go reading, story dramatization, or partner reading as I do with the other groups. I think they need the page-by-page guidance but I did hear Chip mumbling something about, "I don't see why we can't read a whole story at our seats like the other groups. We're second graders, too!" as he returned to his seat the other day. Of course, he is right. I don't like treating this group differently but they do need more guidance and direction. I wonder if there is something else I can do to let them read more on their own. I think I will ask Mrs. Wise if she has any suggestions.

We began SQUIRT again after the holidays, every day, right after lunch. I now get my children settled with their books before we set the timer and I am forcing myself to be a good model and read too. (It's not that I don't like to read because I do. It's all those papers to grade and lessons to plan!) We started with five minutes again and I made a SQUIRT chart. It is hanging at the front of the room and is a long sheet of paper marked off in days and months. Along the side, the minutes are marked off in 5- to 15-minute segments. Each day we color our bar graph to show how many minutes we are reading. In just this one month, our bar graph shows that we have increased a minute at a time from five minutes to eight minutes. The children are already begging to go to nine minutes. They love to see the bar graph growing. I am going to increase the time very gradually, however, so that we don't have the trouble we had before.

SSR

Though my classroom control techniques are improving, and it is so much easier to accomplish our work, there are still many problems. I hate to sound like a fishwife yelling at the children, but sometimes that seems to be the only way to deal with a situation. In extreme cases, I send a child from the room to stand in the hallway until he or she is in control. At other times I send a child to stand facing the chalkboard for a period of time. Unfortunately, the last child I had do that was Mike. He was to stand there quietly until I told him he could return to his seat. I sat down with a reading group, my back to Mike, and worked with them until I noticed children giggling and pointing to the spot behind me where I had positioned Mike. I turned around and saw that he was imitating a monkey for the benefit of the other children, so I drew a circle on the board and told him to keep his face toward that circle. He did, but as soon as I got my group back to work again, there were more

Discipline

snickers around the room. Knowing it must be Mike I turned to find he had drawn a caricature of me on the board, using the circle I had drawn for my head. Not a bad job for a little kid, I remember thinking, right before it hit me that he had defied me again.

That afternoon, I talked to Mrs. Wise about how I could let Paul's group read some stories on their own as the other groups do and, of course, I ended up telling her my latest "Mike story." She said that after hearing about Mike all year she was considering retiring a year early so that she wouldn't have to spend her last teaching year with Mike! I was horrified to think that someone like Mrs. Wise would worry about discipline and told her so. She responded, "You are going to worry about discipline for as long as you teach. I have to run out early this afternoon and haven't helped you much with your problems. Why don't you come over and have dinner with me tomorrow night. We can have a long, uninterrupted chat then." Of course I accepted. We had a lovely, relaxed dinner during which she steered me away from school topics whenever I brought them up. As we were stacking the dishes, she told me that she knew I wanted to discuss school, but that her own philosophy of life prevented her from doing so. "We live with school so much of our lives as it is that I force myself to forget it, or at least not discuss it, during dinner. There are so many disturbing things about school that they can ruin your digestion!"

Why, I could hardly believe that this woman with more than 20 years of teaching experience could still have troubles in school! That made me feel better.

After dinner, though, we did talk. She suggested that I find a book at the primer level and that one day each week, I assign Paul's group a story to read silently at their seats from this easier book.

"That's a marvelous idea," I responded, "It will also be good for Paul, Daisy, and Mike who really should be reading in a primer all the time."

"In that case," she suggested, "why not meet with them another day each week and do some instruction in the primer-level book." I told her I would love to but I couldn't imagine when I could do it. I showed her my schedule (which I had in my car. I keep all my teaching stuff in the car. At least I am never idle in traffic jams!) and she suggested that perhaps I could let Danielle's group go to the library one day each week during their group time.

"Miss Page is always willing to help the children and she especially loves to introduce the precocious ones to the wonders of reference books." I could then use that time to meet with Paul, Daisy, and Mike. I must admit that I know Danielle's group needs much more reading than is provided in their basal reader. I will talk to Miss Page about this tomorrow.

We talked about discipline, too, and particularly about Mike. Mrs. Wise seems to think I am handling him about as well as he can be handled! "Make sure he knows the rules. Withdraw privileges as necessary.

Keep giving him chances to be responsible and show him he will not get the best of you," she advised. "Some children are difficult and we must continue to be firm and fair with them. No system will work for everyone but it sounds like what you are doing is working quite well for most of your children most of the time. You are having a good year for a first-year teacher. And they will get better."

As I was trying to absorb the fact that Mrs. Wise seemed to have such faith in me, the doorbell rang. Mrs. Wise went to answer it and I gathered up my things. Mrs. Wise then returned with her neighbor, a new doctoral student at the university. She introduced me to Mr. Horatio Flame, who said, "Just call me Red." We chatted for quite awhile and I got home much later than I usually do on a school night. As I was driving home I realized that we had talked for over an hour about things other than teaching. What a wonderful feeling! Red seems like a really nice guy. I wonder why he just happened to drop in like that. Surely, it was just a coincidence that he came while I was there ????

February

As you can see by my schedule (see page 362), there have been some changes made! Each morning, I start the day by reading something to the whole class. This was one of the things which was getting left out so I decided if I did it first thing, it would get done. Mrs. Wise has convinced me that if I teach these children to read and they never do read, I have wasted all that effort! Besides, why should the children put forth all the effort required to learn to read if they don't know what marvelous adventures and ideas are contained in books. At 8:45, we do Words on the Wall. I stole this idea from Mrs. Wright. Each Monday, I add ten new words. I choose the words from those which the children misspell in their writing and in their workbooks. I also let children suggest words they would like to learn to spell. I have put the words on the wall above the chalkboard. We now have 40 and we should have 160 by the end of the year. The children enjoy their spelling test each day. I have found that some children (Butch, Mike, Mort, Alexander, and Daisy, to be specific) were not putting forth their best effort to find the words and spell them correctly. Other children wanted me to grade their tests each day! I told them that I had my "hands full" right now but I would try to think of some way to grade some of them. It was Red (who knows nothing about teaching, thank goodness) who came up with the brilliant idea. "Why not have five checkers in a box," he suggested one night as I was telling him my problem while he was, as usual, whomping me at checkers, "four red ones and one black one. When the children have finished their tests and exchanged and checked them, let one child close her eyes and pick a checker. If a red checker comes out, this was only a practice

Wall Vocabulary

Miss Nouveau's After-Christmas Schedule

	8:30–8:45	8:45–9:00	9:00–9:25	9:30–9:55	10:00	10:15–10:40	10:45–11:10
Monday	READ TO WHOLE CLASS	WORDS ON THE WALL	Meet Mike's group; Larry's group—centers; Horace's group—seatwork	Meet Larry's group; Mike's group seatwork; Horace's group centers	SNACK	WHOLE CLASS WRITING	Meet Horace's group; Mike's group—centers; Larry's group—seatwork
Tuesday	(→)	(→)	Same as Monday	Same as Monday except Larry's group—lib. Meet, Paul Daisy, Mike	(→)	(→)	Same as Monday
Wednesday	(→)	(→)	Children choose which of four groups they want to work with, prepare story dramatization, choral reading, play, pictures or other story-response activities for Friday		(→)	(→)	Same as Monday
Thursday	(→)	(→)			(→)	(→)	Whole-class listening comprehension activity
Friday	(→)	(→)	Children share response activities from Thursday's groups		(→)	(→)	Children choose favorite story for editing and rewriting and/or do art

(TRANSITION periods occur between segments; arrows (→) indicate activities carried across the week.)

test. If the black one comes out, however, this was 'the real thing' and you can collect them, verify that they are correctly checked and record them in your grade book." I told Red he would be a wonderful teacher, he is so creative, but he declares he hasn't "the stomach for it."

At any rate, we now use his checkers system. It is super! All the children, including Mike, put forth their best efforts each day because they never know when it will count. They love to have the black checker come out because, if they try, they can do well and this helps their grades. I am going to try this system in the afternoon when we practice addition and subtraction facts. Each day, we will have a five-minute timed practice, exchange and check papers, and then see if it counts or not by having a blindfolded child select a checker. This will give the children the practice they need without putting an impossible grading burden on me.

On Mondays, Tuesdays, and Wednesdays, I meet with my three reading groups. (Except that on Tuesdays, Larry's group goes to the library and works with Miss Page while I give special instruction at the primer level to Mike, Daisy, and Paul). I meet Mike's group first and then have their seatwork time immediately following. They have their center time after snack time and I check to see that they have it done and reasonably well done or they don't go to centers! The children in Horace's group are more dependable so I have them do their seatwork first, then go to centers, and then meet with me. I don't have time to check and make sure they all have their work done before they go to centers but I do suspend their center time for the following day if they are not getting their seatwork done. Mort, however, must check with me each day before going to centers. He simply won't do his work without this immediate consequence. Larry's group always do their work. (Except for Roberta, who is too smart for her own good. I check with her first thing in the morning before her group goes to centers). Larry's group begin their morning in centers, then meet with me or Miss Page, and then have their seatwork time to prepare for the next day's group. This system is working so well, I can't believe it. I thought I didn't have time to have centers but now I can see I don't have time not to. I assign a reasonable amount of seatwork, mostly preparation for silent reading of and follow-up to stories, to each group and they spend a part of each morning with me, part doing seatwork, and part in the centers.

My centers are quite simple. I have a math center in which I have collected a lot of math manipulatives, an art center in which I put a different art medium each week, a game center in which I put a different game (Candyland, Old Maid, Chutes and Ladders, for example) each week, a listening-viewing center in which I set up some tape-filmstrips Miss Page suggested the children might enjoy, and a classroom library. The children choose which three of the centers they would like to go to and sign up for these on Monday. They go to a different center on Monday,

Organization

Centers

Tuesday, and Wednesday, and thus can go to three of the five. The current complaint is that they can't go to all five centers!

Choice Groups

On Thursdays, I do not meet with the reading groups. Rather, the children choose which of four groups they want to work with. Each group reads or listens to a book or story and then prepares something to share with the whole class on Friday. They choose according to what the book or story is and they make their choices on Wednesday afternoon. This gives me a chance to decide, depending on who chooses which, whether they will read silently, read in partners, listen to a tape I make, or listen to someone in the group read. If, for example, I know that a book or story is much too hard for some of the children who chose it to read, I either make a tape of that story or, if the choosers of that story include an exceptionally popular, good oral reader (such as Larry, Roberta, or Danielle), I will let that person read the story to the group. If, on the other hand, the children who chose the book or story are capable of reading it, I either have them each read it silently or have them read it orally in partners.

Literature Response

After reading or listening to the book or story, the groups prepare some way of sharing it with the rest of the class. So far, I have told them how to prepare this story sharing and have had all the groups share in the same way. I hope, however, that as they are taught more literature response activities, and become better at preparing these, they will be able to decide how they want to share the story. Maybe by May. So far, these literature response activities which I have used with the children include puppetry, lap stories, acetate stories, maps, and display ads [see pp. 122–129]. The children love being able to choose which group they will be in. I select four stories or books which lend themselves to the literature response activity I want to have them do, and display these in the reading corner on Monday. By Wednesday, many of the better readers have read all four books or stories so that they can choose "the best one." I take turns about who gets to choose first and allow seven people to choose each book or story. The groups thusly formed are usually quite heterogeneous and the children enjoy getting to work with their friends who are in different reading groups on Monday, Tuesday, and Wednesday. While the groups are reading/listening to their stories or books and preparing their literature response activities, I circulate and give help as needed. During this time, I find that I can relax and enjoy the children since I am not directly involved in teaching them. I learn so much about them when I have a few minutes to listen to them!

Writing

I also have Mrs. Wise, who gave me the idea for the choice groups and literature response activities on Thursdays, to thank for the whole-class writing activity we do each day from 10:15 to 10:40. When I visited Mrs. Wise's classroom, I was amazed at how much writing her children did and at how well they wrote. Mrs. Wise told me that she believes writing helps children become better readers as well as better writers.

She showed me how the two processes, reading and writing, are reciprocal. "Once you can write in a particular way," she remarked, "You can better understand something you are reading which is written in the same way." Mrs. Wise showed me samples of her children's writing which included poetry, letters, and informational writing as well as stories.

Each day at 10:15, the children and I write. (Children need to see that adults write in the same way they need to see that adults read. Maybe I should ask Mr Topps or even Red to come and write while we write so that the boys will see that writing is something adult males do!) We first brainstorm a list of words we might need to write about our topic. Of course, I use my timer to limit our brainstorming session to three minutes. It is amazing how much they can think of in three minutes when that timer is clicking away the seconds. I write the words they suggest on half-sheets of chart paper. Here is the brainstorm chart of words they did before writing about "What My Teacher Was Like at My Age" (see p. 366).

You should have seen what great stories they came up with. They all wanted to read theirs. This has become the biggest problem recently. We take about five minutes to get ready and brainstorm the words. The children then write for ten minutes. (For some children this is just a beginning. They often continue to work on their story later in the day.) By the time they stop and we get ready, there are only about seven or eight minutes left to share and everyone wants to read his or her creation. We must stop at 10:40 so that we can get ready for our groups or whole-class listening activity but many of the children grumble when they don't get a chance to read their masterpieces. There must be a creative way to solve this problem. I shall have to ask Mrs. Wise about it. On second thought, I may ask Red tonight. He knows nothing about teaching but has the most creative mind!

March

I forgot to mention in last month's journal how much I learned from the parent-teacher conferences I had in February. Everyone except Paul and Jeff had a parent (or other relative) come. I was so much more at ease because I knew I was doing a better job. I wasn't on the defensive waiting for them to ask me something I didn't know or expecting them to attack me for something I wasn't doing. Rather, I was relaxed (relatively!) and we had good conversations about their children. Most of the parents expressed their pleasure at what I was doing with their children. I think this may have been a reflection of how relieved they were that things have gotten much better as the year has gone on. Mike's mother is quite worried about him and says she can hardly handle him at home. I told her that he is making some progress and seems to be able to learn

What My Teacher Was Like at My Age	
Miss Nouveau	spanked
Cathy	played a trick
Catherine	fell in the mud
mean	was too tall
talked a lot	was nice
laughed a lot	was pretty
got in trouble in school	lived in a trailer
her mother	curious
her dad	cute
her teacher	had freckles

when he settles down long enough. I suggested that she read some easy-to-read books at home with Mike each night and let him chime in when he knows a word. She said she would try but that she practically had to "rope" him to get him settled down long enough to eat, never mind anything else. When she left, I thought, "I shall be more patient with Mike. I imagine that that woman must deal with his energy for as many waking hours as I do each day, and all day on Saturdays, Sundays, and holidays."

Many parents expressed their pleasure with the "nice writing" the children bring home every two weeks. Mandy's mother declared that Mandy had decided to become a writer and keeps a writing notebook at home in which she writes faithfully. She told me that the children liked writing each day and especially like my pulling the popsicle sticks out of the hat to see which children get to read their stories. (This was Red's solution to the problem of everyone wanting to read and not enough time.) When the timer signals the end of the ten-minute writing time, the children who wish to read their story put the popsicle stick with their name on it in a special container. I pull the popsicle sticks out and those children whose names come out get to read their stories. The children love the drama of wondering whose stick will come out and are very good listeners as they know we will get to pull more sticks in the allotted time if I don't have to interrupt constantly and ask them to be good listeners.

Writing

Each Friday, one-half of the children pick their favorite story from the ones they have written and put in their folders during the past two weeks. They then rewrite and illustrate this story. I let one-half do it each Friday morning because I can only work with so many in a short period of time. The other children who are not rewriting have an assignment to do and then get to do art along with the children who are rewriting.

To do the proofreading and rewriting, we go through a three-step process. First, I meet with the 12 (or 13, depending on the week) children who bring the selection they have chosen to rewrite. I have them look for one "mechanical" thing and see if they can find an example of that and fix it in their story. "You all know that people's names begin with a capital letter. Who can find a person's name in their story which needs a capital letter?" or, "You all know that when we write exactly what a person says, we put quotation marks around what they said. Who can find something that someone said and put quotation marks around it?" This changes the focus from finding something you didn't do or did wrong to finding something in your writing which is special. The children love to find that they have a person's name or a direct quote which needs fixing, and to fix it and share it with us.

After they have looked for one mechanical thing, fixed it, and shared it with the group, they are ready for the second step. In this step they get with their proofreading partner and the partners each read the other's story aloud. I have assigned the proofreading partners so that they are similar in their stage of writing development. Pat, for example, is Danielle's partner. Manuel is Steve's partner. I am the partner for Paul, who cannot do more than copy the words on the brainstormed chart, and for Daisy and Mike who are at the same stage of development but who can't stand to work with each other. The partners read each other's story aloud and the person whose story it is fixes things at the suggestion of the partner. The child who wrote, "I saw one my way to skool," will read this as, "I was on my way to school," because that is what that child intended to say. The proofreading partner, however, will read what is there and the writer will hear the need for some correction. (I wonder if the reason I can't proofread my own typing is because I read what I think is there???)

When the partners have proofed each other's papers, they are ready for the final step. They bring the story to me and I go over it with them. I very quickly correct the most obvious errors, "You need a capital *M* here. *Where* has an *h* in it." etc. The writer then copies his or her masterpiece on good paper in the best handwriting and often using colored thin-line markers. Art is then done to complement the writing and all children's art and rewritten stories are displayed on my "Art and Writing" bulletin board. They stay there until the next Friday when the other half of the class rewrites and creates illustrations to go with their stories. These stories and art then replace the ones which have been up for a week and the ones which have been displayed for a week are taken home by their proud creators.

The children are developing a lot of pride in their writing. I think that is because, doing it every day, they are getting so much better at it. The Words on the Wall help them so much with spelling (as does the chart of brainstormed words). Even after the three-step proofreading and rewriting process, the rewritten versions are seldom perfect. But, they are much improved and generally readable, and you can't expect perfection from second graders! The fact that every child's story is displayed with that child's name for a week seems to give them extra motivation to rewrite them well and neatly. Even Mike, who could care less about almost everything academic, was heard to remark last week, "No matter what this looks like, old Freckles will put this up and everyone will get to see it for a week, so I'll do the best I can."

Listening Comprehension

The whole-class listening comprehension lessons on Thursdays are going better. In step one of the lesson, I always give them one purpose for listening. Often I have them make an every-pupil-response card (I took that idea from Mrs. Wright) before they listen which they can show me after listening to demonstrate their comprehension. I try to bring in short newspaper and magazine articles of interest to the children and do listening comprehension activities around these. I hope in this way to demonstrate the importance of reading in the real world and develop their knowledge of what is happening in the world as I develop their listening comprehension abilities.

This morning, I brought a magazine article on poisonous plants from which I read them some excerpts. I began as always by setting the purpose for listening: "This morning you are going to listen to learn about some plants you have probably seen which are poisonous and others which are perfectly harmless." I then had them write *OK* on one side of a computer card (Mrs. Wright's neighbor now keeps me supplied, too) and draw the poison symbol on the other side. "After I have read some parts of this magazine article to you, I will name six plants and you will show me you know whether or not they are poisonous by showing me the OK or the poison symbol on your card."

For the second step of my listening comprehension lesson, I read them the appropriate parts and they listened. Next, I named the six plants and they showed the appropriate side of their card. Almost all the children showed the appropriate side each time and I always responded to the children showing the correct response as Mrs. Wright does. Mrs. Wright has such a common-sense approach to her teaching. "You get the point across as well by saying, 'Yes, Carl has the poison sign showing because holly berries can be poisonous,' as by noticing someone with the wrong side showing, and the children who are right get good attention and the wrong ones are not necessarily embarrassed," is what Mrs. Wright would have said if she had observed my lesson.

The children and I then agreed that they had listened well today. We knew that was so because they had been able to do what I had asked them to do when I set the purpose for listening.

To follow up this listening comprehension lesson, I had them go home and ask their parents what poisonous plants they knew about. The children and parents enjoy homework assignments like this. Mrs. Smith commented during the conference that they often got out their encyclopedia at home to look up information or resolve controversy about a particular "find out more about this from your parents" homework assignment.

SQUIRT is working so well now! The children and I enjoy the read- **SSR** ing immensely and we love to watch our progress on the bar graph. We are now up to 11 minutes daily, which is still too short for some of the children. They continue reading after the majority of the class goes back to other activities. I am so glad that Mr. Topps straightened me out on this.

Red, who is working to put himself through his doctoral program, has offered to come to school early next month to show the children the musical instruments that he plays. He is the leader of a rock band that he calls "Red and the Flamers." I know that Mike and many of the others will be enthralled with his presentation as well as with his personality, which matches his gorgeous, curly auburn hair. I realize how busy he is—and am delighted he is willing to talk to the class.

April

Red's appearance was enormously successful! We discussed rock bands, and I was amazed at how knowledgeable these young children are about rock groups. Mike was fascinated with the drums. Red had brought an amplifier along as well, and we just caught Butch in time; he had plugged in the electric guitar and was ready to strum—full blast!

After Red left, I had the children tell me about his visit and I wrote what they told me on chart paper. We read it over together, cut apart some of the sentences, and relocated them in the correct order of occurrence. Here is what they came up with. (Hilda reminded me that Mrs. Wright always put their names after their own sentences.)

Language Experience

Mr. Flame of "Red and the Flamers" came to our class. (Alex)
It was really cool, man! (Mike)
He showed a variety of instruments. (Larry)
Some of us danced when he played. (Rita)
I almost played the electric guitar. (Butch)
It sound good. (Paul)
He asked Miss Nouveau for an aspirin before he left. (Mandy)

Reading Comprehension

This month, I have tried several new (to me) teaching strategies I discovered in a *Reading Teacher* article by Spiegel (May, 1981). In this article, Spiegel points out that the important parts of a reading comprehension lesson can be done using a variety of other formats. I was particularly intrigued by the DR-TA (Directed Reading-Thinking Activity) because the children make predictions about what will take place in the story and thus the children rather than I are setting their purposes for reading.

DR-TA

I tried out my first DR-TA with Larry's group. They are the most cooperative and easiest to work with so I often try new things with them first. By the time I do the strategies with Paul's group, I have most of the kinks worked out and I can do them automatically and thus concentrate all my attention on keeping the children in that motley group with me. Larry's group was going to read a story about a whale who moved to a new zoo. We surveyed the pictures and headings and had a general discussion about animals and people adjusting to new surroundings. I then asked the children to guess what would happen in the story. As they made predictions, I listed them. Their prereading hunches were:

1. The whale will be unhappy. (Rita)
2. The whale will get sick. (Pat)
3. The whale will almost die. (Roberta)
4. The veterinarian will have the water in the tank tested. (Larry)
5. The whale misses his family. (Mandy)
6. The whale will get well. (Hilda)
7. And they will all live happily ever after. (Danielle)

Once they had made these predictions and I had recorded each and put their names after them as Roberta suggested, they returned to their seats to read the story and determine which of the predictions were true and which were not. They were told to number a sheet of paper from 1 to 7 and next to each number write "yes" or "no" and a page number which they thought confirmed or disconfirmed the prediction. When the group gathered back together, we went through each prediction and decided if it had been confirmed or disconfirmed. For each prediction the children believed had been confirmed, a child read the portion of the story aloud which supported this prediction.

Larry's group really enjoyed doing this DR-TA. In fact, they have asked to "make guesses" before every story. I am limiting it, however, because I don't want the children to tire of it and because there are a variety of ways to lead them through stories so that they become better comprehenders and readers. I plan to try some of the other alternatives suggested by Spiegel. I am particularly intrigued by the "Expectation **Expecta-** Outline" in which children tell what they expect to learn from a piece of **tion** informational text. I plan to use this strategy when Larry's group gets to **Outline** the selection on bees. "What questions do you think may be answered as you read the selection on bees?" I will ask. When the children have listed some possible questions ("Why do bees sting?" "How do bees sting?" "How do bees make honey?") we will categorize the questions ("sting" and "honey" are two possible categories). The children will then read the story to see which questions are answered. When we get together again, we will share the answers and let the children read the part aloud which provides these answers. I will then let the children spend part of their library time on Tuesday using the reference sources in the library to see if they can find answers to the unanswered questions. I shall have to ask Miss Page to let them take those reference books out of the library for a brief time so that they can verify their answers to the group.

As I write this down, I realize that the expectation outline is similar to the DR-TA in many ways. The children set their purposes, read silently to satisfy those purposes, and then read orally to verify what they have found. It makes more sense to ask, "What are some questions you think will be answered?" rather than, "What do you think will happen?" when reading informational text. Informational text tells us about things and thus often answers questions. Things happen in stories!

I have also done DR-TA's with Horace's group and Paul's group. The **DR-TA** children in Paul's group had a lot of trouble coming up with predictions. For a story about a boy whose bike disappeared, they predicted:

His bike is gone. (Chip)
He will find it. (Mike)
He will not. (Daisy)
He will get a whipping. (Jeff)

They then read the story and had difficulty accepting the fact that what happened was not, in all cases, what they had predicted. Daisy insisted that, "He didn't really find it." (Whatever that means!) Jeff said, "He probably got a whipping but didn't want to tell you." I am going to continue to do DR-TA's with this group at least once every two weeks because I know that the ability to make predictions and then confirm or disconfirm them based on the text is crucial to reading comprehension but getting them to do it is like pulling teeth. I think I shall have them make some predictions based only on the pictures and title and then read half the story, confirm or disconfirm the first set of predictions, and then make new predictions before reading the second half of the story. Maybe that will work better.

Imitative Reading   Speaking of Paul's group, I have begun doing Imitative Reading with them. Imitative reading is a fancy name for having the children read a story enough times so that they can read it easily and fluently, "like a good reader." I know that silent reading is what is most important, but I got so tired of Paul's group's poor oral reading. Even when they had read the story to themselves, they read aloud   one   word   at   a   time (like this is typed). I got so tired of telling them to "read with expression" and my telling them didn't seem to do any good. One day, Miss Port was visiting while Paul's group was doing partner reading. That afternoon, she popped in with some easy-to-read books and tapes. "Those children in that poor little Paul's group need a lot of practice with some really easy books," she suggested. "They spend so much of their effort figuring out the words, they don't have much attention left over to consider the meaning of what they read. Besides, reading has always been slow and hard for them and by now they are used to reading one   word   at   a   time." She then explained to me that I should let each child in Paul's group pick one of these easy-to-read books and sign up for a time each day to listen to the book. The child was to listen to the book until he or she could read the book without the aid of the tape recording. Then, the child would sign up to read the book to me and, assuming that the child could indeed read the book well, that child could choose another book-tape combination.

So far, so good! Chip has read four of the easy-to-read books. He listens to them at his signed-up time each day and then will often come in first thing in the morning or stay a little late in the afternoon to listen to them. I am keeping a chart of the books they have read and Chip is now ahead of the others. Daisy is not happy with me, however. She listens to the book-tape one time and then signs up to read it to me. Of course, she can't, and I send her back with instructions to listen to it at least two more times before she signs up to read to me again. Mike's mother has bought him a tape recorder and he takes his book-tape home every night. Even he seems pleased that he can easily read, cover-to-cover, three books and seems motivated to read some more. If Chip had a tape recorder at home, there would be no stopping him!

The children do seem to be reading more fluently and with more expression now, at least for the easy-to-read books they have listened along with. I may be too optimistic but I think I can detect some improvement in their oral reading of the stories in their basal readers. I think that by listening to the tape of the easy-to-read book often enough, they get to the point where they can easily identify the words and anticipate what is coming next and they have, probably for the first time, the experience of reading like a good reader. I am going to start my word-by-word readers right off next year with imitative reading.

May

We had to add on to our SQUIRT chart, for we have reached 16 minutes of SQUIRT time! I never thought last fall that I would be here in May, and I probably wouldn't have been if Mr. Topps and the others hadn't helped me isolate my problems and correct them. I certainly never thought that I would see my class sitting still and reading attentively for 16 straight minutes and liking it! In some ways it has been a long year, but in others it has been too short. How I wish I could have begun my current reading program earlier!

Anticipating next year and the first day of school (it just has to be better!), I asked the children to think back over the year and all of the things we have done. I wrote their comments on the chalkboard and we filled it in no time! I had no idea that we had done so many things or that the children could remember them.

The next instructions that I gave them were to pretend that they were their own desks. As the desk, they were to write a letter to whoever would be sitting in that seat next year. They were to give the new second graders an idea about what to expect during the new school year. We would leave the letters in the desks and surprise the new children with them in the fall. The children seemed excited about the project and eagerly began to write. Here is a copy of the letter that Roberta wrote:

> Hi, Kid,
>
> You're pretty lucky to be starting second grade already. And, boy, will you have fun. Especially sitting at this desk. This is where Roberta Marie Smith sat last year, and she had fun. This year you will learn to read harder books and you'll do your workbook (if you're better than Roberta). Have a good time, kid, 'cause it won't last long. Soon you'll have to go to third grade where they really have hard work to do! Maybe I can ask Roberta's desk in third grade to write to you, too.
>
> Love,
> Clarence, your desk

We have added to the supply this year with children's paperbacks. The children and I receive brochures every month from two companies which publish inexpensive, high-quality children's books. The children take their individual brochures home and bring back the completed order forms with the necessary money. I mail these and add the bonus books, one of which we get for each ten books the children order. Then we all eagerly await the arrival of our new books. In this way, I have added about 25 new books to our classroom library.

All in all, it has turned out to be a very good year for me and, I think, for almost all my children. Most of my discipline problems have lessened as I established some routines and began to give the children interesting and varied things to do. The new seating arrangement, a group-meeting place, and the timer have really helped too. I still have some days when I wonder why I ever wanted to be a teacher. Mike is most difficult to handle and my promises to myself to be firm and patient with him just seem to dissolve when I am faced with one of his regular disruptions. He tells me they are moving right after school is out. Some third-grade teacher somewhere will have her hands full next year. I am sorry he is moving because I am sure Mrs. Wise would be able to calm him down. Paul is another one of my failures. He seems to be perking up and making some progress and then he goes into a somber, depressed state during which he might as well not be here. I don't know what is going to happen to him. And Daisy—I never thought I would teach a child and not come to love that child but I can't find anything lovable about Daisy. Maybe Mrs. Wise can get through to her, too. I have such faith in that lady. I would never have made it through the year without her.

I *have* made it through the year, however, and I will be ready for next year. I told Mrs. Wright the other day that if I learned as much every year I taught as I have this first year, I would never have to fear getting stale and bored. She said that teaching was many things, some positive and some not so positive, but that she had never found it to be boring. Red says that one thing he learned this year was that in teaching, there are so many intriguing problems to be solved! I guess that if I can continue to view my crises as "intriguing problems to be solved" I will someday be a good, capable, creative teacher.

THE STUDENT TEACHING SEMINAR

Miss Nouveau, veteran of one year in the classroom, had been asked by Dr. Link to talk with her student teachers at their weekly seminar. At first, she had protested that she was the last person who should be asked. After all, she was still learning herself, and she didn't think she had anything of significance to contribute.

Dr. Link explained that several students in the class had asked her to find a first-year teacher who would talk to them. They wanted to know what it was *really* like when one started teaching. While teachers like Mrs. Wise could contribute a great deal to the seminar, they had been teaching too long to focus honestly on the first year of teaching. And, she added, she had been observing Miss Nouveau's progress throughout the year, and was pleased with the growth that had been taking place. Miss Nouveau finally consented to address the class, "But," she cautioned, "I'm not promising that it will be any good."

"If you just tell them what you have lived through this past year," Dr. Link replied, "they will be more than satisfied."

And that, she resolved, was precisely what she would do. These students would find out the real truth from her before they had to live through it themselves! She requested that they meet in her room.

The afternoon of the seminar, Miss Nouveau stood at the back of her room while Dr. Link greeted the carefree students. After Dr. Link had introduced her, she began her talk by saying, "To paraphrase an old television program,'I Led One Life.' For me, that life was school." She then related her inaccurate judgments, errors in placement, discipline problems, and poor assignments she had made. As she spoke, she noted looks of disbelief turning to looks of pity and fear as she related anecdote after anecdote. Not wanting to discourage them, however, Miss Nouveau then began to relate the positive things that had happened to her and the consequent changes she had made in her program since Christmas. When she finished, several hands went up for questions.

"If you knew you weren't doing very well in October, how come you kept right on doing things wrong? I mean if *I* were doing something I knew was wrong, I wouldn't just keep on!"

"Well," answered Miss Nouveau, with a smile, "maybe you would and maybe you wouldn't. I would have thought that same way a year ago, but it's so different when you're actually there day after day with the children and you know you're totally responsible for their instruction. There's neither the opportunity nor the knowledge to do it any other way! I was fortunate, though, to be in a school with a principal who cared, other teachers who helped me, and an elementary supervisor who showed me alternatives. Though they were all busier than I was, they gave freely of their time and advice. If it hadn't been for them, I know I would have resigned at Christmas."

"What would have helped you, though, before you got to your first year of teaching?" another student asked.

"If only I had been given more experience in classrooms prior to my student teaching, then I could have spent student teaching time learning more about classroom management. The better prepared you are when you enter your student teaching, the better you will be at the end of it. Also, if my reading-language arts course had been more activity oriented, I would have been better prepared to evaluate and teach the children."

Another student raised his hand to ask, "Could you just summarize for us a few of the most important things that you learned this year?"

Miss Nouveau thought for a moment before replying, "I suppose that one of the most important things I learned was how to get kids to the bathroom." The class exploded into laughter. "You laugh! But when it happens to you, it won't be so funny!" She smiled at them and began again. "Another thing was locating the school storeroom. It's often a goldmine of books and materials just lying there, gathering dust. Also, I learned that I must have some time for myself. One reason I was so depressed last fall, I'm sure, was that I had no time to do things that I had always done and that I enjoyed doing. I regret very much some of the things I did this year, and if I could be granted one wish it would be that I could repeat this school year knowing at the beginning what I know now!"

"How are you going to start next year, since obviously you won't repeat what has been done?"

"I thought you might ask that," responded Miss Nouveau confidently. "As a matter of fact, I have given a lot of thought to that and I think I am prepared to get next year off to a better start. I will begin the year right off with my horseshoe seating arrangement. I even know from watching the first graders which children will get the ends of the horseshoe! I will give an IRI to all the children but I will only count errors which change the meaning and that way will not penalize fluent readers like Larry for having their eyes out ahead of their voices as all good readers do. I will form my reading groups according to the instructional levels I find and I will make sure that the lowest group spends some time in an instructional-level book and some time in an independent-level book each week. I will also have 'choice groups' at least one day each week.

"When I meet with my groups, I will make sure that they have purposeful silent reading. I will not do round-robin oral reading but rather will use some of the alternatives such as stop-and-go reading and partner reading to provide them with oral reading practice. I will try to remember to use every-pupil-response activities whenever possible, both because they help to keep the children involved and attentive and because they allow me to diagnose in an informal, ongoing manner who is learning what (and who is not!). Never again will I make the mistake of trying to do everything in the teacher's manual. Rather, I will pick those activities which a particular group needs and can profit from at that time. Since I will be timing my groups for 25 minutes each day, I will have to decide which things the children need to be with me to do, which they can do independently before and after meeting with me, and which to leave out altogether.

"Finally, I hope that I will remember that I am a Libran and try to be true to my Libran nature. I shall balance my day and instruction with whole-group, small-group, and individual instruction. I will also remember that reading instruction does not go on solely when the children are reading in their basal reader. I will read to the children each day and have them write each day. I will do regular listening comprehension lessons. I even hope to help them become better readers during science and social studies as they read informational text."

As Miss Nouveau paused to catch her breath, Dr. Link interrupted to say that she regretted having to announce that the seminar time was up. Miss Nouveau and most of the students turned in astonishment to view the clock and confirm that indeed an entire hour had fled past. "Just like teaching," observed Miss Nouveau, "when you are thinking about what you have to say and do, it seems like there is an enormous amount of time to fill. But, when you start doing it, there is never enough time." The students chuckled. A few stayed afterward to talk privately with Miss Nouveau. Dr. Link looked on proudly!

12 | Mrs. Wise

THE PARENT MEETING

Mrs. Wise walked around the room, carefully placing materials for the parents to examine when they arrived for the meeting later that evening. She went about the task methodically, for she had been having parent meetings for most of her 28 years as a teacher, long before they became an "in" thing to do. As a matter of fact, she was the one who had suggested to Mr. Topps, some ten years before, that these meetings become a regular part of the school routine. She had also initiated the parent conferences which everyone now held twice yearly. There were those who called her an innovator and those who said it was amazing that a woman of her years could be so up-to-date! Mrs. Wise chuckled over that one! She told them all that it had nothing to do with innovation or age—she simply knew what her children needed and how *she* could best teach them.

She was always exhilarated by these meetings, as she was by the parent conferences. It was astonishing how much one could learn about a child in half-hour conferences with the parents. She made the parents feel relaxed by sitting in a chair beside them rather than in the more formal position behind the desk. She had acquired a knack for knowing what to say and how to say it that helped put parents at their ease and yet elicited from them the maximum amount of information about the child. Tonight, however, she was to meet the parents *en masse*. She enjoyed explaining what she and their children were going to be doing, for she loved teaching. She was not looking forward to the day in the near future when she would be retiring.

Shortly before 8:00 P.M., the parents began to arrive. Mrs. Wise didn't begin the meeting until 8:15, however, for long years of experience had taught her that many parents would arrive late no matter when the meeting was to begin. At least most of them would be there by the time she started.

"Hello. Some of you I know quite well because I have had other children of yours. Some of you are new to me as I am to you. I certainly hope that we will become well acquainted this year. I want to urge you *all* to come visit the classroom. I have only two requirements: (1) that you let me know in advance when you want to come, so that I can let you know whether or not it is convenient, and (2) that you plan to stay at least an hour, so that the children will settle down and forget that you are here so that you can really see the program. I warn you! You may be put to work though. Any extra hands in my class can and probably will be used. Just ask Mr. Topps! I'm sure that is why he has been avoiding my classroom for the last couple of years!"

She paused for breath and to let the laughter die down. "We, at this school, decided many years ago that we felt strongly enough about the place of children's literature and children's writing in the curriculum that we would make a concerted effort to incorporate them into our classrooms. I have developed my entire reading and language arts program around books for children and children's own writings. In order to make reading and writing situations as natural as possible, I have implemented an individualized program. Let me explain to you how it works.

"I have hundreds of books in this room; many of them belong to the room, many belong to me, and quite a few belong to your children. I classify the books into three large groupings: below average for *my* students, average for *my* students, and above average for *my* students. The books are color coded for these three groupings, so that children will know which groups of books they may choose from to read. Your children are on a five-day cycle: one day they read on the tape recorder allowing me to evaluate oral reading skills, another day they confer with me so that I can work on specific individual problems and teach comprehension, and for three days they read intensively. When your child finishes a book, he or she writes the title in a booklet. After five books have been read, the child chooses one of the five to report on. Few children choose the traditional, formal, written book report, for there are so many other ways they can indicate that they have understood and enjoyed a book.

"Children's reading assignments are recorded on a card like this file card. It lists the date, the assignment, and the evaluation of the assignment. Each child has a file folder which has a stapled sheet inside on which I record language arts assignments, the date completed, and the evaluation of those assignments.

"In order to develop their writing skills, I have a structured series of lessons for them to follow that takes them from whole-group, oral compositions to being able to write independent pieces. Additionally, paper and pencils and writing stimuli abound in the classroom along with the encouragement to use 'free time' for writing activities."

She looked at the parents sitting before her and said, "I think that's enough talking for me. Why don't we get some refreshments and come back here for a question-and-answer period in five minutes. I don't know about you, but I could use a cup of tea right now."

The parents drifted out into the hall where Mrs. Wise had set up the coffee pot and hot water for tea. As soon as the five minutes were up, Mrs. Wise resumed the meeting by asking if there were any questions, comments or concerns.

MR. PESKINS: Mrs. Wise, this all sounds so, so busy! How are you going to be able to do all of these things at once? Won't children be running wildly around the room while you're in conferences? And I don't just mean my Butch, either.

MRS. WISE: It is my contention that if we give children meaningful tasks at their individual levels of ability, we reduce the probability of that occurring. Besides, they have assignments to be working on while I work with individuals or groups. They might be working at their seats, at learning centers, in the hall, or in the library. I have never yet had a child run "wildly around the room."

MR. MARTIN: But what about the other part of the question? How can you meet with all of these children one-to-one? Isn't that what individualizing instruction means?

MRS. WISE: To me, individualizing instruction means providing children with what they need, when they need it. Therefore, some instruction will be 1 to 1, some will be 1 to 5, and some will be 1 to 24.

MRS. FIELD: Daphne came home and told me that she didn't have to write about books when she finished. I thought that she was just telling me a story! I always had to write book reports in school. How else will you know if they've read their books?

MRS. WISE: But didn't you dread doing those written book reports? I know that I did, even though I always did rather well on them. I remember how sorry I felt for a friend of mine who was not quite as good at writing as I was. There are other ways: dramatizing the most important ideas, "selling the book" to friends by convincing them that this is the greatest book ever written, or painting a picture that expresses a mood. These techniques require children to evaluate a work of literature, not merely regurgitate it.

MRS. SMITH: But how will you keep track of all these children? They are doing so many different things.

MRS. WISE: The children will keep many of their own records, which is a big help to me. In addition, I have the assignment cards and sheets which tell me exactly who is doing what. I keep track of what the children have learned and what they still need to be taught.

MRS. PENN: Well, I for one have every confidence in you, Mrs. Wise. I am convinced that Pat and every other child in this room will come to love reading.

MRS. WISE: Are there any more questions? If not, thank you and good night. I hope you'll visit us soon.

MONTHLY LOGS

September

Now that this busy summer is over, climaxed by Miss Nouveau's marriage in August, I'm ready to begin my last year of teaching. I've been around a long time—I've seen fads come and go in education, and I have observed the cyclical nature of these fads—the whole-word approach, phonics, altered alphabets, and others. I am, I suppose, reluctant to change, but the program that I have developed for my students is one that I am comfortable with and one that has proven itself to me. I don't need to constantly search and try out new methods. Years ago I read about individualizing instruction through children's literature, and this is the technique I have continued to use.

I always assess the children before I begin instruction as well as doing on-going assessment. So many teachers have indicated to me that they could not carry through with the individualization plans which they had established. With further questioning, I often discover that they either have not tested the children to see what they know and what they need to know so that they can plan intelligently, or they have simply taken the same old material and put the children through it at different rates. Both of these are contrary to the nature and spirit of individualization. **Assessment**

In general, individualization refers to self-paced, self-selected instruction. However, there are as many systems as there are teachers who individualize. The system that I have used for years with my students is one that allows me more control. And, in the beginning of the year, there is more control than there is at the end. When children first come into my room, they have often been through a basal reading program that is highly structured and sequenced. One of the most difficult tasks I face, therefore, is weaning them away from an overdependence upon the teacher for instruction.

These children have had fewer problems adapting to my program than some classes because Miss Nouveau, or rather Mrs. Flame, did an excellent job with them toward the end of the year. Still, they do not know how to go about selecting a book which would not be too easy or too difficult. Also, the children don't yet have the reading stamina that it takes to have a full-fledged individualized program going. They don't know how to prepare for a reading conference, and to many of them, their individual work folders are still somewhat baffling. I noticed many of these things immediately. **Routines**

On the first day of school, I gave each child a file folder in which to keep assignments. Initially, all the children are given the same work papers so that I can assess skills and work habits. This information, in conjunction with that obtained from an Informal Reading Inventory, gives me an indication of the child's general level of functioning. I give an IRI in September and again in May as a means of measuring reading growth.

Assessment

As part of my initial testing, I like to give the children an interest inventory as well. As a matter of fact, that is one of the work papers which they find in the folders on the first day. I walk around the room while they are working on it so that I can identify those children who are unable to read the inventory and therefore need to have someone read it to them. I soon discovered that children like Larry, Pat, Hilda, and Roberta were quite willing to be amanuenses for children such as Butch, Chip, and Paul. They were a great help. Questions such as, "You are going to be living all alone on the moon for one year. You can take only a few things with you. What three things will you take?" and, "I sometimes feel ____," produce many clues to the needs, perceptions, and values of children. With some of this information in mind, I can help the children to find reading materials and work assignments that will be both interesting and informative. I do, however, use the information with caution, for years ago, after assessing a certain child's interest inventory, I gleefully brought several books to the child about things which he had indicated an interest in. After looking through the stack before him, the child pushed them all aside. "Why, Clarence," I remonstrated, "these are all about cars and football which you said that you liked. Why don't you want to read one of them?" He glanced up at me and told me, "Well, 'cause I likes to play 'em, don't mean I likes to read 'em. Does you have any scary stories? I likes 'em!"

Another time, I searched for reading materials in another child's interest area of the Civil War. He *wanted* to read about it, but I could find very few materials written on his low reading level. These experiences have tended to make me somewhat cautious in use of an interest inventory, though I still feel that it can yield much information that will prove helpful.

Routines

This month we have been working toward independence. That is, the first part of the month was highly structured by me—"Do this." "Tape now." "See me at ____." In this way, I helped the children to learn the routines. They soon knew that they would have to tape record once a week, confer with me once a week, read intensively for three days, work on their folders, and meet for skill group instruction. At the beginning of the third week, I gave each child a ditto paper that had the five days marked off with time slots. On Monday of that week, we spent time filling in the day's plan. I reminded them that they would have to sign up on the chalkboard for a conference as well, since I could only meet with a certain number of them each day. At this time, too, I assigned each of them a day of the week for taping their oral reading, and thereafter each student knew on which day he or she was to tape.

On the day that the child chooses to have a conference, he or she comes to see me early in the morning. I indicate the purpose for which he or she is to read during the morning reading time. For example, I indicate whether to read for main ideas, details or sequence. In that way the child has a structure around which to build the given work time. Being able to choose a book and read it silently was one of the major accomplishments for many children during this month, though there are still some who cannot accomplish this. Children tend to browse too long or select too quickly so that they find the book they selected too hard or not appealing. One morning we just had "browse time" so that they could peruse some books for future selection. That really did seem to help. Also, children suggest books to their friends. ARRF (Average Reader Readability Formula) has helped, too. The books in my classroom have been arranged in three major categories—too easy for my average third grader, just right, and too hard—by means of ARRF (Cunningham, 1976). ARRF is an alternative to the readability formulas currently available. The plan is that you choose an average reader from your class, 100 books, and two hours of time. Horace Middleman was willing to be my guinea pig when I told him that I needed the help of someone just like *him* to assist me with a job that I couldn't do myself. Well, that intrigued him, for many children get the idea—perhaps from teachers themselves—that teachers are omnipotent. I explained that his job would be to go through the books and choose a page near the middle of each book. He was then to read some of it aloud and with my help he would determine if the book was too easy, just right, or too hard for third graders and then place it in the appropriate pile. Once the piles were finished, Horace helped me to color code them by placing one of three different colors of tape on the binding: blue was "easy," green was "average," and orange was "hard." Now my books are codified for this year; of course one must go through the same process every year to tailor the book groupings to an individual class.

Larry (whom the children are beginning to call "Ace"), Danielle, and Pat may choose from any books in the classroom. Paul, Mort, Daisy, Jeff, and Chip will find greatest success with the "easy" books. The others will be reading the "average" books, though sometimes they may dip into the "easy" or "hard" ones. These are not inflexible categories, for sometimes interest will carry children through materials that are too hard by standard criteria. One child I taught was fascinated with tales about the Knights of the Round Table. Unfortunately for him, there were not many of these tales written on his second-grade reading level. We did get the easiest ones that we could, though, and he and I struggled through them. He used the dictionary and me constantly, but refused my offer of finding him simpler, though less interesting, reading. He taught me a great lesson.

The children have had some difficulty adjusting to being responsible

Compre-hension

Library Corner

Routines

for their own time. They see that they have a folder of work to do, but they also notice that there is no set time for them to work on it. Butch came to me the third day of school and asked me when he was to do the work because, "I don't see it nowhere on the chalkboard." I explained to him (again—for I had gone over this with the entire class) that he could plan when to complete the assignments written there. He must plan around his other responsibilities, such as taping and having a conference, but other than that the time was his to plan. At the end of the week Manuel, Mitch, Butch, Paul, Chip, Daisy, Carl, and Mort had not completed their assignments. Realizing what I should have seen immediately, I told them that they were to be my special helpers for some of the room jobs that needed doing (watering plants, feeding animals, and various other tasks). The only restriction was that they were to complete at least two assignments before doing a job, and that the job must be completed by 9:30 A.M. This plan helped to get them organized so that they had some sort of goal that they could aim for. Carl, however, did not do well with this system. We sat down and talked about his problems during the third week of school, and he told me that he just couldn't seem to get going on a task. I asked him if he would like to try an experiment. When he agreed, I told him that when he got his folder every day, he should select one assignment and come to tell me how long he thought it might take him to do the task. I then set my timer for that period of time and he raced against the clock to complete the job. Sometimes he became careless when he knew that time was nearly up, but a little talk about the importance of doing well the first time, rather than having to redo the assignment took care of this problem for him.

Mitch had a different kind of problem with his work. He was so easily distracted by what the other children were doing and so easily tempted to join in with them or bully them that I tried the tack of offering him an "office." One corner of the room is relatively quiet, so I moved a desk and chair there. I told Mitch that sometimes I would have some things for him to do that would require privacy and quiet, and I would like him to have such a place available. Immediately after I told him about this and showed him the office, I asked him to correct a few work papers for me with the teacher's key. He felt very important, sitting there with my —his—grading pencil. The next day, I gave him some more work to do for me in his office. After he finished it, he brought the papers over to me and asked what I did with his office when I wasn't having him work there. I told him that it just remained empty, but that if he would ever like to go over there and work on his other things that would be fine with me. I told him I realized that sometimes things got to be a little exciting in the room, making it difficult for him to do his own work. Needless to say, for days afterward he took nearly all of his work over to that corner. After the novelty wore off and he no longer went there, I would sometimes drop by his desk and ask if he wanted to go the office to work.

He usually agreed to do so, but that is probably because I never ordered him to go there. It was always his choice.

Manuel has taken to coming to sit beside me while I am working with an individual or a group. He brings his work there and sits quietly, doing his assignments. I asked him after this had happened several times why he came when he rarely had any questions. He responded with the wisdom that children have that he knew he could not work by himself at his seat; he just needed to be closer to me. So, if I didn't mind, he would like to come sit near me whenever he felt that he couldn't get his work done at his seat. I wonder what his response would have been had I suggested that he sit near me?

These children who have been through basals are unaccustomed to sitting and reading for long periods at this time of the year, so, rather than the large blocks of reading time which I will have later in the year, I have broken up the time with social studies. After an hour of reading, assignments, centers, taping, and so forth, the children put away their things and we do an activity-oriented social studies lesson. This helps the children to relax from their long periods of concentration, and allows them to talk and release pent-up energy in a constructive way. After the lesson, we go back to our reading-language block for an hour and then to lunch. I intend to increase gradually the time for the first reading period by delaying the start of social studies as I find the children more able to cope with the longer periods. Eventually, the entire two hours will be in one block.

Many children were anxious about the skill groupings. They wondered why they were in a skill group with children who had not been with them in reading group the year before. I relieved their anxiety about this by showing them my card for sorting them into groups (see illustration on p. 392). After that, they were fascinated with the device and would gather around to see whose names came up.

Comprehension Reading Conferences

Conferences, too, frightened them, for they had not had to be responsible for an entire story or book before. In second grade they could depend upon some group support and could learn from the group discussions—now they were on their own! I tried to make their first sessions with me as easy as possible, so that they would come to enjoy and look forward to conference time. I wanted them to see that I really did care what they thought about an instance in the book or what they felt about the entire book. Sometimes it is unnecessary to ask a child how he or she feels about a particular story, for facial expressions or the way the book is held tells more than words. Do we really need to ask comprehension questions when a child closes *Sounder* (Armstrong 1969), clutches it in his or her arms, and sheds tears because there is no more to read?

Writing

I have really been making use of my "writing machine" to create lessons for the children's writing experiences. I call it a writing machine because I can generate a variety and balance of lesson plans with this

	Persuasion	Exposition	Narration	Description
Concrete objects				
Passage starters				
Pictures				
Story retellings				

system. I became very aware, early in my teaching, that it is too easy to give children story starters. The children are comfortable with stories and can write them more easily than any other form of writing. When I caught myself lapsing into the story-starter rut, I formed a grid like the one below so that I would provide opportunities for children to try writing in different modes. That, of course, does not mean that they are all able to write in the modes I planned, but at least they are getting exposure to the modes through listening to their successful peers.

I sit down with my "machine" and plan 16 lessons, 1 for each box on the grid. Sometimes it takes me several days to do the 16 plans, so I always begin working on a new set of 16 in plenty of time so I never run out. I don't, of course, use those terms with the children since they are only for my own planning. I tell them that today they are to form an opinion about something and try to convince others of their ideas (persuasion), or they are to explain how to do something so that someone else could also do it or understand it (exposition), or that they are to have characters in their story who talk to one another and help the story be developed (narration), or they are to tell about how someone or something looks, feels, smells, etc. (description).

I have found the lessons easy to work on and rather a challenge to try to come up with some good lessons interesting to children. A couple of examples that will help show how the core of the lesson develops follow. Let's say that I'm going to have a *persuasion* lesson with a *passage starter*:

Point of view: Children have too much recess time at school.

Have children decide if they think they get too much or too little recess time at school. Have them list their reasons for their opinion. Try to convince others, in writing, using their reasons.

Or for an *exposition* lesson with a *story retelling*:

Read a story which describes the adventures of foxes in the wilderness.

Have children tell about the animals by telling what they eat, where they live, what animals they are related to, how they feel about living in groups (with families or others), and what animals are their friends and enemies.

Clearly, these are only the beginnings of lessons, but once I have 16 of them in this form, I begin putting them into lesson plan format. Sometimes I decide that I really want to try to develop children's abilities with one of the modes, such as persuasion. Persuasive writing is very difficult for most children. In order to focus on that mode and its characteristics, I will group 4 persuasive lessons as the last of a group of 16 lessons (having randomly assigned the other 12 lessons) and add 4 persuasive lessons from my new group of 16 lessons. Having eight lessons in a row dealing with persuasive writing begins to get to them as well as through to them! We're all ready for a change after that, but it does help as an occasional technique. Most of the time, I just put the lessons into a stack and shuffle them so that they come up randomly—fun for me and them!

October

The children are all on their reading cycles now, and things are going more smoothly than they did last month. Other teachers frequently ask me how I can have time to do an individualized program, and I must reply that organization is half the battle. In fact, an individualized program is self-perpetuating, once begun, and I don't think I could return children to the traditional reading groups even if I wanted to. Besides, I enjoy it, and if this is to be my last year of teaching, I want to enjoy it!

As with many teachers, I think I would rather come to school ill and teach than to have a substitute. I think I can do a better job *sick* than many substitutes can do *well*! And this type of a program is more easily done than explained, so that my lesson plan book, so graciously provided by the school system, is a lovely book for keeping track of social studies, science, and other subjects as well as giving me a place to write down dates for staff meetings and hair appointments. But, for the purpose of recording my individualized math and language arts plans, it is totally inadequate. Those assignments are written on file cards and in work folders. You can perhaps anticipate the problems that a substitute—even a good one—might have. One day, Mr. Topps *sent* me home! I had come to school with a sinus headache that increased in intensity as the day wore on, and by lunch I was miserable. He told me that he had already called Mrs. Payne and that she would be arriving soon to take over the class—I was to leave immediately! Imagine speaking to me like that! Why, I'm old enough to be his mother! Anyway, I went back to the room and told the children I would be leaving, and that Mrs. Payne would be coming. Holding my head, I told them to help her figure out the day: "You all know what to do and where your work is."

They all survived the day, but it was rough on Mrs. Payne *and* the children because she wasn't about to trust what the children told *her* to do! She insisted that they all sit in their seats and she passed out copies of the same basal reader (wonder where she found 24 copies?) to each child! They had a round-robin reading lesson, each child taking a turn reading out loud from the book to the rest of the class. Then she made each one write a summary of what he or she had read and listened to. She graded them before she left that evening—conscientious soul that she is—and left them for me to distribute the next day. I was appalled! The letter grades ranged from *A* to *F*! Paul, Daisy, Jeff, Chip, and Butch all received *F*. She said that she was grading them on their oral reading as well as on their summaries, and that these children had failed miserably in reading the third-grade book and in writing a comprehensible paper on it!

Routines The children are still at the stage where they are planning day by day what their activities are to be, though this month we are working toward two and three-day plans; I hope that in November they will get to the point where they are planning for the entire week. In their planning, they must allow time for reading, work folders, and skill groups. They are to spend time at various centers created around the room, too. On two days a week, they must allow time for tape recording and for conferences with me. When a book is finished, they must allow time for the completion of a project built around that book. As you can see, even as they achieve the ability to plan for the entire week, they must still be flexible since events occur which alter the schedule.

I have a highly structured individualized program since that is the type of program with which I am most comfortable. I want the children to use the tape recorder at least once a week, and each child is assigned one day for taping, so that I have a sample of oral reading skills. I make notes of the words misread, fluency, and phrasing. I assign them a day so that I never have more than five oral readings a day to check. In addition, if there is any question in my mind after evaluating their tape recordings, I can further check on these skills when they come to me for a conference.

They are to read intensively for three days, but it is up to the children which three days of the week they will do that. In addition, they choose which day they will meet with me and sign up on the sheet by my table. I can only meet with six children a day, so they try to plan ahead. I've noticed some striking individual differences among the children in that respect. Betty, who likes her life organized and balanced whenever possible, reads on Monday; Tuesday, she tapes; Wednesday, she reads; Thursday, she confers with me; and on Friday, she reads.

Butch, who likes to delay things as much as possible, likes to read for the first three days, then he wants a conference, and on Friday he finally tapes. And so it goes; within the limits which I have established the children choose a schedule which best fits their individual personalities.

Let me describe a typical morning. The children began to arrive at about 8:30 A.M. and from then until 8:45 they played games with one another, read, or worked in some of the centers. Between 8:45 and 9:00, attendance was taken, the lunch count tallied, and the children listened to me read some poems.

Work actually began at 9:00 A.M. Horace got his work folder from the box where I store them, and to which he will returned it when he was done for the day. He checked to see if this was a taping day for him and decided if he wanted to sign up for a conference with me. (He did.) He got his reading book from the shelf where we store the ones currently being read and took his materials to his seat to work. During this "settling in" time, I wandered around the room, assisting the children in beginning their work and helping to clarify instructions and to locate materials.

At 9:10, I went to my small desk where I confer with children. I use a child's desk so that I am at their level; this helps keep the atmosphere relaxed. I noted that five children had signed up to meet with me. Rita wanted to see me at 9:15, Horace at 9:45, Steve at 10:00, Anthony at 10:15, and Betty at 10:45. Between reading conferences, I scheduled skill groups and wrote on the chalkboard the names of the children for each group with the time that I wanted to see them. Skill groups generally last five to ten minutes, so I saw that I could fit in several today. I noticed, too, that Alex, Pat, Chip, Manuel, and Steve had signed up to record their reading.

While I was having skill groups and conferences, children back at their seats began folder work. Sometimes the work assignments send the children into the various center which I have set up in the classroom (see sample assignment sheets for Paul, Hilda, and Larry). When their work is completed, the children can also *choose* to go to centers, where there is a wide range of materials and activities for them. Every center includes assignment cards which direct the children in some specific activity, or instruct them in other activities, such as games. The cards give varying assignments. For example, Paul must do "listening card #9," which is:

Compre-hension—Listening

Put the tape of *Sylvester and the Magic Pebble* (Steig, 1969) in the recorder.
Get the book from the shelf.
Listen to the story and turn the pages when you hear the bell.
After the story is over, put the book and tape away.
Make a picture of the part of the story which you liked best.

Paul

DATE	ASSIGNMENT	EVALUATION
Oct. 4–8	Listening Center—Card 9.	
	Math Center—Cards 4 and 5.	
	Retell story on tape.	
	Alphabet Matching Game.	
	Cut pictures from magazines for *Bb*, *Ff*, *Pp*, *Ss*, *Tt* (sheets included).	
	Listening Center—6 and 10.	
	Science Box 3—magnets.	
	Read *Hop on Pop* to Daphne.	

Hilda

DATE	ASSIGNMENT	EVALUATION
Oct. 4–8	"Silly Sentence" game with Horace, Joyce, Steve.	
	Tape a story for Listening Center—make an activity card.	
	Math Center—Card 52.	
	Math Center—Card 54.	
	Math Center—Card 59.	
	Listening Center—Card 16, 19, 21.	
	Create a puppet play for *Charlottes's Web*.	
	Write a mystery story.	

Larry

DATE	ASSIGNMENT	EVALUATION
Oct. 4–8	Listening Center—Card 32.	
	Math Center—Card 78.	
	Math Center—Card 82.	
	Math Center—Card 87.	
	Make thesaurus entries for these words: *big, little, cute, nice*.	
	Choose a story to read to kindergarten and make flannel board characters to tell story with.	
	Make a crossword puzzle on autumn.	

**Meaning
Vocabulary**

One of Larry's assignments kept him in his seat for a while, for he had to come up with a crossword puzzle which he put on a ditto master and duplicated for the other children to do if they wished. If they had any questions, I directed them to Larry, since he had been the one to design it. He loved being "teacher." I've been having children make ditto papers for other children to do for a long time, and they enjoy it. In fact, they enjoy it so much that last week even Butch told me he wanted to make a ditto. Although he couldn't yet design a crossword puzzle or anything like that, he devised a train for the class to finish. I approved his plan, and he made it into a ditto. How proud he was when he handed it out to the other children. And how pleased he was to run the ditto machine!

Make the rest of the trane and put on a sentense.

by Butch

**Comprehension
Reading
Conference**

When I meet with individual children for a conference, we discuss the kinds of things that are happening in the book they are reading and why some of those things might be happening. Often, I ask the child to imagine himself or herself as a character in the book and to decide what he or she would do in a particular situation. We also work on phrasing and fluency, and plan what the student's reporting project is to be for the book once it is completed. Conferences are generally five to ten minutes long. During the conference, I check the child's work folder and discuss his or her progress. I don't normally deal with phonics skills or some of the other language arts areas, such as writing, in conferences, for I have small, flexible skills groupings for that purpose. During the conference and during my review of the tape, I make notes on the individual child's file card (which lists the date, the assignment, and my evaluation of the work). I make notes while the child is with me, for it is too easy to forget to write something down later. Because I share my notes with the child, he or she is not worried about what I am writing.

Comprehension Questioning

Since it concerns the child the most, I feel that it is my responsibility to discuss what the child does well, and what needs to be worked on. One technique I use to help improve the childrens' questioning abilities is to have them ask me questions about a reading passage. They enjoy "playing teacher" and are delighted if I seem to have trouble answering their questions. After they finish with a question, I say something like, "Now, if I were you, I would have asked...," and employ one of the higher conceptualization levels. In this way, I am providing them with a real model of questioning. I have found that almost all of the children improve their questioning techniques by the end of the year.

Word Identification— Skill Groups

The skill groups to which they come are formed by means of cards like the one that I have shown. The cards have areas I want to teach written around the outside edges. A hole has been punched above each skill so that a knitting stitch holder can be readily inserted. I form a temporary skill group by inserting my knitting stitch holder (which looks like a giant safety pin) into a stack of the same color skill cards. I lock the holder and shake. The cards that fall off are those of children who have already mastered the skill. Those which remain on the holder indicate the children to whom I must teach that skill. In this way, I can quickly find which children need to work on a particular skill and I can keep up with their progress. When children are proficient in an area, a second hole is punched, opening the top edge (see first three boxes in the illustration). Note that one corner has been clipped; that is so that the cards for the same skills can be grouped together right side up, and errors in grouping don't result.

Card #1

Name:

Date begun:

Date finished:

Comments:

I have the skills on the various cards listed by difficulty, so that I can look at an individual child's card and see just where that child is on the skill ladder. Because there are several different skill cards, I have made each different skill card a different color. Some of the cards look like the illustrated card, except that they don't have teaching areas written in. That is for two reasons: (1) if I want to add to the skill program, I can, and (2) I can deal with skills which I cannot describe in that little space: I can write a numeral in the space and code them to skills indicated on the back.

Another organizational device that I use is the work folder. I bought bright-colored folders, at the office supply store, one for each child. On the inside front cover, I stapled a sheet of paper for their assignments. Again, I listed the date, assignment, and evaluation of the assignment. I also listed each child's work so that both they and I knew what things they were to be working on. Their assignments might be work papers, writing assignments, working in centers on specific things ("Do activity card #9 in the listening center."), being assigned to play an instructional game with another child, or creating an instructional material, such as a crossword puzzle.

Routines— Work Folders

I have really been emphasizing the stages of writing with the children. Any time I present a formal writing assignment to them we go through a prewriting stage that includes discussion of the ideas and points of view that they might take. For part of last month, I followed up this prewriting stage with whole-group oral composition, a sort of language experience passage. When they seemed to feel comfortable with that, I put groups of six together in order to do small-group oral compositions, with one of the students in the group acting as the stenographer. They discovered on their own (well, with maybe a *little* help) that during the actual writing stage, they had ideas which hadn't occurred to them during the prewriting discussion. They found themselves making changes and editing their group efforts. These small groups have continued into this month. In the past I have rotated students into different writing groups so that they would not be always working with the same children. This year, however, I decided to try keeping the same groups together for about a month so that they could get to know one another's strengths and weaknesses. They seem to me to be much more cohesive and supportive groups, overall, than the students have been in other years. I am going to encourage them to meet informally over the next month to share their writings with one another. Who knows how that will go?

Writing

November

A new student has arrived—Tanana—and I am afraid that she will have some rather severe adjustment problems. Tanana is an Eskimo child and is so accustomed to wilderness and freedom that she must be finding her new life here rather confining. I have asked two of the girls, Daphne and Betty, to be her special friends until she becomes acclimatized. Those two girls are very outgoing and friendly, and will help Tanana feel at home here.

Writing   Tanana, like many of the others, has difficulty writing stories, so I created two story stimulants that I thought might help. One is a deck of cards that is divided into three equal parts. Each part has a colored line drawn along one edge, to distinguish it from the others. All those with a red line are characters; those with blue are situations; and those with green are places. The cards are separated into three piles and then a child draws a card from each pile. The child must then make up a story using those elements. Alex told a hilarious one when he drew the cards that indicated that his story would be about *a bear, sleeping, in my bed.* Very imaginative child! I must make a note of that on the anecdotal record card which I keep on him and on all of the children. I find that when it comes time for conferences and written reports, I have a much easier time if I have dated records indicating some of the things that I note.

The other device is a golden egg that originally served as a container for nylon hosiery. Inside the egg I have placed many story starters this month. (Later on there will be story middles and story endings.) An example is, "The boy lay quietly, trying not to let the sound of his pounding heart drown out the sounds that he thought were coming from behind his closed bedroom door. Finally, he worked up enough courage to get out of bed, cross the room, and fling open the door. He couldn't believe his eyes! There before him was ...." That kind of starter can spur children on to writing, for who would not be caught up in the excitement? Well, I must admit that Mort was only mildly interested, though Daisy seemed very excited by some of the story starters, particularly the ones that she thought had violence in them. I'm very concerned about her social and academic growth, and I must make an appointment to speak with her mother soon.

I really do think I am seeing improvement in the children's writing skills. We actually have three kinds of writing activities going on, so I suppose the fact that they are becoming better writers has to be related to the amount of practice and feedback they get on their writing. The three writing activities are those which I structure as formal writing lessons using my writing machine creations. With these lessons, I prepare a lesson plan that includes three parts: prewriting activities, writing the composition, and postwriting activities. The second type of writing which takes place is stimulated by devices such as the two I described above. They are stimulators but not full blown lesson plans. The third type is when I direct a student to do some writing in response to something read or experienced in one of the other curricular areas such as reading or social studies. Obviously, writing on self-selected topics is encouraged as a way to spend any other uncommitted time in the classroom.

The children are now enjoying many books and I thought it was time to have them think of some ways to let me know that they had enjoyed their reading other than the ways which I had suggested to them. At first they protested by asking how else they could report on their books, other than the suggestions which I had made. "Fine, I'm glad that you like them, but there are so many other ways to show that you love a book, let's see if we can list them. First, though, tell me the ones I have suggested so that we don't get confused."

Literature Response Activities

1. Make a painting which shows how you felt when you finished your book.
2. Make up a different story ending.
3. Make a diorama showing the characters or a favorite scene.
4. Make a play of some of the most important scenes.
5. Produce a book jacket which shows some of the best scenes, and write a short version on the front and back flaps.
6. Present a puppet show to the class based on the book.
7. Write a letter to the author, telling what you most enjoyed about the book and why.
8. Create a new character for the book. Why is the character necessary? What is the result of adding this character to the book?

Several of the children said, "But with all of those, why do we need to think up more? You've got all the good ones!" I told the children I knew they could think of some good ones, put them into groups of six, and told them that part of their morning work would be to contribute new ideas to our list. I then set the timer and told them that they had only 20 minutes to complete this assignment.

There was instantly a hum of activity in the room. Children formed their groups in various parts of the room to insure the privacy they felt they needed. When the timer rang, I told the children that they were to select one person from their group to report to the class on what they had discovered. As is usual, the natural leaders in the class were chosen: Horace, Larry, Hilda, Roberta, and Danielle. Here is a composite of their ideas as they finally appeared on our chart:

9. Turn the poem you read into a play.
10. Turn the poem you read into a story.
11. Turn the story you read into a play.
12. Turn the story you read into a poem.
13. Turn the play you read into a story.
14. Turn the play you read into a poem.

15. Tell a lap story for the class.
16. Make finger puppets from egg carton dividers. Tell the story.
17. One of the main characters has asked you to spend the night. What kinds of things will you do? What will you talk about?
18. Dress up like one of the characters in the book. Why do you wear those clothes?

When the list was finished, Joyce asked if there was anything else the class could do. Couldn't *someone, sometime*, think up *something* else to do? I assured her that that was exactly what I was hoping would happen, for the whole point of this was just to get them started thinking about ways to help others to enjoy their books.

December

Literature Response Activities
This was a busy and exciting month, but we have accomplished many things. One of the things that we did was to add to our list of book reportings. I found an old copy of *Elementary English* which had an article by Arlene Pillar on "Individualizing Book Reviews" (1975). I asked a committee of students to go through the article and select some activities which they thought might be interesting from among the 30 listed in the article. They chose these:

19. You are the interviewer on a television talk show and will have one of the main characters in the book you have just read as your guest. List the questions you would like to ask. For as many of these as possible, write what you think the character might answer.
20. King Kong has just climbed through your bedroom window. He is trying madly to rip apart the book you have just finished reading. You must act very quickly and defend it. Convince him not to destroy it by citing incidents that you enjoyed. Prove to him that this book is worth keeping.
21. Invite one of the characters in your book to dinner. Tell him or her why you have selected them above the others. Then, leave a note for your mother describing the person and including a few "do's and don'ts" for her to follow so that guest will feel right at home.
22. You are a fortune teller and have been asked to predict what each of the characters in your book will be doing ten years after the story ends. Think of what each one is like (his or her personality, talents, likes and dislikes) before you answer the question.
23. You are a television commercial writer and have been asked to write a commercial advertising this book to the American Public. In not more than two paragraphs, since commercial time is expensive, tell why your book should be read.
24. Since you have the power to transform the major characters in your

book into animals and choose to do so, decide upon an animal for each based upon personality traits. Write a letter to each telling why he or she is similar to the animal selected.

25. You are a real estate agent and want to sell a family a house in the neighborhood in which your book takes place. As part of the job, you must inform your clients about the community, the kinds of people living there, the existing organizations, the types of jobs available, and the schools. Make your description brief and to the point or else you may lose the interest of your clients.

26. The President of the United States wants you to tell him one thing that the character in your book discovered about life which all Americans should know in order to make this a better world. Write him a *brief* letter about this "lesson of life." Remember, the President is busy!

27. You are a famous astronaut flying a secret mission to Mars. Certain that there are Martians on the planet, you must be prepared to convince them that Earth people are friendly. Mission Control wants you to bring along the book you have just finished reading to help you show episodes with helpful and friendly citizens. What would you choose to share?

Betty, who had been on the committee, announced to the class that these additions improved our original list immensely. Others asked me if they could see the article, too, so I suppose that they will be supplementing these 27 on the list with others as the year progresses.

The children in my class decided to go on a hunt for books which had been awarded one of the two major awards in children's literature. I was reading *Island of the Blue Dolphins* (O'Dell, 1960) to them after they came in from lunch recess when I happened to mention to them that this book was a Newbery winner. "A new berry winner?" asked Carl. "Why? Because of all the fruit she eats?"

I explained then about John Newbery and the award which had been established in his honor for books of high literary quality. While I was on the subject, I also told them of the Caldecott Award which was established in Randolph Caldecott's honor to recognize superior illustrations in children's books. As I was doing so I was reminded of something I had read that stated perhaps we ought to have a "Caldebery" or a "Newcott" award for the books which *children* like, for the other awards are selected by adults who think they can choose books which children will enjoy most. Very often the best books are chosen, but it is also true that many times children prefer the runners-up, or even books not nominated, more than the winners of the Newbery and Caldecott awards.

The children decided then that they would very much like to see how many award-winning books our school possessed. I told them that I

Literature Response Activity— Research

would provide them with a list of all the winners and runners-up since the time that the awards began. With this list in hand, the children decided that it would be easier if they divided into groups that could check the books in the rooms and in the school library. They decided that they would need six groups:

Kindergarten and library: Alex, Betty, Daisy, and Jeff
First grade: Butch, Daphne, Carl, and Danielle
Second grade: Chip, Hilda, Horace, and Anthony
Third grade: Joyce, Pat, Tanana, and Manuel
Fourth grade: Larry, Mitch, Roberta, and Paul
Fifth grade: Mandy, Mort, Rita, Steve, and Alexander

Each group was given a copy of the list and told to make an appointment with the teachers to check their bookshelves when it would be convenient. They asked me if we might bring the books to our room for comparison. I told them that they could if they could find a place to store the books from each room *separately* and would label each room's stack of books carefully. Some of the children expressed interest in doing more reading from some of these books—it's an interesting phenomenon that the books from another classroom are more appealing!

A young woman walked into the midst of all this confusion one day as the children were organizing the books that they had gathered. There were books on the floor, on tables, desks, window sills, and in boxes— what a mess! Mr. Topps told me that she had introduced herself to him and that she had asked to meet me. It seems that Miss Young is to be my student teacher next quarter. At least she will be if the mess didn't scare her off! She said that she just wanted to meet me and learn if there was anything that she could do during the holiday break to prepare herself for student teaching in my class. Well, I was flabbergasted! The fact that she took the time to come to see me now gave the impression that this young woman was going to be an exceptional student teacher! I gave her some packets of materials that I had prepared for a substitute after that last awful experience with Mrs. Payne, and explained my goals, policies, and program. I also told her that I hoped she had a strong background in children's literature and suggested some children's books she might read during the Christmas vacation.

Meanwhile, back at the stacks! The children found that the school owned nearly every one of the award books; however, they were so scattered that no teacher knew which of the books was available. As a result, there were several copies of some books throughout the school and none of others. They compiled a list of all these books with an indication of which rooms they were in. They made it on a ditto so that they could duplicate copies for all of the teachers and one for the library.

After we had finished with that project, some of the children were

Literature Response Activity

talking about several of the books that they_had discovered. The ones that especially intrigued them were the Caldecott winners. Mandy said, "You know, I always thought that those were just books for little kids. But some of them are so interesting!"

Daphne asked, "Couldn't we make plays out of those and give them to the other classes for a Christmas present?" Cries of "Yeah! Yeah!" rang through the room. Mort was the only dissenter.

"Why not a Hanukkah present?" he inquired.

"Well, let's make it a Happy Holidays present," I mediated. This was accepted and we set to work. The children decided that they would keep their original groupings and each group would devise a play for the grade level with which they had worked before. They became as excited about this as they were about the approaching holiday season, so that December became a little harried!

Another helpful holiday deed was sending volunteers from my class **Writing** to Miss Launch's kindergarten room to write down the children's dictated letters to Santa. I don't know if it's just the thought of Santa's coming or if there really is a change occurring, but both Butch and Mitch have been extremely helpful and kind this month. I *fervently* hope that it will last!

I've also had to add pages to some of the children's word books this **Sight** month. Each child has a book divided into the sections for the 26 **Words** alphabet letters. In each section, they have been writing all of the new words that they have been learning this year, either through their reading or by asking me to spell some word that holds special appeal, like "vampire" or "groovy." The words are then available to the children later for writing purposes, or, if they encounter them in their reading but cannot remember what a particular word is, the position of the word on the page often triggers their memories. They go through their books often, showing their words to others and getting ideas for new words by seeing what their friends have collected.

I must close this month off rather hurriedly as I have to catch my holiday flight to the Bahamas! Happy Piña Colada to you!

January

Well, my expectations about this term's student teacher seem to be supported by her deeds. Miss Young is a most eager young woman, staying late in the afternoon to complete a bulletin board or game that she is making for the children. The children have for the most part become quite attached to her. Her special friend seems to be Joyce. Joyce and Miss Young talk at great length on the playground, and I have noticed that Joyce is beginning to get really involved with her work. She doesn't need to be reminded to do it, and even seeks extra things to do now. Part of the reason might be that Miss Young had discovered Joyce's interest in witchcraft and the supernatural, and that she has been bringing some of Zilpha Keatley Snyder's books for Joyce to read. She especially enjoyed *The Egypt Game* (1967) and *The Changeling* (1970). Right now she is reading *Below the Root* (1975), a book which I found fascinating. Joyce is really growing up!

Miss Young also taught the children how to construct hardcover books. The children were enchanted with this opportunity to make "real" books. I am including the instructions here so that I won't lose them.

Bookmaking

1. To make a twelve-page book, fold three sheets of typing paper in half. Fold one more sheet in half and place it behind the others.
2. Sew the pages together on the fold either by hand or by using the longest stitch on a sewing machine.
3. Cut two pieces of cardboard that are 9″ × 6″ each.
4. Cut one piece of colored or printed adhesive paper that is approximately 10½″ × 13″. Peel off the paper backing.
5. Place the cardboard on the sticky side of the adhesive plastic cover, allowing ⅛″ between the two pieces of cardboard.
6. Fold the edges of the adhesive plastic over onto the cardboard, snipping corners when necessary in order to make "hospital corners."
7. Lay the pages of the book on the cardboard. Glue the back of the extra sheet to the cardboard on both sides. Allow to dry.
8. The book is now ready to be written and drawn in. Longer books can be made by using more pages. For each sheet of typing paper used, four book pages are made.

After the children had mastered the process, they decided to make books for the kindergarten children. They brought in all kinds of brightly colored, plastic adhesive paper which they could use for the covers of the books. Then a delegation took several samples of their completed books to the kindergarten room. They told the children that if they wanted to write really good stories, then, they, the third graders, would be back to help them make their stories into books! They made the same offer to the first graders, for they knew that Mrs. Wright had her students writing many stories. I let Miss Young continue to be in charge of the project, and though it took nearly a month to complete, the children—all of them—were pleased with the results. Miss Young also thought that it had gone well; however, she did comment, "But the next time I see a roll of adhesive plastic will be *too* soon!"

Skill Groups— Punctuation

I have had Miss Young help me plan and teach some of the skill groups, for she will be taking them over very soon. I wanted her to see some of the activities and materials which she might be able to use. One group that she observed was composed of Manuel, Mitch, Alex, Carl, Steve, and Mort. They were working with punctuation marks. For those children who showed mastery of the exclamation point, period, and question mark, Miss Young was to prepare the next day's lesson on quotation marks and commas. I began the lesson by putting the three punctuation marks on my portable chalkboard and asking the pupils if they could tell me what any one of them was and/or what it meant. Steve commented that he knew "the curly one" meant that someone had asked a question and so it was called a question mark. Mitch knew that "the dot" meant that a sentence was over, and that it was called something that he couldn't remember. Manuel and Mort said "period" together. None of them knew what the next one was called, though several said that they had noticed it sometimes when reading. In response to that, I wrote these three forms of the same sentence on the board:

1. The house is on fire.
2. The house is on fire?
3. The house is on fire!

I asked if anyone could read the sentence for me in three different ways, reminding them that number one would be read in a normal tone, as though they were saying, "Please pass the bread."

Alex decided to try it. He read all three exactly the same way except that he kept his voice lower for the first one. He read them all as if they had an exclamation point. I had turned the tape recorder on when Alex began so that we could play it back and let him hear himself. (Incidentally, I have found this to be very helpful in eliminating many of the errors that children make orally, for they can hear themselves as others hear them.) Alex, after listening to the play-back, admitted that his three readings were not really different. Carl decided to take a chance now. He, too, read them all as if they had exclamation points. I stopped the tape and let the group hear it. They agreed that they had been read alike.

"What is it about that sentence that makes you want to read it as if you were excited?"

Alex said, "Well, it would be dumb to say it like, 'The house is on fire,' because nobody would come help you."

"Right. And the mark of punctuation which we use to show excitement, fear, anger, and other strong emotions is this one—the exclamation point. Listen to me read these sentences now." I taped mine, too, for them to hear.

"When would I say it like number 2?"

Carl replied, "Well, maybe you didn't know if you heard it right." I nodded and Steve asked to read them, and then Manuel did. They read quite well.

"Now, I'm going to read a sentence to you. Write on your magic slates (for this we use plastic coffee can lids and transparency pencils so that they can be easily erased and used again) the punctuation mark which I am using." I proceeded to say several sentences. After saying one, I paused long enough for them to write one of the punctuation marks. After they had written what they considered to be the proper one, they individually showed it to me. If the correct mark had been made, I showed my coffee can lid with the happy face drawn on it. If I didn't show the happy face, the pupil tried again. If the child was still in error, I helped him or her hear what I had said and showed the proper mark on the chalkboard.

"Now I am going to show you a mark, one at a time, and you must think of a sentence for that mark." I marked a blank coffee can lid with one of the three marks. We did this activity for two minutes and then I sent the boys back to their other work. Miss Young commented, "You did so many different things in just seven minutes—I timed you! How can you get so much done?"

I told her that I try to focus on exactly what needs to be taught so that we don't waste time. The children respond well when they expect the lesson to be interesting (because of the frequent changes of pace) and that it will not be too difficult (for I always review what they already know and build from there). She promised to try to come up with a lesson that would do as well, and an admirable job she did, I must say, for her first effort.

I met with Dr. Link after school a couple of times this month to discuss the progress that Miss Young was making. I told her I had been favorably impressed initially, and that she had indeed lived up to those first impressions. Dr. Link was pleased to hear that Miss Young was so involved in the classroom, for some supervising teachers like to have their student teachers just observe for the first weeks.

"Those people must be better organized than I am, then," I told her, "for I can use every pair of hands I can get, particularly when they are such capable ones."

I admitted that I was giving Miss Young more responsibility than I usually give to student teachers so early in the quarter, but that she seemed to be enjoying it. In addition, she and I share many of the same interests, and she had asked if she could begin planning a poetry project for March as her final large assignment. I am eager to get some new ideas from this one! It's a rare student teacher who hasn't taught me something during tenure in my classroom.

February

Complaints! Complaints! Several of the children are upset because in order to find a book dealing with a particular interest of theirs, they must search through all of the books in the room. "Why can't it be like the library?" is the cry heard more and more frequently. So this month I challenged them: "Why can't it be?" We discussed how to find books in the library and what kind of a system is used. I said I was tired of searching, too, and if they could come up with a plan, we would try it. Several days later, the children asked if we could get the entire class together for a discussion. When the entire class had assembled, Larry and Mandy took over. They told the group that they had been asking questions of the librarian and had learned from her that books are divided into categories like history and science. Then within those categories, the authors' names are arranged alphabetically. That is the system, basically, that our school library uses, but Miss Page had told them that she didn't think that they wanted their system to be so complex. "Just divide the books into categories and they will be much easier to locate," she told them, "and the addition of new books will be much simpler."

"What's the first step, Ace?" asked Hilda, who always likes to be prepared.

"Well, the first step," Miss Page explained, "is to make sure that somebody has read all of the books in the room." Groans from the children as they looked over the bookshelves loaded with at least 200 books.

"But how can we do *that*?" Carl asked.

"My guess is that we nearly *have* done that. Wouldn't you agree, Mrs. Wise?" asked Larry. At my nod of agreement, he continued, "The first thing to do is find out which books have been read and which ones still need to be read. Mandy and I got some file cards from Mrs. Wise. You are to go to the shelves, find some of the books that you have read, and write the name of the book and the author on the top line. Later, when they are all done, we'll sit down and decide in which categories they belong. We'll all work at the same time so that we don't get several copies of cards on the same book."

"You know what I wish we could do?" asked Tanana. "I wish that we could know what the book is going to be about before we choose it. I know that Mrs. Wise lets us choose another one if we don't like what we get, but sometimes I waste a lot of time trying to find one I like."

"How about this, you guys?" Roberta spoke up. "Why don't we leave the card in the book when we finish, sticking up out of the top like this? Then when we're all done, those who have read a book get together and think up one or two sentences telling what the book is about."

Remarks of "Yeah!" and "Neat!" were heard around the group,

Library Corner— Card Catalogue

though I could see Mitch and Butch grimacing at the idea of the extra work that this would mean.

"How are you going to show what kind of book it is?" I asked. "How will people know that it is an animal book when they get it off the shelf?"

"Well, we could write on the outside like they do in the library," said Pat. "We could use numerals, like all the books with the numeral *one* would be animal stories. Something like that."

"Good idea, Pat. I think that would work very well. Then we could have a chart in the room in case anyone forgets what a numeral stands for. And we could put all of the *ones* together, all of the *twos* together, and like that," replied Larry.

And so we did. It took the children weeks to get the system organized, materials read, cards made and filed, but they have produced a system that will be used by scores of other children in this room, whoever their teacher might be. I regret that I will not be around next year to reap the benefits of all this work.

This is a most unusual class; in fact, it is *the* most unusual blend of children that I have encountered in my years of teaching. However, they seem to have a great deal of group cooperative spirit (the result, no doubt, of all the team effort that previous teachers have encouraged), so **Dictionary** I suggested to them that it might be a good time to make a classroom dictionary. We would include all the words in their word books in the same way that they are listed in the regular dictionary. Butch, foreseeing more work ahead, asked why we needed to do this since we already had five different dictionaries in the room. Pat, Daphne, Betty, and Tanana hushed him up with an "It'll be fun!" His look said that he was *not* convinced.

"You're right, of course, Butch. It will be a great deal of work, but I'm hoping that you will all learn more about a dictionary and how to use it by actually constructing one. I think that it will be fun, too!"

How did we begin? First, the children formed four groups of five or six children. Each child brought his or her word book to the group. Next they went through all of the *Aa* words and listed them alphabetically. There was one bad moment when Daisy didn't want anyone to use her word *apple* because it was *her* word and she liked it! She actually *hit* three of the children who insisted that they had to include the word. I noticed the first blow and got across the room to her group by the time she had struck the third child. When the children explained the problem to me, I took Daisy over to the shelf where we kept the other dictionaries and turned to the word *apple* in each of them. I showed her that while she may have a special feeling for the word, it indeed was not only her word. It belonged to all of us, but because she liked it so much, she could think up a nice sentence using the word to go into the dictionary.

The next thing that they did after they had gone through all of the words in their books and had alphabetized them was to send one representative from each large group with the list to make a master list for the class. They eliminated duplicates and came up with a final copy with the hundreds of words that the children had learned throughout the year. Needless to say, when the children saw this mammoth list, they were astonished. They had no idea that they had learned so many new words since September. They retained another aspect from their original group word lists; beside each word that they wrote on the list, they put the initials of the first three children who had learned that word. Those three children were to be responsible for the definition, any illustrations they might feel necessary, and a sentence to illustrate the meaning of that particular word. I was somewhat hesitant to allow them to do this, for I thought of children like Paul and Chip who never learn a word first! But I was wrong. The dictionary, being a list of the words learned by the children, included the words that Chip and Paul were learning to read, and since most of the others had learned the word *farm* long ago, it was a word that Chip and Paul could work on this year. When the children completed this task, they asked Mrs. Mainstay in the office to type it for them in dictionary format, and, being the dear lady that she is, she readily complied. The children then selected a bookbinding committee to do the various steps involved in making a hardbound copy of their book. They were quite proud of it, especially when Mr. Topps, showing visitors around the school, pointed it out and told them how long and hard the children had worked on it. Butch took special pride in the book and was always first at the door when visitors arrived so that he could bring it to them as soon as Mr. Topps mentioned it. He would always say, "Well, it took us a long time, but it was fun."

March

Miss Young has become invaluable to me, and I told Dr. Link that I was not going to let her go! She laughed at me, of course, and said that if I felt that strongly, perhaps I would be willing to recommend her for my position which would become vacant with my retirement this June. I assured her that I would certainly do that, for Miss Young has been the *best* student teacher I have ever had. It is rather nice to think that someone who spends so many hours with the children working on their classroom catalogue system might be able to benefit from it next year. She is so creative, willing, and sympathetic to the students! And yet she doesn't let that sympathy interfere with providing them with the best possible instruction: she feels quite sad about Chip's home situation, but it is one that we can do nothing about, since his family is too proud to accept welfare. But, we can't let that interfere with doing what we can for him: providing him with the best possible education.

Miss Young has become a real expert at managing her time so that she can confer with five children and meet with six skill groups within a one-and-one-half-hour reading period. With both of us working, team-teaching style, we can accomplish even more, so I was reluctant to give her the experience that she needed in handling the entire day by herself. But, I did allow her two weeks, of course, so that she had a small taste of what it would be like to be totally responsible for a class.

Writing
During those two weeks—her last two weeks with us—she had the children making "shape books." Chip made a "hand book" in the shape of a large hand. The illustrations were photos made with an inexpensive Polaroid camera as well as others cut out from magazines. All were pictures of hands doing various things. The illustrations were labeled with descriptions of the hands' actions. One picture had a man's hands playing a piano, and the sentence said, "Hands can make music." Another showed a lady cuddling a baby, and was entitled "Hands can love you, too." Horace made a "foot book" using the same technique. Several other children found shape books to be an entertaining exercise.

Poetry
Another project of Miss Young's was the long-awaited poetry unit. I knew that these children had had quite a lot of exposure to poetry. They had had much poetry read to them, and they had, in turn, created many poems of their own. I knew that they were ripe for the kinds of activities that Miss Young had in mind for them.

Topical Word Sets
She began the poetry unit by reading to the children from Mary O'Neill's beautiful *Hailstones and Halibut Bones* (1961), a collection of poems about colors. After reading a couple of her favorites and one of mine ("What is Purple?"), she discussed with them the fact that Mary O'Neill is saying that colors are not only things, but also feelings, moods, smells, and sounds. Then she took a stack of colored construction paper from her table and asked the children to form groups of five or six and told them that each group would receive one color sheet. They were then to list all the things that the color could be, feel like, smell like, sound like, or make them feel like within the five minutes that the timer would be set for. They began to discuss furiously and to list all of these qualities while she sat calmly reading more of the book (presenting all the while a good model for the children). When the timer rang, there were some groans of "Oh, no! Not yet! Let us put down some more." She asked each group to choose someone who could read the completed list to the rest of the class. One which I thought was particularly good was this one by Rita, Jeff, Manuel, Mort, Pat, and Steve. Their color was white:

lacy snowflakes	glaring light	refrigerator door
frosty window pane	anger	fear
unfriendly	coldness	sweet apple inside
crunchy ice cube	fluffy whipped cream	winter morning breath
hot mashed potatoes	a story before it's written	clouds above

Poetry

She told the children that poetry creates images and that those images do not need to be done with rhymes. She said that she was sure that the children could create a poem from what they had listed. She said, "Let me see if *I* can try to make one." And this is it:

> Lacy snowflakes
> Against my window pane.
> Fluffy whipped cream
> Coldness from clouds above.

The children were enthralled, as was I, with this creation. Immediately, each group set to work to create a poem. Miss Young had explained to me that she wanted the children to have many experiences in writing group poems before they attempted to write individual ones. She told me that she had come to love poetry only within the last few years, that she had dreaded and hated it before. She was sure that that was because of the way in which her teachers had dealt with it—not as something to be loved, treasured, and enjoyed, but rather as something to be analyzed, dissected, and criticized. She had vowed that she would do her best to help her students learn to enjoy poetry at an early age. A format which she used with them involved the "diamante" form that Iris Tiedt (1970) had developed. It is as follows:

> noun
> adjective, adjective
> participle, participle, participle
> noun,   noun,   noun,   noun
> participle, participle, participle
> adjective, adjective
> noun

The first and last words are to be opposites, and images build on the first noun through the two nouns in the middle. The transition is made here to building images for the last noun. The poem below is one written by the class.

> Father
> Strong, kind
> Working, resting, loving
> Bed, baby, boy, Mommie
> Working, working, working,
> Tired, busy
> Mother.

Miss Young also had the children complete the following phrases, and with the unifying factor of "The year" repeated at the end of the poem, she found that even the less capable children could produce a poem of worth.

> The year...
> The fall...
> The winter...
> The spring...
> The summer...
> The year...

I knew that the poetry unit had been successful when I noticed that the previously untouched poetry books in the class library became the most demanded ones and when scraps of poetry began to appear in the margins of work papers. The children recited poetry to one another at the playground! If only they keep this enthusiasm!

April

My, how the time is passing now. With April over, only one more full month of school remains. I always begin to panic at this time of the year, wondering if I will accomplish all that needs to be done. Oh well, done or not, the year *will* end! I've started to go through my file cabinets so that I won't be here all summer, trying to move out of this room. One accumulates a lot in 28 years.

Routines While cleaning, I came upon the file folder for individualization I compiled the year that I first began to become discontented with what I had been doing, and was searching for something more satisfying for myself and the children. I had read a lot of articles in my professional journals, attended workshops, and taken courses at the university. I tried, then, to put all of the information together in a way that I could deal with it. I thought that I was ready after we returned from our Easter break (in March of that year). There was still enough time to work out some of the problems and to give it a fair try, realizing that if it didn't work, I wouldn't have wasted an entire year of the children's time. I began with my "top" reading group. I suppose that was because they had already completed the traditional third-grade curriculum and were actually just marking time. I called them together and told them that I wanted to begin an experiment with them. I told them that I had been looking into different ways to teach reading, and I wondered if they would like to help me try it out. I implemented, essentially, the same plan that I have explained in this journal.

Grouping I was most eager for them to tell me what they thought of it after we had been at it for a month, so I called the original group together and asked them for comments and suggestions. One suggestion was that they be allowed to work in groups, for I had them all working independently so that there was little interaction among them. I agreed, and some of the group activities described in this journal are the results of their suggestions. They also wanted more entertaining things to do, for I, in my eagerness to provide them with a good skills reinforcement program, had given them stacks of ditto papers to do every day and very little for pleasure. They were interacting with the material in only a limited way—read the book, answer questions about the book, do a ditto on parts of speech. I promised that I would find some other ways to teach and provide practice. This whole thing became more complex than I had ever anticipated. I changed many of my ideas about teaching reading that spring, and began to be, I felt, a much better teacher. After years of teaching I was finally beginning to be concerned about the children and *how* they learned as well as *what* they learned.

With the children's suggestions implemented, I decided to individualize the middle group of readers as well. Since I had the first ten children going strong, I was sure that I could handle eight more. Well, I did it, but for a week or so I thought I would go crazy! All of those assignments to check every night and then more to make up for the next day! Finally one evening I asked myself why I continued to punish myself that way. Unless this "treadmill to oblivion" was to be my entire life—correcting work and assigning more so that I would have something to do the next night—I had to find an alternative. But what was it? The work had to be checked, but *why* did it have to be checked? The answer: so that the children would have reinforcement for the things that they knew and so that they could see through their errors what they didn't know. It suddenly became apparent that it would be more useful to them if the children corrected their own work. So that is what I let them do. I made self-corrective as many of the materials in the learning centers as I could. When the children did some work papers, the key was made available to them, and they did the correcting. I still saw some of these papers, for I did need to evaluate their work, but it was not necessary to mark a paper in order to evaluate it. Besides, the unit tests that I gave and the skill tests that I devised gave me information about the children's progress so that I did, indeed, know their respective strengths and weaknesses. With things running smoothly, I was able to individualize the "low" group, also, so that I had all the children working more or less independently—and happily.

How I wish that Miss Young had been around that year to help me. If she had been available, I could have been using "LAP's" all these years. She introduced me to the concept and produced a few of them during her quarter in the room. A LAP is a "Learning Activity Packet" that includes a pretest over material in the packet, activities to teach and reinforce, and a posttest to determine how well each child has mastered

Routines

the materials. She did an excellent unit on "Nyms"—synonyms, antonyms, and homonyms. The pretest had a page with exercises like the following:

Choose the homonym pairs in each row:

her	hair	hare	chair
sore	chore	soak	soar
flour	shower	flower	floor

Match antonym pairs:

hot	ugly
beautiful	laugh
cry	cold

Write two synomyms for the following words:
pretty
said
good

After she evaluated the child's strengths and weaknesses, she assigned certain of the activities within the packet. After those were checked by the child and after he or she felt that the concepts had been mastered, he or she asked to take the posttest. If the child did well, another packet was assigned. If, however, he or she still had areas of weakness, Miss Young had prepared alternative activities to review an area without going over the same work. Some of her packets included a tape which the children could drop into a recorder and then listen to the instructions. These were especially helpful for those with inadequate reading skills, but I think that all of the children benefitted from the ones they used, for it was one more valuable listening exercise for them.

Before I was introduced to LAP's I had another system which worked rather well for me. I went through all of the old workbooks in the school storeroom, tore the pages out of their covers, and sorted them according to skills. In addition, I had a lot of sample workbooks and activity cards that publishers' salespeople had given me. Usable materials also went into skill piles. When I had gathered everything available to me (ditto masters, directions for games, etc.), I labeled file folders and stored the materials in the appropriate folders. Then when I wanted to teach the suffix *ly*, I went to that particular folder and got the materials that I needed. They were all there together and ready for use. I think that if I were going to teach another year, I would use a combination of my file folders and those LAP's. Dittoes and workbook materials can provide opportunities for children to practice the skills I have been teaching. Though these materials do not themselves teach children what they need to learn, they nevertheless allow me to provide frequent and varied practice when I couple them with materials I have designed and planned.

May

More drawer and file cabinet sorting this month. I came across an old cardboard folder in which I found pictures, stories, poems, plays, and other nice things done by my students over the past 28 years. Here is the picture that Cathy drew after her mother died and she had such a hard time adjusting to it. And here's the story that David wrote to give me for my birthday. All of these are reminders of all the wonderful children who have taught me as much as I ever taught them. I should throw them away, for I can't possibly keep all of these remembrances of years gone by—and yet, how can I possibly discard the souvenirs of so many years of my life?

Assessment

In this last busy month, I called for parental help to administer the IRI's to the children again. I do this as a further gauge on what they have accomplished. I also have a mother help me by administering a basic sight word list to the children. They all should have this list mastered by the end of third grade, but, unfortunately, some do not. In the file that is passed on to the next teacher, I will include with the written evaluation each child's skill cards and the Dolch test so that the teacher will know which skills and words still need to be worked on.

Book Selection

To help the children become even more independent, I have taught them to use Jeannette Veatch's "rule of thumb" (1966). They can determine if a book is too difficult for them by turning to a full page somewhere near the middle of the book and choosing a paragraph of about 100 words. As they read, they may encounter words they do not know, so when the first one is met, the thumb of one hand is extended from a closed fist; when the second one is encountered, the next finger is extended, and so on. If all five fingers are extended by the end of the paragraph, that book is probably too difficult. They are instructed to make another selection. Most of the children find that this system works quite well for them, but for some few it's not a good system. Mitch finds it difficult to admit, even to himself, that a book that he has chosen from a shelf may be too hard. He "fudges" by starting over if he runs out of fingers. Daisy doesn't know that she has made any errors, so, consequently, she ends up with books that she is unable to read. She substitutes words, but since she still has difficulty with even literal comprehension, she is unaware that what she says does not make sense.

Writing— Group Product

Even though almost all of the writing done by the children these past couple of months is individually written and only periodically shared with and evaluated by other children, I have tried a couple of ideas with them that they really enjoy. These writing activities require that the children be active readers as well as writers.

One type of writing is called the traveling tale. All the children in the classroom sit at their seats with pencil and paper waiting for me to give the start signal. When I say, "Write!" the children begin writing anything they would like to write in any format we have used during the year. Some begin a letter, others start a description of a pet owned, and still others may enumerate the physical attributes of one of our classroom animals. I allow children three minutes for this initial writing. At the end of three minutes, I say, "Pass," and the papers are sent to the person to the left. "Write," I say, and they begin to add to the writing they have just received. After one minute they pass the papers again. Each time they get a new paper, I add on a half minute for writing so that they have time to read what was written as well as to add new lines. After they are again back to three minutes of writing, I tell them that this is the last pass and they are to add an ending to what they have received. At the end of the three minutes, I ask for volunteers to read any paper they have which they think is particularly good.

Children really like this activity because of the surprise element and the anonymity. They also love to find out how their initial starter was finished. I like it for other reasons. With the traveling tale, children do just a bit more reading (and every little bit helps). They have to adjust their thinking every couple of minutes for the new task at hand. Many children need opportunities to practice this ability to shift gears. Children are being exposed to many different styles and qualities of writing with the traveling tale. This modeling allows them to participate in better writing than many would be able to do wholly independently. Another reason I like the traveling tale is that it is a form of writing which children enjoy and ask to do. In fact, I have noticed small groups of children congregating in a corner of the room and trying traveling tales on their own with the aid of the kitchen timer.

Writing— Group Product

Another almost equally popular type of writing activity is the written conversation. For this one I group children into pairs or triplets and tell them they cannot talk. They can only write down what they want to tell the other or others in the group. Amid much giggling and eager anticipation, reading and writing do occur. For some of the children, written conversations are a killjoy; they had heard from older siblings that writing notes in school was one of the forbidden acts and that dire consequences befell those who were caught. If a teacher encouraged them to write notes, what fun was there left in the world? They'll just have to cope!

Writing

Reading and writing are so clearly related that I do not see how I could teach were I not constantly using one to reinforce the other. Children become better readers by reading what they themselves and others have written; by the same token, they also become better writers through practice, exposures to the writings of others, and evaluation of their own writing.

With the good start they were given by previous teachers, particularly Mrs. Flame who inaugurated a biweekly writing plan with this group, they were receptive to increasing their writing skills. Such receptivity has paid off. Each one of the children whom I had a conference with this month was amazed at the improvement in writing as demonstrated by the weekly samples I had collected this year. The difference between September and May was astonishing whether the child was Paul or whether it was Danielle. Even those who considered themselves poor writers, as Butch does, could see the remarkable progress made. "Hey, Mrs. Wise," he approached me late in the day we had had the conference. "If you was just gonna throw them papers away, I could maybe take them to my house and do it for you." And, no doubt, share them with his father on their way to the trash! Congratulations, Butch! They're all yours.

THE THIRD-GRADE MEETING

Mrs. Wise smiled as Miss Port departed. There were many teachers who felt considerable fear of that small but dynamic Miss Port whenever she entered their classrooms. Not Mrs. Wise! She remembered when Miss Port had been *her* student teacher some 14 or 15 years ago. It was on Mrs. Wise's recommendation that the school system had hired Miss Port and had later promoted her to the position of Elementary Supervisor. Now Mrs. Wise was smiling, for she had just been asked if she would present the program for the final meeting of the third-grade teachers. "My valedictory," she thought. "Oh, well. I suppose they had to ask me now, since I won't be here next year. I was hoping, though, that I could get away without even attending, let alone being the program!" After 28 years of these meetings, she was *ready* to retire; she had often said that the meetings were things she would never miss about school!

But now to plan what to do! She began by going through some of the materials which she had selected for this final meeting, dragging out samples of cards and charts that she had used during this past year. She had asked to have the meeting in her own room so that she would not have to transport all of her paraphernalia across town to the room in the Administration Building, where these meetings were usually held. Here she would show the other teachers the learning centers which occupy the children's time, as well as the card catalogue system that the children had devised. She sat down to plan the meeting for the following week.

One week later, Mrs. Wise was completely organized and ready for the meeting. She greeted the teachers who entered her room and then began the meeting by expressing her pleasure at seeing all her old friends and acknowledging her sincere delight at the interest they had shown in her program. She told them that she was eager to share with them the kind of program that she had been using for many years. Some of those present had visited her classroom in the past and she invited them to make any comments which they felt were pertinent.

"First of all, it is important to emphasize that individualized reading instruction is not a *method* of teaching. Rather, it incorporates parts of many methods. Furthermore, individualization does not mean instruction on a one-to-one basis. This is a common fallacy. Individualization means *providing children with what they need, when they need it.* Therefore, it can mean teaching 1 to 1 or 1 to 5 or 1 to 30. The point is that the *children* are central to what is being taught, not a curriculum.

"Another factor to keep in mind is that, for most of us, it is better to begin gradually when initiating my kind of program. Until I had worked out many of the details, I only had my 'top' reading group involved in the individualized program. It was only after I felt more confident that I included the rest of the children in the program.

"I want to emphasize that I have learned that you *must* provide group activities for the children. It is so easy, really, to isolate the children, to make them so independent of the others that they don't develop the cooperative spirit that is so necessary if they are to make their contributions to society. We tend to give children their work folders and books, send them off to do their own work, and be sadly unaware of the social damage that we may be inflicting upon them. We are, after all, social creatures, and it is just as much our responsibility as teachers to consider that aspect of children's education as it is to provide for the basic academics."

Mrs. Wise then showed the assembled teachers her skill cards ("they operate on the same system as computer key-sort cards"), samples of work folders and assignments, the reading cards on which she kept notes on a child's progress, and the other materials that she used in her daily teaching. She described the conferences and the skill group meetings, the learning centers, the testing, and the games. She then told them that long ago she had given up correcting every one of the assignments *herself.* That statement caused several sidelong glances, and one of the teachers challenged her.

"Maydelle Wise! Do you mean to tell us that you let the *children* mark their papers? I wouldn't dare to try that! Why I'd have children cheating all over the place."

"Yes, you probably would, if you think of it in those terms. Children respond as they are expected to respond. I had few instances of cheating, though there were many instances in which the children, feeling frustrated and concerned, 'forgot' to mark errors. Those instances fortunately occurred early in my experimentation. I discovered that what was actually causing the tension was that the work that I had assigned was too difficult. Once I had planned an instructional program for each child that fit his or her special needs, there was no longer a problem. Letting children know that you trust them and expect them to accept some of the responsibility for their own learning is a most important step. They respond well to this, at least in *my* experience, which, as you all know, has been considerable!"

Mrs. Wise went on to tell them that in order to help children choose books which they might enjoy, she had administered an "interest inventory." It was not complex, and she had devised it after examining several that she had found in journals and books. She had also found that she needed to organize herself, and so she had devised a materials-skills checklist that enabled her to sort out her various materials. This had taken a lot of time, but it had been easily augmented once the initial work had been completed. One of the teachers asked her how it was done, and she drew a diagram on the board to illustrate. The top of the paper was divided into skill areas; the left side listed all the materials she had available for use, either from her own supplies or from those of a cooperative teacher in another grade. Then she marked all of the skills that a particular material would deal with. This had a twofold purpose: first, she could see at a glance all of the materials which she had available for a specific skill, and second, she could see those areas for which she needed to find or develop materials. She had found, she said, that her teaching materials were inadequate in the areas of listening and study skills. If she had not made the checklist, she might not have realized this fact and might have gone on to this day wondering why her students had weaknesses in these areas. Since she had known her for many years, Mrs. Wise was not at all surprised when an older teacher, Agatha Nostic, declared, "It seems to me that you spent far too much time testing your class. How could you get any teaching done?"

"But my dear, how can you teach children until you know what it is that you *must* teach them? What a waste of your time and theirs to go over material which is already known, and how frustrating for you and them to try to deal with material that is too hard. Surely you see the absurdity of it? After careful assessment, I have a notion of what they know and what they need to learn. From there on, it's relatively easy."

"But didn't you repeat yourself a lot? I mean, it seems to me that it is more economical to introduce a new concept to everyone at the same time."

"But, Agatha," Mrs. Wise replied, "don't *you* repeat yourself? Do all of the children master a concept when it is introduced? I found out many years ago that if I introduced something to the entire class that they were not all ready for, I then had to spend the next few months going over and over the same thing for some of the children, trying to drive it into their heads. However, if I waited until they were ready to learn the concept, then the teaching and the learning were less difficult."

"One thing that I didn't understand was how you could get through with a conference in just five to ten minutes. I take 30 minutes for a reading group and I *still* feel that I haven't accomplished much."

"Agatha, if your reading groups are anything like the ones I have had, my guess is that you spend a lot of the time in noninstructional roles. 'Eyes on the book, Johnny.' 'Sue, do you know where we are?' 'No voices, please; Mary is reading.' 'Hands on the table and out of your desk, Jake.' Does that all sound familiar? Of course it does! I had a student teacher make a chart of my teaching behaviors on a certain day, and I was appalled at how much time I was spending disciplining or trying to gain the attention of bored and/or frustrated children. That was another thing that led me to try individualization. With only two of us, the child and myself, who is there to show off *for*? If attention begins to wander, I am immediately aware of it. Five minutes of good, solid, individual instruction is worth more than 30 minutes of interrupted and incomplete instruction in a group."

Mrs. Wise paused to notice the nods of agreement around the room. She had had the feeling when she began that some of these teachers were not very sympathetic to what she was doing, but now there was a noticeable change. Several of the teachers wanted to know how to begin her program. She showed them some of the materials that she had developed in her program. She recommended that they read professional journals since there is much helpful information in them which is practical and realistic.

She began to gather up her materials, preparatory to leaving the meeting, when Miss Port, with a grin on her face, told her to sit down, for the best part of the meeting was yet to come. And through the door, borne by two of her oldest friends, came a cake of mammoth proportions. The inscription read "Good-by, Mrs. Wise. We will miss you." She was stunned and unable to speak for a moment, but one of her friends thought she heard her mutter under her breath. "I'd rather have a martini!"

13 | Ms. Maverick

THE PARENT MEETING

Ms. Maverick greeted most of the parents by name as they entered the door of her fourth-grade classroom. Five years before, she had known no one in this community and had missed the easy familiarity she had established with the residents of the small mountain community where she had taught during her first three years.

"Welcome," she began. "As most of you know from our annual book fairs, I am Ms. Maverick. I am pleased to see so many parents here tonight. Usually, there is a tremendous turnout of parents for the kindergarten and first-grade meetings, but attendance decreases as the grade level of the children increases. You are to be commended for your continuing interest in the education of your children.

"Tonight, rather than talk at you about the reading program we pursue in this room, I am going to engage your participation in a learning activity similar to many of the lessons your children will be participating in. I would like you now to think back on all your activities over the past week and to try to remember all the things you had to read in order to get along in your daily lives. You see, reading is such a constant activity that often we read without realizing it. We are aware that we are cooking or traveling or working without realizing that reading is an integral part of all these activities. Tonight, I want you to tell me all the things you have read this week that were not books or magazines and, as you list these things for me, I will write them up here on the board."

At first there was silence as the parents adjusted their expectations to include their active participation in the meeting and began to think about what they had read that was neither a book nor a magazine. Mrs. Penn broke the silence by volunteering that she had read a map to get over to the state capital for a special meeting of a citizen's action group. Ms. Maverick wrote *map* on the board and then waited. Mr. Moore said that he had read the revised criminal rights statutes which had come in the mail to the police department. Mrs. Smith said that she had read the electric bill. Everyone groaned, the group relaxed, and suggestions came faster than Ms. Maverick could record them: *traffic signs, clocks, pat-*

Functional Reading

417

terns, *exit signs, blueprints, phone books, letters, sales ads, the dials on the stove, directions on a varnish can.* In ten minutes, Ms. Maverick had the board filled and the parents had "experienced" reading as a survival skill.

"You know, I have always been a reader and thought how unfortunate people were who couldn't read," Mrs. Penn volunteered. "But I never realized how downright impossible it would be to get along in the world if I couldn't read."

Daphne's grandmother recounted, "Once I was in the grocery store and a man came up to me with a can of soup in his hand and asked me what kind it was. I just assumed he had left his spectacles at home, but perhaps he couldn't read the label. They don't put pictures on the cans the way they used to, you know." Her husband added, "You can't be a successful farmer these days if you don't know how to read!"

Ms. Maverick agreed. "That's right, there are very few jobs you could hold these days that don't require some reading ability. So often, wanting the best for our children, we point out to them that they must do well in school if they want to grow up to be lawyers or doctors. Many children, however, aspire to the 'exciting' occupations: they want to be truck drivers, police officers, medical technicians, beauticians. Little do they realize the reading demands of these jobs.

"My most important reading goal for your children is that they experience reading as a survival skill. To accomplish this, I do exercises with them like the one I just did with you tonight. I also provide them with 'real world' reading materials. I have some of these 'real world' materials displayed here on this table and I will be encouraging the children to bring in reading material they find of interest."

The parents looked over to the table and saw displayed there two daily newspapers, several different magazines, a driver's license manual, maps, menus, pamphlets, telephone books, catalogues, games, and directions for constructing various objects.

"For the final part of my 'reading is real' scenario, I plan to invite people engaged in various jobs to come in and talk with my children about what they must read to do well in their jobs. I haven't done this before but I think it will make a more lasting impression if the children hear people explain the reading needs of their jobs. This is one area in which I am seeking your help this year. I won't ask you to volunteer now, but if you could spare a half-hour to come and talk to the children about your job and its reading demands, please stay a minute after the meeting and leave me your name and the best time for you to come."

Ms. Maverick looked at the clock and realized that she had already used most of her meeting time. ("This is a consistent problem in an activity approach to learning," she thought. "It always takes more time.") She then hurried on to explain the other three components of her reading program.

"While the 'reading is real' component is an important part of our reading program in this room, it is certainly not the total program. In fact, it is only one side of my four-sided reading approach. A second side of the approach is SQUIRT.

SSR

"Reading is considered important enough so that we take time out each and every day to do it. Presently in our class we are reading for 15 minutes, and I hope that we will be up to 25 minutes by the end of the year. During SQUIRT time your children have intensive sustained practice in reading in material of their choice. I believe strongly in the concept of SQUIRT because it just makes so much sense. All of you know that to be good at anything, you have to learn to do it *and* you have to practice doing it. You wouldn't expect anyone to be a good driver who had just taken driving lessons but had never practiced driving. I believe that our daily SQUIRT time insures the practice half of the instruction-practice partnership which is essential for learning anything.

"The third part of my reading approach is what I call my 'integrated curriculum block.' I do not separate the subjects so that math is taught for 45 minutes, followed by 45 minutes of reading, language, science, and social studies. It seems so much more economical to spend the reading, language, and math time engaged in reading, writing, and doing math problems that relate to the real world topics of social studies and science. So each morning from 9:00 to 11:00 we have our block time. During this time we are practicing our language and math skills as we investigate a topic from the social studies or science curriculum.

Integrated Curriculum

"For the next several months, we will be busy finding out about our state, which is the major social studies topic in fourth grade. We will be reading from all kinds of sources to find out more about the history, geography, politics, and economics of our state. During this morning block time, I will be especially concerned with improving your children's comprehension and helping them build rich concepts and increase their meaning vocabulary stores [see pp. 76–80].

"The final part of the reading approach is our afternoon skills time. Many fourth graders have not yet mastered the word identification skills essential to successful reading. Each afternoon from 1:15 to 2:00 the children work individually or in small groups on those skills they most need to master. During this time we work not only on reading skills but also on the other language skills and basic math skills. By the time children reach fourth grade, there are great differences among them. During this afternoon skills time, I work with each child to focus on his or her own individual needs."

Skills

Ms. Maverick finished her last sentence hurriedly and apologized for going over the allotted 30 minutes. She thanked them for coming and said that she would answer any questions they might have individually if they would stay for a moment after the others left. She reminded them that she really hoped some of them would come and talk with her class about the reading needs of their jobs and also asked for volunteers to drive the class on field trips.

To her surprise, she had six volunteers to come and speak to her class. Mr. Peskins, who was a truck driver, said he had come to five of these meetings over the years and that this was the most interesting one he could remember. He said he would be glad to come and bring all his maps, routing sheets, and delivery orders. Mr. Moore, the chief of police, also volunteered, as did Mr. Smith, who worked for the gas and electric company. Mrs. Tomás said that she and her husband ran a diner and that one of them would come. She apologized for Mr. Tomás's absence. "Someone has to be there all the time, you know, so we just take turns coming to these meetings. This year it's my turn."

Mandy's parents, both of whom were musicians, volunteered to come together. The last to leave was Steve's mother. She said she didn't usually like to talk in front of groups of people but that she had never thought of how important reading was before. Since she is a waitress she could bring the menus and order pads from her restaurant and let the children pretend to be either waitresses or waiters and customers. That way she could help and wouldn't need to talk too much! Ms. Maverick assured her that that would be delightful and signed her up for the following Tuesday!

MONTHLY LOGS

September

What an unusual class of children this is! I thought that over the seven years I have taught I had seen every possible combination of children but this class disproves that theory. Of course, I expect to find great differences among children by the time they get to fourth grade, but I have never before seen the range represented by the span between Paul and Daisy, who read almost nothing, and Larry who qualitatively reads almost as well as I do, and quantitatively reads more than I do. Then there are the personality differences. Roberta cannot do the right thing no matter how hard she tries, and Betty, her twin sister, can't do anything wrong. Joyce and Hilda are both very capable and intelligent but they are so independent.

I am pleased, however, with the adjustments most of the children have made to my program. I always enjoy getting Mrs. Wise's children because they have had so much experience working together in groups. It is still a shock to me to see someone else teaching in her room next door.

I am especially pleased with Daisy. According to her records, she just never got anything done. She is working now, although I think she is doing it for me rather than for herself. Each time she does anything, she comes to me for approval. I pat her on the head because I want her to establish the habit of sitting down and accomplishing something, but I am trying to help her develop some internal feedback. Yesterday she brought me a picture she had painted. I said, "Yes, it is lovely. Didn't it feel good to do it?" I have a feeling this is going to be a year-long process, however; I have seldom seen a child with so little intrinsic motivation. For the moment, I am thankful that she is working for whatever reason. Her reading and math skills are awful. Paul is the only one who is more deficient in skills than Daisy. I must talk to his mother. When I did the sociogram, not only did no one choose to be in Paul's car but Paul couldn't even make any choices about whom he wanted to go with. He never speaks up during class, and I have never seen him playing on the playground. If I can't get his mother to come to school this year, I will go and visit her.

Mort is a pill! If I hear that child sigh and say, "Well, it doesn't matter. I don't care," one more time I may lose my composure and shake him! Except I know it wouldn't do any good. Yesterday I said to him, "Mort, what do you do when you go home after school?"

He replied, "Oh, mostly I just sit around and get bored. Sometimes I watch television." As far as I can tell he has no friends, no interests, and no aspirations! I guess I should think of him as "a real challenge."

I now have each child working on an individual program during the afternoon skills block time. Most of the children spend at least some of their time on math facts. Paul and Daisy still have not mastered the addition and subtraction facts. Butch, Carl, Tanana, Alex, and Danielle need a little more work on subtraction and will soon be ready for multiplication. The rest, with the exception of Steve, Larry, and Anthony, who have learned them, are working on multiplication facts, the big computational hurdle in fourth grade. **Skills**

I used a sample of the revised A and P Sight Word List to make sure that the children could immediately recognize these common words. All but Paul, Daisy, Chip, and Butch knew them. I am working with them to learn the ones they don't know [see pp. 45–48]. I also have these four reading in some first- and second-grade high-interest, low-vocabulary books and am conferencing with them about this reading. Many of the children still have difficulty decoding polysyllabic words. I have heard about a game called "Mystery Word Match" which helps children learn some polysyllabic sight words and also helps them learn to decode polysyllabic words by comparing unknown polysyllabic words to known polysyllabic words. It sound like fun and I am going to try it during this afternoon skills time. [See pp. 70–72.]

While we have not actually begun the unit on our state this month, we have done some readiness activities in preparation for this unit. One of the concepts which is very difficult for young children to grasp is the **Concept Development— Timeline** notion of time and sequence. Last year I had my class construct a time-line showing the important events in our state and their corresponding dates. While the children learned from this activity, it was very difficult for them to conceptualize the differences in time. Last year's class never understood that the spaces between the depicted events were proportional to the actual time lapsed between these events.

In order to provide readiness for the state timeline and to help the children relate time passage and sequence to their own lives, I had the children make a timeline depicting the important events in their lives. I began by having the children put their chairs in a circle and asking them to think about all the important things that had happened in their lives. The children were all eager to respond and everyone had something to share since the subject was one they all knew lots about. Rita recalled her first trip to the library when the librarian told her she was too young to have a library card. Tanana remembered moving to our state and how scared she was when she first came to Mrs. Wise's class-room. Larry recalled the first Hardy Boys book he had read. When all the children had contributed something to the discussion, I suggested that we might create some "lifelines" to show all the important events which had already taken place in their lives. I showed them how we could use string and little slips of paper with words and illustrations to depict our individual histories.

The children were most enthusiastic, so we began right then. I gave each of the children a long sheet of paper and asked them to put their birthdate in the top left corner and the current date in the bottom left corner. Although many of the children knew the month and day on which they were born, only Larry, Pat, and Hilda knew the year of their birth. I then asked the others how they thought they could figure out the year in which they were born. After some discussion, they worked out the mechanics of subtracting how old they were from the current date and filled in the year on the chart they were making. In the meantime, I demonstrated by making my chart on the board. Next to my birthdate, I wrote "Ms. Maverick was born" and next to the current date, I wrote, "Ms. Maverick is helping her children to make their own lifelines." The children then followed my example and put appropriate entries next to their own names.

They then listed the important events in their lives. I told them not to worry too much at this point about the date or the order but just try to get down about eight to ten events. Most children had no trouble at all listing a dozen events. Paul, however, needed a great deal of help with this and I fear his lifeline represents my thinking more than his. When the children had finished listing the events, I asked them how they thought we could find out the approximate date of each event. Several suggested their parents kept lists of everything and that if they could take the charts home that night, they could fill in many of the dates.

The others suggested they could fill in by knowing in what order they happened in relation to the events with known dates.

The next day they returned with dates and many more events filled in on their charts. We then cut the charts and arranged the events into the proper order. Next began the construction of the actual lifelines. Since all of the children in the class were either eight or nine years old, we decided to cut the strings either nine or ten feet long. In that way, each foot could represent a year. Any events which happened in the same year would be placed close to one another. If there were a year or two in which no events occurred, that would be represented by the unfilled space for that year. We also agreed that since we were going to hang these around the room for others to read, we should try to spell the words correctly and to use readable handwriting. Each child then measured and cut his or her string and marked it off in one-foot lengths. They also cut and measured strips of colored paper to 3″ × 6″ dimensions. While the children were doing this, I acted as editor, helping children correct the spelling and punctuation on their charted events so that they could copy them correctly on their lifeline slips.

Somehow, it all got done! The children illustrated the events and taped the slips to the strings. Those who finished first helped the others. The lifelines now hang below the windows and the chalkboards, and whenever the children have a spare moment, they can be seen reading their own or someone else's life history. This activity, which started out as readiness for our state's timeline, had value in and of itself. The children helped one another and learned more about one another. They learned that we share many common experiences and that other experiences are unique to each individual. They do seem to have a better sense of time sequence and proportion, and they have certainly practiced their math, reading, and writing skills. I will do this again next year!

FIND A CHILD

Construct your own lifeline. Then help a child or group of children to construct theirs. How does this activity provide for practice in math and reading and writing?

The other readiness activity this month was constructing a map of the school. We will do a lot of work with maps when we begin the actual study of our state next month and for many children this is their first exposure to maps. Again, I wanted them to relate maps to their own lifespace before asking them to generalize to the less tangible world outside. After a discussion about maps and what would be involved in constructing a map of our school, we walked around the whole building

Concept Development— Maps

to observe what we would include in our map. The children suggested, and I listed on the board, all the things we might want to include in a map of our school. I then grouped the children in pairs and each pair took responsibility for going to a particular classroom or area of the building, measuring that area, and constructing that part of the map. When all the children reassembled with their measurements, we measured the total length and width of the building and then decided what proportion of that length and width the various rooms comprised. For a while, it looked as if we had a lot less total space in what we had measured than what there actually was in the building. Larry was the one who realized we had forgotten to consider the space taken up by the hallways! After measuring these, we were able to decide on a scale. Each pair of children cut from colored paper the model for the room or area they had measured and labeled it appropriately. We then pasted the individual rooms on a piece of appropriately sized poster board and, six days after we started, had our map of the school. Well, actually, we only had it for a day or two before it was commandeered! Mr. Topps noticed it when he came in to read with our class during SQUIRT time and remarked that we had done a first-rate job and that this map was just the thing he needed to hang outside the office so that visitors could find their way around. He asked if he could "borrow" it for a while. The children all autographed it, and it now hangs outside the office.

October

Unit Development

We are now off and running on our state unit. Each unit actually has three overlapping phases. At the beginning, I provide the children with a great deal of input from many different sources. During most of this first phase we work together as a whole class, building some interest and motivation for the unit, becoming familiar with new and specialized vocabulary terms, and discovering enough informaton so that we can begin to raise some questions to which we can seek answers. During the second phase of the unit, while we continue many whole class activities, the children are also doing extensive reading, listening, and viewing, either individually or in small groups. Finally, they engage in several culminating activities which help them to organize and synthesize the information gained during the unit.

Concept Development

Throughout the unit, we do a variety of activities designed to foster concept development and to increase the store of words for which they have rich meanings. As much as possible, I try to provide direct experience for concept and meaning vocabulary development. We take field trips to the source of real places, objects, people, and events and the children and I are always on the lookout for things to bring into the classroom which will make new words and unfamiliar concepts real to us. Of course, we cannot go to see or bring everything into the classroom, so I rely on pictures, filmstrips, and other visual aids to provide indirect experience. When I introduce new vocabulary to the children, I always try to put these words in topical word sets. During our state unit, I will begin topical word sets for maps, state government, and places to visit. These topical word sets become part of our wall vocabulary. The children learn to read and spell them as well as develop rich meanings for them. [See pp. 80–82.]

Topical Word Sets

My kickoff motivator for this unit was a large white outline map of our state which I had drawn by projecting the image of an overhead transparency map onto the bulletin board at the rear of the room. After tracing the projected image, I cut along the outline and stapled the giant white map to the red-backed bulletin board. I did this all late one night so that the children's attention would be drawn immediately to the giant blank white map against the bright read background. Of course, they noticed it immediately and were intrigued by its size and blankness. Several correctly guessed that it was an outline map of our state. I had the children move their chairs closer to the board and began to lead them in a discussion of our state. Little by little, in response to their comments and questions, I wrote the name of a particular landmark in its proper location. I let the children help me decide where these landmarks should go by consulting several maps which I spread out on the floor as we talked. At the end of this initial motivating session we had (1) located our town, the state capital, several other cities, lakes, and rivers, (2) talked about what went on at the capital and began to use words such as *governor, lieutenant governor, legislators, laws, and taxes*, (3) used directional words such as *north, south, east*, and *west* and noted these directions above, below, and on the appropriate sides of our map, and (4) begun to discuss various places that the children had lived, visited, or had some other connection with.

I told them that as we studied our state we would use again and again many of the words we had used in our talk. They would need to be able to read the words in order to find out more about our state and they would need to be able to spell them in order to be able to write about it. Mitch, Jeff, and Daisy didn't look too happy at the thought of additional work, so I smiled reassuringly as I picked up a black marker and several half-sheets of different colored construction paper and let them help me remember the "special" words we had used that morning. I then let them watch me print these words on the colored slips of paper. As I was doing so, I remarked about the relative length and distinctive features of the words, pronounced the words carefully and had the children pronounce each word after me. I then had Mitch climb on a chair and tape the words to the wall above the bulletin board. I noted that we had eleven words to start with and that we would add more as we continued

Wall Vocabulary

Concept Development

to study about our state. I then prepared the children for our following morning's activities by showing them a little color-headed pin and a triangular shaped slip of paper. On the triangular slip, I printed in tiny letters

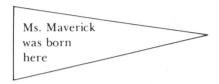

and pinned this slip to our map high in the northwestern corner. Next to the pinned flag I wrote the name of the community in which I was born. The children were fascinated and all wanted to make little flags. I assured them that that was tomorrow's activity and that, in the meantime, they should look at the maps and try to figure out places they had been to or knew of to put flags on them. I also suggested that they talk with their parents and perhaps even look at a map with them to determine such family history information as their parents' birthplaces, where aunts and uncles lived, and the names and locations of places they had visited. For the rest of the day, there was always someone at the back of the room looking at our giant map and investigating the smaller ones which I had placed on a table under the bulletin board.

The next day the children came bursting into the room loaded with maps and family histories they had brought from home. We immediately gathered in the back of the room and the children began to spread out their maps, sharing the information they had with one another and trying to locate the places they wanted to flag on our giant map. While still giant, our map was no longer blank. It was covered with place names and flags, all of which the children had some personal affiliation with. We even have a flag marking the city to which Mike had moved. Mrs. Flame would be happy to see that. She still worries about how Mike is doing. We also added the names of several neighboring towns and a few lakes and rivers to our wall vocabulary, which now has eighteen words.

Wall Vocabulary

The interest and excitement generated by the giant map motivator has grown throughout this month as have the number of words in our wall vocabulary. We now have 32 words up there and as I use these words again and again in different contexts, I try to remember to point to the words and remind the children of the other contexts in which we used them. We take five minutes each morning to practice spelling the words on our wall vocabulary. Each child takes out a sheet of paper and numbers it from one to ten. I then call out ten of the words from the words on the wall. As I call each word, the children are allowed and, indeed, encouraged to look up at the wall and find the word and then write it on their papers. The trick to this technique is that they can't actually copy the words since they must look up and then down at their papers and then up again. In order to do this they have to be trying to take a mental picture of the word and then reproduce this mental picture. When all ten words have been called out, the children check their own papers as I repeat each word and spell it aloud, letter by letter. Most days, all the children get nine or ten right and because they are so successful at it, they love to do it. The other day during recess it rained and when they were trying to decide on an indoor game, Horace suggested that we do the spelling words again! I couldn't believe it, but that's what they "played" with Horace being the teacher and calling out the words. From now on, once the children are very familiar with the words, as they are now, I shall let the children take turns "being teacher" and calling out the words. Strange—I always think I am allowing the children as much participation as is possible and then discover something else that I am doing that the children could do with benefit.

I have done several whole-class directed reading lessons this month. Through these lessons, I help them increase their knowledge about our state and work on increasing their vocabularies and improving their comprehension skills at the same time. To do these, I select part of a newspaper or magazine article or a short selection from a book and type it using Mrs. Wright's primary typewriter. I then run the typed sheet through the machine in the office to make a transparency. Using my overhead projector for group comprehension lessons has several advantages: If the passage I select is unusually difficult to read, I can change a few of the words or omit sections to make it more readable. I don't waste a lot of paper making 25 copies of the same story, and I can focus the attention of the children where I want it. I do, however, always show the children the source of the original article so that they know that what they are reading is "something real." **Comprehension— Directed Reading Lesson**

I begin my preparation for the lesson by identifying any words or concepts I think will present difficulty for many of my children. I make a distinction between unknown words and unfamiliar concepts. In the first directed reading lesson, for example, the subject was "things to do in our state." I had taken this article from the magazine section of the Sunday newspaper. Two concepts which I thought would not be familiar to most of my children were *rapids* and *currents*. In both cases, most of my children would probably be able to identify the words but would not have a meaning for those words appropriate to the particular contexts in which they were being used. The word *current* they might associate with the term "current events," and for *rapids*, while they might have the concept of speed, they would probably not readily associate this concept with fast-moving water. **Concept Development**

In addition to the two relatively unfamiliar concepts, *current* and *rapids*, I also identified several words for which most of my children would have listening-meaning concepts but which they would not be able to identify in print. These unknown words for the "things to do in our state" selection included *reflection* and *parachute*. In both cases, I was quite sure that the children would have a concept for these words once they were able to identify them but doubted that the "big word decoding skills" of most of my children would allow them to figure out the pronunciation of these familiar concepts but unknown words.

Having identified several unfamiliar concepts and unknown words, I then decided what to do about them. Sometimes, I built meanings for unfamiliar concepts or told them the pronunciation of unknown words before they read the story. More often, however, I alerted the children to the existence of these unfamiliar concepts or unknown words, and challenged them to see if they could figure out what a word was or what the concept meant as they read the selection. This encouraged the children to use the context to figure out the meaning and/or pronunciation of words. This is what I did with *current, rapids, reflection*, and *parachute*. I wrote these four words on the board and asked a volunteer to pronounce *current* and *rapids*. Betty gladly pronounced them. I then asked them if anyone could give me a meaning for *current* or *rapids*. Manuel suggested that current has something to do with electricity and Steve said that it means "like in 'current events.'" For *rapids*, Roberta said that "without the *s* it means fast." I told them that the definitions they had given were right but that, as I hoped they knew, words have many different meanings and that the words *current* and *rapids* in the selection we were about to read had meanings different from the ones they knew. I then told them that, as they were reading the selection, I wanted them to see if they could figure out what these different meanings might be. I hinted to them that the other words and sentences near the words *current* and *rapids* would give them the clues they needed to solve the mystery. To add another element of mystery, I pointed to *reflection* and *parachute* and told the children *not* to pronounce the words. I told them that these two words were different from *current* and *rapids* in that they knew what these second two words meant but hadn't yet learned to identify them in print. I suggested that as with *current* and *rapids*, the words close to *reflection* and *parachute* would allow them to solve the mystery. Once the children had read the selection, they explained what they thought *current* and *rapids* meant in this context, identified the other words which had let them figure that out, and compared these meanings for the words with the meanings they already knew. Many of the children had also figured out the unknown words, *reflection* and *parachute*, and explained which other words had led them to solve the mystery.

Purposes for Reading

Having identified and decided what to do about any unknown words or unfamiliar concepts, I then decided for what purpose I was going to have the children read the selection. In a directed reading activity, my goal is always that the children are better at reading for a specific purpose after reading the selection than they were prior to reading the selection. Sometimes, I work on improving their literal comprehension. I may decide that after reading the selection, we will put the events of the selection in order, or that we will read in order to answer the fact questions: Who? What? When? Where? How? For other selections, I may decide that we will work on being able to state main ideas in our own words.

I teach many lessons designed to sharpen the children's inferential comprehension ability. In these lessons, I show them only a portion of the text and ask them to predict what will happen next. I write these predictions on the board and let the children vote to decide which one they consider most likely to occur. I then display enough of the text so that they can check their predictions. Finally, I ask the children who made the correct prediction to read me the words in the passage that allowed them to make the correct prediction. In this way, the children who are not very good at inferring see that inferences are based on something that is directly stated in the text.

Inferential Comprehension

The first year I taught, I referred to inferential comprehension as "reading between the lines." One day, I watched one boy squinting at his book and then peering over the shoulder of the boy in front of him who could "read between the lines." It suddenly occurred to me that, from a child's vantage point, it was conceivable that he believed that there was something between the lines that he couldn't see or that was only between the lines of other people's books. Since then I have stopped using that particular phrase. I have begun to ask those who can make inferences to point out the words in the text on which they based their inferences. This allows the children who can't make inferences to begin to observe the way the process works in the minds of those who can.

Finally, I teach some lessons designed to help children become more critical readers. During these lessons, I ask the children to read in order to make judgments or evaluations, and I stress that their judgments are decided on the basis of their own value systems and that there are no right or wrong answers to these judgment questions.

Critical Reading

For the "things to do in our state" lesson, I decided to focus the children's attention on the main ideas of each paragraph. I displayed only the portion of the text which mentioned a particular place and asked the children to read so that when they finished they could tell me in a sentence what the main attraction was at each place. First, I let the children read silently. When most appeared to have finished, I let a volunteer read the section aloud. In this way, Paul, Daisy, and the others whose reading skills are still very limited could get the content of the selection and participate in the comprehension activity.

Main Ideas

After each section was read silently and then orally, I asked a child to tell me in one sentence what the main thing was that most people went there to see. I then made a list on the board which gave each place name and the sentence describing its main attraction. When we had completed reading about the eight places, I read over the list I had made on the board and pointed out to the children that, in addition to being the main attraction, these sentences were also the main ideas of each paragraph. Main ideas, like main attractions, are the most important ideas (attractions); the ideas (attractions) most people would like to re-member after reading (visiting) a paragraph (place). While we will con-tinue to work on identifying and stating main ideas all year, this lesson was a good one to begin with because it helped to make the concept of main idea a little more concrete.

As a follow-up to this directed reading lesson, I put the children in eight groups. Each group was to make a little flag for one of the eight places we had read about, write the place name and the main attraction on the flag, locate the place using the ever-growing supply of maps we now had in the room, and pin the flag to our giant map, which was no longer blank.

TRY IT OUT

Find a short selection. Use a primary typewriter to type it and make a transparency. Decide what word and concept problems this selection would present for most of the children at a particular grade level. Decide what you would do about those word and concept problems. Decide what area of comprehension you would try to strengthen by having a class read the selection. Set your purposes for reading and divide the selection to show which parts you would display together. Plan a follow-up activity.

Concept Develop-ment—Direct Experience

We have taken two field trips this month. For the first, we went to visit the local newspaper. I bring daily copies of both the local and capi-tal newspapers to school each morning, and, since we began the unit on our state, the children have become quite interested in them. Before we took the field trip, I had the children put their chairs in a circle and we began to talk about the local newspaper and to formulate some ques-tions to ask Ms. Daley, the editor. I listed these questions on a large sheet of chart paper and, on our return, we checked the chart to see how many of our questions had been answered.

We then got out a local map and looked at the various routes we could take to get from our school to the newspaper office. We tried to de-cide which route would be the shortest and which would be the quickest. Since there was much disagreement about the best route, I asked the children how we might plan an experiment to find out. After much discussion, the following plan was arrived at. Each of the four cars (Mrs. Penn, Mrs. Smith, and Daphne's grandfather had volunteered to drive) would take a different route. One person in each car would be responsible for writing down the beginning and ending mileage. Another person would time the trips. The other riders in the car would keep track of the number of lights, stop signs, intersections, and so on. It was agreed, of course, that each driver would drive carefully and obey all speed limits.

Finally, Friday arrived! The four cars set out at the same time. Mrs. Smith arrived first, but Mrs. Penn had taken the shortest route. I, of course, arrived last and my passengers were not too pleased about that, especially Butch!

The receptionist took us on a tour around the buildings and then took us to Ms. Daley's office. The children behaved very well and, because they had discussed and planned before coming, asked some very good questions. I was just beginning to relax and pat myself on the back for preparing them so well when the inevitable happened. A reporter came into Ms. Daley's office with some copy. She introduced him to the children and asked them if they had any questions. Hilda asked him a question about a story she had read recently in the paper and as he was answering her question, he turned to Ms. Daley and said, "Why don't you take them down into the morgue and show them some of the dead ones?" Roberta's head twitched with excitement; Betty fainted! The reporter quickly explained that the newspaper morgue had "dead" newspapers, not dead bodies, while Mrs. Smith and I revived Betty. A striking example of the multiple meanings of common words!

We then did go into the morgue, however, and spent a long time there. Ms. Daley showed us the newspapers which recorded such historic events as the end of the Civil War, the Lincoln and Kennedy assassinations, and the state's celebration of its 100th birthday. She pointed out the difference between history books which are written long after the actual events have occurred, and newspaper accounts which are written immediately. She also pointed out how newspapers are one very important source of historical data. The children were particularly impressed when she showed them a copy of a biography of a famous general and explained that the writer of that book had spent many days in this very morgue doing research about our town where this general had grown up.

Upon our return from the newspaper, we looked at our collected data, computed the mileages and times, decided that the shortest route in distance was not the quickest route and discussed reasons why this was so. We also looked to see which of our questions had been answered and decided that six had been answered quite thoroughly, three partially, and two not at all. Finally, each child composed a short note to Ms. Daley thanking her for her time and telling her what he or she had found most interesting about the visit. Here is Roberta's letter:

Dear Ms. Daley,

Thank you for letting us come down to visit your newspaper. There was lots to see and I can only apologize for Betty's fainting in your office. She is always doing things like that and I can't understand why. The dead newspapers were interesting but I would have liked to have seen some dead bodies since I never have. Being a newspaper lady I bet you have seen hundreds of them.

Sincerely,
Roberta Smith

Our other field trip this month was to the county seat. This was an all-day field trip, and we packed a picnic lunch. Thank goodness it didn't rain! We prepared for this one as we had for the newspaper office, by having discussions and coming up with a list of questions we wanted answered. This time, Hilda wrote down the list to make sure that we came back with at least a partial answer to all our questions.

In the morning we visited the county court house. When we got to the county clerk's office, a young couple was waiting to get a marriage license. All the boys plus Pat and Roberta thought that was hysterical. The children were most fascinated by the sheriff. They wanted to know what happened when a person got arrested and what a sheriff and his deputies did. The sheriff showed them the county map, which was very detailed, and helped them to locate our school and some of their homes.

When we went into the court, the judge was hearing a traffic case. He revoked the license of a person arrested for driving recklessly and speeding. This impressed the children greatly. When we got to the tax assessor's office, Hilda was busily checking her list to see what we might have forgotten to ask. When her question was finally asked, it came out as, "We want to know how you decide how much taxes everyone should pay and my Dad says you must be a friend of our next door neighbor's because his house is twice as big as ours and he pays less taxes!"

That afternoon we toured the county historical museum. The children were especially intrigued by the original state flag and the lists of names of all the men who had died in the major wars we have fought. The restored log cabin behind the museum added much realism to our study of how people used to live in our state and, of course, the children were fascinated by the Indian artifacts.

Upon our return, we made a list of all the people we had visited or seen in the court house and what their functions were. We also referred to our question chart and, with Hilda's help, did indeed have at least a partial answer to all the questions we had raised. I then helped the children form five groups. Each group composed a letter thanking one of the people who helped us on our visit.

November

What a great month this has been! Normally, we don't go to the state capital. It is almost a two-hour trip, and the legislature is usually not in session during the fall when we are studying our state. Three weeks ago, however, the legislature was called into special session in order to consider a new water pollution bill. Everyone in the state has been debating this issue for some time now, but it took a tragedy to get the legislators moving. Four weeks ago, five people died in a small downstate industrial town. The cause of death was determined to be the high level of industrial chemical wastes in the water—way above the standards already set, but never enforced. The antipollution forces were able to rally support around this emotional issue and the governor called the legislature into special session to consider a more stringent water pollution bill with provisions for enforcement and severe penalties for lack of compliance.

The children came back to school on the Monday after the five people had died and they were all upset. Many of them brought the various newspaper stories and related the discussions they had had about this issue at home. The children, unlike the adult population, were almost unanimous in their insistence that the water pollution standards be much stricter. Not being burdened with financial responsibilities, they could see the need for clean water much more clearly than they could understand the financial strain the new controls would put on industry and, if industry is to be believed, the entire state population.

Of course, we put our chairs in a circle immediately and discussed the problem. I tried to raise questions and interject information which would allow them to consider the issue in its broadest terms. Many of the children were unclear about words like *chemicals* and *bacteria* and I began to make mental notes on which words we might want to explore more fully and add to our wall vocabulary. Later, I decided that the subject was such an important one and the children were so naturally motivated that a unit on ecology and pollution would be first on our agenda after Christmas.

Concept Development—Need for

It was Mrs. Penn who suggested that we take the children to the state capital. She came in after school that very afternoon and told me that she would be going over to meet with a citizen's action group later in the week and that she would be glad to make all the arrangements at the capital and to be one of our drivers. She added that she had seen Mrs. Smith that morning and had mentioned the possibility to her and that Mrs. Smith had agreed it would be a great experience for the children to see the legislature in session and that she, too, would be willing to drive. I told Mrs. Penn that I would talk it over with the children but that I was all for it!

The children, of course, were most excited. In addition to the general excitement of going on a trip that long and being "at the capital" was the excitement generated by the knowledge that Ms. Maverick had never taken any of her other classes to the state capital. They were not just doing the same trips all the other fourth grades did—they were doing something very special and very grown-up. As I watched their delight in this specialness, I vowed to try to think of something special for each class of children I taught.

The preparations for the trip took most of the month and many of the activities which I had planned for this middle part of the unit went by the boards. The transportation problem was solved by Mrs. Penn, who, in addition to commandeering Mandy's father as our fourth driver, also arranged for our tour through the capitol and our visit to the gallery while the legislators were debating. And she got our local representative to agree to come up to the gallery when the session broke for lunch and talk with us and answer our questions. Our list of questions for Mr. Stans took three sheets of chart paper and Hilda thought she would never get them all copied in her notebook.

Lunch was a problem. We were going to leave at 7:30 A.M. so that we could get there, park, and go on a 10 A.M. tour through the capitol building and be in the gallery from 11 A.M. to noon. A picnic lunch was a little risky at this time of year, and I thought it would be good for all the children to have the experience of eating in a real restaurant. They had all eaten at fast food drive-ins, but many of them had not been to a restaurant, ordered from a menu, or paid their own bill plus tax and tip! The problem with taking them to a restaurant, of course, was that many of them could not come up with the money and that many families who would come up with the money really couldn't afford it.

As I was thinking about the lunch problem, I was also gathering up the week's supply of newspapers to take them to the recycling drop point. I then remembered that some organizations had collected money for various causes by having paper and aluminum drives. It occurred to me that if our class could collect paper and aluminum for recycling as well as collect deposit bottles for return to the grocery stores, we might make enough money for everyone to have lunch. We might also become more personally "pollution conscious."

In three weeks, we collected hundreds of pounds of paper and aluminum and returned $27.80 worth of bottles to the grocery stores. Several parents made voluntary donations to our lunch fund and we ended up with $83.00. The children thought this was a fortune until we divided by 25 and realized that each person's share of the fortune was only $3.32

Chip said that even that seemed like a fortune to him, and quickly went to work figuring out how many bags of peanuts that would buy!

Mrs. Penn had found an inexpensive restaurant close to the capitol which was equipped for people in wheelchairs like Danielle and had arranged for the 29 of us to eat there. She had also gotten several sample menus and from these each child figured out the various combinations of food he or she could buy with $2.78 (which is what each child actually had to spend after paying the 4 percent sales tax and 15 percent tip).

In order to prepare them for their visit to the capitol and the legislature, I showed a film entitled "Your State Government" which is put out by the State Chamber of Commerce and the State Department of Education. Just as when I am going to have the class read something, I often do a directed reading lesson with them; when I am going to show them a film, I do a directed viewing lesson. First, I prepare my lesson just as I would a directed reading lesson. After previewing the film, I determine which unfamiliar concepts I want to teach and whether I will help them to build these concepts before, during, or after the film. Often the film provides indirect experience for words which I cannot provide direct experience for. I stop the film at the appropriate frame, and discuss the picture which makes real the unfamiliar word or concept.

Concept Development— Indirect Experience

I then determine my purposes for having them view the film and decide how much of the film I will show at a time. Unless it is strictly for entertainment, I never show a film all the way through. Rather, I set the purpose for viewing a particular segment, stop the film and discuss the fulfillment of that purpose, set another purpose and begin the film again. If the film is one which the children seem to especially enjoy, I will often show it over again the following day in its entirety. I then try to think of an appropriate follow-up activity to the film. My purpose in this follow-up activity is to help the children organize and synthesize the new information gained from the film.

Mr. Peskins came this month before we went to the capital. He brought his routing slips and maps and talked to the children about all the reading he has to do in his job as a truck driver. The children were quite impressed! He also showed us the best route to take to the capital and told us some interesting things to watch for on the way.

Functional Reading

The actual trip was exhausting but very exciting. We left promptly at 7:30 A.M. I provided some apples and crackers for each car so that the children could have a little snack when we first got there. The woman who escorted us on our tour through the capital was very sweet and very pretty, so Betty and Daphne have decided to be tour guides when they grow up! Of course, while we were in the gallery, one of the "anti-the-more-stringent-bill" legislators was talking and the children were quite upset. I think they did begin to get some notion, however, that there are always two legitimate, defensible points of view. Mr. Stans was great!

He spent almost 30 minutes talking with us. He commended the children on their paper/aluminum/bottle collection and told them that another way they could make a difference was by getting in the habit of writing to their legislator and letting him or her know how they felt. Larry asked him if telegrams weren't "a more effective medium than letters." Mr. Stans agreed that legislators really notice when their constituents sacrifice time, trouble, and money to send telegrams expressing their views. He then gave us his address and promised to come to visit our class when he was next in our town.

Lunch was fun! The children were well prepared and most knew exactly what they wanted. The only person who overspent was Daisy. I didn't realize it at the time but Mandy's father had to bail her out with 34 cents. I told him he should have left her to wash dishes! We got back to the school at 4:30 P.M.

The next day as we began to discuss our trip and what we had learned, the children were all anxious to write to Mr. Stans. Larry suggested that in addition to our individual letters, we pool any money left from lunch and send a telegram from the whole class. His suggestion was applauded and the telegram writing practice that followed was great fun and a lesson in getting your money's worth of words.

TRY IT OUT

Here is the telegram Ms. Maverick's class finally decided to send to Mr. Stans. How was this a good language activity? What might the children have learned about words and sentences from doing this activity? Do you think the children worked on this in small groups or as individuals? Why?

> MR STANS STOP   FOURTH GRADERS AND
> TEACHER WANT BILL 7384 PASSED STOP
> CLEAN WATER NOW STOP

December

Concept Development— Projects

This month marked not only the end of the year, but also the end of our state unit. No small feat, I can assure you! For culminating activities on this unit, I decided to have small groups work on several different activities: a timeline, a relief map, a mural, a historical drama, and a book about our state. I described the projects to the entire class, letting them know what they would be doing on each. I then had the children write down their first and second choices for the project on which they wanted to work.

Steve, Mitch, Butch, Hilda, Alexander, and Jeff worked on the relief map. Actually I probably should add Ms. Maverick to that roster since I had to help this group more than any of the others. The children had already had many experiences with all kinds of maps throughout this unit, but constructing this relief map was still a big job. (When they had finished—finally!—the map was amazingly accurate.) I then sat down with the group and had them tell me the materials needed and steps to follow in making a relief map. This served as a good language and directions-writing activity for the group, and the chart we made will help us in making relief maps in the future.

Making a Relief Map*

Materials Needed:

opaque projector	oil paint
contour map of area	varnish
sheet of paper	paintbrush
plyboard four feet long and	screen
cut as wide as needed	sawdust
nails	wallpaper paste powder
hammer	two-gallon pail

Steps:
1. Put the contour map in the opaque projector.
2. Put the plyboard in the chalktray.
3. Project the contour map onto the plyboard.
4. Trace the outline and all the markings onto the board.
5. Cover the board with a sheet of paper.
6. Trace the contour map on the paper like you did the board.
7. Decide what the highest point would be on your map and that will be three inches high.
8. Divide to figure out the scale.
9. Using the scale and the sheet of paper on which you traced the contour map, decide how high in inches each area should be built. Write these heights on the right place on the paper.
10. Hammer nails into the board along the contour lines.
11. Paint rivers and lakes on the board with blue oil paint.
12. Let blue paint dry. Then varnish.
13. Screen the sawdust.
14. Mix four quarts of sawdust with one quart of wallpaper paste powder.
15. Add just enough water so it can be shaped.
16. Build the map one layer at a time using the nails as a guide.

* Adapted from Preston (1968).

17. When it is all built and dry, varnish the whole map.
18. Paint the rivers and lakes blue again.
19. Paint the other areas.

Paul, Manuel, Chip, Anthony, and Carl worked on constructing a timeline for our state. The completion of this project was, indeed, much facilitated by the experience of making the lifelines which they had done in September. They began by listing important events in our state's history and verifying the dates on which they occurred. Miss Page, our librarian, helped them to find some of the references they needed for this part of the project. They then decided to use a twenty-foot piece of string and to let each foot represent ten years. While Paul was not much help on the researching end, he did work diligently to copy the dates and events onto the markers which would go along the line.

Rita, Mandy, Danielle, Larry, and Horace made a lovely bound book entitled *Facts You Should Know about Our State*. They took much of the information we had gained from our discussions, reading, films, and field trips and wrote several topical stories. They also included maps, pictures of the state flower and bird, and representations of the several flags our state has had. Mrs. Mainstay was nice enough to type up their stories and I helped them to make a title page and a table of contents. They then bound it with a lovely cloth cover, as they had learned to do from Mrs. Wise, and took it to the library to show to Miss Page. You can imagine their delight when she told them it looked good enough to be a library book. The children asked if it could really *be* a library book, so Miss Page pasted a pocket in the back, typed up a card, gave it an appropriate number, made a card for the card file, and shelved it with the other books about our state. Needless to say it doesn't stay on that shelf long. Every child in our room wants to check it out to read, and now they are all asking to make their own bound books to put in the library. Perhaps after the first of the year, we will begin keeping writing notebooks in preparation for such a large project!

Mort, Tanana, Betty, and Daphne did the mural which covers the side of the room. This mural depicts the changes in the way people lived, traveled, and dressed in our state over the past 200 years. Again, Miss Page's help was invaluable in steering this group to reference works which contained many pictures. She also arranged for this group to view several filmstrips, including one film which helped them be accurate in their representations.

The drama group, Roberta, Alex, Pat, Daisy, and Joyce, presented several short skits representing significant events in our state's history. The funniest one was their skit of the legislators debating the new water pollution bill. Pat was the "anti" senator and Roberta, Alex, Daisy, and Joyce sat and booed and hissed as she spoke.

TRY IT OUT

Ms. Maverick sees the relief map, timeline, book, mural, and dramatizations as activities which help the children synthesize and organize the information they have learned throughout the unit. These activities also extend and review the major concepts and meaning vocabulary which the children have learned. In addition, these activities serve as vehicles for growth in communication, computational, and social skills. For each culminating activity, list the ways in which it (1) served as a synthesizer and organizer, (2) helped extend and review concepts and meaning vocabulary, and (3) served as a vehicle for skills growth. Then, think up another culminating activity she could have done and list its contribution to the three areas.

While these culminating activities occupied much of our time and energies this month, we did do some other things. We are now up to 18 minutes of SQUIRT time each day, and many of the children are choosing to read from the our state books, magazines, pamphlets, brochures, and maps displayed on the back table. We have had lots of fun devising math word problems for each other to solve. The ground rules were that (1) each word problem had to involve our state in some way, and (2) the person who made up the problem had to be able to solve it. The children worked out the problems at odd times during the day, and then, just before lunch, five children would come and write their problems on the board. The rest of us would then work at solving the problems. The children learned that writing clearly stated mathematical word problems which contain all the information needed to solve them is a difficult task.

We had a whole-school party on the day before school let out for the holidays. Mr. Sweep, the custodian, was retiring after being here since the day the school opened 27 years ago. While we were all sad to see him leave, that sadness, for me, was lightened by the knowledge that Mr. Moppet, Chip's father, needed the job so badly. He has been out of work for months, and he and his family were too proud to accept "charity." I have, however, been seeing to it that Chip has some breakfast when he gets here in the morning and, now that his father is the school custodian, I know they will be all right.

Oh, I almost forgot! I am going to have a student teacher. I don't know quite what to expect, however. Dr. Link was here at the beginning of the month and told me about a young man named Donald Ditto. It seems that Donald started his student teaching in the fall but just couldn't get along with the teacher with whom they placed him. He dropped out of the program and was going to drop out of school entirely with only student teaching left to complete! Dr. Link assures me that the young man really has potential and that he had just been poorly matched with a very rigid teacher. At any rate, Dr. Link thinks he will be able to work with my program and that he will make a contribution. I hope she's right—for his sake as well as for mine. I guess we will just have to wait and see what this new year brings!

January

Mr. Ditto has been with us all month now and he is terrific! I am just so glad Dr. Link convinced him to give teaching another try and brought him out here. He has a very quiet, easy-going manner with the kids and will never be a disciplinarian, but the children respect and cooperate with him. He never talks about his other student teaching experience, but I'll just bet that in addition to the inherent problems created by matching him with an authoritarian teacher, he also experienced difficulties because of the expectations of what a male teacher is supposed to be like. I imagine that both the students and the other teachers expected him to behave like a drill sergeant. Mr. Ditto has no top sergeant qualities about him. I like him.

Our unit for most of this month has been on ecology. It has been a lot of fun, and I found many ways to help the children become involved in the community. We discussed interviewing techniques and constructed a little questionnaire to find out what people are doing about energy conservation and pollution. The children interviewed neighbors, relatives, and business owners, and we prepared a report, sort of a miniature Harris poll, which we distributed to all the people interviewed. Newspapers, magazines, and television broadcasts provided much of the input for this unit because this information needs to be the most current available.

During one of our initial sessions, the children and I decided on some categories under the general heading of ecology and began a bulletin board for each of these subtopics. The children brought newspaper and magazine articles and pictures, shared them with the class, and put them on the appropriate board. I made tape recordings of the nightly national and local newscasts and played back for the children those parts which applied to our study. I also arranged for many members of the community who are involved in specific ecological concerns to come in and talk with us about their particular involvement. As a culmination to this unit, the children and I drafted a list of recommendations for conserving energy and preventing pollution which we sent to Ms. Daley. The letter was published with all the children's names under it. The children were pleased, but their parents were ecstatic! Copies of that paper with its 15 suggestions for conserving energy and preventing pollution have gone to doting aunts and grandparents all around the country.

The children are very careful not to waste anything, anymore, and are quick to point out wasteful habits in others. Sometimes these others are not so pleased to have their faults aired in public. One day in the cafeteria, Mrs. Flame took her tray up to deposit it. She hadn't even touched her roll or her cake. Butch informed her that if she didn't want to eat something, she shouldn't take it in the first place!

My "book board" is off to a successful start. I selected 50 titles from our classroom library that are at a variety of reading levels and that are generally popular with my fourth graders. I then wrote these titles on sheets of white paper and covered the back bulletin board with them. I had Chip, Mort, and Paul measure and cut red, blue, and yellow construction paper into 10 cm × 5 cm rectangles. These rectangles were put into pockets I made along the bottom of the bulletin board. Now that all was ready, I gathered my children together and announced a new contest. In this contest, books, not people, were going to be the winners. Together, we read the titles of the 50 books. Among these were books a few of my children had already read and they commented briefly on them. I then explained that whenever they read one of these 50 books, they were to decide what color best describes the book. If it was "super—a book everyone should read," they would put their name on a red rectangle and attach this rectangle to the appropriate white sheet. If the book was "awful—boring—a waste of time," they would put their name on a yellow rectangle and attach this rectangle. Of course, if the book was "OK—enjoyable or informative but nothing super special," that book would get a blue rectangle with their name on it. "From time to time," I explained, "we will have discussions during which you can tell us why you think a certain book rated a red or a yellow."

Literature Response Activity

The board has only been there four weeks and already there are many red, yellow, and blue autographed rectangles attached to several of the books. The children love to see their names and ratings attached to the books. When they see a book with several red rectangles, they all try to get it and read it. One book has three yellow rectangles. Now everyone is reading it to see if it is "really that bad!" Pat has rounded up extra copies of several books from the public library and Danielle's dad bought her several paperback titles at the bookstore.

The book board is a new idea I tried this year and so far I am delighted with the results. The children are motivated to read and attach their ratings to the books. I have seen classrooms in which the number of books read by each child was kept up with and in some cases rewarded with T-shirts or records. While I think it does encourage some children to read, I also have noticed that some children start reading only very short books or very easy books. The goal seems to become the number of books read rather than the enjoyment and appreciation of the books. Because the book board keeps up with how many children have read and how they rated each book rather than how many books each child has read, children are motivated to read many books but not to just accumulate titles. We have had two book discussions so far. Both were lively interchanges in which some children tried to convince others that the book was really a "red" or really a "yellow." I was reminded of the deadly dull oral book reports I had my students do during my first year of teaching. How could I have done that???

Skills

The children are progressing quite well in their afternoon skills work. Butch, Chip, and Daisy have learned the words on the A and P list. Paul knows most of the words most of the time (and almost none at other times!). Alex, Carl, Mitch, Roberta, and Alexander are learning to spell some words on the A and P list that they could read but had spelled incorrectly in their writing. Betty, Daphne, Tanana, and Anthony are working on cursive handwriting. Larry, Horace, Pat, Anthony, and Steve are now working together on a project. Miss Page, the librarian, is teaching them to locate information and how to use basic reference works.

Comprehension Lesson— GRP

I also tried a different comprehension lesson plan this month—the guided reading procedure.

To begin with, I chose a short selection from a magazine article on one city's successful attempt to clean up its waterways. I had this passage typed and duplicated and gave it to the entire class with the instructions to "read to remember everything." After approximately ten minutes when I observed that most of the children had finished the selection, I told them that if they had finished, they should turn the selection face down on their desks and that if they had not yet finished they should continue reading until they were finished. I then asked them what they remembered from their reading and recorded everything they told me on the chalkboard, numbering each response. Every once in a while, when their responses seemed to stop, I would say, "Listen as I read what we already have on the board and see if you can remember anything else." Eventually they had exhausted their memories. I asked them to listen again as I reread what was on the board and told them that when I had finished reading I would allow them one minute to reread portions of the article to correct any inconsistencies or misinformation recorded on the board.

There was, of course, some misinformation on the board, and the children couldn't wait to get back to the text to prove it. When Hilda said, "Number 27 is not right. It should be...," I responded, "Can you read me the part of the text which lets you know that?" Hilda then read that part aloud to verify her statement and the class agreed that number 27 was indeed incorrect. We then corrected it. In addition to correcting misinformation, the children added other bits of information they had missed or forgotten during the first reading.

Next, I asked them to listen again as I read the information on the board, but this time they were to listen and try to decide which ideas seemed to be the main ideas, the most important ideas, the ideas they would like to remember or tell someone else if that someone asked them what the story had been all about. I phrased "main idea" in this way so that the children began to conceptualize that very elusive concept of main idea. After I read the items one final time, several children suggested what seemed to be the main ideas, and I circled them. Different children had different notions about which were really the main ideas, but I circled all they suggested and then reminded them that we could all agree that each item on the board was written in the text. Choosing the main ideas was, to some extent, I explained, a matter of personal judgment: "What is most important to one person may not be most important to someone else." If the children had asked me to circle an inordinately large number of items, I would have done so, and as we finished, I would have said something like, "Now, as you know, not everyone would agree on which ideas are the most important. If I had to select the main ideas here, I believe I would select numbers 4, 6, an 27." I would then read those three items and explain that these three seemed to me to tell what the selection was primarily about, and that the other items explain these three. In this way, I would try to model for them the complex process of selecting main ideas.

Finally, I asked them to take out a sheet of paper and number it from one to five. While they were doing this, I erased the board. I then read them five true-false items I had constructed prior to the lesson. The children responded by putting a *T* or *F* on their papers. When we had finished the five-item quiz, I reread the items and we decided whether each was true or false. Each child checked his or her own paper.

The children then recorded the number they got correct by coloring in the appropriate area on a graph. One week later, I gave them a delayed-retention test on the information contained in the selection. I used five different true-false items but I tried to make the two tests equally difficult. Needless to say, the children did not do nearly as well on the second test. This is exactly what I wanted them to observe. To us, as adults, it is obvious that unless we make an effort and review information, we forget. Children, however, are quite unaware of this natural phenomenon. Last week, in fact, when I gave them the delayed test and they did not do nearly as well as on the first test, they accused me of making harder items for the second test. No explaining of mine could convince them otherwise. Mr. Ditto settled the controversy by suggesting that next time I should make up all ten items ahead of time and put them in a hat. One child would then reach in and select five items which would be used for the immediate retention test and the others would be put away for the test one week later. I thought that was a brilliant suggestion, and I already have the ten questions made up for the guided reading procedure I plan to do tomorrow.

The guided reading procedure was developed by Professor Anthony

Manzo (1975) who addressed a seminar I attended at the university last summer on the subject of comprehension. His theory is that many children do not comprehend a lot of what they read because they don't have many stored facts to which they can compare, contrast, and relate information being read. He suggests that if guided reading procedures are done every two weeks with a delayed retention test in the intervening week, children will, after several procedures, begin to develop a mind-set to try to remember more of what they read. About the fourth time they sit down to read a selection with the direction, "Read to remember everything," a little voice inside their heads begins to say, "Hey, now I am going to remember this stuff well enough so that I can do as well on the test a week from now as I do on the one today." This is when, it is hypothesized, teachers begin to see some improvement in long-term memory of information read. Over the course of a year's time, it is hoped that this mind-set to remember what you read will transfer to material being read at times other than guided reading procedure times. As this continues, the child increases his or her store of facts with which to think about what is being read.

I don't know how it will work, but I do plan to do a guided reading procedure every two weeks for the rest of the year and see what happens. I was at first concerned about giving everyone the same selection when I know that children like Daisy, Chip, and Paul couldn't read it. But Dr. Manzo pointed out that if the nonreaders sit quietly and look as if they are reading for the ten minutes and then listen carefully as the readers tell what they have remembered, they too will get the information and be able to do well on the test. This is the reason the test should be true-false. In this way, even the nonreaders in the class can learn the information and be successful. It seems to be working. Daisy got four right on the first test, and Chip got all five. He was so proud of himself. As you can see from his chart, Chip has an unusually good memory. He only missed one item on the delayed test.

February

What a strange month this has been! January, February, and March are supposed to be the calm, uninterrupted "teaching months" but so far they, like the rest of the year, have been extraordinary! I guess it all started when the legislature held the special session and we made our unexpected trip to the capital. The new water pollution bill was passed, by the way, and the timeline committee added this momentous occasion as another event on their state timeline. Mr. Stans did come to visit our class as he had promised, and expressed astonishment at the children's political sophistication.

Then, Mr. Ditto came when I wasn't expecting to get a student

Chip's Progress Chart

Guided Reading Procedure

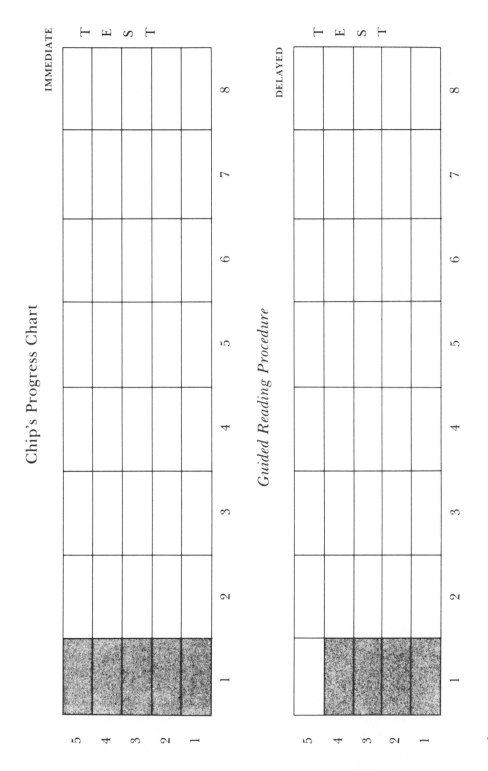

445

teacher this year, and, as a result of his being here, I have been asked to leave my class in March and go to the university! It seems that one of the professors over there has been in the hospital for months and they are very shorthanded. She had been scheduled to teach a special seminar on the integrated curriculum during the spring quarter and there is no one else who can teach it. Dr. Link's plan is that Mr. Ditto should take over my class for the rest of the year and I should go to the university. She had already discussed this with Mr. Topps and the university administration before she let me in on her plans, so I guess the decision is mine. My first instinct was to say "no" immediately. How could I leave my children in the middle of the year? But, upon reflection, I had to admit that, with the exception of Daisy, the children would thrive under Mr. Ditto's continued tutelage. Next, I thought, "But I can't teach a university seminar. What could I tell them? How would I teach it?" But then I remembered some of the terrible graduate classes I sat through when I was working on my master's degree and I remembered wondering if the professors who taught our college classes could survive, let alone thrive, in a class of real children. At least I could bring some realism to that seminar. I am tempted...and I have one week in which to decide!

Content-area Language Experience   We have now completed four guided reading procedures and the children do, indeed, seem to be increasing their long-term memory of what they read. This month, I tried some "translation writing" experiences with Paul, Daisy, Butch, Jeff, Chip, Joyce, and Tanana. I got the notion for translation writing when I was reading through an old book which I stumbled across (Burton, 1952). Being curious about what educational methods were being expounded in the forties, I perused the book. One chapter was on the unit approach to teaching which, while different in several ways, bears some striking similarities to what I call my "integrated approach." In one chapter, a fifth-grade teacher describes some of the activities which she did with the children as part of her "colonial life unit." One of these activities she called "cooperative stories." To do a cooperative story, she sat down with the children who were not very able readers, read a portion of a book to them, and then had them tell her what they heard. She then recorded what they told her on the board and had them copy that "cooperative story" into their notebooks. In this way, the less able readers constructed a textbook at their own reading level.

As I was reading this, I thought of Paul, Daisy, Butch, Jeff, and Chip, whose reading skills are still not sophisticated enough to read the complex materials which we often need to read to gain information for our units. I vowed to try what I termed "translation writing" with them. I worried, however, that if I took these particular five children to work with me while the rest of the class worked with Mr. Ditto, the five I was working with might feel segregated because they don't read as well. I then hit upon the idea of including Joyce and Tanana in the group. While Joyce is a very good reader, her oral expression skills are not nearly as sophisticated. Tanana, while also a good reader, is hesitant to speak out in front of the group. I knew that with Joyce and Tanana added to the original five, no one would even think to label my translation writing group as a "slow group."

The lessons were fun. I, unlike the teacher in the forties, did not have the children copy the story into their notebooks. Rather, I wrote it as they all sat around the table, then I typed it and had seven copies made. Thank goodness for some aspects of modern technology! The other children were intrigued and the members of my group read their stories to everyone. Now, of course, everyone wants to do it. Hilda remarked that this was "just like we used to do in first grade." Roberta informed her that the topics we were discussing were, as Mr. Stans had said, "sophisticated!" [See pp. 163–165.]

February was also parent conference month. I made it a point to include Mr. Ditto in all the conferences, both because he needs to build confidence in dealing with parents, and because, if I leave, I want the parents to have met him. Daisy's mother will be furious if I leave. She just bragged and bragged about how well Daisy has done this year and how much more ladylike she has become. She is convinced that Daisy's only problem has been that she hasn't had a good teacher before!

Paul's mother didn't come, of course. The more I thought about that woman and that poor child the madder I got. So finally I determined that if she wasn't going to come and see us, I was going to go and see her. Mr. Ditto concurred and asked to come with me.

I wrote her a letter, which she ignored, asking her when would be a good time to visit. I then called her one evening and just about insisted that we had to talk with her and that we were coming. Finally she agreed, and last Thursday evening, we went! It was quite sad, really. She was stone sober and the house was modest but tidy. She invited us into the living room. The chairs and sofa all had new covers on them. She served us coffee and cookies. We then talked, or attempted to talk, with her. Mostly, she sat chain-smoking and nodding her head. She, like Paul, looked ready to burst into tears at any moment. She kept saying that it was hard to raise a child all alone and that she prays each night that Paul's father will come home. She said that Paul is a good boy and that he doesn't run around the neighborhood with the other hoodlums! She wishes there were some nice children around that he could be friends with. I asked her if she would go with Paul to the family services clinic and she said that she really wasn't very well and that she just couldn't depend on feeling well enough to do anything like that on a regular basis. Finally, we left. I drove Mr. Ditto home and as he got out of the car, he said, "You know, it's even worse now because I don't have anyone to hate. That poor woman is doing the best she can!"

March

I have always heard the expression, "Two heads are better than one." Now I know it was referring to two teachers' heads! I really didn't realize how much I would miss Ms. Maverick, I was so excited about being able to stay with this class. But I do miss her. She comes in every Thursday afternoon and we plan activities together, but that is not the same as having her here every day. Just having another adult around sometimes is important, but I guess most teachers have to do it all, all day, every day, by themselves. Maybe I'll team teach with someone next year! I guess the success of that would depend on who that "someone" is!

This month has gone well. Ms. Maverick seems pleased with what we've done here while she's been working at the university. Fortunately, she left all her materials here for me to use. I can see that if I try to do this type of program next year, I will have to spend quite a lot of time over the summer gathering materials on the topics around which I plan to build units. (Each week Ms. Maverick comes to our planning session and gathers up something to take with her and share with her students. She brings it back the next week, however, and so far I have not had to spend a great deal of time hunting material).

So far the children have adapted exceedingly well to the change. They miss Ms. Maverick, however, and, for the first week, they were more unruly than usual. Ms. Maverick had warned me, however, that they would test me after she left, so I was prepared. I made a special effort to be fair and firm, and to continue the usual routines. In spite of my resolve, there were occasional laments of, "Ms. Maverick never did it that way!"

Daisy is the only one who seems damaged, perhaps even in some permanent way, by Ms. Maverick's leaving. Ms. Maverick is very worried about her, and even invited Daisy to her house after school to try to minimize the trauma. Daisy's mother refused to let Daisy go, however, and even wrote a very angry note to the school board concerning Ms. Maverick's unprofessional behavior in leaving her class. I try to be nice to Daisy and not to push her too much, but she simply does not respond positively. Her dislike of me is quite apparent. I just don't know what to do. I hope that by being gentle and patient, she will eventually come around.

Chip, on the other hand, is a delight! I can almost see him growing each day—physically as well as mentally. He has grown several inches since Christmas and has put on several pounds. He has learned all the words on the A and P sight word list and is beginning to get involved with books! We are now up to 21 minutes of SQUIRT time each day. Chip loves mystery stories and folk tales and takes a book home almost every night.

Comprehension Lesson— Listening Reading Transfer

While I have tried to follow our routines just as we did when Ms. Maverick was here, I have experimented with a new teaching strategy.

For some time now, I have been curious about why children seem to understand what they listen to so much better than what they read. Even when they can read most of the words, they often have a great deal of difficulty reading for a specific purpose. I discussed this with a friend who is still a student, and she suggested I try listening-reading transfer lessons (Cunningham, 1975). To do a listening-reading transfer lesson, the teacher uses two selections (or two sections of one long selection; I chose selections which related to our unit). One of these selections is read to the children and the other is used for them to read. From these selections, I identified several unfamiliar concepts in the selection that I was going to read to them, as well as some unknown words and unfamiliar concepts in the one they were going to read. I also decided what to do about these unfamiliar concepts and unknown words: as often as possible I try to lead the children to derive the meaning of unfamiliar concepts and the pronunciation of unfamiliar words from the context of the story, in order to encourage them to become independent readers. Usually, I write the unfamiliar concepts or unknown words on the board and ask them to see if they can figure out the meaning/pronunciation of these words. Often, after listening to or reading the selection and determining what the word seems to mean because of the way it is used and because of the other words around it, we look up the word in the dictionary, read the several definitions, and decide which one applies. We then compare our guess against the dictionary definitions and usually decide that the context of the story gave us a rather good notion of at least one meaning for that word.

Next, I decide on a purpose for having the students listen to or read the selection. To facilitate the transfer from listening to reading, I set the same purpose for both the listening and the reading part of the activity.

Last week I taught a listening-reading transfer lesson designed to help the children improve their sequencing abilities. I began by putting the word *rectify* on the board and asking the children to listen for this word as I read the selection and to try to figure out its meaning by the way it was used and by the other words in the story. I then taped to the chalkboard several sentence strips on which I had written the major events of the story. I read these events to the children and set the purpose for listening. "Listen as I read so you can help me put these events, which are now jumbled, into the order in which they occur in the story." After listening to the story, the children helped me rearrange the strips to put the events in their proper order and explained how they knew which should go first, second, and so on. We then discussed how *rectify* was used and several children suggested that it must mean "to fix something." We determined that the other words which let us know that *rectify* had to do with fixing were broken, repair, and breakdown. Hilda then looked up *rectify* in the dictionary and read us the appropriate dictionary definition. We added *rectify* to our wall vocabulary as part of our

Things People Do topical word set. This ended the listening part of the listening-reading transfer lesson.

On the following day, I gave the children a selection to read and a dittoed sheet on which I had written the major events of that story. I then put the words *candid* and *sword* on the board. I pronounced *candid* for them and told them that the other words in the selection would help them figure out part of the meaning for *candid*. I told them that they all knew the meaning for the other word, but that many of them might not recognize it immediately and be able to pronounce it. I told them that as they read they would be able to figure out what the word was. Having alerted them to one unfamiliar concept and one unknown word, I then reminded them of the listening lesson we had done the day before and how we had reordered the events of the story after listening to it.

"That is exactly what I want you to do today, only today, instead of listening to me read, you will read the story and reorder the events. First, read the list of events, then read the story. Then use your scissors to cut the events into strips and reorder them just as we did with the strips on the board yesterday."

The children immediately formed reading pairs. These pairs have been set up for months now, and each pair contains a good reader and a less able one. This works out amazingly well and allows me to occasionally give the whole class the same selection to read. After reading the events and then the selection, the children cut and pasted the events in order. We then discussed the order and the reasoning behind that order, and noted that *sword* was what a knight carried, and that to be *candid* was to be outspoken or frank. *Candid* was added to our Describing People topical word set. Finally, I helped the children to observe that what they can do after listening, they can do after reading.

I have also done a listening-reading transfer lesson in which the children selected a main idea for each paragraph, and, next week, I plan to do one in which they match certain causes with certain effects. Ms. Maverick says she always preached that a teacher must teach for transfer and that she can't imagine why she never thought about doing that. (It seems so obvious once you do think about it.)

April

Our unit this month has been on Alaska. Ms. Maverick and I have long been concerned about helping Tanana adapt to our culture, and it occurred to us last month that one way to help her feel more comfortable with us would be for us to learn more about her and her home. Tanana was a great resource during this unit and helped us empathize with native Alaskans who see their traditional ways threatened by the advance of civilization.

After talking with Mrs. Wright, the first-grade teacher, I decided to try a "List, Group, and Label" lesson as a kickoff to our unit. I asked the children to tell me all the words they thought of when they heard the word *Alaska*, and listed these on the board. When the children had exhausted their Alaska vocabulary, I read the entire list to them and asked them to listen as I was reading for any that seemed to go together in some way. Mrs. Wright had suggested that the next step was to let individual children list the things they felt went together, tell why they put them together, and give a label to that group. I did this, but in order to get greater participation, I let each child write on a slip of paper the items he or she wanted to put together. Individuals then read their lists and responded to my questions on why they had put those words together and what they would call that group. When each child who desired to had read his or her group to us, had explained the reason for grouping, and had labeled the group, I suggested that each one of them make another group which was different from any they had already made. We then repeated the explaining and labeling process with these second groups.

This seems to be a very effective technique to use to begin a unit. I learned what kind of prior knowledge and preconceptions the children had about Alaska, and they began thinking about Alaska and using the specialized vocabulary: *caribou, Aleuts, pipeline*. I also think it helps their classification skills, and, thus, their thinking skills. I plan to begin many units with a "List, Group, and Label" lesson.

One thing that I tried this month was not quite successful, at least not at first. Ms. Maverick had always had the children in small groups to discuss various topics, so, of course, I planned for some small-group discussions, too. The first ones were awful. I let them form their own groups and told them to discuss the pro's and con's of Alaska's development. Absolutely nothing happened! They just sat there and looked at each other! When I told Ms. Maverick of my failure, she said, "The one direction which will ensure no discussion is to tell them 'Discuss!' If you want them to discuss, give them some concrete task to do which will require discussion for its successful resolution." She also suggested that I form groups which will remain constant over a period of several weeks so that the children in those groups will develop some group pride in what they accomplish. She further suggested that we spread the rowdy ones, the leaders, the quiet ones, and the "outcasts" among the groups. These are the five groups we formed.

Concept Development—List, Group, Label

Concept Development—Group Discussions

Daisy	Paul	Butch	Mitch	Mort
Alex	*Betty	Carl	Chip	Daphne
*Rita	Hilda	*Joyce	*Pat	Horace
Larry	Manuel	Roberta	Tanana	*Mandy
Alexander	Anthony	Steve	Danielle	Jeff

We then planned the following structured discussion. The children were told which group they would be in and where their group would meet (the four corners and the center of the room). They then practiced getting quickly into their groups and ready to begin. Once they were in their groups, I gave them a card with their names on it and explained that the person whose name had a star next to it would be the recorder for that group for the day and would do all the writing for the group. (We picked the recorders according to their ability in spelling and writing.)

I then gave each group index cards and a felt marker and told them they had five minutes to list the resources of Alaska. They were asked to write only one resource on each index card because they would use the cards later. Since they had seen a film a few days before on Alaska's resources, and many had read about Alaska's resources in various source books, they had no difficulty thinking of resources. When the timer rang to signal the end of the five minutes, each group had a stack of cards and was still talking!

Next, I gave them two large sheets of construction paper and some tape. On the top of one sheet of construction paper, I had written "Resources which will be used up" and on the other, "Resources which will last forever." I explained the concept of renewable and nonrenewable resources to them, and gave them a few examples from our local resources. I then gave them ten minutes to tape each of their index cards to one of the construction paper sheets. The discussion which ensued was lively and topical! Ms. Maverick had been right again. Once they had a task to do which required discussion and a strict time limit in which to complete that task, there was no dawdling or silence. (Never again will I instruct a group to "discuss" unless, of course, I want a few rare moments of silence in this otherwise noisy room.) Once the ten minutes were up, we displayed the charts and compared the results. When two groups had put the same resource in two different categories, the groups explained their reasoning, and if we could come to any resolution, the resource was changed to the appropriate chart. In several cases, we decided we would have to do a little research to resolve a controversy—an unexpected bonus of our first successful discussion!

I have been continuing the guided reading procedures as Ms. Maverick began them, but have also initiated guided listening procedures. Every other week, we do a full procedure in which the children have ten minutes to read a selection, list what they remember, skim the selection to verify or correct inconsistencies, identify main ideas, and complete a five-item nonreading quiz. In the intervening week, we do the delayed retention quiz. The children have increased in their ability to remember information over a one-week time span and they are very proud of this growth, which is vividly displayed on their guided reading procedure charts.

I got to thinking that if the procedure was good for reading, it should also be good for listening! Last week, I tried it. I had planned to read to the class an editorial from an Alaskan newspaper. I brought a tape recorder to class and asked the children to listen to remember everything. I then read them the editorial and taped my reading. Once finished, I asked them what they remembered and listed what they told me on the board. When they had exhausted their memories, I replayed the tape, telling them to listen to make sure the information on the board was correct, and to raise their hands to stop the tape if they heard anything which contradicted the information on the board. They found several pieces of incorrect information and seemed to really enjoy this new strategy. We then circled main ideas, and I gave them a quiz. They all wanted to know if I was going to give them a delayed quiz next week and if they were going to keep a chart. I hadn't planned to be this systematic about it, but they seem to want to! They certainly did listen attentively and knew what that editorial said. I think I will do guided listening procedures on the off-week for guided reading procedures. I wonder what Ms. Maverick will say when I tell her about this!

Listening Comprehension— GLP

May

What a terrific month this has been. I started the month a little "down," realizing that this year was ending with so much left undone and that I still had to find a job for next year. I knew I would never find a school like this one. I had made up my mind, however, that I believed in the integrated approach to teaching, and that I would move elsewhere to find a school which would allow me to follow through on my beliefs.

You can imagine my surprise when, as I was relaying my concerns and convictions to Ms. Maverick, she informed me that she knew just the principal I ought to talk to—Mr. Topps! While conducting the seminar at the university, Ms. Maverick had become even more convinced of her approach to teaching and to children, and had decided that she would stay on at the university as a graduate student in administration and supervision so that she could get her principal's certificate. Although Mr. Topps was sorry to lose her, he agreed that the principal could be an effective change-agent in the schools, and admitted that this factor had weighed heavily in his decision to become a principal. I, of course, quickly applied for Ms. Maverick's job, and although the school board has not yet acted officially, Mr. Topps assured me that they will approve his recommendation. So, I have found a job in a school which will let me teach according to my beliefs! Ms. Maverick has even agreed to leave most of her materials here. While I am delighted at this turn of events, I am also somewhat apprehensive. Even with her materials, planning this program all alone and starting a whole new class of children in this approach will not be easy.

Ms. Maverick was away at a national reading meeting at the beginning of the month, and since then has been busy finishing up her seminar. The annual book fair thus became totally my responsibility. And while I survived and it got done, it was not as well planned as I would have liked. We ordered the books for the fair from several publishers of paperback books. We got catalogues and the children met in groups to decide how many copies of each title they thought we might sell. (Fortunately, the publishers take back and credit us for any books which are not sold!) Once the books were ordered, we began to plan how to organize and promote our sale. As is traditional, the books are first put on display for sale on the evening of the last parent's meeting. My children wrote flyers encouraging the parents to come to the final meeting and informing them that many good, inexpensive paperback books would be on sale that evening. Parents were encouraged to buy the books for their children to have something new and exciting to read during the long summer months.

We then made posters which were hung in the various classrooms of our school and in the local supermarket and drugstore. A group of children composed an announcement about the book fair which they sent to the newspaper, and another group composed an announcement which was read several times a day on the local radio station.

With our advertisement campaign well under way, we began to plan how we would organize ourselves for the actual sale. After much discussion, it was decided that we would divide all the books according to topic and display them on cafeteria tables set up in the halls. We then began a lengthy classification procedure during which we looked at the titles of the books we had ordered and tried to place them in appropriate categories. After several days of discussion and argument about what the categories should be, I saw that we were getting nowhere except closer to the night of the fair. Obviously I had to provide some direction or we weren't going to make it! I then sat down with the lists and established eight categories, plus a ninth category for miscellaneous books. The next day I wrote the category names on the board and had the children get into the groups they had been in for the ordering. Each group took nine sheets of paper, put the name of one category on each sheet, and decided in which category each book they had ordered belonged. While we did have several disagreements and a lot of books relegated to "miscellaneous," we finally got our lists made. The children made a first or second choice for which books they would like to sell, and I formed them into groups of two or three based on these choices.

When the books finally arrived (only one day ahead of the fair!), it was a fairly easy job to sort them and put them in piles according to category. Then, on the afternoon of the fair, each group set up their displays. Several children who lived quite far away and I stayed at school until the parents arrived at 7:00 P.M., watching over our displays, doing some last minute "advertisement," and eating the three pizzas I had ordered. (The ones who had gone home for supper were not too pleased when the ones who stayed bragged about having pizza for supper, but you just can't please everyone no matter how hard you try!)

We sold books out in the hall that evening to the parents and all the next morning to the children who came out of their classrooms at scheduled times. We then took the 100-plus books we had left back to our room, put them on the back table, and sold about 20 more to children and teachers during the remainder of that week. Finally, on Friday, we boxed up the unsold books and shipped them back to the companies from which they had come. We also totaled our money and figured which books we would order with the profits. We decided that each child could order one free bonus book, and that with the remainder of the profits we would order books for the classroom's already large paperback library. I didn't know until I was almost through with this project that I would be in charge of it again next year!

TRY IT OUT

Mr. Ditto obviously found the book fair a lot of work and found that it took more planning than he had anticipated. What did the children learn as they were planning and implementing the book fair? Specifically, what language, reading, math, and social skills were they practicing? Can you think of ways that planning and carrying out the book fair improved the children's thinking abilities? List these and then decide if you think the time and effort was well spent. Remember the added bonuses—books for the whole school to read over the summer, extra books for Mr. Ditto's classroom library, and good public relations for the school with the parents and community.

We have been having SQUIRT time for 24 minutes for the last two weeks of this month. While this is a minute short of the 25 minutes Ms. Maverick thought they could reach. I think it is quite a long time for fourth graders to sit still and read intently. I am proud of them!

Since Ms. Maverick was invited to the university, people in the school system have suddenly become curious about her approach to teaching. She has been asked to address the final meeting of one of the local professional organizations and has requested that I join her on the podium. At first I protested that I had nothing to say to teachers that they would be willing to listen to, but Ms. Maverick argued that I could answer some of their questions about beginning to teach with this method. When I hesitated, she asked whether I felt strange about going because I knew that my first supervising teacher and many of the other teachers in that school would be there. I had to admit that I wasn't looking forward to meeting those people who represented my failure as a teacher. She said that that was exactly the point: I was not a failure—simply misplaced—and that was precisely the reason I should be present at the meeting, even if I didn't say a word. I have had my orders and am going, and I have even begun to think I may enjoy it!

THE PROFESSIONAL MEETING

Mrs. Wright called the meeting to order, made a few business announcements, and then said, "As many of you know, I use what is essentially a language experience approach to help my first graders bridge the gap between the language they speak and reading the language of others. While I believe in this method for beginning readers, I realize that there are many valid approaches to the teaching of reading and that each teacher's approach must be one he or she is comfortable with and one which meets the needs of the children being taught. I have for the past five years been able to observe the results of Ms. Maverick's integrated curriculum. Often she teaches in fourth grade a group of children I had in first grade, and I am always pleased to watch these children grow in independence, self-awareness, and real-world concern under Ms. Maverick's direction. I must confess that until this year when Mr. Ditto took over Ms. Maverick's class and carried on just as she always had, I thought that Ms. Maverick's teaching method was really peculiar to her own style and personality. I have seen, however, that this was not the case, and that given the desire and the will, one can learn to teach an integrated curriculum. It gives me great personal pleasure, therefore, to introduce to you this afternoon my friend and colleague, Ms. Maverick, and her protégé, Mr. Ditto."

Ms. Maverick rose, but before she began her address made a confession to Mrs. Wright: "I must admit, Mrs. Wright, that I always thought your teaching was peculiar to *your* style and personality!" As the group nodded their appreciation of this humorous but candid confession, Ms. Maverick began her presentation.

"One of the main reasons why I teach an integrated curriculum is that there are never, for me, enough hours in the teaching day. When I help my children become better readers, more precise language users, and more competent mathematicians as they learn science and social studies content, I get almost twice the mileage out of my instructional time. I believe this is a principle which can be applied to learners of any age. Today, rather than lecture you about the wisdom of this economy, I am going to demonstrate it with you.

"While I use many teaching strategies in my integrated curriculum, a new one which I have tried out this year and which I am most impressed with is the guided reading procedure. Mr. Ditto is presently passing out to you copies of a summary of my instructional program which I wrote. I would like you to read this summary to remember *everything*. When you have completed reading this, I will demonstrate for you the steps in the guided reading procedure."

Ms. Maverick then sat down and after a few moments the teachers realized that she did indeed intend for them to read the summary and they settled down to do so. When most of the teachers had completed the summary, Ms. Maverick reminded them of the purpose she had set for reading and asked them what they remembered. At first no one responded, but Mrs. Flame finally said: "You have a four-sided plan. Reading is real. SQUIRT. Skills time and the integrated block activity." Ms. Maverick smiled and wrote Mrs. Flame's responses on the board. Slowly, others began to volunteer bits and pieces of what they remembered reading. Ms. Maverick recorded their contributions, numbering each as she went along:

1. Each unit has three phases.
2. In the beginning phase, you provide much input and try to build interest in the topic being studied.
3. As much as possible, you use real-world reading materials from newspapers and magazines.
4. You do lots of directed reading activities with the whole class and the reading material on an overhead transparency.
5. At the end of each unit you do activities which help the children to synthesize and organize what they read.
6. You have a block of time in the afternoon when you teach reading and math skills.

Once the teachers got going, they, just like the children, were able to fill the board with their pooled remembrances from the summary they had read. Ms. Maverick continued through the steps of the procedure with them, having them go back to the summary for one minute to correct any inconsistencies or supply missing information, identifying the main ideas, and then giving them a five-item, true-false quiz.

When she had finished the whole procedure, she explained to them the rationale for the guided reading procedure, that it was intended primarily to help children increase their long-term memory of what they read. She explained how Mr. Ditto had adapted this procedure to listening, and reported that the procedures did indeed seem to be effective in helping the children develop a mind set to remember more of what they read and heard. She showed them Chip's GRP progress chart which she had brought along.

"What I have just done with you is what I try to do with my children," Ms. Maverick went on to explain. "There was some content which

I wanted to teach you—in this case, a summary of how my integrated curriculum works. At the same time, I wanted to help you increase your repertoire of teaching skills, so I used the guided reading procedure to teach you about my instructional program. Hopefully, you have experienced in the last 40 minutes the kind of economy teaching I practice in my classroom."

The teachers seemed much warmer and more interested than they had when the meeting started, and Ms. Maverick reaffirmed her faith in the belief that a good teaching strategy is appropriate for learners of any age. Although there was not much time remaining, several questions were asked and answered. In one of the questions, an elderly teacher referred to Ms. Maverick's integrated approach as a radical approach. Ms. Maverick informed her that while her own version of it had certain unique characteristics, the notion that learning should be integrated was hardly new. She went on to cite references for this fact. She told them that Henry Morrison in 1931 had first pointed out the need for some external organization of subject matter to achieve internal learning products, and that he had condemned the fragmenting of the curriculum.

A young teacher indicated that he was very interested in trying the integrated curriculum approach, but that the intermediate grades in his school were departmentalized, allowing him only 45 minutes of reading time for each of six classes. Ms. Maverick indicated to him that one of the greatest values of the self-contained classroom, as she saw it, was that teaching of the different subject areas could be integrated, but that he certainly could include SQUIRT and some "reading is real" activities during his reading period.

The final question had to do with beginning an integrated curriculum, and, since the time had nearly elapsed, Ms. Maverick referred the questioner to Mr. Ditto and informed the audience that both she and Mr. Ditto would be glad to stay and talk with anyone individually after the meeting. Ms. Maverick was delighted to observe that Mr. Ditto was still excitedly talking with a group of young teachers after everyone else had cleared out and gone home.

14 | Mr. Dunn

THE PARENT MEETING

Ed Dunn sat at his desk waiting for the parents to arrive. A few years before at this time he had been nervously rehearsing an almost-memorized speech, but this night he was more confident. His first year of teaching had begun as a challenge, and he soon found himself floundering. Many of his students had difficulty reading their textbooks, and he had no idea what to do for them. He tried teaching phonics during reading class, but the students hated it, calling it babyish and boring. Happily, with help and guidance from Mr. Topps and other teachers, he began to catch up with the challenge. He planned activities that allowed all the students some measure of success. For instance, using brightly colored paper to hide the books' real grade level, he covered easy content texts that he had found in the materials room. By the end of the year, he had survived, if not thrived, and he believed that the students, too, had learned something.

Over the summers, Ed had taken several graduate courses in reading at the university. While there, he had asked specific questions of many professors and graduate students. He had read several books and articles beyond those assigned to him and had participated actively in his courses. In short, he had attempted to learn everything he could about teaching reading to intermediate-grade students.

This year, especially, he felt that he was ready. He had learned many ways to provide materials and activities that took into account the many reading levels that inevitably are found in fifth grade. He had discovered that reading instruction actually could be provided while students read materials in content areas such as social studies, science, and math. And he came to realize that students required opportunities to read independently for their own purposes. Now he was to welcome the parents of this year's class and tell them about the reading program he had planned for their children.

After everyone had arrived and was seated, he began: "Good evening and welcome to your child's fifth-grade classroom. I am Ed Dunn, and I hope to get to know all of you as I teach your children this year. So far

459

we are still learning each other's names, but they do seem to be an interesting group.

"During this meeting, I hope to give you an overview of what we will be doing to improve reading, since that is the backbone of all our studies. Even in math, fifth graders need to be able to follow written directions and to deal successfully with word problems. And in the middle school next year, your children will be expected to read well enough to be independent learners.

"Mr. Ditto and I have talked at some length about the type of reading program your children had with Ms. Maverick and him last year. I was very impressed with their reading-to-learn approach. To some degree, my general approach to reading instruction can be seen as an extension of theirs. However, I intend to follow the traditional divisions among the content areas. By this I mean that we have periods of the day set aside specifically for literature, language arts, math, social studies, and science. This basically is the way your children will spend their school days in middle school, high school, and—if they go on—in college. I am introducing them to this format this year. The difference, of course, is that I teach all the subjects as we stay in our self-contained classroom.

"One of the most important reading goals that I have for your children is to begin them on the road to selective reading. Let me give you an example of what I mean by selective reading."

Mr. Dunn displayed the following short paragraph which he had written on an overhead transparency:

A man named Eric Thorvaldsson came to the island in 982 A.D. Eric had been exiled from Iceland for three years for killing another man. When he returned to Iceland, he wanted settlers to be eager to go to this land, so he made it sound attractive by calling it Greenland!

He turned to the parents. "What are some of the things you must do in order to learn this information?"

After some silence, Mrs. Penn raised her hand. "We have to get a basic understanding of the passage, but I know there's more to it than that."

Mr. Moppett spoke out. "When I was in school, I simply memorized all of the information. I usually got A's and B's on the tests because I could produce practically anything the teacher wanted. Of course, I promptly forgot most everything I had memorized as soon as the test was over, too."

The parents obviously could relate to Mr. Moppett's confession as Mr. Dunn noted many of them smiling and nodding their heads in agreement.

"That's exactly what I hope to keep your children away from in my class as I work on selective reading," Mr. Dunn said. "In the passage I've displayed overhead for you, there is quite a bit of information. Students could memorize facts such as the date Eric first came to Greenland, Eric's last name, the length of his exile, and so on. However, in January we will begin extensive lessons on helping students independently determine what is important. This is the key to selective reading. It takes a long time for students to acquire this ability because determining what is important depends on numerous factors."

At this point, a woman dressed in a plain housedress raised her hand, stood up, and began speaking. "Mr. Dunn, I'm Daphne's grandmother. Don't misunderstand me, please. Mr. Fields and I have been very happy with Daphne's progress at Merritt Elementary, and we've liked all her teachers. But from what we read in the newspaper, it seems like all anyone needs to improve their reading is some good old phonics. Does this other stuff really matter?"

Remembering when he had thought the same thing, Mr. Dunn began, "There's no doubt that children must learn to identify words if they are going to learn how to read. But some children are 'word callers'. I taught a couple of them last year. One of my students could read orally from a fifth-grade book without missing a word, but he couldn't understand what he was reading even from a third-grade book. To say that he needed more phonics, as I did at first, was to doom him to being a poor reader.

"By the time someone reads as well as the average fifth or sixth grader, that person usually can identify most of the words in what he or she reads. To some extent, then, if we don't teach a child to attend to important information or develop meaning vocabulary, then we allow the child simply to become an 'advanced word caller'!"

Mr. Dunn turned and wrote on the chalkboard the following sentence:

Blabble forsh ibe zummer.

"I'll bet that all of you and most of your children could pronounce these 'words' that I just wrote on the board. But as you can tell, you simply would be producing sounds that have no meaning. A big part of my program is to continue emphasizing the meaning and not the sounds of what your children read."

This seemed to satisfy everyone, so Ed Dunn continued. "Two other important goals that I have this year are to help your children learn from their content area reading materials and to help them become independent learners. For example, we will study a unit on matter and energy in science, and there are many concepts in this unit that your children probably have never encountered before. It's my job to help this class learn about things in this unit such as conductors, insulators, convection currents, waves, energy chains, collision systems, and many other concepts that probably are unfamiliar. The reading materials that Miss Launch and Mrs. Wright used in the primary grades generally contained information which your children had directly experienced inside or outside of class. But the emphasis now is on reading materials that contain new, unfamiliar information.

"And not only do the youngsters need help understanding new ideas, they are expected to remember those ideas, too. If you'll think back, after Miss Launch and Mrs. Wright had finished with a reading passage, they didn't check at a later date to see if your children had remembered the information in that passage. The information certainly was worthwhile, but in general it dealt with familiar things and the children did not need to spend time learning it. But now in fifth grade the emphasis is on learning as well as remembering unfamiliar information."

Ed Dunn paused for a second to see if the group were still with him. They seemed to be, so he pressed on to what he thought would be brand new to them.

"I must confess to you that I am of two minds when it comes to helping students learn from their texts. First of all, I want to carefully guide your children through their materials so they know what information is important and how to deal with that information. I have a pretty good idea of what I think should be learned, and I want to make sure that all of it is highlighted. Because of this, I tend to be the one to tell the class what to read or listen for, and I then ask questions that call for extra thinking about that information. Often I will lecture or show a film that gets at the desired information. Unfortunately, there's a problem with this. The problem with this approach is that if I always choose the materials, always set the purposes for reading, and always follow up those purposes, then my students come to depend totally on me for guidance. They learn a good deal of information, but they become dependent learners. And one of the goals that I mentioned to you earlier is to help your children become *independent* learners.

"Independent learners choose their own materials for learning, set their own purposes, and follow up those purposes by themselves. In order to reach this goal, while your children are in my fifth-grade class they will ask questions just about as often as they will answer questions. They will look in the library, in our classroom, and at home for materials that provide the information they seek. And they will report to me and to their classmates the new information they have acquired. This is all part of becoming independent learners. Of course, I will help them learn how to do these things, but they will be allowed toward the end of the year to pursue topics largely on their own.

"The reason I am of two minds when it comes to helping students learn from their texts is because I know that I should not continually direct my class's reading. But I often worry that they will miss important information if I'm not out there telling them exactly what to look for. In other words, I want to direct your children's reading, but I also want to let them learn how to discover information by themselves. I believe that I can strike the correct balance, although I must admit that sometimes that balance is hard to find."

Ed Dunn was relieved. He thought he had done a fairly good job summarizing the complex program which he had spent so much time designing and setting. He purposely had left out discussion of his plans for designing lessons that fit the reading levels of all his students even though he would spend the first few months of school doing just that. He believed what he had just covered was of more interest to the parents. He waited for a response.

Mrs. Penn broke the silence for everyone. "Mr. Dunn, we are all thankful that our children are here in Merritt Elementary, and we know that the program you have planned for our children will continue to help them grow as they have in the past. Basically, I think I know what you mean about teaching reading along with content-area subjects, selective reading, learning from text, and developing independent learners. Although we don't always understand the philosophies behind what you do for our children, we do know that they are happy and learning here."

"I'd like to second that," spoke up a woman at the back. "We left here when Mike was about to start third grade. We are very glad to be back. Mike is a handful but at least here we know everyone will work with him. Miss Nouveau worked wonders with him and I know you, Mr. Dunn, will be able to help him behave and learn."

Few questions seemed necessary after that, and the meeting came quickly to an end. Mr. Dunn left even more determined to improve the ability of all his students.

MONTHLY LOGS

September

What a month this has been! Establishing a classroom routine and set of expectations always takes time because the children simply don't know what to do or what "this year's teacher's" expectations are. This group of students, as usual, tested the limits of acceptable behavior in order to find out just what those limits are. I've found that as long as I maintain consistent, firm guidelines about what I expect with regard to classroom behavior, and as long as I provide reasonably stimulating lessons that allow the children to succeed, then the class runs rather successfully.

Mike, Butch, and Daisy tried to take over the class at first, but,

Routines

Mr. Dunn's Daily Class Schedule

Time	Activity
8:30– 8:40	Plan the day
8:45– 9:30	Reading/Literature
9:35–10:20	Language Arts
10:25–10:35	SSR
10:40–11:25	Math
11:30–12:15	Lunch/Recess
12:20–12:35	Music
12:40– 1:25	Science
1:30– 1:45	Journal Writing
1:50– 2:35	Social Studies
2:35– 2:45	Close the day

without overreacting, I continued to remind them of what I wanted them to do. I watched for signs of trouble and tried to prevent problems. I ignored what I could, and when I made an assignment I insisted that they stay with it.

My schedule shows how I divided the day. Believe me, I stuck to this schedule! We study five main subject areas: reading/literature, language arts, math, science, and social studies. I use textbooks as the backbone for the content areas of science and social studies, but whenever possible I bring into the classroom other printed materials, A-V materials, concrete objects, and guest speakers. I refer to all these sources of information as *collateral sources*. This means that all are equally important. In fact, the main contribution of the textbooks seems to be that they are rather complete reference sources for the topics we cover in class. They are not the only sources.

When I passed out the textbooks in each of the five areas, I got quite a variety of responses from the children. For instance, Danielle immediately began poring over the pages of each book. Reading does seem to provide her an outlet. Hilda pulled out her eraser and began cleaning up her books before placing them carefully in her desk. Conversely, when I distributed the social studies texts, Mike and Butch pulled out their pencils and began drawing mustaches, crossed eyes, and big ears on George Washington and Abraham Lincoln who grace the covers of our books. Although I could remember doing the same thing when I was their age, I still informed them in no uncertain terms that such action was unacceptable in my room. They grumbled, but they erased their "artwork."

Content-Area Reading

In social studies and science I plan lessons that develop understanding of the information and that improve reading abilities at the same time [see pp. 136–138]. In effect, I use these materials just as if they were written for formal reading instruction. If a key word is defined clearly by the context, then I have the class figure out what the word means from the context. If a passage we are reading is organized clearly, then I have the class portray that organization through webbing, structured overviews, or outlining. In addition, I design activities that allow students to work at their independent reading levels. Most of these activities are completed in centers with materials written at various levels of difficulty so different children complete different sets of activities.

Our mornings are devoted to the subjects which mainly call for learning how to do things. Reading/literature, language arts, and math fill up this time. I carry over skills from one of these areas to another throughout the day. For example, if we're studying capitalization in language arts, then occasionally we notice what is capitalized in the books we read and the writing we do in reading/literature, math, social studies, and science.

The time set aside for reading/literature is devoted to two general types of readers. One type consists of students who are reading above, at, or only slightly below grade level. I mainly want to improve these students' meaning vocabularies, and I want to help them become active readers of literature. I provide these students a lot of material they can readily read but which call for thoughtful responses. For example, we spend a good bit of time discussing the motives that underly characters' actions.

The other general type of reader that I identify consists of those students who have major difficulties. I gave some thought about how I would identify students with "major difficulties" and made the decision that a student who is reading at the 3^1 level in the beginning of fifth grade has them. It's my job to find out what the difficulties are and do something directly to help each child overcome them. Poor readers, those who have major difficulties, require a closer look and a specific program that gets after whatever is holding them back. In the time set aside specifically for reading/literature, I attempt to do just that.

My language arts and math programs are based on presenting a common topic to the class and then pursuing that topic at levels which are appropriate for the children. For example, if we're doing subtraction, then I do whole-class presentations to get everyone thinking about "taking away." However, the children work on their own or in small groups with problems and exercises that are appropriate for their ability levels.

The children seem to be able to cope all right with my division of the subject areas. In fact, I overheard Chip and Carl talking about how neat it was that they were studying subjects just like the high school kids do. However, Roberta pointed out to me that they studied things "together" in Ms. Maverick's room. I agreed that that was a good way to do it, and then I tried to explain how I intended to tie together reading and language arts, especially, with science and social studies. The expression on her face after we talked indicated that I hadn't totally convinced her. We'll see.

SSR

SSR, music, and journal writing fill up the other time blocks during the day. Sustained Silent Reading (SSR) is what I call SQUIRT. My "young adults" resented the term SQUIRT although most of them do expect and even seem to enjoy the opportunity to read silently on their own for a certain time period. I'm sure this is the result of the programs these children have been through in their earlier grades here at Merritt Elementary.

Functional Reading

I really enjoy listening to music, although I don't play any instruments nor do I sing especially well. I think most youngsters like music, too, and can benefit from it, so I scheduled a part of each day for it. During the 15 minutes we have for music, we simply take out our song books and sing. I start off by choosing a student to select a song for the class to sing. After everyone sings the song, the original student chooses someone else—usually a friend—who selects another song for us. For example, I started out one music session calling on Joyce. She chose "When Johnny Comes Marching Home" for us to sing. She then called on Roberta who had us sing "On Top of Old Smokey." When Roberta called on Larry there were some murmurs among the class because a girl actually had called on a boy. I get some useful information about friendships while this selecting goes on, the children settle down after an invigorating recess, and they are reading and interpreting lyrics as they sing the various songs.

Content Journal Writing

Our 15 minute journal writing session got off to a rather poor start, but I intend to stay with it for a while. I explained to the class how they needed to write on their own during journal writing just as they needed to read on their own during SSR. I also explained the rationale for doing content journal writing [see pp. 167–168]. But when the time first came to write, Butch kept saying that he didn't know what to write about. This complaint was picked up by Mike almost immediately, and I could see others agreeing. As a result, I got hot on the program and told them specifically to write what they thought Vasco da Gama's sailors thought about as they sailed around Africa. This kept the class going, but I wish I hadn't had to assign a specific topic as I ended up doing that first time.

Diagnosis

One of the most important things I did this month was begin my ongoing classroom diagnosis. Mort and Paul put forth very little effort in completing the social studies and science activities I assigned, but at least they did not disturb others who were working. I suspected that those two had difficulty reading and writing and that that difficulty caused them to appear lazy and uncaring. But I wasn't sure. That's why I spent part of the second week of school doing group diagnosis with our content-area reading materials. I wanted to determine who required adjustments to the assignments.

The group diagnosis that I use relies quite a bit on common sense. I simply have students complete an assignment that is roughly typical of the type of assignment that I would make with that text during the year. However, the difference is that I look at the students' performance as a measure of how well they can deal with the materials, not as a measure of the grade they should receive. This is an inventory, not a test.

To construct a group reading inventory, I took the basic textbook that we have for each of our five subjects, and I identified an appropriate selection from the second 50 pages. Each selection had a beginning, middle, and end; that is, each selection stood by itself. For each section I wrote questions that were the same type that would normally occur during a regular class. In fact, my questions covered the topics that would receive emphasis if I were actually teaching them. One of the other fifth-grade teachers might ask different questions that emphasize different aspects of the passage, but that is to be expected. The point is that I conducted this group diagnosis the same way as I would conduct a regular class lesson.

After the class completed one of the group inventories, I took it home at night for evaluation. Last year I graded each paper and then compared percentages to see who fell into the 90s, 80s, 70s, 60s, and below. However, this year I evaluated the papers holistically because all of my questions called for short-answer, essay-type responses rather than responses that called for circling letters or underlining words.

To do holistic evaluation, I first read all the papers rather quickly one time in order to gain an overall perspective. Then I went through the papers again and sorted them into four piles according to how well they satisfied the assignment. I took care not to let handwriting influence my judgments; clear handwriting does not always indicate clear thinking, and vice versa. After obtaining four piles, I read the papers a final time and rank ordered them. I now had tentative information to help me determine how well each student could meet certain outcomes with each textbook.

Based on my group reading inventory in social studies, I came up with a tentative list of students and their ability to benefit from working with the classroom social studies text. My holistic scoring of the group reading inventory for our social studies textbook indicated that I have four students who cannot be expected to learn from it. Daisy, Jeff, Mike, and Paul appear to need special lessons and materials if they are to use reading in order to develop their understanding of social studies. If I don't provide them special lessons and materials, then they are doomed to two situations: (1) frustration with an incomprehensible text, and (2) reliance on listening to class lectures and presentations, and viewing films or other media in order to obtain information.

I seem to have 14 students who can be expected to learn from our text and increase their reading abilities while doing so as long as they receive some direct guidance from me. I realize that learning from text is not an all-or-nothing affair and that students can acquire some knowledge, even from quite difficult materials. However, it seems that this group of 14 children will learn the most information and best improve their reading abilities at the same time if I provide them clear guidance before and after they read.

The remaining eight students look as though they will be able to understand the text with ease. They still will require my help to lead them to even better understanding and insight into what they read. But from what I can tell, they should have little difficulty with my typical assignments based on the text.

I will observe my students' reading abilities throughout the year, but for the present I have a tentative idea of their relative levels. In a week or two I intend to take aside some of the students who appear to have major reading difficulties and administer an Informal Reading In-

Tentative Ranking of Abilities to Benefit from Instruction with Social Studies Textbook

Relative Ability	Student
Independent level (little guidance)	Betty Danielle Hilda Larry Mandy Pat Rita Roberta
Instructional level (some guidance)	Alex Anthony Carl Chip Daphne Horace Joyce Manuel Mitch Steve
Instructional level (much guidance)	Alexander Butch Mort Tanana
Frustration level (needs accommodation)	Daisy Jeff Mike Paul

ventory (IRI). This will give me a better picture of their reading levels, and it will help pinpoint what is holding them back.

Sometime in October I will look at the permanent files of those students who I am especially concerned about, and perhaps I will talk with some of their past teachers. I like to form my own opinions first, however, before I solicit other people's opinions about my students.

TRY IT OUT

Read the section in Chapter 6 of this book entitled "Question: What is the Child's Instructional Level?" [See pp. 183–194.] Compare the suggestions in that section with Mr. Dunn's procedures for matching students with his textbooks. What does Mr. Dunn do that is specifically described in that section? What does he do that is not specified in that section?

October

As I get to know my students better, I always am amazed how different they are! Larry has an exceptionally quick mind, and his knowledge of the world is actually astounding. Occasionally I wonder if he couldn't teach the class. The students ask him for help as often and as willingly as they ask me.

Mike either cannot or will not stay at any task or in any one place for more than a minute or two. He does not defy me, but he does require constant reminding.

Betty, Tanana, Daphne, and Joyce are fast friends, which is not unusual of course, but individually they are such diverse people. Betty is a perfectionist who almost always succeeds. Tanana's interest in nature has dominated all her other interests. Daphne has a tremendous imagination. And Joyce has proven to be quite popular. She inevitably is called on more than once during music to choose a song.

We got off to a good start this month working on different reading-writing activities in social studies and science because of the care I took getting into them. I always am careful to keep my class together as a large group during the first few weeks of school. This allows the students to learn what my limits are in regard to acceptable behavior, and it allows the class routine to become established. After a time, I gradually begin allowing the students to control their own learning activities. This is a year-long process, and some classes go further than others in assuming self control. The procedure I follow was described quite well in an article I read years ago entitled "The Half-Open Classroom: Controlled Options in Reading," by Earle and Morley (1974).

Half-Open Classroom

The way I "opened up" my science period is a good example of getting to a half-open classroom. The first few weeks were spent exploring our class science textbook, noting its table of contents, skimming through the chapters, and becoming familiar with the special parts of the book such as its index, glossary, and footnoting system. Other available science materials were introduced, also. I then began whole-class lessons on our first unit of study which dealt with motion.

When reading materials were used, I always prepared students for the reading, set specific purposes, and discussed the material afterwards to make sure that the purposes had been met. Activities such as DR-TA, Possible Sentences, [see p. 101], and GRP were conducted to help guide the class through the material.

When reading-writing tasks were assigned, I made them one at a time and held everyone responsible for each one. As expected, some students did better than others. Larry and Pat turned in papers that could have been displayed in a showcase, Alexander had some terrific insights but they were not stated very clearly, and Tanana and Daisy appeared to jot down whatever came to their minds. As a group, my students worked on these assignments in a rather perfunctory way.

Later in the month, we watched a film and a filmstrip on motion and I read aloud a short article on "Our Friendly Moving Machines." Then I listed four reading-writing activities on the board:

1. Draw arrows around a diagram of an airplane wing that show the direction and relative amounts of force pushing on the wing.
2. List names of pictured machines.
3. Construct a "web" of the information that is contained in the article "Our Friendly Moving Machines." (See Mr. Dunn for a copy of the article and a taped version of it.)
4. Complete the experiment described on page 83 of our science textbook.

"But Mr. Dunn, some of those activities have nothing to do with our textbook!" Hilda patiently explained to me.

"That's right. They all are connected to our study of motion, but they include a variety of materials. Try it, you'll like it," I assured her. "But wait 'til you hear the real surprise."

I then told the class that they were all responsible for completing all four activities, but that each student could choose the order in which to complete them. Friday of that week was set as the due date for the four projects.

This small bit of choice-making was handled quite well by most students. (Again, they do reflect their previous training!) The biggest exception was Mort who told me that he chose not to do any of the assignments. However, I reminded him firmly that he could choose the *order* of doing them and not the actual doing of them. I think he got the message.

After the class became accustomed to choosing the order of my reading-writing activities during science period, I extended this procedure to the other subject areas. I had different due dates for the various projects in the different areas so that I didn't get totally snowed evaluating papers that came in all at once. I will need to see about cutting down on the paper load, though. I am sure that planning creative lessons for which the students give each other feedback is time better spent than my evaluating uncreative lessons. Somehow I need to get the youngsters in on the act.

A committee of girls who apparently had taken an hour to pose their question met me after lunch one day. Betty, Mandy, and Roberta came up and wanted to talk about our music period. **Functional Reading**

"Mr. Dunn, we like singing after lunch, but we're not too crazy about the songs you have for us. They're too old fashioned," complained Mandy.

Well, I thought that the songs in their songbooks like "America the Beautiful" were rather nice, but I could see their point. When we brought this up with the whole class, we decided that they could bring in song lyrics on their own, and I would duplicate them for everybody. My only caution was that the song needed to be "singable" by a group. Some of the top 40 numbers are just a little too fast and complicated for unsophisticated group singing.

Our short time set aside specifically for music is a high point of the day. We get a nice group feeling after each session, and the afternoons do seem to go by quite pleasantly. Sometimes we discuss the lyrics of a song. I brought in some folk songs from the 1960s, played a recorded version of them, we sang them, and then we talked about them. There wasn't much to say about "Puff, the Magic Dragon," but we did talk at some length about "Blowin' in the Wind." I hate to let them know that we're actually studying poetry at these times, but we are.

This month I was able to complete my IRI's of the four students I had selected for further testing on the basis of my group inventories. The one thing I did that is not always done with IRI's is obtain a level of listening comprehension. This measure helps me determine how well students can understand passages that are read to them. A child who has high listening comprehension but low word identification and reading comprehension scores generally is considered to be a child who can benefit the most from reading instruction. Children with relatively low levels of listening comprehension still can benefit from reading instruction, but they also require extra attention to overall language comprehension and background information. **Diagnosis**

When I had determined the word identification and reading comprehension levels for the student, I obtained a listening comprehension level. Beginning at his or her reading comprehension level, I read the listening comprehension passages to the student and then asked eight questions which had been constructed the same way as the questions for the reading comprehension passages. The student's listening comprehension level was the highest level at which he or she answered six or more of the eight questions before failing to do so on two basal passages in a row.

The information which I obtained from the IRI's helped me to plan lessons during reading period for Daisy, Jeff, Mike, and Paul. I made a chart entitled "Tentative Profiles Obtained from Informal Reading Inventory" so I could compare the three major aspects of reading ability for each child. Based on these findings, on my analysis of the types of errors that each child made, and on my observation of the children in class, I set up a general program for each child.

Tentative Profiles Obtained from Informal Reading Inventory

Name	Word Identification Level	Reading Comprehension Level	Listening Comprehension Level
Daisy	2^2	3^1	4
Jeff	5	3^2	3^2
Mike	1^2	2^2	5
Paul	2^1	2^1	2^1

Daisy: Clear expectations and goals are to be included. Daisy certainly has the capacity to improve her reading, but her personality and attitude seem to be holding her back. Place her in a 3^1 book and hold her to it.

Jeff: Emphasize interest and knowledge about the world. Jeff has good word identification abilities, but he needs help expanding his background of information. Start independent projects with a variety of informational books, biographies, and realistic fiction.

Mike: Attention to the words seems to be needed here. Mike is a bright and verbal boy, but he is too restless to take the time to visually analyze print. In order to build some responsibility and basic word recognition abilities, have Mike work with a child in a lower grade who needs much of the same word analysis abilities.

Paul: An even profile here, but depressed scores in all areas. Seems to catch on slowly. Try to get Paul and Daisy to work together in a "study-buddy" arrangement where they share responsibility for each other. If Paul becomes overpowered by Daisy, get him into an individual program.

November

This class and I are moving steadily toward a balance among whole-class, small-group, and individual projects. In general, I want to be in front of the whole class presenting lessons, leading discussions, and providing directions about one-third of the time. I like to spend another third of my time circulating about the class, dealing with individual problems that occur as students work through their various assignments. Finally, I want to spend the other approximately one-third of my time instructing students in small groups and individually.

My small-group and individual instruction calls for me to get with selected students and lead them through a lesson. In reading/literature period, for example, I frequently sit with a group and review the vocabulary in a short story. In math, I might sit with some students and help them compose word problems that fit the mathematical operation we are studying at that time. In social studies, I frequently review vocabulary with students, and I have presented several specific lessons on reading maps to those who are ready for such instruction.

The key to maintaining this balanced instruction is to ease students into working responsibly on their own. And in all five subject areas, my students are choosing the order in which to complete their assigned tasks. In fact, the children had been completing their activities in whichever order they chose and turning them in by the deadline quite well, so this month I began allowing the children to choose among the tasks.

It was Larry who pointed out to me that the time had come to begin allowing more decision making. "I would like to try this experiment in page 115 of our science text, Mr. Dunn," he said, "but you have us doing this other one. Would you mind if I did the one on my own?"

Did I ever love that question!

The next day, I told the class that they could choose any three of the four activities listed on the board. They were to complete the activities in whatever order they liked. They could do all four if they wanted, but the assignment was to complete three. I purposely included activities that varied in difficulty. This way, students like Paul and Daisy could participate fully with the class on easier tasks, and students like Larry and Hilda could be challenged by more difficult tasks.

I offered choices this month in the subject areas other than science, too. The tasks were always related to the central topic we were studying, but they varied according to how difficult they were and the type of ability they required. I regularly offered the choice of reading and responding to some material other than the basic material being used. In social studies, for instance, we studied the Middle Ages. For one assignment, the class could choose to read one of three short stories that were

Half-Open Classroom

about King Arthur and the Knights of the Round Table. The stories ranged in difficulty from about a third-grade level to seventh-grade level. After reading their story, each child could respond to it by either writing a summary, drawing a picture of their favorite scene, or describing how Camelot differed from our town. I made it very clear that this was one task for them, but that they could decide among variations within the task. I should mention, too, that we had worked on summarizing in our language arts period, so everybody had at least an idea of what to do if they chose that activity.

A big problem that I encountered again this month with offering choices is the lack of appropriate materials for my students. It's tough finding things that relate to the same topic but that are written at different levels for each subject area. I continually am on the lookout for materials that contain pertinent information but that don't frustrate my various readers. My filing drawers are filling up now, and I am sure they will become more full as I continue teaching.

I tape recorded many crucial passages from the different textbooks, but this is not the best answer to my problem. Alexander needed this help, but his hearing loss interfered with him listening to the tape with a group. He needed to listen to it on his own. Jeff, Paul, and Daisy rarely could understand even the taped version of the text. The material was just too dense. So actually my taped portions of the books were most appropriate for Butch, Mort, Tanana, and Mike. And goodness knows the difficulty they had working together! I will continue using the tapes, but I know that my best hope is to locate easy-reading materials for these students.

I did adjust my students' assignments by varying the purposes, amounts of text, and degrees of response structure while working with one passage. [See pp. 155–158.] This way they all worked on the same text, but they dealt with that text differently. Next month, I'll begin translation writing with those who need it. [See pp. 446–447.]

Routines   Although my attempts to create a half-open classroom are mostly successful, there have been some hitches. Chip turned in a summary of a story for reading/literature that looked suspiciously similar to one Horace had turned in a few days earlier. I confronted the two of them and was ready to launch into a big discussion about cheating when the looks on their faces stopped me.

"Honest, Mr. Dunn, I wrote that on my own," said Chip. He went on to explain that he and Horace had read the same story and that they had talked about it, but he maintained that he had written his summary independently.

After some more talking, I realized that I had accused them unjustly, and so I apologized. Luckily, they were mature enough to realize that even teachers make mistakes. I'll bet that if I had wrongly accused Daisy of cheating she would never have let me forget it!

The thing that especially bothered me about that episode with Chip and Horace is that I really want my students to work together. In fact, two, three, or even four students often work together and turn in a joint project. Copying and cheating can be a problem if one makes a big deal about grading every piece of paper that comes in and if a lot of work-sheet-type, circle-the-correct-answer assignments are made. But copying and cheating seem to be less of a problem in classrooms that encourage cooperation and allow somewhat creative responses.

"Test formation" has become my best remedy for the occasional kid who does tend to use somebody else's answer. I use test formation when I want to be absolutely sure that the children's products come only from each child. Tanana told me about test formation, saying that it was the way they took tests at her old school. I first tried it when I administered the group inventory in social studies last month, and I intend to use it more and more often. In test formation, the children spread throughout the room, and each child sits at an isolated position. I moved a few children at first just to make sure that they could not easily see another's paper. I explained to them that I occasionally needed an uncontaminated measure of their performance so that I would know exactly how they were doing. We discussed the differences between an inventory (when I want to find out what they know for the purpose of planning lessons) and a test (when I want to find out what they know for the purpose of assigning a grade). I then explained that I would not even trust my own mother in the seating arrangement we normally used because even she would not be able to resist sneaking a quick peek at another's paper. Thus, I said flatly, "When I need to take inventory or administer a test, the class needs to get into test formation." They seem to have accepted this procedure.

This month closed with a visit from Daphne's grandmother. Mrs. Field was concerned that Daphne was developing some very bad habits. **Reading Interests** "Mr. Dunn, maybe you can help us decide what to do. This fall my husband and I have noticed that Daphne is hard to get up in the morning. Every year before, she's always jumped right out of bed. The other night I went to her room after midnight and there she was under the cover with a flashlight reading a Nancy Drew book!

"I asked the public librarian and she said that Daphne has checked out over 15 of them in the past two months. We want her to read better books than that. What do you think we ought to do?"

I tried to reassure her. "Daphne has been reading Nancy Drew books in SSR every day since school started. Frankly, I think you should encourage her to read even more."

Mrs. Field frowned slightly. "You mean you allow them to read those series? Aren't all the books alike, anyway?"

"Series books have some positive attributes," I explained. "They interest many children in reading. Once the reading habit is formed, books of greater literary quality can be introduced. These books also provide lots of easy reading which is the way many children practice the skills they have learned in reading instructional time at school. Don't worry, every good reader I've known read both comic books and one or more juvenile series at Daphne's age. If these books didn't cause them to be good readers, they at least didn't prevent them from becoming good readers.

"I would suggest that you give Daphne time to read before she goes to bed so that she won't miss her sleep. I agree with you that she needs proper rest, but please don't be alarmed about these mysteries."

I haven't heard any more about it, but Daphne has continued to read Nancy Drew during SSR. Whether that 15 minutes a day is all the Nancy Drew she gets is another question!

Many of the other students have locked onto a favorite author or two and are reading them exclusively. Betty, Tanana, Daphne, and Joyce have discovered Judy Blume's books; Horace, Mitch, and Alex are going through Edgar Rice Burroughs' old Tarzan of the Apes series; and Mandy and Pat are trading stories by Richard Peck.

December

My attempts in the five subject areas to achieve a balance among whole-class, group, and individual instruction has been moving steadily this month. I still move gradually because I've seen some quite chaotic classes where the teacher one day simply opened everything up to learning centers and individualization without preparing the class. If anything, I may prepare the class for independence too slowly.

But whatever the case, most of my students have been working quite well choosing their own assignments and finishing them in the order they choose. Consequently, I have become better and better able to work with small groups and individuals. I'm sure that much of the reason for this group cooperation is the fact that my materials and assignments have been adjusted to allow practically every student a good deal of success. By easing this class into making choices with materials and assignments that they can handle, I am able to work more effectively with small groups and individuals. Furthermore, students require materials that are written at appropriate levels if they are to learn the information and also improve their abilities to learn. Easing students into a half-open classroom situation allows them the opportunity to deal with such materials.

Meaning Vocabulary—Topical Word Sets

In fact, I've been able to spend extra time emphasizing meaning vocabulary in the subject areas now that the class is working so smoothly. This month I used capsule vocabulary (Crist, 1975) to develop understanding of geometry terms during math period. For the first part of the lesson, we sat as a group and discussed the topic of geometry. I had selected the following ten words which the group needed to know:

Geometry Terms for Capsule Vocabulary

point	plane
polygon	perpendicular
line segment	ray
angle	triangle
parallel	line

As we discussed geometry, I made a conscious effort to introduce the ten terms in meaningful context even though I had to occasionally force the conversation in order to allow the word to fit. "The wall in front of me can be considered a *plane*," I said at one point. "The wall behind me is a *parallel plane*, then, and the walls on either sides are *perpendicular planes*." The students copied these words into their math notebooks, and we continued using them in discussion until everyone felt that they understood their meanings.

In the second part of the lesson, the students paired off for one-to-one talk sessions. The requirement was that each student use each one of the new words in a meaningful context at least once while talking to the other. For instance, I overheard this part of the conversation between Manuel and Steve:

MANUEL: Yesterday, when we played softball during recess the ball came off my bat at a funny *angle*. It didn't go *parallel* to the ground; it went straight up.

STEVE: Yeah, it almost went *perpendicular* to the ground. As for me, I hit a ball that broke the *plane* between second base and third base. I actually got a hit into left field!

MANUEL: Uh, huh. Well, I played second base, and I was looking at the base paths. Did you realize that some form a *ray*? Well they do! The one going from second to first, and the one going from second to third form *rays*. What do you think about that?

I always set a timer when we do one-to-one conversations like this because they tend to get a little looney if I allow them to just go on and on. But when the children know that they only have a little time, they usually work in a much more concentrated manner. Indeed, Larry and Danielle really got going, and I'm sure that they each used each term at least four times in entirely different contexts.

After applying the new terms in conversation, each student then wrote a short paper using all the new words in a meaningful context. Sometimes I collect the papers and check them for proper inclusion of the specific words, and sometimes I have the original one-to-one pairs look over each one's paper for proper use of the words. With this lesson, I include reading, writing, speaking, and listening development along with the math content which I am responsible to teach.

Meaning Vocabulary— Webbing

In order to review the ten geometry terms a few days after our capsule vocabulary lesson, I had the students web them [see pp. 151–152]. We still are at this basic level of organizing information, although after Christmas I intend to jack up the pace of instruction in organization. I had the students form their pair groupings again and web the ten words. Since we've been webbing terms in all the subjects since September, this was a fairly easy task for most children. Anthony and Steve, my whizzes in math and science but who are so-so in the other areas, produced a logical web.

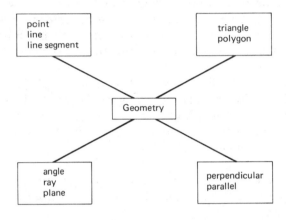

Geometry Web

Both boys were able to explain why they grouped the words that way, and they could justify different groupings, also.

Adjusting Instruction

Good news! I think a breakthrough is being made with Mike! That child certainly has his good and bad days, but lately his good days are beginning to outnumber his bad ones. Just last week he made it through an entire day without picking on Rita even once! I'm sure that there are a number of reasons for this change in his behavior, but I believe his tutoring the second grader is part of it. After administering the IRI, I found that word identification was his major weakness. He knew surprisingly few words at sight, and his use of context plus initial sound was weak. His listening comprehension scores indicated that he certainly knew the meanings of lots of words and that he could process the information he received. I looked into his permanent file for some additional information and saw that he was not here at Merritt for third and fourth grade. As a result, we don't know what type of instruction he was getting out of state. The file did confirm the fact that he could be a bit of a behavioral problem.

With my information about Mike, I decided to see about having him tutor a younger child. I figured this way Mike could work with quite easy reading materials and still save face. I also thought that the responsibility of caring for a younger child might help him mature a bit. However, when I contacted Mrs. Flame about my proposal, she was dubious, to say the least.

"Mr. Dunn," she exclaimed, "you don't realize the nights I spent in tears because of the mean things Mike had done in my classroom!"

She eventually agreed that we could set up Mike with a second grader who had some reading abilities but who could benefit from some extra individual attention with word identification. (I do believe that Mrs. Flame has come a long way since her first year of teaching as Miss Nouveau!) We established a three-day-a-week schedule for Mike and Jimmy, the boy to be tutored. Mrs. Flame provides lessons for the boys for two days; the third day is devoted to Mike reading books aloud that Jimmy wants to hear. All I can say is that having special responsibility for another person and being able to work comfortably with easy materials without losing self-esteem seems to have given Mike a boost that he sorely needed.

My other youngsters with "major difficulties" in reading are involved in their special programs during our 8:45 to 9:30 reading/literature period, too, but changes with them are not so obvious as with Mike. Jeff is reading and comparing animal stories at present. Since his word identification is rather well developed, we decided that he would read about a certain topic and that we would get together once a week in order to compare the information he is learning. Miss Page, the librarian, was able to help Jeff find a good number of books and magazines about animals since that was the topic he chose. He reads and we discuss animal books such as *The Wounded Wolf* (George, 1978), *Little Rascal* (North, 1965), *Tyrannosaurus Rex* (Selsam, 1978), and *Snails* (Zim, 1975) along with informative magazines like *Ranger Rick** and *National Geographic World** that often contain features on animals.

Daisy and Paul were started in a rather structured program largely because they seem to need clear goals and tangible evidence of progress. Daisy, especially, won't budge unless she knows exactly what she is to do. She then will do the activity at a minimal level of acceptability. On the other hand, Paul is willing to extend himself, but he seems to get lost once he does so. He will read a passage all the way through, but

* See Appendix B.

then he has great difficulty manipulating the ideas in a thoughtful or creative way.

The program I've devised for them is based largely on materials from high-interest, low-vocabulary book series and on collections of high-low short stories and informational passages. The high-low book series consists of hard cover books made up of about eight chapters each, with word identification and comprehension activities that correspond to each chapter. I have a chart for Daisy and Paul to keep in their personal folders. They fill in a section of the chart each time that they complete a chapter of the book and its corresponding activities. After finishing an entire book, they choose and complete at least one written composition and one artistic response.

In addition, Paul and Daisy regularly choose at least one short story or informational passage from a high-low collection to read on their own and discuss with me. I meet with these two at least once a week for about 20 minutes in order to discuss what they have chosen and to provide specific word identification and comprehension instruction with those materials. The "dynamic duo" typically take something away from our sessions to complete as follow-up and practice to my instruction.

During SSR I have noticed that Mike, Jeff, Daisy, and Paul have had some difficulty locating materials to read. We do have a stack of comic books, but few students choose them any more. In fact, Butch and Mort are about the only students who still read them. My students with "major difficulties" seem content to flip through magazines and the newspaper. I've suggested that they try some of the high-low paperback novels that are available, but none of the four have yet taken me up on them.

Content Journal Writing

Our content journal writing is going a bit more smoothly than it did at first. I still need to suggest topics and specific perspectives on a topic for many of the students to write about, but about half of the class can get started on their own. I have not collected the journals for any type of evaluation, although I do occasionally ask to see somebody's just to check on the quantity of writing. I have noticed that my own writing during this period has improved in fluency, and I imagine that my students' writing has improved, also.

Although I want my class to write about either science or social studies topics during our content journal writing time, they are including personal topics in their journals, too. This fact burst to light last week in class when Roberta slugged Butch. We had quite some turmoil there when Butch hit Roberta back and they started yelling at each other. I got everything settled down, marched the two outside, and got the explanation: Roberta had written in her journal that she "liked" Mitch, and Butch had read her journal and was telling everyone about it. Butch and I had a long talk about private property, he apologized to Roberta, and life in the fifth grade became settled once again.

January

January often seemed like September: it felt as though we were starting anew. The first few days after the holidays were a bit hectic as we reestablished the routine that was so carefully nurtured the first four months of school. After a while, though, everyone got back into the swing of things, and I was able to regain my balance among large-group, small-group, and individual instruction.

Comprehension Lesson

January typically is a time to begin teaching new things or begin approaching instruction differently. In my case, this month signaled the beginning of my attempts to develop my students' abilities to learn independently. Up to this time, in the subject areas I had been deciding what materials the students should read and the purposes they should have for reading them. Even though I had allowed my students to choose many of their materials and activities, I was the one who dictated what the possible materials and activities would be.

In order to help develop independent learners, I focussed first on teaching students to select important information on their own. My plan for doing this began in the second week of January. One day during reading/literature period I kept the class together and showed them a picture of an aircraft carrier that I had cut out of a magazine. "If I had a book about aircraft carriers, what could I learn?" I asked. At first everyone was quiet because they were somewhat used to being told what they would be learning.

Finally, Larry spoke up, "I think we could learn how something that big and heavy can float on top of the water."

Pat thought she would learn the name of the carrier and how many sailors it held.

Mitch was tentative, but he finally blurted out, "We could learn whether the ship can get close enough to shore so the guns and airplanes can blow up a town!"

When the time was up for suggesting what we might learn about aircraft carriers, I explained how each student could become a better reader by following this same procedure with material that they were reading.

After putting the picture away, I presented a short, expository passage that was about the U.S. Navy's battleships. We surveyed the passage as we normally did before reading any informative materials, and then I asked the class, "What do you think you can learn from this passage?" I listed their responses on the chalkboard. Because this activity was so similar to what we had just done with the picture, the responses came much more easily.

"I think we can learn how many ships the navy has," ventured Alex.

Larry was sure that we would learn something about the U.S. Navy's submarines because he noted the picture of one along the side of one page and he saw the subheading entitled "Submarine Warfare." When I probed for a specific aspect to learn, he decided that we probably could learn the advantages and disadvantages of submarines versus surface craft.

Roberta suggested that we could learn when women first were allowed to join the navy, even though she could not point out any evidence in the passage that indicated coverage of that topic.

After the children listed what they thought could be learned from the passage, I read it to them. This way, everybody was able to receive the information, and they finished receiving it at the identical time. We then followed up the list on the board by noting which items actually were covered in the passage.

During the next few days during reading/literature period, I conducted this same activity using another passage with groups of randomly assigned students. They seemed to become rather good at determining what they thought they could learn from the passages.

As a follow up, I had the class get into test formation, and I put up an overhead transparency that was made from a page in the social studies textbook. My question to the class was, "What do you think you can learn from this passage?" I collected the papers and took them home in order to see who needed further work with anticipating meaning from a passage.

Meaning Vocabulary— Morphemes   Although I've been emphasizing anticipating meaning throughout the subject areas, I continue to place a large emphasis upon meaning vocabulary. We do capsule vocabulary lessons frequently, and I always have students first determine the meaning of new, unfamiliar terms by noting the information that is contained in the passage about those terms. We spend time relating past experiences and previously encountered concepts to the new concepts encountered in passages. Word origins are discussed (Betty informed us just recently that "boycott" comes from a British army officer, C. C. Boycott, who was the first victim of this tactic), and the special meanings of technical terms are pointed out. For example, while studying "Coal Mining and Steel Manufacturing" in social studies we encountered that troublesome term, "coke." I brought in a piece of charcoal as a rough example of this substance. I explained that coke is distilled from coal and that it can produce the terrific heat necessary to separate iron ore from waste rock. After this rather thorough explanation and demonstration, Jeff volunteered the opinion that he would never drink another coke now that he knew where it came from. I'm still not sure if he was kidding or not!

One vocabulary activity that we regularly pursue during subject matter instruction is to note words that contain frequently occurring morphemes. Rather than use the terms *morpheme, prefix, root, suffix, contraction,* and *compound,* we use the phrase *meaningful word part.* Whenever I am introducing or reviewing subject area vocabulary that contains meaningful word parts, I point them out. Sometimes I simply underline the meaningful parts if the words are written on the chalkboard, and sometimes I ask a group of students to identify the parts in words that have them. I always point out how that part contributes to the formation of the word. For example, one of the geometry terms that we studied last December contained a meaningful word part that occurred in other words frequently enough to warrant attention, so I pointed out that part to the class. I underlined the *tri* in *triangle* and pointed out how it contributed to the meaning of the word. Next, I listed *tricycle* and *triplane* underneath *triangle* in order to reinforce the way *tri* functioned. We constructed sentences with the words to keep this exercise meaningful. Then, as one of the choice activities for this unit, the students were to list at least five words that contained *tri* as a meaningful part and make up sentences that included their words.

Alexander and Steve got together and produced the following list:

"Tri" Words

trilogy	triplet
tricycle	triannual
trio	trilingual
triple	

Later I put these words on the board, and we noted how the pronunciation of the part could change drastically, but that the meaning stayed the same. Hilda was quick to point out that the *tri* in *trilogy, triple,* and *triplet* was pronounced one way, that it was pronounced another way in *trio,* and still another way in *tricyle, triannual,* and *trilingual.*

Daisy got a little angry with me because she had recorded *trial, tribe,* and *trigger* among her *tri* words. When I explained to her that *tri* did not refer to "three" in those words, she became sullen. What a shame! I have shown this class that *father* is not made up of *fat* and *her* and that looking for meaningful word parts doesn't always work. I've tried to demonstrate how this word-analysis technique is useful when it is used while attending to the context of a passage. Looking for meaningful word parts doesn't always help students figure out words, but pronouncing words, recognizing them at sight, and attending to the way they are used in a passage don't work in isolation, either. However, word analysis techniques are worthwhile when readers learn to let them interact with each other. Besides, meaningful word parts frequently occur in technical, content area vocabulary, and noting them helps students get a handle on the new terms.

I was totally surprised when Larry, Horace, and Danielle took *poly* from our geometry term *polygon* and created a list of *poly* words. They came up with *polygamy, polyester, polyglot,* and *polyhedron.* They were quite proud of themselves and assured me that they understood the meanings of all their terms. They just might! I had decided not to introduce *poly* to my fifth graders for what I thought was a good reason. Even though *poly* occurs frequently as a meaningful part in many words, those words are rarely encountered by students in the fifth grade. If I were teaching ninth grade math or science, then I probably would have presented it. At present, highlighting more common, meaningful parts such as *tri* allows students to attend to that particular element, and it helps children become accustomed to noting meaningful word parts.

TRY IT OUT

See how the vocabulary in a subject matter textbook for the fifth grade can present students a serious challenge. In order to do this, locate an appropriate text and mark off any ten pages. Then identify the terms that you would need to introduce to your students [see p. 139]. What direct and indirect experiences could you call on to connect those terms with your students' lives? Which terms contain morphemes that you think would help students?

February

Reading Interests

Paula Danziger has been discovered. I had noticed that our class singing after lunch had been wearing down a bit and that the class seemed to be losing interest in it. During the holiday season we had done great justice to all the traditional carols from "Deck the Halls," to "O Tannenbaum," to "God Rest You Merry, Gentlemen." But that was over now. There still were some favorite songs such as "Where Have All the Flowers Gone?" and "Ode to Billy Joe," but after about the one-hundreth rendition even they had become stale. In order to maintain interest and keep the "group commonality" time intact, I decided to read a book to the class one chapter per day.

I first chose Judy Blume's *Tales of a Fourth Grade Nothing* (1976), and the class loved it. Even though several students had read it already, they listened and laughed along with the others. *Superfudge* (1980) came next, and it, too, was a hit. After I read the first chapter of Paula Danziger's *The Cat Ate My Gymsuit* (1975), Pat, Rita, and Joyce came up and wanted to know if she had written any other books. When I told them about her other books, they wanted to go immediately to the library and check out *The Pistachio Prescription* (1978), *Can You Sue Your Parents for Malpractice?* (1979), and *There's a Bat in Bunk Five* (1980). So now there is a new craze for Paula Danziger books.

I still am amazed at how people select one author and read everything which that person has written. This seems true for series as well as nonseries books that are written by the same person. For example, during SSR I've noticed that Daphne still is reading her Nancy Drew stories. Horace, Mitch, and Alex switched from Tarzan of the Apes stories and are now into Lloyd Alexander's Chronicles of Prydain. And Mandy and Pat have discovered Tolkein.

Another interesting point about these fifth-graders' reading interests is their fascination with informative books. Butch has been perusing *Tell Me Why* books, and he does take the time to really study some of the entries. Anthony has his own collection of science-oriented books at home which he brings in, and Paul has taken to an easy reading collection of animal books that is well illustrated and documented. Students at this age do like to read to learn as well as to be entertained.

My plan for developing independent learners is continuing still. The directed reading and listening activities that I do with the whole class and small groups is devoted more and more to helping them articulate what information deserves attention. I want them to decide beforehand, and afterward, what they should attend to in a passage. The activities I conducted last month on anticipating meaning with the U.S. Navy passages is one way to get children to do this.

Comprehension Lesson

One activity, The Mag Bag, that we did during language arts period got the class quite involved in independent learning. This idea came from an article I had read in the *Journal of Reading* (Adams, 1980). To begin, I brought in duplicate copies of popular magazines. The class divided themselves into groups based on interests such as sports, fashion, and the environment, and each group went through the magazines and found an article they thought interesting. After locating an appropriate article, they had three tasks. First, they created a poster to advertise the article. Headlines, blurbs, and pictures were included in the posters. (I brought in duplicate copies of the magazines partly because they had to be cut up to make these posters.) Second, the students prepared a 6″ × 8″ file card that contained complete bibliographic information about the article. Of course, I gave them a model of how to cite the articles. An identical number was written on the poster and on the card so other students could match them later. Finally, on the back of the cards each group wrote a question or two that would guide a person's reading of the article. For instance, Horace and Mitch worked together on an article about the human heart. They decided that the most important information in the article was about heart attack, so they asked two questions: "What are the most common causes of heart attacks?" and "What can people do to guard against heart attacks?"

After preparing the posters and file cards, these two items and complete, original issues of the magazines were placed in the classroom library area. The file cards were placed in a box by numbers. This way, just before SSR, students could study the posters to locate an article that seemed interesting. Then they noted the number of the poster, got its corresponding file card, and used the bibliographic information on the card to locate the correct magazine. This was a good precursor to locating information in the library, and it got the class to independently figure what was important in the articles.

Another activity that got at attending to important information used index cards, also. After guiding the class through a science passage about invertebrates in the ocean, the students formed pairs. To begin this activity, each person wrote four questions which they thought dealt with the most important information in the passage. For instance, Joyce wrote the following questions:

1. What are sponges?
2. How do jellyfish get food?
3. How do sea anemones get food?
4. Why is a coral really an animal?

After writing the questions, the partners traded cards and attempted to answer each other's questions. Then, after writing down their answers, the partners decided which questions would be best for a whole-class quiz. They rank-ordered their questions and turned them in to me. As promised, I gave a short quiz the next day using the class's own questions.

That day Tanana came up to me and complimented me for allowing them to write their own questions. I asked why she liked doing it, and her reply showed a lot of insight.

"For the first time I felt like I was in charge of the book," she said. "I had to decide what we needed to know; I couldn't just wait for you to tell us what to study for."

I knew that I had my curriculum guide to help me lead this class to the important information, and I knew I had my own opinions about what was important, but Tanana's mature comment helped remind me that children need to develop this ability for themselves.

March

Unit Development— Locating Information This was the month to emphasize locating information independently. We continued our study of the ocean during science period, and as a group we watched films and filmstrips, read passages from the text and from magazines I had saved, discussed our various experiences at the beach, and did several activities such as guided reading procedure and webbing. In addition, I listed five activities for independent work and allowed the students to choose any three. The final thing they were to do was choose any animal that lived in the ocean, gather all the information they could about that animal, and write a report on it. This last assignment was the culmination of much preparation. To prepare the class for their individual reports, I listed categories of information about animals so that the class would know what to look for and so their reports would be well organized. The following list of categories was put on the board:

Information about Ocean Animals

Type of animal (fish, mammal, mollusk?)
Appearance (How big is it? What does it look like?)
Location (Where is it found? Describe its habitat.)
Eating habits (What does it eat? How does it eat?)
Relation to humans (How does it help or harm humans?)

After describing these categories of information, I passed out copies of an ocean animal report that was completed last year in my class. This provided a model for this year's class. Everyone seemed to be obtaining a fairly good idea of what to look for. Since we had worked on selecting important information in passages throughout the past few months, I figured most students would be able to identify what should be included in each category from what they were reading. And since we had done several one-paragraph essays [see pp. 165–166], I figured most students would be able to write fairly well-formed paragraphs for each of the five categories of information. The missing component of this project was the ability to locate materials that contained appropriate information about particular animals. With this in mind, I told them all to remember which animal they had chosen to study, but that we had some preliminary things to learn. Then I turned to Miss Page, our librarian, for help.

Miss Page said we could have a 45-minute period each afternoon in the library for two weeks to work on our projects. But first, she said, she would show the class how to locate information. On our first day in the library, she taught the class for me and introduced the concept of subject indices. First, everyone was given a xeroxed copy of the index of a book on animals. To see if everyone could use an index, she dictated ten topics for each student to find. She gave topics such as "skeleton," "teeth," and "veins" and the students wrote down the page numbers where information on each topic could be found. Everyone then traded papers, and she read out the correct page numbers. No one missed any, of course, since this task only required the ability to locate a word and the ability to copy its corresponding page number.

Next, she showed them the *Reader's Guide to Periodical Literature*. As they grouped around her, she took a topic suggested by a student and looked it up for them as they watched. This task, too, seemed simple enough. She gave another list of topics, and the class spent the rest of the period writing down bibliographic information of the articles that were found under Miss Page's topics.

At the beginning of the next day in the library, Miss Page checked the students' references for the topics she had provided. Eventually, everyone had listed the correct materials which the *Reader's Guide* listed under the topics. Then she showed how to obtain the various magazines and journals from the library's collection.

"Hey, Mr. Dunn," Mitch called, "this system works almost like our 'Mag Bag' system."

"You're catching on," I thought to myself.

Finally, Miss Page demonstrated the use of the card catalogue. This time students suggested topics for which she searched and showed them what she found. If a subject were not listed, she asked for another one and searched for it. Most of the class was used to going to the card catalogue to locate a book by its title or author, but using the card catalogue by subject was a new task for most students.

At the end of the lesson, everyone was asked to write the answers to two questions:

1. How are the index of a book, the *Reader's Guide to Periodical Literature*, and the card catalogue alike?
2. How is each one different from the other two?

When all the students were finished writing, we discussed the answers to the two questions.

Following this lesson, Miss Page and I figured that this group of students had the prerequisites for locating information in a library. They knew what subject indices were and the principle on which they work. And they knew how to use the *Reader's Guide* and the card catalogue.

For the next few days, either Miss Page or I helped the students locate a book given as a source by the card catalogue, or a periodical given to them by consulting the *Reader's Guide*. We were into our ocean animals research full blast now. Most of the students could already find books by their Dewey Decimal System or Library of Congress number, which reflected their experience with this and other libraries.

The class seemed to enjoy this time in the library. They had used the library many times for obtaining books for pleasure reading, but now they seemed to feel rather grown up using it for obtaining information. Even Mike paid close attention to Miss Page's directions about how to locate information. He likes to know how things work, and learning how the library worked was no exception. This group had located information within materials such as encyclopedias, atlases, other textbooks, and newpapers before, but learning how to obtain those reference books in the first place was new to them.

A problem did arise, however, with selecting topic words. Chip wanted to investigate conches because his grandfather had brought him a conch shell from the Indian Ocean. He had that shell on top of his dresser in his bedroom, so he knew that there was such a thing. However, he couldn't find *conch* listed in either the *Reader's Guide* or the card catalogue.

"Now what am I supposed to do?" he moaned. "I'm stuck."

I helped Chip locate information about conches by going through the key words *shellfish* and *mollusk*, and then I raised Chip's predicament with Miss Page. She agreed that predicting key words to locate information was a problem and suggested that I prepare a lesson to develop that ability. I mentioned that I thought that she might have a "predicting key words" lesson handy, but she assured me in her good natured way that she didn't.

"Mr. Dunn," she said, "I'd love to help you, but I'm afraid you'll have to do this one on your own. I am totally inundated trying to keep up with my cataloguing. But be a dear, do let me know what you come up with . I'm sure it will be very useful to me in the future."

"Boy, is she smooth!" I thought. "Not only do I need to come up with an entirely new lesson, but I need to share it with her. I guess flattery *will* get you everywhere."

Like many abilities that are part of reading to learn, the ability to predict key words for locating information is a complex one. The lesson I used to develop this ability had two parts. First, the class tried to think of all the possibilities for key words given a particular topic. Then they tried to determine which of those possibilities would most likely yield the desired information.

The sample topic we chose was last month's holiday, Valentine's Day. Using a chalkboard, they brain-stormed all the possible key words which, regardless of source used, might yield information about Valentine's Day. We listed the following possible key words:

Valentine's Day Key Words

hearts	Cupid
St. Valentine	romance
Valentine's Day	February
holidays	February 14
love	red
candy	saints
greeting cards	

After compiling the list, we considered each item as a possible key word for use in researching Valentine's Day. After the discussion, everyone wrote down three topic words to consult and handed in these choices. I sorted the ballots and placed votes by the items in our list as they had been chosen by the group.

Four possible key words received the most votes by far: *St. Valentine, Valentine's Day, holidays,* and *February 14.* As a group, we then discussed why these four might be better than the others.

The follow-up activity for this lesson was to go the library with the key words the class had selected, and to use those key words to see if information could be found about that topic. Alexander, Manuel, and Carl were selected, and they reported the next day that there was a wealth of information about Valentine's Day under *Valentine's Day* and *holidays* in the *Reader's Guide,* card catalogue, and various encyclopedias. Thank goodness!

This month closed with the students' written reports on ocean animals being one of the highlights. Within the limits I had set, they had selected their own topics, organized their search, located appropriate sources of information, gathered the important data, and reported it in one paper. Of course, the finished products varied in quality quite a bit, but even my students with the weakest reading and writing abilities had the opportunity to learn independently from printed materials.

TRY IT OUT

Mr. Dunn's unit on ocean animals differs from Ms. Maverick's unit on the students' home state. How are these units different? How are they similar? Also, compare Mr. Dunn's procedures with the suggestions contained in the section of Chapter 5 entitled "Unit Approaches." Finally, if you were presenting a unit of study on ocean animals to a class of fifth-grade students, what might you do that differs from the activities Mr. Dunn describes?

This was the month of caterpillar jokes! What monster have I created?

Early in the month during science class we were discussing the four stages of metamorphosis of certain insects. As a part of this lesson, Butch and Mitch each brought in live caterpillars in a jar. In a moment of weakness, I asked the class, with a straight face, "What do you call a baby caterpillar?"

When no one responded, I answered, "A kitty-pillar!"

Everyone laughed loudly at the joke, and we went back to discussing insect development. Before long, Horace raised his hand, "When does a caterpillar go the fastest?" After a short pause, he said, "When it's being chased by a dogerpillar!" This, of course, brought a new round of laughter.

Ever since, during recess, lunch, and, occasionally, in class there has been an epidemic of caterpillar joke telling. Some of my favorites have been these:

Q: What did the caterpillar say when it climbed into its cocoon?
A: See you next moth!

Q: What do you call a caterpillar who finks on his friends?
A: A dirty ratterpillar!

Q: Where do crazy caterpillars go?
A: To the cuckoo-n.

Q: What is green and breaks into your house?
A: A caterpillar burglar.

There were many more. Why children at this age love jokes like these, I don't know. When I was in the fifth grade, we told elephant and grape jokes. (Why was the elephant hiding in the grape tree? He had welched on a bet and gotten himself into a jam.)

I thought about a way to capitalize on this interest in caterpillar jokes and decided that a graffiti bulletin board would be my best bet. I planned to wait until the middle of April to put up a sheet of white construction paper on the back wall. This would be a nice end-of-the-year type of activity. There would be the opportunity for movement and the intrigue of seeing what new inscriptions were written on the board.

April

April began with a controversy over a book. I was reading *The Little Fishes* by Erik Haugaard (1967) each day after lunch. Never have I had such interest in a book on the part of the students. It is a sad tale about orphan beggars in Italy during World War II, and it is beautifully told. When I read it, everyone was totally still and quiet. It was not unusual to see tears in certain eyes when the story became especially intense.

Censorship

One day when we were a little over half finished with the book, an office messenger brought a note from Mrs. Mainstay. Daisy's mother had called and wanted permission to visit our room while I read aloud to the class. Of course, I returned a message to the office that she was welcome to come.

The next day, just as I opened *The Little Fishes* at our place and began reading, there was a knock on the classroom door. The door opened and in came Daisy's mother. Naturally, she was welcomed and given a chair; then I continued with our reading. Some of what I read included a part in which the main characters are captured by a cruel and unscrupulous man. The students were on the edge of their seats, including

Daisy. Even Paul seemed interested in what was going on. In the middle of my reading, Daisy's mother stood and stalked out of the room. I didn't hesitate in my reading. Daisy sat glued to her chair.

Within a few minutes, I was called to the office. When I arrived, Mr. Topps and Daisy's mother were there. I went in and closed the door.

Daisy's mother was seething as Mr. Topps turned to me. "Mr. Dunn, Daisy's mother is disturbed about the book you are reading to your students." Facing her, he said, "Would you please tell us your objection to the book."

"I certainly will! I try to protect Daisy against this kind of book. When she told me what she was hearing at school, I just had to hear it for myself."

"And what is she hearing?" asked Mr. Topps.

"About beggars and wars and cruel people. Sad, unhappy stories. Children are supposed to be happy. They should always have what they need to be happy."

("And be spoiled and lazy like Daisy," I thought, but didn't say.)

Mr. Topps paused momentarily and then explained. "If you do not want Daisy to hear the rest of the book, she may come to the office during that time and study her lessons here. Meanwhile, I will read a copy of the book and I recommend that you do the same. When you have read the book, if you are still concerned about it, you may come and we will discuss it."

I left the office and returned to my classroom. From then on, when I was to read from the book, Daisy had to go to the office and sit. I felt sorry for her. She didn't have to hear anything unhappy; she only had to be unhappy.

Locating Information   As a follow-up to developing abilities to predict key words for locating information, I brought in a collection of telephone books that Ma Bell had graciously donated. I listed the types of phone calls I wanted to make, and the class found the page numbers in the yellow pages where I should look. For instance, the class discovered that to locate a doctor, one looked under the key word *physician*; to locate a kitchen oven, one looked under *ranges and stoves*; and to locate a store that sold baseballs, one looked under *sporting goods*. I discovered that my "predicting key words" lesson actually was a good lesson on organizing information. It's amazing how so many language arts abilities are interrelated!

Unit Development   Independent research projects were conducted in social studies this month according to the same general plan which we followed in science. I still was rather directive about the general topic and the report format, but there was enough room for individual decisions that allowed each final product to be unique. The general topic this time was the 50 United States, and each student chose a different one to investigate.

Again, we set out a common outline so that everybody would work toward the same general goal. However, this time I had the class decide what specific aspects of the topic deserved investigation. I knew they had studied a unit on our home state last year in Ms. Maverick's class, so I thought they would be in a good position to decide on those aspects.

Mort suggested researching amusement parks in the 50 states, and Daisy wanted to do restaurants.

"Very funny," I replied. "Let me give you a better perspective on why you are investigating your state. Let's say that your family is going to move out of our state, but they haven't decided where to go. They have asked you to help. Your mission, class, should you decide to accept it, is to convince your family either to move to or else avoid the state you have chosen."

Well, this livened things up a bit because this new perspective helped them focus their thinking. After all, "doing" a state is a rather global and abstract task; convincing your family of the relative desirability of moving somewhere is a much more compelling endeavor.

"We need to find out about the weather," Tanana volunteered. "My family likes the cold."

"What about deer hunting?" asked Mitch. "My dad won't go anywhere unless he will be able to take us hunting."

Larry suggested that we had better find out what the job situation was since that was important, and Jeff wanted us to be sure to figure out how far the state was from where we lived. He gets carsick. Mike, the old pro who actually had done some moving, offered the fact that we should find out about the various cities so we would know exactly where to move once we had gotten to the state.

We kept this up for five minutes, and then we organized the categories of information on the chalkboard. Again, these categories allowed each student to pursue an individual topic within a set of common guidelines. We decided that the following areas deserved special attention:

Information about the State

Location (How far away from our state is it? How long would it take to travel to by car? Where is it in relation to neighboring states?)

Weather (What are the temperature ranges in various locations? Is it warmer or colder than where we are already?)

Industry (How easily could your father and/or mother find a job?)

Major cities (Where are the major cities? Which city seems best for your family?)

Vacation spots (Where could you go within the state for a weekend visit?)

With these categories of information in mind, we descended upon Miss Page once again. However, this time the group had a much better notion of how to locate the information that would satisfy their particular reasons for reading.

After about ten minutes in the library, Betty and Hilda came up to me with a question that revealed a great idea. "Can we write to our states requesting information about these five areas?"

"Of course!" I thought, "Why didn't I think of that?"

Talk about activity. Addresses for state and city chambers of commerce were located, letters were drafted, newspapers were being consulted for weather reports, and a multitude of reference books and trade books were checked out for information about specific states. Students were even using our social studies textbook as a reference, which probably is its best use.

I did get with Mike, Jeff, Paul, and Daisy at individual times in order to provide as much direction as possible. These four, and a few others in the class, easily got lost in such research projects. I made certain that they got off letters to their respective chambers of commerce and helped them locate understandable materials about their states. Luckily, there were such materials! I also made a deal with each of the students: if three of the five areas were investigated thoroughly, then that would be enough.

"You certainly can do all five, but you don't need to," I told Daisy.

"Why? Because I'm dumb?" she asked.

"You're not dumb, Daisy, but you do have some difficulty reading and writing. And I would rather see a few things done well than a lot of things done sloppily," I replied.

The final products this time were much more elaborate than the science research projects! When the class worked on ocean animals, they were rather intent on completing in a straightforward fashion the outline which I had presented. But this time many students completed the outline through some rather creative means. Mandy and Pat teamed up and put together a travel brochure of their state that was patterned after the ones they received in the mail. Several students produced relief maps of their states following the procedure they had learned in Ms. Maverick's class. Posters of vacation spots were in evidence everywhere. Everyone turned in a written report dealing with the areas of investigation, but the compositions were directed toward their parents and guardians rather than me. Most students wrote their reports as personal letters to their families detailing the advantages and disadvantages of moving to their chosen state. I believe the class found this perspective more meaningful, and I do know that their writing was better planned and more complete than usual.

Writing Reports

"Since these final reports are going home," I told the class, "I want them to be as letter perfect as possible. Here's how to do that. Choose a partner that you can work with and have that person read your paper for proper spelling and sentence construction. In other words, find someone, trade papers, and edit each other's paper. Then I'll take a final look at your edited papers."

Most of the final projects were in quite good shape, although Paul and Mort submitted papers with room for much improvement. Paul's report basically consisted of the promotional materials he had received in the mail. But at least he had received them and arranged them! He was after me every day after we had mailed his request to see if he had gotten anything. He was elated when the fat envelope finally came with his name on it. (I bet a personal subscription to a magazine or comic book would do him much good.) Mort just went through the motions with this project. I wish I knew how to motivate that guy!

READ SOME MORE ABOUT THIS

If you were in Mr. Dunn's position, what additional things might you do to motivate Mort? Consult the following references in order to list ways to stimulate Mort to become actively involved in reading:

Ciani, A. J., Ed. *Motivating reluctant readers*. Newark, Del.: International Reading Association, 1981.

Noland, R. G. and Craft, L. H. Methods to motivate the reluctant reader. *Journal of Reading*, 1976, 19, 387–391.

The practice we had writing one-paragraph essays during the year paid off during these independent projects. Most students were able to focus their writing on one topic at a time during their letter writing. My task, then, was to show them how to organize their specific topics so that they logically followed each other within their letters. We already had listed the five main categories of information, so I went around to individuals and helped them organize their topics/paragraphs within each category. For instance, Horace had chosen a large state, so I helped him list the cities in order of importance under the heading "Major Cities." One thing I have learned from these projects is that reading abilities alone do not make students good researchers. There are quite a few written composition abilities that need to be developed, also.

I ran into Mr. Topps after school the other day, and I asked him what had ever happened about Daisy's mother, if she had come back or called.

Censorship

"No, Ed, I think we defused that situation pretty well. Censorship is a deforming and incurable disease, and, once caught, there is little that can be done about it. The main thing that can be done to prevent it is to have parents place their faith in the school, and to handle individual complaints in a firm and reasonable manner the way I tried to in this case. Once people come hunting for ideas and books to censor, it no longer is possible to have a good instructional program.

"As long as you are able to point out specific and worthwhile reasons for using the materials you do, then we should be in good shape. If matters do get any worse, then you might list the books you intend to read to your whole class and the time period when each book will be presented. We'll send that timetable out to each child's parents or guardians. They have the responsibility, then, to read the books. If they want their child removed from your class while a certain book is being read, then I guess they have that right. But first, let's wait and see if any other parents complain."

I wanted to say "Thank you for standing by me," but Mr. Topps was already walking toward a child who was waving at him and thoroughly enjoying being noticed by the school principal.

May

When spring comes, the sap rises, and it has certainly risen in my students! Pat and Horace are obviously in love, and Rita is constantly following Larry around and writing him notes. Daisy seems to have her eye on Mitch, but he pays absolutely no attention to her.

Literature Response Activity   In reading/literature period, we completed a unit on prejudice that went over rather well. I began this unit by reading *Roll of Thunder, Hear My Cry* by Mildred Taylor (1978) to the whole class. Most students seemed to realize for the first time not only how pervasive prejudice can be, but also how an author can present a theme such as prejudice through a novel. Afterward, I set out multiple copies of various short novels and short stories for the class. For instance, William Armstrong's novel *Sounder* (1969), was made available, and Shirley Jackson's short story, "After You, My Dear Alphonse (1943)," was provided.

The students' assignment was basically the same in all cases. They were to write a short paper or else explain to me verbally the instances of prejudice which the materials portrayed. This assignment had been modeled beforehand with *Roll of Thunder, Hear My Cry* when I displayed a short composition one of last year's students had written about the prejudice Cassie encountered in that story. By providing this model, everyone had an idea of how to write their own composition. This lesson was similar to the research projects we had done in science and social studies. The students knew what to read for and how to report what they read, and they were able to choose materials that were written at various levels of difficulty. The difference between this lesson and the two others was that here I located the materials to be read, and the project was shorter. No one complained about that.

Note Taking   We did one final activity this month to continue developing abilities to learn independently. I called it an "open-notes" quiz. We had practiced writing notes that corresponded to outlines of passages throughout the year [see pp. 166–167], so the idea of note taking was familiar to the class. Indeed, the independent projects they had undertaken with ocean animals and the 50 United States had called for note taking to be applied. This particular application activity began with me telling everyone that they would have a quiz on a section of the science textbook that dealt with the formation of mountains. They were to be able to compare the effects of volcanic action, folding, and faulting on mountain formations. However, they had time to take notes on the section of the text that dealt with mountain formations, and they could use those notes during the quiz. I met in a part of the room with whoever wanted to read the section orally and decide as a group what notes to make. Most of the class found this activity worthwhile, especially after they all did so well on the quiz.

The graffiti bulletin board turned out to be a good idea for this time of the year. It gave the class an opportunity to express themselves, and they did so in a clever way. The students began writing their names beside their contributions so they would get proper exposure for their creation. Some of the jokes were quite witty:

Q: What do you call a caterpillar who eats hamburgers?
A: A pattykiller. (Horace)

Q: Where does a caterpillar go to wash up?
A: A larva-tory. (Mitch)

Q: What did the caterpillar aunts say about their baby niece?
A: What a cute-rpillar. (Joyce)

Q: Why was the cocoon embarrassed?
A: Because his butterfly was open. (Butch)

When I saw Butch's contribution, I had to do a little soul searching. I didn't want to become a censor, especially after my episode with Daisy's mother. But I didn't intend to let my students use improper language in front of me and gain my implicit approval, either. I finally decided that Butch's joke was no more offensive than a lot of prime time television jokes which parents allowed in their homes, so I let it go.

Diagnosis

I took a careful look this month at the four students who had special reading programs this year in order to estimate the impact my individual plans had on them. I administered an IRI that was equivalent to the one I had given originally. That is, I obtained measures of each student's word identification, reading comprehension, and listening comprehension abilities with word lists and passages that were equally difficult but different than the ones they had seen in October. By far, Mike demonstrated the greatest improvement. Frankly, I'm not sure if I'm more pleased with his change in behavior or his change in reading abilities. Working on reading with Jimmy, the second grader, seemed to help Mike grow up. He needed some real responsibility. His word identification moved up to a 3^2 level, and he understood the fourth-reader passage satisfactorily. He read fluently until he came upon some rather unfamiliar words that he simply couldn't figure out. Mike still has quite a bit of catching up to do, but he certainly appears to be on the right track. And Mrs. Flame reports that Jimmy made good progress this year, too, although she thought Mike clearly had progressed the most. In tutor-tutee relationships, the tutor often does show the most improvement.

Jeff's scores showed improvement although not as dramatically as Mike's. Jeff stayed with his independent projects throughout the school year, and his reading and listening comprehension levels did go up a year. However, I can't truthfully say that his reading abilities have actually improved. His scores may have gone up simply because he learned so many new words and gained so much new information. At least that's part of developing good readers in school! If anything, Jeff can now locate a lot of new material to read.

Paul's profile remained uniformly depressed, although he seemed to have improved slightly in all areas. Apparently I didn't find the key to unlock the world of reading for him, but my continued attention helped him progress at his even, slow pace. He's becoming a better reader, but it's a terrifically slow process. I shudder when I think what his self image and his reading abilities would be if he had not been in as caring and professional a situation as we have here at Merritt.

And Daisy. I am beginning to see some positive things for her in the future. During the past few months she seems to have begun assuming a bit of direction and self-motivation. She put a little more effort than usual into her science and social studies research projects this spring. And during SSR she began reading real books rather than thumbing slowly through the old magazines and comic books we had. The books she got into were Daphne's Nancy Drew favorites, but at least she's reading. It's likely that her individual program which led her through complete books was the stimulus. Her IRI scores are at the juncture between fourth- and fifth-grade level, and that's not too bad for her. All of her teachers thought that she could read better if she would only extend herself to the task. Well, it looks as though she's beginning to do so.

In all, this class seemed to have become accustomed to independently learning from text. They chose individual assignments that called for learning as part of my half-open classroom, they spent a good deal of time learning how to select important information, and they were led through two rather extensive research projects. A good amount of time was spent developing their understanding of topics, concepts, and verbal labels. I think these students definitely are ready for middle school!

THE MEETING AT THE MIDDLE SCHOOL

Ed Dunn sat quietly by Mr. Topps as the middle school language arts teachers filed into the small meeting room at their school. The expressions on their faces indicated that they were as excited about going on vacation as he. They were smiling and kidding each other about what they would do with their upcoming vacation. For most of them, it seemed that their families and summer school at the university would take much of their time, and they were enthusiastic about the change.

Mr. Topps had known since April that he would be the new principal at Upton Hill, and he was meeting with small groups of teachers at that school ever since. He thought the meetings would help make for a smoother transition, and, so far, everyone agreed.

When all the teachers were present, Mr. Topps closed the door and introduced Mr. Dunn. "Ed has done an excellent job with his students this year and I wanted him to share some of his ideas with you. He has emphasized some of the areas with which you teachers are most concerned."

Ed, in his usual serious and businesslike manner, stood to address these teachers. "To demonstrate how my type of reading program fits in with other types, it might be useful to talk about stages in the development of reading ability. I believe there are four stages in that development:

1. The reading readiness stage
2. The beginning reading stage
3. The intermediate reading stage
4. The reading-to-learn stage

"The reading readiness stage begins at the birth of the child, continues through the development of oral language, and ends when the child knows what reading is, knows what it is for, and desires to learn how to do it. A kindergarten program like Miss Launch teaches at our school is really an attempt to bring this stage to a successful completion.

"Upon completion of the readiness stage, the child is able to benefit from formal reading instruction. For some children, the beginning reading stage starts in kindergarten; for others, it does not start until much later. A first-grade teacher like our Mrs. Wright would have most of her students at this stage, although she would still have some students at the readiness stage.

"The beginning reading stage is over when material exists which the student can and does read silently without instruction or help from anyone. Mrs. Wright tells me that many of her students are reading pre-primer and primer stories independently by the end of the first grade.

"The intermediate reading stage continues from the first successful attempts at independent, silent reading until students become quite adept at seeking out, selecting, and self-pacing their reading through a variety of books. Most second and third graders are becoming more sophisticated in their ability to read this way.

"However, if students are to thrive academically, they must become able to learn from what they read independently. Mr. Ditto, who currently teaches fourth grade at Merritt School, tries to take students from the intermediate reading stage into the reading-to-learn stage.

"Now we have reached the point where I come in. By the time many of my students reach fifth grade, they have had such excellent instruction year after year that they have reached the reading-to-learn stage. Given an assignment or study question, they are able to comprehend and recall information from written material. In part, my job is to continue developing students' abilities along this line. This is quite important because of the huge volume of literature, language arts, math, science, and social studies content which my students are expected to learn.

"In addition, I attempt to help students determine for themselves what information in a passage deserves attention. I believe that we want students to take what they read and independently decide what to learn. If I continue asking all the questions and setting all the purposes, then the class comes to depend totally on me to tell them what is important in a passage. I lead my class through many activities and two substantial research projects in order to develop this ability to independently decide what is important to learn. But I have not finished the job.

"Our elementary school students still require the ability to ask their own questions and seek their own answers. I always provided a general topic, and specific guidelines for organizing information as my class read in order to learn. But when they reach middle school, they will be expected to do many of these same tasks totally independently."

Mr. Dunn sat down. One of the language arts teachers spoke up, "I have a question, Mr. Dunn. What do you do when you have students who are at different stages of development in their reading ability?"

"Miss Stern," Ed responded, "you've raised the issue that probably causes the most difficulty in classrooms. It would be an unusual class without students from several stages. In my class this year, for example, I had at least two students still in the beginning reading stage, and two others still in the intermediate reading stage. Of course, the other students who were able to read to learn did so with widely varying degrees of success. "There are several approaches to differentiating instruction, and instruction must be differentiated to some degree if students at various stages of reading development are to benefit from school.

"In essence, I followed a dual approach. On one hand, I varied the tasks that were required with a single material. If a passage from the textbook were assigned, then I tape recorded the passage for those who needed it. I provided extra guidance through the text for those who needed it, too. Students often paired up to work on the textbook assignments together. But on the other hand, I varied the materials as often as possible. The textbook was quite difficult, so we read magazine articles, library books, and newspaper clippings. We completed research projects with materials from the classroom, from the library, and from the mails. I made every attempt to locate readable, outside information that dealt with the topics we were studying in our subject areas.

"As for my students with major reading difficulties, I tested them individually to determine what was holding them back. I then set up individual plans to be followed during a special time of the day that got at the cause of their reading difficulty."

Mr. Topps interrupted at this time to make a final comment because it was time to end the meeting.

"At Merritt Elementary School we help all students become the most successful readers that is possible. We try to provide the right instruction with the right materials at the right time. We think we do a good job helping students learn from what they read and become more and more responsive to what they read. But our students only begin their journey into the world of print while they are with us in elementary school. They will continue their journey while they attend middle school, high school, and beyond. We have provided them a solid foundation of reading abilities and attitudes, but they will never be finished adding to those abilities and attitudes."

References

Chapter 1

Allen, R. V. and Allen, C. *Language experiences in reading*: *Teachers' resource book*. Chicago: Encyclopedia Brittanica Press, 1966.

Chomsky, C. Write first, read later. *Childhood Education*, 1971, 47, 296–299.

Chomsky, C. Approaching reading through invented spelling. In L. B. Resnick and P. A. Weaver, Eds., *Theory and practice of early reading*, vol. 2. Hillsdale, N.J: Erlbaum, 1979.

Clay, M. M. Early childhood and cultural diversity in New Zealand. *The Reading Teacher*, 1976, 29, 333–342.

Clay, M. M. *Reading: The patterning of complex behavior*. Exeter, N.H.: Heinemann Educational Books, 1979.

Durkin, D. *Teaching young children to read*, 3rd ed. Boston: Allyn and Bacon, 1980.

Durrell, D. D., Nicholson, A., Olson, A. V., Gavel, S. R., and Linehan, E. B. Success in first grade reading. *Journal of Education*, 1958, 140(3), 2–48.

Gambrell, L. B., and Wilson, R. M. *28 Ways to help your child be a better reader*. Paoli, Pa.: Instructo/McGraw-Hill, 1977.

Mayer, M. *A boy, a dog, and a frog*. New York: Dial Press, 1967.

Morris, D. Beginning readers' concept of word. In E. H. Henderson and J. W. Beers, Eds. *Developmental and cognitive aspects of learning to spell: A reflection of word knowledge*, Newark, Del.: International Reading Association, 1980.

Read, C. Preschool children's knowledge of English phonology. *Harvard Educational Review*, 1971, 41, 1–34.

Read, C. *Children's categorization of speech sounds in English*. Urbana, Ill.: National Council of Teachers of English, 1975.

Slepian, J. B. and Seidler, A. G. *The hungry thing*. New York: Scholastic Book Services, 1971.

Stauffer, R. G. *The language experience approach to the teaching of reading*. New York: Harper and Row, 1970.

Steiner, C. *I am Andy*. New York: Knopf, 1961.

Taylor, J. Making sense: The basic skill in reading. *Language Arts*, 1977, 54, 668–672.

Templeton, S. What is a word? In E. H. Henderson and J. W. Beers, Eds., *Developmental and cognitive aspects of learning to spell: A reflection of word knowledge*. Newark, Del.: International Reading Association, 1980.

Tierney, R. J. and Mosenthal, J. A critical look at macro-analyses of text. *Perspectives on Reading Research and Instruction, Twenty-ninth Yearbook of the National Reading Conference*, 1980, 29, 126–130.

Waterhouse, L. H., Fischer, K. M., and Ryan, E. B. *Language awareness and reading*. Newark, Del.: International Reading Association, 1980.

Chapter 2

Artley, A. S. Phonics revisited. *Language Arts*, 54, 1977, 121–126.

Cunningham, P. Teaching were, with, what, and other 'four-letter words.' *The Reading Teacher*, 34, 1980, 160–163.

Dolch, E. *Problems in reading*. Champaign, Ill.: Garrard Press, 1948.

Durkin, D. *Teaching young children to read*, 3rd ed. Boston, Mass.: Allyn and Bacon, 1980.

Goodman, K. S. Reading: A psycholinguistic guessing game. *Journal of the Reading Specialist*, 1967, 6, 126–135. Reprinted in H. Singer and R. B. Ruddell, Eds., *Theoretical models and processes of reading*, 2nd ed. Newark, Del.: International Reading Association, 1976.

Harris, A. J. and Sipay, E. R. *How to increase reading ability*, 7th ed. New York: Longman, 1980.

Heilman, A. W. *Phonics in proper perspective*, 4th ed. Columbus, Ohio: Charles E. Merrill, 1981.

Horn, E. A. Principles of method in teaching spelling as derived from scientific investigation, chap. II. *Eighteenth Yearbook, Part II, National Society for the Study of Education*. Bloomington, Ill.: Public School Publishing Company, 1919.

Otto, W. and Chester, R. Sight words for beginning readers. *Journal of Educational Research*, 1972, 65, 435–43.

Chapter 3

Anderson, R. C. The notion of schemata and the educational enterprise: General discussion of the conference. In R. C. Anderson, R. J. Spiro, and W. E. Montague Eds., *Schooling and the acquisition of knowledge*. Hillsdale, N. J.: Erlbaum, 1977.

Anderson, R. C. Schema-directed processes in language comprehension. In A. M. Lesgold, J. W. Pellegrino, S. D. Falkbema, and S. R. Glaser, Eds., *Cognitive psychology and instruction*. New York: Plenum Press, 1978.

Beck, I. L., McKeorun, M. G., Mc Caslin, E. S., and Burkes, A. M. *Instructional dimensions that may affect reading comprehension: Examples from two commercial reading programs*. Learning Research and Development Center, University of Pittsburgh, 1979.

Britton, B. K. Use of cognitive capacity in reading: Effects of processing information from text for immediate recall and retention. *Journal of Reading Behavior*, 1980, 12, 129–137.

Britton, B. K., Holdredge, T. S., and Westbrook, R. D. Reading and cognitive capacity usage: Effects of text difficulty. *Journal of Experimental Psychology: Human Learning and Memory*, 1978, 4, 582–591.

Britton, B. K., Zieglar, R., and Westbrook, R. D. Use of cognitive capacity in reading easy and difficult text: Two tests of an allocation of attention hypothesis. *Journal of Reading Behavior*, 1980, 12, 23–30.

Cooper, J. L. *The effect of adjustment of basal reading materials on reading achievement*. Unpublished doctoral dissertation, Boston University, 1952.

Durkin, D. What classroom observations reveal about reading comprehension. *Reading Research Quarterly*, 1978–1979, 14, 481–533.

Durkin, D. Reading comprehension instruction in five basal reader series. *Reading Research Quarterly*, 1981, 16, 515–544.

Ekwall, E. E. Should repetitions be counted as errors? *The Reading Teacher*, 1974, 27, 365–367.

Ekwall, E. E. *Diagnosis and remediation of the disabled reader*. Boston: Allyn and Bacon, 1976.

Ferguson, G. A. *Statistical analysis in psychology and education*, 3rd ed. New York: McGraw-Hill, 1971.

Johnson, D. and Pearson, P. D. *Teaching reading vocabulary*. New York: Holt, Rinehart and Winston, 1978.

Jorgenson, G. W. Relationship of classroom behavior to the accuracy of the match between material difficulty and student ability. *Journal of Educational Psychology*, 1977, 69, 24–32.

Lake, M. L. Improve the dictionary's image. *Elementary English*, 1971, 48, 363–365.

Rumelhart, D. E. Schemata: The building blocks of cognition. In R. J. Spiro, B. C. Bruce, & W. F. Brewer, Eds., *Theoretical issues in reading comprehension*. Hillsdale, N. J.: Erlbaum, 1980.

Strange, M. Instructional implications of a conceptual theory of reading comprehension. *The Reading Teacher*, 1980, 34, 391–397.

Taba, H. *Teachers' handbook for elementary social studies*. Palo Alto, Calif.: Addison-Wesley, 1967.

Thorndike, E. L. Reading as reasoning: A study of mistakes in paragraph reading. *The Journal of Educational Psychology*, 1917, 8, 323–332.

Vaughn, S., Crawley, S., and Mountain, L. A multiple-modality approach to word study: Vocabulary scavenger hunts. *The Reading Teacher*, 1979, 32, 434–437.

Chapter 4

Professional Sources:

Allington, R. L. If they don't read much, how they ever gonna get food? *Journal of Reading*, 1977, 21, 57–61.

Anderson, W., and Groff, P. *A new look at children's literature*. Belmont, Calif.: Wadsworth, 1972.

Huck, C. *Children's literature in the elementary school*, 3rd ed. New York: Holt, Rinehart and Winston, 1979.

Hunt, L. C. Six steps to the individualized reading program (IRP). *Elementary English*, 1971, 48, 27–32.

McConaughy, S. H. Using story structure in the classroom. *Language Arts*, 1980, 57, 157–165.

Moore, J. C., Jones, C. J., and Miller, D. C. What we know after a decade of sustained silent reading. *The Reading Teacher*, 1980, 33, 445–450.

Rosenblatt, L. M. *Literature as exploration*, rev. ed. New York: Noble and Noble, 1968.

Sutherland, Z., Monson, D. L., and Arbuthnot, M. H., *Children and books*, 6th ed. Glenview, Ill.: Scott, Foresman, 1981.

Children's Books:

Berenstain, S., and Berenstain, J. *Inside, outside, upside down*. New York: Random House, 1968.

Blume, J. *Superfudge*. New York: E. P. Dutton, 1980.

Branley, F. M. *Flash, crash, rumble, and roll*. New York: Thomas Y. Crowell, 1964.

Burch, R. *Queenie Peavy*. New York: Viking, 1966.

Carroll, L. *Alice's adventures in Wonderland*. New York: Franklin Watts, 1966.

Chernoff, G. T. *Just a box?* New York: Scholastic Book Services, 1971.

Cobb, V. *More science experiments you can eat.* New York: Lippincott, 1979.

Garelick, M. *What's inside?* New York: Scholastic Book Services, 1968.

George, J. *My side of the mountain,* New York: E. P. Dutton, 1959.

Ginsburg, M. *Mushroom in the rain.* New York: Macmillan, 1974.

Hughes, L. April rainsong. In *The dream keeper and other poems.* New York: Alfred A. Knopf, 1932.

Jackson, J., and Perlmutter, W. *The endless pavement.* New York: Seabury, 1973.

Kipling, R. *The elephant's child.* From the *Just so stories.* New York: Doubleday, 1952.

L'Engle, M. *A wrinkle in time.* New York: Farrar, Straus, and Giroux, 1962.

Leokum, A. *Still more tell me why.* New York: Grosset and Dunlap, 1968.

Lobel, A. *Frog and toad together.* New York: Harper and Row, 1972.

Milne, A. A. *Winnie-the-Pooh.* New York: E. P. Dutton, 1926.

Rawls, W. *Where the red fern grows.* New York: Doubleday, 1961.

Sendak, M. *Where the wild things are.* New York: Harper and Row, 1963.

Schulevitz, U. *Dawn.* New York: Farrar, Straus and Giroux, 1974.

Speare, E. G. *The witch of Blackbird Pond.* Boston: Houghton Mifflin, 1958.

Sperry, A. *Call it courage.* New York: Macmillan, 1940.

Taylor, M. D. *Roll of thunder, hear my cry.* New York: Dial Press, 1976.

Viorst, J. *Alexander and the terrible, horrible, no good, very bad day.* New York: Atheneum, 1975.

White, E. B. *Charlotte's web.* New York: Harper and Row, 1952.

Wiese, K. *You can write Chinese.* New York: Viking, 1945.

Wise, W. *In the time of the dinosaurs.* New York: Scholastic Book Services, 1963.

Zemach, H., and Zemach, K. *The princess and the froggie.* New York: Farrar, Straus and Giroux, 1975.

Zweifel, F. *Pickle in the middle and other easy snacks.* New York: Harper and Row, 1979.

Chapter 5

Anderson, T. H. and Armbruster, B. B. *Studying.* Technical Report No. 155. Urbana: University of Illinois, Center for the Study of Reading, January, 1980.

Barron, R. F. Research for the classroom teacher: Recent developments on the structured overview as an advance organizer. In H. L. Herber and J. D. Riley, Eds., *Research in reading in the content areas: the fourth report.* Syracuse, N.Y.: Reading and Language Arts Center, Syracuse University, 1979.

Barufaldi, J. P., Ladd, G. T. and Moses, A. J. *Heath science.* Lexington, Mass.: D. C. Heath, 1981.

Britton, J., Burgess, T., Martin, N., McLeod, A. and Rosen, H. *The development of writing abilities: 11–18.* London: Macmillan Education, 1975.

Daigon, A. Rhetorically based and rhetorically deficient tasks: An explanation. In J. A. Meagher and W. D. Page, Eds., *Language centered reading instruction.* Storrs, Conn.: The Reading-Language Arts Center, The University of Connecticut, 1980.

Earle, R. A. and Morley, R. The half-open classroom. *Journal of Reading,* 1974, 18, 131–135.

Fulwiler, T. Journals across the disciplines. *English Journal,* 1980, 69, 14–19.

Greene, F. P. Radio reading. In C. Pennock, Ed. Reading comprehension at four linguistic levels. Newark, Del.: International Reading Association, 1979.

Herber, H. L. *Teaching reading in content areas*, 2nd ed. Englewood Cliffs, N.J.: Prentice-Hall, 1978.

Joyce, B. and Weil, M. *Models of teaching*. Englewood Cliffs, N. J.: Prentice-Hall, 1972.

McKee, P. *The teaching of reading in the elementary school*. Boston: Houghton Mifflin, 1948.

Moore, D. W. and Arthur, S. V. Possible sentences. In J. E. Readence, E. K. Dishner, and T. W. Bean, Eds. *Reading in the content areas: Improving classroom instruction*. Dubuque, Iowa: Kendall/Hunt, 1981.

Postman, N. *Teaching as a conserving activity*. New York: Delacorte Press, 1979.

Preston, R. C. and Clymer, E. *Communities at work*. Boston: D. C. Heath, 1964.

Stauffer, R. G. *Teaching reading as a thinking process*. New York: Harper and Row, 1969.

Weener, P. Notetaking and student verbalization as instrumental learning activities. *Instructional Science*, 1974, 3, 51–74.

Chapter 6

Betts, E. A. *Foundations of reading instruction, with emphasis on differentiated guidance*. New York: American Book Company, 1946.

Botel, M. *How to teach reading*. Chicago, Ill.: Follett Educational Corporation. 1968.

Cooper, J. L. The effect of adjustment of basal reading materials on reading achievement. Unpublished doctoral dissertation, Boston University, 1952.

Goodman, K. S. Reading: A Psycholinguistic Guessing Game. In H. Singer and R. B. Ruddell, Eds., *Theoretical models and processes of reading*. Newark, Del.: International Reading Association, 1970, pp. 259–72.

Goodman, Y. M. and Burke, C. L. *The reading miscue inventory*. New York: Macmillan, 1972.

Nunnally, J. C. *Psychometric theory*. New York: McGraw-Hill, 1967, pp. 172, 175.

Pikulski, John. A critical review: Informal reading inventories. *The Reading Teacher*, 1974 28, 2, 141–51.

Powell, William R. Reappraising the criteria for interpreting informal inventories. In D. De Boer, Ed., *Reading diagnosis and evaluation*. Newark, Del.: International Reading Association, 1970, pp. 100–09.

Spache, G. D. *Diagnastic reading scales*, rev. ed. Monterey, Calif: CTB/McGraw-Hill, 1972.

Tuinman, J. J. Asking reading-dependent questions. *Journal of Reading*, 1971, 14, 5, 289–92, 336.

Chapter 8

Anderson, R. C. Schema-directed processes in language comprehension. In A. M. Lesgold, J. W. Pellegrino, S. D. Fakkema, and R. Glaser, Eds., *Cognitive psychology and instruction*. New York: Plenum Press, 1978.

Baron, J. Mechanisms for pronouncing printed words: Use and acquisition. In D. LaBerge and S. J. Samuels, Eds., *Basic processes in reading*: *Perception and comprehension*. Potomac, Md.: Erlbaum, 1976.

Diehl, W. A. and Mikulecky, L. The nature of reading at work. *Journal of Reading*, 1980, 24, 221–227.

Frederiksen, C. H. Representing logical and semantic structure of knowledge acquired from discourse. *Cognitive Psychology*, 1975, 7, 371–458.

Grimes, J. E. *The thread of discourse*. The Hague, Netherlands: Mouton, 1975.

Halliday, M. A. K. *Language as a social semiotic*: *The social interpretation of language and meaning*. Baltimore, Md.: University Park Press, 1978.

Halliday, M. A. K., and Hasan, R. *Cohesion in English*. London: Longman, 1976.

Chapter 9

Aardema, V. *Why mosquitoes buzz in people's ears*. New York: Dial, 1975.

Burton, R. *The elephant's nest*. New York: Harper and Row, 1979.

Cuyler, M. *The all-around pumpkin book*. New York: Holt, Rinehart and Winston, 1980.

Ginsburg, M. *Mushroom in the rain*. New York: Macmillan, 1974.

Hogrogian, N. *One fine day*. New York: Macmillan, 1971.

Lansky, V. *The taming of the C. A. N. D. Y. monster*. Wayzata, Minn.: Meadowbrook Press, 1978.

LeSeig, T. *Ten apples up on top*. New York: Random House, 1961.

Lionni, L. *In the rabbitgarden*. New York: Pantheon, 1975.

O'Neill, M. *Hailstones and halibut bones*. New York: Doubleday, 1961.

Sendak, M. *Where the wild things are*. New York: Harper and Row, 1963.

Seuss, Dr. *Green eggs and ham*. New York: Random House, 1960.

Slepian, J. B. and Seidler, A. G. *The hungry thing*. New York: Scholastic, 1971.

Steiner, C. *I am Andy*. New York: Knopf, 1961.

Ungerer, T. *Crictor*. New York: Harper and Row, 1958.

Chapter 10

Taba, H. *Teachers' handbook for elementary social studies*. Palo Alto, Calif.: Addison-Wesley, 1967.

Chapter 11

Hardin, B. and Bernstein, B. Twelve reading ideas we know and love. *Teacher*, 1978, 95, 49–51.

Spiegel, D. L. Six alternatives to the directed reading activity. *The Reading Teacher*, 1981, 34, 914–920.

Chapter 12

Armstrong, W. *Sounder*. New York: Harper and Row, 1969.

Cunningham, P. ARRF! A book that fits! *The Reading Teacher*, 1976, 30, 206–07.

O'Dell, S. *Island of the blue dolphins*. New York: Houghton-Mifflin, 1960.

O'Neill, M. *Hailstones and halibut bones*. New York: Doubleday, 1961.

Pillar, A. Individualizing book reviews. *Elementary English*, 1975, 52, 467–469.

Snyder, Z. K. *The Egypt game*. New York: Atheneum, 1967.

———. *The changeling*. New York: Atheneum, 1970.

———. *Below the root*. New York: Atheneum, 1975.

Steig, W. *Sylvester and the magic pebble*. New York: Simon and Schuster, 1969.

Tiedt, I. Exploring poetry patterns. *Elementary English*, 1970, 47, 1083–1084.

Veatch, J. *Reading in the elementary school*. New York: Ronald Press, 1966.

Chapter 13

Burton, W. H. *The guidance of learning activities*. New York: Appleton-Century-Crofts, 1952.

Cunningham, P. M. Transferring comprehension from listening to reading. *The Reading Teacher*, 1975, 29, 169–172.

Manzo, A. V. Guided reading procedure. *Journal of Reading*, 1975, 18, 287–291.

Morrison, H. C. *The practices of teaching in the secondary school*. Chicago: University of Chicago Press, 1931.

Preston, R. C. *Teaching social studies in the elementary school*, New York: Holt, Rinehart and Winston, 1968.

Chapter 14

Adams, J. S. The mag bag. *Journal of Reading*, 1980, 23, 294–295.

Armstrong, W. H. *Sounder*. New York: Harper and Row, 1969.

Blume, J. *Superfudge*. New York: E. P. Dutton, 1980.

Blume, J. *Tales of a fourth grade nothing*. New York: Dell, 1976.

Crist, B. I. One capsule a week—a painless remedy for vocabulary ills. *Journal of Reading*, 1975, 19, 147–149.

Danziger, P. *The cat ate my gymsuit*. New York: Dell, 1975.

Danziger, P. *The pistachio prescription*. New York: Delacorte, 1978.

Danziger, P. *Can you sue your parents for malpractice*? New York: Delacorte, 1979.

Danziger, P. *There's a bat in bunk five*. New York: Delacorte, 1980.

Earle, R. A., and Morley, R. The half-open classroom: Controlled options in reading. *Journal of Reading*, 1974, 18, 131–135.

George, J. *The wounded wolf*. New York: Harper and Row, 1978.

Haugaard, E. *The little fishes*. Boston: Houghton Mifflin, 1967.

Jackson, S. After you, My Dear Alphonse. *The New Yorker*, 1943, 18, 51–53.

North, S. *Little rascal*. New York: E. P. Dutton, 1965.

Selsam, M. *Tyrannosaurus Rex*. New York: Harper and Row, 1978.

Taylor, M. *Roll of thunder, hear my cry*. New York: Bantam, 1978.

Zim, H., and Kranz, L. *Snails*. New York: William Morrow, 1975.

Appendix A

BOOKS ABOUT CHILDREN'S BOOKS AND WAYS TO USE CHILDREN'S BOOKS

Anderson, W. and Groff, P. *A new look at children's literature*. Belmot, Calif.: Wadsworth, 1972.

Association for Childhood Education International. *The world in children's picture books*. Washington, D.C. 1968.

Bettelheim, B. *The uses of enchantment*. New York: Alfred A. Knopf, 1976.

Bleich, D. Readings and feelings: *An introduction to subjective criticism*. Urbana, Ill.: National Council of Teachers of English, 1975.

Carlson, R. K. *Enrichment ideas*, 2nd ed. Dubuque, Iowa: William C. Brown, 1976.

Chambers, D. W. *The oral tradition: Storytelling and creative drama*, 2nd ed. Dubuque, Iowa: William C. Brown, 1977.

Cianciolo, P. *Illustrations in children's books*, 2nd ed. Dubuque, Iowa: William C. Brown, 1976.

Fader, D., Duggins, J., Finn, T., and McNeil, E. *The new hooked on books*. New York: Berkley Publishing Corporation, 1976.

Fisher, M. *Who's who in children's books*. New York: Holt, Rinehart and Winston, 1975.

Hopkins, L. B. *Books are by people*. New York: Citation Press, 1969.

Hopkins, L. B. *More books by more people*. New York: Citation Press, 1974.

Huck, C. *Children's literature in the elementary school*, 3rd ed., updated. New York: Holt, Rinehart and Winston, 1979.

Lamme, L. L., Ed. *Learning to love literature: Preschool through grade 3*. Urbana, Ill.: National Council of Teachers of English, 1981.

Larrick, N. *A parent's guide to children's reading*, 4th ed. New York: Doubleday, 1975.

Lonsdale, B. J. and MacKintosh, H. K. *Children experience literature*. New York: Random House, 1973.

Monson, D. L. and McClenathan, D. K., Eds. *Developing active readers: Ideas for parents, teachers, and librarians*. Newark, Del.: International Reading Association, 1979.

Monson, D. L. and Peltola, B. J. *Research in children's literature: An annotated bibliography*. Newark, Del.: International Reading Association, 1976.

Reasoner, C. F. *Releasing children to literature*. New York: Dell, 1968.

Reasoner, C. F. *Where the readers are*. New York: Dell, 1972.

Reasoner, C. F. *When children read*. New York: Dell, 1975.

Rudman, M. K. *Children's literature: An issues approach*. Lexington, Mass.: D. C. Heath, 1976.

Shapiro, J. E., Ed. *Using literature and poetry affectively*. Newark, Del.: International Reading Association, 1979.

Smith, D. V. *The children's literary heritage*. Urbana, Ill.: National Council of Teachers of English, 1964.

Spiegel, D. L. *Reading for pleasure: Guidelines*. Newark, Del.: International Reading Association, 1981.

Sutherland, Z., Monson, D. L., and Arbuthnot, M. H. *Children and books*, 6th ed. Glenview, Ill.: Scott, Foresman, 1981.

VanScoy, K. and Whitehead, R. *Literature games*. Belmont, Calif.: Fearon Publishers, 1971.

Weiss, M. J. *From writers to students: The pleasures and pains of writing*. Newark, Del.: International Reading Association, 1979.

White, M. L., Ed. *Adventuring with books: A booklist for pre-K—Grade 6*. Urbana, Ill.: National Council of Teachers of English, 1981.

White, V. L. and Schulte, E. S., Eds. *Books about children's books: An annotated bibliography*. Newark, Del.: International Reading Association, 1979.

PERIODICALS THAT CONTAIN INFORMATION ABOUT CHILDREN'S BOOKS AND WAYS TO USE CHILDREN'S BOOKS

Booklist
American Library Association
Subscription and Order Service
50 East Huron Street
Chicago, Ill. 60611

The Horn Book Magazine
The Horn Book, Inc.
Park Square Building
31 St. James Avenue
Boston. Mass. 02116

The Kobrin Letter
The Kobrin Letter
732 North Greer Road
Palo Alto, Calif. 94303

Language Arts
National Council of Teachers of English
Subscription Service
1111 Kenyon Road
Urbana, Ill. 61801

The Reading Teacher
International Reading Association
800 Barksdale Road
P. O. Box 8139
Newark, Del. 19711

School Library Journal
R. R. Bowker Co.
Subscription Department
P. O. Box 67
Whitinsville, Mass. 01588

Top of the News
American Library Association
Subscription and Order Service
50 East Huron Street
Chicago, Ill. 60611

Appendix B

PERIODICALS FOR CHILDREN

The American Girl
Girl Scouts of the U.S.A.
830 Third Avenue
New York, N.Y. 10022

American Junior Red Cross News
American National Red Cross
17 and D Streets, N. W.
Washington, D.C. 20006

Arts and Activities
Jones Publishing Co.
8150 North Central Park Avenue
Skokie, Ill. 60076

Boy's Life
Boy Scouts of America
1325 Walnut Hill Lane
Irving, Texas 75062

Calling All Girls
Parents' Institute, Inc.
52 Vanderbilt Avenue
New York, N.Y. 10017

Child Life Magazine
Child Life, Inc.
36 Federal Street
Boston, Mass. 02110

Children's Digest
Parents' Magazine Press, Inc.
52 Vanderbilt Avenue
New York, N.Y. 10017

Children's Playcraft
Children's Playcraft Subscription
Office
Bergenfield, N.J. 07621

Children's Playmate Magazine
Children's Playmate Magazine,
Inc.
3025 East 75th Street
Cleveland, Ohio 44104

Cricket
Open Court Publishing Co.
1058 8th Street
LaSalle, Ill. 61301

Current Health
Curriculum Innovations, Inc.
3500 Western Avenue
Highland Park, Ill. 60035

Ebony Jr.
Johnson Publishing Co.
820 South Michigan Avenue
Chicago, Ill. 60605

The Electric Company Magazine
Children's Television Workshop
The Electric Company Magazine
P. O. Box 2929
Boulder, Colo. 80322

Golden Magazine
Western Publishing Company, Inc.
1220 Mound Avenue
Racine, Wisc. 53404

Highlights for Children
Highlights for Children
2300 West Fifth Avenue
Columbus, Ohio 43216

Humpty Dumpty's Magazine for
Little Children
Parents Magazine Press
52 Vanderbilt Avenue
New York, N.Y. 10017

Jack and Jill
Curtis Publishing Co.
Independence Square
Philadelphia, Pa. 19105

Junior Natural History
American Museum of Natural
History
Central Park West at 79th Street
New York, N.Y. 10024

Kids Magazine
Kids Magazine
Box 3041
Grand Central Station
New York, N.Y. 10025

Model Airplane News
Air Age, Inc.
551 Fifth Avenue
New York, N.Y. 10017

National Geographic World
National Geographic Society
17th and M Streets, N. W.
Washington, D.C. 20036

Odyssey
Astromedia Corp.
411 East Mason Street
P. O. Box 92788
Milwaukee, Wisc. 53202

Peck-of-Fun
Clapper Publishing Company
P. O. Box 568
Park Ridge, Ill. 60068

Penny Power
Consumers Union
Fulfillment Division
Box 1909
Marion, Ohio 43305

Plays: The Drama Magazine for
Young People
Plays, Inc.
8 Arlington Street
Boston, Mass. 02116

Ranger Rick
National Wildlife Federation
8925 Leesburg Pike
Vienna, Va. 22180

Sesame Street Magazine
Children's Television Workshop
Sesame Street Magazine
P. O. Box 2896
Boulder, Colo. 80322

Scienceland
Scienceland Magazine
501 5th Avenue, Suite 2102
New York, N.Y. 10017

Summertime
Scholastic Magazines, Inc.
33 West 42nd Street
New York, N.Y. 10036

3-2-1 Contact: A Science Magazine
Children's Television Workshop
3-2-1 Contact Magazine
P. O. Box 2933
Boulder, Colo. 80322

The Weewish Tree
American Indian Historical
Society
1451 Masonic Avenue
San Francisco, Calif. 94117

Young Americans
Strong Publications, Inc.
Box 1399
Grand Central Station
New York, N.Y. 10025

Young Athlete
Young Athlete, Inc.
1601 114th Avenue, S. E.
Bellevue, Wash. 98004

Index